Economics of the Family

The NBER's research in population and family economics is one of five programs in the NBER Center for Economic Analysis of Human Behavior and Social Institutions. This research program has been supported since 1970 by a grant from the Ford Foundation and since 1972 by a grant from the National Institute of Child Health and Human Development. As a part of that program, NBER co-sponsored with the Population Council two conferences held in June 1972 and June 1973 under the chairmanship of Theodore W. Schultz. This volume contains papers discussed at those conferences.

Economics of the Family
Marriage, Children, and Human Capital

Edited by Theodore W. Schultz

A Conference Report
of the National Bureau
of Economic Research

Published for the
National Bureau of Economic Research

by

The University of Chicago Press
Chicago and London

The University of Chicago Press, Chicago 60637
The University of Chicago Press, Ltd., London

International Standard Book Number: 0-226-74085-4
Library of Congress Catalog Card Number: 73-81484

National Bureau of Economic Research, 1974

Relation of the National Bureau Directors to Publications Reporting Conference Proceedings

Since the present volume is a record of conference proceedings, it has been exempted from the rules governing submission of manuscripts to, and critical review by, the Board of Directors of the National Bureau.

(Resolution adopted July 6, 1948, as revised November 21, 1949, and April 20, 1968)

Contents

Prefatory Note

During the past decade a small group of economists have been analyzing the fertility behavior of the family, using the concepts of human capital and of the allocation of time. These studies led to the development of the household production function and to the representation of the family as an important decision-making entity in allocating the scarce resources at its disposal in household production for current consumption and investment in children.

I have had the privilege of organizing two conferences, in 1972 and in 1973. These conferences were sponsored by the National Bureau of Economic Research and the Population Council, a joint enterprise set into motion by Victor Fuchs. This book brings together the two sets of studies which I edited and which were first published as supplements to the *Journal of Political Economy*, "New Economic Approaches to Fertility," March/April 1973, and "Marriage, Family Human Capital, and Fertility," March/April 1974. Gary S. Becker has kindly given permission to include the first part of his "A Theory of Marriage" which appeared in the July/August 1973 *Journal of Political Economy*.

I am very much indebted to Mrs. Virginia K. Thurner for her competent editorial assistance.

THEODORE W. SCHULTZ

October 1974

Part One

In Search of New Approaches

Fertility and Economic Values

Theodore W. Schultz

University of Chicago

Women and men who are mated in marriage prefer to have their own children. Their preference is strong and clear in the family behavior of parents. They sacrifice much to have their own children. Most of the costs (sacrifices) in having children and in caring for them during their infant years is borne by mothers. In an economic context, the scarce resource that matters most at this early stage in the marriage cycle is the time that mothers devote to their children. It follows that, in analyzing the economics of fertility, the economic value of the time of women is a major factor affecting fertility. I shall first present a brief economic perspective of the value of children and I shall then consider broadly the effects of the high price of human time on the number and quality of children and indicate the population equilibrium implications.

I. The Value of Children

In bringing economics to bear on procreation and children, a new dialogue between data and theory has begun. The studies in this book are a part of that dialogue. Whereas Malthus assumed that the price of children would remain constant, these studies argue that the cost of children increases with the rise in price of human time. We now see that fertility is affected by prices as well as by income and by the formation of human capital in children. We also see that the human capital embodied in adults, especially in women, affects fertility and the supply of labor. Recent developments in economic analysis provide some testable hypotheses. The empirical endeavors, as expected, disclose important new unsettled questions underscoring the fact that the work has just begun in understanding the mechanisms that account for changes over time.

I am indebted to Gary S. Becker, Yoram Ben-Porath, Dennis De Tray, Gregg Lewis, Marc Nerlove, Margaret Reid, T. Paul Schultz, and Robert Willis for their helpful suggestions to gain clarity and cogency.

3

In assessing the contributions of these studies, it would be premature to look for policy implications. The implications that matter at this stage of this work are primarily analytical. To see the setting of the problems that are on the agenda calls for an economic perspective which entails some elementary, albeit fundamental considerations. Although these considerations might be taken for granted, I shall elaborate on them to make sure that they are not overlooked. Fertility means children, and children are an important part of the standard of living of most families. Most married couples want their own children, and they proceed to bear and rear them. What is not clear is that parents derive satisfactions and productive services from their children and that the sacrifices made by parents in bearing children and in the investment they make in the care, health, and education of their children are in substantial part deliberate family decisions.

I anticipate that many sensitive, thoughtful people will be offended by these studies of fertility because they may see them as debasing the family and motherhood. These highly personal activities and purposes of parents may seem to be far beyond the realm of the economic calculus. I repeatedly expressed the same concern about this sensitive issue when I began to apply the concept of human capital to education. It, too, could be viewed as debasing the cultural purposes of education. I pointed out with care and at length that investment in education is fully consistent in serving cultural purposes in acquiring future cultural satisfactions along with the earnings associated with schooling and higher education. The same basic logic is applicable in this endeavor in explaining the sacrifices that parents make in acquiring the personal satisfactions and productive services that they derive from their children.

The analytical core of these studies rests on the economic postulate that the reproductive behavior of parents is in large part a response to the underlying preferences of parents for children. Given the state of the birth control technology and the various classes of uncertainty associated with contraception, infant mortality, the health and fecundity of the parents, and the income and wage rates parents expect to realize over their life cycles, these preferences are constrained by the parents' resources and the associated alternative economic opportunities in using their resources. In turn, these resources imply sacrifices, measured in terms of opportunity costs that parents must be prepared to make in acquiring the future satisfactions and productive service they expect to realize from children.

It could, of course, be argued that parents are nevertheless indifferent to these and all other economic considerations when it comes to having children, on the grounds that children are in considerable part the unintended outcome of sexual activity, that parents in general do not engage in any practical family planning, and that the lifetime resource constraints are not known to parents with enough certainty to influence their decisions at the time they bear their children. I shall not, at this point, enter upon the reasons for not accepting this line of argument because of the evidence to the contrary that emerges from these studies. I shall instead proceed on the postulate that parents respond to economic considerations in the children they bear and rear and that parents equate the marginal sacrifices and satisfactions, including the productive services they expect from children, in arriving at the value of children to them. Thus, in thinking about the economics of fertility, social cost and benefits aside, the analytical key in determining the value of children to their parents is in the interactions between the supply and demand factors that influence these family decisions.

Growth economists, to the extent that they have dealt with fertility, have featured the gross economic *effects* of population growth, leaving to biologists, sociologists, and demographers the task of explaining the increases in the size of the human population. This concentration on such gross effects is understandable in view of the fact that the factors determining population growth have been a major unsettled part of economic theory. The concept of an optimum population has not been fruitful. Modern growth theory, with some notable exceptions, treats increases in the size of the population as an exogenous variable, although in classical economics it was (following Malthus) an endogenous variable. The Malthusian assumption about bearing and rearing children in response to economic growth led, of course, to the long-standing dismal economic perspective with respect to the population consequences of the accumulation of capital and of any advances in the techniques of production. While economists no longer accept the subsistence standard of living as invariant over time in view of the widely observed rise in standards of living that has occurred with the rise in real family income associated with economic growth, the recent proliferation of doomsday literature featuring the population bomb, produced mainly by a few biologists, rests basically on the early Malthusian notions of reproductive behavior.

Meanwhile, demographers have done much in clarifying the complexity of population data and in examining in depth particular differences among classes of parents in their fertility behavior (Ryder and Westoff 1971, and others). Moreover, demographers know that the population projections that are based on their well-standardized data are tenuous projections even for the short run, for they know that these projections do not rest on any theory of population growth. Demographers are asking key questions, however, on which the economist would be well advised to ponder: What is the explanation of the rapid adoption of the pill? What accounts for the fluctuations in the birth rates in countries in which the economy is highly developed?[1] In my view, the most important question they are asking is:

---

[1] This question has been mainly on Richard Easterlin's research agenda (1968, 1969).

What is the explanation of the *demographic transition,* that is, how do we explain the economic and social processes and family behavior that accounts for the marked decline from very high birth and death rates to modern very low birth and death rates? It is obvious that the theory which treats population growth as an exogenous variable is of no help in answering these questions.

I shall restrict the rest of my comments first to the recent advances in economic analyses that have made these new approaches possible. The economic picture that emerges will then be sketched briefly, and finally, I will consider some of the implications of these studies for future economic thinking and work.

A. Advances in Economic Analysis

There are four developments in economic analysis that are relevant here: the investment in human capital; the theory to treat a heretofore neglected basic attribute in the allocation of human time; the household production function; and a view of the family that encompasses both consumer choice and household production decisions, including the bearing and rearing of children.

Investment in human capital, as we know, rests on the proposition that there are certain expenditures (sacrifices) that are made deliberately to create productive stocks, embodied in human beings, that provide services over future periods. These services consist of producer services revealed in future earnings and of consumer services that accrue to the individual as satisfactions over his lifetime.[2]

Children are here viewed as forms of human capital. From the point of view of the sacrifices that are made in bearing and rearing them, parents in rich countries acquire mainly future personal satisfactions from them,

---

[2] Professor Harry Johnson has summarized the producer attributes of human capital succinctly as follows: "The contribution of human capital to the productive process is developed by a process of investment (which means simply the sacrifice of current resources for future returns) incurred in the formal education system and through on-the-job training, and that this investment yields its returns over the lifetime of the individual concerned. . . . The concept of human capital has tremendous integrative power, in that it provides a unifying principle for the consistent explanation of many phenomena of the labour market. Perhaps its most fundamental implication, from the point of view of social thought, is that the worker in an advanced industrial economy is typically a very considerable capitalist. . . . A second implication, which is extremely relevant to the broad question of social and economic inequality, is that the economic rewards for alternative occupations and careers need to be compared in terms of lifetime income profiles, and not in terms of the highest annual income earned in the course of the career. . . . A third implication, also relevant to the question of inequality, is that in their choices among alternative possible careers, new entrants to the labour force face the same problems of assembling information, assessing risks, evaluating returns, and obtaining the resources for investment, as do prospective investors in material capital equipment or in stocks and shares" (Johnson 1968, pp. 7–8).

while in poor countries children also contribute substantially to the future real income of their parents by the work that children do in the household and on the farm and by the food and shelter they provide for their parents when they no longer are able to provide these for themselves. Children are in a very important sense the *poor man's capital*. It is becoming clear that the investment in children is in many ways akin to the investment in home-grown trees for their beauty and fruit. A very young child is highly labor-intensive in terms of cost, and the rewards are wholly psychic in terms of utility. As a child becomes a teen-ager, the additional cost borne by the parents involves less labor intensiveness and the rewards, especially in poor countries, consist in increasing part of useful work that the teen-ager performs.

The second important advance in economic analysis is in the treatment of human time in allocative decisions with respect to both market and non-market activities (Becker 1965). The linkage between human capital and this concept of time allocation is strong and clear. The usefulness of the new concept of human time is not restricted to work in the labor market for it is also applicable to work in the household. With respect to the household the individual, predominantly the housewife, allocates her time in part in choosing and shopping for consumer goods and in part in using them in household production leading to consumption. Then, too, consumption per se also requires time. The central principle of this advance in analysis is that in reality each consumer service has two prices attached to it: (1) a money price, as in traditional theory of consumer choice, and (2) a time cost of acquiring the consumer goods and processing them in the household; and the time cost that is involved in consuming the services obtained from this household activity.

It is obvious that bearing a child and caring for the infant child are normally highly labor-intensive activities on the part of the mother. What has not been clear is the difference in the value of time of mothers in bearing and rearing children asssociated with the difference in the human capital of mothers. The studies that follow contribute substantially in clari-fying this relationship.

There is, then, the treatment of the economics of household production. This household production function is an outgrowth of the concepts of human capital and of the value of human time. It provides a comprehensive ap-proach to the nonmarket activities of the household, an approach that was foreshadowed by the much earlier work of Margaret Reid (1934). The dis-tinctive merit of Becker's 1965 formulation of a theory of the allocation of human time is in accounting for the use of the time of individuals in house-hold production activities. Clearly, the housewife is not only allocating her time in choosing among consumer goods and in acquiring them, but she also engages in altering these goods as she processes and prepares them for con-sumption. The household production function is for this purpose a useful analytical tool.[3] A further development of the household production function is now called for. Empirical analysis indicates that the production of a child (children) differs importantly in terms of inputs of time and of the services of purchased goods depending upon the age of the child (children).

The fourth advance is envisioning the family as a decision-making unit not only in maximizing its utility in consumption but also in determining the allocation of human time and of goods in the production activities of the household. In terms of economic analysis, the family as a decision-making unit with respect to household production is here viewed as an application of theory of the firm in traditional economic theory. In this view of the family, the assumption is made that the welfare of each member of the family is normally integrated into a unified family welfare function,[4] that there are "overheads," and that shadow (nonmarket) prices play an important role in the family's producer and consumer activities, including the bearing and rearing of children.

B. The Emerging Economic Picture

Each of the studies in this book should be viewed as a progress report on research that has been underway for some time. As studies, none has been done in splendid isolation, for there has been much communication among these economists; and, as might be expected, they all use essentially the same economic language. It is also clear from the fairly extensive list of references that a number of other economists are likewise engaged in research in this area.

Admittedly, the theory is restricted by its static economic assumptions, from which it nevertheless derives a good deal of analytical power; it cannot yet, however, cope adequately with the lifetime behavior of parents with respect to the many diverse investments they make in the health, education, on-the-job training, travel, and marriage of their children and with respect to the transfer of property via inheritance. The core of the theory is designed primarily to analyze the effects of the differences in the price of the time of parents that enter directly and indirectly into the production of children. The static theory at hand still lumps together first all expenditures on children and then all satisfactions from children that occur over the life cycle. It does not disentangle the early and later parts of this cycle in determining the relative importance of the two parts. In my thinking, important parts of the changes in fertility over time, changes that are related to the rise in the expenditures on children, are consequences of long-term developments with respect to the economic value of education, job opportunities, the incentives to migrate toward better

---

[3] The usefulness of this analytical tool is suggested by its applications in analyzing the derived demand for health, leisure, durable goods, transportation, and here in ascertaining the derived demand for children.

[4] I shall return to this issue in Section C.

economic locations, the opportunities to reduce infant mortality, and the improvements in contraceptive techniques and the decline in their cost, along with the secular rise in family income. The treatment of these and other secular developments, including the rates at which families adjust their fertility to these various types of disequilibria, is as yet beyond the scope of the theory.

Admittedly, also, the empirical analysis is subject to serious data limitations and to some econometric complexities that remain unsolved. Data are always hard to come by when it comes to testing economic hypotheses. Better data, however, for these purposes can undoubtedly be "made." Then, too, although there have been major advances in the development of econometric techniques, some of them are not as yet common property among economists; meanwhile new unsolved econometric problems keep cropping up.

Turning to the empirical part, the responses of parents to differences in relative prices inducing substitution are evident. Specifically, the negative effects of increases in price of the mother's time on the number of children leaves little room for doubt that there is a role for economics in analyzing fertility. When education is used as a measure of the price of her time, the task of untangling the several different influences of education presents difficulties which I shall consider presently.

The responses of parents to differences in income and to changes in income over time are very difficult to get at. There is, however, an unwarranted tendency to treat the estimates at hand as weak and ambiguous for the wrong reason. These income effects are not for theory to decide any more so than in the case of the income elasticity of the demand, say, for food. The wrong reason is in the belief that the partial effect of income must be to increase fertility.

In my view, the determination of these income effects will depend ultimately on data. But it is exceedingly difficult to determine empirically the effects of income while holding the price of time and goods constant. It is even more difficult to measure correctly the true family wealth over its life cycle. To do it using ex post data is up against the fact that what is needed are the ex ante expectations of the time path of the family income streams over the life cycle with the appropriate weights of these expectations at different stages in the life cycle with due regard for risk and discounting. Static models are unable to account for revisions of these expectations and for the adjustments that parents make to unexpected income changes along the life-cycle path. Furthermore, the effect of changes in the ratio of quality per child to the number of children may cause the relative price of numbers of children to rise as income rises even when the price of time is held constant.[5] My interpretation of the Becker-Lewis paper herein is that it supports this inference.

[5] The latter part of this paragraph owes much to a clarifying comment from Robert Willis.

More generally and fundamentally, with respect to the interaction between quality per child and number of children, is the overall constraint of family resources in the sense that additional numbers of children necessarily implies fewer resources to draw upon to invest in quality per child.

The ongoing research here under consideration presents a major challenge in untangling and isolating the various functions that the education of parents performs in household-family behavior as it influences fertility. The education of parents, notably that of the mother, appears to be an omnibus. It affects the choice of mates in marriage. It may affect the parents' preferences for children. It assuredly affects the earnings of women who enter the labor force. It evidently affects the productivity of mothers in the work they perform in the household, including the rearing of their children. It probably affects the incidence of child mortality, and it undoubtedly affects the ability of parents to control the number of births. The task of specifying and identifying each of these attributes of the parents' education in the family context is beset with analytical difficulties on a par with the difficulties that continue to plague the economic analysis of growth in coping with the advances in technology.

I am impressed by the evidence that the relationship between additional schooling of mothers and the number of children is strongly negative for the early years of schooling of mothers. But, why this relationship should not continue for additional education at the higher levels is a puzzle.[6] In view of the importance of this relationship in determining public policy in support of elementary schooling, a special effort is called for, both in making sure of the empirical inferences and in resolving the apparent puzzle.

Analytically, I deem it to be a real advance to treat children as a heterogeneous stock of human capital. Clearly, a child less than age 3 is a very different component of human capital, both in terms of costs which consist largely of the value of the mother's time and in terms of psychic satisfactions that parents derive from so young a child, compared with an older child who has become a teen-ager. As I noted at the outset, a very young child is highly labor-intensive measured in terms of the input of the mother's time. As the child becomes older, he becomes less and less labor-intensive and more costly in terms of other family resources that are required for the schooling and other activities that enhance his acquired abilities.

The problem of determining the allocation of family resources as between quality per child and numbers of children looms large. It deservedly is high on the agenda.

There is too little explicit analysis of the investments by parents in the abilities that children acquire from education, on-the-job experi-

---

[6] Ben-Porath and Willis attempt in their papers herein to provide some possible explanations of this puzzle.

ence, travel, and other activities that enhance the capacities of children; these are investments from which the family benefits and which it can afford by drawing on family resources, in addition to the mother's time, through dissaving during the early stage of the family life cycle, especially so in the advanced, modern economies such as Israel and the United States.

The rate of child mortality in the United States is not only low, but the difference in this rate among the white families has become sufficiently small so that variations in their child mortality are no longer a significant factor in fertility behavior. But the decline in child mortality currently underway in most poor countries is in all probability an important variable to which parents are responding with lags as they become informed and are prepared to act, given the state of the information that appears relevant to their fertility decisions.

Last, one of the more important new insights pertains to the economics of the supply of and demand for contraception techniques. Would that we had estimates of the rates at which the superior and cheaper contraceptive techniques are adopted. The indications are that this information will tell a story that is in many respects comparable to that of farmers in a number of poor countries in their adoption of new, superior varieties of wheat, rice, and other crops that has set into motion the so-called Green Revolution. The responses of parents in adopting these contraceptive techniques is also further support of the economic postulate that parents are not indifferent in their fertility behavior to changes in economic conditions.

C. Prospects

Are we, as Norman Ryder suggests (in Part 2), destroying the idea of a family? On the contrary, we are enlarging and enriching the role of the family as it is envisioned in the new home economics. The assumption that the family integrates the welfare of its members into an internally consistent family-utility function attributes a role to the family that undoubtedly exceeds its capacity as a social institution. Thus, one of the unsettled issues for future work is an approach for treating the individual utility functions of the husband, wife, and older children.

The family is indeed one of the basic social institutions that has been fortified legally as it has evolved culturally. Ryder is correct in noting that "society intervenes, in obvious and in subtle ways." With regard to the family's social functions, there has been a persistent concern with respect to marriage, procreation, and children. The family is for these reasons a concept that is basically in the domain of anthropologists, of sociologists, and of legal scholars, and all of them contribute to demographic studies. Can economists also contribute, in view of the advances in economic analysis made possible by concepts of human capital, the value of human time, the household production function, and the family as a decision-making unit in consumption and in household production? What are the prospects that these new approaches will contribute significantly in explaining marriage, fertility, and the investment in children?

The prospects would not be promising if it were true that virtually all that has been and could be learned using these economic approaches is already known by scholars in other disciplines. While it would be presumptuous to proclaim that an economic theory of population is in prospect, it is not to be ruled out at this stage. The more modest prospects, which are nevertheless important, are of two parts: (1) the substantive contributions already at hand, and (2) the potentially rewarding research opportunities that these approaches afford.

The substantive contributions that I have featured in the preceding section along with others that are reported in the several papers that follow are new and important. We see that the household-family unit responds to changes in relative prices in the manner implied by the economic theory, that the most important price in the production of children during the early years of each child is the price of the mother's time, that there is substitution in the family context between the quality embodied in children and the quantity (number) of children, that the investment in the quality of children looms large as family income rises, that additional schooling at the lower level of education of mothers has a strong negative effect on family fertility, and that the response to superior and cheap contraceptive techniques is clearly subject to economic analysis.

Furthermore, these studies are a rich source of economic hypotheses that have as yet not been tested and of ideas and speculations worthy of much more economic thinking. Most of the research opportunities that I see are mentioned in the preceding section. I shall, therefore, restrict further comments to several specific ways of getting at some of the unexplored issues and at some of the long-term economic developments that may have substantial explanatory power in accounting for the observed changes in fertility over periods of two and more family cycles.

The static household-family models can be extended to take account explicitly of the array of consumer durables that enter into the household production function and of the ready-made consumer items that save on the time of housewives. The acquisition of consumer durables by borrowing funds during the childbearing and rearing stage of the family cycle can also be made an integral part of these models. I would expect that as the education of the parents increases, we will observe a significant positive effect in acquiring borrowed funds more cheaply and in the effectiveness with which parents manage their investment portfolio, including their investment in children. Hired household help is included in some of these studies but it probably requires substantially more attention in analyzing empirically the economic behavior of parents in allocating their own time to children who are no longer infants. I am convinced that these extensions of these models will produce additional worthwhile insights even where the empirical applications are restricted to cross-sectional data and one date in time.

Important parts of these models patently call for cross-sectional data covering in sequence several dates encompassing the family life cycle from marriage and presumably until the children are really on their own, inasmuch as most of the investment in children made by parents occurs after the childbearing period is over. In this endeavor, it will be necessary to account for the savings and the accumulation of assets by the household-family along with the borrowed funds that the family acquires, thereby enhancing the current resources it has available, resources that are used in part to purchase labor-saving consumer items and in part to finance investments in the quality of the children.

As we proceed beyond the stationary economic state, we enter an uncharted frontier. Our analytical maps do not tell us how to proceed. The typical family that we observe, especially in rich countries, lives and has lived in an economy in which economic conditions are and have been changing substantially over time. As these changes occur, thinking in terms of economics, there presumably are responses—responses in the age at which marriage occurs, responses in spacing and numbers of children, and responses in the amount of family resources devoted to investment in children. Furthermore, before these families have fully adjusted and have arrived at an equilibrium with respect to any given economic change, additional unexpected changes will have occurred. Thus, the families we observe are seldom, if ever, in a state of economic equilibrium. This uncharted frontier is beset with all manner of disequilibria. Economic theory, capable of coping with them in the family context, is very much wanted.

It is, of course, possible to improvise by endeavoring to analyze each of these major changes one at a time and, in doing so, abstract from the other changes. Admittedly, there are severe limitations to this procedure; it may, however, provide enough additional information to apply a comprehensive simultaneous economic model encompassing family decisions over the life cycle under changing economic conditions.

In my thinking, research priority should be given to the economic attributes of the following changes to determine the extent to which they influence marriage, fertility, and investment in children: (1) improvements in the technology of contraceptive goods and services reckoned in terms of their effectiveness and their cost to the family; (2) improvements and the declines in the price of labor-saving consumer items; (3) changes in the economic opportunities of investing in the education of children; (4) changes in the labor-market opportunities (a) for women and (b) for teen-agers; (5) changes in the reduction in labor-market earnings that are a consequence of the curtailment of on-the-job training during the period when women leave the labor force to bear and to take care of a child (children); (6) the decline in the cost of reducing infant mortality, a change that currently characterizes mainly the developments underway in poor countries; and (7) the changes in the location of job opportunities associated with economic growth that require geographical migration of youth and of established families (T. W. Schultz 1972a).

As a framework to guide one's thinking in accounting for these various economic changes over time and the economic interactions among them, a model of the type developed by Marc Nerlove and T. Paul Schultz (1970) is an appropriate instrument in charting this frontier. In my view, the empirical usefulness of this model, however, is dependent upon our acquiring a substantial amount of new information with respect to each of the major changes that I have listed.

II. The High Value of Human Time: Population Equilibrium

A child, as the studies in this book show, is doubly time intensive. Having and rearing a child entails much time on the part of the mother. Enjoying the pleasures derived from a child also requires much time. Thus, in the impersonal language of economics, a child is a labor-intensive entity in terms of costs (sacrifices) and also in terms of consumption time. Moreover, although modernization has contributed much to increasing the value of human time, and in spite of all the advances in knowledge and all of the new techniques used in household production, children continue to be highly labor intensive for parents and especially so for women, whether they live in poor or rich countries. Herein lies the lesson of this part of my paper.

My aim is to develop the basic underlying propositions on which Nerlove's paper at the end of this volume rests. Since his approach to the high price of human time parallels my recent work, as he notes, my analysis complements his. I shall first consider two widely different population equilibrium concepts; in support of the second concept I shall extend the explanation of the secular increases in the value of human time. I shall then take a critical look at the usefulness of the household model in analyzing the fertility in countries characterized by high birth and death rates and by substantial increases in national income in a context where the level of the economic value of human time is very low and not increasing much.

A.

The idea of a population equilibrium is here viewed strictly as an analytical concept to guide economic thinking in deriving testable propositions pertaining to fertility. As an analytical device there is no presumption that any population ever has arrived or will arrive at a precise equilibrium. In this respect the concept of a population equilibrium is on a par with the many other equilibrium concepts that abound in economic analysis.

Two very different concepts of a population equilibrium can now be formulated. They may be viewed as types at the two extremes with respect to the state of the economy. The first rests on the proposition that the equilibrium is basically a consequence of increases in the price of the services of natural resources relative to capital and labor (wages). The underlying proposition of the second concept is that the equilibrium is determined predominantly by increases in the price of human time relative to that of materials. The per capita income implication of the first is subsistence and that of the second a high standard of living.

The first concept, as it was envisaged by the early English economists, has long been a standard part of economics. It assumes that the supply of land is fixed and that diminishing returns gradually increase the price of food as a consequence of population growth. Gains in productivity from capital are exhausted by this process. This concept can, of course, be extended to encompass the results of the recent macrosystem models that purport to show the limits of the earth in accommodating population growth. These models are not restricted solely by the availability of land to produce food, since they also include the physical limits set by the availability of minerals, energy, and space for people. The fertility behavior of people in these models is crudely Malthusian; population growth stops (suddenly) as a consequence of the inevitable food, energy, and space crisis. Within the Ricardian framework, this concept is a logical conception of a population equilibrium. It is a dismal view of human behavior that has long been an important idea in social thought.

The foundation of the second concept is the high price of human time relative to the price of the services of material factors and goods. The concept rests on the proposition that the state of the economy is such that the economic role of the services of natural resources and of intermediate material products is small relative to the role of the services of human agents in production and in consumption, in the sense that the value of the contribution of materials to human satisfactions is small compared with that of human agents. In the context of such an economy, the opportunity costs of bearing children is high and the investment in their human capital is large. The welfare implications of this concept are unmistakably optimistic because the gains in productivity from the accumulation of human and nonhuman capital are transformed into high standards of living supported by high per capita income. Advances in useful knowledge, embodied in human and nonhuman capital, have gradually destroyed the assumption of the fixed supply of the "original properties of the soil." In the process, it is the scarcity of human time and its high value that dominate, and it is the "fixed supply of human time" consisting of 24 hours per day and of a man's lifetime that becomes the critical factor in analyzing the economic behavior of people, including their fertility.

Empirically, there is an abundance of evidence which shows that the price of human time accounts for most of the costs in a modern economy. The upward tendency of real wages and salaries, including fringe benefits, of earnings foregone by mature students, and of the value of the time of housewives relative to the price of materials is well documented.[7] Economic theory implies, and we observe, that material goods are substituted for human time by firms and by households. Received theory, however, is silent on the effects of the high and rising price of human time on pure consumption, although consumption obviously entails time. In my thinking, the ultimate economic limit of affluence (economic growth) is not in the scarcity of material goods but in the scarcity of human time for consumption.[8]

Theoretically, the critical postulate assumes that there is a dynamic process that determines the increases in the price of human time relative to the price of the services of the nonhuman factors and that this process tends toward an equilibrium. The dynamic part is the economic key to the following four issues: (1) the relative increase in investment in human capital augmenting the quality of human beings, (2) the relatively high price of all labor time–intensive goods and other sources of labor–intensive satisfactions, including children, thus leading to the substitution of quality for numbers of children, (3) the relatively cheap material goods that are not labor-intensive, and (4) the scarcity of the time for consumption, setting the ultimate limit to the satisfactions that can be derived from materials provided by economic growth.

Although it is obvious that the economic value of human time is high in the affluent countries that have a modern economy, it is not obvious why these economies have developed the demand for and supply of human abilities that have such a high value in terms of earnings and satisfactions that people derive from them. I shall elaborate on these developments (see T. W. Schultz 1972*b*, 1973) and examine some of their basic aspects.

My approach to the persistent secular increase in the economic value of human time consists of a highly simplified framework to get at the supply and demand developments that appear to be determining the rise

---

[7] Evidence, for example, on long-term changes in wages and salaries relative to rent paid for the services of farmland in the United States shows that the total real compensation per hour at work of all manufacturing-production workers increased between 1929 and 1970 more than twice as much as did the rent on farm real estate per acre, similarly adjusted, under the assumption that rents tended to parallel the changes in the price of farm real estate per acre (T. W. Schultz 1972*b*).

[8] The approach outlined in this paragraph and a considerable part of the argument that follows appear in my Woody Thompson lecture to the Midwest Economics Association, "Explanation and Interpretations of the Increasing Value of Human Time" (T. W. Schultz 1973).

of the price of human time in the context of the modernizing processes. The developments explaining the increases in the supply of the quality attributes of human agents are fairly clear, whereas the developments underlying the increases in the demand for these quality attributes are still not clear. Recent advances in economic analysis (summarized in T. W. Schultz 1972a) provide the major parts of the theory for determining the supply of these quality attributes. They treat the useful abilities that people acquire as forms of human capital. The investment in these abilities is taken to be in response to favorable investment opportunities, and thus the increases in the supply depend on current expenditures (sacrifices) made by individuals, by families, and by public bodies on education, health, job training, the search for information, and geographical migration to take advantage of better jobs or of better consumption opportunities. These expenditures (sacrifices) are presumably made deliberately with an eye to future satisfactions and earnings. The theory of the allocation of time and the household production model are of special importance in analyzing the incentives and responses of people in acquiring education and job training, in enhancing their health, in searching for information, and in altering their fertility, including the substitution of quality for numbers of children. Thus, these supply responses to the increases in the economic incentives associated with modernization are not hard to comprehend. The human capital literature abounds with studies dealing with aspects of these supply responses.

But these human capital studies have not explained the secular increases in the demand for these quality attributes of human agents. The clue to this unresolved puzzle is concealed in two basic factual issues. The first of these is that diminishing returns to capital have not occurred generally, despite the vast accumulation of capital in the advanced economies. The second is the relatively high rate at which the formation of human capital has occurred. Of the two, the first is fundamental, and the resolution of it provides a solution for the second. In my thinking, the key to both is in that part of the economic process that increases the stock of useful knowledge.[9] It is the acquisition, adoption, and efficient utilization of this knowledge that have provided *the decisive new sources of investment opportunities* that have maintained the growth process and have kept the returns to capital from diminishing over time. Furthermore, these additions to the stock of knowledge have been relatively more favorable in increasing the investment opportunities in the quality at-

---

[9] Simon Kuznets in his Nobel Prize lecture, which appeared in the June 1973 *American Economic Review* under the title "Modern Economic Growth: Findings and Reflections" (Kuznets 1973), also attributes a major role to the additions in knowledge in this context. He argues that the last two centuries have been periods during which there has occurred "enormous accumulation in the contribution to the stock of useful knowledge by basic and applied research" (p. 251).

tributes of human agents than in the quality components of material agents of production. The investment incentives that are revealed by the inequalities in these investment opportunities, as they occur over time, are the mainspring in this process.

In an all-inclusive view of these investment opportunities, the knowledge-producing sector must also be included. It is not a trivial sector in modern countries, nor is it exogenous. Research is an organized activity that requires specific, expensive, scarce resources. Although research is costly, recent studies, most of them devoted to analyzing the rates of return to investment in organized agricultural research, show very high social rates of return.

With respect to this investment process, economists could have been spared much aimless wandering had they perceived the implications of the concept of capital as Marshall sketched it for us. His predecessors had formulated the concept of the "state of the productive arts," and they then proceeded to develop the core of economic theory under the assumption that these arts remained constant. It was an ingenious simplification, and their theory was in general relevant to a wide array of problems of their day. But industrialization undermined this simplifying assumption, and Marshall saw it clearly and cogently. In his treatment of the agents of production, he extended the concept of labor to include work with our hands and our heads. It should be noted with care that his concept of capital "consists in great part of knowledge and organization; and of this some part is private property and the other part is not. *Knowledge is our most powerful engine of production. . . .* Organization aids knowledge. . . . The distinction between public and private property in knowledge and organization is of great and growing importance: in some respects of more importance than that between public and private property in material things."[10] In not seeing the implications of Marshall's remarkable insights, economists have wandered for years in the wilderness of capital confined to material goods.

Thus, in a nutshell, the persistent increase in the demand for the high-quality services of human agents is a function of the additions to the stock of useful knowledge.[11] The complexities of the additions to this knowledge have been much greater in recent, modern economic growth than during early, relatively simple industrialization. The rate at which the stock of useful knowledge has increased has also been higher than the rate at which it grew during the early stages of modernization.

This approach has broad integrative power in that it provides a unifying

---

10 Marshall (1930, bk. 4, chap. 1, pp. 138–39); the italics are mine.

11 The argument in support of this summary statement appears in previous works (T. W. Schultz 1972b, 1973). It is anticipated in chaps. 1 and 2 in my *Investment in Human Capital: The Role of Education and Research* (1971). Chapter 12 treats the "Allocation of Resources to Research."

principle for a consistent explanation of the allocation of investment resources encompassing both human and nonhuman capital as modernization proceeds. From it we derive important empirical implications that can be tested against data. It implies that the value of human time increases relative to the cost of investment resources.[12] It implies that the relative share of national income accruing to labor increases over time.[13] It implies that there is a special premium for the allocative ability of both males and females in managing firms[14] and households and in allocating their own time, including investments in themselves. It also implies that as the value of the time of mothers increases, fertility declines.[15] These implications are derived from the dynamic process, not from a model of the economy that has arrived at a general equilibrium.

The concept of a general economic equilibrium in this context is necessary, however, as an analytical guide. It is an assumed economic state toward which this modernization process tends. Given this state, there would be no inequalities among investment opportunities. The high price of human time would be stable in the sense that it is no longer increasing relative to other factor service prices. There would be no incentive to make additional investments in human capital or in the knowledge-producing sector, as a consequence of the completion of the modernization process, and advances in knowledge would no longer augment the productivity of human time within firms and households; presumably, virtually all of the value added in production would be contributed by the input of human time. The basic economic constraint that determines the upper limits of modernization (economic growth) in this equilibrium model is the increasing scarcity of human time for consumption. The underlying logic can be put very simply: modernization increases the consumption stream; consumption requires human time; advances in knowledge, whether they are embodied in material capital or in human capital, are severely limited in the extent to which they can alleviate the scarcity of human time for consumption.

For the purpose at hand, the bearing and rearing of children is a very labor-intensive activity; the satisfactions that parents derive from their children is a large part of their "standard of living," and the process of

[12] A simplified approach to this implication is to treat the cost of investment resources as constant under the assumptions that the "normal" long-term real rate of interest remains constant and that, from an increasing amount of capital embodied in human beings, people derive earnings and satisfactions commensurate with the going rate of interest.

[13] As the earnings from the increasing stock of human capital rise relative to income acquired from property assets.

[14] As a consequence of the dynamics of the economy, the premium for allocative ability, distinguished from the ability of people to do useful work, is substantial (see Welch 1970; Fane 1972; Huffman 1972; Khaldi 1972).

[15] Nerlove's subtle and incisive treatment of the interactions between the high value of time and fertility lays the groundwork for new thinking with respect to this important implication.

enjoying these satisfactions requires much time, the economic value of which, in this context, is very high.

B.

Turning to fertility behavior in the low-income countries, the household model as it now stands has not been developed to treat the particular classes of circumstances that constrain the household in these countries. These are countries in which illiteracy abounds, human time is cheap, and the income opportunities that women have outside the home are mainly not jobs in the labor market. Furthermore, infant mortality is high, life expectancy at birth is low, debilitation during the adult years is substantial for reasons of inadequate nutrition and endemic diseases, and the availability of modern contraceptive techniques, including information about them, is, in general, wanting. These classes of circumstances are not as yet at home in the household model.

The difficulty here is not that economic theory is pointless in explaining fertility behavior in the low-income countries. On the contrary, in principle basic economic thinking is fully as applicable to the poor as it is to the rich countries. As a case in point, I have long argued (T. W. Schultz 1964) that the theory of the firm is analytically as powerful in the allocation of resources of poor, small, illiterate farmers in the less-developed countries as it is in determining the allocative efficiency of farmers, say, in Iowa. The usefulness of this theory is now widely recognized because of many recent successful applications. The same argument holds for a fully developed theory of the household. As yet, however, the part of this theory that has been applied to the United States, Israel, and Japan is a special and narrow part of what I envisage as a general theory of the household. Once the additional parts of this theory have been formulated, its usefulness in analyzing household activities in low-income countries will not be in doubt, assuming that it is also extended to treat the effects of economy-wide dynamic development.

Households in low-income countries perform, in fact, a substantially larger economic role than they do in high-income countries. The value of home production is not only large relative to the total family income, it is also produced predominantly by family labor and only in small part by purchased inputs, because in low-income countries the purchased material goods that households can acquire are very high in price relative to the economic value of the time of members of the household. With regard to the costs of children, children are labor-intensive during their infancy regardless of the country's level of income. In low-income countries, however, the mother's time is cheap in a context where health services, nutrition, and education for the children are dear. The satisfactions and producer services that parents derive from their children are in large measure from an assured number of children to provide help for household work and for family endeavors consisting mostly of farm work and to provide food and shelter for the parents during their old age and only in small measure from human capital that enhances the acquired quality of children. These particular economic constraints on the household are not treated in the part of the theory that has been applied in these fertility studies restricted to rich countries.

As an overview, the interactions between the changes in the economy and the economic role of the household including fertility are probably more important in most of these developing countries than in the advanced countries. With respect to which of the two concepts of a population equilibrium is the more relevant in guiding our economic thinking in explaining the fertility behavior in the low-income countries, my view is that it is the second concept. My reason for opting for this concept is that the now-popular doomsday literature is not a valid characterization of the direction toward which the economy of such countries is moving. The crude Malthusian view of fertility does not apply; these countries are not headed toward a population equilibrium that is being imposed on them by diminishing returns from natural resources. Per capita income is in general not falling in these countries. Measured in terms of living conditions, there are appreciable gains, as is evident from improvements in health and from longer life expectancy. Moreover, birth rates are falling and substantially so in an increasing number of low-income countries. Although they are far from arriving at the second type of population equilibrium, they are moving toward it, and it is therefore analytically the relevant concept.

In the first part of this paper I expressed my concern that our estimates of the price and income effects on fertility may be subject to considerable error for reasons of changes in the economy over time, changes that are not taken into account in these studies. The changes that are taking place in the low-income countries appear to me to be even more important than those in the developed countries, and if this is true, it will be imperative to extend our economic approaches in ways that will make these changes an integral part of the theory and its application. The most pervasive change is in the improvement of health. Estimates of life expectancy from time of birth are rising at a high rate relative to the further rise in the rich countries. The decline in infant mortality must have important fertility implications. Along with somewhat better nutrition, the marked decline in debilitating diseases during adulthood must have some price and income effects on household activities, including fertility. The fact that in some parts of poor countries, in the Punjab of India, for example, many girls are now enrolled in schools is an important change in this context. Then, too, there is some progress in increasing the supply of information about modern contraceptive techniques and in subsidizing the supply of contraceptives. While all of these changes are occurring, the quality of the labor force is slowly rising as is the value of human time.

One measure of the fruitfulness of these studies is in the agenda of unfinished research that the papers and comments produce. There is a couplet by Robert Frost bearing on research. Let me paraphrase it:

> We sit around the circle and suppose
> The Secret sits in the middle and knows.

Part Two

Economics of Family Fertility

Economic Theory of Fertility Behavior

Robert J. Willis

Graduate School, City University of New York, and National Bureau of Economic Research

Until the past decade or so, economists tended to believe that the determinants of fertility are largely noneconomic or, at least, that the analysis of fertility is outside the scope of economic theory.[1] In part, these beliefs

This is a substantially revised version of a paper of the same title, which, in its earlier form, is the first chapter of my University of Washington Ph.D. dissertation. I have accrued a substantial debt to too many individuals who have contributed to the evolution of the ideas in this paper to acknowledge them all individually. I would like especially to thank John Floyd, who first suggested to me that economic analysis might be applied to population, Jon Rasmussen, who contributed importantly to the mathematical development of the paper, and Warren Sanderson, whose contribution to my thinking on fertility behavior is so ubiquitous that I can only reluctantly absolve him from responsibility for any errors or inadequacies in this paper. My debt to Yoram Ben-Porath will be apparent from his paper in this book. T. W. Schultz, Gary Becker, and H. Gregg Lewis made valuable suggestions for improving the final draft of this paper. I would also like to acknowledge the excellent research and programming assistance of C. Ates Dagli. Work on this paper was supported by a Ford Foundation grant to the National Bureau of Economic Research, for study of the economics of population. Earlier, I was aided by a Ford Foundation dissertation fellowship and by Wesleyan University.

[1] Becker (1960) argued that fertility could be analyzed within an economic framework. He emphasized the connection between income and fertility which he believed to be positive under conditions in which birth control knowledge was equalized across income classes. He also distinguished, importantly, between the cost and quality of children, arguing that the latter but not the former is subject to parental choice. This distinction remains a matter of controversy. Efforts were made in the sixties to investigate empirically the relationship between income and fertility over time and cross-sectionally, with mixed results in the sense that income did not seem to have a consistent positive or negative effect on fertility, nor did the magnitude of the effect of income seem to be large (see, e.g., Adelman 1963; Freedman 1963; Silver 1965, 1966; Freedman and Coombs 1966a, 1966b; Friedlander and Silver 1967; Easterlin 1968, 1969). Mincer (1963) shifted the emphasis of the economic approach from income effects to the effects on fertility of variation in the cost of children by showing that the opportunity cost of the wife's time as measured by the wife's wage rate was negatively related to fertility. The allocation of time between home and market and within the home was also discussed by Mincer (1962a), and a formal theory of time allocation was provided by Becker (1965). Becker's theory of time allocation has

25

were fostered because the neo-Malthusian proposition that increases in income tend to stimulate fertility conflicted with the facts that income growth has been accompanied by secular decline of fertility and that family income is inversely associated with cross-section fertility differentials in the industrialized countries.[2]

More fundamentally, economists have neglected fertility behavior because it has been difficult to incorporate it rigorously into the traditional theory of consumer choice. Recent extensions of economic theory to cope with human capital, allocation of time, and nonmarket household behavior now make possible the analysis of fertility as well as other traditionally demographic, sociological, and bio-medical aspects of behavior such as marriage, divorce, birth control, child-rearing practices, schooling, and health along with more conventional economic variables such as income, consumption, saving, and labor-force behavior within a unified choice-theoretic framework.

This framework might be called the "economic theory of the family." In it, the family is treated as a complex social institution in which the interdependent and overlapping life-cycle behavior of family members and the family unit as a whole is determined by the interaction of the preferences and capacities of its members with the social and economic environment they face currently and expect to face in the future. Clearly, no single tractable, intelligible, or testable model of the full range of family life-cycle behavior is yet feasible. At best, the present state of the economic theory of the family provides a framework within which a large class of models may be developed and their implications tested against one another as well as against hypotheses derived from other, more comprehensive theoretical frameworks.

I present a static economic theory of lifetime marital fertility within the context of this new economic approach to family behavior. The theoretical model is developed under a set of restrictive assumptions designed to make it analytically tractable and capable of yielding implications which may be tested with individual data on the number of children born to recent cohorts of American women who have completed their fertility. The model also has implications for child "quality," which is

---

heavily influenced models of fertility, child quality, and related aspects of household behavior by T. P. Schultz (1969), Nerlove and Schultz (1970), and Sanderson and Willis (1971), as well as a number of unpublished studies. Empirical tests in these studies lend support to Mincer's finding that increases in the cost of the wife's time tend to reduce fertility while the effect of income is more problematic.

[2] After World War II many of these countries experienced an upswing in fertility which, in the United States, is known as the postwar "baby boom." The U.S. birth rate peaked in 1957 and has followed a declining path since then to a current level lower than the previous minimum reach in the 1930s. The inverse association of income and cross-section fertility differentials also changed in the postwar period to a more U-shaped pattern in which the fertility of the middle-income classes tends to be lower than that of either the lowest or highest classes.

defined as a function of the resources parents devote to each child, and for the wife's lifetime market earnings capacity and labor supply.

1.   Fertility as a Form of Economic Behavior

A number of characteristics of fertility behavior have made it difficult to analyze fertility within a choice-theoretic framework: (1) Childbearing and child rearing are nonmarket activities in which there are few transaction prices to provide information to the outside observer about the cost of children to suppliers or the value of children to suppliers. Parents are both demanders and suppliers of children. (2) Children and competing household activities both require the expenditure of parental time in addition to money. (3) The parental obligation to a child tends to be a long-term one, extending, sometimes, beyond the parents' lifetimes. (4) The wide variation of parental expenditures of time and money on bearing and rearing children observed from family to family and culture to culture suggests that the parents' obligations to children do not entail an exogenously determined program of expenditures per child. Rather, within the scope of laws and mores, parents may exercise considerable discretion in their expenditures in an attempt to shape the characteristics and activities of children in accordance with parental desires. The concept of the cost of children contains unavoidable ambiguity unless discretionary expenditures on what may be termed "child quality" are explicitly included in the analysis. (5) The motives for having children may include both the direct satisfaction children are expected to provide their parents and the indirect satisfaction they may render by working in the household or family business or by remitting money income to their parents. Thus, fertility is motivated by consumption, saving, or investment considerations. (6) Parents cannot exercise direct control over the number and timing of children they will bear and rear to maturity. A couple may only attempt to influence the monthly probability of conception and, given conception, the probability that a pregnancy will terminate in a live birth. Similarly, the probability of survival of a child will depend on choices made by parents as well as on environmental conditions outside their control. Imperfect fertility control and child mortality and morbidity pose additional constraints on family fertility behavior and add further dimensions to family choice. (7) Finally, there are difficulties in defining the appropriate unit of analysis. Decisions to have children and decisions concerning age at marriage and the characteristics and preferences of the marital partners are closely intertwined. Moreover, as children mature, they may have an independent effect on family decisions.

The principal problem to be resolved in analyzing fertility as a form of economic behavior is how to define conceptually satisfactory measures of the costs and satisfactions of children to their parents in a manner consistent with the distinctive characteristics of fertility behavior just listed. The required measure of cost is one that corresponds to the concept of opportunity cost, that is, the value to parents of the opportunities foregone in having an additional child; and the required concept of satisfaction is one that specifies the characteristics of children that give rise to utility.

In order to focus on these problems in the simplest possible context, the theoretical model presented here abstracts from the sequential and stochastic nature of the family's economic and demographic life cycle. A one-period comparative static framework will be used in which a husband and wife of given ages and characteristics are considered to adopt, at the outset of marriage, a utility-maximizing lifetime plan for childbearing, for expenditures of time and money on children, and for other sources of parental satisfaction not related to children. The utility function being maximized reflects the tastes and preferences of all family members as they are taken into account by the husband and wife, who are assumed to make all family decisions. The couple will be assumed to have perfect and costless control over their fertility and to possess perfect foresight concerning all relevant demographic and economic variables over the course of their marriage, so that the lifetime plan adopted ex ante at marriage coincides with ex post observations of their completed fertility.

The new approach to consumer theory suggested by Lancaster (1966) and especially the pioneering work of Becker, Mincer, and others on the allocation of time and human capital provide a theoretical framework within which the costs and satisfactions of children to their parents may be formulated in a more satisfactory way than is possible within the conventional theory of consumer choice.[3] Becker (1965) and Lancaster (1966) argue that a family's utility is not received directly from its consumption of market goods or leisure, as it is in conventional models. Instead, Becker assumes that the family combines time supplied by family members with goods and services purchased in the market to produce within the household the more basic "commodities" which are the true objects of utility. For example, rather than assume that medical care is purchased because it yields satisfaction directly, it may be assumed that medical care along with other purchased goods and services, the individual's own time, and the time of other family members combine to produce the commodity "good health," which is the actual source of utility.[4]

In general, family utility is considered to be a function of a vector of nonmarketable, home-produced commodities such as good health, entertainment, nutrition, and, as I will suggest, satisfaction from children.

---

[3] For a survey of the application of these ideas to a variety of problems in the field of human resources, see T. W. Schultz (1972a).

[4] See Grossman (1972a) for an application of this analysis to the demand for health. He analyzes health both as as a consumption and as an investment commodity.

This utility function, whose properties reflect the family's tastes or preferences, is defined by Becker on the n vector of commodities Z and may be written as

$$U(Z) \qquad Z = (Z_i) \qquad i = 1, \ldots, n. \tag{1}$$

It is assumed that the family will behave as if it attempts to maximize (1) subject to its limited capacity to produce Z_i.

The validity of this assumption has been discussed by Samuelson (1956). In general terms, a family may be regarded as a collection of individuals whose common welfare is a function of the utility of each of its v members so that in place of (1) we may write a Bergson-Samuelson "family welfare function" of the form

$$W = W(U^1, U^2, \ldots, U^v), \tag{2}$$

where the $U^j(j = 1, \ldots, v)$ is the level of utility of family member j. Assuming that the family attempts to maximize W, that $U^j = U^j(Z_{ij})$, and that

$$Z_i = \sum_j Z_{ij},$$

Samuelson proved that the family will behave as if it were an individual attempting to maximize (1). The condition $U^j = U^j(Z_{ij})$ implies that an individual family member's utility is independent of the level of utility of any other family member, and the condition

$$Z_i = \sum_j Z_{ij}$$

means that an additional unit of Z_i allocated to family member j must be subtracted from the consumption of other family members. Thus, Samuelson's proof that a family may be treated as if it were an individual maximizing a utility function such as (1) assumes no interdependency in utility among family members and no jointness in consumption.

But these are precisely the factors most responsible for the existence of the family as the predominant social institution in which individuals live. As Samuelson wrote (1956, pp. 9–10):

> Where the family is concerned the phenomenon of altruism in-
> evitably raises its head: if we can speak at all of the indifference
> curves of any one member, we must admit that his tastes and
> marginal rates of substitution are contaminated by the goods
> that other members consume. These Veblen-Duesenberry ex-
> ternal consumption effects are the essence of family life. They
> require us to build up an interpersonal theory that sounds more
> like welfare economics than like positive demand analysis. Such
> problems of home economics are, abstractly conceived, exactly

of the same logical character as the general problem of government and social welfare.

Samuelson's emphasis can be reversed, however. The family exists as an institution because, given altruism and the nonmarket mechanisms by which it is able to allocate commodities and welfare among its members, it has both the incentive and the capacity to resolve allocative problems involving public goods, externalities, and the like that in impersonal markets inevitably lead to market imperfections. The capacity of the family to resolve these problems efficiently provides a basis for a positive theory of family behavior, because, given efficient allocation, the family will tend to respond systematically to changes in the position or shape of the constraints it faces. Consequently, for many purposes, it may be assumed, as it is in this paper, that the family behaves as if it is attempting to maximize a utility function of the type in (1).

It is assumed in Becker's model that each of the commodities Z_i is produced according to a household production function with inputs of an m vector of market goods and services, x_i, and vector of time inputs, t_i, of the v family members. The set of household production functions, f^i, may be written

$$Z_i = f^i(t_i, x_i), \quad t_i \geqslant 0, x_i \geqslant 0,$$

$$t_i = (t_{ij}), \qquad j = 1, \ldots, v, \qquad (3)$$

$$x_i = (x_{ik}), \qquad k = 1, \ldots, m.$$

The properties of these household production functions may be said to be determined by the state of the family's consumption technology in exactly the same sense that the properties of conventional production functions of firms are said to be determined by the state of standard production technology.

It is natural, within this framework, to consider those characteristics of children that provide satisfaction (or dissatisfaction) to their parents as commodities produced with time and goods according to household production functions. The relevant dimensions of child characteristics and the processes by which parents may alter them are inherently complex matters about which there is much ignorance (especially among parents). Fortunately, the traditions of economics permit the economic actors to solve the difficult problems.

In this spirit, it is assumed that a couple may choose to bear up to a maximum of $\overline{N}$ children and that the vector of utility-generating characteristics of a given child may be aggregated into the commodity Q_i, which will be called the "quality" of the ith child. Each child's quality is produced according to a household production function of the form

$$Q_i = f^i(t_i, x_i), \qquad i = 1, \ldots, \overline{N}, \qquad (4)$$

where t_i and x_i are, respectively, vectors of purchased goods and family members' time devoted to the ith child.[5]

It is assumed that the marginal products of time and goods in the production of Q_i are positive but diminishing and that the ith child is born if $Q_i > 0$ and is averted if $Q_i = 0$, where the index i indicates the order of birth. The production functions for child quality imply that the parents may increase the satisfaction they derive from a given child by increasing the resources devoted to the child and that a given level of child quality may be obtained with alternative combinations of time and goods. The efficient or least-cost input combination will depend on the relative prices of time of individual family members and on the relative prices of market goods and services.

As specified in (4), the production functions for child quality need not be the same across birth orders. For example, the "technology" of producing child quality in the first child may differ from that appropriate to the second child because of interactions between the children, because parents may apply lessons learned from the first child to rearing the second child, or because some inputs are jointly productive for both children. Heterogeneity in technology implies that for a given set of input prices, the marginal costs of augmenting the Q_i may differ and that there will tend to be changes in their relative costs with respect to changes in relative input prices. This formulation also allows the Q_i to be imperfect substitutes or complements for one another in consumption, assuming that they enter as separate arguments into the family utility function. The effect of changes in the prices of time and goods or in the total resources of the family would, in general, result in changes in the input mix used to produce child quality, changes in the relative and absolute levels of quality of each child, and, most important from the standpoint of this study, changes in the number of children born.

The advantages of this rather general and flexible formulation of the problem of child quality are, for the purposes at hand, outweighed by the disadvantages of its analytical complexity and the lack of data necessary to place appropriate restrictions on the production functions for child quality or to test the implications of intuitively plausible restrictions. An analytically simpler specification which will prove to have testable implications is derived, given the following assumptions: (1) the production

---

[5] This concept of child quality need bear no connection with an outsider's judgment of the physical, intellectual, or personal characteristics of higher-quality compared with lower-quality children; it merely reflects the parents' judgment about the optimal quantity of resources to be devoted to each child. This disclaimer does not rule out the possibility that parents do affect the characteristics of their children or that child characteristics are unrelated to child quality. Indeed, an investigation of the connection between resources devoted to children and child characteristics would seem amply justified on empirical grounds (see, e.g., Wray 1971) and in terms of its relevance for the implications of policies designed to affect fertility. Some work in this direction has been done already by De Tray (1972a).

functions for child quality, f^i, are linearly homogeneous and identical, (2) there is no joint production of child quality,[6] and (3) parents choose an equal level of child quality for each child born.

Under these assumptions, the production function for the quality per child, Q, may be written as the linearly homogeneous function

$$Q = f(t_c/N, x_c/N), \tag{5}$$

where t_c and x_c are, respectively, the vectors of the total amount of time and goods devoted to all children during the parents' lifetime and N is the total number of children born, so that t_c/N and x_c/N are the amount of time and goods devoted to each child. Multiplying (5) by N, we may write

$$C = NQ = f(t_c, x_c), \tag{6}$$

where C, the total amount of child quality, will be called "child services."[7] It is assumed that N and Q enter as separate arguments into the family utility function.

In addition to utility derived from the number and quality of children, parents derive satisfaction from many other sources. These other sources of satisfaction which are unrelated to the number and quality of children will be expressed as the aggregate commodity, S, which is assumed to be produced according to the following linearly homogeneous household production function:

$$S = g(t_s, x_s), \tag{7}$$

where t_s and x_s are, respectively, vectors of time and goods devoted to S production. It is assumed that inputs to S do not jointly produce child quality. It should be noted that S embodies all sources of satisfaction to the husband and wife other than those arising from their children. Thus, the family utility function, which is written as

$$U = U(N, Q, S), \tag{8}$$

is a function of the number and quality of children as well as the parents' other sources of satisfaction.

The level of utility the family may achieve is limited by its capacity to produce C ($= NQ$) and S. Given its state of consumption technology as embodied in the properties of household production functions, the pro-

---

[6] There is joint production if a unit of time or goods devoted to the production of Q_i simultaneously increases or decreases the output of Q_j ($j \neq i$). See Grossman (1971) for a theoretical analysis of joint production in the household.

[7] A multiplicative treatment of quality-quantity relationships similar to that specified in eq. (6) is given, in the general case, by Theil (1952) and, for children, by Becker (1960). Neither, however, used the concept of a household production function as a basis for the relationship, nor did they consider time inputs. The more complex specification involving separate production functions for each child was adopted by Sanderson in a life-cycle model of fertility described in Sanderson and Willis (1971, pp. 34–42).

ductive capacity of the family is limited by its lifetime supplies of time and goods. The model is further simplified by assuming (1) that only the husband and wife contribute market earnings to family income,[8] (2) that only the wife's time is productive at home, and (3) that the structure of relative market prices remains fixed, so that the Hicks composite commodity theorem may be used to justify treating goods inputs as an aggregate good, x, with a price index, p.

Under these assumptions, the family's input of purchased goods is limited by its lifetime money income (or money wealth),

$$Y = px, \tag{9}$$

which, in turn, is equal to the sum of its nonlabor wealth, V, and the lifetime market earnings of the husband and wife. Since the husband's time is assumed unproductive at home, he will have an incentive to work "full time" in the market during marriage. His lifetime earnings and the family's nonlabor wealth together will be called the husband's lifetime income or wealth, H, and will be treated as an exogenous variable. The family's lifetime income and expenditure equation may be written as

$$Y = H + wL = px, \tag{10}$$

where w is the average hourly market wage received by the wife and L is the number of hours she works in the labor market during marriage. The amount of the wife's time available for home production, t, is equal to her life-span after marriage, T, minus (marital) lifetime hours of market work, L. Thus, the time constraint may be written

$$T = t + L, \tag{11}$$

where T is considered exogenous.

Since joint production of C and S is ruled out, it follows that a unit of goods or the wife's time devoted to C production must be subtracted from S production so that

$$x = x_c + x_s \tag{12}$$

and

$$t = t_c + t_x = \rho_c x_c + \rho_s x_s, \tag{13}$$

where x_c and t_c are inputs of goods and time to children, x_s and t_s are inputs of goods and time to S, and $\rho_c = t_c/x_c$ and $\rho_s = t_s x_s$ are, respectively, the time intensities of C and S production.

The structure of the model is completed by considering the determinants

---

[8] It is assumed, in other words, that children do not remit any money income to their parents. The lifetime earnings of children, which depend partly on the time and goods devoted to them by their parents, may be considered as a component of child quality (see De Tray 1972a).

of the wife's lifetime market earnings. Her average market wage, w (defined as equal to her lifetime earnings divided by her lifetime hours of work) is determined by an earnings (capacity) function of the form

$$w = w\,(L, \kappa),\tag{14}$$

where κ is a shift parameter which is assumed to increase w. The earnings function may be regarded as a reduced-form equation embodying the solution to the wife's optimal program of human capital accumulation for each possible level of her lifetime labor supply, L.[9] The parameter κ represents her initial stock of human capital at the outset of marriage (and an associated exogenous time rate of depreciation on that stock during marriage). The dependence of the wife's average wage on her lifetime labor supply reflects the interaction of the supply and demand for postmarital investments in human capital. Generally, it may be expected that $\partial w / \partial L = w_L$ will be positive. Thus, the return from any given postmarital investment which increases the wife's market earnings capacity increases with the number of hours she plans to work over her lifetime, so that the larger L is, the more likely investment is to be undertaken and the higher the wife's average wage will be.[10] An additional factor that would tend to make w_L positive is that "learning by doing" forestalls depreciation of the initial human capital stock or leads to its augmentation.[11] Since the wife's lifetime labor supply, L, is subject to choice, it follows that her average wage, w, is an endogenous variable in the model.[12]

[9] Compared with males, relatively little is known about the effects of investment in human capital on the market (or nonmarket) productivity of females, particularly in the post school and postmarital phases of the life cycle. Empirically, the life-cycle profile of male wage rates, particularly better-educated males, tends to rise quite steeply with age while the life-cycle profile of married women's wages tend to be much flatter, even for college-educated women. Strong theoretical and empirical support has been offered in favor of the hypothesis that the rising profile of male earnings is a function of labor market experience and investment in human capital, against the alternative hypothesis that it is merely caused by a maturation process (see, especially, the theoretical and empirical work of Mincer, particularly his 1970a paper and 1974b book and the theoretical work of Ben-Porath [1967] and Becker [1964, 1967]). The relative flatness of married female wage profiles is consistent with the human-capital interpretation of life-cycle wage rates because of their much lower levels of lifetime labor-force participation, because their periods of greatest participation are relatively late in the life cycle after childbearing, and because, with rapid growth of female labor-force participation across cohorts, cross-section age profiles are a progressively downward-biased approximation to the life-cycle profile of women of a given cohort. An interesting piece of evidence supporting this view is Fuchs's (1971) finding that the wage profile of single (never married) women, who have much higher participation rates than married women, has a shape closer to that of males than to that of married females. Whatever its past importance, it is likely that continued growth in the married female labor-force attachment will make postmarital investment in human capital of increasing importance in the future.

[10] See Lindsay (1971) for further discussion of a static, lifetime model of human capital and labor supply.

[11] Michael and Lazear (1971) emphasize this point, using the terminology "negative user cost" instead of learning by doing.

[12] The husband's earnings capacity could be similarly discussed. However, since his

The family's capacity to obtain satisfaction from the number and quality of its children and from S is limited by its consumption technology, its endowments of wife's time and nonlabor income, and the earnings capacities of the husband and wife. The constraint on the family's production and consumption of commodities may be written in implicit form as the production-possibility function

$$\phi\,(NQ, S, H, \kappa, T) = 0. \tag{15}$$

This function may be interpreted as follows. For preassigned levels of the exogenous variables H, κ, and T and for a preassigned output level of S, the production-possibility function gives the maximum attainable output of $NQ\,(= C)$.

The assumption that the production-possibility function is the relevant constraint on family behavior implies that the family allocates its resources optimally. The family allocates its resources between C and S production by choosing vectors of wife's time inputs (t^*_c, t^*_s) and market goods (x^*_c, x^*_s) corresponding to a commodity vector (N^*, Q^*, S^*) satisfying (15), that maximize the output of C for any given output of S. Like a small economy in a world of many countries, the family need not be self-sufficient. Although commodities N, Q, and S are nontradeable, the family does "export" the time of the husband and wife to the labor market and, in return, it "imports" goods from the market at terms of trade determined by market prices for labor and goods and by earnings capacities of husband and wife. Thus, the family must also choose the optimal supplies of wife's home time, t^*, and market goods, x^*, by choosing her optimal lifetime labor supply, L^*.[13] Finally, the optimal commodity vector (N^*, Q^*, S^*) is the one that maximizes the family utility function (8).

It is well known from the principle of duality that the optimal physical allocation of commodities and factors implies an optimal set of shadow prices which reflect the marginal opportunity costs of commodities and factors in consumption and production. The value of the family's real lifetime consumption or "full wealth," to use Becker's term, evaluated in terms of shadow prices of commodities is

$$I = \pi_c NQ + \pi_s S = \pi_c C + \pi_s S, \tag{16}$$

where I is full wealth and π_c and π_s are the shadow prices of C and S. In order to measure real rather than nominal full wealth, S is chosen as the numeraire commodity and π_s, its shadow price, is set equal to unity.

The duality between optimal consumption and production of N, Q, and S and the optimal shadow prices, π_c and π_s, is seen readily by noting that

---

lifetime hours of work are assumed to be exogenous, it follows that his lifetime program of human capital accumulation and lifetime income are also exogenous.

[13] Recall that the husband's time is assumed to be unproductive at home, so that it is "exported" to the labor market at any positive price.

the one-stage process of maximizing utility subject to the production-possibility function is equivalent to the two-stage process of (1) minimizing the "expenditure" of full wealth subject to production possibilities and (2) maximizing utility subject to the (minimum) full wealth constraint. By considering the optimization process in two stages rather than one, it is possible to analyze the supply and demand sides of family behavior separately even though they are determined simultaneously. The linkage between supply and demand is given by the family's full wealth, I, and the shadow price of children, π_c. In the second stage, the family demands for N, Q, and S may be derived as functions of I and π_c, and in the first stage, I and π_c may be expressed as functions of the exogenous variables H, κ, and T. For example, the effect of a change in husband's lifetime income on fertility may be analyzed by its effect on I and π_c and, in turn, the effect of these changes in I and π_c on demand for N.

My analysis of the theoretical structure will follow this two-stage scheme. Demand functions for N, Q, and S will then be derived subject to the full wealth constraint (sec. 2), followed by analysis of the properties of the production-possibility function and its implications for full wealth and the opportunity cost of children (sec. 3). In section 4, I examine the family's desired fertility and wife's lifetime labor supply in full (general) equilibrium of supply and demand. Finally, the empirical implications of the model will be considered and some tests of these implications with U.S. census data reported.

2. Fertility Demand and the Demand for Child Quality

The family's demand functions for number of children, child quality, and S may be written as follows:

$$N = N(I, \pi_c, \pi_s), \tag{17}$$

$$Q = Q(I, \pi_c, \pi_s), \tag{18}$$

$$S = S(I, \pi_c, \pi_s), \tag{19}$$

and, since $C = NQ$,

$$C = C(I, \pi_c, \pi_s) \quad = N(I, \pi_c, \pi_s)\, Q(I, \pi_c, \pi_s), \tag{20}$$

where the family's full wealth, I, and the shadow price of children, π_c, are treated as parameters and the shadow price of the parents' standard of living, π_s, is treated as a numeraire and set equal to 1. These demand functions are derived in Part A of the Mathematical Appendix by maximizing the family utility function (8) subject to its full-wealth constraint (16).

The first-order conditions for utility maximization in (A1) of the Mathematical Appendix may be solved for the Lagrange multiplier, $-\lambda$, to obtain the marginal equalities

$$-\lambda = \frac{U_N}{\pi_c Q} = \frac{U_Q}{\pi_c N} = \frac{U_S}{\pi_s}. \tag{21}$$

The interpretation of (21) is that the family equates the ratios of the marginal utilities of the number of children, quality per child, and parents' standard of living to its respective marginal costs, where $\pi_{cQ} = p_N$ is the marginal cost of an additional child of given quality, $\pi_{cN} = p_Q$ is the marginal cost of raising the quality per child given the number of children, and $\pi_s = 1$ is the marginal cost of the parents' standard of living. Thus, parents not only balance the satisfactions they receive from their children against those received from all other sources not related to children (satisfactions from S), but they also must decide whether to augment their satisfaction from children at the "extensive" margin by having another child or at the "intensive" margin by adding to the quality of a given number of children.

Because of the multiplicative relationship between the number and quality of children, there are interesting differences between the properties of the demand functions for N and Q and the properties of more conventional demand functions in which the commodities enter the budget constraint additively.[14] Let the wealth elasticities ϵ_N, ϵ_Q, ϵ_c, and ϵ_s be defined as the percentage change in N, Q, C, or S demanded per percentage increase in I, holding π_c constant. In the Mathematical Appendix, it is shown that

$$\alpha(\epsilon_N + \epsilon_Q) + (1 - \alpha)\epsilon_S = 1 \tag{A7}$$

and

$$\epsilon_C = \epsilon_N + \epsilon_Q, \tag{A8}$$

where $\alpha = \pi_c NQ/I$ is the share of I devoted to children. Becker (1960) speculated that all of these wealth elasticities are positive but that the quality elasticity, ϵ_Q, is likely to be substantially larger than the quantity elasticity, ϵ_N, because high-income families are observed to have only slightly larger or even smaller numbers of children than low-income families, but they tend to spend much more on each child. This conjecture,

[14] The discussion here will focus on the "observed" wealth and price elasticities of demand for N, Q, and S as distinguished from the "true" elasticities discussed herein by Becker and Lewis. The difference between the observed and true elasticities stems from the measure of wealth implied by the multiplicative model and the conventional measure implied by an additive model. To take the simplest case, suppose children are the only source of wealth, so that $I = \pi_c NQ$. Conventionally, a doubling of N and Q would be said to double full wealth and the wealth elasticities of N and Q would each be equal to unity. However, in order to double N and Q, I must be quadrupled so that the equiproportionate increase in N and Q resulting from a quadrupling of I results in observed wealth elasticities of one-half. I am grateful to Becker and Lewis for permitting me to see their notes on quality-quantity models and for helpful discussions which have greatly improved the treatment of quality and quantity in this paper. Any errors remaining are mine.

he pointed out, is also consistent with evidence that the quality elasticity of demand for consumer durables, such as automobiles, is generally found to be substantially higher than the quantity elasticity.

A theoretical basis for substantial differences in quality and quantity elasticities, given some propensity for tastes to be biased toward N or Q, lies in the fact that relative costs of N and Q do not remain constant when π_c is held constant unless N and Q change equiproportionately. Thus, the relative marginal costs of N and Q are $p_N/p_Q = \pi_c Q/\pi_c N = Q/N$. Assuming tastes are biased relatively toward Q, increases in I will tend to increase Q/N, thereby increasing the cost of numbers relative to quality of children, which induces a substitution effect toward Q and away from N. This is illustrated in figure 1, in which the initial equilibrium in the (N, Q)-plane is achieved at the tangency of the indifference curve, U_0, and the rectangular hyperbola, $C_0 = NQ$, at point a. Assume that an increase in income leads the family to increase its output of C to C_1 and that its new choice of N and Q is to the left of the ray Oad at point c. Had the relative costs of N and Q remained the same as they were at a, the new equilibrium point, remaining on the new indifference curve, U_1, would be at b rather than c, with a smaller consumption of Q and a larger consumption of N. It is even possible, in this case, for the wealth elasticity of number of children, ϵ_N, to be negative without N being, in the conventional sense, an inferior commodity.

The substitution effects on N and Q caused by changes in π_c, holding utility constant, also differ from those in demand functions derived from an additive constraint, because the marginal costs of N and Q, $p_N = Q\pi_c$ and $P_Q = N\pi_c$, cannot be varied independently.

In the Mathematical Appendix, it is shown in equation (A14) that $\eta_N + \eta_Q = \eta_C < 0$, where η_N, η_Q, and η_C are, respectively, the compensated

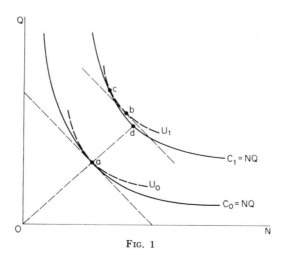

FIG. 1

substitution elasticities of N, Q, and C with respect to π_c.[15] It is possible, therefore, for an increase in π_c to increase either N or Q but not both. In equations (A19)–(A21) it is shown that η_N and η_Q may be expressed as follows under the pretense that p_N and p_Q may be varied independently:

$$\eta_N = \eta_{NN} + \eta_{NQ}, \eta_{NN} < 0;$$

$$\eta_Q = \eta_{QQ} + \eta_{NQ}, \eta_{QQ} < 0;$$

and

$$\eta_C = \eta_{NN} + 2\eta_{NQ} + \eta_{QQ} < 0,$$

where η_{NN} and η_{QQ} are own-substitution elasticities which measure the percentage change in N (or Q) caused by a given percentage change in p_N (or p_Q), holding utility, p_Q (or p_N), and p_S constant and where $\eta_{NQ} = \eta_{QN}$ are cross-substitution elasticities which measure the percentage change in N (or Q) caused by a given percentage change in p_Q (or p_N), also holding utility and the other prices constant. As η_{NQ} is positive or negative, N and Q are said to be substitutes or complements.

The signs of η_N and η_Q depend on whether N and Q are substitutes or complements and, if they are substitutes, on the relative magnitudes of the negative own effects, η_{NN} and η_{QQ}, and the positive cross effect, η_{NQ}. Since the issues to be resolved in order to derive hypotheses about the signs of η_N and η_Q depend on the nature of family tastes, economic theory as such has little to say. Some clues, however, may be found by judging the implications of alternative assumptions about η_{NN}, η_{QQ}, and η_{NQ} for the relationships among N, Q, and S in terms of their sociological and intuitive plausibility.

For example, if N and Q are complements, both η_N and η_Q would be negative. This would imply that an increase in π_c would reduce both N and Q and would increase S. This implication would be objectionable to those persons including Duesenberry (1960) and Blake (1968) who have argued that parents either cannot or will not choose child quality independently of their own standard of living. They argue, in effect, that Q and S should usually move in the same direction. The thrust of this argument may be accommodated by assuming that N and Q are substitutes and that η_{QQ} and η_{NQ} are roughly equal in absolute magnitude so that η_Q is near zero or even positive, which would imply, of course, that η_N is negative. This also implies that substitution in consumption between N and S is easier than between Q and S and, indeed, that Q and S are complements if η_Q is positive. This also seems consistent with the sociological argument.[16] These sociological considerations suggest the hypotheses that η_N is negative and that η_Q is small in magnitude and possibly positive.

---

[15] This result was first proved by Theil (1952).

[16] The following relationships hold between own elasticities and cross-elasticities of N with Q and S and of Q with N and S:

There is also an interesting implication of this analysis for the demographic impact of changes in the cost of fertility control. Willis (1971) shows that the (shadow) marginal cost of fertility control, π_f, defined as the additional fertility-control cost incurred per birth averted, acts as a per unit subsidy to childbearing. That is, a couple may reduce their fertility control costs by π_f by having an additional birth so that the full marginal cost of an additional child becomes $p_N = \pi_c Q - \pi_f$. This implies that a decrease in π_f caused by, say, an improvement in birth control technology will increase p_N, leaving p_Q and p_S unaffected. Thus, the effect of a change in π_f is

$$\frac{\partial N}{\partial \pi_f} = \frac{\partial N}{\partial p_N} \frac{\partial p_N}{\partial \pi_f},$$

which, in elasticity form, is

$$\eta_{Nf} = -\eta_{NN} \left(\frac{\pi_f}{\pi_c Q - \pi_f} \right).$$

If η_{NQ} is positive and η_N is negative, it follows that $|\eta_{NN}| > |\eta_N|$, so that a given percentage increase in p_N caused by an improvement in fertility control will cause a larger decrease in fertility than an equal change caused by an increase in π_c. Moreover, the effect of a given decrease in π_f will be larger the smaller $\pi_c Q$ is. While this may suggest that the demographic impact of improved birth control technology would be greatest among low-income groups, such a conclusion is unwarranted until it is known how the change in technology affects π_f in different income groups. It is beyond my scope here to explore the determinants of fertility-control costs which doubtless include a large element of psychic cost in addition to costs in time and money. Thus, for present purposes, let us revert to our former assumption of perfect and costless fertility control.

The results of the preceding analysis of the demand side of the theoretical model of fertility behavior suggest the hypothesis that the observed wealth elasticity of demand for the number of children, ϵ_N, is likely to be small and possibly negative even though N is not an inferior commodity in the conventional sense. The other main hypothesis, which resulted from a

$$\gamma(\eta_{NN} + \eta_{NQ}) + (1 - \gamma)\, \eta_{NS} = 0,$$

$$\gamma(\eta_{QQ} + \eta_{QN}) + (1 - \gamma)\, \eta_{QS} = 0,$$

where γ is the share of full wealth devoted to children and η_{NS} and η_{QS} are, respectively, the cross-elasticities of N and Q with respect to p_N and p_Q. Assume that $\eta_Q = \eta_{QQ} + \eta_{QN} = 0$. It follows that η_{QS} must also equal zero, indicating that there is no substitutability between Q and S. If η_Q is positive, it follows that Q and S are complements, since η_{NS} must then be positive. Since, in either of these cases, $\eta_N = \eta_{NN} + \eta_{NQ}$ must be negative, it follows that η_{NS} is positive, so that N and S are substitutes. I am indebted to Lewis for pointing out these implications to me.

combination of economic analysis and sociological considerations, is that the compensated effect of an increase in π_c, the opportunity cost of child services in terms of parents' standard of living, will tend to reduce fertility so that η_N is expected to be negative. The next step is to analyze the supply side of the model in order to derive the relationship between I and π_c and the exogenous variables H, κ, and T.

3. The Supply of Child Services and the Allocation of Time

The family's capacity to produce and consume N, Q, and S is given by its production-possibility function (eq. [15]). If (15) is the effective constraint on family behavior, the implication is that the supplies of wife's home time and market goods are allocated efficiently between the production of C ($=NQ$) and S, and that, through the family's choice of the level of the wife's lifetime labor supply, an optimal mix of the supplies of time and goods is achieved.

The duality between optimal allocation of resources and optimal shadow prices may be exploited to facilitate the analysis of the production-possibility function. It was noted earlier that the family may be considered to minimize the cost of its consumption by minimizing its "expenditures" of full wealth subject to the constraint of its production-possibilities function. The condition for minimum cost is

$$-\frac{dS}{dC} = \pi_c/\pi_s = \pi_c = \phi_c/\phi_s,$$

where $-(\partial S/\partial C)$ is the opportunity cost of an additional unit of C in terms of the amount of S foregone, ϕ_c/ϕ_s is the marginal rate of transformation along the production-possibility function, and $\pi_c/\pi_s = \pi_c$ is equal to the marginal rate of substitution in consumption between S and C.

Efficient allocation of family resources depends on the fulfillment of certain marginal productivity conditions. Because the production functions for C and S, (6) and (7), are assumed to be linearly homogeneous functions of inputs of wife's time and market goods, the marginal products of these two factors are functions solely of the input ratios or time intensities, $\rho_c = t_c/x_c$ and $\rho_s = t_s/x_s$. Thus, (6) and (7) may be written as $C = x_c F(\rho_c)$ and $S = x_s G(\rho_s)$, where their first derivatives, F' and G', are positive and their second derivatives, F'' and G'' are negative, indicating that the marginal product of wife's time is positive but diminishing.

Production within the home will be optimized when the value of the marginal product (VMP) of each factor is equal to its shadow price and when the ratio of the marginal products of the two factors in the production of each commodity is equal to the ratio of shadow factor prices. These conditions permit the addition of three equations to the model. The shadow price of the wife's time is equal to the VMP of her time in the production of C and S:

$$\hat{w} = \pi_c F' = G'; \tag{22}$$

the VMP of market goods is

$$\hat{p} = \pi_c(F - \rho_c F') = G - \rho_s G' = 1; \tag{23}$$

and the ratios of the marginal products of time and goods are equal to the ratio of the shadow factor prices,

$$\frac{\hat{w}}{\hat{p}} = \hat{w} = \frac{F'}{F - \rho_c F'} = \frac{G'}{G - \rho_c G'} , \tag{24}$$

where S is taken to be the numeraire commodity, so that $\pi_s = 1$, and the market and shadow prices of market goods, p and $\hat{p}$, are also set equal to 1.

Since $\pi_s = \hat{p} = p = 1$, the family's full wealth and the opportunity cost of children, π_c, are measured in dollars of constant purchasing power and the wife's shadow price of time, $\hat{w}$, is measured in dollars per hour, the same unit in which her market wage is measured. The wife's price of time, $\hat{w}$, plays a central role in the allocation of her time between home and market, in the allocation of resources within the home, and through its relationship with π_c, in the division of consumption among the number of children, child quality, and other sources of satisfaction.

The linkage between $\hat{w}$ and π_c is provided by the famous Stolper-Samuelson theorem, which states that there will be a one-to-one monotonic correspondence between factor and commodity prices in a two-factor (time and goods), two-commodity (children and standard of living) general-equilibrium system if the following conditions are met: (a) the commodity production functions are linearly homogeneous, (b) the factor intensities (factor-input ratios) of the two commodities differ, and (c) the sign of the factor-intensity ordering is invariant over all possible values of the factor-price ratio (see Stolper and Samuelson 1941). If condition (c) fails to hold and there exist so-called factor-intensity reversals, the monotonicity of the correspondence between factor and product prices will be destroyed. In this case, the Stolper-Samuelson theorem will hold locally, with the sign of the change in factor prices caused by a change in product prices (or vice versa) depending on the difference in factor intensities prevailing in that locality.[17]

In terms of the present model, (a) has already been assumed to be true and (c) will be satisfied if $\rho_c \neq \rho_s$ for all possible values of $\hat{w}$. The Stolper-Samuelson theorem implies that the elasticity of π_c with respect to $\hat{w}$ is

[17] See Samuelson (1949) for a discussion of factor-intensity reversals.

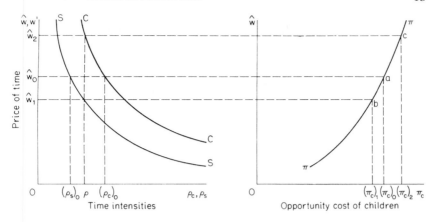

FIG. 2

$e = k_c [(\rho_c - \rho_s)/\rho_c]$, where $k_c = \hat{w}t_c/(\hat{w}t_c + \hat{p}x_c)$ is the share of wife's time cost in the total cost of children and $(\rho_c - \rho_s)/\rho_c$ is the percentage difference in the time intensities of C and S.[18] Since it is the product of two terms, each smaller than 1 in absolute value, e must also be smaller than unity in absolute value. On the basis of evidence cited later, it is assumed that children are more time intensive than S (i.e., $\rho_c > \rho_s$), so that e is positive and increases in $\hat{w}$ will tend to increase π_c.

The relationships between factor intensities, ρ_c and ρ_s, and the shadow factor and commodity prices, $\hat{w}$ and π_c, may be illustrated by a diagram introduced by Samuelson (1949). In the left panel of figure 2, the "substitution curve," CC, plots the locus of points satisfying $\hat{w} = F'/(F - \rho_c F')$ in (24). Curve CC slopes downward because, as the wife's price of time rises, the family switches to progressively less time-intensive methods of producing C, so that ρ_c falls as $\hat{w}$ increases. The elasticity of CC is equal to σ_c, the elasticity of substitution of the C production function. If time and goods must be used in fixed proportion ($\sigma_c = 0$), CC is vertical; if t_c and x_c are perfect substitutes ($\sigma_c = \infty$), CC is horizontal; and if they are imperfect substitutes ($0 < \sigma_c < \infty$), CC will slope downward as drawn.[19]

[18] This elasticity is derived by forming a simultaneous system from (22)–(24) in which π_c, ρ_c, and ρ_s are endogenous and $\hat{w}$ is treated as exogenous. Totally differentiating this system, the solution

$$\frac{\partial \pi_c}{\partial \hat{w}} = \rho_c - \rho_s$$

is obtained, which is written in elasticity form in the text.

[19] It should be emphasized that t_c is the wife's own time and that purchased time such as that of a babysitter is a component of purchased market goods, x_c. Since CC is not horizontal, it is implied that purchased time is an imperfect substitute for a

A similar substitution curve for S production, satisfying $\hat{w} = G'/(G - \rho_s G')$ in (24), is indicated by the curve SS. It is everywhere drawn to the left of CC to conform to the assumption that children are more time intensive than S, and its elasticity is equal to σ_s. The diagram is completed with the Stolper-Samuelson relationship, drawn as the inelastic, positively sloped curve, $\pi\pi$, in the right panel of figure 2. It slopes upward because of the assumption that $\rho_c > \rho_s$. Since (24) requires that $\hat{w}$ be equal in C and S production, it can be seen that each level of the price of time (e.g., $\hat{w}_0$) corresponds to a pair of optimal time intensities [e.g., $(\rho_c)_0$ and $(\rho_s)_0$] and to a given value of the opportunity cost of children [e.g., $(\pi_c)_0$].[20]

The allocation of the wife's time between home production $(t = t_c + t_s)$ and market work $(L = T - t)$ depends on the opportunity cost of an additional hour of market work in terms of the value of home production foregone. Assume, for the moment, that the wife may work any number of hours during marriage at a constant wage rate, w', and that her price of time when she does no market work $(L = 0)$ is $\hat{w}_0$ in figure 2. If $w' < \hat{w}_0$, it will be optimal for the wife to supply no market labor, because the dollar value of commodity production sacrificed by withdrawing an hour of her time from direct input into home production exceeds the gain from the added goods input obtained from her additional market earnings. If $w' > \hat{w}_0$, optimality requires that she supply labor to the market until ρ_c and ρ_s are reduced sufficiently to raise her price of time at home to equality with her market wage. Thus, the weak inequality

$$\hat{w} \geq w' \tag{25}$$

may be added to the model.

It was argued earlier that the wife's lifetime market earnings capacity depends on her initial stock of human capital at the outset of marriage, κ, and on the additional human capital she accumulates during marriage through postmarital investment, which, in turn, is an increasing function of her lifetime labor supply, L, so that her lifetime earnings are $wL = w(L, \kappa) L$, where w is her average lifetime wage and $w(L, \kappa)$ is her earnings (capacity) function specified in (14). The value of an additional hour of work during marriage, which is called the marginal wage rate, w', is given by the first derivative of wL with respect to L as follows:

---

wife's time in raising children. It should also be pointed out that k_c, the share of wife's time in the total cost of children, will increase with $\hat{w}$ if $\sigma_c < 1$, will decrease if $\sigma_c > 1$, and will remain constant if $\sigma_c = 1$. Analogous remarks also pertain to S production.

[20] Time-intensity reversals, which would disrupt the one-to-one correspondence between π_c and $\hat{w}$ and change the sign of e, may be visualized in fig. 1 by imagining CC and SS to intersect at one or more points. Given that $\rho_c > \rho_s$ at, say, the median level of $\hat{w}$ in a population, the likelihood of a reversal depends on the magnitude of $\rho_c - \rho_s$, the difference between σ_c and σ_s, and the range of variation of $\hat{w}$ in the population. If there is one reversal (intersection), it will occur below the median $\hat{w}$ if $\sigma_c < \sigma_s$ and above the median if $\sigma_c > \sigma_s$; π_c will be negatively related to $\hat{w}$ for sufficiently low $\hat{w}$ in the former case and for sufficiently high $\hat{w}$ in the latter case.

$$w' = w + w_L L, \tag{26}$$

where w_L reflects the increased earnings capacity the wife finds it worth-while to acquire when her lifetime labor supply increases. Since she will stop investing if increasing costs or diminishing returns are sufficient to reduce her average wage with further investment, w_L must be greater than or equal to zero.[21]

Optimal allocation of time between home and market requires the wife to adjust her lifetime labor supply so as to equate her price of time, $\hat{w}$, and her marginal wage, w'. This implies that her price of time will tend to exceed her average wage and, more importantly, that the price of time will tend to be an endogenous variable, dependent on the choice of L. The change in w' with respect to L is $w'' = 2w_L + w_{LL}L$. For low levels of the labor supply, w'' will be positive and w' will be an increasing function of L. If the average wage has a maximum, however, the marginal wage will reach a maximum before this point and begin declining while the average is still rising. Thus, w'' may become zero or negative for sufficiently large values of L.

The production-possibility function (15) is determined by the simultaneous solution of the set of equations embodying the household production functions for C and S, the time and goods constraints, the wife's earnings function, and the conditions for efficient allocation of time and goods within the home and efficient allocation of the wife's time between home production and market work. Gathering these equations together and renumbering them for convenience, we can determine the family's production-possibility function by the following 10 equations and one weak inequality:

$$C = x_c F(\rho_c), \tag{27.1}$$

$$S = x_s G(\rho_s), \tag{27.2}$$

$$T = L + \rho_c x_c + \rho_s x_s, \tag{27.3}$$

$$px = x = H + wL, \tag{27.4}$$

$$x = x_c + x_s, \tag{27.5}$$

$$\pi_c F' = G' = \hat{w}, \tag{27.6}$$

$$\pi_c(F - \rho_c F') = G - \rho_s G' = p = 1, \tag{27.7}$$

$$\hat{w} = \hat{w}/\hat{p} = \frac{F'}{F - \rho_c F'} = \frac{G'}{G - \rho_s G'}, \tag{27.8}$$

[21] It is possible for w_L to be negative if physical and mental strain from long hours of work reduce the average wage associated with a given stock of human capital. Such positive "user costs" are the converse of the negative user costs stemming from learning by doing which were mentioned earlier (n. 11 above).

$$w = w\,(L, \kappa) \tag{27.9}$$

$$w' = w + w_L L, \tag{27.10}$$

$$\hat{w} \geqslant w'. \tag{27.11}$$

The endogenous variables of the model are: $C =$ output of child services, $S =$ output of all other sources of satisfaction, $L =$ lifetime labor supply of wife after marriage, $x =$ total quantity of market goods, $x_c =$ goods used in C, $x_s =$ goods used in S, $\rho_c = t_c/x_c =$ time goods ratio in C production, $\rho_s = t_s/x_s =$ time goods ratio in S production, $w =$ wife's average lifetime market wage, $w' =$ wife's marginal lifetime market wage, $\hat{w} =$ wife's shadow price of time or home wage, and $\pi_c = \pi_c/\pi_s =$ marginal opportunity cost or shadow price of child services.

The exogenous variables are: $H =$ the husband's lifetime income, $\kappa =$ the wife's stock of human capital at the outset of marriage, and $T =$ the life-span of the wife after marriage.

The following market and shadow prices are set equal to unity: $p =$ the market price of goods, $\hat{p} =$ the shadow price of goods, and $\pi_s =$ the shadow price of S.

The system (27.1)–(27.11) constitutes a household-level general-equilibrium system whose properties depend on whether or not the wife works in the labor market. If she does work (i.e., $L > 0$), $\hat{w} = w'$ in (27.11) and the general-equilibrium system is composed of 11 equations, (27.1)–(27.11), in 12 unknowns (C, S, L, x, x_c, x_s, ρ_c, ρ_s, w, w', $\hat{w}$, and π_c). If the wife does not work (i.e., $L = 0$), (27.11) becomes the strong inequality $\hat{w} > w'$ and equations (27.9) and (27.10) become irrelevant. In this case, the system is composed of eight equations, (27.1)–(27.8), in nine unknowns (C, S, x, x_c, x_s, ρ_c, ρ_s, $\hat{w}$, and π_c). In either case, the number of unknowns exceeds the number of equations by one. This degree of freedom represents the scope of family choice: given the family's choice of the level of C (or S), the level of S (or C) and the equilibrium values of the other endogenous variables will be determined simultaneously. The system is closed in the full model by the family's choice of the utility-maximizing combination of C ($= NQ$) and S. For now, the system may be closed by treating S as a parameter in order to focus attention on the supply side of the model.

The two general-equilibrium systems, (27.1)–(27.11) if the wife works and (27.1)–(27.8) if she does not work, may be solved for the equilibrium values of each of the endogenous variables as functions of the exogenous variables of the system: H, κ, and T if the wife works and H and T if she does not. The properties of these "reduced form" equations depend on the properties of the "structural" equations of the general-equilibrium systems, particularly the properties of the household production functions for C and S in (27.1) and (27.2) and the earnings-capacity function of the wife in (27.9).

Among the reduced-form equations, the most important are the production-possibility functions which constrain the family's consumption possibilities and subject to which the family attempts to maximize its utility. If the value of the wife's time at home exceeds her marginal market wage so that she does no market work, the production-possibility function may be written in implicit form as

$$C = K(S, H, T) \tag{28}$$

and will be called the K-type constraint. If the wife's marginal market wage is sufficient to cause her to enter the labor market, the production-possibility function may be written in implicit form as

$$C = J(S, H, \kappa, T) \tag{29}$$

and will be called the J-type constraint. Taken together, the K- and J-type constraints constitute the constraint on household consumption and production possibilities over all possible values of the exogenous variables H, κ, and T. The full constraint may be written

$$0 = \phi(NQ, S, H, \kappa, T) = \begin{cases} -C + K(S, H, T); & \hat{w} > w' \\ -C + J(S, H, \kappa, T); & \hat{w} = w' \end{cases}. \tag{30}$$

The condition for the family to face a K-type constraint (i.e., $\hat{w} > w'$) is also the condition for the wife to remain out of the labor force (i.e., $L = 0$); conversely, the condition for the family to face a J-type constraint (i.e., $\hat{w} = w'$) is also the condition for the wife to participate in the labor force (i.e., $L > 0$). Thus, the properties of the constraint faced by the family are determined simultaneously with the wife's labor-force participation decision. Since $\hat{w}$ and w' are also endogenous variables, it follows that the participation decision will be a function of the exogenous variables H, κ, and T and the family's choice of S (and C).

Let us define the wife's lifetime labor-force participation function as

$$R = R(S, H, \kappa, T), \tag{31}$$

where $R = 0$ if $\hat{w} > w'$ and $R = 1$ if $\hat{w} = w'$. If the wife is out of the labor force, her price of time, $\hat{w}$, is determined by values of S, H, and T, and at $L = 0$, the value of her (potential) marginal wage rate, w', is simply an increasing function of her initial human capital stock, κ. Consequently, for given values of S, H, and T, the larger κ is, the more likely it will be that $R = 1$ and that the family will face a J-type constraint. It will be shown shortly that $\hat{w}$ is an increasing function of H, a decreasing function of T, and, provided that children are more time intensive than S, a decreasing function of S. It follows that R is more likely to equal 1 and that the family is more likely to face a J-type constraint, *ceteris paribus*, the smaller H is and the larger T and S are. If R is interpreted as a continuous cumulative probability function (e.g., $0 \leqslant R \leqslant 1$) rather than as a dichotomous step function, this discussion implies the following signs for the partial derivatives of R: $R_S > 0$, $R_H < 0$, $R_\kappa > 0$, and $R_T > 0$.

The shape of the production-possibility function ϕ in (30) and the manner in which its shape and position change when the exogenous variables H, κ, and T change depend on whether the wife participates in the labor market and, if she does work, on whether her marginal market wage is a constant or varies with her lifetime labor supply because of post-marital investment in human capital. The slope of ϕ at any given point, $\partial C/\partial S = -(1/\pi_c)$, measures the reciprocal of the opportunity cost of children.[22] The shape of ϕ in the neighborhood of a given point depends on the sign of the second partial derivative, $\phi_{SS} = (1/\pi_c)^2/(\partial \pi_c/\partial S)$, which measures the change in the opportunity cost of children, π_c, given a change in S along the production-possibility curve. As ϕ_{SS} is negative, zero, or positive, the curve will be concave, linear, or convex to the origin. The amount by which ϕ shifts, given a change in H, κ, or T, is measured by the first partial derivatives, ϕ_H, ϕ_κ, and ϕ_T, and the change in its slope (i.e., the change in π_c) by the second partials, ϕ_{SH}, $\phi_{S\kappa}$, and ϕ_{ST}.

These first and second partial derivatives of ϕ are derived in Parts B and C of the Mathematical Appendix for three forms of the production-possibility function: (i) the K-type constraint (wife does not work); (ii) the J^*-type constraint (wife works at a constant marginal wage, w'); and (iii) the J-type constraint (wife works and her marginal wage, w', varies with her lifetime labor supply, L). The shapes of the K-, J^*-, and J-type constraints are determined, respectively, by the signs of the second partial derivatives, K_{SS}, J^*_{SS}, and J_{SS}, in (C9), (C14), and (C18) in the Mathematical Appendix. In what follows, these results are interpreted diagrammatically.

If the wife does not work, the family's total supplies of goods and time are fixed (i.e., $x = H$, $t = T$) and the K-type production-possibility curve has the conventional "bowed-out" shape of $K_0a'K_0$ in figure 3 if it is assumed that the time intensities, ρ_c and ρ_s, are not equal. The reason for the bowed-out shape and its connection with the opportunity cost of children, the wife's price of time, and her labor supply may be explained with the aid of figure 2.

Since the slope of $K_0a'K_0$ at any given point is equal to $-\pi_c$, it can be seen that the upper and lower limits of π_c correspond, respectively, to the slope of the constraint at the maximum output of C and at the maximum output of S. Let $\rho = t/x = T/H$ (in fig. 2) be the ratio of the total supplies of time and goods corresponding to the fixed-resource endowment underlying $K_0a'K_0$ in figure 3. Each point on $K_0a'K_0$ must satisfy $\rho = k\rho_c + (1 - k)\rho_s$, where $k = x_c/x$ is the share of goods devoted to children. The output of C along $K_0a'K_0$ ranges from zero when $k = 0$ and $\rho = \rho_s$

---

[22] For ease of interpretation, the production-possibility curves in fig. 3 have been drawn with C on the horizontal axis so that their slopes are $\partial S/\partial C = -\pi_c$.

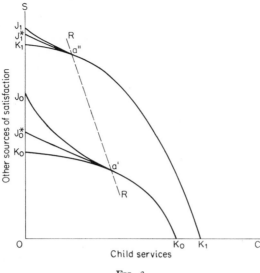

FIG. 3

to a maximum when $k = 1$ and $\rho = \rho_c$. If $\rho_c > \rho_s$, as is assumed in figure 2, the price of time ranges from a minimum of $\hat{w}$, when $\rho = \rho_s$, to a maximum of $\hat{w}_2$, when $\rho = \rho_c$, because relatively more goods and less time are released from S production than can be reabsorbed in increasing C production at existing levels of ρ_c and ρ_s. Consequently, both ρ_c and ρ_s must fall, implying that $\hat{w}$ must rise as C increases and, because the cost of time is more important in C than in S, that the opportunity cost of children must increase as well from a minimum of $(\pi_c)_1$ to a maximum of $(\pi_c)_2$. Had it been assumed, instead, that $\rho_c < \rho_s$, the price of time would decrease as the output of C increased, but π_c would still increase because the cost of goods would be relatively more important in C than in S.

While the hypothesis that children are relatively time intensive has some intuitive appeal, its most important support is its consistency with the negative relationship between the number of children in the household and the labor-force participation rates and hours of work of married women which has been found in many empirical studies of female labor-force behavior (e.g., Mincer 1962*a;* Cain 1966; Bowen and Finegan 1969). The wife's labor-force participation decision depends on whether her marginal wage, w', exceeds her price of time, $\hat{w}$, at $L = 0$. From figure 2, it can be seen that the wife will never work if w' is less than the lower limit of the price of time, $\hat{w}_1$; that she will always do some market work if w' exceeds the upper limit of the price of time, $\hat{w}_2$; and that if w' falls within these limits, the participation decision depends on the value of $\hat{w}$ implied by the family's choice of C and S. If children were assumed to be relatively goods intensive, this would imply, *ceteris paribus,* that childless women would have the lowest participation rates and that, as C increases and $\hat{w}$ declines, participation rates would rise. Of course, these implications are counterfactual. If, conversely, children are assumed to be relatively time intensive, the predicted negative relationship between C ($=NQ$) and the wife's labor supply is consistent with the negative relationship between N and the labor supply if an increase in N is not wholly offset by a decrease in Q.[23]

The form of the constraint faced by the family depends on the wife's labor-force participation decision. If she does participate, the shape of the J-type constraint depends on the relationship between her marginal market wage, w', and her lifetime labor supply, L, implied by the properties of her lifetime earnings function (14) and on the negative relationship between C and L implied by the assumption that children are relatively time intensive. The family faces a K-type constraint over the full range of its production possibilities if the wife's marginal market wage is less than her minimum price of time corresponding to $C = 0$ and $\rho = \rho_s$; it faces a J^*- or J-type constraint over the full range if w' exceeds her maximum $\hat{w}$ when $S = 0$ and $\rho = \rho_c$, and it faces a mixed constraint if $\hat{w}_{min} < w' < \hat{w}_{max}$.

Two mixed constraints are illustrated in figure 3 by $K_0a'J^*_0$ and $K_0a'J_0$, each of which is tangent to the K-type constraint $K_0a'K_0$ at point a'. Point a' in figure 3 is assumed to correspond to point a in figure 2 so that the common slope of the three production-possibility curves at a' is assumed to equal $(\pi_c)_0$ at point a. It is implied from figure 2 that the time/goods ratios correspond to points a' and are $(\rho_c)_0$ and $(\rho_s)_0$ and that the wife's price of time is $\hat{w}_0$. Point a' is a point of mutual tangency if it is assumed that point a corresponds to the threshold value of the wife's labor-force participation function R in (31) such that (i) the wife is not working ($L = 0$) and (ii) her price of time is equal to her marginal market wage ($\hat{w}_0 = w'_0$).

If the family chooses relatively large outputs of C to the right of a', the price of time rises above w'_0, the wife remains out of the labor force, and the family faces a K-type constraint over the segment $a'K_0$. If it

[23] Two results of recent research on married women's labor supply bear on the model of this paper. Leibowitz (1972) has found that additional young children cause more highly educated women to withdraw from the labor force more than do women with less education. One explanation for this might be that the more highly educated women have children of higher quality, so that a given increase in N causes a larger increase in C for them than for the less educated women. Smith (1972a), using a different body of data and a somewhat different empirical technique, was unable to obtain Leibowitz's result. The second result, obtained by Smith and by Landsberger (1971), among others, is that, *ceteris paribus*, the negative effect of additional children on the wife's labor supply is attenuated as the children age, becoming possibly positive for teen-age children. This suggests the hypothesis that children become relatively less time intensive as they age, eventually becoming relatively goods intensive. While this hypothesis cannot be incorporated into the static, lifetime framework of the present model, it was incorporated by Warren Sanderson into a dynamic life-cycle model of fertility behavior described in Sanderson and Willis (1971).

chooses relatively small outputs of C to the left of a', the price of time tends to fall below w'_0, which leads the wife to withdraw time from home production in order to supply labor to the market. If her marginal wage remains constant at w'_0, the opportunity cost of children must also remain constant at $(\pi_c)_0$, so that the constraint is the linear segment $a'J*_0$ in figure 3. The amount by which $a'J*_0$ lies above $K_0a'K_0$ and to the left of a' in figure 3 represents the "gains from trade" to the family from "exporting" the wife's time to the labor market in order to "import" additional market goods.

Postmarital investment in human capital opens the possibility of additional gains from trade through improvements in the wife's lifetime earnings capacity as illustrated by the "bowed-in" segment of the constraint, $a'J_0$, to the left of point a' in figure 3. As the output of C decreases to the left of point a', the wife's optimal labor supply and optimal investment in human capital both increase, causing w' to rise above w'_0. As long as w' is an increasing function of L (i.e., $w'' = 2w_L + w_{LL}L > 0$), the price of time and the opportunity cost of children will decrease as the output of C increases, causing the J-type constraint to be convex to the origin as it is in figure 3. At a sufficiently high level of the labor supply, it is possible that w' will reach a maximum and begin to decrease with further increases in L (i.e., $w'' \leqslant 0$). In this case, not depicted in figure 3, the J-type constraint will have an inflection point and become concave to the origin as C becomes sufficiently small.

The family's desired levels of fertility, child quality, and the parents' standard of living depend on the interaction of the family's tastes and on the constraints that it faces. More precisely, the family's optimal consumption of N, Q, and S and the production of C ($=NQ$) and S are determined simultaneously by maximizing utility subject to the production-possibility constraint. The solution of this household-level general-equilibrium system implies, simultaneously, solutions for the wife's optimal labor supply and postmarital investment in human capital and optimal lifetime allocations of her home time and market goods between C and S production.

The solution of this household-level general-equilibrium system may be expressed as a set of reduced-form equations relating the optimal quantity of each of the endogenous variables of the model to the values of the exogenous variables. This set of equations consists of (1) a set of final consumption demand functions for N, Q, C ($=NQ$), and S, (2) a set of derived input demand functions for t, t_c, t_s, x, x_c, and x_s, (3) a derived labor supply function for L, and (4) a threshold function for the wife's labor-force participation, R. Each of these is a function of the exogenous variables H, κ, and T.

The hypotheses about family behavior that can be derived from this model are embodied in the properties of these reduced-form demand and supply functions. These properties depend, in turn, on the form of the constraint faced by the family and on the hypotheses about the nature of the family, its goals, and the capacities of its members which are embedded in the specification of the utility function, household production functions, and earnings functions.

According to the model, changes in family behavior are in response to changes in the family's lifetime economic circumstances resulting from a change in the husband's lifetime income, H, the wife's initial stock of human capital, κ, or her lifespan after marriage, T. Changes in these variables (1) change the family's full wealth, I, by shifting the production-possibility curve, (2) change the opportunity cost of children, π_c, by changing its slope, and (3) if the wife's labor-force status is altered, change the form of the constraint the family faces from a K- to a J^*- or J-type constraint or vice versa. It follows that the effect of a change in a given exogenous variable on each endogenous variable may be resolved into the sum of a wealth effect caused by a change in I and a substitution effect caused by a change in π_c. The effect of changes in the exogenous variables on I and π_c depends on the form of the production-possibility function in the neighborhood of the initial equilibrium. Because of this, the form of the demand and supply functions depends on the value of the wife's labor-force participation function, R, which determines whether the family faces a K-type or a J^*- or J-type constraint. Since R is also determined by the values of the exogenous variables, the participation function is an integral part of the demand and supply functions.

In the next section, the empirical hypotheses for family fertility behavior implied by the model will be developed in detail. The same line of analysis may also be used to obtain the empirical implications of the model for other aspects of family behavior, such as the demand for child quality or the derived demand for time or goods inputs to children.

4.   Desired Fertility and Wife's Labor-Force Participation

The theoretical model of family behavior presented in this paper implies the following model of fertility demand:

$$N = \begin{cases} N^0(H, T) & \text{if} \quad R = 0 \\ N^1(H, \kappa, T) & \text{if} \quad R = 1 \end{cases},$$

$$R = R(S^0(H, T), H, \kappa, T), \tag{32}$$

where N^0 is the family's demand function for number of children if the wife does not work ($R = 0$) and the family faces a K-type demand function; N^1 is the fertility demand function if the wife does work ($R = 1$) and the family faces a J- or J^*-type constraint; and R is the wife's labor-force participation function in which the demand function for S under a K-type constraint, $S^0(H, T)$, has been substituted for S in (31). Before the properties of N^0, N^1, and R are investigated, (32) will be reformulated more suitably for empirical purposes.

Although the theoretical model has concentrated on a single hypothetical family, its empirical implications must be tested with data on a population of families. This population may be considered to be made up of a mixture of families, some proportion of whom face a J^*- or J-type constraint and the remaining proportion of whom face a K-type constraint. Since the demand relationships, N^1 and N^0, between fertility and measures of H, κ, and T are expected to differ in the two groups because of differences in the properties of the J- or J^*- and K-type constraints, it may seem tempting to test for these differences by comparing the estimated relationships from a sample of families containing nonworking wives with those from a sample containing working wives.

Unfortunately, this straightforward procedure is valid only under the highly implausible assumptions that each family has identical tastes and consumption technology, that each wife has an identical earnings function, and that there are no accidental births. Otherwise, the sampling procedure tends to select families by their tastes for children, contraceptive efficacy, and so on because, *ceteris paribus*, those women who have more children are also less likely to work. Moreover, since the labor-force participation function, R, in (32) is a function of H, κ, and T, the degree of selectivity will depend on which portion of (H, κ, T)-space is being considered. For example, women with high potential market wage rates (high levels of κ) may work even though their families desire more children than the average family in the same circumstances, while women with lower κ and the same strong taste for children do not work. Thus, the proportion of families with above-average tastes for children in the sample containing working wives will tend to be positively correlated with κ, *ceteris paribus*, even though the taste for children is uncorrelated with κ in the population as a whole.

An alternative approach is to consider the form of the relationship between N and the exogenous variables H, κ, and T that would be expected on the basis of the model of individual fertility behavior in (32) if the relationship were estimated with data on a sample of families containing both working and nonworking wives. Again, the sample population may be considered to contain a mixture of families, of which some proportion faces a J^*- or J-type constraint and the remaining proportion faces a K-type constraint. The proportion of the two groups in the population as whole are, respectively, $\bar{R}$ and 1-$\bar{R}$, where $\bar{R}$, the percentage of working wives in the population, may be called the average lifetime labor-force participation rate of married women. Since $\bar{R}$ varies with H, κ, and T, the proportions of the mixture of demand functions of each type (N^0 and N^1) will vary across subpopulations whose mean levels of H, κ, and T vary. Thus, the general fertility demand function may be written as a mixture of the two special demand functions as follows:

$$N = N(H, \kappa, T) = \bar{R} N^1(H, \kappa, T) + (1 - \bar{R}) N^0(H, T) + u, \quad (33)$$

where $\bar{R} = \bar{R}(S^0[H, T], H, \kappa, T)$ is the conditional mean of wives' labor-force participation rates given the values of H, κ, and T, and u is an error term. It is assumed that variations in the parameters of the structural equations of the model (such as the utility function or household production functions) among families in the population are such that u is normally distributed with mean zero and constant variance and is independent of the exogenous variables. If this assumption can be maintained, the "mixture model" in (33) may be used to test the implications of the theoretical model.

The implications of the mixture model depend on the signs of the partial derivatives of its constituent functions: the two demand functions, N^0 and N^1, and the labor-force participation function, $\bar{R}$. The partial derivatives of the demand function are derived rigorously in Part D of the Mathematical Appendix, where it is shown in equation (D22) that these partial derivatives (in elasticity form) may be decomposed into the sum of substitution and wealth effects as follows:

$$\delta_{Ni} = \eta_N e_i + \epsilon_N \gamma_i, \qquad i = H, \kappa, T,$$

where δ_{Ni} is the elasticity of N with respect to the ith exogenous variable; η_N is the compensated elasticity of N with respect to π_c; e_i is the elasticity of π_c with respect to the ith exogenous variable, given the form of the constraint; ϵ_N is the wealth elasticity of N; and γ_i is the elasticity of full wealth with respect to the ith exogenous variable.[24] In section 2, it was argued that η_N is negative and the ϵ_N may be either positive or negative but, in either case, it is likely to be small in magnitude. For convenience in exposition, it will be assumed that ϵ_N is positive. The sign of δ_N under each form of the constraint and the derivatives of $\bar{R}$ will be discussed below.

Assume that the wife is not working, so that the family faces a K-type constraint such as $K_0 a' K_0$ in figure 3 and that its initial equilibrium level of number and quality of children and S correspond to the output of C and S at point a'. Because the wife's initial (and postmarital) stock of human capital is assumed to leave her home productivity unaffected, variations in κ do not affect the K-type constraint and, therefore, do not affect desired fertility.[25]

---

[24] The signs of the compensated substitution elasticities for N, Q, C, and S with respect to each exogenous variable under each type constraint are tabulated in table A1 in the Mathematical Appendix.

[25] This assumption is an obvious candidate for relaxation. From an analytical standpoint, the simplest way to do so is to assume that increases in human capital increase

An increase in the husband's lifetime income, H, increases the family's supply of goods ($x = H$) but leaves the supply of wife's time unaffected ($t = T$), while in T, the wife's life-span after marriage, increases the supply of time without affecting the supply of goods. An important property of the K-type constraint is that an increase in the supply of goods (time) will tend to raise (lower) the opportunity cost of children unless the output of C (S) falls absolutely by a sufficient amount. This property, often called Rybczynski's theorem, follows from the assumption that $\rho_c > \rho_s$.[26] It is illustrated for the case of an increase in the supply of goods caused by an increase in H in figure 3 by the asymmetric outward shift in the K-type constraint from $K_0 a' K_0$ to $K_1 a'' K_1$, where the slopes of the two curves at points a' and a'' are equal and the output of C at a'' is smaller than the output of C at a'.

Unless C is sufficiently inferior in consumption (i.e., unless the wealth elasticity of C, ϵ_C, is sufficiently negative), the new equilibrium point on $K_1 a'' K_1$ must be to the right of point a'' and the slope of the constraint at the new equilibrium must be steeper than it was at the initial equilibrium at a' on $K_0 a' K_0$. Since the slope of the constraint equals $-\pi_c$, it follows that an increase in H increases both full wealth, I, and the opportunity cost of children, π_c. Consequently, the wealth effect in favor of fertility is offset by a substitution effect against fertility when the wife does not work so that N^0_H, the partial derivative of N^0 with respect to H, may be either positive or negative. Since the effect of an increase in T is to reduce π_c, N^0_T is unambiguously positive.

If the wife works at a constant marginal wage and the family faces a J^*-type constraint, an increase in H or T simply shifts the constraint out without changing its slope, because the wife adjusts her labor supply in order to keep her price of time, $\hat{w}$, from becoming unequal to her marginal wage, w'. In this case, H and T cause no substitution effects, so that N^1_H and N^1_T are positive because the wealth elasticity, ϵ_N, is assumed to be positive. An increase in H causes the wife to reduce her labor supply and an increase in T causes her to increase L. If w' is an increasing function of L and the family faces a J-type constraint, it follows that w' and π_c will fall as H increases and rise as T increases. In this case, the substitution

---

the wife's productivity neutrally, raising the marginal products of time and goods equally in both C and S production. In this case, because $\hat{w}$ is equal to the ratio of the marginal products in each activity, $\hat{w}$ and π_c would be invariant with respect to κ. An increase in κ would simply shift any of the types of production-possibility functions out homothetically, thereby increasing full wealth and causing wealth effects on consumption. An endless variety of nonneutral effects could be posited which would also affect π_c and $\hat{w}$ in any direction desired. Unless a theory of "bias" is provided, it is not clear that the undoubtedly realistic hypothesis that human capital affects non-market productivity has any empirically falsifiable implications.

[26] See Rybczynski (1955). Jones (1965) has shown that the Rybczynski theorem and the Stolper-Samuelson theorem bear a dual relationship to one another.

effect reinforces the wealth effect of H so that $N^1{}_H$ becomes more positive and offsets the wealth effect of T and $N^1{}_T$ becomes ambiguous in sign. The substitution effects caused by H and T are of opposite sign when the wife works and when she does not.[27] An increase in the wife's initial stock of human capital, κ, tends to increase her marginal wage rate, w', and, therefore, to increase the opportunity cost of children, causing a substitution effect against children. Unless her labor supply curve is backward bending, the increase in κ will tend to increase L, which will further increase w' and π_c if the family faces a J-type constraint. The increase in κ also increases full wealth by an amount related to the level of the wife's labor supply. In general, it will be assumed that the positive wealth effect of κ does not offset the negative substitution effect so that $N^1{}_\kappa$ is hypothesized to be negative.

The effects of H, κ, and T on the labor-force participation rates of wives are given by the partial derivatives of $\bar{R}$ in (33). Variation in $\bar{R}$ depends on the relative change of the wife's marginal wage rate, w', and her price of time, $\hat{w}$, both evaluated at $L = 0$ (i.e., when she is not working). The proportion $\bar{R}$ will increase if w' increases, holding $\hat{w}$ constant, or if $\hat{w}$ decreases, holding w' constant. Since an increase in the wife's initial stock of human capital, κ, increases w', $\bar{R}_\kappa$ is positive. It was shown earlier that an increase in H increases π_c when the wife is not working. It follows that it also increases $\hat{w}$ so that R_H is negative. By the same token, increases in T decrease π_c so that R_T is positive.

The empirical implications of the mixture model in (33) follow from the signs of its partial derivatives with respect to H, κ, and T. For theoretical reasons, however, the implications of changes in T will not be tested. Variations in T may be caused by variations either in longevity or in age at marriage, with the latter being the only source which is of practical importance. So far, it has been assumed implicitly that age at marriage is an exogenous variable. Since bearing and rearing children is one of the principal reasons for marriage, this is an untenable assumption. Thus, accidental births sometimes hasten marriage, while averting them may prolong the single state. Moreover, if children are time intensive and time is cheaper earlier in life, those who wish to have more children will have an economic (as well as a biological) incentive to marry earlier. Thus, both accidental births and the taste for children are likely to be negatively correlated with age at marriage, which is contrary to the assumption that the error term, u, is independent of T.

The general form of the mixture model in (33) cannot be estimated. One way to obtain a function that can be estimated is to take a Taylor series expansion of (33) about the mean values of H and κ and estimate

[27] If w' is a decreasing function of L ($w'' < 0$), as it might be among working wives whose optimal labor supplies are large, the substitution effects caused by increases in H and T become negative and positive, respectively.

the coefficients of the resulting polynomial in H and κ as an approximation to (33). A more intuitive but operationally equivalent procedure is to consider each of the constituent functions of (33) (i.e., $\bar{R}$, N^0, and N^1) to be polynomials of degree r, in which case the mixture function will be a polynomial of degree $2r$ whose coefficients will be functions of the coefficients of the constituent functions.

In the simplest plausible case, N^0, N^1, and $\bar{R}$ are each assumed to be linear functions, as follows:

$$N^0(H) = a_0 + a_1H, \qquad\qquad a_1 = N^0{}_H \gtrless 0$$

$$N^1(H, \kappa) = b_0 + b_1H + b_2\kappa, \qquad b_1 = N^1{}_H > 0, b_2 = N^1{}_\kappa < 0,$$

$$\bar{R}(H, \kappa) = c_0 + c_1H + c_2\kappa, \qquad c_1 = \bar{R}_H < 0, c_2 = \bar{R}_\kappa > 0.$$

The mixture model is then the following quadratic equation:

$$N(H, \kappa) = d_0 + d_1H + d_2\kappa + d_3H\kappa + d_4H^2 + d_5\kappa^2, \qquad (34)$$

where

$$d_0 = c_0b_0 + a_0(1 - c_0),$$

$$d_1 = c_0(N^1{}_H - N^0{}_H) + (b_0 - a_0)\bar{R}_H + N^0{}_H,$$

$$d_2 = c_0N^1{}_\kappa + (b_0 - a_0)\bar{R}_\kappa,$$

$$d_3 = \bar{R}_HN^1{}_\kappa + (N^1{}_H - N^0{}_H)\bar{R}_\kappa > 0,$$

$$d_4 = (N^1{}_H - N^0{}_H)\bar{R}_H < 0,$$

$$d_5 = \bar{R}_\kappa N^1{}_\kappa < 0.$$

There are no a priori expectations for the signs of the constant term, d_0, or for the coefficients of the first-degree terms, d_1 and d_2, because each involves the constant terms of the constituent equations, a_0, b_0, and c_0, whose signs are not predicted by the theory. The implications of the theory do, however, lead to a priori expectations of the signs of the second-degree coefficients, d_3, d_4, and d_5, as indicated above.

The signs of the coefficients of the squared terms, d_4 and d_5, and of the interaction term, d_3, reflect the differential impact of variations in H and κ on the opportunity cost of children between families in which wives work and families in which wives do not work, together with changes in the proportions of the two types of family caused by variation in H and κ on the labor-force participation rate of married women. The reason that d_5, the coefficient of κ^2, is negative is that increases in κ raise the participation rate ($\bar{R}_\kappa > 0$) and that, among working wives, increases in κ raise the cost of children and depress fertility. An increase in H causes wealth effects in both groups, but it increases π_c among nonworking wives and either lowers

π_c or leaves it unchanged among working wives, so that $N^1{}_H - N^0{}_H$, which measures the algebraic difference between the substitution effects in the two groups, is positive. The reason that d_5, the coefficient of H^2, is negative is that an increase in H reduces participation ($\overline{R}_H < 0$), reducing the proportion of families in which H causes a negative substitution effect and increasing the proportion in which it causes a positive substitution effect. The coefficient of the interaction term, d_3, is positive because increases in H reduce the proportion of families in which κ causes a negative substitution effect (i.e., $\overline{R}_H N^1{}_\kappa > 0$) and because increases in κ reduce the proportion of families in which H causes a substitution effect against fertility (i.e., $\overline{R}_\kappa$ ($N^1{}_H - N^0{}_H > 0$).

The nonlinearity of the mixture model implies that the effects of changing income and female wage rates on fertility behavior will vary in strength and even in sign with the prevailing levels of income and wage rates. This implication is consistent with the apparent ambiguity of the effect of income on fertility so often noted by students of fertility behavior.

5. Empirical Results

The results of an attempt to test the implications of the mixture model with data on American families from the 1960 census 1/1,000 sample follow. Unfortunately, of the three second-degree coefficients of the mixture model in (34), only d_3, the coefficient of the interaction term, $H\kappa$, may be estimated unless the theoretical variables, H and κ, can be measured empirically up to a linear transformation.[28] Given the unavoidable imprecision of the definition of the theoretical variables, "husband's lifetime income" and "wife's initial stock of human capital," it is difficult to see how one might hope to do better empirically than to measure them up to positive monotonic transformation. Accordingly, the model that will be estimated is the "interaction model"

$$N = d^*{}_0 + d^*{}_1 H + d^*{}_2 \kappa + d^*{}_3 H\kappa + u^*, \qquad (35)$$

in which the variables H^2 and κ^2 are omitted. In general, since the truncated model in (35) is a misspecification of the full quadratic model, the coefficients of (35) will not be unbiased estimates of their counterparts in (34).[29]

[28] To see this, let $H = m(y)$, where y is the empirical measure of H and m is a positive monotonic transformation (i.e., its first derivative, m', is positive for all y). Substituting for H in the general fertility demand function, (33), we have $N = N [m(y), \kappa]$. The signs of the first partial derivative with respect to y and the second cross-partial are unchanged by the transformation ($N_y m'$ and $N_{y\kappa} = N_{H\kappa} m'$), but the second partial with respect to y is of arbitrary sign ($N_{yy} = N_{HH} m' + N_H m''$) unless m'' is zero, in which case m is a linear transformation. The same argument holds for empirical measures of κ.

[29] The effect of omitting H^2 and κ^2 causes the estimated interaction coefficient, $d^*{}_3$,

Before the empirical results are discussed, another measurement problem must be considered. Any empirical measure of H or κ is likely to measure the "true" variable with a random error. For example, husband's current income is almost certainly an error-ridden measure of the income variable relevant to fertility decisions. Childbearing takes place relatively early in the marital life cycle, and completed fertility and husband's income are usually observed much later. The income variable relevant to childbearing decisions presumably involves the shape and height of the husband's life-cycle income profile as the family expects it to be at the time these decisions are taken. Since the husband's current income is observed long after these decisions have been made, it is likely to be a poor measure of the relevant variable and its regression coefficient a biased estimate (probably toward zero) of the true coefficient.[30]

In an earlier paper, an apparently successful effort was made to alleviate the problem of errors in variables in estimating the interaction model by using weighted cell means as observations where the grouping scheme was chosen in such a way, as, hopefully, to be uncorrelated with the error and correlated with the true measure of husband's lifetime income (see Sanderson and Willis 1971, pp. 35–37 and n. 1). Here, in a different approach to the problem, I use estimates, by occupation, of life-cycle earnings functions of males of a form suggested by Mincer (1970a, 1974b) to predict the income of husbands as a function of their education, labor market experience, cohort, weeks worked, size of place, and whether or not they reside in the South.[31]

Warren Sanderson and I (1971) attempted to test the interaction model with grouped data from seven independent subsamples consisting of three successive 10-year cohorts (1896–1925) from the 1960 census and four successive 5-year cohorts (1881–1900) from the 1940 census. An interaction regression of the form in (35) was estimated in each subsample, using weighted cell means of husband's income and wife's education as measures of H and κ. In each of the seven regressions, the coefficient of the interaction term, d^*_3, was positive and statistically significant and the coefficients of husband's income and wife's education, d^*_1 and d^*_2, were negative and significant. Rather surprisingly, the estimated coefficients of the inter-

---

to be downward biased ($d^*_3 < d_3 > 0$). The reason for this is that H and κ (measured by wife's education) are positively correlated, so that the positive effect on fertility of high levels of H and κ measured by d_3 tends to be offset by the negative effect of high levels of H and κ measured by d_4 and d_5. The bias of d^*_0, d^*_1, and d^*_2 is not certain.

[30] See Theil (1971, pp. 607–15) for a discussion of the problem of errors in the variables.

[31] These earnings functions were estimated from a pooled sample of married males age 18–65 from the 1960 census 1/1,000 sample and from the 1967 Survey of Economic Opportunity (SEO). A description of these regressions and their estimated coefficients is available from the author on request.

action model appeared to be sufficiently stable across the cohorts of 1881–85 to 1916–25 for us to suggest "that it may be possible to apply our model to the explanation of trends in cohort fertility as well as to the explanation of cross-section differentials within cohorts" (p. 36).

We were surprised, for it would seem to be beyond the scope of the static theory underlying the interaction model to explain the effect on cohort fertility trends of the complex dynamic changes that took place in the American economy in the period 1881–1965, when these women were born, married, and bore their children. The static theory would appear to be better suited to the explanation of differential fertility within closely adjoining cohorts whose historical experience is held more or less constant by their common years of birth.

In the empirical work reported in this paper, a crude attempt has been made to see more directly whether the interaction model can help explain trends in cohort fertility as well as differential fertility within cohorts. The data consist of a sample of 9,169 white women age 35–64 in 1960, married once, living with husbands, and living in urban areas at the time of the 1960 census (see table 1 for summary statistics of sample). These women, born 1896–1925, are essentially the same women from the 1960 census used in the Sanderson and Willis (1971) regressions just discussed.

A pure trend equation is estimated from the census sample data to provide a benchmark against which to measure the impact of the economic variables in the interaction model. Since this trend was first declining and then rising among the cohorts of 1896–1925, a quadratic trend function is fitted by regressing wife's cohort and cohort squared (the birth cohort of 1925 is set equal to zero) on the reported total number of children born to her. In this regression, reported in line 1 of table 2, the coefficients of both the linear and squared terms are positive and statistically significant.

TABLE 1

SUMMARY STATISTICS ON SAMPLE OF URBAN WHITE WOMEN MARRIED ONCE,
LIVING WITH HUSBAND: 1960 CENSUS 1/1,000 SAMPLE
(NUMBER OF OBSERVATIONS = 9,169)

Variable	Mean	Standard Deviation
Total number of children born	2.2650	1.7780
Cohort (1925 = 0)	−10.6900	7.4310
Cohort^2	169.4840	191.9660
ED	10.5190	2.8990
H(NOW) ($1,000)	6.7651	5.3936
H(40) ($1,000)	4.2929	2.1407
H(NOW) ED	75.1466	75.2934
H(40) ED	47.8497	31.7309
SMSA (=1, 2, 3, 4)	2.6100	1.6130

TABLE 2

REGRESSIONS ON COMPLETED FERTILITY OF URBAN WHITE WOMEN AGE 35–64, MARRIED ONCE, LIVING WITH HUSBAND: 1960 CENSUS 1/1,000 SAMPLE

Concept H, κ	Cohort	Cohort^2	d^*_1 (H)	d^*_2 (κ)	d^*_3 ($H\kappa$)	SMSA	Constant	R^2
1. Pure trend	.05596 .00834 (6.65)	.00150 .00032 (4.66)	...	...	...	...	2.60838	.00854
2. H(NOW) ED	.05983 .00824 (7.09)	.00132 .00032 (4.13)	−.06898 .01687 (4.09)	−.14206 .00991 (14.31)	.00617 .00131 (4.71)	−.08111 .01135 (7.15)	4.38947	.04389
3. H(40) ED	.06004 .00831 (7.23)	.00124 .00032 (3.88)	−.24836 .03381 (7.35)	−.17572 .01258 (13.97)	.02023 .00276 (7.33)	−.07243 .01173 (6.17)	4.83269	.04656

NOTE.—See table 1 for summary statistics of sample; t-ratios are reported in parentheses.

The minimum level of cohort fertility, as computed from the trend equation, was reached by the cohort of 1906.

Two alternative measures of husband's lifetime income are used in the estimates of the fertility demand equations. The first, H(NOW) (see table 2) is equal to the husband's reported 1959 income. As already discussed, H(NOW) is likely to be an error-ridden measure of husband's lifetime income, particularly since the husbands in the sample range in age from their early thirties to retirement age. It is used for purposes of comparison with the alternative measure, H(40), which is the husband's income at age 40 as predicted on the basis of his occupation, education, labor market experience, cohort, race, residence in the South, and size of urban area from the life-cycle earnings functions described earlier. In addition to its econometric advantages, the use of H(40) has the advantage of permitting the choice of a given point on the life-cycle income profile in order to provide a comparable measure of income for men whose current ages differ considerably.[32] Both variables have the great disadvantage of being ex post measures of income, which may provide a distorted measure of the ex ante expectation of lifetime income on which fertility decisions are based.

The wife's years of schooling, ED, is used to measure κ, her stock of human capital at the outset of marriage. Although all of the effects of education except its effect on the market earnings capacity of the wife have been ruled out by assumption, it is recognized that education may well have a systematic effect on tastes, efficacy of fertility control, or efficiency in household production. This should be borne in mind when the regression results are considered.

The estimates of the interaction model using H(NOW) and H(40) are reported, respectively, in lines 2 and 3 of table 2. In each regression, the variable, Standard Metropolitan Statistical Areas (SMSA), has been added to hold the influence of the size of urban area constant, and the variables "Cohort" and "Cohort²" have been added so that the effect of the economic variables on cohort fertility trends may be assessed.

The coefficients of husband's income and wife's education, d^*_3, and d^*_2, are negative, and the coefficients of the interaction term, d^*_3, are positive in each regression; all coefficients are statistically significant. The absolute magnitudes of the coefficients involving H(NOW) are considerably smaller in magnitude and have lower t-ratios than the corresponding coefficients of the regression involving H(40).[33] This result supports the belief that

[32] The method of grouping used in Sanderson and Willis (1971) and the auxiliary regression method used here may both be considered as alternative applications of the method of instrumental variables to the problem of errors in the variables. The advantage of the latter method over grouping is that it preserves degrees of freedom and permits the use of a linear combination of a large number of instruments (the regressors in the earnings function); see Malinvaud (1966, p. 606).

[33] Comparisons between the magnitudes of the coefficients involving the two measures of H should be adjusted for differences in their means, which are reported in table 1. Since the mean of H(NOW) is 1.56 times the mean of H(40), the coefficient

TABLE 3

COMPUTED ELASTICITIES OF FERTILITY WITH RESPECT TO H(40) AND ED FROM
REGRESSION 3, TABLE 2

WIFE'S EDUCATION	HUSBAND'S INCOME		
	Mean	High	Low
Mean:			
η_H	−.0674	−.101	−.0338
η_{ED}	−.412	−.181	−.614
High:			
η_H	.0438	.0656	.0219
η_{ED}	−.526	−.270	−.783
Low:			
η_H	−.179	−.268	−.0895
η_{ED}	−.299	−.153	−.445

NOTE.—High husband's income and low husband's income refer to points one standard deviation above and below mean [H(40)], respectively. The same definitions are used for wife's education.

a longer-run, lifetime concept of income is relevant to fertility behavior.

The interaction model helps explain the U-shaped relationship between fertility and cross-section measures of husband's lifetime income that emerged in the United States and some European countries after World War II.[34] The effect of H(40) on fertility is

$$\frac{\partial N}{\partial H(40)} = d*_1 + d*_3 \, \text{ED},$$

where $d*_1$ is negative and $d*_3$ is positive. As the level of wife's education (ED) surpasses about 12 years of schooling, the sign of the "income effect" changes from negative to positive. Thus, in populations or subpopulations in which wife's education levels are low, the effect of income on fertility tends to be negative, and it becomes positive as these levels grow. For effect of variations in the level of H(40) and ED on the elasticities of fertility with respect to husband's income and wife's education, see table 3. These elasticities are computed at the sample mean of H(40) and ED and at one standard deviation above and below the mean for each variable.

The estimates of $d*_1$, $d*_2$, and $d*_3$ using individual data across cohorts are consistent in sign and magnitude with the corresponding estimates within cohorts reported in Sanderson and Willis (1971) and described earlier. Despite this, it appears that my suggestion that the interaction

of H(NOW) is 39 percent of the coefficient of H(40) and the coefficient of H(NOW) ED is 48 percent of the coefficient of H(40) ED after the appropriate adjustment is made.

[34] The interaction model also performs quite well with Israeli data, as Ben-Porath reports in this volume.

model may be used to help explain cohort fertility trends is unwarranted, at least when static ex post measures of the exogenous variables are used. Ideally, if the interaction model fully explained cohort fertility trends, the coefficients of the trend terms, "Cohort" and "Cohort^2," would fall to zero. In fact, these coefficients are not substantially changed by the addition of the economic variables.

6. Conclusion

The restrictions placed on the specification of the individual equations of the structural model of fertility behavior that I have presented and on the structure as a whole represent a drastic simplification of the complex interconnections among fertility, family formation, and family behavior. Consideration of these restrictions and the manner in which they may be relaxed or changed suggests that the present model is only one particularly simple member of a large class of economic models of individual fertility behavior which share the common framework of the economic theory of the family. Thus, the static lifetime framework of the present model could be changed to a dynamic life-cycle framework. The assumptions of (1) perfect fertility control could be removed in favor of a theory of imperfect fertility control, (2) exogenous date of marriage and characteristics of marital partners could be replaced by a theory of marriage, and (3) exogenously determined efficiency in household production could be relaxed by applying the theory of investment in human capital to nonmarket efficiency, and so on. Work under way on a number of such models promises to provide a rich source of alternative hypotheses about fertility behavior and, simultaneously, about many other aspects of family behavior.

Recognition that there are potentially many alternative economic models of fertility behavior must influence any assessment of the empirical importance of economic variables on fertility as expressed in the present model. On the basis of evidence presented in this paper, it appears that the interaction model captures an important empirical regularity in the cross-section relationship between fertility and measures of husband's income and wife's education that has become apparent in the emergence of a U-shaped relationship between fertility and income which has been observed in many advanced countries in the past 25 years and which was an incipient relation at the lower levels of income and education prevailing in earlier periods. This empirical regularity is also consistent with the predictions of the theoretical model of fertility demand developed in this paper and must, therefore, be counted as evidence in its favor. To reiterate the position Ben-Porath has taken in his paper in this volume, caution must be exercised in accepting the explanation of fertility behavior provided by this model, because the mechanism by which the empirical regularity is generated need not correspond exactly or even chiefly to the one posited in the theoretical model. If scientific progress consists in large part of the process of rejecting hypotheses, it follows that progress will be impeded if hypotheses are not proposed. It is in this spirit that the hypotheses implied by the theoretical model of this paper are advanced.

Mathematical Appendix

A. Derivation and Properties of Demand Functions Subject to Full-Wealth Constraint

The demand functions for N, Q, and S are derived by maximizing the utility function (eq. [8]) subject to the full wealth constraint (eq. [16]), where I, π_c, and π_s are treated as parameters. Maximizing the Lagrangian expression,

$$U(N, Q, S) + \lambda(\pi_c NQ + \pi_s S - I),$$

where λ is a Lagrange multiplier $(\lambda < 0)$, we obtain the following first-order conditions for a maximum:

$$U_N + \lambda \pi_c Q = 0,$$
$$U_Q + \lambda \pi_c N = 0,$$
$$U_s + \lambda \pi_s = 0,$$
$$\pi_c NQ + \pi_s S - I = 0.$$
(A1)

The quantities of N, Q, and S demanded as functions of the parameters I, π_c, and π_s may be obtained by solving (A1) simultaneously. These solutions, expressed in implicit form, are the demand functions for N, Q, S, and C $(=NQ)$ in equations (17)–(20).

The properties of these demand functions may be obtained by totally differentiating the first-order conditions (A1) to obtain the following set of simultaneous linear differential equations written in matrix form:

$$\begin{bmatrix} U_{NN} & U_{NQ} + \lambda\pi_c & U_{NS} & Q\pi_c \\ U_{QN} + \lambda\pi_c & U_{QQ} & U_{QS} & N\pi_c \\ U_{SN} & U_{SQ} & U_{SS} & \pi_s \\ Q\pi_c & N\pi_c & \pi_s & 0 \end{bmatrix} \begin{bmatrix} dN \\ dQ \\ dS \\ d\lambda \end{bmatrix} = \begin{bmatrix} -\lambda Q & 0 & 0 \\ -\lambda N & 0 & 0 \\ 0 & -\lambda & 0 \\ -NQ & -S & 1 \end{bmatrix} \begin{bmatrix} d\pi_c \\ d\pi_s \\ dI \end{bmatrix}.$$
(A2)

Among the second-order or sufficient conditions for utility maximization are $\Delta < 0$, Δ_{11}, Δ_{22}, and $\Delta_{33} > 0$, where Δ is the determinant of the bordered Hessian matrix on the left in (A2) and Δ_{11}, Δ_{22}, and Δ_{33} are the cofactors of the elements of the principal diagonal.

Holding π_s constant and solving for the differentials dN, dQ, and dS by Cramer's rule, we obtain

$$dN = 1/\Delta[-\lambda(Q\Delta_{11} - N\Delta_{21})d\pi_c - \Delta_{41}(dI - NQd\pi_c)], \quad (A3)$$

$$dQ = 1/\Delta[-\lambda(-Q\Delta_{12} + N\Delta_{22})d\pi_c + \Delta_{42}(dI - NQd\pi_c)], \quad (A4)$$

$$dS = 1/\Delta[-\lambda(Q\Delta_{13} - N\Delta_{23})d\pi_c - \Delta_{43}(dI - NQd\pi_c)], \quad (A5)$$

and, since $C = NQ$ and $dC = QdN + NdQ$,

$$dC = 1/\Delta [-\lambda (Q^2\Delta_{11} + N^2\Delta_{22} - 2NQ\Delta_{12}) \tag{A6}$$

$$+ (-Q\Delta_{41} + N\Delta_{42})(dI - NQd\pi_c)].$$

The wealth effects, obtained by setting $d\pi_c$ equal to zero in (A3)–(A6), involve the cofactors $-\Delta_{41}$, Δ_{42}, and Δ_{43}, none of the signs of which are restricted by the second-order conditions. However, the following relationships hold (a) the weighted sum of the wealth effects equal unity, and (b) the weighted sum of the wealth effects on N and Q equals the wealth effect on C. In elasticity form, these two propositions may be expressed as follows:

$$\gamma(\epsilon_N + \epsilon_Q) + (1 - \gamma)\epsilon_S = 1, \tag{A7}$$

$$\epsilon_N + \epsilon_Q = \epsilon_C, \tag{A8}$$

where $\gamma = \pi_c NQ/I$ is the share of full wealth accounted for by expenditures on children and ϵ_N, ϵ_Q, ϵ_S, ϵ_C are, respectively, the wealth elasticities of demand for N, Q, S, and C.

The compensated substitution effects are obtained from (A3)–(A6) by evaluating the partial derivatives of N, Q, S, and C with respect to π_c, holding utility constant by setting $(dI - NQd\pi_c)$ equal to zero. To simplify the interpretation of these effects, the following right-hand expressions will be substituted for their left-hand counterparts in (A5) and (A6): $Q\Delta_{13} - N\Delta_{23} = -\pi_s/\pi_c \Delta_{33}$ and $Q^2\Delta_{11} + N^2\Delta_{22} - 2NQ\Delta_{12} = (\pi_s/\pi_c)^2\Delta_{33}$. The compensated substitution effects, written in elasticity form, are

$$\eta_N = (-\lambda\pi_c/\Delta)(Q/N\Delta_{11} - \Delta_{21}), \tag{A9}$$

$$\eta_Q = (-\lambda\pi_c/\Delta)(N/Q\Delta_{22} - \Delta_{12}), \tag{A10}$$

$$\eta_S = (\lambda\pi_c/S)(\Delta_{33}/\Delta) > 0, \tag{A11}$$

$$\eta_C = (-\lambda\pi_s^2/\pi_c C)(\Delta_{33}/\Delta) < 0. \tag{A12}$$

The second-order conditions imply that η_S is positive and η_C is negative such that

$$\gamma\eta_C + (1 - \gamma)\eta_S = 0, \tag{A13}$$

where γ is the share of full wealth devoted to children. Since the signs of $\Delta_{12} = \Delta_{21}$ are not restricted by the second-order conditions, the signs of η_N and η_Q are ambiguous. However, they must sum to a negative number, since

$$\eta_N + \eta_Q = \eta_C < 0. \tag{A14}$$

The conditions for both η_N and η_Q to be negative or for one or the other (but not both) to be positive may be seen by considering the price effects embedded in (A9) and (A10) as if they had been generated by a conventional linear full wealth constraint, $I = p_N N + p_Q Q + p_S S$, which is tangent to the actual nonlinear full wealth constraint, $I = \pi_c NQ + \pi_s S$, at the initial point of equilibrium. The prices in the linear constraint are defined as $p_N = \pi_c Q$, $p_Q = \pi_c N$, and $p_S = \pi_s$.

Although, from their definitions, it is apparent that p_N and p_Q cannot vary independently, we shall pretend for a moment that they do. Under this pretense, the left side of (A2) remains the same and the right side becomes $(-\lambda dp_N -\lambda dp_Q -\lambda dp_S I)'$. The following compensated own-substitution effects, written in elasticity form, are restricted by the second-order conditions to be negative:

$$\frac{\partial N}{\partial p_N}\frac{p_N}{N} = \eta_{NN} = (-\lambda \pi_c Q/N)(\Delta_{11}/\Delta) < 0, \tag{A15}$$

$$\frac{\partial Q}{\partial p_Q}\frac{p_Q}{Q} = \eta_{QQ} = (-\lambda \pi_c N/Q)(\Delta_{22}/\Delta) < 0. \tag{A16}$$

The compensated cross-price effects, in elasticity form, are written as follows:

$$\frac{\partial N}{\partial p_Q}\frac{p_Q}{N} = \eta_{NQ} = \lambda \pi_c (\Delta_{21}/\Delta), \tag{A17}$$

$$\frac{\partial Q}{\partial p_N}\frac{p_N}{Q} = \eta_{QN} = \lambda \pi_c (\Delta_{12}/\Delta). \tag{A18}$$

Since $\Delta_{21} = \Delta_{12}$, it is clear that $\eta_{NQ} = \eta_{QN}$. If N and Q are substitutes, η_{NQ} is positive, and if they are complements, η_{NQ} is negative.

In fact, a change in π_c affects both p_N and p_Q so that, for example,

$$\frac{\partial N}{\partial \pi_c} = \frac{\partial N}{\partial p_N}\frac{\partial p_N}{\partial \pi_c} + \frac{\partial N}{\partial p_Q}\frac{\partial p_Q}{\partial \pi_c}.$$

Thus, substituting (A15) and (A17) into (A9) and (A16), (A18) into (A10), we have

$$\eta_N = \eta_{NN} + \eta_{NQ}, \tag{A19}$$

$$\eta_Q = \eta_{QQ} + \eta_{QN}, \tag{A20}$$

where, from (A14),

$$\eta_C = \eta_N + \eta_Q = \eta_{NN} + 2\eta_{NQ} + \eta_{QQ} < 0. \tag{A21}$$

B. Partial Derivatives of the K-Type Constraint

The household's production-possibility constraint when the wife does no market work was obtained by implicitly solving the simultaneous equation system (27.1)–(27.8) to obtain the K-type constraint $C = K(S, H, T)$. The partial derivatives of this function may be found by totally differentiating (27.1)–(27.8) to obtain a set of simultaneous linear differential equations that may be solved for the differential dC as a function of the differentials of the independent variables. This task is simpler if appropriate substitutions are made to reduce the number of equations and unknowns to four and if the production functions are written in their general form, $C = f(t_c, x_c)$ and $S = g(t_s, x_s)$. The partial derivatives of these functions are then written as $\partial C/\partial t_c = f_1$; $\partial C/\partial x_c = f_2$; $\partial S/\partial t_s = g_1$; $\partial S/\partial x_s = g_2$; and so on.

The four-equation system to which (27.1)–(27.8) is reduced is

$$-C + f(t_c, x_c) = 0, \tag{B1}$$

$$g(T - t_c, H - x_c) = 0, \tag{B2}$$

$$\pi_c f_1 - g_1 = 0, \tag{B3}$$

$$\pi_c f_2 - g_2 = 0. \tag{B4}$$

Taking the total differential of (B1)–(B4) and writing the result in matrix form, we obtain

$$
\begin{bmatrix}
-1 & -f_1 & -f_2 & 0 \\
0 & -g_1 & -g_2 & 0 \\
0 & \pi_c f_{11} + g_{11} & \pi_c f_{12} + g_{12} & f_1 \\
0 & \pi_c f_{12} + g_{12} & \pi_c f_{22} + g_{22} & f_2
\end{bmatrix}
\begin{bmatrix}
dC \\
dt_c \\
dx_c \\
d\pi_c
\end{bmatrix}
$$

$$
=
\begin{bmatrix}
0 & 0 & 0 \\
-g_2 & -g_1 & 1 \\
g_{12} & g_{11} & 0 \\
g_{22} & g_{21} & 0
\end{bmatrix}
\begin{bmatrix}
dH \\
dT \\
dS
\end{bmatrix}. \tag{B5}
$$

Let the determinant of the 4×4 matrix on the left be A and let the cofactor of its element a_{ij} be $A_{ij}(-1)^{i+j}$.

Solving (B5) by Cramer's rule, we can give the first partial derivatives of the K-type constraint as follows:

$$\frac{\partial C}{\partial S} = K_S = -A_{21}/A = -1/\pi_c, \tag{B6}$$

$$\frac{\partial C}{\partial H} = K_H = 1/A(g_2 A_{21} + g_{12} A_{31} - g_{22} A_{41}) = 1/\pi_c, \tag{B7}$$

$$\frac{\partial C}{\partial T} = K_T = 1/A(g_1 A_{21} + g_{11} A_{31} - g_{21} A_{41}) = \hat{w}/\pi_c. \tag{B8}$$

Expressing the partial derivatives of the production functions $f(t_c, x_c)$ and $g(t_s, x_s)$ in terms of simple derivatives of the functions $F(\rho_c)$ and $G(\rho_s)$, we can give the second partial derivatives of the K-type constraint as follows:

$$\frac{\partial^2 C}{\partial S^2} = K_{SS} = (1/\pi_c)^2 \frac{\partial \pi_c}{\partial S} = (1/\pi_c)^2 (A_{24}/A)$$

$$= -(1/\pi_c)^2 \frac{\pi_c F'' G'' (\rho_c - \rho_s)^2}{x_c x_s A} < 0, \tag{B9}$$

$$\frac{\partial^2 C}{\partial S \partial H} = K_{SH} = (1/\pi_c)^2 \frac{\partial \pi_c}{\partial H} = (1/\pi_c)^2$$

$$(g_2 A_{24} - g_{12} A_{34} + g_{22} A_{44})(1/A) \tag{B10}$$

$$= -(1/\pi_c)^2 \frac{\pi_c F'' G'' (\rho_c - \rho_s)}{x_c x_s A} > 0,$$

$$\frac{\partial^2 C}{\partial S \partial T} = K_{ST} = (1/\pi)^2 \frac{\partial \pi_c}{\partial T} = (1/\pi_c)^2$$

$$(-g_1 A_{24} - g_{11} A_{34} + g_{12} A_{44})(1/A) \qquad \text{(B11)}$$

$$= -(1/\pi_c)^2 \frac{\pi_c \rho_c F'' G'' (\rho_c - \rho_s)}{x_c x_s A} < 0,$$

where

$$A = -\frac{F''}{x_c}(\rho_c \hat{w} + 1)^2 - \frac{G''}{x_s}(\rho_s \hat{w} + 1)^2 > 0.$$

C. Partial Derivatives of the J-Type Constraint

The production-possibility function when the wife does some market work is obtained by solving the simultaneous equation system (27.1)–(27.11). The solution is the J-type constraint, which is written in implicit form as $C = J(S, H, \kappa, T)$. Again, the full system may be reduced by substitution to the following system of five equations in five unknowns:

$$-C + f(t_c, x_c) = 0, \qquad \text{(C1)}$$

$$g(T - L - t_c, H + wL - x_c) = S, \qquad \text{(C2)}$$

$$\pi_c f_1 - g_1 = 0, \qquad \text{(C3)}$$

$$\pi_c f_2 - g_2 = 0, \qquad \text{(C4)}$$

$$f_1 / f_2 - w' = 0. \qquad \text{(C5)}$$

This system differs from the system (B1)–(B4) underlying the K-type constraint only in the addition of equation (C5) and in the addition of a term involving the labor supply, L, into the arguments of the production function g.

By totally differentiating the (C1)–(C5) system, the following system is obtained:

$$
\begin{bmatrix}
-1 & f_1 & f_2 & 0 & 0 \\
0 & -g_1 & -g_2 & 0 & -g_1 + w'g_2 \\
0 & \pi_c f_{11} + g_{11} & \pi_c f_{12} + g_{12} & f_1 & g_{11} - w'g_{12} \\
0 & \pi_c f_{12} + g_{12} & \pi_c f_{22} + g_{22} & f_2 & g_{22} - w'g_{22} \\
0 & \dfrac{f_{11}f_2 - f_{21}f_1}{(f_2)^2} & \dfrac{f_{12}f_2 - f_{22}f_1}{(f_2)^2} & 0 & -w''
\end{bmatrix}
\begin{bmatrix}
dC \\ dt_c \\ dx_c \\ d\pi_c \\ dL
\end{bmatrix}
$$

(C6)

$$
=
\begin{bmatrix}
0 & 0 & 0 & 0 \\
1 & -g_2 & -g_1 & -w\kappa L g_2 \\
0 & g_{12} & g_{11} & w_\kappa L g_{12} \\
0 & g_{22} & g_{21} & w_\kappa L g_{22} \\
0 & 0 & 0 & w_\kappa + w_{L\kappa} L
\end{bmatrix}
\begin{bmatrix}
dS \\ dH \\ dT \\ d\kappa
\end{bmatrix}.
$$

Let the determinant of the matrix on the left in (C6) be B and let the cofactor of its element b_{ij} be $B_{ij}(-1)^{i+j}$.

It may be observed that the cofactor B_{55} of the element w'' is equal to the determinant A in (5), from which it follows that

$$B = B^* - w''A, \tag{C7}$$

where

$$B^* = -\frac{f_{11}f_2 - f_{12}f_1}{(f_2)^2}B_{52} + \frac{f_{12}f_2 - f_{22}f_1}{(f_2)^2}B_{53}.$$

Similarly, it follows that

$$B_{ij}(-1)^{i+j} = (B^*{}_{ij} - w''A_{ij})(-1)^{i+j}, \tag{C8}$$

where $i, j = 1, \ldots, 4$.

The element w'' $(=2w_L + Lw_{LL})$ is zero if the wife's market wage is independent of her lifetime hours of work. In this case, her market wage, $w' = w(\kappa)$, is a parameter whose value depends solely on her initial stock of human capital, κ, and the partial derivatives of the J-type constraint depend only on B^* and the $B^*{}_{ij}$. Let the J-type constraint in this special case be

$$C = J^*(S, H, \kappa, T). \tag{C9}$$

The first partial derivatives of J^* are

$$\frac{\partial C}{\partial S} = J^*{}_S = -B^*{}_{21}/B^* = -1/\pi_c; \tag{C10}$$

$$\frac{\partial C}{\partial H} = J^*{}_H = (1/B^*)(g_2B^*{}_{21} + g_{12}B^*{}_{31} - g_{22}B^*{}_{41}) = 1/\pi_c; \tag{C11}$$

$$\frac{\partial C}{\partial \kappa} = J^*{}_\kappa = (w_\kappa L/B^*)(g_2B^*{}_{21} + g_{12}B^*{}_{31} - g_{22}B^*{}_{41})$$
$$+ w_\kappa(B^*{}_{51}/B^*) = w_\kappa L/\pi_c; \tag{C12}$$

$$\frac{\partial C}{\partial T} = J^*{}_T = 1/B^*(g_1B^*{}_{21} + g_{11}B^*{}_{31} - g_{21}B^*{}_{41}) = w'/\pi_c. \tag{C13}$$

The second partial derivatives of J^* are

$$\frac{\partial^2 C}{\partial S^2} = J^*{}_{SS} = (1/\pi_c)^2 \frac{\partial \pi_c}{\partial S} = (1/\pi_c)^2(B^*{}_{24}/B^*) = 0, \tag{C14}$$

$$\frac{\partial^2 C}{\partial S \partial H} = J^*{}_{SH} = (1/\pi_c)^2 \frac{\partial \pi_c}{\partial H}$$
$$= (1/\pi_c)^2(-g_2B^*{}_{24} - g_{12}B^*{}_{34} + g_{22}B^*{}_{44})(1/B^*) = 0, \tag{C15}$$

$$\frac{\partial^2 C}{\partial S \partial \kappa} = J^*{}_{S\kappa} = (1/\pi_c)^2 \frac{\partial \pi_c}{\partial \kappa} = (w_\kappa L/\pi^2{}_c)(-g_2B^*{}_{24} - g_{12}B^*{}_{34}$$
$$+ g_{22}B^*{}_{44})(1/B^*) + w_\kappa(-B^*{}_{54}/B^*) \tag{C16}$$
$$= (1/\pi_c F)^2 w_\kappa w'(\rho_c - \rho_s) > 0,$$

$$\frac{\partial^2 C}{\partial S \partial T} = J^*{}_{ST} = (1/\pi_c)^2 \frac{\partial \pi_c}{\partial T} = (1/\pi_c)^2(-g_1 B^*{}_{24} - g_{11} B^*{}_{34}$$

$$+ g_{22} B^*{}_{44})(1/B^*) = 0. \tag{C17}$$

If the wife's market wage is affected by her lifetime hours of work because of postmarital investment in human capital (or for any other reason), w'' will not equal zero. In specifying the signs of the following partial derivatives of the J-type constraint, it will be assumed that w'' is positive, as it would tend to be if postmartial investment provided the major source of dependence between w' and L, but the results are also relevant to the converse assumption of negative w''.

The partial derivatives of J may be expressed in terms of the partial derivatives of the K- and J^*-type constraints by utilizing the relationships in (C7) and (C8). The first partial derivatives of J are identical to those of J^* and will not be repeated. The second partials of J are

$$\frac{\partial^2 C}{\partial S^2} = J_{SS} = -w''(A/B) \, K_{SS} > 0, \tag{C18}$$

$$\frac{\partial^2 C}{\partial S \partial H} = J_{SH} = -w''(A/B) \, K_{SH} < 0, \tag{C19}$$

$$\frac{\partial^2 C}{\partial S \partial T} = J_{ST} = -w''(A/B) \, K_{ST} > 0, \tag{C20}$$

$$\frac{\partial^2 C}{\partial S \partial \kappa} = J_{S\kappa} = -w'' w_\kappa L(A/B) \, K_{SH} + (1 + \frac{w_{L\kappa}}{w_\kappa} L)(B^*/B) \, J^*{}_{S\kappa}. \tag{C21}$$

The sign of $J_{S\kappa}$ is ambiguous because the term on the left involving K_{SH} is negative and the term on the right involving $J^*{}_{S\kappa}$ is positive.

D. *The Derivation and Properties of the Demand Functions for* N, Q, *and* S

Let the general production-possibility constraint faced by the family be

$$\Phi(C, S, H, \kappa, T) = 0, \tag{D1}$$

where, if the wife works in the market, $\Phi = -NQ + J(S, H, \kappa, T)$, $R = 1$; and, if she does no market work, $\Phi = -NQ + K(S, H, T)$, $R = 0$. The family is assumed to maximize the Lagrangian function $U(N, Q, S) + \lambda \, \Phi(C, S, H, \kappa, T)$, where λ is a Lagrange multiplier. The first-order conditions are

$$U_N + \lambda Q \Phi_c = 0,$$

$$U_Q + \lambda N \Phi_c = 0,$$

$$U_S + \lambda \Phi_s = 0, \tag{D2}$$

$$\Phi = 0.$$

The ratio $-\Phi_c/\Phi_s$ is the marginal rate of transformation between S and C along the production-possibility function, and in equilibrium, it is equal to the marginal rate of substitution in consumption, $-\pi_c/\pi_s$. Accordingly, in what follows, let $\Phi_c = \pi_c$ and $\Phi_s = \pi_s (=1)$, where these magnitudes can be interpreted as equilibrium values.

Corresponding to the general maximization problem involving the constraint Φ and to the particular problems involving the K- and J-type constraints, define, respectively, a general fertility demand function,

$$N = N(H, \kappa, T), \tag{D3}$$

a demand function when the wife does no market work,

$$N = N^0(H, T), \qquad R = 0, \tag{D4}$$

and a demand function when the wife does work,

$$N = N^1(H, \kappa, T), \qquad R = 1. \tag{D5}$$

Also define with similar notation general and special demand functions for Q and S

The properties of these demand functions may be examined by totally differentiating the first-order conditions (D2) to obtain

$$
\begin{bmatrix}
U_{NN} & U_{NQ} + \lambda\pi_c & U_{NS} & Q\pi_c \\
U_{QN} + \lambda\pi_c & U_{QQ} & U_{QS} & N\pi_c \\
U_{SN} & U_{SQ} & U_{SS} + \lambda\Phi_{SS} & \pi_s \\
Q\pi_c & N\pi_c & \pi_s & 0
\end{bmatrix}
\begin{bmatrix}
dN \\
dQ \\
dS \\
d\lambda
\end{bmatrix}
\tag{D6}
$$

$$
=
\begin{bmatrix}
0 & 0 & 0 \\
0 & 0 & 0 \\
-\lambda\Phi_{SH} & -\lambda\Phi_{S\kappa} & -\lambda\Phi_{ST} \\
-\Phi_H & -\Phi_\kappa & -\Phi_T
\end{bmatrix}
\begin{bmatrix}
dH \\
d\kappa \\
dT
\end{bmatrix}.
$$

The second-order conditions for a maximum require that $D < 0$ and D_{11}, D_{22}, and $D_{33} > 0$, where D is the determinant of the bordered Hessian on the left in (D6) and D_{11}, D_{22}, and D_{33} are the cofactors of the elements of the principal diagonal.

Introducing the dummy argument α_i $(i = H, \kappa, T)$, we can solve (D6) by Cramer's rule to obtain the following partial derivatives of the general fertility demand function, (D3):

$$\frac{\partial N}{\partial \alpha_i} = (-\lambda D_{31}/D)\ \Phi_{si} + (-D_{41}/D)(-\Phi_i). \tag{D7}$$

In the conventional manner, the total effect on demand of a change in α_i may be expressed as the sum of a compensated substitution effect and a wealth effect.

The compensated substitution effect is obtained where utility is held constant by setting the total differential of the utility function equal to zero (i.e., $dU = U_N dN + U_Q dQ + U_S dS = 0$). The first-order conditions of (D2) imply that $U_N = U_S(Q\pi_c/\pi_s)$ and $U_Q = U_S(N\pi_c/\pi_c)$, from which it follows, by substitution into dU, that $Q\pi_c dN + N\pi_c dQ + \pi_s dS = 0$ when utility is held constant. The last equation of (D6) is $Q\pi_c dN + N\pi_c dQ + \pi_s dS = -\Phi_i$. Thus, if we set Φ_i equal to zero in (D7) to hold utility constant, the compensated substitution effect is

$$\frac{\partial N}{\partial \alpha_i} = (-\lambda D_{31}/D)\Phi_{si}, \tag{D8}$$

where $\partial N/\partial \alpha_i$ is understood to be evaluated with utility, instead of α_j $(j \neq i)$ being held constant. From the analysis of the second partial derivatives of the production-possibility functions, it is known that $\Phi_{si} = \pi^2_c(\partial \pi_c/\partial \alpha_i)$. Consequently, by the chain rule, it follows that

$$\frac{\partial N}{\partial \alpha_i} = \frac{\partial N}{\partial \pi_c}\frac{\partial \pi_c}{\partial \alpha_i},$$

where $\partial N/\partial \pi_c = -\lambda D_{31}/D$. Thus, in elasticity terms, the compensated substitution effect on fertility of a change in α_i, η_{Ni}, is the product of the compensated price elasticity of demand for N, η_{lN}, and the elasticity of π_c with respect to α_i, e_i, where

$$e_i = \frac{\alpha_i}{\pi_c}\frac{\partial \pi_c}{\partial \alpha_i} = \pi_c \alpha_i \Phi_{si}. \tag{D9}$$

An equivalent argument may be made with respect to the compensated substitution effects of a change in α_i on Q and S, so that the following relationships may be expressed:

$$\eta_{Ni} = \eta_N e_i, \tag{D10}$$

$$\eta_{Qi} = \eta_Q e_i, \tag{D11}$$

$$\eta_{Si} = \eta_S e_i, \tag{D12}$$

$$\eta_{Ci} = (\eta_N + \eta_Q) e_i. \tag{D13}$$

In section 3, it was found that $\eta_c < 0$ and $\eta_s > 0$ and, less certainly, that $\eta_N < 0$ and $\eta_Q > 0$. Given these signs, the signs of compensated substitution effects will depend on the signs of the e_i, which in turn will depend on which of the α_i (H, κ, or T) is being considered and which type of constraint (K, J^*, or J) the family is facing. The signs of these substitution elasticities are tabulated in table A1.

The wealth effects on fertility are defined as the partial derivatives of N with respect to α_i, holding π_c constant. If we set

$$\Phi_{si} = \pi_c^2 \frac{\partial \pi_c}{\partial \alpha_i}$$

equal to zero in (D1), the wealth effects are

$$\frac{\partial N}{\partial \alpha_i} = (-D_{41}/D)(-\Phi_i). \tag{D14}$$

TABLE A1

Signs of Compensated Substitution Elasticities N, Q, C, and S with
Respect to H, κ, and T by Type of Constraint

Compensated Elasticity	Type of Constraint		
	K	$J*$	J
Fertility (N):			
η_{NH}	−	0	+
$\eta_{N\kappa}$	0	−	−
η_{NT}	+	0	−
Child quality (Q):			
η_{QH}	+	0	−
$\eta_{Q\kappa}$	0	+	+
η_{QT}	−	0	+
Child services (C):			
η_{CH}	−	0	+
$\eta_{C\kappa}$	0	−	−
η_{CT}	+	0	−
Other sources of satisfaction (S):			
η_{SH}	+	0	−
$\eta_{S\kappa}$	0	+	+
η_{ST}	−	0	+

The change in the family's full wealth, $I = \pi_c C + \pi_s S$, given a change in α_i and holding prices constant, is

$$\frac{\partial I}{\partial \alpha_i} = \frac{\partial I}{\partial C}\frac{\partial C}{\partial \alpha_i},$$

where $\partial I/\partial C = \pi_c$ and $\partial C/\partial \alpha_i = -\Phi_i$. Thus, by the chain rule, the wealth effect may be expressed as

$$\frac{\partial N}{\partial \alpha_i} = -\frac{\partial N}{\partial I}\frac{\partial I}{\partial \alpha_i},$$

where $\partial N/\partial I = -D_{41}/D$ and $\partial I/\partial \alpha_i = -\pi_c\Phi_i$.
Again, an equivalent argument may be made for the wealth effects on Q, C, and S caused by a change in α_i. Thus, the wealth elasticities may be written

$$\epsilon_{Ni} = \epsilon_N \gamma_i, \tag{D15}$$

$$\epsilon_{Qi} = \epsilon_Q \gamma_i, \tag{D16}$$

$$\epsilon_{Ci} = (\epsilon_N + \epsilon_Q)\alpha_i, \tag{D17}$$

$$\epsilon_{Si} = \epsilon_S \gamma_i, \tag{D18}$$

where

$$\gamma_i = \frac{\alpha_i}{I}\frac{\partial I}{\partial \alpha_i} = (-\pi_c \alpha_i/I)\Phi_i$$

is the elasticity of full wealth with respect to α_i and ϵ_N, ϵ_Q, ϵ_C, and ϵ_S are, respectively, the wealth elasticities of demand for fertility, child quality, child services, and other sources of satisfaction. From the first partial derivatives of the K J* and J-type constraints, it is easily seen that the γ_i are simply

$$\gamma_H = H/I, \tag{D19}$$

$$\gamma_K = w_K L/I, \tag{D20}$$

$$\gamma_T = \hat{w}T/I. \tag{D21}$$

The total effect on consumption of a change in γ_i is the sum of the compensated substitution effect and the wealth effect. In elasticity terms, these total elasticities are

$$\delta_N = \eta_N e_i + \epsilon_N \gamma_i, \tag{D22}$$

$$\delta_Q = \eta_Q e_i + \epsilon_N \gamma_i, \tag{D23}$$

$$\delta_C = (\eta_N + \eta_Q) e_i + (\epsilon_N + \epsilon_Q) \gamma_i, \tag{D24}$$

$$\delta_S = \eta_S e_i + \epsilon_S \gamma_i. \tag{D25}$$

Comment

Norman B. Ryder

Office of Population Research, Princeton University

Let me abuse the invitation to discuss the paper by Robert Willis by taking the opportunity to unload a few thoughts on the new home economics and related concerns. Although it is basically presumptuous for an outsider (even one who was once inside) to try to tell a group of professionals what they are really doing or ought to be doing, it may be that noninvolvement in the rituals and routines of the work in question can provide a clarity of vision. If the outcome is mere heresy, it can at least be readily dismissed as the obvious consequence of ignorance.

I think of economics as playing a central and unique role within the complex of the sciences of behavior—central because its area of expertise is the calculus of choice, and choice is ubiquitous and ineluctable in all behavior; unique because its contribution is primarily (maybe exclusively) a deductive one. I think of the principles of economics as ultimately tautological derivations from a branch of applied mathematics. These comments are in no sense denigrating; I perceive demography, which is my lifeblood, to have the same formal characteristics. No act of an individual or group is without an economic dimension, although many classes of action have been underexposed to the risk of an economist's scrutiny because they do not pass through the marketplace. What goes on in the family is an obvious case in point. The subject calls for an expansion of the power and reach of the calculus of choice beyond merely money-valued resources into the economies of time, energy, emotional commitment, and the like.

So economists have entered the home and declared that children can be thought of as purchases by parents and that the time the wife spends on domestic affairs has an opportunity cost. True enough. But to build the new home economics on a solid foundation, so that the other social scientists interested in the family will be forced to pay attention, it is necessary to specify those ways in which the purchase of a child is distinctive from the purchases of those kinds of commodity on which economics has developed its discipline to date—and those ways in which the decision by the

76

wife to divide her time between the world inside and the world outside the home is a peculiarly constrained choice.

I suggest the simple but fundamental proposition that the replacement of a continually aging citizenry by new recruits is much too important to the entire body politic to tolerate untrammeled individual choice to hold sway. On this issue, as on so many others, the society intervenes, in obvious and in subtle ways, to ensure that the outcome, at least in the aggregate, makes sense on the society's behalf. These constraints on choice are what sociologists call norms. Just as no act is devoid of economic content, so no act is devoid of normative content. Norms are not just another discipline's jargon for tastes and preferences; the distinction is crucial between them, because the terms point in entirely different research directions. When tastes and preferences are employed for some purpose more elevating than circular reasoning, they promote research into the properties of individuals, whereas norms are properties of organized groups which individuals pay heed to in their actions to the extent that they have been successfully socialized into membership in the groups. Nor are norms arbitrary in their shape: they are institutionalized solutions to pervasive problems, and if they do not make sense, the group suffers the consequences. Were these norms fixed in time and space, one could readily take them as given (meaning essentially to forget them), but they vary from culture to culture, from subculture to subculture, from class to class, and they vary through time. Only when the time perspective of the economist is very short can they safely be neglected. So thoroughly are they embedded in our lives that they verge on the invisible, and this is one of the major sources of their strength. Yet that creates great research difficulties for the sociologist and provokes great impatience in the nonsociologist. Now no economist would fail to take into account various biological properties which condition behavior, like early dependence or limited reproductive span. Sociocultural properties play the same kind of role.

Willis presents a model within a framework of the economic theory of the family, but he proceeds about this important task by systematically destroying the idea of a family. The family in its skeleton form consists of a flow of person-years through time, encompassing the adult lifetime of one male and one female and the nonadult lifetimes of a varying number of children (including zero). The members of the family are bound to each other by contract, with clear specifications, *inter alia,* of the directions and amounts of flows of resources and services from one to another member. Willis has collapsed time into the instant of initial decision, he has defined the parents as subjects and the children as objects, he has denied the members the right to take satisfaction in the satisfaction of others, he has merged the husband and wife into a single utility function of the individual type—in short, he has solved the problems of family economics by dissolving the family. To give one specific example: there is no characteristic of the child save perhaps the requirement of the expenditure of time as well as other resources that makes the model any different from one concerned with any other purchase. Willis presents a good list of the recalcitrant characteristics of fertility behavior, but the job of coping with those characteristics from an economic standpoint remains undone. Almost the only concession to the family as a concept—and that regrettably an unwittingly sexist position—is to assign the husband to the labor force full time and permit the wife to be assigned to the labor force some proportion of time (from 0 to 1).

I am incompetent to evaluate the merits of the economic model Willis presents, but I feel less abashed by that circumstance than would ordinarily be the case because, as I have suggested, I cannot perceive its special relevance for fertility. But there are some empirical results, and they suggest some observations. Willis examines the determinants of parity for white women age 35–64, married once, husband present, in urban areas in 1960. Why each of these implicit choices was made is unexplained. It seems regrettable to destroy variance by restricting the examination to urban whites; the use of an age limit as low as 35 unfortunately reduces variance still further (because, although fertility beyond age 35 is small in toto, it bulks large as a source of differentials); many interesting kinds of families get short shrift by the restriction to stable unions; and the particular epoch of our history associated with these cohorts is the trough of a cycle, so that the relationships observed may be quite different from observations around a peak or observations independent of cycle altogether.

Willis presents his regression equation in the following form: $P = 4.83269 - 0.24386*I - 0.17572*E + 0.02023*E*I - 0.07243*S$, where P is parity, I is estimated income of husband at age 40, E is education of wife, and S is the size of urban area of residence. This may be reformulated by assigning S its mean value and subsuming it in the constant term (Willis gives us no reason to be interested in S) and by dividing the coefficients of E and I by the coefficient of $E*I$. Collecting terms and doing a little rounding, I obtain $P = 2.5 + 0.02*(8.7 - I)*(12.3 - E)$. The mean of I, which is in thousands of dollars, is 4.3; the mean of E, which is in years of schooling completed, is 10.5. The rephrased regression suggests the presence of threshold values for income and education; it also leads into a favorite theme of some sociologists, that of status inconsistency, since the low parities are produced by combinations of high income and low education, on the one hand, and low income and high education, on the other. The reformulated regression indicates the way in which the partial of P with respect to I depends on E and the partial of P with respect to E depends on I.

The cluster of relationships which leads Willis to his regression are: The proportion of women working varies directly with the education of wife and inversely with the income of husband; for the working woman, fertility varies inversely with education of wife; for the nonworking woman, fertility varies inversely with income of husband. Implicit is the empirical tendency for the education of wife to vary directly with the income of husband. The only one of these relationships with which I find any difficulty is the inverse relationship of fertility with husband's income for the nonworking woman. I suggest that a more plausible version would be that fertility varies inversely with wife's education for the nonworking woman. The point is that I believe the alternative opportunity cost of children rises with the wife's education, whether she is thinking of market or nonmarket pursuits. I recognize that Willis intended her education as a surrogate for her lifetime earning capacity, but the data are blind to the concepts of the theorist, and wife's education means whatever it means, which to me is a lot more than merely earning capacity. Similarly, the dependent variable, completed (or nearly completed) parity, is presumably thought of as a consequence of the initial game plan. I think the results of a generation of fertility research suggest that variations in parity are more likely to reflect variations in the efficacy of fertility regulation than variations in intention. The use of a regression equation to estimate husband's income at age 40 is an interesting innovation. Unfortunately, it has the consequence of erasing from the system one kind of income variable which has been found to affect fertility, that is, the deviation of one's income from what would be expected on the basis of one's occupation, education, and so forth.

Were I designing research on fertility, from an economic standpoint, I think it would be advisable to consider the aspects of the reproductive process which are most clearly discretionary. One of these is the age of the wife (and husband) at birth of the first child. More precisely, that should be the age at birth of the first intended child. There is substantial variance in this. It would appear to be related in obvious ways to current and prospective income, as well as to the education of the wife and her work history, and it is of extraordinary importance demographically (in terms of its consequences for variations in the birth rate, in the short run, and for variations in the ultimate size of the population, in the long run). A second focus would be the decision as to whether or not to have a third child. On that decision hangs the balance between growth or decline in population size. Such was the central concern of the Princeton Fertility Study, by Westoff and others. The yield from their economic inputs was meager, but their staff did not include an economist. A third suggestion is examination of the temporal interdependency of the work history and the procreative history of the wife, because of its potential bearing on the initiation and termination of childbearing as well as on the length of birth interval. Again, it is important to distinguish carefully those acts of procreation which occur by design from those which occur by accident (and

are accordingly presumably the focus for another kind of model altogether). The final discretionary point which may deserve increasing
attention in the future, although it has largely been proscribed in the
past, is the decision as to whether to have children at all (and quite apart
from whether or not marriage occurs). The proportion voluntarily infertile
seems now to be rising, and the norms defining women's roles are under
concerted attack.

While I would be reluctant to dissuade Willis and others from attempts
at model building such as the present one—since I work in a theoretically
impoverished area and regret it—it does seem to me that some redirection
of energies is requisite to the further development of the economic theory
of fertility. What seems most needed is information, collected according to
the specifications of economists, about the behavior with which their models
purport to be concerned. Demographers survived for centuries on official
registration and enumeration data, but only in the last few decades
have they faced the realization that they have to create their own data to
test their own theories. In my judgment, the economic theory of fertility is
too important to rely on secondhand data, devised for other purposes, from
the U.S. census, or even from our National Fertility Study.

Interaction between Quantity and Quality of Children

Gary S. Becker and H. Gregg Lewis

University of Chicago

Students of human fertility have been aware for a long time that there may be some special relation between the number (quantity) of children ever born to a family and the "quality" of their children as perceived by others if not by the parents. One need only cite the negative correlation between quantity and quality of children per family so often observed in both cross-section and time-series data. One of us (Becker 1960) more than a decade ago stressed the importance for understanding fertility (quantity) of the interaction between quantity and quality, and we are pleased to note that this interaction is emphasized in this book, and especially by De Tray and Willis.

Some economists have argued that the negative relation between quantity and quality often observed is a consequence of a low substitution elasticity in a family's utility function between parents' consumption or level of living and that of their children (see, e.g., Duesenberry 1960; Willis 1969). The approach followed by De Tray in this volume is different, but it makes equally special assumptions about the substitution between quantity and quality in the utility function and in household production.

We want to argue here that one can go a long way toward understanding data on the interaction between quantity and quality as well as on quantity or quality alone without assuming that, either in the utility function or in household production, quantity and quality are more closely related than any two commodities chosen at random. The analysis that follows is sketchy and incomplete, mainly because we have only recently developed this line of argument.

The key feature in our analysis is that the shadow price of children with respect to their number (i.e., the cost of an additional child, holding their quality constant) is greater the higher their quality is. Similarly, the shadow price of children with respect to their quality (i.e., the cost of a unit increase in quality, holding number constant) is greater, the greater the number of children. Furthermore, with appropriate change of language, the same may be said of the other commodities consumed by the family. However, to simplify the analysis in this paper, we make the quantity-quality distinction only for children. Thus, to illustrate our reasoning, we specify the following simple utility function:

$$U = U(n, q, y), \qquad (1)$$

where n is the number of children, q their quality (assumed to be the same for all of the children), and y the rate of consumption of all other commodities. We start out with a simple budget restraint:

$$I = nq\pi + y\pi_y, \qquad (2)$$

where I is full income, π is the price of nq, and π_y is the price of y. We make no special assumptions about the elasticities of substitution among n, q, and y, either in the utility function or in the household production functions that underlie the π's.

The first-order conditions for maximizing the utility function subject to the budget restraint are:

$$MU_n = \lambda q\pi = \lambda p_n; \; MU_q = \lambda n\pi = \lambda p_q; \; MU_y = \lambda\pi_y = \lambda p_y, \qquad (3)$$

where the MU's are the marginal utilities, the p's are marginal costs or shadow prices, and λ is the marginal utility of money income. The important point is that the shadow price of children with respect to number (p_n) is positively related to q, the level of quality, and the shadow price with respect to quality (p_q) is positively related to n, the number of children. The economic interpretation is that an increase in quality is more expensive if there are more children because the increase has to apply to more units; similarly, an increase in quantity is more expensive if the children are of higher quality, because higher-quality children cost more.

These equilibrium conditions (3) together with the second-order conditions can be found in several places in the literature on quantity and quality (see, e.g., Houthakker 1952; Theil 1952; Becker 1960; and Willis's paper in this volume), but a number of their important implications for income and price effects apparently have not been explored.

1. Income Effects

Let the "true" income elasticities of demand for the number (n) and quality (q) of children and for all other commodities (y) be η_n, η_q, and η_y, respectively. These elasticities are derived in the usual way by changing "income" while holding constant the "prices" of n, q, and y. The appropriate prices for this purpose are the shadow prices (marginal costs)

p_n, p_q, and p_y, whose ratios in equilibrium (see eq. [3]) are equal to the marginal rates of substitution in the utility function. The appropriate income concept is the total "expenditure" on n, q, and y calculated at these shadow prices; that is, the correct measure of income for this purpose is

$$R = np_n + qp_q + yp_y = I + nq\pi. \tag{4}$$

It is well known that the mean value of the true income elasticities is unity; that is:

$$1 = \frac{np_n}{R}\eta_n + \frac{qp_q}{R}\eta_q + \frac{yp_y}{R}\eta_y. \tag{5}$$

Consider, however, the "observed" income elasticities, which we denote by $\bar{\eta}_n$, $\bar{\eta}_q$, and $\bar{\eta}_y$, derived by changing I while holding π and π_y constant. It follows directly from the budget restraint (2) and the definitions of the p's in (3) that the similarly weighted mean of the observed income elasticities is $I/R = I/(I + nq\pi)$, which is less than unity; that is:

$$1 > \frac{I}{R} = \frac{I}{I + nq\pi} = \frac{np_n}{R}\bar{\eta}_n + \frac{qp_q}{R}\bar{\eta}_q + \frac{yp_y}{R}\bar{\eta}_y. \tag{6}$$

That is, on the average, the observed elasticities are smaller than the true elasticities in the ratio I/R. The economic explanation for this downward bias is simple. The direct effect of the increase in I, holding the π's but not the p's constant, in general is to increase n, q, and y. However, increases in n and q cause the shadow prices p_n and p_q to rise. Thus, the percentage increase in real income in the sense of R deflated by an index of the p's is less than the percentage increase in money income I.

This price effect of an increase in money income resembles somewhat the price effect resulting from a rise in money income caused by a rise in wage rates. The increase, in ratio terms, is less in real income than in money income, because the costs of producing commodities in the household are increased by the rise in the price of time (see Becker 1965).[1]

We think that it is plausible to assume that the true income elasticity with respect to quality (η_q) is substantially larger than that with respect to quantity (η_n). Because of the downward bias in the observed elasticities and the effect on prices, the observed elasticity for quantity ($\bar{\eta}_n$) may be negative even though the true elasticity (η_n) is not. Assume for simplicity

---

[1] This price effect, however, does offer a correction to the argument advanced by Becker (1960), and followed by many others, that the price of children is the same for the rich as for the poor (aside from the cost-of-time argument), even though the rich choose more expensive children. The relevant price of children with respect to their number *is* higher for the rich precisely because they choose more expensive children. Similarly, the relevant price of cars, houses, or other goods is higher for the rich because they choose more expensive varieties.

that $\eta_n = 0$. Let income I increase while holding π and π_y constant. The direct effect of the increase in I is to increase q (and y) while leaving n unchanged. But then the shadow price with respect to quantity ($p_n = q\pi$) will rise while the shadow price of quality ($p_q = n\pi$) and that of y($p_y = \pi_y$) are unchanged, causing q and y to be substituted for n, and therefore n will decline.

More generally, when the utility function and budget restraints are those given above in equations (1) and (2), the observed income elasticities for quantity and quality are related to the corresponding true elasticities as follows:[2]

$$\frac{D\bar{\eta}_n}{1-k} = (1 - k\sigma_{nq})\eta_n - (1 - k)\bar{\sigma}_n\eta_q;$$

$$\frac{D\bar{\eta}_q}{1-k} = (1 - k\sigma_{nq})\eta_q - (1 - k)\bar{\sigma}_q\eta_n,$$

$$(7)$$

where

$$\left\{ \begin{array}{l} k \equiv \dfrac{nq\pi}{R} \ ; \ (1 - k)\bar{\sigma}_n = k\sigma_{nq} + (1 - 2k)\sigma_{ny}; \ (1 - k)\bar{\sigma}_q \\[2mm] = k\sigma_{nq} + (1 - 2k)\sigma_{qy}; \\[2mm] D \equiv (1 - k\sigma_{nq})^2 - (1 - k)^2\bar{\sigma}_n\bar{\sigma}_q. \end{array} \right. \quad (8)$$

The σ's are the familiar Allen partial elasticities of substitution in the utility function; the $\bar{\sigma}$'s are averages of the σ's, and they must be positive; D and $(1 - k\sigma_{nq})$ are positive by the second-order conditions. Equations (7) verify that the observed quantity elasticity ($\bar{\eta}_n$) may be negative even when the true quantity elasticity (η_n) is positive. Furthermore, if $\eta_q > \eta_n$, as we assume, $\bar{\eta}_q > \bar{\eta}_n$ unless q is a much better substitute than n for y, for it follows from (7) and (8) that

$$\frac{D}{1-k}(\bar{\eta}_q - \bar{\eta}_n) = \eta_q - \eta_n + (1 - 2k)(\sigma_{ny}\eta_q - \sigma_{qy}\eta_n). \quad (9)$$

Moreover, $\bar{\eta}_q$ may exceed $\bar{\eta}_n$ by more than η_q exceeds η_n; that is, the downward bias in $\bar{\eta}_q$ may be less than that in $\bar{\eta}_n$. This is easily seen for the case in which $\sigma_{nq} = \sigma_{ny} = \sigma_{qy} = \sigma$. Then D, which is positive, is equal to $(1 - \sigma)[1 + \sigma(1 - 2k)]$ and $\bar{\eta}_q - \bar{\eta}_n = (1 - k)(\eta_q - \eta_n)/(1 - \sigma)$, so that $\bar{\eta}_q - \bar{\eta}_n > \eta_q - \eta_n$ if $\sigma > k$. Indeed, $\bar{\eta}_q$ may even exceed η_q, as may be seen from (7) and (8) by assuming $\eta_n = 0$ and $\sigma_{nq} = \sigma_{ny} = \sigma_{qy} = \sigma$. Then $\bar{\eta}_q = (1 - k)(1 - k\sigma)\eta_q/(1 - \sigma)[1 + \sigma(1 - 2k)]$, which will exceed η_q if, for example, $k = \frac{1}{3}$ and $\sigma = \frac{3}{4}$.

---

[2] See the Mathematical Appendix to this paper.

Even if η_n were constant, $\bar{\eta}_n$ need not be, since the latter depends not only on η_n but also on the substitution elasticities and the share of $nq\pi$ in money income I $(nq\pi/I = k/(1 - k))$. For example, if η_q declines as income I rises—a plausible assumption, we think—$\bar{\eta}_n$ would tend to rise with income, even with constant η_n, and, of course, η_n may rise with income, contributing to the increase in $\bar{\eta}_n$. Indeed, $\bar{\eta}_n$ could be negative at lower levels of income and positive at higher levels, the pattern observed in some fertility data.[3]

2. Price Effects

Before discussing price effects, we generalize the budget constraint (2) slightly as follows:

$$I = n\pi_n + nq\pi + q\pi_q + yp_y \qquad (10)$$

so that the shadow prices or marginal costs are now

$$p_n = \pi_n + q\pi; \; p_q = \pi_q + n\pi; \; p_y = \pi_y. \qquad (11)$$

These shadow prices for n and q each contain a "fixed" component: π_n in p_n and π_q in p_q. The component $n\pi_n$ in child costs consists of costs that depend on quantity but not on quality. Contraception costs and prenatal child costs (such as maternity care) are moderately good examples. Similarly, the component $q\pi_q$ depends on quality but not quantity, and thus has the attributes of a "public good," or a better expression is a "family good." Perhaps some aspects of training in the home and the "handing down" of some clothing are reasonable examples. We assume that the fixed component is more important for quantity than for quality, that is, $n\pi_n > q\pi_q$.

a) First consider the pure substitution effects of an increase in π_n induced, say, by an exogenous improvement in contraceptive technique. Since this increases the shadow price of quantity (p_n) relative to both the shadow price of quality (p_q) and the shadow price of $y(p_y)$, n would fall. But the fall in numbers reduces the shadow price of quality $(p_q = \pi_q + n\pi)$, which induces substitution in favor of quality. The outcome would be not only a fall in quantity but also a relatively large rise in quality— relative, that is, to other commodities—without assuming that quantity and quality are better substitutes than any two commodities chosen at random. Exactly the same result holds if π_q falls, say, because of an increase in the education of parents. The fall in p_q induces an increase in quality, which in turn induces an increase in the shadow price of quantity $(p_n = \pi_n + q\pi)$ and thus a relatively large decrease in quantity.

Consequently, both De Tray's finding (in his paper which follows) that an

[3] See the discussion and alternative explanation of this finding earlier in Willis's paper.

increase in the education of mothers has a strong positive effect on the quality and a strong negative effect on the number of their children, and the common belief that important advances in birth control knowledge not only significantly reduce the number of children but also significantly increase their quality, are consistent with the preceding analysis. Quantity and quality are closely related, because the shadow price of quality depends on quantity and the shadow price of quantity depends on quality. We repeat that no special assumptions about substitution in household production or consumption are required to derive a special relation between quantity and quality.

b) Now consider the pure substitution effects of equal percentage increases in π_n, π_q, and π due, say, to increases in wage rates. To put the argument in extreme form, assume $\pi_q = 0$ and $\pi_n > 0$. The equal increases in π_n, π_q, and π relative to $\pi_y = p_y$ can be treated simply as a relative fall in $\pi_y = p_y$. A fall in p_y initially would induce equal percentage declines in n and q if they were equally good substitutes for y. However, since the equal percentage declines in n and q would lower p_q more than p_n, n would fall relative to q. Thus, the income-compensated elasticity of quantity with respect to equal percentage changes in π_n, π_q and π tends to be greater numerically than the corresponding elasticity for quality. De Tray finds that an increase in women's wage rates reduces the number of children by a much bigger percentage than the quality of children.

This difference is, of course, accentuated if quantity is a better substitute than quality for other commodities, which we think is a plausible, though special, assumption. For then a fall in p_y directly induces a fall in n relative to q, which accentuates the decline in p_q relative to p_n.

We conclude, therefore, that the observed price elasticity of quantity exceeds that of quality, just the opposite of our conclusion for observed income elasticities.[4] This reversal of the quantity-quality ordering for price and income elasticities is not only a somewhat unexpected implication of the analysis, but also gives a consistent interpretation to the findings of De Tray and others.

Of course, most of our discussion applies not only to the interaction between the quantity and quality of children, but also to the quantity and quality of cars, houses, food, tea, education, publications, and large numbers of other goods. The observed price and income elasticities of quantity and quality will differ in predictable directions from the "true" elasticities. A systematic analysis and reconsideration of the interaction between quan-

---

[4] This conclusion about income elasticities, derived from the budget restraint (2), is modified somewhat when the budget restraint is of the more general form (10), since the shadow price of quality is less sensitive to any given percentage change in quality than the price of quality is to a change in quantity. Conceivably then, $\bar{\eta}_n$ could be greater than $\bar{\eta}_q$ at the same time that $\eta_n < \eta_q$, but we consider this unlikely, since η_q is probably much greater than η_n.

tity and quality of all goods from the viewpoint of this paper should be quite rewarding.

Mathematical Appendix

The budget restraints specified in equations (2) and (10) are not linear in n and q. It is precisely this nonlinearity, of course, that leads to the "interaction between quantity and quality" that we discuss in this paper.

The derivation of the elasticities of the demand functions for number of children (n) and child quality (q) can be carried in a direct fashion by differentiating the budget restraint and the first-order conditions. Because of the nonlinearity of the budget restraint, however, if this direct mode of derivation is followed, it is all too easy to lose sight of the underlying income and substitution elasticities in the utility function. Hence, we follow an indirect approach that makes use of quite familiar propositions in demand theory.

First, we replace the curvilinear budget surface given in equation (10) by a plane surface by adding $nq\pi$ to both sides:

$$I + nq\pi = n(\pi_n + q\pi) + q(\pi_q + n\pi) + y\pi_y \tag{A1}$$

$$R = np_n + qp_q + yp_y. \tag{A2}$$

where

$$R = I + nq\pi = I/(1-k); \quad k \equiv nq\pi/R. \tag{A3}$$

The two income concepts I and R differ by the nonlinear term $nq\pi$ in the budget restraint.

Define

$$k_i \equiv \frac{ip_i}{R}, \quad i = n, q, y; \quad k_n + k_q + k_y = 1. \tag{A4}$$

It is well known that the true income elasticities (η_n, η_q, and η_y) must satisfy the relation

$$1 = k_n\eta_n + k_q\eta_q + k_y\eta_y. \tag{A5}$$

The observed income elasticities ($\bar{\eta}_n$, $\bar{\eta}_q$, $\bar{\eta}_y$) obtained by changing full income I while holding the π's constant, however, must satisfy

$$1 - k = -\frac{I}{R} = k_n\bar{\eta}_n + k_q\bar{\eta}_q + k_y\bar{\eta}_y. \tag{A6}$$

Equation (A6) may be verified by differentiating the budget restraint (10) logarithmically with respect to I, holding the π's constant, and then using equations (A3) and (A4). Thus, the observed elasticities, on the average, are smaller than the true elasticities in the ratio $1 - k = I/R$.

We now define two household price indexes $\bar{\pi}$ and $\bar{p}$ in differential form as follows:

$$
\left\{
\begin{aligned}
E\bar{\pi} &\equiv \frac{y\pi_y}{I} E\pi_y + \frac{n\pi_n}{I} E\pi_n + \frac{q\pi_q}{I} E\pi_q + \frac{nq\pi}{I} E\pi \\
&= \frac{1}{1-k} [k_y E\pi_y + (k_n - k)E\pi_n + (k_q - k)E\pi_q + kE\pi],
\end{aligned}
\right.
\tag{A7}
$$

$$E\bar{p} \equiv k_y Ep_y + k_n Ep_n + k_q Ep_q, \tag{A8}$$

where the symbol E denotes the natural logarithmic differential operator dln.

Since $p_y = \pi_y$, $p_n = \pi_n + q\pi$, and $p_q = \pi_q + \eta_\pi$, it follows that

$$Ep_y = E\pi_y; \; Ep_n = \frac{(k_n - k)E\pi_n + k(E\pi + Eq)}{k_n};$$

$$Ep_q = \frac{(k_q - k)E\pi_q + k(E\pi + En)}{k_q}. \tag{A9}$$

Substitute these results (A9) into (A8) and then use (A7) to obtain

$$E\bar{p} = (1 - k)E\bar{\pi} + kEnq\pi. \tag{A10}$$

Now differentiate (A3) logarithmically:

$$ER = (1 - k)EI + kEnq\pi. \tag{A11}$$

Subtract (A10) from (A11):

$$E(R/\bar{p}) = (1 - k)E(I/\bar{\pi}). \tag{A12}$$

When I is increased, holding the π's constant, real income $R/\bar{p}$ increases in the smaller ratio $1 - k = I/R$. This is the economic basis of the downward bias in the observed income elasticities relative to the true income elasticities.

We now turn to the derivation of the observed income and substitution elasticities. We make use of the well-known propositions that

$$\begin{cases} En = \eta_n E(R/\bar{p}) + k_y \sigma_{ny} Ep_y - (1 - k_n)\bar{\sigma}_n Ep_n + k_q \sigma_{nq} Ep_q, \\ Eq = \eta_q E(R/\bar{p}) + k_y \sigma_{qy} Ep_y + k_n \sigma_{nq} Ep_n - (1 - k_q)\bar{\sigma}_q Ep_q, \\ (1 - k_n)\bar{\sigma}_n \equiv k_y \sigma_{ny} + k_q \sigma_{nq}; \; (1 - k_q)\bar{\sigma}_q \equiv k_y \sigma_{qy} + k_n \sigma_{nq}, \end{cases} \tag{A13}$$

where the σ's are the Allen partial elasticities of substitution in the utility function. Notice that $\bar{\sigma}_n$ is the average elasticity of substitution of n against y and q and that $\bar{\sigma}_q$ is the similar elasticity for q against y and n.

We first derive the observed income elasticities $\bar{\eta}_n$ and $\bar{\eta}_q$ by letting I change while the π's are constant. Because the π's are constant, it follows from (A9) and (A12) that

$$Ep_y = 0; \; Ep_n = \frac{kEq}{k_n}, \; Ep_q = \frac{kEn}{k_q}; \; E(R/\bar{p}) = (1 - k)EI. \tag{A14}$$

Substitute (A14) into (A13) and collect terms to obtain

$$\begin{cases} (1 - k\sigma_{nq})\bar{\eta}_n + \frac{k(1 - k_n)\bar{\sigma}_n}{k_n}\bar{\eta}_q = (1 - k)\eta_n \\ \frac{k(1 - k_q)\bar{\sigma}_q}{k_q}\bar{\eta}_n + (1 - k\sigma_{nq})\bar{\eta}_q = (1 - k)\eta_q. \end{cases} \tag{A15}$$

Solve these two equations for $\bar{\eta}_n$ and $\bar{\eta}_q$:

$$\left\{ \begin{array}{l} \dfrac{D\bar{\eta}_n}{1-k} = (1 - k\sigma_{nq})\eta_n - \dfrac{k(1-k_n)\bar{\sigma}_n}{k_n}\eta_q, \\[2mm] \dfrac{D\bar{\eta}_q}{1-k} = (1 - k\sigma_{nq})\eta_q - \dfrac{k(1-k_q)\bar{\sigma}_q}{k_q}\eta_n, \\[2mm] D \equiv (1 - k\dot{\sigma}_{nq})^2 - \dfrac{k^2(1-k_n)(1-k_q)\bar{\sigma}_n\bar{\sigma}_q}{k_n k_q}, \end{array} \right. \tag{A16}$$

where D and $(1 - k\sigma_{nq})$ must be positive by the second-order conditions.

In the section on income effects, we used the simpler budget restraint (2) rather than (10), so that we assumed that $k_n = k_q = k$; equations (7) and (8) are simply equations (A16) when $k_n = k_q = k$. The only proposition in that section that needs qualification when the budget restraint is (10) is the proposition that $\bar{\eta}_q - \bar{\eta}_n$ has the sign of $\eta_q - \eta_n$ unless σ_{qy} is much larger than σ_{ny}. Let $\sigma_{ny} = \sigma_{qy} = \sigma_{nq} = \sigma$ in (A16). Then

$$\frac{D(\bar{\eta}_q - \bar{\eta}_n)}{1-k} = (1 - 2k\sigma)(\eta_q - \eta_n) + \frac{k\sigma}{k_n k_q}(k_q\eta_q - k_n\eta_n), \tag{A17}$$

where $(1 - 2k\sigma)$ must be positive by the second-order conditions. In the section on price effects, we assume that $k_n - k_q = n\pi_n - q\pi_q/R$ is positive. But then if η_q/η_n is sufficiently smaller than k_n/k_q, $\bar{\eta}_q - \bar{\eta}_n$ will have a sign opposite that of $\eta_q - \eta_n$. We have noted this qualification and commented on it (see n. 4 above).

We turn now to the income-compensated elasticities of quantity and quality with respect to the π's, deriving them in essentially the same manner as the income elasticities. We consider first the elasticities with respect to π_n and π_q:

$$\left\{ \begin{array}{l} D\bar{\eta}_{i\pi_i}{}^{(s)} = -\dfrac{(k_i - k)(1-k_i)\bar{\sigma}_i}{k_i}, \quad i = n, q, \\[3mm] D\bar{\eta}_{i\pi_j}{}^{(s)} = (k_j - k)\left[\sigma_{nq}(1 - k\sigma_{nq}) + \dfrac{k(1-k_i)(1-k_j)\bar{\sigma}_i\bar{\sigma}_j}{k_i k_j} \right], \\[3mm] \hspace{7cm} i \neq j = n, q. \end{array} \right. \tag{A18}$$

When $\sigma_{ny} = \sigma_{qy} = \sigma_{nq} = \sigma$, these simplify to

$$\left\{ \begin{array}{l} D\bar{\eta}_{i\pi_i}{}^{(s)} = -\dfrac{(k_i - k)(1-k_i)\sigma}{k_i}, \quad i = n, q, \\[3mm] D\bar{\eta}_{i\pi_j}{}^{(s)} = \dfrac{(k_j - k)\sigma}{k_i k_j}(k_i k_j + k k_y\sigma), \quad i \neq j = n, q, \quad (A19) \\[3mm] D = (1 - 2k\sigma) - \dfrac{k_y(k\sigma)^2}{k_n k_q}. \end{array} \right.$$

Both observed "own price" elasticities, $\bar{\eta}_{n\pi_n}{}^{(s)}$ and $\bar{\eta}_{q\pi_q}{}^{(s)}$ are negative, and the sign of $|\bar{\eta}_{n\pi_n}{}^{(s)}| - |\bar{\eta}_{q\pi_q}{}^{(s)}|$ is ambiguous even when it is assumed that

$\sigma_{ny} = \sigma_{qy} = \sigma_{nq} = \sigma$ and that $k_n - k_q > 0$. However, if π_q is small relative to p_q, $|\bar{\eta}_{n\pi_n}{}^{(s)}|$ will exceed $|\bar{\eta}_{q\pi_q}{}^{(s)}|$. The observed cross-elasticities, $\bar{\eta}_{n\pi_q}{}^{(s)}$ and $\bar{\eta}_{q\pi_n}{}^{(s)}$, are positive if $\sigma_{nq} > 0$, and $\bar{\eta}_{q\pi_n}{}^{(s)}$ exceeds $\bar{\eta}_{n\pi_q}{}^{(s)}$ if $k_n > k_q$, as we assume. The cross-partial derivatives, however, are equal:

$$\frac{\partial n}{\partial \pi_q} = \frac{\partial q}{\partial \pi_n} = \frac{nq}{R}\left[\sigma_{nq}(1 - k\sigma_{nq}) + \frac{k(1-k_n)(1-k_q)\bar{\sigma}_n\bar{\sigma}_q}{k_n k_q} \right]$$

(A20)

where the derivatives are income-compensated.

The observed elasticities with respect to $\pi_y = p_y$ are

$$\frac{D\bar{\eta}_{i\pi_y}}{k_y} = \sigma_{iy}(1 - k\sigma_{nq}) - \sigma_{jy}k(k_j\sigma_{nq} + k_y\sigma_{iy})/k_i, \; i \neq j = n, q,$$

(A21)

from which it follows that

$$\left[\begin{aligned} \frac{D}{k_y}(\bar{\eta}_{n\pi_y}{}^{(s)} &- \bar{\eta}_{q\pi_y}{}^{(s)}) = (\sigma_{ny} - \sigma_{qy})(1 - k\sigma_{nq}) \\ &+ \frac{k\sigma_{nq}}{k_n k_q}(k_n{}^2\sigma_{ny} - k_q{}^2\sigma_{qy}) + \frac{kk_y\sigma_{ny}\sigma_{qy}}{k_n k_q}(k_n - k_q). \end{aligned} \right.$$

(A22)

Thus, if the σ's are equal and if $k_n > k_q$, the quantity elasticity ($\bar{\eta}_{n\pi_y}{}^{(s)}$) exceeds the quality elasticity ($\bar{\eta}_{q\pi_y}{}^{(s)}$); this difference is increased if $\sigma_{ny} > \sigma_{qy}$, a special, though plausible, assumption.

The observed elasticities with respect to equal percentage changes in π_n, π_q, and π are simply those with respect to π_y but with signs changed. Thus, the demand functions for n and q are homogeneous of degree zero in I and the π's, just as they are in the shadow income (R) and the shadow prices (p's).

Child Quality and the Demand for Children

Dennis N. De Tray

RAND Corporation

I. Introduction

The past decade has brought a substantial increase in economic analyses of phenomena outside the traditional realm of economics. An already sizable portion of such effort has been directed toward the determinants of desired fertility and family size.[1] In this paper, I will first consider the degree to which pure economic theory can, or cannot, predict changes in completed fertility. The second, and the major emphasis of the study, is the way in which households produce the household commodity "child services."[2] I argue that households can increase their production of child services either by increasing numbers of children (quantity) or by increasing the resource investment (quality) in existing children. Further, quantity and quality are postulated to be substitutes in the household's production function for child services. After presenting an economic model of desired family size, emphasizing the substitutability of numbers of children and child quality, I will discuss several of the model's important parameters and then offer an empirical formulation based on data from U.S. counties.

This paper is drawn from a more comprehensive study (De Tray 1972*a*) published by the RAND Corporation. I have benefited greatly from many people's comments and criticisms on earlier drafts, and would especially like to thank Gary Becker, Yoram Ben-Porath, Glen Cain, Marc Nerlove, T. Paul Schultz, T. W. Schultz, and Finis Welch for their many helpful suggestions, not all of which have been incorporated in this paper. I, of course, am solely responsible for any remaining errors. The work for this paper was financed in part by grants to the University of Chicago from the National Institute of Mental Health and the Rockefeller Foundation, and by a grant to the RAND Corporation from the Rockefeller Foundation. Views expressed in this paper are mine and not those of any organization with which I am affiliated.

[1] See, for example, Becker (1960), Schultz (1969), Willis (1969), Ben-Porath (1970*a*), Nerlove and Schultz (1970), and Michael (1970).

[2] Familiarity with the terminology of the "household production function" model (Becker 1965; Lancaster 1966) is assumed throughout this paper. For a more detailed description of this model, see De Tray (1972*a*).

II. Toward an Economic Model of Desired Family Size

Children are viewed in this model as home-produced durable assets from whom parents consume a flow of services. This flow varies with both biological units of children (numbers) and with the resource intensity (quality) with which children are raised. No distinction is made between consumer-durable and producer-durable aspects of children in the formal model, although the effect of a positive opportunity cost for child-time (children having value as produced durables) is explored (Section III).

The utility function underlying household behavior has arguments "child services" and a composite commodity, Z, representing all other household production-consumption activities. The household utility function can be written as

$$U = U(C, Z), \tag{1}$$

where C is the stock of child services.

This study is concerned only with households' determination of the desired stocks of children and not with optimal timing patterns. The model is, therefore, of the one-period, static-state variety in which the household is assumed to make all lifetime decisions at one point in time and to have correctly gauged lifetime conditions. Strictly speaking, it is not C but the flow of services from C that enters the household utility function. However, in order to write the utility function as in equation (1), C need only be measured in "efficiency units," so that total services derived are proportional to the stock.

Assume that all inputs into the various production processes are perfectly divisible and all production functions homogeneous of degree one.[3] The amount of Z produced and consumed by the household depends on the quantities of time and purchased goods the household allocates to that production process, the state of household technology, and the efficiency with which that production process is undertaken. Inputs may be classified into three categories: male (husband's) time (t_m), female (wife's) time (t_f), and market goods and services (X).[4] The efficiency effect is assumed to be a function of the environment in which production takes place, which, in turn, depends primarily on husband's and wife's education.

The production of C is not accomplished directly through inputs of time and goods but by way of two home-produced factors, numbers of children

---

[3] The analysis is complicated, but the major results remain unchanged for homogeneous production functions of degrees other than one.

[4] To simplify the model, households are assumed to consist of a husband, a wife, and children only; that is, other adult members are not considered. Also, throughout this study, the terms "male time" and "female time" are used interchangeably with "husband's time" and "wife's time" and should not be confused with *hired* male and female time.

(N), and child quality (Q).[5] The complete household production framework can be summarized by the following four equations:[6]

$$C = C(N, Q); \tag{2}$$

$$N = N(t_{m,N}, t_{f,N}, X_N; \beta, \gamma); \tag{3}$$

$$Q = Q(t_{m,Q}, t_{f,Q}, X_Q; \beta, \gamma); \tag{4}$$

$$Z = Z(t_{m,Z}, t_{f,Z}, X_Z; \beta, \gamma), \tag{5}$$

where $t_{i,j} = $ total time of the ith household member in the production of the jth commodity or input $(i = $ male or female, and $j = Z$, N, or $Q)$; $\beta = $ generalized index of husband's efficiency in nonmarket production; $\gamma = $ generalized index of wife's efficiency in nonmarket production; and $X_j = $ market goods and services in the jth production process.

The form of the production framework may, at first, seem arbitrary in that N and Q might well be viewed as household commodities, thus eliminating equation (2). However, the relationship between N and Z would then be conceptually similar to that between N and Q. The model is formulated to emphasize that this may not be the case; that is, a special relationship exists between N and Q that does not exist between N and any other household commodity. In fact, the constant-returns-to-scale assumption restricts the pure derived income elasticities of N and Q to equality in this production framework; and thus the model has at least one testable prediction that separates it from alternative forms. More will be said below on this rather unusual feature of the model.

In arriving at desired lifetime levels of C and Z, households maximize equation (1) subject not only to the technological constraint implied by equations (2)–(5) but also to total available lifetime resources. With respect to market goods and services, the household can spend no more than the total earnings of all members plus any initial endowment or wealth transfers (inheritance, dowries, and so on). That is,

$$X_C \cdot P_C + X_Z \cdot P_Z \leqslant Y_m + Y_f + V, \tag{6}$$

where $X_j = $ market goods and services in the jth production process, $P_j = $ per unit price of X_j, $Y_i = $ lifetime market (wage) earnings of the ith household member, and $V = $ non-wage related income.

The household is also constrained in the time available for work and household production. If T_m and T_f represent total time of husband and wife respectively, then

---

[5] For this discussion, quality may be thought of as the resource intensity with which children are produced. The same notion is found in both Becker (1960) and Michael (1970).

[6] Note that the form of the equations implies that each production process is independent—joint production is ruled out. Given the previous assumption of perfectly divisible inputs, this is not a further restriction of the model (see Grossman 1971). However, since the earlier assumption is unrealistic in certain important respects, in Section III are mentioned possible effects of externalities, joint production, and so on, although the model is not formally amended to take these factors into account.

$$
\left.\begin{array}{l}
T_m = L_m + t_{m,c} + t_{m,z} \\
T_f = L_f + t_{f,c} + t_{f,z}
\end{array}\right\}, \tag{7}
$$

where $t_{i,j}$, as before, is time of the ith household member in the jth production process, and L_i indicates time spent in the market place (working).

Since time can be exchanged for goods at the market wage rate, the two constraints (eqq. [6], [7]) can be combined into the following "full wealth" or lifetime resource constraint:

$$
\begin{aligned}
I &= \pi_Z \cdot Z + \pi_C \cdot C \\
&= T_m \cdot W_m + T_f \cdot W_f + V, \tag{8}
\end{aligned}
$$

where $I =$ household full wealth, $\pi_j =$ shadow price to the household of the jth commodity, $W_m =$ male lifetime wage rate (per unit time), and $W_f =$ female lifetime wage rate (per unit time).

The framework set out above is structured to emphasize the possibility that households can substitute quality for numbers of children in their production of child services. It has also been left unrestricted to illustrate that even in the simplified framework of equations (1)–(8), there are serious problems involved in predicting, a priori, changes in *numbers of children*.

The following equation, derived in detail in the Appendix, illustrates the complexity of determining changes in the demand for N for given changes in exogenous or predetermined variables in the system:[7]

$$
\begin{aligned}
EN ={}& (V/I)\eta EV \\
&- \alpha_{X_N}\{\alpha[k\eta + (1-k)\sigma] + (1-\alpha)\sigma^*\}EP_N \\
&+ \alpha_{X_Q}(1-\alpha)[\sigma^* - k\eta - (1-k)\sigma]EP_Q \\
&+ \alpha_{X_Z}(1-k)(\sigma-\eta)EP_Z \tag{9} \\
&+ [(1-\alpha)\sigma^*(\alpha_{t_{m,Q}} - \alpha_{t_{m,N}}) + (1-k)\sigma(\alpha_{t_{m,z}} - \alpha_{t_{m,c}}) \\
&\qquad\qquad\qquad\qquad\qquad\qquad\qquad + (Y_m/I)\eta]EW_m \\
&+ [(1-\alpha)\sigma^*(\alpha_{t_{f,Q}} - \alpha_{t_{f,N}}) + (1-k)\sigma(\alpha_{t_{f,z}} - \alpha_{t_{f,c}}) \\
&\qquad\qquad\qquad\qquad\qquad\qquad\qquad + (Y_f/I)\eta]EW_f \\
&+ \{(1-\alpha)\sigma^*(\mu_{N,\beta} - \mu_{Q,\beta}) + (1-k)\sigma(\mu_{C,\beta} - \mu_{Z,\beta}) \\
&\qquad\qquad\qquad\qquad\qquad + \eta[k\mu_{C,\beta} + (1-k)\mu_{Z,\beta}]\}E\beta \\
&+ \{(1-\alpha)\sigma^*(\mu_{N,\gamma} - \mu_{Q,\gamma}) + (1-k)\sigma(\mu_{C,\gamma} - \mu_{Z,\gamma}) \\
&\qquad\qquad\qquad\qquad\qquad + \eta[k\mu_{C,\gamma} + (1-k)\mu_{Z,\gamma}]\}E\gamma,
\end{aligned}
$$

where $E = d(\log)$ operator (percentage change); $V =$ non–wage-related

---

[7] A multitude of simultaneity problems have been brushed aside in this statement. Probably the most important is the interdependence of the market wage rate and the amount of time spent in the home, an especially severe problem for women. For a recent attempt to deal with this, see Nerlove and Schultz (1970).

income; $I = $ full wealth; $\eta = $ income elasticity of C, child services; $\alpha = $ the share of expenditures on N in total expenditures on C, that is, $(\pi_N \cdot N)/(\pi_C \cdot C)$; $\sigma^* = $ the elasticity of substitution between N and Q in the production of C; $\alpha_{i,j} = $ the share of expenditures on the ith input in total expenditures on the jth output, where $i = X$, t_m, t_f and $j = N$, Q, Z, C; $k = $ the share of total expenditures on C in full wealth, I; $\sigma = $ substitution elasticity between C and Z in $U(C,Z)$; $P_i = $ price of market goods and services, X_i; $Y_i = $ lifetime market earnings of the ith household member; $W_i = $ wage of the ith family member; and $\mu_{i,j} = $ the partial elasticity of the ith output with respect to the educational level of the jth household member, $i = N$, Q, C, Z, and $j = \beta, \gamma$.

Although formidable in appearance, this expression is not difficult to interpret. Each line represents the "weighted" effect on N of a change in one price, wealth, or productivity variable. Note that with the exception of two variables (V and P_N), the signs of the elasticity coefficients are ambiguous. An increase in V will increase the demand for N if N is a normal good, and an increase in P_N will lead to a reduction in the demand for N. All other coefficients depend on (1) the relative importance of various inputs in the household production functions (as measured by their share in total production costs), (2) the degree to which male and female efficiency affects various production functions, and (3) relative household expenditures on C and Z. Unless one is willing to speculate on the magnitudes of these weights and efficiency effects, no a priori conclusions on fertility behavior can be drawn from the model.

A similar equation can be derived for child quality, with equally discouraging results. However, restricting the analysis to the *relative* amounts of N and Q improves the situation somewhat. Either from the above model, or more simply from a variant of the definition of the elasticity of substitution,[8] the following relationship for the percentage change in the ratio of Q to C can be derived:

$$E(Q/N) = EQ - EN = \sigma^*[(\alpha_{t_m,N} - \alpha_{t_m,Q})EW_m + (\alpha_{t_f,N} - \alpha_{t_f,Q})EW_f$$
$$+ (\alpha_{X_N})EP_N - (\alpha_{X_Q})EP_Q - (\mu_{N,\beta} - \mu_{Q,\beta})E\beta - (\mu_{N,\gamma} - \mu_{Q,\gamma})E\gamma],$$

$$(10)$$

where the variables are defined as in equation (9).

If equation (10) were estimatable, several interesting aspects of the model could be explored. Most important, the model assumes that derived

---

[8] The elasticity of substitution between N and Q can be written as $\sigma^* = [E (Q/N)]/[E (C_N/C_Q)]$, where C_Q and C_N are representatively the marginal products of Q and N in production of C. But, in equilibrium, $\pi_N/\pi_Q = C_N/C_Q$; therefore, $\sigma^* = [E (Q/N)]/[E(\pi_N/\pi_Q)] = [EQ-EN]/[E\pi_N-E\pi_Q]$, or $EQ-EN = \sigma^* (E\pi_N-E\pi_Q)$. The rest of the proof consists simply of breaking $E\pi_N$ and $E\pi_Q$ into their constituent parts (see the Appendix for this last step).

pure income elasticities for N and Q are equal. This assumption runs counter to findings of studies in the demand for household durables and to previous speculations on the observed negative relationship between numbers of children and household income. The formulation has a clear, refutable hypothesis that changes in household full wealth will leave the ratio of Q to N unaffected. Furthermore, it has the advantage of concentrating its explanatory power upon pure price effects.

There are several other important features of the model. One is the separation of price of time (wage rates) and education effects. The model assumes that education can affect household decisions independent of its well-known effect on wage rates. Thus it is meaningful to speak of the effect of a change in education levels holding market time values constant. Serious empirical problems raised by this treatment are discussed below.[9]

Another feature of the model is that the husband and wife are treated symmetrically. Both are permitted either to work in the market place or to engage in household commodity production. Whether one or both choose to specialize depends especially upon the wage of the husband relative to that of the wife and the value of each spouse's time in home production.

III. Supporting Evidence and Related Issues

I want to summarize a detailed but nonrigorous discussion (see De Tray 1972a) of important parameters of the model just presented. I will first try to establish bounds for parameters associated with adult household members and then bounds for child-related parameters, and to indicate throughout the implications these "estimates" have for the model.

Adult Time and Adult Education

Much of the ambiguity in signs of the coefficients of education (9) stems from a lack of information on relative weights for various inputs. It has often been assumed (see, e.g., Willis 1969) that since men spend less time in the home than women, expenditure shares in household production for male time are less than for female time. This assumption is seldom questioned even though male wages are above female wages in most households.[10] If $\alpha_{t_{i,z}}$ represents the expenditure share of the ith individual's time in all household production, then it is not obvious a priori which is larger, $\alpha_{t_{m,z}}$ or $\alpha_{t_{f,z}}$.

---

[9] To be sure, there are some conceptual problems; again (see n. 7) they involve the simultaneous nature of the household decision-making process. For example, a woman's decision on the number of years of schooling she chooses to receive in general will not be independent of the number of children she wants.

[10] Based on the Office of Economic Opportunity's Survey of Economic Opportunity, the husband's wage exceeded that of the wife in 81 percent of the households in which both spouses were working.

That male time in production of child services (however defined) is less important than female time is even more generally accepted.[11] This seems indisputable at early ages, say for children under 6 years, but one must be cautious in extending this proposition to lifetime considerations. In the notation of equation (9), $\alpha_{t_{m,c}}$ and $\alpha_{t_{f,c}}$ are concerned with *lifetime* allocation of time by husbands and wives and not merely time allocation during the first few years of a child's life; but, for simplicity, $\alpha_{t_{f,c}}$ will be assumed larger than $\alpha_{t_{m,c}}$.

This model further complicates the analysis of the role of time by assuming that children are produced with two time-using inputs, quality (Q) and numbers (N). Although the direct evidence is scarce (De Tray 1972a), there are scattered indications of the relative importance of husband's and wife's time in the production both of child services and of Q and N.

Differences in allocation of time by men and women over the life cycle appear to substantiate the assumption that child-services production is, indeed, more female time-intensive than male time-intensive. In his work on time allocation by households, Smith (1972a) finds that with an increase in the number of young children in the household, men work more hours per year, but women substantially reduce the hours they work in the labor market. The effect of older children is less clear and does not rule out a reversal of intensities as children grow up.

Other studies of labor-force behavior (Cohen, Rea, and Lerman 1970; Leibowitz 1974) also shed some light on the underlying production functions for Q and N. A most important finding of these studies for this paper concerns the effect of children on time spent working by women with differing educational levels. Increasing a wife's educational level appears to increase the time (per child) she reallocates from market work to child rearing even though highly educated women, on the average, have higher market wage rates than do women with less education.

This behavior is open to several interpretations. One could argue that highly educated women (or households they reside in) desire high-quality children, and that the differential labor-force behavior of women by education class is indicative of the female time-intensity of child quality. This explanation has the prediction that, holding all other factors constant, increasing the wife's wage will reduce child quality more than numbers of children.

An alternative explanation, also consistent with the observed behavior, stresses the role of education as an efficiency (entrepreneurial) factor in household production. In this argument,[12] more-educated women are more

[11] Willis (1969), for example, assumes that the role of male time in production of child services is sufficiently small to be ignored.

[12] Again, see De Tray (1972a) for the details of this argument and a discussion of related issues such as birth control knowledge, simultaneity problems, and so on.

efficient at producing child quality *relative* to numbers of children. Furthermore, an increase in female education is not factor neutral in its effects
on marginal products of inputs into the production of Q, but increases the
value of female time more than the value of other inputs. If this is true,
highly educated women will tend to allocate more time per child to child-
services production, and produce more quality-intensive children than
women with less education. This explanation of female labor-force behavior can be summarized as follows:

$$\alpha_{t_f,N} > \alpha_{t_f,Q};$$
$$\mu_{C,\gamma} > \mu_{C,\beta};$$
$$\mu_{Q,\gamma} > \mu_{N,\gamma}.$$

Note that an increase in female wages does not tend to reduce quality
per child. Which of these hypotheses better fits the data will be taken up
in Section IV.

Child-related Factors

Child-Time

No mention has been made as yet of the effect of child-time, or its value, on
the household decision-making process. The formal model does not rule
out producer-durable aspects of children, but there has been no systematic
treatment of this characteristic. However, this factor has been an important
consideration in past models of desired family size and thus requires some
discussion.

Variation in the value of child-time has often been called upon as one
explanation of urban-rural fertility differences. The gist of the argument is
that farm children are a financial asset to their parents but city children are
not; therefore, farm families will desire larger numbers of children than
households in an urban environment, other things being equal. Note that
the emphasis is on the market (work) value of child-time. As the household
production model emphasizes, time can usually be productively employed
within the household as well. One implication of the traditional argument,
therefore, is that the elasticity of substitution between child time and
"hired" time is larger than that between child-time and adult home-time.
If this were not true, parents who live in urban areas could substitute the
child-time for their own time in the home, enabling them to allocate more
hours to work.[13] Thus, in household production models rural child-time

[13] The argument does not preclude the farm environment from having *any* effect
on desired fertility; it simply reduces the expected magnitude of the effect. In fact,
one would predict that the increase in the range of alternative uses for child-time
caused by establishing a family business such as farming would have a positive effect
on desired fertility. But, unless the new alternative significantly increased the value
of child-time to the household, the expected magnitude of the effect would not be
large.

plays conceptually much the same role as urban child-time in the household decision-making process, reducing the expected difference from this source.[14]

The farm setting may affect more than just expected returns from child-time. It may alter the price of both time and market goods and services inputs into children so as to lower the shadow price of child services relative to other household production-consumption. For example, living on a farm may reduce the cost of female time in household production even if the wife's market-productivity level is unchanged. The reduction stems from increased opportunity for joint production which a family-operated business permits. In essence, a farm wife can work and participate in home production simultaneously, reducing the opportunity cost of female time in household production.[15] If this is true, then female time-intensive commodities (C) will become more attractive to a farm household.

Price effects may also encourage farm families to substitute numbers of children for child quality *within* their production of child services. Goods inputs into the production of N—for example, basic food and shelter—are probably cheap in rural areas relative to purchased inputs into the production of Q—for example, schooling,[16] books, and travel. Under these circumstances, farm families would find Q a costly means of increasing child services and would choose to hold relatively large proportions of that commodity in the form of numbers of children.

If π_i^r is the marginal cost of the ith commodity or input in rural areas, and π_i^u is similarly defined for urban areas, then this discussion implies the following:[17]

$$\frac{\pi_N^r}{\pi_Q^r} < \frac{\pi_N^u}{\pi_Q^u}.$$

Infant Mortality

The discussion so far has treated both N and Q as expected values, ignoring such problems as uncertainty and poor forecasting. The effect of infant mortality on desired family size requires elaboration, however, since in the empirical formulation of the model the proxy for desired family size is not net of expected infant losses. To correct for this, the usual procedure is

[14] Large differences cannot be ruled out, given the empirical nature of the issue. The purpose of the statement is to emphasize that the matter is one of degree, not of direction.

[15] Glen Cain has pointed out that farm children may require less supervision, that is, are less time-intensive, than urban children and consequently are less costly from that standpoint also.

[16] The case for schooling seems clear from Finis Welch's work (1966) on quality of education. Welch found that rural areas were at a disadvantage compared with more densely populated areas in the production of "education" because rural schools were too small to take advantage of the apparently large economies of scale in education production.

[17] For given levels of Q and N.

to enter a measure of infant or child mortality as an independent variable in regressions on desired numbers of children. Traditionally, the predicted sign for this variable has been positive, based on the argument that high infant mortality causes parents to bear a relatively large number of children to ensure a given number surviving to adulthood. Note that in this theory the implicit assumption that leads to the predicted positive relationship is that, other things being equal, all parents desire the same number of surviving children, regardless of the infant mortality levels they expect. To justify this assumption, either the demand for surviving children must be perfectly inelastic, or the cost of an infant death must be zero. It is unlikely that either of these conditions holds; in fact, economic theory would lead us to argue that one factor on which parents base their "target" family size is expected losses from infant deaths or, more accurately, the costs associated with these losses. Thus, whether an increase in infant mortality raises or lowers observed numbers of children-ever-born will depend in part on the costs associated with infant deaths (both pecuniary and psychic), and on the elasticity of demand for surviving children.

As O'Hara (1972) points out, other forces, specifically the substitution between Q and N in the household's production of child services, may encourage parents to have large numbers of children, holding other things constant, in a regime of high infant mortality. The important distinction, however, is that these forces do not imply the strong "replacement" relationship that the traditional argument does. To summarize, if Pr represents the probability that an infant will survive to adulthood, then,

$$\frac{\partial N}{\partial Pr} \gtrless 0;$$

$$\frac{\partial\, Q/N}{\partial\, Pr} > 0.$$

Summary and Predictions of the Model

Although the model and subsequent discussion result in few unambiguous predictions,[18] we are left with strong expectations on the signs of certain coefficients in equations (9) and (10).

In equation (9), female variables should "dominate" male variables. The effect of a change in female education or wage rates should be larger in absolute terms and contribute more to the explanatory power of the estimated equation than changes in male education or wages. Furthermore, since the female wage coefficient contains large negative substitution effects, and that for the male does not, the former should be arithmetically smaller

---

[18] In fact, in equation (9), if (as is true) separate measures of the price of market goods and services inputs into Q and N are not available, the only remaining prediction is that an increase in non–wage-related income should increase the demand for N.

than the latter. If both C and N are female time-intensive, the sign for the female wage coefficient should, in fact, be negative.

Along similar lines, the sign of the female education coefficient should reflect the nonneutral efficiency effect of that variable on the production of N and Q, and thus should be arithmetically smaller than the male education coefficient. Again the female coefficient is likely to be negative if the differential efficiency effect is a significant factor.

Since the primary purpose of equation (10) is a qualitative estimate of the relative shares of inputs into N and Q, predictions are less apropos than for equation (9). Nonetheless, the theory and discussion imply two propositions. First, if the effect of female education is predominantly on the production efficiency of Q, then $\mu_{Q,\gamma} - \mu_{N,\gamma}$ should be positive. Second, household full wealth (or non–wage-related income) should have no effect on the relative level of Q to N.

If the model is a useful representation of household decisions about desired family size, we would also expect certain consistencies in the behavior of variables *between* the two equations. One has already been mentioned—female education should have a negative coefficient in equation (9) and a positive one in equation (10). Another is that the coefficient for female wage rate should be arithmetically smaller in equation (9) than (10), because of the female time-intensity of child services in general. A third is that the index of the price of market goods and services used in the estimations should exhibit consistent behavior in both equations.

The most important implied consistency from the standpoint of testing this particular form of the fertility model, however, is that for the behavior of household full wealth in the two equations. As equation (9) indicates, a non–wage-related increase in full wealth should unambiguously increase the demand for numbers of children. In contrast, that same variable in equation (10) should have neither positive nor negative effects on the dependent variable, since it is assumed to affect N and Q equally.

IV. An Empirical Formulation of the Model

The results of a preliminary empirical investigation of the derived-demand equations for numbers of children (9) and quality per child (10) follow. The estimates are based on aggregate data drawn from a cross section of U.S. counties.

The Data[19]

The regression sample consists of 555 counties randomly selected from the approximately 3,300 counties of the continental United States; the primary

---

[19] A more detailed description of the data, including a list of the counties in the sample, is given in De Tray (1972a).

data source is the 1960 U.S. *Census of Population* (U.S., Bureau of the Census 1963*b*). Since these data are cross-sectional, they have a number of shortcomings. First, they fail to capture the dynamic nature of the decision-making process. Second, for the women who make up the sample, relevant values of the variables are those 10–20 years prior to 1960.[20] Third, the theory yields equations whose form requires that the variables be expressed in percentage changes, while the data are measures of levels.[21]

The Variables

The two dependent variables in the theoretical framework are numbers of children, N, and quality per child, Q/N. The numbers-of-children variable has a relatively close empirical counterpart, children-ever-born to women of sufficient age to have completed families.[22] For this analysis women aged 35–44 were chosen as the group with essentially completed fertility.[23]

Constructing an operational measure of child quality is a more difficult task. One approximate measure, in one sense of the term, is the expected full wealth of the child. The best available statistic summarizing a child's future economic prospects is the amount of education that child will receive. With the additional assumption that parents base their expectations on current conditions, quality per child is empirically estimated by the following formula:

$$\text{EXPED}_j = \sum_{i=1}^{n} \left(\frac{\text{ENR}_{i,j}}{\text{POP}_{i,j}} \right) \left(\frac{\text{EDEXP}_j}{\sum_{i=1}^{N} \text{POP}_{i,j}} \right),$$

where EXPED_j = expected public school investment per child in dollars for the jth county; $\text{ENR}_{i,j}$ = number enrolled in school in the ith age group of the jth county; $\text{POP}_{i,j}$ = population in the ith age group of the

[20] This problem may not be too severe, given the time-invariant nature of the variables used in the study.

[21] This transition does not affect the expected sign of the coefficients, however. The fundamental assumption required is that the parameters are constant over the entire range of the activity in question.

[22] One problem with this measure is that desired family size and completed family size may differ. The most often cited example of this is that poorly educated, low-income households do not have sufficient birth control knowledge to limit children to the desired number. Although this view cannot be ruled out, the regression results offer little support for it.

[23] This choice was governed by the fact that this is the oldest age group for which the Census gives children-ever-born figures at the county level in 1960. One might argue, however, that some women in the group may plan to have additional children. If this were particularly true for women who postponed having children in order to participate in another time-intensive activity, attending college, then female education and children-ever-born would exhibit a spurious negative correlation. Fortunately, this does not appear to be true. (See De Tray [1972*a*] or Sutton and Wunderlich [1967] for evidence supporting this statement.)

jth county; and $\mathrm{EDEXP}_j =$ total public educational expenditures by the jth county. The variable EXPED measures, in dollars, the county public educational investment each child is expected to receive. The first term on the right-hand side is the expected number of years of schooling per child. It is calculated under the assumption that each child of the ith age group who is enrolled in school receives 1 year of schooling for each year the age group spans. The second term is the expected county expenditure on education per child per year.[24]

In theory, enrollment and population for each year, say between the ages of 5 and 19, is required to calculate this measure accurately. In practice, the years were grouped, since the Census does not report enrollment by individual years.[25]

A point of clarification may be necessary here. In the theoretical model, child quality includes all investments in children, whereas the operational measure of that variable appears to capture only those investments that occur outside the home. The assumption implicit in the transition is that total child quality is highly positively correlated with expected public school investment at the county level.

This variable obviously has a number of other shortcomings. The most serious involve the expenditure component. Its political nature will make it suspect for some; it contains both current expenditures and capital investments; it may poorly reflect the quality of education being produced (Welch 1966);[26] it fails to capture either private school or college investments in children, two areas where much of the variation in child quality may be occurring. To the extent that these criticisms are valid, they will tend to increase the error with which EXPED measures quality per child. If capital expenditures are randomly distributed among counties, their inclusion in the EXPED variable will reduce the explanatory power of the regressions and increase the standard errors associated with the estimated coefficients. The exclusion of private school and college inputs into the

---

[24] County educational expenditures are calculated from data in the 1962 *County and City Data Book* (U.S., Bureau of the Census 1962). The data are in the form of total county government expenditures and the percentage of those expenditures classified as educational.

[25] The 1960 Census reported enrollment at the county level for the following age groups: 5 and 6, 7–13, 14 and 15, 16 and 17, 18 and 19. Population estimates were available in machine-readable form only in five-year groups except for 14-year-olds. The final formula for each county, therefore, took the following form:

$$\mathrm{EXPED} = \left[9 \left(\frac{\mathrm{ENR}_{5\text{--}13}}{\mathrm{POP}_{5\text{--}13}} \right) + 6 \left(\frac{\mathrm{ENR}_{14\text{--}19}}{\mathrm{POP}_{14\text{--}19}} \right) \right] \left(\frac{\mathrm{EDEXP}}{\mathrm{POP}_{5\text{--}19}} \right),$$

where 9 and 6 are the maximum possible years of schooling for each age grouping.

[26] As mentioned earlier, Welch (1966) found that rural schools were often less efficient at producing education than their urban counterparts; thus, higher school expenditures in rural areas did not always mean higher educational output. Since the analysis attempts to remove this rural effect, the problem is somewhat mitigated here.

educational process will reduce overall variation in EXPED and understate the amount of education received in "high-quality" counties, biasing estimated coefficients toward zero.

The independent variables are more straightforward.[27] Male and female efficiency parameters, β and γ, are measured by median years of schooling of adults aged 25 and over. Since wage rates by sex are not currently available at the county level, median earnings are used to measure these variables. Male earnings and male wage rates are sufficiently highly correlated, at both the aggregate and the household level, so that earnings are a respectable proxy for wage rates. The same, unfortunately, is not true for female earnings and wages. Smith's (1972a) work points toward virtually no correlation between wages and earnings for individual women over their lifetimes; however, at the highly aggregate state level, this correlation is almost as strong as that for men.[28] Even though the state sample should more closely approximate the county sample than the individual data used by Smith, the lack of wage rates by sex is a serious shortcoming of the county data.

A second very serious problem with using observed earnings and even actual wage rates to measure the value of the wife's time in the market place was alluded to in Section II. Neither the level of wages a woman can command in the market place nor, certainly, her market earnings are independent of the number of children she has or wants to have in the future. Thus, as is well known, ordinary least-squares (OLS) regression techniques may yield seriously biased estimates of the impact of female wages on desired children. I attempt to correct this shortcoming of the OLS estimates by using two-stage least-squares (TSLS) techniques, but the results are not encouraging.[29]

Other income (V in the model) has traditionally been difficult to measure. The Census does not enumerate other income separately but does record median male and female earnings and median income. Unfortunately, since base populations for these figures differ, it is not meaningful either to calculate other income by subtracting earnings from total income[30] or to enter all three measures in the same regression.

----

[27] One overall shortcoming, however, is that none of the independent variables is age-specific. See De Tray (1972a) for a discussion of this problem. As will be seen, an attempt is made to overcome this problem through two-stage least-squares estimation techniques.

[28] The simple correlation for the 48 contiguous states between male earnings and male wages is 0.91; that same correlation for women is 0.88. The wage figures were taken from Social Security full-time (four-quarter) earnings data (U.S., Department of Health, Education and Welfare 1968b).

[29] Professor Ashenfelter's comment on this paper was written before the TSLS estimates were available, but I doubt that the gist of his remarks would have changed had he seen them.

[30] In fact, this procedure would lead to a negative average value for other income.

The proxy chosen for other income is the median value of housing in each county.[31] Housing expenditures and family size may, of course, be related in ways other than through the postulated wealth effect. For example, it could be argued that households with large numbers of children will spend more on housing because they require more space, other things being equal.[32] A positive partial correlation between numbers of children and housing value might therefore stem from this "scale" effect rather than from a positive wealth effect. The available empirical evidence indicates that this is not the case. The results of three separate investigations (Reid 1962; Moeller 1970, p. 83; and De Tray 1972a, p. 57) confirm that expenditures on housing appear to be independent of number of children in the household, when other factors are held constant.

The number of infant deaths per 1,000 live births is included in the regressions to account for exogenous variation in the expected survival rate of children, thus allowing children-ever-born to be interpreted as completed family size.

The last three variables measure the general economic and social structure of each county. They are: percentage of the population living in urban areas, percentage of the population that is rural, and percentage of the population that is nonwhite. The first two are included in an attempt to account for cross-sectional variation in the price of market goods and services;[33] the last, to account for differences (if any) not captured by the other variables in the economic opportunities and constraints faced by nonwhites.

Table 1 contains a description of the variables, table 2 has summary statistics, and table 3 gives weighted summary statistics. Table 4 is a simple correlation matrix for the variables. The "weighted" means and standard deviations are based on the original sample weighted by the square root of the female population aged 35–44.[34]

[31] Median value of housing and median income are highly correlated: the simple correlation between these variables for this sample is 0.82.

[32] Of course, "more space" and "larger housing expenditures" are not synonymous terms. In order to increase their physical living space, families may reduce the overall quality of their housing, thus keeping housing expenditures constant.

[33] Two measures of "ruralness" were used originally, one being percentage of the population classified as rural farm, and the other, the percentage of the employed population working in agriculture. Initial estimates contained only the rural-farm measure. A problem of interpretation arose with this variable in that any increase in the percentage of the population classified as rural farm while holding constant percentage of the population classified as urban implies that the only remaining sector, percentage rural nonfarm, must be decreasing. However, since both measures performed very similarly, only the rural-farm results are reported here.

[34] The weighting factors are chosen so that the moment matrix will be weighted by the denominator of the dependent variable. Since both weighting factors (women aged 35–44 and population aged 5–19) yield similar weighted summary statistics, only one set is presented.

TABLE 1

THE REGRESSION VARIABLES

Variable Name	Conceptual Equivalent	Description
CEB35*	N	Children-ever-born per 1,000 married women aged 35–44, in 1960
EXPED*	Q/N	Expected public school investment per child ($) (see text for formula), 1960
EDM	β	Median years of schooling for men aged 25+, 1960
EDF	γ	Median years of schooling for women, aged 25+, 1960
MALEARN*	W_m	Median earnings ($) of males who had earnings in 1959
FEMEARN*	W_f	Median earnings ($) of women who had earnings in 1959
HSEVAL*	I	Median value of housing ($), 1960
INFDTH	...	Infant deaths per 1,000 live births, 1960
URBAN	P_N/P_Q	Population (%) living in towns of 2,500 inhabitants or more, 1960
RURAL	P_Q/P_N	Population (%) living on farms, 1960
RACE	...	Population (%) nonwhite, 1960

* Variable entered in log form.

The Results[35]

The results of the regression analysis are presented in table 5. As the model of Section II indicates, the two dependent variables, children-ever-born and the expected schooling investment per child, as well as all mea-

TABLE 2

SUMMARY STATISTICS

Variable	Mean	SD	Minimum	Maximum
CEB 35	3,116.3	568.6	1,962.0	5,346.0
EXPED	2,758.3	1,180.0	323.0	8,872.1
EDM	9.11	1.44	4.9	12.6
EDF	9.98	1.52	5.7	12.6
MALEARN	3,366.1	1,119.6	913.0	6,546.0
FEMEARN	1,575.0	517.4	442.0	3,343.0
HSEVAL	8,014.1	2,882.9	5,000.0	20,200.0
INFDTH	27.5	11.4	0.0	72.5
URBAN	34.0	27.6	0.0	100.0
RURAL	21.6	15.3	0.0	67.2
RACE	11.4	17.4	0.0	76.0

[35] An analysis of the residuals of the two sets of regressions was also undertaken. The results indicate no particular underlying relationship between the CEB35 and the EXPED regressions (see De Tray 1972a).

TABLE 3
WEIGHTED SUMMARY STATISTICS

Variable	Mean	SD	Minimum	Maximum
CEB 35	2,613.5	457.1	1,962.0	5,346.0
EXPED	3,027.2	982.0	323.0	8,872.1
EDM	10.3	1.34	4.9	12.6
EDF	10.8	1.22	5.7	12.6
MALEARN	4,653.0	1,093.8	913.0	6,546.0
FEMEARN	2,333.0	631.7	443.0	3,343.0
HSEVAL	12,953.0	4,346.9	5,000.0	20,200.0
INFDTH	25.5	6.48	0.0	72.5
URBAN	71.8	28.0	0.0	100.0
RURAL	6.81	11.19	0.0	67.2
RACE	11.3	11.7	0.0	76.0

NOTE.—Each observation is weighted by the square root of the female population aged 35–44.

TABLE 4
SIMPLE CORRELATION MATRIX

Variable	EXPED	EDM	EDF	MALEARN	FEMEARN
CEB 35	−0.28	−0.60	−0.53	−0.58	−0.63
EXPED	...	0.43	0.55	0.48	0.25
EDM	...	...	0.91	0.81	0.58
EDF	...	...	...	0.73	0.46
MALEARN ..	...	...	...	...	0.74
FEMEARN ..	...	...	...	...	...
HSEVAL	...	...	...	...	...
INFDTH	...	...	...	...	...
URBAN	...	...	...	...	...
RURAL	...	...	...	...	...

TABLE 4 (*Continued*)

Variable	HSEVAL	INFDTH	URBAN	RURAL	RACE
CEB 35	−0.45	0.33	−0.43	0.36	0.43
EXPED	0.25	−0.29	0.07	−0.06	−0.41
EDM	0.71	−0.37	0.49	−0.39	−0.51
EDF	0.62	−0.38	0.36	−0.24	−0.49
MALEARN ..	0.76	−0.33	0.60	−0.61	−0.49
FEMEARN ..	0.64	−0.27	0.49	−0.50	−0.43
HSEVAL	...	−0.24	0.64	−0.46	−0.22
INFDTH	...	...	−0.05	−0.03	0.49
URBAN	...	...	...	−0.61	−0.09
RURAL	...	...	...	...	0.05

TABLE 5

THE REGRESSION RESULTS

| | DEPENDENT VARIABLE | | | |
| | CEB35† | | EXPED† | |
INDEPENDENT VARIABLE*	OLS‡	TSLS‡	OLS§	TSLS§
EDM: median years of schooling, male	0.0077 (0.74)	0.0046 (0.28)	−0.068 (1.77)	−0.064 (1.51)
EDF: median years of schooling, female	−0.030 (3.19) [0.32]	−0.060 (4.23) [0.64]	0.092 (2.65) [0.99]	0.11 (2.84) [1.2]
HSEVAL: median value of housing†	0.065 (2.73) [0.07]	0.39 (6.12) [0.39]	0.073 (0.81) ...	0.28 (1.58) ...
MALEARN: median earnings, male†	0.074 (2.12) [0.07]	0.28 (3.27) [0.23]	0.90 (6.96) [0.9]	0.37 (1.56) ...
FEMEARN: median earnings, female†	−0.30 (12.5) [0.30]	−0.86 (13.2) [0.86]	−0.11 (1.23) ...	−0.11 (0.67) ...
INFDTH: infant death rate	0.0009 (1.24) ...	0.0010 (0.94) ...	−0.0048 (1.95) [0.12]	−0.0060 (2.28) [0.15]
URBAN: % urban	−0.0022 (7.69) [0.16]	−0.0027 (5.54) [0.17]	−0.0001 (0.09) ...	−0.0003 (0.22) ...
RURAL: % rural-farm	0.0011 (1.74) ...	−0.0015 (1.34) ...	0.0070 (3.04) [0.05]	0.0015 (0.50) ...
RACE: % nonwhite	−0.0005 (1.12)	−0.0037 (4.44)	−0.0027 (1.67)	−0.0060 (2.74)
CONSTANT	9.33 (41.1)	9.38 (19.8)	0.347 (0.41)	2.88 (2.20)
R^2	0.75	...	0.47	...
F	169	10.83	51.1	2.67
N	516	516	527	527

* For description of variables, see table 1; t-ratios given in parentheses; elasticity at mean given in brackets (absolute value; given only for coefficients with t-ratios ≧ 1.95).
† Variable enters regressions in log form.
‡ Weighted by square root of female population, ages 35 to 44.
§ Weighted by square root of population, ages 5 to 19.

sures of earnings and full wealth, are used in log form. Following Mincer's work,[36] years of schooling for men and women enter as normal numbers, as do infant deaths and the three measures of county characteristics, percentage of the population urban, rural, and nonwhite.

[36] See, e.g., Mincer (1974a), where he summarizes much of his previous published and unpublished work and once again states the rationale for using years of schooling rather than the log of that number in equations explaining wage differences.

For comparison, TSLS estimates treating male and female earnings and house value as endogenous are also given in this table.[37] These results do not appear to solve the simultaneous-bias problem as had originally been hoped.

Numbers of Children (CEB35)

The OLS coefficients for the CEB35 regressions are remarkably strong, especially in view of the severe multicollinearity among the variables.[38] The statistically weakest coefficient is that for male education. This may be partly because of the close correlation of this variable with both female education and male earnings; it may also indicate that with earnings, full wealth, and female education held constant, changes in male education have little effect on numbers of children. The female education coefficient is strongly negative, with an elasticity at the mean of approximately -0.3. In the past it has been argued that education is a proxy for either price of time (female education) or permanent wealth (male education), or that education captures differences in contraceptive knowledge. With respect to the first of these, an attempt has been made to remove wealth and time-price effects. The continued existence of a significant negative coefficient for female education and a very weak positive coefficient for male education indicates that these variables may have effects on numbers of children that are not associated with either wealth or relative prices. This result is consistent with the earlier contention that increasing female education increases the efficiency with which child quality can be produced but has little effect on the production technology of numbers of children.

The alternative education-contraception hypothesis is difficult to disprove, particularly in aggregate data such as these. It is my opinion, based on my own work and that of others, that the strength of the female-education coefficient is not attributable to differences in contraceptive knowledge across the U.S. population, but the case is far from proven either way.

Increases in median value of housing have a small but significant positive effect on CEB35. In her housing-income study Reid (1962) found the pure income elasticity for housing expenditures to be around 2.0. If this latter measure is taken as correct, the HSEVAL coefficient implies on

[37] See n. 29 in this regard. The excluded "exogenous" variables are percentage of the population with less than 5 years of schooling and with 12 years or more of schooling (educational distribution parameters), percentage of the population in different age categories (21-plus and over 65), median age of population, and several measures of parent background such as percentage foreign born and percentage whose parents were foreign born.

[38] The various tests for multicollinearity suggested in Farrar and Glauber (1967) were applied to the regressions. The worst problem occurred, as one might suspect, between male and female education.

the average an income (full-wealth) elasticity for numbers of children of 0.12.

Although the simple correlation between male and female earnings is quite high (0.73), the effects of these variables on CEB35 differ considerably. An increase in male earnings has a positive effect on children-ever-born, but an increase in female earnings has a strong negative effect. Elasticities associated with these variables are 0.09 for male earnings and −0.30 for female earnings. These results are consistent with previous findings and my discussion of these variables above. Numbers of children, as well as child services in general, have long been assumed to be female time-intensive; therefore, an increase in the price of female time causes households to substitute away from both numbers of children and child services.[39] If the opposite is true for men, that is, that the share of male time in the production of both N and C is small relative to the share of male time in other household commodities (Z), then an increase in the price of male time will bring about a substitution toward both N and C.

The coefficient of the infant-death-rate variable is never significantly different from zero. In part, this may be due to the offsetting effects associated with this variable (see discussion above).[40]

The variables URBAN and RURAL behave as predicted under the assumption that they measure variations in the price of market goods and services. An increase in percentage urban lowers the desired number of children, but a similar change in percentage rural increases the desired number of children.

In the past, demographers and sociologists have implied that nonwhites produce more children than whites, other things being equal. The coefficient for RACE contradicts this belief.[41] If education levels and earnings are held constant, increasing the percentage nonwhite in a country has, if anything, a weak negative effect on children-ever-born.

Table 6 illustrates the reasonable magnitude of effects on predicted numbers of children-ever-born associated with plausible changes in certain variables.[42] If the OLS estimates are valid, a rather strong assumption

---

[39] Again, the reader must be cautioned about the simultaneous nature of the female-earnings variable. The OLS regression technique used in this report is not capable of distinguishing the effect of earnings on desired children from that of children on female earnings. Therefore, this coefficient may contain a serious simultaneous bias. The degree to which the TSLS estimates solve this problem is discussed later in the text.

[40] It may also reflect the fact that the expected infant mortality rates on which women 40 years old in 1960 based their fertility decisions were those of 1940 or so, not those of 1960.

[41] However, see Gardner's paper in this book for evidence that contradicts this finding.

[42] The choice of the "plausible changes" was not entirely arbitrary. In each case, the 1960 values for the variables were increased or decreased by the percentage change for comparable variables between 1950 and 1960; thus, the "prediction" is for decen-

TABLE 6

PREDICTED DECENNIAL CHANGE IN CHILDREN-EVER-BORN PER WOMAN AGED 35–44

Initial predicted value (1960)*	2.66 children-ever-born
Changes in exogenous variables:†	
Female education	+14%
House value (full wealth)	+39%‡
Male earnings	+43%‡
Female earnings	+42%‡
% population urban	+12%
% population rural-farm	−55%
New predicted value*	2.36 children-ever-born
Change in childen-ever-born	−11.5%

* Calculated using first two significant digits of OLS coefficient only. TSLS estimates yielded similar net results even though individual coefficients differ.
† Based on 1950–60 changes for comparable variables.
‡ Represent *real*, not nominal, changes.

given the inadequacies of the data, zero population growth is, so to speak, just around the corner. The postulated changes in the variables indicate a reduction in predicted family size from 2.7 children per woman to 2.4 over a 10-year period.

Quality per Child (EXPED)

The proxy chosen for quality per child (EXPED) is an admittedly crude first attempt to quantify that potentially important variable. The results of the regressions on public school expenditures should, therefore, be viewed with much more skepticism than those for the number of children. It seems likely that problems caused by the level of aggregation and simultaneous bias may be even more severe than those encountered in the CEB35 results. Finally, even though the EXPED regressions are open to several alternative, and reasonably plausible, explanations, they will be discussed as if the proxy variables do measure what they are supposed to measure.

Male education (EDM) and percentage of the population rural (RURAL) exhibit what appears to be anomalous behavior. The male-education coefficient is insignificant or negative, implying that either (1) the effects of that variable are approximately the same both for numbers of children and for child quality, or (2) if anything, male education contributes more to the production efficiency of numbers of children than to the efficiency with which child quality is produced.

As for the RURAL measure, it was argued during the discussion of the CEB35 results that URBAN and RURAL captured cross-sectional variation in the price of market goods and services. Implicit in this statement is

nial, not annual, changes in the variables. Note that only those variables with statistically significant coefficients were changed.

the presumption that in rural counties those market goods and services that are primary inputs into numbers of children will be cheap relative to goods and services entering child-quality production. This, in turn, implies that the coefficient for RURAL in the EXPED regressions should be negative; in fact, this coefficient is strongly positive.

Part of the solution of this puzzle may be found in Welch's (1966) work on quality in education, where he observes that educational expenditures are, in and of themselves, poor indicators of the quality of education being produced by schools. He attributes this to the existence of "economies of scale" in the educational process. In essence, his argument is that schools in sparsely populated areas suffer because their facilities fall well below the optimal size.[43] If this is true, rural areas are likely to receive less education per dollar expenditure than more densely populated urban areas.

These scale effects will at minimum cause EXPED to overestimate quality per child in rural areas. The positive coefficient for RURAL may be a result of this latter phenomenon plus the fact that education, earnings, and income are being held constant. In other words, if the rural population has tastes similar to those of the urban population for quality per child as measured by EXPED, then, with prices and income held constant, rural counties are likely to have relatively high educational expenditures per eligible population to partly offset the inefficiencies of their school systems.

Female education has a strong positive sign, as would be expected from the earlier efficiency arguments and the partial correlation of female education in the children-ever-born regressions. Since quality does not appear to be particularly female time-intensive compared with numbers of children (the OLS coefficient for female earnings is not significant in the EXPED regression), this finding lends support to the "efficiency" (as opposed to time-intensity) explanation of the observed differences by educational class in female labor-force participation.

It is tempting to interpret the insignificant coefficients for HSEVAL as indicating that derived income elasticities for Q (total quality in children) and for N (numbers of children) are equal in size.[44] This interpretation supports the quantity-quality substitution hypothesis and the particular functional forms chosen for the model. Indeed, it is surprising that EXPED and HSEVAL are not positively related if for no other reason than that school expenditures are usually derived from property taxes. However, it is always difficult to attach precise meaning to insignificant coefficients; therefore, this finding must be viewed with considerable caution.

---

[43] Also, Welch points out that a significant fraction of rural educational expenditures went for transportation, which, again, implies that rural school dollars "buy" less education than urban school dollars.

[44] That is, EXPED is a proxy of Q/N (the relative amount of Q to N), which is invariant with respect to scale (nonwage income) effects.

As in the CEB35 regression, male and female earnings have very different effects on quality per child. The strength and size of the positive male-earnings coefficient make its theoretical interpretation suspect. According to theory, this result implies that male time is used more heavily in quantity than in quality production.

The strong negative coefficient for infant death rates is consistent with the theory that the higher the probability of a child's dying, the less likely parents are to invest large amounts of resources in that child (see O'Hara 1972). The statistical strength of this coefficient may also be a function of the fact that the rate at which infants survive is not, as has been traditionally assumed, always exogenous to household decisions. The more resources invested in a child, the more likely that child is to survive. But the more resources a household invests in children, the higher the "quality" of those children. Thus infant mortality and expected school expenditures may both measure child quality; it is not surprising, therefore, that they are strongly related.

TSLS Estimates

One question is why I concentrate on OLS results when TSLS estimates should yield less biased coefficients. One simple answer is that my two-stage estimates are not included in this paper. A second more substantive reason is that for these data the TSLS techniques apparently do not do what they were expected to do, that is, solve the simultaneous-bias problem. If an OLS estimate of, say, the impact of female earnings on children-ever-born seriously overstates the size of that effect, then TSLS techniques should produce a reduced estimate of the female-earnings coefficient. As equation (2) confirms, female earnings have a larger impact on numbers of children in the TSLS regressions than in the OLS results. It seems likely, then, that the TSLS procedures simply yield more error-free measures of the included endogenous variables, but do little to reduce simultaneous bias.

Summary of Empirical Results

Both sets of regressions (CEB35 and EXPED) imply that production of child services is dominated by women. The role of men seems to be primarily as suppliers of market goods and services, but this part of the picture is still unclear.

Female earnings are the single most important factor in the completed-family-size regressions in terms of both magnitude of effect and statistical significance. Other variables having a significant negative effect on children-ever-born are female education and the degree to which a county is urban. On the other hand, median value of housing as a proxy for full wealth and male earnings exerts a positive influence on desired numbers of children.

In addition, the children-ever-born regressions indicate that (1) the full-wealth elasticity for numbers of children is probably positive but small, and (2) when economic differences are accounted for, race may play virtually no role in determining family size.

The regressions on quality per child are weaker than those for numbers of children. In part, this must stem from the proxy variable used in the regressions (expected county public school investment), which undoubtedly contains large errors of measurement. The very tentative findings from these regressions are, first, that female education increases the relative efficiency with which child quality is produced, thereby reducing its effective real price, and, second, that the derived income elasticities for numbers of children and for child quality appear to be equal. Also, although it is not a prediction of the theory, the behavior of the rural and race measures is consistent with the hypothesis that there is little difference in "tastes" for child quality either between rural and urban residents or between whites and nonwhites, other things being equal.

Appendix

Derivation of the Model[45]

Let the household utility function be represented by

$$U = U(C,Z),\tag{A1}$$

where C is child services and Z is everything else. Production functions for C and Z are assumed to be linear homogeneous, with average costs of π_C and π_Z, respectively. The household budget constraint may then be written as

$$I = \pi_Z \cdot Z + \pi_C \cdot C,\tag{A2}$$

where R is a measure of the household's full wealth. Under the assumptions of linear homogeneity, changes in the demand for C can be written

$$EC = \eta EI - [k\eta + (1-k)\sigma]E\pi_C + (1-k)(\sigma - \eta)E\pi_Z,\tag{A3}$$

where the E operator denotes percentage change (for example, $EC = d[\log C]$ $= [1/C]dC$); η is the income (wealth) elasticity of the demand for C; σ is the elasticity of substitution between C and Z in $U(C,Z)$; and k is the share of full wealth spent on C $(=[\pi_C \cdot C]/I)$.

The production function for C takes the form

$$C = C(Q,N),\tag{A4}$$

where Q = child-quality input and N = child-body input. Since equation (A4) is linear homogeneous,

$$E\pi_C = \alpha E\pi_N + (1-\alpha)E\pi_Q,\tag{A5}$$

where π_Q = per-unit "rent" of the stock of quality, Q; π_N = per-unit "rent" of the stock of child bodies, N; and $\alpha = \pi_N \cdot N/\pi_C \cdot C$.

[45] Professor H. Gregg Lewis first put me on this particular tack and supplied an outline of the derivation.

From the definition of the elasticity of substitution between two factors of production and from the fact that in equilibrium $(\pi_N)/(\pi_Q) = MP_N/MP_Q$ (the ratio of the prices of N and Q must equal the ratio of their respective marginal products in the production of C),

$$EC - EN = \sigma^* (E\pi_N - E\pi_C), \tag{A6}$$

where $\sigma^* =$ elasticity of substitution between N and Q in the production of C. Therefore, from (A3), (A5), and (A6),

$$EN = \eta EI - \{\alpha[k\eta + (1-k)\sigma] + (1-\alpha)\sigma^*\}E\pi_N$$
$$+ (1-\alpha)[\sigma^* - k\eta - (1-k)\sigma]E\pi_Q$$
$$+ (1-k)(\sigma - \eta)E\pi_Z. \tag{A7}$$

Full wealth is defined as

$$I = V + W^*_m + W^*_f, \tag{A8}$$

where $V =$ property wealth, $W^*_f =$ lifetime possible wage earnings of the female $(T_f \cdot W_f)$, and $W^*_m =$ lifetime possible wage earnings of the male $(T_m \cdot W_m)$. From equation (A8),

$$EI = \frac{V}{I} EV + \frac{W^*_f}{I} EW^*_f + \frac{W^*_m}{I} EW^*_m. \tag{A9}$$

Again, the E operator signifies percentage change.

As with C, the production functions for N, Q, and Z are linear homogeneous; each takes as inputs three factors, that is,

$$Q = Q(t_{m,Q}, t_{f,Q}, X_Q; \beta, \gamma),$$
$$N = N(t_{m,N}, t_{f,N}, X_N; \beta, \gamma), \tag{A10}$$
$$Z = Z(t_{m,Z}, t_{f,Z}, x_Z; \beta, \gamma),$$

where $t_{m,N}$, $t_{m,Q}$, and $t_{m,Z}$ are time of male in the production of N, Q, and Z, respectively, and $t_{f,N}$, $t_{f,Q}$, and $t_{f,Z}$ are market-goods inputs into the production of N, Q, and Z. The environmental variables β and γ represent the husband's and the wife's "quality," respectively, and are a function of the amount of formal schooling each has received. The male's time has a price of W_m; the female's time, a price of W_f; and the market goods have prices of P_N, P_Q, and P_Z, respectively. From these equations it follows that

$$E\pi_N = \alpha_{t_{m,N}}EW_m + \alpha_{t_{f,N}}EW_f + \alpha_{x_N}EP_N - \mu_{N,\beta}E\beta - \mu_{N,\gamma}E\gamma;$$
$$E\pi_Q = \alpha_{t_{m,Q}}EW_m + \alpha_{t_{f,Q}}EW_f + \alpha_{x_Q}EP_Q - \mu_{Q,\beta}E\beta - \mu_{Q,\gamma}E\gamma;$$
$$E\pi_Z = \alpha_{t_{m,Z}}EW_m + \alpha_{t_{f,Z}}EW_f + \alpha_{x_Z}EP_Z - \mu_{Z,\beta}E\beta - \mu_{Z,\gamma}E\gamma, \tag{A11}$$

where $\alpha_{t_{m,N}} = (t_{m,N} \cdot W_m)/\pi_N \cdot N)$ and the other α's are similarly defined, and $\mu_{N,\beta}$ is the partial elasticity of N with respect to β, with similar definitions for the other μ's.

Now, combining (A9) and (A11) with (A7), the following expression for the percentage change in N is obtained:

$$
\begin{aligned}
EN = (V/I)\eta EV \\
- \alpha_{X_N} \{\alpha[k\eta + (1-k)\sigma] + (1-\alpha)\sigma^*\}EP_N \\
+ \alpha_{X_Q} (1-\alpha)[\sigma^* - k\eta - (1-k)\sigma]EP_Q \\
+ \alpha_{X_Z} (1-k)(\sigma - \eta)EP_Z \quad\quad\quad\quad\quad\quad\quad\quad \text{(A12)} \\
+ [(1-\alpha)\sigma^*(\alpha_{t_m,Q} - \alpha_{t_m,N}) + (1-k)\sigma(\alpha_{t_m,Z} - \alpha_{t_m,C}) \\
+ (Y_m/I)\eta]EW_m \\
+ [(1-\alpha)\sigma^*(\alpha_{t_f,Q} - \alpha_{t_f,N}) + (1-k)\sigma(\alpha_{t_f,Z} - \alpha_{t_f,C}) \\
+ (Y_f/I)\eta]EW_f \\
+ \{(1-\alpha)\sigma^*(\mu_{N,\beta} - \mu_{Q,\beta}) + (1-k)\sigma(\mu_{C,\beta} - \mu_{Z,\beta}) \\
+ \eta[k\mu_{C,\beta} + (1-k)\mu_{Z,\beta}]\}E\beta \\
+ \{(1-\alpha)\sigma^*(\mu_{N,\gamma} - \mu_{Q,\gamma}) + (1-k)\sigma(\mu_{C,\gamma} - \mu_{Z,\gamma}) \\
+ \eta[k\mu_{C,\gamma} + (1-k)\mu_{Z,\gamma}]\}E\gamma.
\end{aligned}
$$

In order to ease the reader's task, nonmnemonic symbols all will be defined here:

E = $d(\log)$ operator (percentage change);

V = non–wage-related income;

I = full wealth;

η = income elasticity of C, child services;

α = the share of expenditures on N in total expenditures on C, that is, $(\pi_N \cdot N)/\pi_C \cdot C$;

σ^* = the elasticity of substitution between N and Q in the production of C;

$\alpha_{i,j}$ = the share of expenditures on the ith input in total expenditures on the jth output, where $i = X, t_m, t_f$, and $j = N, Q, Z, C$;

k = the share of total expenditures on C in full wealth, I;

σ = substitution elasticity between C and Z in $U(C,Z)$;

P_i = price of market goods and services X_i;

Y_i = lifetime market earnings of the ith household member, $i = m,f$;

W_i = wage rate of ith household member; and

$\mu_{i,j}$ = the partial elasticity of the ith output with respect to the educational levels of the jth household member, $i = N, Q, C, Z$ and $j = \beta,\gamma$.

Comment

Orley Ashenfelter

Princeton University

When an important social issue emerges that does not fall into the traditional domain of economic analysis, there is always some uneasiness about the usefulness of economists' applying their tools in the new domain. Since I believe that economic tools are useful in the analysis of social problems, it is my own view that it is important for economists' methods to be extended into these "nontraditional" fields as far as possible, and I interpret the works of Becker and Mincer cited so frequently throughout this conference as among the original efforts to do this. Moreover, in a subject as important as the economic determinants of fertility control, I find somewhat shortsighted the comments of those economists who argue that the explanations for most of the variation in birth rates or family size are noneconomic or sociological factors. For even if it is true that the historical explained variance for economic variables is small, this position ignores the fact that most of the social programs of interest to economists in recent years—including negative income taxes, demo-grants, and housing allowances—change the income and effective wage rates that many families in some economic strata will face, and that any careful analysis of the social and economic consequences of these programs should include an objective appraisal of their long-run effects on population size. The ability to obtain such an appraisal is presumably the long-run goal of the economic analysis of population.

At the same time, it seems important to me that when economic tools are applied in unfamiliar terrain, the work should be done with special clarity and without any exaggeration of their power to obtain rigorous predictions concerning observable variables. In addition, our standards for evidence regarding the validity of hypotheses should, if anything, be stronger than in more traditional areas. On both of these grounds Dennis De Tray's paper leaves something to be desired.

As to the underlying theory, it is essentially an application of the

117

classical theory of consumer choice to the demand for children. In order to test the usefulness of this theory, one presumably should first clarify its implications, which, though limited, are nevertheless powerful, even in this case. On the one hand, for example, one could observe the demand for some commodity that is clearly and directly related to childbearing, as, for example, the cost of maternity services, and estimate the income-compensated effect of a change in the price of these services on the demand for them, which the theory would predict is negative. Alternatively, one could observe the demand for two goods or services thought to be related in utility to the demand for children in order to test whether the income-compensated cross-price effects were equal, which is also an unambiguous prediction from the theory. Instead, De Tray attempts to determine the empirical importance of changes in the wage rate of the wife on the demand for children, following up the interesting observation by several economists that the wife's nonmarket time and the family's demand for children may be economic complements. Unfortunately, unless we assume that *all* of the wife's nonmarket time must be used for child rearing, we cannot *predict* that complementarity will be the case, just as we cannot predict that the effect of a pure (nonlabor) income increase will be to increase the demand for children. We are thus left with a useful theoretical framework, but not much else.

As to the empirical estimates, these are based on intercounty differences in the number of children-ever-born to women aged 35–44 and on the expected expenditure on public schooling, the latter presumed to be a proxy for the expected quality of children. As they stand, I find these empirical results far from convincing of the case De Tray intends to make. Concentrating, for example, on the effort to estimate the extent of the complementarity between the wife's nonmarket time and the family's demand for children, one would presumably want to regress completed family size on some permanent wage level. Unfortunately, however, the observed wage rate suffers from the deficiency that it is determined in part by the extent of labor-market experience that a woman has had, and the latter is clearly smaller for women who have larger families. There is thus likely to be a strong negative correlation between completed family size and observed wage rate, but with the causation running from the former to the latter.[1] This problem would clearly be solved satisfactorily only in a simultaneous-equations framework, but some estimates of the likely biases in De Tray's results might be inferred by using some of the standard methods for analysis of specification error. In practice, however, it is not entirely clear how useful this exercise would be with De Tray's data, since the independent variable in his regressions is not the wage rate of women

[1] See, e.g., Oaxaca (1971) for estimates from microeconomic data that purport to show this latter relationship and for an explicit discussion of the effect of labor-force experience on the wage rates of women.

but their annual earnings. Now, it is well known that the labor-force participation and weeks worked of women with children are lower than those of women without. Since annual earnings are the product of the wage rate and annual hours, it follows that the number of children a woman has and her annual earnings are likely to have a strong negative correlation, but again with the causation running from the former to the latter. Analyzing the compound effect of these biases is likely to be difficult, particularly when another variable—namely, house value—that is also jointly determined with the demand for children and the demand for the nonmarket time of the wife, is included on the right-hand side of the regression equation.

Though interesting, it will take better data and a more complete model before De Tray's results are likely to convince very many economists that we have reliable estimates of the basic parameters in the application of economic analysis to the determination of family size.

Education and the Derived Demand for Children

Robert T. Michael

University of California, Los Angeles, and National Bureau of Economic Research

I. Introduction

A negative correlation across households between parent's education and completed fertility is one of the most widely and frequently observed relationships in the empirical literature on human fertility behavior. In this paper I utilize the emerging economic theory of household behavior, which is also employed in other papers in this volume, to formulate an explanation for this observed negative correlation. In particular, the paper has two objectives: (1) to consider the mechanisms through which a couple's level of education might affect their fertility and (2) to document the effects of education on one of these mechanisms that is an aspect of fertility control—the choice of a contraceptive technique.

The following section briefly outlines the theoretical framework, and in Section III I discuss the mechanisms through which education's influence may operate. Throughout, the discussion is restricted to channels of influence from education to fertility; that is, the reverse causation is ruled out by assumption. The specific focus of this discussion should not be interpreted as an assertion of the exclusiveness or the primacy of education's influence on fertility. Section IV considers the fertility-control decision in greater detail. It also reports on my initial empirical work with the 1965 National Fertility Study, a nationwide sociological survey of 5,600 U.S. women undertaken by the Office of Population Research at

I would like to thank Gary S. Becker, Barry R. Chiswick, Victor R. Fuchs, Reuben Gronau, Michael Grossman, Edward P. Lazear, Jacob Mincer, Norman B. Ryder, T. W. Schultz, T. Paul Schultz, and Robert J. Willis for constructive suggestions on this project, and Anne O. Stevens for her able research assistance. Margaret G. Reid's discussion of an earlier draft has been helpful to me. I would like also to thank the Office of Population Research at Princeton University and Professor Charles F. Westoff in particular for making available to me data tapes from the 1965 National Fertility Survey. My work has been supported by a grant from the Ford Foundation to the National Bureau of Economic Research for study of the economics of population.

Princeton University. The paper does not attempt to set out an explicit, formal model with precise, testable implications, but rather attempts to explore channels of influence in a relatively flexible analytical context.

II. The Theoretical Considerations

To delineate mechanisms through which a couple's education affects their fertility behavior requires a framework in which that behavior can be analyzed. Since the choice of a framework determines the structure in which the analysis takes place, it thereby influences the nature of the mechanisms emphasized. Fortunately, the theory of human fertility behavior emerging from pioneering work on a theory of household behavior by Becker (1960, 1965) and Mincer (1962a, 1963) is clearly useful both in predicting broad patterns of completed fertility and in analyzing other dimensions of fertility. Since other studies reported herein, notably Willis's, develop specific and detailed versions of this model, I intend to limit my exposition to a few particular points.

i) *An Analytical Framework*
Assume the household has the intertemporal utility function

$$U = u(Z_{1t}, Z_{2t}, \ldots, Z_{nt}), \quad t = 1, \ldots, h, \tag{1}$$

where Z_{it} is the amount of the commodity i consumed in period t and where each commodity in each period is produced according to a household production function

$$Z_i = f_i(x_i, T_{ij}), \tag{2}$$

where x_i represents purchased market goods and T_{ij} is the jth household member's time used in the production and enjoyment of Z_i. An essential feature of these commodities is that their production and enjoyment are inseparable; thus, these commodities cannot be exchanged among households.

The household is assumed to maximize equation (1) subject to the production-function constraints as in equation (2), a money-income constraint,

$$\sum_{t=1}^{h} \sum_{i=1}^{n} x_{it} \frac{p_{it}}{(1+r)^t} = \sum_t \sum_j \left[\frac{W_{jt}}{(1+r)^t} (Tw_{jt}) + \frac{V_{jt}}{(1+r)^t} \right], \tag{3}$$

and a time-budget constraint,

$$\sum_{i=1}^{n} T_{ij} + Tw_j = T \qquad \text{for all } j, \tag{4}$$

where i is an index over the n commodities, j is an index over the adult family members, r is the household's rate of time discount, p_i is the market price of good x_i, W_j is the real wage rate of individual j, Tw_j is the time spent at work by individual j, V_j is the property income of individual j, and T is the total time available to each individual per period.

In applying this typical representation of the household production-function model to the household's fertility behavior, we consider two of the production processes in equation (2) more explicitly. The analysis will be for a single period of time. First, assume that one of the commodities, say Z_1, is "family life" and is related to the stream of satisfaction obtained from the couple's offspring. More specifically, for a single time period

$$Z_1 = f_1(x_1, T_{1j}, C), \tag{5}$$

where x_1 and T_{1j} are the goods and the adult's own time, which are combined with a flow of "child services," C, to produce the stream Z_1, which enters the household's utility function. The C, then, is an intermediate product used in f_1 and is itself produced from the quality-adjusted stock of children in the household.

It will be assumed that C is proportional to the number of offspring in the household, N:

$$C = \alpha N \tag{6}$$

where the factor of proportionality varies across households but is assumed to be constant among children within a given household. The N is a stock of offspring or children, and C is a flow of services per unit of time. The term α therefore indicates the rate of flow per unit of the stock. The "quality" of the household's children is then defined to be monotonically related to α, $Q = \Phi(\alpha)$, $\Phi' > 0$, and although α can in principle be objectively determined, the scaling of Q is arbitrary. The production function for Q is assumed to be

$$Q = \theta(x_Q, T_{Qj}; e), \tag{7}$$

where x and T are direct inputs of goods and own time and e represents the household environment to which the child is exposed. This latter variable will be discussed more extensively below.

A second commodity in the utility function which is analytically related to the level of N (the household's number of children) is the commodity "sexual gratification." This commodity, designated as Z_2, is also produced by one of the household production functions in equation (2) using both purchased inputs and the couple's own time. The relationship between Z_2 and N results from the effects of the level of production of Z_2 upon the price of acquiring a unit of N. Abstracting from the uncertainties associated with the acquisition by a consumer of any durable good, "children" as a durable good is subject to a rather unique risk: the uncertainty of conception. Given a positive level of production of Z_2, a fecund couple is exposed to a positive probability of conception. That probability is affected by the couple's age, fecundity at each given age, and its coital frequency. The couple may expend resources of time and money to alter (raise or lower) this probability. Thus P, the probability of a conception per unit of time, will be treated as the outcome of a distinct production process:

$$P = f_3(x_p, T_p; Z_2, F),\qquad(8)$$

where F is the couple's unadjusted fecundity. By definition, $\partial P/\partial F > 0$, and there is evidence suggesting $\partial P/\partial Z_2 > 0$.[1] The direct expenditure on the probability of conception, G, will be defined as the expenditure at a given level of Z_2 and F:

$$G\big|_{Z_2,F} = \Pi_P(P - P^*) = x_P p_x + T_P p_T,\qquad(9)$$

where Π_P is the price of a unit change in P and P^* is the level of P which would exist at the given levels of Z_2 and F if no effort were made to affect the level of P. For example, for a fecund couple, P^* may be equal to 0.20 per month, but with an expenditure of money and time on a contraceptive method, the couple may be able to lower its monthly probability of conception, P, to .05. Similarly, a subfecund couple with a given level of Z_2 and a given (low) level of F may have a monthly birth probability, P^*, equal to .10, but by an expenditure on medical advice and the use of some of their own time in following that advice, they may be able to raise P to, say, .25. Since G, the total expenditure on the probability P, is nonnegative, Π_P is negative or positive, depending on whether the couple is expending resources to lower P below P^* or to raise P above P^*:

$$\Pi_P \lessgtr 0 \text{ as } P \gtrless P^*.\qquad(10)$$

In the case of contraception, the negative price of a unit of P simply reflects the fact that the intermediate good being produced is a reduction in

---

[1] Potter, Sagi, and Westoff (1962, p. 54) indicate that, for couples using no contraception during the interval prior to the first pregnancy, as coital frequency rose from under twice, to twice, to three or more times per week, the mean period required for a conception fell from 11.0 months, to 7.1 months, to 6.6 months. Earlier, MacLeod and Gold (1953, p. 29) found a strong positive relationship between coital frequency and the time required for conception. Using husband's age-specific data, they found that the percentage of couples with conception occurring in less than 6 months rose with coital frequency. For example, for husbands under age 25, as frequency rose from less than twice a week, to two to three times, to three to four times, to four or more times a week, the percentages rose from 37.5, to 70.6, to 83.9, to 94.6. They conclude: "The frequency of intercourse is a strong determining factor in ease of conception, no matter what the age of the husband" (p. 29). For a brief statement of the expected effects of differences in coital frequency on childbearing, in a simple mathematical model of births as a perpetual renewal process, see Keyfitz (1971). Although the commodity Z_2 is not defined exclusively in terms of coital frequency, the two are positively related, so the evidence cited here suggests $dP/dZ_2 > 0$.

P; that is, x_P and T_P have negative marginal products in f_3 since they are used in an effort to reduce P.

Given an appropriately explicit set of assumptions about the nature of the household production functions, cost curves, and utility function, we can specify a relatively complete model of household fertility behavior. The decisions to construct such a model in a static or in a dynamic framework and to suppress or to include any particular production relationship (such as the production of Z_2), any intermediate stage of production (such as the production of Q), or any simultaneous or joint production (such as the relationship between Z_2 and P) depend, of course, upon the specific purpose of the analysis. The household production function framework itself is not wedded to any particular formulation. At one level, it simply provides a means by which the complexities of observed fertility behavior can be sorted out and an economic language in which the various interrelationships can be discussed.

ii) *The Fertility-Control Decision*

To illustrate an application of this framework, consider the family's decision regarding fertility control. It will be assumed for now that the decision makers suffer from a particular type of myopia: specifically, although they consider long-run repercussions of their fertility-control decision in terms of future costs and benefits of children, they do not make long-run fertility-control plans. Thus, the assumption is that the couple does not determine an optimal fertility-control strategy: in each period an independent decision is made with respect to fertility control.

The first stage in the fertility-control decision is the determination of the net benefit from an additional child. The net benefit, B, is computed from the stream of costs and benefits attributable to the child over time; it may be positive or negative (see Appendix). The term B is functionally related to all the arguments in the completed-fertility demand function and simply represents the household's effective excess demand for children at the prices, income level, level of production of complements and substitutes, and so on, which are implicit in the calculation of B. If B is positive, the household's excess demand for children is positive and the couple may seek to raise their probability of conception. If, on the other hand, B is negative, the couple may engage in fertility control.[2]

---

[2] It was pointed out above that the level of production of Z_2 is positively related to the probability of conception P. If the first-order condition for the optimal level of production of Z_2 is considered (see Appendix):

$$\frac{\partial L}{\partial Z_2} = MU_2 - \lambda \left(-B \frac{\partial N}{\partial P} \frac{\partial P}{\partial Z_2} + \Pi_2 \right) = 0,$$

where B is defined as in (A4) and Π_2 is the direct marginal cost of Z_2. So the shadow price of Z_2 in a given period, π_2, is equal to the term in parentheses above. Since both derivatives in the above equation are positive, the shadow price of Z_2 is higher than its direct marginal cost when B is negative. That is, when the net benefit from

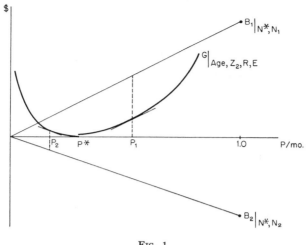

FIG. 1

Furthermore, it is assumed that there is a cost function G representing the total cost to the household of producing various levels of the probability P. This cost curve is presumably functionally related to the parents' age and coital frequency and their religion and level of education. Thus, from these two monetary relationships, B and G, the optimal level of P for a given period can be determined. Figure 1 depicts hypothetical G and B functions for a couple with a specific age, level of production of Z_2, religion, education, parity (current number of children), and effective completed-fertility demand. If the parents demand, say, four children and their current parity is two, then perhaps $B = B_1$. In this case, the marginal cost and marginal benefit of altering the probability of conception are equated at a level P_1. Since $B_1 > 0$, the couple would produce a $P > P^*$. If, instead, the same parents' current parity were, say, five children, then perhaps their $B = B_2$. In this case, the couple would engage in fertility control up to the point of equality between the marginal-cost and marginal-benefit functions (P_2 in fig. 1). Thus, $P_i \lesseqgtr P^*$ when $B_i \lesseqgtr 0$.

III.   Channels of Influence

The household is viewed as maximizing a utility function subject to a money-wealth constraint, a time constraint for each adult, and a set of

---

an additional child is negative, the shadow price of sexual gratification is higher than its direct cost, and symmetrically, when the net benefit is positive, the shadow price is lower than the direct cost (for an extended discussion of this joint production issue, see Grossman [1971]). In the former case the household is induced to reduce its effective demand for Z_2 (or to substitute toward less coitus-intensive means of production); in the latter case the household is induced to increase the quantity demanded of Z_2.

household production functions. By definition, the parents' education level may influence their fertility behavior by affecting any of these four relationships.

Before these relationships are discussed, the term "education," which is so frequently used to mean so many different things, needs defining. An individual attends school for a period of time, and the "number of years of schooling," S, is an objectively quantifiable number. As a product or outcome of that schooling, knowledge and physical and mental skills are acquired. The accumulated stock of knowledge and the acquired physical and mental skills constitute productive human capital. These stocks of knowledge and skills acquired from schooling are here defined as "education." Thus, education is human capital, but education does not necessarily represent the individual's entire stock of human capital, since this capital may also be acquired from activities other than schooling.[3] While education is analytically a particular portion of one's stock of human capital, empirically it is generally measured by years of schooling completed. Our theories indicate how human capital, E, might affect behavior, but we investigate how years of schooling, S, are correlated with observed behavior.

i) *The Utility Function*

Economists have neither developed for themselves nor had available from other behavioral sciences a viable theory about the formation of preferences or the determinants of "tastes." Schooling represents exposure to a differentiated type of experience. If experience influences preferences, then education may affect preferences in some as yet unspecified manner. Economists have dealt with the implications of differences in, say, risk or time preferences,[4] but until a theory of the formation of preferences is available, little can be said, a priori, about the relationship between education and tastes or about the possible influence of education on the preference function.

ii) *The Wealth Constraint*

The influence of education on fertility through the money-wealth constraint has been much explored. The other papers in this volume focus predominantly upon the effects on completed fertility of differences in

---

[3] For an important attempt to distinguish operationally between schooling, education, and human capital, see Welch (1966). For a thorough discussion of the concept of health capital, see Grossman (1972b).

[4] If the evidence on average rates of return to successive levels of schooling (see T. W. Schultz [1972a]) reflects differential marginal rates of time discount by education level, then the higher one's education, the longer one's time horizon. A longer time horizon, however, may simply reflect consideration of longer-run effects or the absence of myopia, and if so, it might be treated as an effect on long-run production functions rather than as a "taste" phenomenon. For the effects of education on money savings behavior and attitudes toward savings objectives, see Solmon (1974).

(1) levels of wealth and (2) value of time of household members. In light of the strong accumulated evidence reported in the human-capital literature of the effects of schooling on wage rates and thus money income, this channel of influence is well established. Investments in education enhance one's earnings capacity, increase one's time value in the labor market, and raise one's full money income. These changes may in turn affect the relative prices of children and child services, and these relative price changes (as well as the changes in wealth) may alter the quantity of child services the household demands. Given an effect of a "pure" income change on the quantity of Z demanded, the effect on the derived demand for N or Q depends upon the nature of the production relationships between N, Q, and C, and between C and Z_1.

In addition to pure income effects from an increase in market wage rates, the marginal time value or the "price of time" also rises with the wage rate for an individual optimally allocating time to the labor market. The effect of an increase in the price of time on the derived demand for children depends upon its effects on the relative prices of intermediate goods and final commodities. As Becker (1965) has emphasized, the effect of a change in the price of time on the relative price of a commodity depends upon its time intensity. In the current literature on human fertility, it is generally assumed that children or child-related consumption is relatively intensive in the wife's time. Thus, increases in her time value raise the price of children and lower the quantity demanded. This is perhaps the key economic explanation for the observed negative relationship between the wife's education level and the (completed) number of children. It should be evident that it is not simply the time intensity of the intermediate product N which is relevant here, but also the time intensity of Q and of Z_1. The time intensity of N relative to Q determines the incentives to substitute in the production of child services, C, while the relative time intensity of Z_1 influences the induced substitution in consumption between commodities.

Differences in the value of time of the husband also affect fertility. The higher the husband's education level, the higher is his time value and thus the greater is his incentive to substitute away from nonmarket activities which are intensive in his time. If, as is frequently assumed, child production uses relatively little of his time, the relative price of child-related production falls as his time value rises. This induced substitution toward N (and perhaps Z_1) as the value of the husband's time rises can help explain the observed phenomenon that the wife's education is generally more negatively related to fertility than is his. Furthermore, in cross-sectional regressions on number of children with two variables representing husband's income and value of wife's time, the often-observed positive effect of the former variable cannot be interpreted as a "pure" income effect, since the increase in the husband's wage rate induces substitution toward the production of children. So the parents' levels of education may affect their fertility behavior by raising income and the value of their time. In addition, there are other, somewhat more subtle, effects on fertility emanating from changes in the income constraint and in the form in which wealth is held.

First, an increase in income results initially in an increase in the ratio of market goods and services to own time in household production. This, in turn, will raise the marginal product of time, given the usual assumptions about the nature of production functions. Only if individuals can exchange some of this additional money income (or these additional units of x) for own time (or T_i) by removing time from the labor market to restore the optimal ratio of x to T will there be no price effects (Becker [1965] explores this point at some length). If, however, an individual were unable to substitute sufficiently (i.e., initially he or she spent no time in the labor market or spent too little time to permit a full adjustment), then the income effect also would represent an increase in the time value of the individual (see Willis's paper in this book for a detailed discussion of this point, as well as Ben-Porath's paper herein).

Second, the nature of the household production function model emphasizes joint production in the household, and one aspect of joint production goes far in resolving the dispute in the literature about the mechanism through which income affects the relative demand for "quality" and number of children. By definition, parents with more income spend more on goods and services, and empirically they spend proportionately more on such items as durable goods, housing, and travel. Many of these expenditures on goods for the couple's own use in various production processes may yield externalities to their children through the children's unavoidable exposure to these goods. Put differently, the purchase of a durable good, say a hi-fi set, may be motivated by the demand for some commodity quite unrelated to children, but once acquired, the item assumes some of the characteristics of a "public good" within the household. The couple's children are necessarily exposed to the good; it represents a part of the environment in which the child lives. If these goods and services which are acquired for the parents' own use are complementary with the direct expenditures used in the production of "quality" in their children, households with larger amounts of these goods and services face a lower marginal cost of child quality, *ceteris paribus*. Thus, the relative price of quality to quantity of children may be lower for wealthier couples.[5] If so, wealthier households would be induced to shift toward fewer, more quality-intensive children, other things held constant.[6]

---

[5] From eq. (7) the marginal products of x_0 and T_0 in the production of quality, θ_x and θ_T, may be affected by the level of e, the environmental variable positively related to the couple's wealth. If $\theta_{x,e} > 0$ and $\theta_{T,e} > 0$, the direct marginal cost of Q is negatively related to e.

[6] Note that the argument here is not that of Duesenberry (1960) and Okun (1960).

A final relative price effect pertains to the form in which one's wealth is held. Education, or human capital in general, is but one form of wealth and is by its nature embedded in the individual. The income flow from human capital cannot be separated from the individual's use of his own time. Consequently, the income or benefit flow from human capital becomes a part of the opportunity cost of one's time. Since the flow of benefits from other capital assets is not so wedded to the individual's time, differences in wealth among individuals do not identically reflect differences in their time value: the proportion of one's wealth held in the form of human capital, as well as the quantity of wealth, affects time values.

Pursuing this point further, if human capital is not homogeneous in the sense that some investments yield benefits in certain specific activities but not in others, and if this "specific" capital depreciates at a rate which is negatively related to its rate of utilization, then the shadow price of one's time incorporates the "user cost" of this capital and may differ among specific uses of one's time.[7] If, for example, time spent in child rearing involves a relatively low rate of utilization of one's knowledge capital and offers relatively little opportunity for additional on-the-job investment, then the user cost of human capital will be particularly high in child rearing.[8] In this case, the couple's education level may be positively related to the shadow price of time used in child rearing, relative even to the shadow price of time used in other household production activities. Obviously, the argument here is no more than a logical possibility, but the point, I think, merits attention. By its nature, human capital is neither a homogeneous nor a static quantity, and the various uses of one's time may embody different rates of depreciation and different investment opportunities which, in turn, affect the opportunity cost of time. Education may affect fertility by altering relative prices subtly, but

---

Their points were, respectively, that the "standard of living of the children is mechanically linked to that of the parents" (p. 234) and "automatically, when parents raise their own level of living . . . quality expenditures per child *must* rise" (p. 236). It is not the case that the "quality" of the child is "mechanically" or "automatically" tied to income: the household could reduce its direct expenditure of time and goods on children and achieve the same level of "quality." It is, rather, that the marginal cost of "quality" is lowered as incomes rise and that the "quantity to quality" mix thus shifts toward "quality." The shift results from a change in relative prices and not from some inexorability.

[7] In discussing the user cost of capital equipment, Keynes (1936) suggests that in normal conditions "the use of equipment brings nearer the date at which replacement is necessary" (p. 73). It is suggested, with respect to physical capital, that the rates of depreciation and utilization are positively related. With regard to human capital, however, it seems more likely that depreciation increases with disuse, implying a negative correlation between its rates of use and depreciation. The "user cost" of capital is higher in uses which represent relatively high net rates of depreciation. For human capital, in contrast to physical capital, such uses are those activities which make little use of the capital.

[8] Michael and Lazear (1971) show that for an individual with a labor-market attachment, the shadow price of nonmarket time is the observed wage foregone plus the net human capital lost through foregone investment opportunities and higher rates of depreciation on existing capital.

perhaps substantially, through these dynamic aspects of the ownership of an array of different human capital assets.

iii) *The Production Function Constraints*

The household faces a set of production function constraints, and its members' education levels may affect these in many ways. Since it is inferred from evidence pertaining to effects on market earnings that education raises one's productive capacity in labor-market activities, it has more recently been argued that education may affect one's productive capacity in nonmarket production activities as well. It might do so either by influencing the choice of productive techniques employed (by improving the couple's capability to acquire, assimilate, and implement knowledge about alternative production techniques) or by affecting the marginal productivity of the inputs used in a given production technique (see Welch [1970] and Michael [1972]). In general, the possible direct influences of education through these productive activities are limitless, since specific effects of education on particular production functions can alter the relative prices of commodities and the relative proficiencies of factors of production, and thereby induce substitution in consumption (between commodities) and substitution in production (between inputs). These shifts can also affect the real income of the household and thereby create "pure" wealth effects (see Michael [1972]).

Focusing upon two production effects which seem, intuitively, to merit particular attention regarding fertility behavior, consider the influence of education on child quality and on fertility control.[9] If the flow of child services per child, α, is directly related to the child's age-adjusted stock of human capital, then it seems plausible that the parents' stock of such capital would be particularly productive in producing human capital in their children.[10] If so, education would be negatively related to the relative

---

[9] That is, the variable E will be added to eqq. (7) and (8) as an additional influence on the environment in which this production takes place: $Q = \theta(x_Q, T_Q; e, E)$ and $P = f_3(x_P, T_P; Z_2, F, E)$.

[10] It has been suggested that education, or human capital in general, may be technologically biased. Specifically, education may raise one's productivity in producing additional human capital more than it improves one's productivity in producing other nonmarket products and, perhaps, more than it improves one's productivity in producing market earnings (see, in particular, Ben-Porath [1970c] and Mincer [1970b]). It is but an extension of this argument to suggest that human capital is relatively technologically biased toward producing human capital in one's children as well. (Current research by Mincer and by Leibowitz, as well as completed work by Leibowitz [1972], pursues this point in the context of preschool investment in children. See also De Tray's paper in this volume.) It should perhaps be pointed out that this contention is not inconsistent with the discussion above. It may well be that education has a disproportionately large effect on lowering the cost of producing human capital in children, but that this production represents a relatively low rate of utilization of the parents' human capital. In short, child rearing by the more-educated may be both quite productive and quite costly.

price of Q, other things constant, inducing technical substitution toward Q in the production of any given level of child services.

Finally, since one of the behavioral attributes often ascribed to education is an awareness of and receptivity to new ideas, and since the production of fertility control encompasses a broad range of techniques of production which require varying degrees of precision in use, this, too, appears to be a productive activity in which education may have a disproportionately strong effect. If education lowers the relative cost of fertility control, *ceteris paribus,* more-educated contracepting couples would choose to produce a relatively lower probability of conception, P. (In fig. 1, if education lowered the slope of the cost curve at all levels of $P < P^*$, then the optimal P would be lower than P_1.)[11] Over extended periods of time, couples exposed to a lower risk of conception would expect fewer conceptions and hence lower fertility on the average, all else equal.

iv) *The Time Constraint*
Consider, finally, the individual household member's time constraint. Expressed in nominal (as distinct from effective) time units, the only way in which this constraint can be altered is by affecting the number of periods to which the constraint applies. If the formation of the household at marriage determines the initial time period of the analysis and if life expectancy determines the time horizon, then the question becomes, How does the couple's education affect the age at marriage and life expectancy? Work on a theory of marriage in the context of a household production function framework is presented below by Becker. The implications from this model for the effects of education on age at marriage will not be pursued here (although some observed correlations are discussed below).

In a recent study of the demand for health, Grossman (1972*b*) analyzed the individual's decision regarding an optimal length of life in the context of a model which treats health as a depreciable capital stock. He showed that the lower the cost of investment in health capital, the longer the optimal length of life, *ceteris paribus.* Empirically, Grossman's evidence suggests that the larger an individual's stock of knowledge capital, as measured by years of formal schooling, the lower his cost of investment in health capital. Hence, one's education level may affect one's time horizon by extending life expectancy, through the endogenous effect of education on the optimal stock of health capital.

v) *Conclusion*
In the context of the household production function framework in which children are viewed as a durable asset, there are several mechanisms

---

[11] Of course, it would be possible for the total cost curve to be lowered without reducing the relevant marginal cost curve. At this point, the specific form of these cost functions is not specified.

through which the couple's education may affect fertility behavior. In addition to the frequently discussed effects through changes in money income and the value of time of household members, effects through the proficiency of household production functions and through indirect changes in relative prices have been emphasized. Effects through the utility function and the length of the couple's time horizon have also been noted.

Too often, the husband's or wife's education level is interpreted in empirical work as a good proxy variable for whatever is of interest to the researcher. As emphasized here, education may affect behavior in many ways. Thus, it seems to me, high priority in empirical research should be given to an attempt to parcel out some of these separate effects and to establish their relative order of importance. The work I report below is a contribution toward that end.

IV. Education and Fertility Control

It has long been argued that more-educated couples have greater access to fertility-control information and are therefore more successful in preventing unwanted pregnancies. Indeed, there is considerable evidence, from sociological surveys in the United States—notably the Growth of American Families (GAF) studies conducted in 1955 and 1960 and the sequel, the National Fertility Studies (NFS), to which I referred earlier as the data base for this study—that standardized, say, for religion or for age, more-educated couples do use contraceptive techniques more extensively, approve of their use more thoroughly, and adopt contraception at an earlier birth interval. Consequently, more-educated couples are more likely to have "completely planned" fertility (as to both the timing and the number of their children) and are less likely to have "excess fertility" or "unwanted" births.[12]

Similar findings are reported for other countries as well. Yaukey (1961) finds, in a study of some 900 Lebanese women, that the use of contraception and particularly the use of appliance methods rise with education. Roberts et al. (1967), utilizing a 1964 survey of 1,500 women of childbearing age in Barbados, found that general knowledge of contraception, the average number of contraceptive methods known per woman who knew of at least one method, and the percentage who had ever used contraception rose with the woman's education level. Broadly comparable findings for India (see Dandekar [1967] and Morrison [1957]), Puerto Rico (see Stycos [1967]), Japan (see Matsunaga [1967]), and Ghana (see Caldwell [1967]), for example, offer supporting evidence of greater use and acceptance of contraception among the relatively better-educated.

---

[12] The principal reports on the 1955, 1960, and 1965 surveys are, respectively, Freedman, Whelpton, and Campbell (1959), Whelpton, Campbell, and Patterson (1966), and Ryder and Westoff (1971).

In studies in less-developed countries, the evidence further indicates that the more educated are also more aware of the possibility of and the methods of contraception.

i) Contraceptive Efficiency

While it may appear intuitively plausible that differences in education level affect knowledge of contraception at a relatively low level of education or at a time when such knowledge is generally not widespread, one might question whether existing differences in education levels in contemporary U.S. data would still reflect much difference in use. Moreover, one might think that with the relatively effective contraceptive methods available in the past decade or so, the specific technique a couple adopted would have little effect on fertility outcome. However, the cumulative effects over extended periods of time of less than near-perfect contraceptive efficiency can indeed have an appreciable influence on expected outcomes. Following Keyfitz (1971), define contraceptive efficiency, e, as the percentage reduction in the monthly birth probability: $e = (P^* - P)/P^*$, where P^* is the monthly probability for the fecund couple with no fertility control and P is the monthly probability with a specific contraceptive technique in use. If a couple used a contraceptive technique which was "only" 90 percent effective, in a 15-year period their expected fertility outcome would be 2.7 births (assuming the period of infertility associated with pregnancy was as long as 17 months; with instantaneous replacement, the expected fertility outcome would be 3.6 conceptions). Or, if a couple used a contraceptive technique which was "only" 99 percent effective, the chance of a conception in a 5-year interval exceeds 10 percent. "Good" (but not perfect) contraception does not provide the long-run protection one might think.[13]

A contraceptive technique, as emphasized above, is a factor of production used along with other factors to reduce the probability of conception. As such, the observed efficiency of the technique should not be treated independently from the complementary factors of production with which it is employed. Comparing the observed effectiveness in use of different contraceptive techniques across households is equivalent to comparing average products, say, of different types of lawn mowers across households. It would be preferable to attempt to standardize for the amount and productivity of the time input (and other inputs) with which the lawn mower or contraceptive is combined. In short, the observed effectiveness in use is affected by the precision and care with which it is used.

Noting this major limitation of such data, consider next the relative observed use effectiveness of the most common techniques of contracep-

---

[13] The chance of a conception is calculated as $1 - (1 - P)^{12Y}$, where Y is the number of years of exposure. There are, of course, assumptions implicit in the calculation, and the relevant figures would be affected by such factors as age, fecundity, and coital frequency. The interested reader is referred to Keyfitz (1971).

TABLE 1

Estimates of Effectiveness of Contraceptive Techniques

Technique	Observed Use Effectiveness R (1)	Monthly Birth Probability P (2)	Contraceptive Efficiency e (3)	Expected Time to Conception (Months) (4)	Probability of a Conception in a 10-Year Period (5)
Pill	1.0	.0008	.9958	1,200	.097
IUD	2.5	.0021	.9896	480	.222
Condom	13.8	.0115	.9425	87	.750
Diaphragm	14.4	.0120	.9400	83	.765
Withdrawal	16.8	.0140	.9300	71	.816
Jelly	18.8	.0157	.9217	64	.850
Foam tablets	20.1	.0168	.9162	60	.868
Suppositories	21.9	.0182	.9088	55	.890
Rhythm	38.5	.0321	.8396	31	.980
Douche	40.3	.0336	.8321	30	.983
No method	...	.2000	.0000	5	1.000

Note.—Col. 1, $R = $ (number of conceptions $\times$ 1,200)/(number of months of exposure); see Tietze (1962). The rates of use effectiveness are estimates derived from several sources. See in particular Tietze (1959b, 1962, 1970). I adjusted the rates obtained from different populations by using relative links from overlapping estimates. Col. 2, $P = (R \div 1{,}200)$. Col. 3, $e = (P^* - P)/P^*$, where P^* is assumed to be .20. Col. 4, Time $= 1/P$. Col. 5, Probability in 10 years $= 1 - (1 - P)^{120}$.

tion. The use effectiveness of each technique is its computed failure rate per 100 years of use and as such reflects its reliability in use by a given sample of couples. It does not reflect the physiological or potential effectiveness of the technique used under ideal circumstances.[14] Table 1 makes use of published estimates of use effectiveness. Although the relatively poor techniques lower the risk of conception per month by more than 80 percent on the average (see col. 3), the expected waiting time until a conception is only $2\frac{1}{2}$ years (col. 4); over a 10-year period the likelihood of an accidental pregnancy is as high as 98 percent (col. 5). So a couple

[14] Tietze has emphasized in several studies the difficulties in estimating the use effectiveness of various contraceptive techniques and the qualifications which must accompany any such estimates. For an excellent discussion of some of these, see Tietze (1959a, 1962) and Potter, McCann, and Sakoda (1970). To illustrate the difficulty, if the computation of contraceptive failure rates includes months of use soon after the termination of pregnancy, the low rates of pregnancy resulting from the natural infertility following delivery will be incorrectly attributed to the technique, biasing downward the estimate of the failure rate. Likewise, a downward bias is also possible if the computation excludes too many months beyond the period of postpartum infertility, since the remaining cohort of users will have excluded the most fecund couples. The use effectiveness, furthermore, will be affected by the distributions of the duration of use among couples and of the parity of couples in the sample, since long-period users are more likely to be less fecund and higher-parity users are generally more careful in their use of contraceptives (see n. 17). The set of estimates in table 1 represents a "ball park" estimate of the relative ranking of the techniques by their observed use effectiveness.

using the rhythm or douche technique at its average observed efficiency cannot expect to avoid conception for long. Even using as effective a technique as the diaphragm or the condom, the typical couple can expect a conception, on the average, after about 7 years of use and faces a probability equal to .75 of incurring a conception in 10 years of exposure.

ii) *Simple Correlates of Interval-specific Contraception Behavior*

The 1965 National Fertility Study that I have used to investigate the selection of contraceptive techniques among households surveyed, nationally, some 5,600 women under age 55, currently married and living with their husbands at the time of the interview (around November 1965) and able to participate in an English-language interview. Interviews of approximately 75 minutes were conducted by specially trained professional female interviewers.[15] Negroes were double-sampled and are dealt with separately in the results reported below.

These data contain information on the specific contraceptive techniques used within separate pregnancy intervals (between marriage and the first pregnancy, between the first and second pregnancy, and so on). In many instances, of course, no technique was used within a given interval. In a small number of instances, no information was obtained. For each of the interval-specific statistics below, these few cases of missing data (typically less than 0.5 percent of the subsample) were deleted, as were cases in which the couple did not have that closed interval.[16]

The first task undertaken with these data, and the only one reported in this paper, was to examine the relationship between the technique selected in a given interval and various economic and demographic variables (in particular, the levels of schooling of the husband and wife). Rather than contend with each specific technique separately, as in a study of the diffusion of specific technological innovations, the techniques were

[15] For a complete description of this data set and its comparability with the earlier GAF surveys and with the 1960 U.S. census and subsequent Current Population Survey data, see Ryder and Westoff (1971). Of the 5,617 observations in the NFS data set, only 1,963 observations have been used in the analysis here (see table 2). The remainder were Catholics (1,271 observations) or non-Catholics under age 25 (806) or over age 40 (1,352) or age 25–40 but designated by race as "other nonwhite" (37 observations). Another 188 observations initially deleted contained either no information on the education level of a spouse or no income information.

[16] Excluding couples that had not "closed" a specific birth interval by a subsequent pregnancy builds in a selectivity bias. While the closed intervals do not necessarily reflect contraceptive failures, the open interval by definition has not been closed by a contraceptive failure. So in successively higher pregnancy intervals, some successful contraceptors will be systematically omitted. The open-ended pregnancy interval, however, has several characteristics which make it somewhat inappropriate to include with the closed intervals. These characteristics include (a) the considerably longer time span of the open interval, (b) the availability of the oral contraceptive near the end of the open interval (the survey date), and (c), most importantly, a somewhat different set of survey questions pertaining to the contraceptive techniques used in the open interval. I intend to study the contraceptive behavior in the open interval but have not yet done so.

collapsed into a single variable defined in terms of the monthly birth probability applicable to that technique. This was done by assigning to each technique its corresponding monthly birth probability from table 1. So, for example, a couple that used a diaphragm in the first pregnancy interval was assigned a value of .0120 (from col. 2 of table 1). This assignment was made for each of the first three closed pregnancy intervals for each household. Couples with no such interval were excluded for purposes of that variable, and couples who used no method in a given interval were assigned a value of .2000 (which is a value often quoted as a typically fecund couple's unadjusted monthly birth probability). For many of the statistics, couples who used no method of contraception in a specific interval were excluded; these statistics are designated below as referring to "users only."

It must be stressed that the average observed use effectiveness of a given contraceptive technique was assigned to each pregnancy interval for each household on the basis of information on the technique the couple used in that interval. So the variable to be examined is *not* the couple's own monthly birth probability computed from its own experience. Rather, the assigned values simply rank the techniques and scale their average effectiveness in a reasonably appropriate manner. This enables us to investigate the selection of a contraceptive technique in terms of its relative average effectiveness.

It should also be emphasized that the unit of analysis here is a pregnancy interval. The lengths of these intervals vary across households and by parity. The procedure used assigns a probability to an interval on the basis of the best technique used in that interval without regard to how extensively or exclusively that technique was used by that couple in that interval. Table 2 indicates mean values for subsamples of the 1965 NFS data. Cell sizes decline in successive pregnancy intervals because households for which the interval has not been closed are excluded. The table reflects a few of the findings from this data set reported by others (see especially Ryder and Westoff [1971]).

Looking at the extent of use of contraception as shown in table 2, there is a systematic reduction in the fraction of women using no contraception from interval to interval for each age-specific and color-specific group. There is not, however, a pronounced tendency for users to use more effective techniques as they progress to successive intervals (i.e., the average probability among "users only" does not decline).[17] Compared

---

[17] This finding is not new. On the basis of the Princeton Study (a longitudinal survey, begun in 1957, of 1,165 urban couples having a second child born in September 1956), Westoff, Potter, and Sagi (1963, pp. 232–35) report that the observed improvement in fertility control across birth intervals "is clearly not a matter of couples shifting from ineffective to effective methods" nor is it related to any important "practice effect" or to a declining fecundity or reduced coital frequency. Instead, the authors suggest that "the chief mechanism in the improvement of contraception

TABLE 2

MEAN VALUES OF SELECTED VARIABLES BY COLOR, AGE, AND PREGNANCY INTERVAL
AS INDICATED (NON-CATHOLIC WOMEN ONLY)

VARIABLE AND PREGNANCY INTERVAL	WHITE WOMEN			BLACK WOMEN		
	25–29	30–34	35–39	25–29	30–34	35–39
All women (cell size)	(466)	(506)	(508)	(160)	(166)	(157)
Income of husband ($)	7,227	8,048	8,532	4,897	4,855	4,615
Education of wife	12.1	11.8	11.8	10.9	10.8	10.3
Education of husband	12.2	11.9	11.8	10.7	10.5	9.5
Total number of births	2.32	2.85	2.92	3.34	3.87	3.95
Number of children intended	2.85	3.06	3.00	3.82	4.28	4.04
Pill: current users (%)	24.2	16.0	9.2	22.5	12.0	5.1
Pill: ever used (%)	38.8	28.7	15.2	30.0	18.1	8.9
Pill: never heard of it (%)	0.9	2.4	2.4	4.4	5.4	11.5
Marriage date	1958	1953	1949	1958	1953	1949
First pregnancy interval (cell size) ...	(431)	(477)	(474)	(146)	(158)	(145)
Used no method (%)	43.2	38.2	36.5	45.2	54.4	60.7
Probability (all)	.0949	.0869	.0832	.1008	.1181	.1292
Probability (users only)	.0150	.0171	.0160	.0190	.0202	.0198
Second pregnancy interval (cell size)	(381)	(431)	(434)	(135)	(137)	(126)
Used no method (%)	27.6	26.4	26.7	31.8	40.9	51.6
Probability (all)	.0665	.0652	.0653	.0763	.0927	.1127
Probability (users only)	.0157	.0168	.0161	.0185	.0185	.0196
Third pregnancy interval (cell size)	(228)	(330)	(317)	(117)	(112)	(109)
Used no method (%)	23.2	26.7	24.9	30.8	34.8	42.2
Probability (all)	.0589	.0654	.0620	.0738	.0823	.0957
Probability (users only)	.0161	.0165	.0162	.0178	.0195	.0195

with whites, blacks tend to have a larger fraction of nonusers and a lower level of contraceptive efficiency among users (keep in mind that such a statement pertains to the choice of techniques only). Of considerable interest is the reduction in nonuse by blacks relative to whites across cohorts.[18]

In examining the relationships between variables within age-, color-, and parity-specific intervals, table 3 indicates various simple correlations between contraceptive-choice variables and income, and education and family-size variables for non-Catholic women. The first three rows reflect some of the usual relationships in terms of positive correlations

appears to be greater regularity of practice." The results in table 2 relate only to the lack of shifting toward more effective techniques on the average. By the procedure of assigning the overall mean use effectiveness to a technique regardless of interval, the differences in actual use effectiveness for specific techniques cannot be observed in the data summarized in table 2.

[18] For the age group 35–39, the ratio of nonuse in the first pregnancy interval for blacks to whites is 1.65 (=60.7 ÷ 36.5) and for the two successive intervals it is 1.93 and 1.70. For the cohort of the ages 25–29, however, this ratio of interval-specific nonuse rates falls to 1.05, 1.14, and 1.33 for respective intervals. That is, the frequency of nonuse of contraception for blacks is considerably reduced by comparison to whites in younger cohorts.

TABLE 3

Simple Correlations* of Selected Variables with Income, Education, and Intended Family-Size Variables, by Color and Age (Non-Catholic Women Only)

	White Women				Black Women			
	Husband's Income	Wife's Education	Husband's Education	Number of Children Intended	Husband's Income	Wife's Education	Husband's Education	Number of Children Intended
A. Women Age 25–29								
All women:	(Cell size = 466)				(Cell size = 160)			
Wife's education	319	...	...	−236	323	...	...	−348
Husband's education	374	647	...	−172	400	630	...	−276
Marriage date	092	514	353	−273	033	305	342	−398
First pregnancy interval:	(Cell size = 431)				(Cell size = 146)			
Used no method†	−112	−236	−271	123	−034	−180	−075	206
Birth probability (all)	−116	−243	−278	126	−044	−190	−095	210
Birth probability (users) ..	−071	−166	−157	072	−224	−180	−366	076
Second pregnancy interval:	(Cell size = 381)				(Cell size = 135)			
Used no method†	−079	−168	−136	159	−145	−270	−139	104
Birth probability (all)	−079	−177	−146	167	−155	−280	−152	103
Birth probability (users) ..	001	−145	−168	132	−157	−163	−189	−008
Third pregnancy interval:	(Cell size = 228)				(Cell size = 117)			
Used no method†	−007	−095	−015	087	−211	−374	−223	201
Birth probability (all)	−005	−106	−021	092	−227	−385	−237	208
Birth probability (users) ..	021	−135	−081	075	−213	−180	−202	099
B. Women Age 30–34								
All women:	(Cell size = 506)				(Cell size = 166)			
Wife's education	380	...	...	−228	353	...	...	−300
Husband's education	491	624	...	−149	442	508	...	−307
Marriage date	092	440	293	−234	319	331	266	−331
First pregnancy interval:	(Cell size = 477)				(Cell size = 158)			
Used no method†	−200	−264	−229	216	−229	−290	−211	118
Birth probability (all)	−206	−273	−237	224	−230	−297	−217	122
Birth probability (users) ..	−117	−180	−147	190	−028	−152	−116	095

TABLE 3 (Continued)

	WHITE WOMEN				BLACK WOMEN			
	Husband's Income	Wife's Education	Husband's Education	Number of Children Intended	Husband's Income	Wife's Education	Husband's Education	Number of Children Intended
Second pregnancy interval:	(Cell size = 431)				(Cell size = 137)			
Used no method†	−171	−260	−190	227	−150	−209	−100	176
Birth probability (all)	−184	−271	−206	236	−169	−226	−120	199
Birth probability (users)	−183	−174	−217	155	−288	−287	−326	394
Third pregnancy interval:	(Cell size = 330)				(Cell size = 112)			
Used no method†	−162	−204	−180	174	−143	−275	−151	209
Birth probability (all)	−175	−221	−198	185	−144	−279	−164	223
Birth probability (users)	−170	−244	−256	190	−024	−058	−172	209

C. Women Age 35–39

	WHITE WOMEN				BLACK WOMEN			
	Husband's Income	Wife's Education	Husband's Education	Number of Children Intended	Husband's Income	Wife's Education	Husband's Education	Number of Children Intended
All women:	(Cell size = 508)				(Cell size = 157)			
Wife's education	330	...	...	−188	357	...	...	−182
Husband's education	526	570	...	−120	399	457	...	−149
Marriage date	048	354	248	−241	026	173	100	−202
First pregnancy interval:	(Cell size = 474)				(Cell size = 145)			
Used no method†	−162	−207	−180	151	−019	−160	−113	025
Birth probability (all)	−170	−218	−188	154	−027	−171	−119	031
Birth probability (users)	−132	−195	−150	062	−163	−249	−131	169
Second pregnancy interval:	(Cell size = 434)				(Cell size = 126)			
Used no method†	−165	−175	−155	141	−075	−103	−171	162
Birth probability (all)	−172	−188	−163	147	−079	−117	−182	168
Birth probability (users)	−104	−187	−113	104	−079	−280	−199	139
Third pregnancy interval:	(Cell size = 317)				(Cell size = 109)			
Used no method†	−051	−135	−124	153	−035	−105	−155	096
Birth probability (all)	−064	−146	−137	159	−035	−110	−166	096
Birth probability (users)	−172	−155	−170	100	010	−092	−157	−000

* The correlations are expressed in units multiplied by 1,000 (i.e., the decimal point has been omitted).
† Dummy variable defined as 1 if no method used in that interval and as zero if any contraceptive method used in that interval.

139

between spouses' education levels and between income and education, and a negative correlation between education (particularly the wife's) and fertility measures. Notice the relatively strong correlation, especially for women and more particularly for whites, between education and marriage date: the more-educated marry at a later date.

The first row in each of the interval-specific sets of rows of table 3 indicates the simple correlation between the column variable and a dummy variable defined as 1 if the couple used no contraceptive method in that interval and zero if a method was used. In every instance, this correlation is negative for the income and education variables and positive for the "intended number of children" variable (for a definition of this latter variable, see n. 20). Holding age, parity, and color constant, couples with higher husband's income or higher wife's education or higher husband's education (separately) are more likely to have used a contraceptive method at some time in the given pregnancy interval. While many of these simple correlations are not high, their consistency over so many groups is corroborative.

The remaining two rows of simple correlations for each pregnancy interval in table 3 are related to the value of the monthly probability assigned to that interval for each couple on the basis of information about the contraceptive method used in that interval. The variable "birth probability (all)" includes the nonusers—those couples who used no method and were assigned the value .2000. Thus, this variable has an essentially bimodal distribution, with many observations at .20 and a distribution of the remainder centered around a value somewhat less than .02. The correlations with the variable defined as "birth probability (users)" exclude all couples who used no method in that specific interval.

Not only is each spouse's education level negatively correlated with nonuse of contraception, but each is also negatively correlated with the probability of birth (or positively correlated with the effectiveness of the technique chosen) among "users only" for every specific birth interval. In other words, there is a consistent systematic selection by more-educated husbands and wives (for each pregnancy interval) of contraceptive techniques which are, on the average, relatively more effective. For whites, the correlations with education tend to decline in successive intervals, relatively more for the dichotomous variable than for the "probability (users)" variable.

To obtain some indication of the relationship between techniques selected in successive pregnancy intervals and between the use and nonuse of contraception in successive pregnancy intervals, simple correlations were computed for pairs of intervals as indicated in table 4. Part A suggests that nonuse is significantly correlated from interval to interval, especially in the later-interval pair. Part B suggests a strong correlation across intervals in the techniques selected (in terms of their average ob-

TABLE 4

SIMPLE CORRELATIONS IN CONTRACEPTIVE BEHAVIOR ACROSS PREGNANCY INTERVALS
WITH RESPECT TO NONUSE (PART A) AND SELECTION OF SPECIFIC TECHNIQUES
AMONG USERS (PART B) (NON-CATHOLIC WOMEN ONLY)

	WHITE WOMEN			BLACK WOMEN		
PREGNANCY INTERVALS	25–29	30–34	35–39	25–29	30–34	35–39
	A. Simple Correlations between Dummy Variables Representing Nonuse in Specified Pregnancy Intervals					
(Cell size)	(228)	(330)	(317)	(116)	(112)	(109)
First and second	421	571	521	567	596	652
First and third	368	439	373	483	531	481
Second and third	698	640	639	627	753	705
Both first and second, and third	632	614	587	632	755	630
First and both second and third	349	487	449	513	543	513
	B. Simple Correlations between Birth Probabilities among Users Only in Specified Pregnancy Intervals					
(Cell size)	(100)	(165)	(165)	(52)	(43)	(38)
First and second	574	662	719	572	548	838
First and third	627	646	690	795	649	834
Second and third	708	733	782	649	726	966

NOTE.—Cell size applies to the entire column for each part. For Part A, couples were excluded if they had not completed the first three birth intervals. For Part B, couples were excluded if they had not used a contraceptive technique in each of the three birth intervals. Correlations are expressed in units multiplied by 1,000 (i.e., decimal point is omitted).

served use effectiveness). The latter correlations appear to be stronger among the later pair of intervals and stronger among the older cohorts.

iii) *Regression Analysis of Interval-specific Contraception Behavior*
Turning to the partial relationships between variables correlated with contraceptive behavior, the earlier analysis (including fig. 1) is helpful. It was stated that B, the present value of the net marginal benefit of a child, is positively related to the household's excess demand for children at that point in time. Define the household's completed-fertility demand as N^* (the outcome from the household's static, completed-fertility demand function) and define the household's current parity as N. All the factors which affect the couple's completed-fertility demand— income, time values, relative productivities, revealed preferences—are incorporated in N^*. It will be assumed that the greater the (positive) discrepancy $(N^* — N)$, the larger the arithmetic value of the term B. This framework, then, is a simple stock-adjustment model, with the benefits from contraception (the negative benefits from an increase in the probability P) negatively related to the discrepancy between the desired and the actual stock of children. The benefits from contraception

continue to increase as the discrepancy $(N^* - N)$ becomes negative. Thus, *ceteris paribus,* we would expect to observe a positive relationship between the couple's monthly birth probability and $(N^* - N)$.

The discussion in Section II also suggests that the cost function of fertility control (the portion of the discontinuous cost curve below point P^*) is presumably related to the couple's fecundity, coital frequency, religion, and education. We will treat the wife's age A as a (negatively related) proxy variable for fecundity and coital frequency, and we expect age, *ceteris paribus,* to be negatively related to the couple's monthly birth probability, P. If education lowers the costs of fertility control, we should expect to observe a negative partial relationship between education, E (measured as the number of years of schooling), and P. If Catholics select a contraceptive technique from a subset of possible techniques, and particularly if the subset excludes the relatively more efficient techniques, the cost of fertility control will be higher for Catholics, *ceteris paribus.* Thus, a dummy variable R (1 if Catholic and zero if non-Catholic) would be expected to be positively related to P.

Combining the effects on P through the benefit and cost functions, the reduced-form equation for the probability P would be

$$P = \psi(N^*, N, A, R, E). \tag{11}$$

In estimating some of these effects empirically, several qualifications must be noted. First, since the structure of the benefit and cost functions has not been made explicit, the form of this reduced-form equation is not given. Consequently, equation (11) has not been estimated directly. Instead, the data have been partitioned by the variables N, A, and R and linear regressions have been run within parity-, age-, and religion-specific groups.[19] In addition, both because of disproportionate representation in the sample and because of an interest in any observed difference in behavior per se, the groups were further partitioned by race. So the regressions reported below pertain to religion-, age-, race-, and parity-specific groups and regress P as a function of the education levels of the spouses and a variable representing N^*.[20]

----

[19] The parity-specific groups are defined in terms of pregnancy intervals rather than live-birth intervals. Some checks on the effects of this distinction are planned. Also, no results are reported for Catholic women, because an analysis has not yet been made. Ryder and Westoff (1971, pp. 244–52) report a similar aspect of these data which does include Catholics.

[20] The variable N^* might be estimated for each subgroup from an auxiliary regression, but for the analysis conducted to date, the variable is defined as either (*a*) the number of children the couple "intends" to have or (*b*) the number of children "wanted" by the wife. The intended number of children was computed by adding to the respondent's current parity her intended number of additional children. (After the woman's current pregnancy status and the couple's current fecundity were determined, the respondent was asked: "Do you intend to have a[nother] child [after the one you are expecting now]?" If the answer was yes, the respondent was then asked: "How many *more* children do you intend to have [not counting your

A second important qualification which must be noted is that the monthly birth probability in the theoretical analysis (eqq. [8]–[11] and fig. 1) is the actual probability produced by the households for themselves, but the dependent variable in the empirical analysis is the probability assigned to that couple from information on the contraceptive technique employed for that pregnancy interval (as discussed above). So while the theoretical discussion sheds light on the partial relationships observed, the regressions do not strictly test the implications of that analysis. The regressions attempt to investigate partial effects on one aspect of fertility-control behavior, namely, the selection of techniques ranked by their average observed use effectiveness.

Table 5 indicates regression results for age- and color-specific non-Catholic women for the first three pregnancy intervals. The dependent variable is the monthly birth probability assigned for each contraceptive technique (the units are multiplied by 1,000). Part A includes couples who used no contraceptive technique in that interval, while Part B excludes the nonusers from the regressions. It would appear from Part A that the wife's education level is quite systematically negatively related to the monthly birth probability: more-educated women, other things constant, achieve a lower risk of conception, on the average, when that risk is measured in terms of the contraceptive technique selected (including no contraception as one of the techniques). The education of the husband also appears to be generally negatively related, but this effect is of smaller magnitude and is more erratic, especially for the youngest age group. As expected, the proxy for N^* is positively related to the monthly birth probability.[21]

While the regressions in Part A include couples who used no contraception in the specific interval, Part B excludes nonusers. Consequently, the mean value of the dependent variable is considerably lower, somewhat below 200 (or a probability of .02), compared with a mean of 600 to

present pregnancy]?" A "don't know" answer resulted in the further question: "Well, what is your best guess?" The resulting total [not additional] births was then considered the number of children intended and is used [tables 5 and 7] as the proxy for N^*. The number of children "wanted" by the wife is a constructed variable based on a rather complicated series of questions. The value is in fact an inference made by Ryder and Westoff and their associates. (Briefly, the variable is defined as the intended number of children for women whose current parity is less than the number intended and as the current parity minus the number of unwanted births [determined from retrospective questions about the circumstances at the time of conception] for all other women [see Ryder and Westoff (1971, p. 93)]. This variable, number of children "wanted" by the wife, is used in table 6.)

[21] In other regressions (not shown here), the two education variables were entered without any additional variables, and the two education variables were entered with variables representing the husband's current income, the wife's current income, and the couple's marriage date (plus appropriate missing-data dummies for the income variables). These results support the conclusion of a generally significant negative effect of the wife's education level and a considerably weaker, somewhat erratic, but generally negative effect of the husband's education level.

TABLE 5

Regressions on Monthly Birth Probability in Specific Pregnancy Intervals for Non-Catholic Women by Age, Color, and User Status (Including and Excluding Nonusers in Each Specific Interval)

I. Women Age 25–29

Color and Pregnancy Interval	A. Contraceptive Users and Nonusers					B. Users Only (Excludes Couples That Used No Method)				
	Number of Observations*	Education of Wife	Education of Husband	Intended Number of Children	R^2 (s.e.e.)†	Number of Observations*	Education of Wife	Education of Husband	Intended Number of Children	R^2 (s.e.e.)†
White women:										
First interval	431 [949] (919)	−44.41 (28.58)‡	−71.96 (21.29)	5.26 (3.64)	.089 880.	245 [150] (77)	−3.99 (3.46)	−2.55 (2.62)	0.31 (0.44)	.033 77.
Second interval	381 [665] (827)	−44.07 (28.53)	−19.55 (20.66)	9.05 (3.67)	.049 810.	276 [157] (79)	−1.84 (3.32)	−4.02 (2.35)	0.86 (0.45)	.043 77.
Third interval	228 [589] (782)	−49.27 (34.17)	20.19 (25.70)	4.27 (4.92)	.018 780.	175 [161] (85)	−5.36 (4.37)	0.02 (3.27)	0.39 (0.69)	.020 85.
Black women:										
First interval	146 [1008] (907)	−84.77 (51.01)	23.64 (41.44)	9.65 (4.78)	.064 887.	80 [190] (96)	5.27 (7.31)	−19.07 (6.21)	−0.04 (0.70)	.140 90.
Second interval	135 [763] (852)	−134.81 (49.99)	7.10 (39.72)	2.13 (4.77)	.080 827.	92 [185] (90)	−4.82 (7.28)	−6.08 (5.53)	−0.27 (0.63)	.042 90.
Third interval	117 [738] (848)	−168.89 (51.41)	−22.86 (40.29)	7.07 (5.00)	.166 785.	81 [178] (91)	−5.64 (7.33)	−6.52 (5.45)	0.40 (0.69)	.054 90.

* Mean and standard deviation (in parentheses) of the dependent variable are bracketed.
† s.e.e. = standard error of estimate.
‡ Standard error in parentheses.

TABLE 5 (*Continued*)

II. Women Age 30–34

Color and Pregnancy Interval	A. Contraceptive Users and Nonusers					B. Users Only (Excludes Couples That Used No Method)				
	Number of Observations*	Education of Wife	Education of Husband	Intended Number of Children	R^2 (s.e.)†	Number of Observations*	Education of Wife	Education of Husband	Intended Number of Children	R^2 (s.e.)†
White women:										
First interval	477 869 (892)	−71.43 (23.68)	−34.37 (18.45)	9.93 (2.63)	.109 845.	295 171 (88)	−4.62 (3.20)	−2.18 (2.41)	1.17 (0.43)	.058 86.
Second interval	431 652 (812)	−73.17 (23.09)	−17.78 (17.59)	9.73 (2.65)	.104 772.	317 168 (85)	−1.28 (3.02)	−6.12 (2.23)	0.95 (0.40)	.067 82.
Third interval	330 654 (816)	−50.54 (27.45)	−29.09 (20.46)	7.10 (3.14)	.070 791.	242 165 (86)	−4.36 (3.55)	−6.12 (2.61)	1.05 (0.47)	.098 82.
Black women:										
First interval	158 1181 (901)	−99.35 (36.30)	−31.98 (33.84)	0.65 (3.10)	.094 866.	72 202 (102)	−5.11 (6.18)	−2.14 (5.63)	0.17 (0.57)	.027 103.
Second interval	137 927 (898)	−74.53 (40.39)	6.64 (37.20)	5.55 (3.70)	.067 878.	81 185 (93)	−4.00 (4.75)	−6.29 (4.64)	1.24 (0.50)	.195 85.
Third interval	112 823 (868)	−101.72 (44.05)	−18.27 (39.75)	7.06 (3.92)	.109 830.	73 195 (100)	1.03 (6.17)	−6.28 (5.54)	0.93 (0.61)	.062 99.

145

TABLE 5 (Continued)

COLOR AND PREGNANCY INTERVAL	A. CONTRACEPTIVE USERS AND NONUSERS					B. USERS ONLY (EXCLUDES COUPLES THAT USED NO METHOD)				
	Number of Observations*	Education of Wife	Education of Husband	Intended Number of Children	R^2 (s.e.)†	Number of Observations*	Education of Wife	Education of Husband	Intended Number of Children	R^2 (s.e.)†
III. Women Age 35–39										
White women:										
First interval ……	474 832 (889)	−59.60 (23.16)	−30.96 (18.01)	5.85 (2.38)	.065 862.	301 160 (83)	−6.26 (2.76)	−1.76 (2.13)	0.19 (0.32)	.041 81.
Second interval ….	434 653 (818)	−47.16 (22.27)	−23.24 (17.25)	5.41 (2.40)	.051 799.	318 161 (82)	−7.00 (2.74)	−0.08 (2.06)	0.43 (0.32)	.041 81.
Third interval ……	317 620 (800)	−28.15 (25.24)	−18.25 (20.15)	6.21 (2.89)	.040 787.	238 162 (84)	−3.25 (3.05)	−3.53 (2.46)	0.46 (0.40)	.040 83.
Black women:										
First interval ……	145 1292 (885)	−63.30 (40.32)	−20.81 (38.78)	−0.21 (2.36)	.031 881.	57 198 (104)	−11.23 (6.98)	0.07 (6.49)	0.60 (0.53)	.085 103.
Second interval ….	126 1127 (908)	1.03 (43.87)	−67.30 (42.36)	4.20 (2.75)	.053 894.	61 196 (100)	−10.82 (6.79)	−3.49 (5.78)	0.32 (0.47)	.093 98.
Third interval ……	109 957 (899)	−11.95 (46.02)	−59.36 (45.27)	1.58 (3.08)	.032 897.	63 195 (101)	−2.45 (6.91)	−6.53 (6.02)	−0.17 (0.50)	.028 102.

1,300 (or a probability of .06–.13) in Part A. Furthermore, the coefficient of variation of the dependent variable in Part B is around .5, while in Part A it is about 1. In Part B, one observes quite consistent, small, negative effects of both education levels, although the coefficients are not often statistically significant. More-educated couples do appear systematically to select contraceptive techniques which are, on the average, more efficient.[22]

The "intended number of children" variable, the proxy for N^*, is generally positive as expected, but it is statistically significant in only about 30 percent of the separate age-, color-, and interval-specific regressions. Since by its definition the "intended number of children" variable (defined in n. 20) is never smaller than a woman's current parity, it may be that the regressions in table 5 suffer from a simultaneity problem: poorer contraceptors achieve higher parities, *ceteris paribus*, so there may be a reverse causation from the dependent variable to the "intended number of children" variable. To overcome this problem somewhat, the regressions in table 6 replace the "intended number of children" variable by the "number of children inferred wanted by the wife" (also defined in n. 20). This variable comes closer to the theoretical concept of N^*, and it is also, by definition, less likely to have been affected by contraceptive behavior in the early pregnancy intervals. Its weakness as a proxy for N^* is its inferential nature: the value is inferred by social scientists on the basis of the respondent's retrospective introspection. Part I of table 6 is comparable to Part II of table 5, for both use precisely the same observations for the same age-, color-, and interval-specific regressions; the latter employs one proxy variable for N^* while Part I of table 6 employs an alternative proxy. In a comparison of Parts A of these two tables, the wife's education effect appears to be somewhat smaller and weaker in Part I of table 6 while the husband's education effect is somewhat stronger and more significant. There appear to be few important differences between Parts B of the two tables. Overall, the differences in the coefficients, in their significance, and in the explanatory power of the regressions appear small.[23]

The economic incentives related to contraception are assumed to be related to $(N^* - N)$ and may in fact be distinctly different (presumably greater) when $(N^* - N) \leqq 0$. As a first approximation to separating the

[22] Using a slope coefficient of -4.0 per year of schooling for each spouse (which is a rough average of the effects for each spouse across estimates in table 5, Part II), an additional 4 years of schooling for each would be expected to lower the monthly birth probability by about .003 on the average. One could then calculate the implied effect on the long-term risks of conception, but I will not do so here because I believe the estimate would be too crude to be meaningful.

[23] While none of the regressions in table 5 or 6 reports intercepts, all regressions included an intercept term. These intercepts, too, appear to be insensitive to whether the proxy for N^* was the "number of children intended" (as in table 5) or the "number of children inferred wanted" (as in table 6).

TABLE 6

REGRESSIONS ON MONTHLY BIRTH PROBABILITY IN SPECIFIC PREGNANCY INTERVALS FOR NON-CATHOLIC WOMEN AGE 30–34 FOR WHOLE SAMPLE AND FOR "CHILD SPACING" COUPLES ONLY, BY COLOR AND BY USER STATUS

COLOR AND PREGNANCY INTERVAL	A. CONTRACEPTIVE USERS AND NONUSERS					B. USERS ONLY (EXCLUDES COUPLES THAT USED NO METHOD)				
	Number of Observations*	Education of Wife	Education of Husband	Number of Children Inferred Wanted by Wife	R^2 (s.e.e.)†	Number of Observations*	Education of Wife	Education of Husband	Number of Children Inferred Wanted by Wife	R^2 (s.e.e.)†
I. Whole Sample										
White women:										
First interval	477 / 869 / (892)	−78.05 (23.56)‡	−37.23 (18.51)	10.00 (3.04)	.102 848.	295 / 171 / (88)	−5.84 (3.13)	−2.04 (2.40)	1.37 (0.45)	.064 86.
Second interval	431 / 652 / (812)	−82.23 (22.97)	−20.17 (17.72)	8.12 (3.01)	.091 777.	317 / 168 / (85)	−2.32 (2.96)	−5.91 (2.23)	0.88 (0.41)	.064 82.
Third interval	330 / 654 / (816)	−58.83 (27.26)	−31.88 (20.55)	4.35 (3.48)	.060 795.	242 / 165 / (86)	−5.60 (3.49)	−5.88 (2.61)	0.80 (0.47)	.089 82.
Black women:										
First interval	158 / 1181 / (901)	−102.99 (35.68)	−27.86 (33.98)	2.61 (3.50)	.097 864.	72 / 202 / (102)	−5.95 (5.79)	−0.70 (5.43)	1.28 (0.60)	.088 100.
Second interval	137 / 927 / (898)	−98.30 (38.74)	16.45 (37.01)	9.16 (3.74)	.092 866.	81 / 185 / (93)	−8.08 (4.69)	−7.61 (4.60)	1.05 (0.50)	.177 86.
Third interval	112 / 823 / (868)	−128.88 (44.52)	−14.38 (40.08)	6.83 (3.76)	.109 830.	73 / 195 / (100)	−2.87 (6.22)	−7.01 (5.46)	1.00 (0.58)	.071 98.

TABLE 6 (*Continued*)

Color and Pregnancy Interval	A. Contraceptive Users and Nonusers					B. Users Only (Excludes Couples That Used No Method)				
	Number of Observations*	Education of Wife	Education of Husband	Number of Children Inferred Wanted by Wife	R^2 (s.e.e.)†	Number of Observations*	Education of Wife	Education of Husband	Number of Children Inferred Wanted by Wife	R^2 (s.e.e.)†
II. Child Spacers Only										
White women:										
First interval	464 [861] (890)	−79.69 (23.68)	−31.00 (18.63)	126.63 (32.38)	.109 843.	289 [171] (88)	−5.76 (3.17)	−1.97 (2.43)	14.49 (4.83)	.063 86.
Second interval	394 [643] (806)	−92.35 (23.73)	−3.95 (18.47)	128.80 (35.47)	.112 763.	292 [169] (85)	−1.31 (3.12)	−6.55 (2.33)	10.02 (4.90)	.065 82.
Third interval	234 [660] (818)	−87.13 (31.90)	−16.06 (23.61)	165.27 (54.10)	.119 773.	171 [166] (86)	−3.64 (4.31)	−6.10 (3.05)	19.83 (7.44)	.107 82.
Black women:										
First interval	140 [1191] (900)	−113.11 (37.78)	−27.77 (36.41)	9.33 (41.05)	.108 859.	63 [202] (103)	−3.53 (6.33)	0.38 (5.82)	16.89 (7.07)	.106 100.
Second interval	110 [960] (905)	−78.15 (45.44)	16.65 (42.63)	107.28 (51.03)	.082 879.	63 [185] (92)	−1.63 (5.07)	−13.15 (4.97)	17.33 (6.14)	.281 80.
Third interval	73 [920] (886)	−142.37 (54.69)	−51.57 (50.08)	27.08 (63.13)	.150 835.	44 [208] (101)	2.35 (8.14)	−8.60 (6.85)	12.25 (9.99)	.074 100.

* Mean and standard deviation (in parentheses) of dependent variable are bracketed.
† s.e.e. = standard error of estimate.
‡ Standard error in parentheses.

149

TABLE 7

REGRESSIONS ON MONTHLY BIRTH PROBABILITY IN FIRST AND THIRD PREGNANCY
INTERVALS FOR NON-CATHOLIC WHITE WOMEN AGE 30–34 BY USER STATUS
(WITH EDUCATION DUMMY VARIABLES)

Pregnancy Interval	HS(W)	COLL(W)	HS(H)	COLL(H)	Number of Children Intended	R^2 s.e.e.
		A. Contraceptive Users and Nonusers				
First interval	−506.11	−261.14			10.22	.102
	(128.02)*	(95.75)			(2.64)	848.
			−375.77	−187.07	11.32	.093
			(110.63)	(88.22)	(2.62)	852.
	−373.72	−196.15	−255.45	−80.68	9.82	.114
	(137.89)	(106.80)	(117.19)	(97.84)	(2.63)	844.
Third interval	−427.09	104.91			7.15	.065
	(143.32)	(116.65)			(3.16)	793.
			−509.07	48.78	7.88	.087
			(119.19)	(99.30)	(3.04)	783.
	−266.15	−129.52	−439.20	116.46	6.35	.099
	(150.10)	(129.13)	(125.13)	(111.28)	(3.13)	781.
		B. Contraceptive Users Only (Excludes Couples That Used No Method)				
First interval	−35.95	−21.70			1.13	.058
	(23.53)	(11.36)			(0.44)	86.
			−1.14	−25.28	1.35	.056
			(17.11)	(10.77)	(0.43)	86.
	−35.70	−12.99	7.55	−18.80	1.14	.066
	(24.85)	(12.76)	(17.96)	(12.01)	(0.44)	86.
Third interval	−47.55	−26.13			0.95	.074
	(20.98)	(13.69)			(0.48)	83.
			−34.02	−30.68	1.21	.091
			(16.73)	(11.79)	(0.45)	82.
	−32.29	−8.39	−25.52	−25.82	0.99	.101
	(21.98)	(15.56)	(17.59)	(13.44)	(0.48)	82.

NOTE.—HS(W) is 1 if wife's schooling level was 1 year of high school or more; COLL(W) is 1 if wife's schooling level was 1 year of college or more; HS(H) and COLL(H) are similarly defined dummy variables for the husband's schooling level.
* Standard error in parentheses.

sample into groups for which $(N^* − N) > 0$ (designated as "child spacers") and $(N^* − N) \leqq 0$, Part II of table 6 reestimates the regressions in the first part of table 6 for the subset "child spacers." That is, for each pregnancy interval, the couple was included in the regressions in the second part of table 6 if and only if the "number of children inferred wanted by the wife" was equal to or greater than the interval number; for example, women who "wanted" two children were excluded from the regressions pertaining to the third interval, and so on.[24]

[24] The sample sizes for the residual subsets (couples for which $[N^* − N] \leqslant 0$) were

Finally, table 7 again makes use of the same observations as does Part II of table 5 and reports regressions for white women for the first and third intervals only, using dummy variables for the education levels of the wife and the husband. In all cases, the high school dummy's coefficient is larger (negative) and stronger than the college dummy's coefficient for the wife's education, and similarly for the husband's education in Part A. That is, the effect of high school education relative to grade school education appears to be greater than the effect of college education relative to high school; the statistical significance of the differences in these pairs of coefficients has not been computed. It clearly is not the case that the negative effects reported for the education coefficients throughout tables 5 and 6 result predominantly from the effects of the high level of schooling (and the high time values) of the most-educated women.

iv) *Conclusion*
The empirical analysis in this section has only begun to investigate observed contraceptive behavior in the context of an economic framework. The results reported here represent initial findings with respect to the selection of contraceptive techniques in low-parity pregnancy intervals for non-Catholic women between the ages of 25 and 40 (in 1965). While the observed effects of the husband's and wife's education levels on the use of contraceptives are often not large and frequently not statistically significant, the effects are quite consistently negative for all age-, color-, and parity-specific regressions. They also appear to be insensitive to the definition of the proxy variable for N^*.

If it is tentatively concluded that the husband's and wife's education levels do have a negative partial effect on the monthly birth probability as defined in this study—that more-educated couples, *ceteris paribus,* select contraceptive techniques which on the average are more effective in preventing pregnancy—the interpretation of this result is not yet clear. One cannot distinguish, by the statistical procedure followed, between two quite distinct interpretations: (1) education lowers contraceptive costs by reducing information costs; and (2) education lowers contraceptive costs by raising the marginal product of the couple's time used in conjunction with any specific contraceptive device. Moreover, an alternative explanation for the observed negative relationship emphasizes an effect of education on the marginal benefit function: (3) "unwanted children" represent a bigger loss to more-educated couples, and hence the more-educated are induced to make a greater effort to prevent timing and quantity failures.

This third explanation, however, requires information about the shape

---

quite small for these low-parity intervals and were not, therefore, analyzed. By the fourth pregnancy interval, however, one would expect to find a sizable number of observations with $(N^* - N) \leqslant 0$; I hope to determine whether the behavior of these couples differs appreciably from the behavior of those for whom $(N^* - N) > 0$.

of the marginal-cost and marginal-benefit functions around the equilibrium at N^*.[25] Also, the use of the interval-specific regressions which include a proxy for the desired number of children is designed to standardize for just such differences in contraceptive motivation. Finally, the finding from the regressions in table 7 that the high school dummy variable has a stronger effect on the monthly birth probability than does the college dummy variable does not support explanation (3). Thus, this interpretation of the observed negative education effects does not seem persuasive.

The results in this paper cannot help us distinguish between the first two explanations, since it is not possible to tell whether better-educated couples (a) select contraceptive techniques which are inherently more effective in use or (b) simply select some techniques systematically and proceed to use them relatively effectively. As long as the selection is systematic—different distributions by education for different techniques— either a differential inherent use effectiveness or a differential effectiveness by education for any given technique could yield the negative effects observed in tables 5, 6, and 7. It would be very useful to analyze the observed use effectiveness of a given technique by education level. This is not feasible with the data I have used here. Other studies, however, do suggest a differential use effectiveness by socioeconomic status (see, e.g., Tietze [1959b], table I, p. 353).

The interpretation of the results reported in this section based on differential knowledge or awareness of contraceptives may seem strained for contemporary U.S. women. It is interesting to note, however, that for the non-Catholic women in the 1965 NFS data, the correlation of wife's and husband's education level with a dummy variable for knowledge of the pill (defined as 1 for women who had never heard of the "pill" at the time of the interview) ranged between $-.10$ and $-.30$ for all six subsamples defined in table 2 for each spouse's education level. So knowledge of new contraceptives may not diffuse uniformly across education groups.[26] For the period of time covered by the data used in the regressions here— primarily from the late 1940s into the early 1960s—there were few changes in contraceptive technology until the pill became available. So it would

---

[25] It is not sufficient simply to argue that the higher price of time of the better-educated couple raises the cost of a child and thereby creates a differential motivation. The child also yields a flow of benefits, and N^* is defined in terms of equality of the marginal-benefit and marginal-cost functions. The economic motivation to avoid an additional child is a function of the differences in the heights of these two marginal curves around their point of intersection.

[26] Since medical care or exposure to medical advice is positively related to income, the simple correlations of the knowledge-of-the-pill dummy variable and the husband's income, which also range between $-.12$ and $-.24$ for the same six color- and age-specific groups, suggest that the information differential may work through this channel. For more information on the use of the pill derived from these data, see Ryder and Westoff (1971, chap. VI).

seem likely that the observed effects result from factors other than differential rates of adoption of new techniques—perhaps differential use effectiveness of a given technique, or perhaps differential knowledge of the different proficiencies of existing techniques. Unlike the survival test applicable to market firms, long-run differences in households' marginal as well as average efficiencies can and do exist, as Wesley Mitchell pointed out several decades ago (1937).

V. Other Dimensions of Fertility Behavior

The empirical results above lend support to the contention that more-educated couples achieve greater contraceptive efficiency. In terms of simple and partial correlations for each of the spouse's education levels, there appears to be a systematic selection of more effective contraceptive techniques by more-educated couples. Over extended periods of time and at high levels of efficacy, comparatively minor differences in contraceptive efficiency imply quite large differences in the risk of conception. If this is so, more-educated couples are exposed to lower risks of undesired conceptions, which would be expected to affect many other dimensions of their observed fertility behavior.

The influence on the completed fertility of more-educated couples is most straightforward. By lowering the costs of avoiding undesired conceptions, more-educated couples, on the average, exhibit lower completed fertility (if the problem of excess fertility dominates the problem of subfecundity in aggregate behavior). Not only may lower contraceptive costs reduce completed fertility, but they may also induce substitution toward quality of children, Q, and away from numbers of children, N, by implicitly raising the price of N relative to the price of Q. Since the shadow price of N is defined net of contraceptive costs, G, a reduction in G raises the price of N and induces substitution toward quality in the production of child services. The Becker-Lewis paper above explores this point in depth.

An effect of education on a couple's risk of conception could also be expected to influence the timing (over the life cycle) and spacing (by birth intervals) of their children. Economists have as yet not devoted much attention to these dimensions of fertility behavior, but the empirical evidence by sociologists suggests that more-educated couples (especially women) tend to marry later and to postpone childbearing longer after marriage begins (see especially Whelpton, Campbell, and Patterson [1966]). A recent (1968) survey of consumer anticipations conducted by the National Bureau of Economic Research and the U.S. Bureau of the Census contained information on the timing and spacing of children by couples in the relatively wealthy suburban households surveyed. These data also suggest that more-educated couples—at relatively high levels of education—begin childbearing at a later age (see Michael [1971a]).

One explanation for this behavior may be that both schooling and child rearing are relatively time-intensive activities, especially for the wife. While engaging in the production of education, one's time value is relatively high, which effectively precludes simultaneously choosing to engage in childbearing. Thus, child production and education production are done sequentially. Add to this an assumption of asymmetry in the effects of the two stocks on the marginal product of time in the production of the other: assume that an acquired stock of education raises the marginal product of time in child rearing more than an acquired stock of children raises the marginal product of time in the production of education. Then one has, perhaps, the beginnings of a theory of the optimal timing of child production. As long as the optimal strategy involves postponement of child rearing, it is facilitated by contraceptive efficiency.

In addition to beginning childbearing later, more-educated couples also appear to space their children closer together (see, e.g., Bumpass and Westoff [1970], chap. 3; Michael [1971]; U.S. Bureau of the Census [1968]). Again, there is no well-developed theory of the optimal spacing of children, although the differential rates of increase in earnings profiles by education levels may be sufficient to imply a negative correlation between education and child-spacing intervals, other things (including child quality) held constant. Contraceptive efficiency is particularly relevant to the child-spacing issue, since a reduction in child spacing for a given number of children implies a longer period of subsequent exposure to the risk of an undesired conception.

Finally, it is of interest to note a tendency for more-educated women to space their children more evenly. Michael (1971) analyzed the absolute and relative variations within the household in the spacing of children and found that for age- and parity-specific groups, more-educated women exhibited a lower variation in the spacing of their children. That is, the standard deviation and the coefficient of variation in the spacing intervals among children within a given household decline, on the average, across households as the wife's education level rises. If the higher variation in spacing among less-educated women reflects outlying spacing-interval observations, these may reflect contraceptive "failures," although this argument is admittedly quite conjectural.

I have explored channels of influence from the couple's levels of education to various dimensions of human fertility in a relatively free format. Obviously, no tightly woven theory of the demand for fertility control or of the optimal timing and spacing of children has been set forth. While different aspects of fertility behavior surely interact with each other, the directions, nature, and magnitudes of these interactions have been considered only in passing. In short, this paper is a progress report on an effort to understand the influence of education on several aspects of observed fertility behavior. I hope that it will help to convince other researchers of the viability of applying the household production function framework to the broad, interesting, and important area of human fertility.

Appendix

The constrained objective function, from equations (1)–(4) may be written

$$L = u[(Z_{it})] - \lambda[\sum_t \sum_i x_{it} p'_{it} - \sum_t \sum_j (W'_{jt} T w_{jt} + V_{jt})]$$

$$- \sum_t \sum_j \lambda_{jt} [\sum_i (T_{ijt} + T w_{jt} - T_{jt})], \qquad (A1)$$

where i, j, and t are indices over commodities, adult household members, and time, respectively, and where a prime represents an appropriate time-discounted value. For the purpose at hand, it will be assumed that all j adults are employed in the labor market at the discounted wage rate W'_{jt} and that the two constraints may thus be collapsed with the shadow price of time λ_{jt}/λ equal at the margin to the wage rate W'_{jt}.

Consider the optimal level of the goods input x_{P_k} in the production of the probability of conception P (see eq. [8]) in time period k. The first-order condition is

$$\frac{\partial L}{\partial x_{P_k}} = \sum_{t=k+1}^{h} \left(\frac{\partial U}{\partial Z_1} \frac{\partial Z_1}{\partial C} \frac{\partial C}{\partial N_{k+1}} \right)_t \frac{\partial N_{k+1}}{\partial P_k} \frac{\partial P_k}{\partial x_{P_k}}$$

$$- \lambda \left[\sum_{t=k+1}^{h} \left(C'_{kt} \frac{\partial N_t}{\partial P_k} \frac{\partial P_k}{\partial x_{P_k}} \right) + \frac{\partial G'_k}{\partial x_{P_k}} \right] = 0, \qquad (A2)$$

where C'_{kt} is the discounted total expenditure in period t on a child born in period k. The inelegant string of partial derivatives simply reflects the chain of influence through which x_P affects utility: x_P affects the probability P and in turn the expected number of children N, which alters the flow of child services and hence the production of Z_1 and, therefore, utility. Equation (A2) can be thus rewritten:

$$\sum_{t=k+1}^{h} \left(\frac{MU_1}{\lambda} MP_C \alpha - C'_k \right)_t \frac{\partial N_{k+1}}{\partial P_k} \cdot \frac{\partial P_k}{\partial x_{P_k}} = \frac{\partial G'_k}{\partial x_{P_k}}. \qquad (A3)$$

The term in parentheses represents the benefits (in constant dollars) of an additional child in period t net of the costs of the child. Summed over time, the term represents the present value of the net marginal benefit of a child. The term will be designated B:

$$B_k = \sum_{t=k+1}^{h} \left(\frac{MU_1}{\lambda} MP_C \alpha - C'_k \right)_t. \qquad (A4)$$

So the first-order conditions for x_P and T_{Pj} are

$$B\left(\frac{\partial N}{\partial P_k}\right) MP_{x_P} = p_{x_P} \quad\text{and}\quad B\left(\frac{\partial N}{\partial P_k}\right) MP_{T_{Pj}} = p_{T_{Pj}}, \quad (A5)$$

where p_{x_P} and $p_{T_{Pj}}$ are the prices of the goods and time used in the production of P.

The term B_k may be positive or negative. If, at time k, the present value of the gross benefit stream from an additional child exceeds the present value of the cost of the child, B_k will be positive. Presumably, the sign of the term B is the analytical analogue of the response to survey questions which seek to determine whether a given pregnancy was "wanted." Abstracting from the costs of fertility control, a child would be "wanted" if $B > 0$ and "unwanted" if $B < 0$. Since $\partial N/\partial P$, the effect of an increase in P on the expected number of children, is positive and the prices of time and market goods are also positive, equation (A5) implies that MP_{x_P} and MP_{T_P} will be positive or negative as B is positive or negative. That is, if $B < 0$, the couple will engage in fertility control by purchasing and using goods and time inputs to reduce P. If, instead, $B > 0$ and an additional child is "wanted," the couple may expend resources to raise P. Expressed differently, from the first-order condition for optimization with respect to P itself,

$$\frac{\partial L}{\partial P_k} = \lambda\left(B_k\frac{\partial N}{\partial P_k} - \frac{\partial G'_k}{\partial P_k}\right) = 0, \quad (A6)$$

or from equation (9),

$$B_k\frac{\partial N}{\partial P_k} = \Pi_{P_k}.$$

So equation (10) can be extended to indicate that if B_k is negative (or positive), P_k is less than (or greater than) P^*_k and Π_{P_k} is negative (or positive).

Comment

Margaret G. Reid

University of Chicago

I. Introduction

The basic assumption of Robert Michael's paper is that each family has a fertility objective and that decisions concerning it are made in the light of a set of constraints that are associated with education of the spouses. Fertility decisions are viewed as flowing from the weighing of benefits of child services against streams of costs. Empirical estimates presented of "education and fertility control" utilize data of the National Fertility Study of 1965, many findings from which are reported by N. B. Ryder and C. F. Westoff (1971). I comment briefly on each of the main sections of the paper and on tests of "wealth" constraints, the feasibility of which is inferred from information secured.

II. Theoretical Considerations

Household models provide an intriguing approach to any consumption analysis. Households are multiproduct firms with an exchange system within them and function in response to market and external nonmarket relationships. Interpretation of Michael's equation (2) fails to recognize activities related to the exchange system within households. All nonmarket activities are not inseparable from the enjoyment of the commodity produced. Failure to differentiate explicitly nonmarket activities of personal utility or enjoyment from those that provide products for another person, or for oneself that might be provided by someone else, is, in my opinion, a source of confusion in a general model of household production functions.

III. Channels of Influence of Education

The influence of education on fertility is assumed to flow through four principal channels, namely, utility, money wealth, a set of household production functions, and time. Michael's review of these is a contribution to all analyses utilizing education as a behavior variable. The heterogeneity of the economic aspects of education is better documented than that of other influences.

a) Michael notes that "until a theory of the formation of preferences is available, little can be said, a priori, about the relationship between education and tastes or about the possible influence of education on the preference function." If knowledge affects preferences, then preferences are modified by exogenous change. Information theory predicts that diffusion of knowledge is affected by channels of information and theories of cultural norms and group identification explain resistance to change. The higher a person's education, the more accessible channels of information tend to be; hence, knowledge of new methods of contraception, such as the pill, will tend to be greater for better-educated couples. Knowledge and use of the pill as of 1965, less than 5 years after its introduction, could be expected to increase with education, to be greater for urban than for farm families, and to have restricted births after the second and third pregnancy intervals more than after the first. Cultural norms and group identification affect birth rates. Existing theories of lags predict that time tends to narrow the effect of their difference as well as that of knowledge among groups. Further innovation in contraceptive techniques may continue to cause differences in contraceptive behavior by education, access to channels of information, and cultural norms.

b) Michael comments briefly on the large literature on human capital. Theoretical models that relate fertility to education through wealth constraints seem well developed. Empirical investigators still search for reliable variables to fill boxes of the theory. So far, attention has concentrated on opportunity costs of time rather than on money costs of quality of children. Even so, money wage rates utilized are often very crude. Those of employed females have considerable measurement error. Even less is known of the supply wage of mothers out of the labor force because of home care of children. Better data on money wealth are, of course, not enough. Purchasing power of money must be considered. Money wages throughout the United States, and probably also within other countries, are likely to be positively correlated with the cost of living.

c) The effect of education on "production-function constraints" is appropriately viewed as "limitless." Economists are, as it were, warned of the maze in which they are likely to be entering in dealing with their ramifications. One production function explicitly dealt with is the effect on efficiency of fertility control due to knowledge and use of new techniques of contraception. Such differential efficiency may, however, be temporary. Diffusion of knowledge has been rapid, and utilization of new techniques calls for little expertise.

Education of mothers tends to increase efficiency of child care. Knowledge of the effects of education awaits identification of quality. Could something be learned from infant mortality with respect to education of mothers, other conditions held constant? Or from the speed of learning of children during early years in school?

d) Discussion of the time constraint first deals with the positive correlation between education and age of marriage of women. This contributes to the negative correlation between education and fertility. This relationship is well documented by other studies. In this study, criteria imposed in testing the effect of contraception on fertility indirectly hold constant the age of marriage. Hence, its effect on fertility is not described.

The time constraint is related to life expectancy without consideration of its relevance to fertility. The discussion does, however, suggest an unexplored area of speculation. Do adults who expect a long life desire more children? They are looking forward to more years in which to enjoy them and their offspring. There are other conditions. For example, does having an additional child restrict leisure that contributes to health, so that parents, as it were, trade an extra year or two of life for themselves for an extra child?

A consideration of life expectancy seems to have been introduced by Michael in the hope of presenting further evidence that education increases efficiency of household production. It undoubtedly contributes. To isolate this effect is a matter of great interest. Attempts at its isolation through examination of longevity seem unlikely to bring much reward, and assuredly have little bearing on birth rates.

IV. Education and Fertility Control

Utilization of an estimate of probability of conception due to the contraceptive technique used is a unique feature of this study. It lends itself to simple and complex quantitative estimates of the type necessary for testing the model presented. The probability of conception is shown to be negatively correlated with the education of wife and husband and positively correlated with the number of children intended. The correlations shown among non-Catholic women by pregnancy interval, age, and race differ considerably between sets of all women and those using contraception. For the first and second pregnancy intervals, the correlation between birth probabilities and education of the wife is appreciably greater for all women than for those using contraception. What conditions account for this? Is effectiveness of contraceptive techniques related to wealth constraints? Wealth, knowledge, and effective use of contraceptive techniques are closely associated.

Economics of the Size of North Carolina Rural Families

Bruce Gardner

North Carolina State University

I. Introduction

One of the best-attested generalizations in demography is the high fertility of rural populations relative to urban ones. For every state of the United States throughout the twentieth century, indeed for practically every Western country since the first half-reliable data have become available, the rule holds (see Jaffe 1942; Okun 1958, p. 94; Petersen 1969, p. 496). It is not viewed in the demographic literature as notably puzzling. Some writers in fact treat the lower fertility of the urbanized population almost as a postulate or definition: low fertility is part of the urban life-style. Neither do economists interested in fertility find larger rural families an especially perplexing phenomenon. Almost everyone would accept at least a loose economic explanation in terms of lower costs and greater pecuniary returns to child rearing on farms.

Probably the most salient fact about the recent history of U.S. rural fertility is the erosion of the rural-urban differential since World War II.[1] There is no lack of plausible explanations. The decline in the value of farm children as old-age support resulting from the extension of Social Security to farm operators, increasing opportunities for labor-force participation by farm women, the general relaxation of those characteristics of rural life traditionally conducive to larger family size—such hypotheses would seem, prima facie, reasonable to most economists. Other social scientists would probably agree by and large, though some might want to put more weight on cultural or "taste" factors—for example, more

I want to thank P. R. Johnson and R. A. Schrimper as well as several authors of papers in this book for their useful criticisms and suggestions.

[1] By the late 1960s the crude birth rate for rural-farm families had even fallen below the urban rate. However, this is partly due to the changing age structure of rural women. Age-specific birth rates of completed family sizes are moving closer together for rural vis-à-vis urban residents, but rural completed fertility remains larger.

rapid and complete diffusion of urban norms and attitudes into rural areas via television and cheaper communication and transportation generally.

It is not easy, however, to demonstrate the importance of these factors, much less to discriminate among them. The recently developed economic theories of fertility based on an allocation of time in a home production model provide a useful framework for dealing with these issues. I begin this paper by discussing briefly the main contributions such a model can make in clarifying conceptually the economic determinants of rural fertility. I then present an analysis of some data pertaining to the fertility behavior of North Carolina rural families.

II. Rural-Farm Home Production

In reviewing the general features of the home production model, some problems that arise in applying the model to cross-sectional data on family size require comment. The dependent variable to be explained is the number of children in completed rural families. This will be referred to as "family size." To treat family size in terms of an economic model is to treat it as a matter of choice in the face of the family's inevitably limited resources. We will not be able to explain those variations in family size that are random or determined by noneconomic factors outside the model.

The size of a completed family is the outcome of many interdependent decisions that are made (and revised) continuously by the family unit. Perhaps the single most helpful feature of the home production model in this context is the relative ease with which it allows one to classify observable variables as endogenous or exogenous. The finding of a stable relationship between two mutually determined variables, say number of children and wife's labor-force participation, would be interesting and worth knowing about. But for purposes both of understanding and prediction it is more satisfying to explain the number of children by means of factors not so likely to be themselves influenced by or determined jointly with family size.[2]

The basic endogenous variables of the home production model, following the now standard terminology, are the "Z's," the "commodities" which enter the utility function. It seems most useful to view children, as is done in the recent work of Willis (1969), Michael (1970), and De Tray

---

[2] For example, one could "explain" higher fertility among farm families in part on the grounds that women on farms are less likely to be in the labor force. But their not being in the labor force is presumably a function of other, exogenous variables having to do with the market for farm-women's labor. A more "fundamental" approach would be to explain *both* fertility and women's labor supply in an explicitly simultaneously determined model like that of Nerlove and Schultz (1970), or, if one wants to use a single-equation approach, by sticking to a reduced form having only exogenous factors as independent variables.

(1972*b*), not as *Z*'s themselves, but as "intermediate commodities" which are inputs in the production of a *Z* called "child services." This term simply refers to whatever it is that people want children for. Nobody has been able to say how to measure the quantity of child services, or even what units they should be measured in. The usefulness of the theoretical work cited is that it avoids the necessity for such measurement; it derives relationships between the directly observable intermediate commodity, number of children, and the exogenous economic variables. This derived-demand approach seems to me an important advance, especially in thinking about the economics of investment in children, that is, in the child's "quality."

The basic exogenous variables are the market prices of goods and time and the endowment of full income or wealth. In addition, the technical conditions of the home production functions themselves are exogenous (though Michael's [1974] treatment of the effects of education on them introduces elements of choice and pushes the exogenous technical conditions back to the production of education). Special conceptual problems are presented by the utility function when it has to represent a family rather than an individual; if it incorporates the children's preferences it has endogenous elements.

The exogenous variables that one might want to consider in explaining rural fertility would include the prices of goods used in child rearing; the wage rates of male, female, and child labor; and the budget constraint. Commonly cited among these as encouraging relatively large rural-farm families are lower prices of child-rearing goods and higher values of children's time.[3] De Tray (1972*b*, p. 46) argues further that high quality children are likely to cost rural-farm families relatively more than they do urban families.

Difficulties in Applying the Model

The first problem in applying the home production model is that it is most rigorously and plausibly stated in static terms whereas the facts we observe are the results of market variables and decisions taken in response to them on dates over a long sequence of time. What, for example, is the appropriate budget constraint? It must ultimately be a wealth constraint, but how and when should it be measured? The human and nonhuman capital possessed by the family at the time we observe its completed size can give a misleading picture; it is even endogenous to the extent that

---

[3] The exogenous aspect should refer to the market for child labor, but for most families there is only a shadow wage for children—their time is used only in the home. For farmers, technical conditions of home production are probably such that additional children do not drive down the shadow wage of children as quickly as for urban families. In other words, there are reasons for expecting greater "economies of scale" (or less diseconomies) in child rearing on farms.

past accumulation has been influenced by the number of children. We would ideally want to know the parents' endowments and expected future income streams at the time family plans are made.

Likewise, we would require schooling and wage rates for the prefamily-completion period if they are to be completely exogenous. The only truly exogenous variables that we can observe contemporaneously with completed family size are age, race, and some other "background" variables. But everyone follows the same age path, and race and original social class are not elements that play any intrinsically important part in the home production model.

We are left with only "base period" endowments and subsequent market prices of goods and time as exogenous variables. A priori, it is difficult to be very confident that these variables will explain a great deal of family-to-family variation in completed fertility. We have only to consider our everyday personal observation of people having greatly varying family sizes that could not have been predicted from our knowledge of differences in their past inheritance and present market conditions. This does not mean of course that economic theories of fertility are unlikely to be useful in predicting changes in fertility in larger population aggregates where economic circumstances vary and other factors are relatively constant. Moreover, such a state of affairs does not necessarily imply that our understanding of fertility behavior would be improved by focusing on noneconomic determinants of fertility. It still could be, and as far as I can see is in fact the case, that explanation via market prices gives results as satisfying as the possible alternatives.[4] In all of this, rural fertility is no different from urban (though it has been argued, generally without direct evidence, that economic motivations in child rearing are more important for farm people). Indeed, in these respects child services are no different in principle from other Z's one might want to investigate.

A second problem concerns not what variables to use but how to specify the model. In this paper the concentration is on prices of time, since it is difficult to measure cross-sectional variations in the prices of goods, and there probably exists less such variation anyway than for the value of time. Willis (1969) has shown that a change in the husband's full-time earnings will affect the value of the wife's time if she spends no time working. This result is analogous to Gronau's proposition (1970b, p. 9) that "an increase in income results in an increase in the intrinsic price of

---

[4] Sometimes it becomes somewhat arbitrary whether we call a variable "economic" or not. For example, farmers who migrate to cities may have larger families than urban natives even though their economic circumstances are essentially the same (although Kiser [1938], trying to isolate this phenomenon, finds no difference in his sample, nor do Goldberg [1958] and Freedman and Slesinger [1961]). This could be interpreted as a noneconomic determinant of differential fertility. On the other hand, if we ask why "tastes for large families" arise for farm people, one plausible answer might be that the behavioral pattern was generated over a long time period by the low price of children, and what we observe in the migrants is a difference between short-run and long-run price elasticities of demand for children.

time" when time spent working is fixed. Moreover, if there are several "kinds of time," each limited in supply, we may observe "corner solutions" in the use of some kinds of time even for women who are in the labor force, with different prices for different kinds of time. In such cases the home production model is complicated by interactions among the various prices which may require a more complex specification for empirical purposes.

Third, following through the derived-demand approach to children yields a model for which a priori predictions about the signs of the coefficients of prices are not intuitively obvious, even without the above interactions. This makes it difficult to test the model, because if a prediction fails we do not know if the variable in question really should be rejected as a determinant of fertility or if we simply made an incorrect restriction of the model so as to make the prediction.

The latter two problems reflect the fact that the theory on the economics of family size has outrun the data available to test it. A few years ago theory was lacking for adequate understanding of even the basic empirical regularities that had been observed, notably the inverse relationship between income and fertility. But as the theory has been advanced, data suitable for observing its implications are becoming harder to find, and the data we do have cannot be interpreted unambiguously in terms of the theory. The situation is rather like a general equilibrium system being worked out within each family; any exogenous change that affects one price affects all prices. Moreover, as the theory advances, fewer of the observed characteristics of a family are taken as exogenous.

In this spirit, then, I will not make any predictions about the signs of coefficients in the regressions to follow, since almost anything could be justified ex post. The hypothesis testing will be of a rather loose sort—to see what light can be thrown upon rural fertility behavior by means of the exogenous variables which the home production model suggests ought to be important. This does not mean, however, that the usefulness of the home production model has to be viewed as a maintained hypothesis throughout. It would look bad for the model, assuming we have the data to specify it adequately, which in this sample I think we do, to find insignificant coefficients on the variables representing the price of children. Failure on rural-farm data would be especially troubling in view of the older sociological literature which found the correlation between economic variables and fertility for families from farm backgrounds to be greater than for native urban families (see Goldberg 1958; Freedman and Slesinger 1961).

III. Analysis of a Sample of North Carolina Rural Families

The basic data for the regression analysis which follows come from two surveys of rural (farm and nonfarm) families in North Carolina. In the first, the Research Triangle Institute of North Carolina surveyed 1,170 families for the U.S. Department of Agriculture in 1968. The sample space was the whole of North Carolina. The sampling methods were quite exhaustive and may have resulted in even better coverage, especially of poor and black families, than has been achieved by the U.S. census (see Research Triangle Institute [RTI] 1971 for details). I surveyed the second sample of 214 rural (farm and nonfarm) residents of Sampson County, North Carolina, in 1971. Though my sampling procedure was less sophisticated than that used in the RTI survey, the original list of names being drawn from the county tax office records, the sample means for age, race, and education appear to be in line with census data for the county (see Gardner 1971).

Neither of these samples was drawn specifically to investigate completed rural fertility; consequently, many observations were not usable because the families were not yet complete when observed or they had been completed too long. This last problem is especially serious in the RTI sample because the survey questionnaire asked only about children living at home during at least some part of the year. By the time parents reach their upper forties, and certainly at older ages, their children start leaving home permanently. My survey questionnaire asked about "children-ever-born" so that this problem did not arise.

Unfortunately there is no way of knowing exactly which families are observed at their completed size. I stratified by age of wife. All families in which the wife was over 49 years old were eliminated. Because even younger wives could have had some children who had left home, I stratified further by means of length of time married. If a woman had been married more than 5 years before the birth of the oldest child reported, the observation was left out on the grounds that I had no precise idea what the true family size was. To avoid eliminating all late-starting families, this rule was not applied if the oldest child reported was 15 years old or younger. Families who reported no children at all presented special problems. Those with wives in their upper forties could easily have had children who had left home. I arbitrarily excluded those in the age group of 46–49. In some of the analysis below *all* women who reported zero children are excluded.

In my own sample, too, even though the problems just discussed did not exist because I asked about children-ever-born, women of 50 years and over were excluded. This was done to be symmetrical with the RTI data, and because many of these older families made childbearing decisions in the 1930s and 1940s under conditions quite different from those facing the rest of the sample but which could not be incorporated in the regression model.

For both samples there was the problem that many younger parents had not completed their families when they were observed. Whatever is done about this fact, it will cause some problems. I simply left out all families in which the wife was less than 30 years old. Because there would still be women in their lower thirties included in the sample who had not yet completed their families, the age of women was added as an independent variable in the regression analysis to try to hold this effect constant.

Finally, 36 families were eliminated because data were missing for some independent variable. These were almost all cases in which no husband was reported present so there was no information on husband's wage and schooling.

In sum, then, the dependent variable is observed for husband-wife families in which the wife is 30–49 years old, with the exclusion of some older women. This leaves 511 families from the original 1,384 covered in the two surveys.

For both samples there is quite complete information on economic variables since both were constructed with a view to measuring the economic status of rural families. For each family there are data on the ages of husband, wife, and children, their schooling, their hours spent working, wage rates, earnings and type of employment for any family members who worked, and income received from all sources, including income in kind from housing they owned and farm-grown food. In addition, the RTI sample has data on consumer durables owned and many items of consumption expenditure.

These data allow us to discriminate between the prices of the husband's time and of the wife's time, which are usually considered to have different effects on the full price of children. Women's value-of-time intensity of child-rearing activities is generally taken to be relatively greater than men's. This condition, if it holds, implies a relatively more negative regression coefficient on wives' than on husbands' price of time.

The market price which is the best observable approximation to the opportunity cost of time in home production is the wage rate that could have been earned. This wage rate is observable for those women who work, but how is it to be measured for those who do not? The only useful data available are the years of schooling attained by them. Age or experience might also be pertinent, but age varies too little in the sample and there are no data on experience. Accordingly, the first regression (presented in table 1) has the wife's schooling as an independent variable, along with the husband's schooling, income, and age of women. The age of women was added to try to adjust for the likelihood that younger wives had not yet completed their childbearing. The coefficient of income is intended to represent a relaxation of the budget constraint, wage rates held constant.

A second set of regressions is estimated for working women. In this case the same independent variables are used but women's wage rates are added. This raises the question: If a woman's schooling is a proxy for the opportunity cost of time in regressions 1 and 2, what is it in regression

TABLE 1

REGRESSION COEFFICIENTS (SHOWING t-VALUES) FOR 511 RURAL NORTH CAROLINA FAMILIES WITH SIZE OF COMPLETED FAMILY AS DEPENDENT VARIABLE

Regression Number	Wife's Schooling	Husband's Schooling	Wife's Age	Race (Nonwhite =1)	Income ($ Thousand)	Wife's Wage	Husband's Wage	R^2
1	−0.14 (3.7)	−0.09 (2.6)	0.04 (3.2)	1.26 (6.0)	0.16 (4.1)	...	...	.19
2	−0.18 (3.3)	−0.06 (1.2)	0.03 (1.6)	1.50 (5.0)	0.15 (2.6)	...	...	.21
3	−0.15 (2.6)	−0.05 (1.0)	0.04 (1.8)	1.41 (4.7)	0.19 (3.2)	−0.43 (2.0)	...	.23
4	−0.15 (2.7)	−0.05 (0.9)	0.03 (1.6)	1.42 (4.7)	0.21 (3.2)	−0.43 (2.0)	−0.06 (0.6)	.23
5	−0.15 (3.8)	−0.09 (2.6)	0.04 (2.8)	1.61 (7.2)	0.25 (5.1)	...	...	.24
6	−0.10 (2.7)	−0.05 (1.5)	0.05 (3.7)	1.26 (5.8)	0.22 (1.8)	...	...	.20
7	−0.14 (3.1)	−0.06 (1.4)	0.05 (3.6)	1.16 (4.8)	0.03 (0.8)	...	...	.19

NOTE.—Regressions 2, 3, and 4 are on 240 families where the wife reported some labor earnings. Regressions 5, 6, and 7 are on the 436 USDA-RTI families only. In regression 5, income is measured by consumption flows as in 1–4. In regression 6, income is nonlabor income only. In regression 7, income is 1967 money income reported (before taxes).

3? One interpretation is that schooling changes a woman's tastes, perhaps decreasing demand for child services or increasing the demand for child quality relative to child numbers. But other possible explanations for this effect arise directly from the home production model. These will be discussed below.

In general, the results of regressions 1–4 seem reasonable. The R^2s in the neighborhood of 20 percent are not bad for observations of individual families. The variables usually considered central to an economic model of fertility—women's schooling, wage rates, and family income—are all significant at the 5 percent level throughout. The elasticities of the number of children with respect to them are: wife's wage, -0.20; wife's schooling, -0.42 to -0.56; and family income, $.26–.35$. Husband's schooling and wage rates have negative signs but are not always significantly different from zero. Race is significant, nonwhites having something over one more child per completed family than whites, other things equal. These latter issues also will be discussed further below.

Note on the income variable.—The RTI data allow three different income measurements to be made: first, total money income (both before and after taxes); second, income from sources other than labor earnings and self-employment; third, a "Fisherian" income measure—current consumption expenditures plus imputed flows to owned consumer durables and housing. Regression coefficients of any of the three should indicate the consequences of relaxing the budget constraint, wage rates held constant.

All of these measures, however, create problems. They are all observed contemporaneously with family size and so are not completely exogenous if having children affects subsequent income. Moreover, the "other-income" measure suffers because over half the sample reported negligible amounts (less than $10.00) of such income. Money income also has serious problems; it is notoriously unstable and ill-measured for rural-farm families. This leaves the third, the "Fisherian" measure, which is the one used in regressions 1–4. This measure could also be appropriately described as an index of "permanent consumption" and, as such, linearly related to permanent income. Also, it seems more likely to be an indicator of the family's expected lifetime-income stream than the other two income measures. Therefore, the permanent-consumption measure may be the best available proxy for the lifetime-budget constraint as seen during the family formation years.

Table 2 presents the simple correlation coefficients among the three alternative income measures, with the sample mean and standard deviation of each. For purposes of comparison of the three as independent variables in explaining family size, the bottom three regressions of table 1 use the alternative income variables. The permanent-consumption measure performs best. Although this variable is highly correlated with money income,

TABLE 2

CORRELATION COEFFICIENTS AMONG ALTERNATIVE INCOME MEASURES, 1968,
IN USDA-RTI SAMPLE OF 436 RURAL FAMILIES

	Nonlabor* Income	Value of† Consumption Flows	Children per Family	M	SD
Money income	.03	.64	−.12	5,502	4,065
Nonlabor income*	...	.12	.07	288	782
Value of consumption† ..	...	...	−.02	5,360	2,286

* Excludes all self-employment income from farm or nonfarm business as well as wage earnings.
† Expenditures on nondurable consumption items and imputed flows to owned housing and consumer durables.

it has a greater t-value (comparing regressions 5 and 7) and yields a higher estimated income elasticity. This probably is a consequence of the errors-in-variables problem with annual money income that has arisen in estimates of consumption functions and in many other contexts.[5] This problem is generally believed to be especially severe for farmers because of the substantially greater variability of their incomes (Reid 1952). Note from table 2 how much greater the standard deviation of money income is than that of consumption in the present sample.

An Alternative Measurement of the Price of Time

Although these data provide more information about some economic determinants of fertility, particularly on wage rates and income, than has usually been the case in other studies, we still have not satisfied the caveats expressed above about using independent variables which are exogenous and timed appropriately. These wages and incomes are observed *after* the family is formed. And they may to some extent depend upon or be mutually determined with family size. One who has no children may choose to work less; one who chooses a larger family also chooses more work, and hence more income. The choice of investing in schooling may be part of the same decision as the choice of a smaller family.

The use of the permanent-consumption measure of the budget con-

[5] The behavior of the husband's-schooling coefficient in comparing regressions 5 and 7 provides some evidence for this interpretation. Husband's schooling may be a reasonably good proxy for the "true" lifetime husband's-income constraint. Therefore, its coefficient is biased in the positive direction when income is left out or poorly measured. In fact, the male-schooling coefficient changes from significantly negative to insignificant as we move from the permanent consumption (regression 5) to annual money income (regression 7) measure. Moreover, other studies, including my own earlier work on state-level aggregate rural-farm populations (1972), show a *positive* sign on male schooling when annual money income is used as the budget constraint.

straint may avoid some of the problems. The most important variable to consider, however, because of its central place in economic theories of fertility, is the women's wage rate. To the extent that wives' schooling holds constant differences in wage rates arising from that source, a substantial fraction of the remaining variation in wage rates in this sample is probably due to variation in experience on the job. But this experience will undoubtedly be negatively correlated with family size. Therefore we will tend to find, *ceteris paribus,* smaller family size associated with higher wage rates of women aged 30–49, whether or not the relative price of children makes a difference in family size via the home production model. While variation in experience might not be all that important in explaining the differences in wage rates observed in this sample, it at least qualifies the extent to which a negative coefficient on women's wage rates can be taken as a confirmation of the allocation-of-time theory of family size.

Of course it is one thing to raise such problems but quite another to do something about them. In what follows I propose to do something by considering the labor market in which the family is located. Instead of measuring the woman's market wage as that which she earns, I shall introduce the average market-wage rates in the area. How does this procedure avoid the possibility of spurious correlation? First, in order for the problem to arise, there must be reasons for variation in family size outside the economic model as specified in the regressions. Such reasons there surely are, since more than 75 percent of the variance in family size is unexplained in table 1. This variance may be conveniently ascribed to "tastes" (though other factors, such as errors in achieving desired family size must play a role, too). Given variance in tastes for children, the experience effect will generate spurious negative correlation between observed wage rates of women and family size. The use of market aggregates reduces this spurious correlation to the extent that variations in tastes cancel out in the aggregation. There may still exist variation in tastes *between* markets, but this should be a much less serious problem. In fact, we have direct evidence on this: namely, the much lower unexplained variation in state or county aggregate-level regressions than in regressions on individual families (R^2 of .7–.8 in De Tray [1972*b*] and Gardner [1972] compared with .2–.3 in table 1 above). Similar results, of course, are observed in many other contexts as we move from aggregate to individual data.

An aggregate market wage has the further advantage of being observable for earlier years when the families sampled were in the process of being formed. This also should make such a wage rate more nearly the exogenous variable that we want.

An average market-wage variable, however, has problems of its own. Since we are dealing entirely with families residing in a single state, one might first of all question how far the market price of time of given quality can vary in this sample; and if the average wage does vary from place to place, which it does, the natural reaction is to attribute the differences to variations in average skills or human capital. Certainly there will be a lot of variation in county cross-sectional wage rates that is not useful for present purposes.

Another problem is even if there does exist more than 'one labor market in North Carolina—even if more than one market price for time of given quality has persisted for many years—how can we tell what the appropriate market area is?

I use counties. This unit was easiest because each family in the sample is identified by county of residence, and there are average market-wage data available by county. The best such data pertaining to the rural population are those of the 1964 *Census of Agriculture* on earnings of farm-operator families in off-farm employment (U.S. Bureau of the Census 1967, vol. 1, pt. 26, county table 7). The data are: (i) aggregate wages and salaries received by persons in farm households; (ii) aggregate days worked off farm by (*a*) farm operators and by (*b*) other persons in farm households; and (iii) aggregate income of persons other than farm operators from off-farm sources. Dividing (i) by (ii) gives an average daily off-farm wage rate. From these data one can also estimate husbands' and wives' wage rates separately. Women's wages are estimated by dividing income (iii) by (ii*b*). Unfortunately, income (iii) includes nonlabor earnings, the amount of which is not given by county but which the census state data (vol. 2, chap. 5, table 23) reveal to be 19 percent for North Carolina. Furthermore, "other persons" includes children who work for wages.

These problems of measurement, together with the variations which undoubtedly exist in the quality of labor from county to county, cause considerable trepidation about the efficiency of the county-wage variable. Nonetheless it still has the advantage in testing the home production model of being a more nearly exogenous market wage. The many sources of error may cause superfluous variation in the county wage and may cause the regression coefficient to be insignificant, but they will not induce a spurious negative correlation between the wage rate and family size. The only evident systematic error is the inclusion of children's earnings. But this will tend to bias the wage coefficient in the positive direction, that is, toward zero. Anyway, this effect may be minimized by what is surely a very high correlation between wives' and children's county average wage rates in off-farm work. Children's wage rates, if we could measure them separately, would probably be a pretty good proxy for wives' wage rates in the county data.

In fact, husbands', wives', and children's wage rates are all probably highly collinear in the county data, so that each could do as a proxy for any other.[6] Therefore, it may not be true that the county wage variable represents wives' time per se. Rather, we are observing something closer to the effect of the price of time-in-general on family size.

Regression results.—The county-wage variable, in addition to providing a more nearly exogenous market-wage rate, has the desirable property of allowing us to observe a market price of time for women who do not work. Thus regressions 8 and 9 of table 3 include all families rather than working-wife families only, as is the case in the corresponding regressions (3 and 4) in table 1. The regression coefficients, *t*-values, and explanatory power of regressions 8 and 9 are all basically similar to regressions 3 and 4. The main differences are: the husband's-wage and schooling variables have become significantly negative and have larger (in absolute value) elasticities in 8 and 9; the elasticity of family size with respect to income increases from around .3 in regressions 3 and 4 to .38 in regressions 8 and 9; the elasticity with respect to the women's wage has increased from —.2 to around —.6 when the exogenous county "women's" wage is substituted for the working women's own particular wage-rate earned.

Regression 9 differs from 8 only in that 9 leaves out all families reporting zero children. The zero-child families present special problems because the inadequacies of the RTI data required some extra adjustments of the families included, as discussed above. In addition, the existence of infertility might mitigate the "choice" aspects of this class, or at least make it a somewhat different kind of choice. However, less than 10 percent of the sample families had zero children, and the regression results are practically identical when these are left out.

The Price of Purchased Time

A surprising aspect of the county-wage variable is that it yields an elasticity greater (in absolute value) than the wife's own wage, whereas all the preceding discussion has suggested an elasticity closer to zero for the county wage. One partial explanation of this result is that the spurious negative correlation between the wife's own wage and family size is empirically negligible. But this cannot explain the absolutely *greater* county-wage elasticity. The most likely explanation is that there is simply less opportunity for substituting hired time for own time when the general wage level rises than when only one's own wage rate rises. This explanation is consistent with the greater elasticity of family size with respect to

---

[6] I estimated men's county-wage rates separately by applying the 19 percent to each county's figures for (iii), subtracting from (i), and dividing by (iia). To the extent that the 19 percent figure varies from county to county, the error in the wives' estimated earnings will induce an error of opposite sign in the husband's earnings. Even so, the correlation coefficient between their estimated wage rates is .74. On state data, free of these problems, it is .93.

TABLE 3

Regression Coefficients (Showing t-Values) for 511 Rural North Carolina Families with Size of Completed Family as Dependent Variable

Regression Number and Coverage	Wife's Schooling	Husband's Schooling	Wife's Age	Race (Nonwhite =1)	Income ($ Thousand)	County Wage	Wife's Wage	Husband's Wage	R^2
8. All families	−0.17 (4.0)	−0.09 (2.2)	0.04 (2.6)	1.26 (5.1)	0.26 (4.8)	−0.020 (3.0)	...	−0.17 (2.2)	.252
9. All families having at least one child	−0.17 (4.0)	−0.08 (2.2)	0.05 (3.5)	1.18 (4.8)	0.20 (3.8)	−0.020 (3.1)	...	−0.16 (2.0)	.270
10. Wife worked	−0.14 (2.1)	−0.03 (0.6)	0.05 (2.2)	1.26 (3.4)	0.16 (2.2)	−0.021 (2.2)	−0.48 (1.8)	−0.15 (1.3)	.269
11. Wife worked	−0.18 (2.8)	−0.04 (0.8)	0.04 (1.6)	1.28 (3.5)	0.15 (2.0)	−0.026 (2.7)	...	−0.19 (1.5)	.263
12. Wife did not work	−0.17 (3.0)	−0.15 (2.7)	0.02 (1.3)	1.30 (3.9)	0.39 (5.1)	−0.014 (1.3)	...	−0.14 (1.5)	.271

women's wages (-0.3 to -0.5) that I found in state-level rural-farm data (1972).

This explanation, however, does not fit straightforwardly into the home production model as utilized up to this point because we have considered only one kind of woman's time. Therefore, there can be only one price of such time in equilibrium, and the own- and county-wage rates are just two different ways of measuring it. However, if we introduce hired time as a different kind of production factor, not a perfect substitute for own time, which can have its own price, then we do have a reason for expecting a more negative elasticity on the aggregate county wage than on the wife's own wage.

This line of thought can be pursued empirically by including both wage rates at once, that is, by adding the wife's own wage as an independent variable to regression 8. This can be done, as in regression 10 of table 3, only for women who worked so that their wage rate is observable. It turns out that, indeed, both wage rates are significantly negative.

Working and Nonworking Wives

Although the county wage is observable for nonworking wives, so that it was possible to include them in regressions 8 and 9, still this wage rate must have a different meaning for them. The marginal value of non-workers' time in home production is presumably greater than the wage rate they could earn. Therefore, variations in the market wage, as long as it stays below their reservation wage, should make little difference to them.

Table 3 presents separate regressions (11 and 12) for working and nonworking wives. The most immediately striking thing about these regressions is their similarity. The model does at least as well at predicting the family size of nonworking as of working wives. It should be noted, however, that the use of a single cross section of data does not give us exactly the division of the sample that we would like. Women working when their families were completed may not have been working in earlier years, and vice versa. Even so, some coefficients are different for the two groups: the county-wage variable is insignificantly different from zero for nonworking wives, and income and husband's schooling are less important in the working-wife regression. A joint test of the significance of the difference between these coefficients, under the maintained hypothesis that the coefficients of all the other variables are the same, allows a rejection of their equality at the 5 percent level.

Farm-Operator Families

The analysis up to this point has made no distinction between rural residents and farmers although there does exist a sizable rural-nonfarm population in the sample. Indeed, only 113 family heads (22 percent) reported farming as their sole source of income. The distinction is useful in exploring rural family size by means of the home production model because rural residence and farm operation probably have different kinds of relative price effects, none of which can be measured directly. Associated with rural residence in general are the prices of goods and public services in rural areas; in addition any "taste" factors in rural family size should be associated with rurality per se rather than the farm occupation; whereas, the hypothesized "economies of scale" arising from a less rapidly declining shadow price of child time as family size increases depends on the use of child time in farm work.

When a dummy variable (constant-term shifter only) is introduced for farm-operator families in regression 8 of table 3, the results are: a regression coefficient on the dummy of 0.46—an average completed farm-family size of about one-half child greater than for other rural families, *ceteris paribus*; a *t*-value of 1.9, indicating 5 percent level of significance; and virtually no change in the coefficients of the other independent variables. The sample means for family size are 3.6 for farmers and 3.1 for nonfarmers. Thus differences in the values of the independent variables of the model explain essentially *none* of the fertility difference between these two groups.

The significance of the farm-operator dummy can only be weak evidence for any particular interpretation of what caused the difference, since there are several alternative explanations which cannot be ruled out. It does seem that the difference between farm families and rural families who are not primarily farmers cannot very well be due to rurality in environment as such, since both subsets came from the same communities. Nor are lower prices of goods that are relatively important in child rearing likely to be the explanation. In fact, the estimates of Pennock (1970) on goods costs for rearing children (given quantities purchased) are slightly *higher* (about 3 percent more for farm than rural-nonfarm children in the South). We are left with: (*a*) the economies of child-time use associated with farm operation and (*b*) the possibility that the relative price of child quality relative to numbers is greater on farms.

Some evidence supporting the latter hypothesis can be extracted from Pennock's data for the South. Her cost figures for food, clothing, and housing are about 1 percent higher for farm than for rural-nonfarm children, while medical care (private expenditures on) education, transportation, and "other" costs are 6 percent higher on farms. Taking the latter as being relatively intensively used in investments in child quality, there is some incentive for production of less quality relative to child numbers on farms.

One-half child per completed family might seem a rather large consequence for such effects as (*a*) and (*b*). But remember that mobility into and out of farming is probably quite easy for this population. If the scale effect exists, people who desire larger families for whatever reason may be attracted to farm operation. To this extent the farm-nonfarm division has endogenous elements.

To investigate further the behavior of farm families, a separate regression, presented in table 4, was estimated for this group. The results differ from the complete-sample regressions: although R^2 is quite a bit higher the coefficient of wife's schooling is insignificant. The coefficient of husband's schooling, however, is strongly negative.

The behavior of family size as the wife's schooling changes can be seen better when dummy variables for schooling classes replace years of schooling entered linearly. The results for five classes are: 0–7 years of schooling, $+1.0$ children relative to 8–11 years ($t = 2.0$); 8 years of schooling, $+0.6$ (0.8); 12 years, $+0.3$ (0.6); and more than 12 years, $+1.3$ (1.9). As will be seen below, the behavior of these farm-operator families as we move from 0–7 through 9–11 years of wife's schooling is the same as for the other families in the sample. The difference is in the effect of 12 and more years of schooling. For farm operators, this group has significantly *larger* families. This results in a U-shaped partial relationship between wife's schooling and family size, which explains why the coefficient on the linear years-of-schooling coefficient is insignificantly different from zero while the dummy variables are not.

Nonwhite Families

Race plays no intrinsic part in the home production model. But since a nonwhite constant-term dummy has been included in every regression presented, it seems pertinent to explore this subject. It was included, of course, because it worked. In these regressions, nonwhites have larger completed families than whites by about 1.3 children, *ceteris paribus*. This result is not surprising; it has been observed in many studies of differential fertility.

How, if at all, can this fact be explained in terms of the home production model? The prospects, prima facie, do not look good. The sample means for completed family size of 2.8 for whites and 4.3 for nonwhites yield a gross difference of 1.5. Every regression estimated attributes most of this 1.5 to the nonwhite dummy, that is, the independent variables included do not come near to explaining the fertility difference.

One complication here is that some of the variables may not measure the same things for nonwhites and whites. This is especially likely for schooling. Eight years of schooling, circa 1945–50, probably yielded less of whatever it is that schooling yields for North Carolina nonwhites than for their white cohorts. Furthermore, it may be that even holding (correctly measured) schooling and age constant, the exogenous county wage rate

TABLE 4

REGRESSION COEFFICIENTS (SHOWING t-VALUES) WITH SIZE OF COMPLETED FAMILIES OF FARM OPERATORS (REGRESSION 13), NONWHITES (REGRESSIONS 14 AND 15), AND COMPLETE SAMPLE (REGRESSION 16) AS THE DEPENDENT VARIABLES (USDA-RTI SAMPLE DATA ONLY)

Regression Number and Coverage	Wife's Schooling	Husband's Schooling	Wife's Age	Race (Nonwhite = 1)	Income ($ Thousand)	County Wage	Wife's Own Wage	Husband's Wage	R^2
13. All farm families (107 obs.)	0.01 (0.1)	−0.25 (3.4)	0.03 (1.1)	1.78 (3.6)	0.34 (3.4)	−0.027 (2.0)	...	...	.36
14. All nonwhites (125 obs.)	−0.32 (3.3)	−0.20 (2.3)	0.04 (1.0)	...	0.50 (2.9)	−0.033 (1.7)	...	−0.18 (0.6)	.31
15. Wives worked (52 obs.)	−0.20 (1.2)	−0.06 (0.4)	0.09 (1.4)	...	0.62 (2.1)	...	−1.3 (1.6)	−0.43 (0.8)	.32
16. All families (436 obs.)	−0.33* (4.5) / −0.11* (2.2)	−0.20* (3.1) / −0.05 (1.2)	0.04*† (2.7) / ...	5.7 (2.8) / ...	0.49* (3.9) / 0.16 (2.9)	−0.035* (2.7) / −0.014 (1.8)	...	...	.28

NOTE.—obs. = observations.
* For the dichotomized variables the upper set refers to coefficients for nonwhites, the lower to whites.
† Wife's age is not dichotomized.

appropriate for whites is not attainable, on average, for nonwhites. Therefore, under the maintained hypothesis that the coefficient of age is the
same, a regression was estimated using a dichotomized white-nonwhite
variable for husband's schooling, wife's schooling, income, and the county
wage.

The results are presented in regression 16 of table 4. An F-test on the
residuals indicates that the regression coefficients as a group are significantly different (at the 5 percent level) for nonwhites. The elasticities of
all the economic variables are larger in absolute value for nonwhites
(though the difference is not so great as appears from the coefficients
because nonwhites have less schooling and income, and larger families at
the mean). This model, however, does not explain much more of the white-
nonwhite difference in family size. This fact cannot be inferred directly
from the coefficient of the nonwhite dummy in regression 16 because the
coefficients differ and the mean values are far from the origin, to which the
5.7 figure refers. Evaluated at the overall sample means, regression 16
predicts nonwhites to have approximately 1.2 more children than whites,
ceteris paribus. Thus, only about 20 percent of the gross racial difference
is explained by this model. The remaining 80 percent could be a matter
of different relative prices facing nonwhites which the model did not
capture, different tastes, or greater differences between actual and desired
family size for nonwhites. There is some evidence that this last difference
does, in fact, exist, namely, the finding that fewer nonwhites practice
family planning while more have children they report as "unwanted."[7]

Schooling and Family Size

Throughout the regression analysis the wife's schooling has been one of the
most consistently significant variables. Moreover, its coefficient has shown
remarkable stability. Though the specification of the model and the sample
of families included varies considerably in regressions 1–12, the elasticity
of family size with respect to wife's schooling never gets far from —0.5.
This is true even when the wife's wage rate is included (compare regression 2 with 4, 9, and 10).

Economists investigating the fertility-schooling relationship via the
home production model have been inclined to view the wife's schooling as
an indicator of the value of her time. But the present results are in a sense
too good for this interpretation because the effect of schooling remains
practically the same when the observed price of the wife's market time is

[7] Kiser, Grabill, and Campbell (1968) found that "white-nonwhite differentials in
planning family size are greatest among couples on farms in the south . . . nearly half
(48 percent) have had more pregnancies than the husband or wife wanted. This is
the highest prevalence of excess fertility for any socioeconomic group in this study"
(p. 49).

held constant. I can think of three ways of fitting this result into the home production model:

The first is that schooling affects the relative price of kinds of time which are specific to home production—that we have a "corner solution" even when the wife is working.

The second interpretation is that increases in schooling, with the wage received held constant, are associated with increased psychic benefits in work time. The appropriate opportunity cost for allocating time to work or home is increasingly understated (or decreasingly overstated) by the market-wage rate as schooling increases.

The third interpretation turns not on specific kinds of time but on specific activities. In particular, we can think along the lines of Michael (1970) of sex and family size as a joint commodity for which schooling increases the productivity of the wife's time more than in other Z-production. (Michael's [1974] model would also allow schooling to reduce family size even with neutral home-time productivity increases. But this would require a negative income elasticity of demand for children, which is inconsistent with the regression results for this population.) An interesting variation on this third way of taking the negative effect of schooling when wage rates are held constant is De Tray's (1972b) hypothesis that schooling increases the productivity of home time relatively more in activities which produce child quality.

There may well be merit in all of these interpretations. Some evidence (see, for example, Gronau 1970b) suggests different values for work and some nonwork time. My problem with such an interpretation as applied to fertility is the seemingly great possibilities for substitution of child-rearing activities among different kinds of time, including hired time. The second interpretation seems most straightforward. The difficulty with it as applied to the present results is that under this interpretation schooling has a bigger impact on the psychic element of work time than it does on market-wage rates. It is true that in this sample the simple correlation coefficient between the wife's schooling and her market wage is low (.24). But it is doubtful that the correlation with psychic returns is any higher.

The results for female schooling as well as the husband's schooling are quite consistent with increasing productivity in child-quality-producing activities over and above the general increases in the productivity of time as schooling increases. Unfortunately, this interpretation is observationally equivalent to the hypothesis that increases in schooling increase parents' desires for high-quality children. But this latter explanation is a matter of tastes; it brings the explanation of the schooling results outside the home production model per se (where it may indeed belong).

The third effect, increasing specifically the productivity of contraceptive activities and thereby reducing the number of children produced "accidentally," seems to have the greatest possibilities for explaining the consistency and magnitude of the wife's-schooling variable within the home production model. On this hypothesis we have some positive, though indirect, evidence: the existence of exceptionally high incidence of excess fertility (unwanted births) among rural southern nonwhites, coupled with the exceptionally high elasticity of family size with respect to wife's education in the regressions for nonwhites (14–15 of table 4).

One further experiment with education is to look at particular levels of schooling by means of dummy variables. Although a dollar is a dollar, years of schooling are not so interchangeable; therefore, suspicion arises about the linear treatment of family size and schooling. Using six classes of wife's schooling in regression 8 instead of years of schooling linearly yielded the following dummy coefficients (with t): 0–4 years of schooling, 1.8 (3.8); 4–7 years, 0.9 (2.9); 8 years, 0.7 (1.9); 12 years, −0.15 (0.6); and 13 or more, −0.08 (0.2). These coefficients measure completed family size relative to those women who completed 1–3 years of high school. The coefficients of the other independent variables are virtually unchanged from regression 8.

These results indicate a nonlinear relationship between schooling and family size. After entering high school, additional education does not reduce family size appreciably, *ceteris paribus*. I would say that this result makes the psychic-wage explanation of schooling's effect less probable. It would seem more likely that psychic-wage increases would be *greater* in moving from 9–11 to 13–16 than from 0–7 to 9–11 years of schooling, considering the moves in occupation that are typically made. But this is only conjecture. Similar considerations make the taste-changing interpretation of schooling less appealing.

The husband's schooling presents problems analogous to those just discussed, but it is not so important a variable in the regression analysis. It is, however, usually significantly negative. Like the wife's schooling, its coefficient is not greatly changed whether wage rates are held constant or not. Here the contraceptive-efficiency explanation seems less likely, but the nonpecuniary work benefits more so. A dummy-variable treatment of male schooling yielded the following coefficients and t-ratios: 0–7 years of schooling, 0.2 (0.6); 8 years, −0.6 (1.7); 12 years, −0.4 (1.3); 13+ years, −1.1 (2.2). For men's schooling there also appears to be nonlinearity, but here it is the *upper* years that are most important.

Interactions

The theoretical point that higher income increases the relative price of kinds of time for which the supply is fixed is a most interesting implication of the home production model. How important are such interactions in the present data?

Some evidence is obtainable from the regressions of table 3 on working and nonworking wives. In the Willis formulation the coefficient on the husband's wage ought to be more negative for the nonworking wives, but with income held constant the husband's wage is presumably a pure relative-price variable. Rather we should look to the income coefficient. But that coefficient is greater, even significantly so, for the nonworking wives. Husband's schooling, however, does act in the way predicted.

Another test suggested is to add interaction terms. Several of these were tried on this sample, but the only one close to significant with a positive sign was that between women's and men's schooling. In any case, this procedure is at best an ambiguous test of the interaction hypothesis, as Ben-Porath points out in this volume. Suppose that the "true" model is nonlinear, say quadratic in one or more variables but contains no interaction terms, and that there exists collinearity among the independent variables. Then an interaction term added to a linear regression will be a proxy for a squared term and may be statistically significant even though the true interaction is zero. Both conditions—nonlinearity and positive correlation (correlation coefficient = .58)—are met in the case of husbands' and wives' schooling in this sample.

To get more direct evidence on interactions, the dummy-variable treatment was extended to a separate classification for various joint combinations of husband's and wife's schooling. This procedure allows a separate set of wife's schooling/family size contrasts to be made for different levels of husband's schooling. For a husband with 0–7 years of schooling, the dummy coefficients (with t-values) are: 0–4 years of wife's schooling, 1.9 (3.9); 5–7 years, 1.3 (3.4); 8 years, 1.0 (2.2); 9–11 years, 0 (basis for contrasts); and 12+ years, 0.3 (1.1). For a husband with 12+ years of schooling, results are: 0–7 years of wife's schooling, 0.8 (1.1); 8 years (only one observation); 9–11 years, 0 (basis for contrast); 12 years, —0.7 (2.3); and 13+ years, —1.0 (2.7). These comparisons are plagued by the collinearity just as the interaction model was. There were no observations of women with 0–4 years of schooling married to men with 12+ years of schooling, and only one of a woman with 13+ years of schooling wed to a man with 0–7. There were only six marriages between men with 12+ years of schooling and women with 0–7, which accounts for the low t on this dummy coefficient even though its value is 0.8.

In order to make more meaningful comparisons, the classes are collapsed to three. The contrasts we then have in number of children by schooling class relative to women and men with 8–11 years of schooling are shown in table 5. Though collinearity still makes it impossible to get as sharp contrasts as one would like, the point estimates of table 5 have interesting implications for interaction and nonlinearity. Both the husband's and the wife's schooling make a difference in family size. But the differences induced by changes in the wife's schooling do not vary much with the husband's schooling—there is no immediately apparent interaction in this

TABLE 5

DIFFERENTIAL EFFECT OF YEARS OF SCHOOLING OF HUSBAND AND WIFE
ON COMPLETED FAMILY SIZE

SCHOOLING OF HUSBAND (YEARS)	SCHOOLING OF WIFE (YEARS)		
	0–7	8–11	12+
0–7	1.18 (62)	0.26 (78)	−0.25 (28)
8–11	0.63 (21)	0.0 (82)	0.29 (37)
12+	0.79 (6)	−0.28 (21)	−0.82 (104)

NOTE.—Income, race, and wage rates are held constant. Basis for all contrasts is the number of children in families in which both husband and wife had 8–11 years of schooling. Number of observations in each cell is in parentheses.

sense. Furthermore, the nonlinearity in the wife's schooling arising from the "flattening out" of the family size/schooling profile has largely disappeared. Thus these data have the interesting property that if you look for interactions alone, you find them; and if you look for nonlinearity alone, you find it; but if you use a general framework that allows the observation of both simultaneously, you find neither. The simple linear, noninteracting treatment of schooling used in the earlier regressions turns out perhaps not to have been egregiously wrong.

IV. Conclusions

The empirical results on the rural North Carolina families yield the following propositions:

1. Increases in the wife's wage, measured either as her own wage-rate earned or as a county average wage rate, reduce completed family size.

2. Increases in family income (measured not in annual money terms but as a "permanent" annual flow of consumption services) increase family size.

3. Increases in the wife's schooling decrease family size. This effect persists and is changed only slightly whether the wife's wage rate is held constant or not.

4. Nonwhite families have 1.2–1.3 more children than whites per completed family, ceteris paribus. Their family sizes are also more responsive to changes in schooling, wage rates, and income than are those for white families in this sample.

5. Farm operators have about 0.4 more children per completed family than rural-nonfarm residents, ceteris paribus.

6. Increases in the price of hired time, holding the wife's own wage rate constant, decrease completed family size.

7. The husband's schooling and wage rate are both negatively related to family size. The negative effect of husband's schooling is significantly

larger for families in which the wife does not work than where she does, as the home production model predicts. However, for nonworking wives, the income elasticity of family size is greater than for working wives.

8. Neither the wife's nor husband's years of schooling are related linearly to family size (though the nonlinearity appears greatly reduced when interaction is allowed between husbands' and wives' schooling). For women, increases from 0–4 through 9–11 years of schooling reduce family size much more than increases from 9–11 through college. The men's nonlinearity is weaker and works in the opposite way; later years of schooling reduce family size by more than earlier ones.

Propositions (1), (2), and (6) are consistent with the predictions of the model. Results (3), (5), (7), and (8) may be plausibly interpreted in terms of the home production model, but alternative explanations cannot be ruled out.

Comment

Glen G. Cain

University of Wisconsin

Most of my discussion pertains to the empirical work presented in Gardner's paper. I have no disagreement with the underlying theory, wherein numbers and quality of children are expected to be related in special and familiar ways to wealth endowments of households and to the market prices which households face. Nor do I disagree with the author's list of difficulties in the empirical estimation of the model—particularly the problem of defining those endowments and prices that are truly exogenous and the difficulties in measuring these variables at the times when decisions are being made. Even if we accept the idea that parents make a "lifetime" decision about the quantity of children they desire, we must work with income and price data that only loosely apply to that "lifetime" period.

At the outset let me say that I find the qualitative results of the empirical work quite acceptable. Gardner obtains positive income effects, negative price effects, a positive effect for farm residents, and other reasonable results in his models predicting family size. But I will question whether the data and the statistical models used are adequate to yield even approximately unbiased measures of these effects.

The Data and the Dependent Variable

The dependent variable is not children-ever-born but rather, in the RTI survey, children present ("some part of the year"). The biases this causes is not clear a priori because there are two biases which may operate in different directions. (1) On the one hand, higher-educated and higher-income people (high SES, for short) tend to marry at later ages than do low-SES people. If we were using a children-ever-born variable, this would mean that at any given age up to the year when the last child is born, the SES relationship to fertility would appear negative, although it need not be negative. (2) On the other hand, the low-SES parents will be younger when their children begin to leave home as they grow up. As a consequence, the numbers of children present will be larger in the older ages, say the late thirties, for the high-SES group, even though the number of children-ever-born may be the same. If, as may be true, the children in low-SES households tend to leave home at earlier ages, the bias understating the numbers of children for these low-SES families increases.[1]

Depending on the frequency of these two types of biases, any positive relation between numbers of children and income would be exaggerated, and any negative relation between education and numbers would be understated; or vice versa.

These biases are illustrated in table 1. With respect to the RTI survey, it appears that bias (2), in which the SES-fertility relation is positively biased, may dominate. In the examples given, there are more ages of the wife when a high-SES woman will show a spuriously larger number of children than the low-SES woman. The table also shows why Gardner had to apply his rule excluding wives whose oldest child over age 15 was born more than 5 years after the date of her marriage. Leaving in such wives would have made bias (2) very large indeed. One additional distortion in this sample is worth mentioning. A special treatment was accorded to women who reported no children present. If these women were under age 46, they were counted as among the childless. As shown in table 1 (see "age 44"), this probably imparts a specific type of bias. Furthermore, all women aged 46–49 with "no children present" were excluded, so even those with "no children-ever-born" were omitted from the sample. One can only speculate on how these excluded cases have affected Gardner's overall results, especially in his tables 3 and 4, where the sample size was often small and complicated interaction variables were analyzed.

The Independent Variables and Their Interpretation

Early in his discussion of the regressions Gardner remarks that education may be standing as a proxy for tastes "against" children. I agree that it might. But is it not also reasonable to expect that the wife's wage rate and the husband's income are also correlated with tastes against children and in favor of market goods? *I* would expect such correlations. It seems to me that this sort of bias is a serious disadvantage when working with disaggregated data in particular.[2]

---

[1] Note that children attending college will probably be counted as "children living at home during at least some part of the year." Such cases would be more common among high-SES families. Also adding to this direction of bias are the higher death rates of children in the low-SES groups, but this may be negligible.

[2] The standard argument is that women differ in a variety of genetic and "personality" characteristics which may be contributing to *both* decisions about desired fertility *and* decisions about wage earning capacities (human capital investments), the choice of a husband regarding his income prospects (and his tastes for children), and so on. Certain aggregations of the data may permit the assumption of a zero variance in tastes, but this would have to be examined. If these tastes are unobservable, the

TABLE 1

CHILDREN PRESENT* BY AGE OF WIFE AND AGE OF MARRIAGE

AGE AT MARRIAGE	Low SES (Age at Marriage = 18)		High SES (Age at Marriage = 23)	
	No. of Children	Age of Oldest	No. of Children	Age of Oldest
18	0	0	. . .	. . .
19	0	0	. . .	. . .
20	1	1	. . .	. . .
21	1	2	. . .	. . .
22	2	3	. . .	. . .
23	2	4	0	0
24	3	5	0	0
25	3	6	1	1
26	4	7	1	2
27	4	8	2	3
28	4	9	2	4
29	4	10	3	5
30†	4	11	3	6
31	4	12	4	7
.	.	.	.	.
.	.	.	.	.
.	.	.	.	.
37	4	18	4	13
38‡	3	17	4	14
39‡	3	18	4	15
40	2§	17	4	16
41	2§	18	4	17
42	1§	17	4	18
43	1§	18	3	17
44‡‖	0	. . .	3	18
45‖	0	. . .	2§	17
46‖	0	. . .	2§	18
47‖	0	. . .	1§	17
48‖	0	. . .	1§	18
49‖	0	. . .	0	. . .

NOTE.—The number of children-ever-born is assumed to be four, spaced 2 years apart, and the children are assumed to leave home at age 18.

* The questionnaire asked about "children still living at home during at least some part of the year."
† At age 30, the low-SES families appear (erroneously) to have a higher measure of children-ever-born.
‡ At ages 38, 39, and 44, the high-SES families appear (erroneously) to have a higher measure of children-ever-born.
§ Wives who would be excluded from the sample because the woman's year of marriage is greater than 5 years earlier than the birth of the oldest child reported (unless the oldest child was less than 16 years old).
‖ Ages when there is an ambiguity regarding "no children present" being taken for "no children-ever-born." In Gardner's treatment of this problem, women aged 46–49 with no children present are excluded entirely, so the spurious positive relation between SES and fertility is observed for the 44-year-old women.

Now consider the specific matter of the income variable used. First, regarding nonlabor income, the problem is not only that the amounts are small and often inaccurately measured, but that they stem from special

"bias" goes unmeasured, and even the existence (or direction) of bias may be in dispute, and the resolution will depend on one's judgment. In cases where some proxy variable serves to measure tastes—stated attitudes, for example—it will probably turn out that these proxies are endogenous and depend on the wage, income, and fertility variables. But, clearly, such simultaneity in the relations does not negate the validity of the general point that the omission of tastes generates a bias in the estimated coefficients of the wage and income variables in models predicting fertility.

sources that may reveal special characteristics of the families. With incomes generally low, as in this sample, dividends, interest, and capital gains are minor. Public assistance in the form of aid to dependent children would introduce a "price effect," but this is probably not important in this sample, since female heads were excluded. Unemployment compensation is a temporary grant that should have no effect on fertility. Disability payments may represent characteristics that have an effect on fertility, but not because of the "pure" income effect. Rent receipts may indicate having a large house, and the rent relation to past fertility behavior may stem from the correlation with housing expenditure rather than from a "pure" income effect.

Second, I am surprised to see consumption expenditures appearing on the right-hand side of the equation that has family size on the left-hand side. For decades econometric work has used family size as a presumed exogenous variable determining consumption and savings decisions.[3] I cannot accept the implicit assumption that consumption expenditures is an exogenous variable determining family size. There are, as Gardner suggests, numerous problems of simultaneity in the fertility model he presents, but this one, which he does not mention, seems to me one of the most serious.

Gardner considers as an innovation the use of an areal aggregate wage rate for wives in their county of residence as an independent variable in a regression with the wife's number of children as dependent variable. After noting the problem of an endogenous "experience" component in the wife's own reported wage, he claims that the area wage is truly exogenous.[4] I would argue against this claim. First, consider the regression of average county fertility rates on average county female wage rates. The potential problem of simultaneity here is that (a) average fertility rates will act as a proxy for average "experience," and the latter affects the average wage; and (b) the average female wage rate will depend on the labor supply of females, which has been admitted to be a variable that is simultaneously determined along with fertility decisions. Now, I claim that the algebra of least-squares fitting produces regression coefficients in Gardner's specification which match just this regression of average county fertility rates on

[3] To cite just one study, although a particularly appropriate one, see H. Watts and J. Tobin (1969). Family size was generally positively related to both stocks of assets and current consumption (more precisely, negatively related to current savings), and precisely these two entities define Gardner's "permanent-consumption" measure of income.

[4] As an aside, I would argue with Gardner's contention that his procedure of dividing days worked into aggregate income tends to bias the wife's wage rate coefficient toward zero. Consider that small-sized families will find it easier to accumulate savings in the form of assets that yield money income. Counties with larger numbers of these types of families will show up with higher wage rates for wives because the numerator includes a lot of nonlabor income. A negative relation between the "wage rate" and fertility is produced which is partly spurious.

average county female wage rates (actually, a regression weighted by the number of observations in each county). Such area regressions are useful, despite the simultaneity problems that arise, but Gardner's specification offers nothing substantively innovative.

Another problem that must be considered—one that is confronted most explicitly when using cross-section area aggregates—is that of selective migration. It seems to me highly plausible that, for example, women who have tastes for market work (or for a "career") *and* for having few children would migrate to areas where they would find better employment opportunities. The measured negative correlation between female earnings (or wages) and numbers of children would then be partly spurious—at least spurious in comparison to the effects of changes in wages on the quantity of children that we would expect to see in a time series. I suggest further that the smaller is the total area from which the population is drawn, the more likely is selective migration a problem since interarea mobility is greater. The use of Standard Metropolitan Statistical Areas (SMSAs), or even counties, in the United States as a whole is better, I believe, than Gardner's use of counties within a single state. (Worse still would be the use of neighborhoods or tracts within a single city.)

I conclude that there are serious problems in accepting the regression coefficients in this paper as even approximately unbiased. The income coefficients appear biased up because of the simultaneity problem, the "tastes" correlation, and because of the sample exclusions and fertility-definitional problem. The wage-rate coefficient appears biased down (too large a negative number) because of the simultaneity problem, the "tastes" correlation, and selective migration phenomena. We have no way of judging the seriousness of these biases, and so my view of the empirical work is reserved: the evidence presented is, however, consistent with the price theoretic models of fertility used in this book.

Economic Analysis of Fertility in Israel

Yoram Ben-Porath

The Hebrew University, Falk Institute, and Harvard University

I. Introduction

I view, in this paper, cross-section evidence on fertility in Israel through a very simple hypothesis based on the links among education, the cost of time of women, and the full price of children. The hypothesis is useful in explaining some aspects of behavior, but important facets of the variation in fertility remain unexplained.

In recent years there have been several attempts to bring the determination of family size within the scope of the economics of household behavior (see Leibenstein 1957; Becker 1960; Mincer 1963; Easterlin 1968, 1969; Schultz 1969; and others).

An economic theory of fertility starts with the postulate that households maximize some utility function in which children and other goods appear as arguments subject to resource constraints in which the prices or the costs of production of the arguments appear. The effect of a change in any variable on the number of children depends on the extent to which it lifts the general resource constraint and induces an income effect and the extent to which it changes relative prices and induces a substitution effect. Recent developments in the theory of the household (particularly by Becker [1965] and Lancaster [1966]) provide a unified framework for handling various aspects of the fertility decision. However, in choosing

This paper is part of a research project at the Falk Institute of Economic Research, Jerusalem, on the economic determinants of fertility. I acknowledge Avner Halevi's very able research assistance. I benefited much from comments by Zvi Griliches as well as conversations with Simon Kuznetz, H. Gregg Lewis, Jacob Mincer, M. Rothschild, T. Paul Schultz, T. W. Schultz, Julian Simon, and many others. Communication with several of the authors in this book was very helpful, and I owe much to Robert J. Willis in particular. The Central Bureau of Statistics supplied data, and the Demographic Center, the Prime Minister's Office, Jerusalem, partly financed this study. I wrote this paper under National Science Foundation grant GS 2762X while visiting at Harvard. None of those acknowledged probably wishes to be responsible for anything in this paper.

a particular specification within this framework, one has to deal with a number of variables that are not directly observable and on which mere speculation could lead more than one way. Alexander Gerschenkron alluded only to one of them when he commented that "in the case of a child the act of shopping has felicific aspects not fully duplicated in buying a car or a refrigerator" (1961, p. 1007).

The most difficult questions have to do with the basic motives for having children, the substance of parent-child relationships in terms of mutual responsibilities, and the associated costs and benefits (see Section VI). The economist's contribution depends on his ability to explain the phenomena in terms of changes in resources and scarcities and to go beyond statements about "taste" differences. Even when one avoids the speculative terrain, these considerations implicitly affect the choice of the dependent variable in the fertility analysis—the "quantity of children demanded." The expected number of surviving adults (or adult-years) would be appropriate according to some motives, while expected child-years or some other measure would be more appropriate under another motive. In this study the choice of fertility variables simply reflects expediency.

An economist is also faced with the (somewhat less frustrating) questions arising because the actual number of children (or any other measure of the quantity demanded) is not equal to what it would have been had people been able to achieve the exact quantity they wanted with full certainty and without extra cost (I am avoiding the distinction between desired and undesired births). Uncertainties associated with the health, virility, and fecundity of the parents, and with contraception and the risks of infant and subsequent mortality, affect the demand for children through their effects on costs and benefits in ways that depend on the risk preferences of the parents.

Much of the economic treatment of fertility has been concerned with the relation between income and fertility, largely in an attempt to discover the expected positive association behind the "mask" of the observed negative association.[1] The emphasis in this paper is on the relation with education. Education of parents is likely to be associated with every aspect of the fertility model. It may affect not only the individual parent's preferences for children and the relative importance of husband's and wife's preferences in family decision making, but also parental productivity in child rearing and in other activities; it may affect the ability to control the number of births as well as reduce the incidence of child mortality. In a dynamic context where households are faced with changes in conditions, people with more education may perceive changes earlier, be able

[1] In addition to the studies already mentioned, see Adelman (1963), Freedman (1963), and Simon (1969).

to form more realistic expectations, and therefore conceive of their "true" optimum earlier than others.

Students of fertility are all aware of the complexity and the richness of the phenomena.[2] There are evidently more aspects and relevant considerations than there are actually measurable variables. The choice of the dividing line between things expressed explicitly in the hypothesis and things relegated to the "residual" or to poststudy speculation is to a degree arbitrary.

The advantage of the simple hypothesis I am using to view evidence in this paper lies in its relative proximity to market phenomena: it minimizes assertions about unobserved relationships. The questions are how far one can go with such a simple tool, and where it fails, what one can learn from this experiment about possible improvements.

After introducing the Israeli context briefly (Section II), I present the following hypothesis in Section III: the demand for children depends on the full income of the household and the full prices of children and other goods. Child rearing, compared with other goods, is intensive in the time of the mother, and therefore the price of children relative to that for other goods moves together with the price of time of women.

Education is assumed to be related to higher cost of time of women, and therefore it is associated with a substitution effect against children. Education is also associated with higher full income; if the substitution effect dominates, one would expect a negative relation between fertility and education of women. Because of the lesser role of men in child rearing, the husband's education is expected to be associated less with such price effects and, perhaps, more with household income.

The evidence (Section IV) shows the expected negative association between fertility and the education of women and an ambiguous relation with the education of men.

A strange pattern emerges, however, in that the relation between fertility and education is steep at the very low levels of education and tends to flatten or even turn up at the top. Section V is devoted mostly to exploring the fertility-education relation as a reflection of the initial hypothesis. Examination of a more sophisticated version of this hypothesis suggested by Willis (1971) does not answer the query posed by this shape of curve. The relation among education of women, the wage rate, and labor supply indicates that at the low levels of education, where the decline in fertility is large, the differentials in labor supply are modest, while at the top educational categories, where differential fertility is modest, the differences in labor supply are large. The possibility of large elasticity of substitution in

---

[2] Roberto Bachi, Dov Friendlander, Judah Matras, Helmut Muhsam, Oscar Schmeltz, and other Israeli demographers have studied various aspects of these questions. See also a recent study by Peled (1969).

child raising and some doubts as to the relative time-intensity assumptions are discussed.

Thus, my impression is that the simple cost-of-time hypothesis, while consistent with some of the evidence, leaves some important aspects of the fertility-education relation unexplained. This is not a statement about the "validity" of the hypothesis, but rather one about its power or robustness —its ability to account for a particular set of facts when other hypotheses are "left out." This is a tentative statement based on limited data and imperfect analysis. Future work will try to improve the analysis of this hypothesis as well as to explore somewhat richer hypotheses (see Section V).

II. The Context

I briefly review here some of the salient characteristics of the Israel case and their implications for analysis of the cross-section data on fertility. A somewhat broader background I presented elsewhere (Ben-Porath 1970a) included some tentative discussion of the time series and the Arab population; the emphasis in this paper is on cross-section differences in the Jewish population.

More than half of the Jews in Israel in 1970 were foreign born. More-over, out of 1,789,000 adult Jews (15 years of age and older), 73 percent were foreign born, and an additional 23 percent had foreign-born fathers (Central Bureau of Statistics 1971, table B/20, pp. 46–47). There is great diversity in place of origin. Slightly more than half of the foreign born in 1970 were natives of Europe and America (EA), mostly of Eastern Europe, and the rest were born in Asia and Africa (AA), mostly in the Arab countries of the Middle East and North Africa. The timing of immigration differed for the two broad groups. As of 1970, about 32 percent of the Europeans and Americans had come before 1948, and another 39 percent had arrived in the period 1948–54. Of the immigrants from Africa and Asia only 7 percent came before 1948 and about 46 percent came in 1948–54. (The period 1948–51 is known as the period of mass immigration, when about half of all the 1948–70 immigrants arrived.) The EA component of the population has thus had a longer average stay in the country.

Both place of birth and recency of arrival show up very clearly in fertility differentials (table 1). The AA women, consistent with the fertility levels of their countries of origin, have much higher levels of fertility than the rest of the Jewish population. Over time, differentials have narrowed—fertility of AA women has declined sharply, and that of the EA group and those born in Israel (IS) showed some increase (among IS, partly reflecting the change in composition by parents' place of birth).

TABLE 1

TOTAL FERTILITY OF JEWISH WOMEN IN ISRAEL BY CONTINENT OF BIRTH AND
PERIOD OF IMMIGRATION: 1960–62 AND 1969

	1960–62	1969
All	3.41	3.39
Israel	2.67	2.95
Asia-Africa, all	5.03	4.22
Immigrated:		
1954 or before	4.69	4.09
1955–60	⎫	4.21
1961–64	⎬ 6.15	4.88
1965 or later	⎭	4.53
Europe-America, all	2.35	2.78
Immigrated:		
1954 or before	2.35	2.79
1955–60	⎫	2.62
1961–64	⎬ 2.40	2.82
1965 or later	⎭	3.79

SOURCE.—Central Bureau of Statistics 1971, table C/26, p. 82.
NOTE.—Total fertility is the sum (unweighted) of age-specific birth for women (all, not only married) aged 15–49.

The cross-section differences by period of immigration reflect both "learning," or adjustment over time, and differences between periods in the composition of immigration by specific countries of origin within each continent.

The main challenge of the Israeli situation, to which this paper can make only a slight contribution, is the understanding of the demographic transition of those coming from less-developed countries of Asia and Africa, together with the fertility behavior of Jews of European origin, who came initially from a low-fertility background and who on the whole had to make a somewhat less dramatic cultural adjustment.

III.   The Wife's Cost of Time

The theory of the allocation of time (Becker 1965) suggests a framework that can accommodate a variety of problems of household behavior. Consider a simple model carved out of this framework which formalizes one of the traditional explanations for the secular decline in fertility.[3] Let:

$C =$ services from children;
$N =$ number of children;
$\overline{Q} =$ a constant;
$S =$ real consumption level of parents;

[3] This is the simplest common denominator of all current microeconomic models of fertility and is a direct application of Becker (1965).

$\pi_j =$ the shadow price of commodity j;
$P =$ price of market goods;
$V =$ nonlabor income;
$I =$ full income;
$t_{ij} =$ time input of individual i into one unit of commodity j;
$T_{ij} =$ total time input of individual i into commodity j;
$T_{iL} =$ total time of individual i in the labor market;
$T_i =$ total time of individual i;
$x_j =$ market goods input into one unit of commodity j;
$X_j =$ market goods input into commodity j;
$E_i =$ education of individual i;
$W_i =$ wage rate of individual i;
$\alpha_{ij} = (t_{ij}W_i)/\pi_j$, the share of the value of i's time in the full price of commodity j;
$i = f,m$, female, male;
$j = N,S$.

Parents are postulated to maximize a utility function:

$$U^*(C, S) = U^*(\overline{Q}N, S) = U(N, S). \tag{1}$$

This maximization is subject to the following constraints—production function for children and the consumption commodity:

$$N = f^N(T_{fN}, T_{mN}, X_N), \tag{2}$$

$$S = f^S(T_{fS}, T_{mS}, X_S). \tag{3}$$

Resource constraints are:

$$T_{iN} + T_{iS} + T_{iL} = T_i, \qquad i = f, m; \tag{4}$$

$$V + T_{mL} W_m + T_{fL} W_f = P(X_N + X_S). \tag{5}$$

Let the production functions exhibit constant returns to scale; thus average and marginal input coefficients are equal. For internal solutions of resource allocations (4) and (5), combine into

$$(t_{fN}W_f + t_{mN}W_m + px_N)N + (t_{fS}W_f + t_{mS}W_m + pX_S)S \tag{6}$$

$$= \pi_N N + \pi_S S = W_f T_f + W_m T_m + V = I.$$

Maximization of utility (eq. [1]) involves equating rates of substitution in consumption to ratio of full prices (7) and adhering to the budget constraint (6).

$$\frac{U_N}{U_S} = \frac{\pi_N}{\pi_S}. \tag{7}$$

Let us now assume that the market wage is a function of education (8):

$$W_i = g_i(E_i) \qquad \frac{\partial W_i}{\partial E_i} > 0, \qquad i = f, m. \tag{8}$$

Education affects the number of children here through its effects on full prices and on full income:

$$\frac{\partial \pi_j}{\partial E_i} = \frac{\partial W_i}{\partial E_i} t_{ij}, \qquad \frac{\partial I}{\partial E_i} = \frac{\partial W_i}{\partial E_i} T_i, \qquad i = f, m; \qquad j = N, S. \tag{9}$$

So the effect of a change in the education of $i = f, m$ is given by (10),

$$\frac{\partial N}{\partial E_i} = \frac{\partial W_i}{\partial E_i} \left(\frac{\partial N}{\partial \pi_N} t_{iN} + \frac{\partial N}{\partial \pi_S} t_{iS} + \frac{\partial N}{\partial I} T_i \right) \tag{10}$$

$$= \frac{\partial W_i}{\partial E_i} \left[\frac{\partial N^*}{\partial \pi_N} t_{iN} + \frac{\partial N^*}{\partial \pi_S} t_{iS} + \frac{\partial N}{\partial I} \left(T_i - N t_{iN} - S t_{iS} \right) \right],$$

where the starred derivatives are the compensated price effects. In elasticity terms,

$$\eta_{NE_i} = \eta_{W_i E_i} \left[\eta^*_{N\pi_N} (\alpha_{iN} - \alpha_{iS}) + \frac{T_{iL} W_i}{I} \eta_{NI} \right], \qquad i = f, m. \tag{11}$$

Consider first the effect of women's education (E_f). If children are more intensive in the value of the mother's time than the consumption good (i.e., $\alpha_{fN} - \alpha_{fS} > 0$) and if the income elasticity of the number of children (η_{NI}) is small, then a negative relation between the number of children and education can be expected.

When men are considered, it is probably reasonable to assume that the α_{mj} are smaller than the α_{fj} and one cannot say much about the difference between them. On the other hand, men contribute relatively more to full income through their earnings $(W_m T_{mL})/I$ so that if the income elasticity η_{NI} is positive, there is greater ambiguity as to the sign of the relation between the number of children and the education of the father.

Mincer's study (1963) of cross-section association between fertility and the wage of women (directly rather than through education) was, to my knowledge, the first exposition and test of essentially this hypothesis, followed by an unpublished paper by Cain and Weininger (1967).

IV. Evidence

I first summarize briefly some of the evidence presented elsewhere (Ben-Porath 1970a, 1970b) relating to the cross-section association between fertility and education in aggregate data (that do not permit analysis of the relation with income).

The theoretical model presented above leads one to expect a larger negative association between the education of wives and fertility than between fertility and education of husbands. A two-way classification of wives by their education and the education of their husbands bears this out. Holding husband's education constant, one gets a clear negative relation between number of children-ever-born and the education of a wife, but when the latter is held constant, no clear relation emerges between fertility and education of the husband.

Also, in cross-section regressions where the observations are mean values for cities, towns, and villages, the median schooling of women has a larger negative coefficient than that of men (the dependent variable is an age-adjusted birth rate). See table 2.

A particularly interesting, albeit inconclusive, result emerges in the regression for kibbutzim. In such a communal social organization, where there is no private budget constraint, where many of the child-raising activities are centralized, and where allocation of women to work is not tied strongly to their education, one would expect the economic mechanism outlined earlier to be much weaker than in the usual case (of course, couples who contemplate leaving the kibbutz will take future conditions into account). In fact, the regression for the kibbutzim was the only one where the coefficient of education of women turned out to be positive, but not significantly so. The very small range of variations in the median years of schooling of women among the kibbutzim is responsible for the inconclusiveness. This can be resolved by studying differences in fertility among individuals in kibbutzim.

Household Data

Introduction

Household data allow a more detailed evaluation of hypotheses and, in the Israeli case, the inclusion of income in the analysis. A cross-section analysis of a problem like ours certainly has many limitations. Individual differences in tastes and abilities may generate the differences in fertility, education, and income, so that the postulated dependence of the first on the latter two cannot be reliably estimated, given the scarcity of truly exogenous instruments to identify the system. (See Nerlove and Schultz [1970] for a brave attempt which illustrates the difficulties involved.)

The single cross-section is particularly inadequate in view of the long span of time involved in the family-formation process. The focus here is on explaining completed family size. Decisions are in fact made on individual children as part of a broader family plan, where the joint decision on an actual child and tentative plans for future children are shaped by presently observed values of the determining variables and expectations about their future levels over the life cycle. Subsequent children are de-

TABLE 2

MULTIPLE REGRESSION OF COMMUNITIES IN ISRAEL, 1961: DEPENDENT VARIABLE, AGE-ADJUSTED BIRTHS

| | CONSTANT TERM (1) | MEDIAN YEARS OF SCHOOLING | | PERCENTAGE OF POPULATION | | | R^2 (7) |
		Men (2)	Women (3)	Born in Europe and America (4)	Moslems (5)	Christians (6)	
Jewish communities except kibbutzim (429):							
1:							
b	2.572	−0.049	−0.132	...	...	...	0.533
t	(26.0)	(2.6)	(10.5)	...	...	...	...
2:							
b	2.599	−0.054	−0.083	−0.010	...	...	0.569
t	(27.2)	(3.0)	(5.7)	(5.9)	...	...	...
Jewish towns* (60):							
3:							
b	1.951	0.079	−0.203	...	...	...	0.603
t	(5.2)	(1.0)	(4.9)	...	...	...	...
4:							
b	1.883	0.096	−0.167	−0.010	...	...	0.646
t	(5.2)	(1.3)	(4.0)	(2.6)	...	...	...
Moshavim,† pre-1948 (112):							
5:							
b	2.124	−0.047	−0.086	...	...	...	0.295
t	(7.6)	(1.0)	(2.8)	...	...	...	...
6:							
b	2.112	−0.043	−0.060	−0.006	...	...	0.314
t	(7.6)	(0.9)	(1.8)	(1.7)	...	...	...

TABLE 2 (*Continued*)

| | CONSTANT TERM (1) | MEDIAN YEARS OF SCHOOLING | | PERCENTAGE OF POPULATION | | | |
		Men (2)	Women (3)	Born in Europe and America (4)	Moslems (5)	Christians (6)	R^2 (7)
Moshavim,† 1948 and later (257):							
7:							
b	2.632	−0.50	−0.137	...	...	...	0.505
t	(21.9)	(2.2)	(8.6)	...	...	...	...
8:							
b	2.668	−0.058	−0.082	−0.011	...	...	0.551
t	(23.2)	(2.7)	(4.4)	(5.1)	...	...	...
Non-Jewish communities‡ (133):							
9:							
b	1.102	0.022	−0.089	...	...	...	0.120
t	(22.2)	(1.8)	(4.2)	...	...	...	...
10:							
b	0.710	0.033	−0.068	...	0.004	0.003	0.159
t	(4.0)	(2.5)	(3.0)	...	(2.3)	(1.7)	...
Kibbutzim (167):							
11:							
b	0.303	0.009	0.046	...	...	...	0.017
t	(0.9)	(0.4)	(1.5)	...	...	...	...
12:							
b	0.652	0.003	0.040	−0.006	...	...	0.051
t	(1.8)	(0.1)	(1.3)	(2.5)	...	...	...

SOURCE.—Actual births by community: unpublished Central Bureau of Statistics data. Independent variables: Central Bureau of Statistics (1963, pt. 2, table 1, and pt. 3, table 2, for cols. 4–6; 1966b, tables 13 and 14, for cols. 2, 3).
NOTE.—The dependent variable is the ratio between (a) number of births (average 1961–62) of the community (e.g., town or village) and (b) the number of births predicted on the basis of women's ages. The predicted number was calculated by multiplying the number of women aged 15–44 (5- and 10-year intervals) by the age-specific birth rate of Jewish women, for all Jewish communities, and of non-Jewish women for all non-Jewish communities. The number of observations is given in parentheses in the stub.
* Includes Jewish population of mixed towns.
† Cooperative rural settlement (all Jewish). The date refers to foundation of settlement.
‡ Includes non-Jewish urban population.

cided upon on the basis of more information, with actual income substituting for part of the previously expected values, while the rest of the expectations are also revised. Cross-section data can give information on completed family size of relatively older couples, but the corresponding earnings or wage data are contemporaneous, realized values that may deviate from the past expected values on the basis of which decisions were made, and which were partly determined by them (e.g., women who decided simultaneously to have children and forego schooling and the learning experience in the labor market).

On the other hand, analysis of the cross section of couples at the prime childbearing ages suffers from lack of information on completed fertility, and issues of spacing are confounded with issues of completed family size (data on expected number of children have not been widely analyzed by economists). Longitudinal data could solve some of the problems and would of course require a more sophisticated analysis.

Data

There is to my knowledge only one source of data that allows analysis of fertility by education and income on an individual household basis in Israel. This is the Family Expenditure Survey 1963/64 (Central Bureau of Statistics 1966a) in which urban wage earners (in communities of 10,000 and over) were sampled, and women were asked, in addition to the usual questions on consumption and income, about the total number children born to them.

The set of observations that I work with has certain defects[4] which I shall ignore in the subsequent analysis. Table 3 presents some of the sample characteristics.

Origin and Immigration Period

The importance of the place of birth and period of immigration has already been stressed. These group differentials may be simply differences in levels of fertility. More likely, they are differences in the coefficients of the independent variables. Even if people were responding identically to these "true" variables, it is plausible that the relation between measured variables and the true variable which they approximate varies among groups.

This affects the analysis in several ways:

a) The sample is divided by place of marriage—those married in Israel

---

[4] The original material was on cards when we got it and was not entirely complete. Also, the tape prepared for us did not include the weights of the individual observations, so the analysis gives equal weight to all individual observations. The survey is described by the Central Bureau of Statistics (1966a).

TABLE 3

MEANS AND STANDARD DEVIATIONS OF VARIABLES USED IN REGRESSIONS—
FAMILY EXPENDITURE SURVEY 1963/64

	ALL COUPLES	MARRIED ABROAD		MARRIED IN ISRAEL (MIS)	
		11 + Years*	15 + Years*	11 + Years*	15 + Years*
No. of households	1,217	455	437	354	201
No. of live births	2.55	3.28	3.29	2.70	2.75
SD	(2.17)	(2.74)	(2.77)	(1.77)	(1.95)
Age of wife	38.1	45.7	46.2	40.3	44.9
SD	(11.5)	(9.9)	(9.8)	(8.8)	(7.8)
Years of marriage	16.4	24.5	25.0	18.1	22.2
SD	(10.5)	(9.3)	(9.1)	(6.8)	(6.4)
Distribution by place of birth and period of immigration:					
ISIS	0.03	...	...	0.06	0.07
ISAA	0.03	...	...	0.03	0.03
ISEA	0.05	...	...	0.04	0.04
AA (1947 or before) ...	0.05	0.01	0.02	0.08	0.09
AA (1948–54)	0.21	0.22	0.22	0.11	0.00
AA (1955 or later)	0.06	0.11	0.10	0.00	0.00
EA (1947 or before) ...	0.23	0.08	0.09	0.51	0.70
EA (1948–54)	0.25	0.37	0.37	0.17	0.07
EA (1955 or later)	0.09	0.21	0.20	0.00	0.00
Total	1.00	1.00	1.00	1.00	1.00
Husband's monthly earnings (IL)	494.7	420.2	421.1	584.3	627.0
SD	(274.2)	(272.6)	(281.0)	(282.4)	(305.1)
Distribution by years of schooling of husband:					
0	0.06	0.10	0.10	0.02	0.01
1–4	0.08	0.12	0.12	0.06	0.03
5–8	0.33	0.35	0.34	0.31	0.26
9–12	0.34	0.28	0.29	0.39	0.40
13+	0.19	0.15	0.15	0.22	0.30
Total	1.00	1.00	1.00	1.00	1.00
Distribution by years of schooling of wife:					
0	0.12	0.18	0.18	0.08	0.07
1–4	0.08	0.10	0.10	0.08	0.04
5–8	0.35	0.37	0.37	0.32	0.29
9–12	0.33	0.30	0.30	0.37	0.42
13+	0.12	0.05	0.05	0.15	0.18
Total	1.00	1.00	1.00	1.00	1.00

NOTE.—The notation for place of birth is: IS = Israel, AA = Asia and Africa, and EA = Europe and America. For those born in Israel, the second two letters indicate place of birth of fathers. Information in parentheses following place of birth of the foreign-born indicates years of immigration to Israel.
* Length of marriage.

(MIS) and those married abroad (MAB). Those married abroad could have had some of their children born abroad, responding to different conditions.[5] Persons married in Israel presumably have had a more common environment for family decision making. In comparing the two groups, MIS and MAB, the following differences should be noted (table 3): Proportionately more members of the MIS sample are of European origin, with only a small fraction of the women born in Asia. They have also immigrated earlier. They have lower fertility and are somewhat younger, the husbands earn more, and both husbands and wives are better educated.

b) Within these place-of-marriage groups dummy variables are used to allow for differences in fertility levels by place of birth and period of immigration. Table 4 shows the following (the benchmark for the dummy variables here is the European- and American-born who immigrated from 1948 to 1954):

Place of birth and period of immigration account for a large proportion of the variance among both MAB and MIS, but more among MAB than MIS. The AA group, particularly the recent immigrants (1955 and later), has much higher fertility than the EA group. Differences are somewhat narrower among MIS. The EA group shows small differentials by period of immigration and has somewhat higher fertility than the Israeli-born.

c) The sample is broken into two groups by origin—European and oriental. The first group includes European-born (EA) and Israeli-born with European-born fathers (ISEA), while oriental origin includes those born in Asia and Africa (AA) and Israelis born to AA fathers (ISAA). The few third-generation Israelis in the sample are left out here.

Years since Marriage and Age

The treatment of the marriage variables is somewhat problematic. Any reasonable theory of marriage will have to state that the decision to marry is at least partly derived from the demand for children. If this is true, then the marriage variable (both as a criterion for dividing the sample and as a variable in the regression) should not be used; if it is used, its estimated coefficients are likely to be biased. In the Israeli population a large fraction of those born abroad went through the world war, migrated, and endured various experiences that might have postponed marriage independently of the demand for children. Thus for some groups the age and length of marriage may indeed be an exogenous variable relevant to the determination of the number of children. (Bumpass [1969] discusses this issue differently.)

Most of the analysis was performed on subsamples of couples who were married 11 or 15 years or more, with age and length of marriage as vari-

---

[5] In future work I hope to be able to follow a suggestion by H. Gregg Lewis to break the sample into those educated in Israel and abroad.

TABLE 4

REGRESSIONS OF NUMBERS OF CHILDREN-EVER-BORN TO COUPLES MARRIED 11+ YEARS, BY PLACE OF MARRIAGE

	ALL (MIS + MAB)			MARRIED IN ISRAEL (MIS)			MARRIED ABROAD (MAB)		
	b	t	R_i^{*2}	b	t	R_i^{*2}	b	t	R_i^{*2}
Constant term	2.69	6.59	...	2.55	5.01	...	2.69	4.15	...
Age of wife	−0.05	4.84		−0.05	3.41		−0.05	3.10	
Years married	0.06	5.63	.07	0.07	4.04	.08	0.06	3.61	.06
Continent of birth and period of immigration:									
ISIS	0.98	2.52		0.99	2.61		...	...	
ISAA	0.80	1.47		0.78	1.55		...	...	
ISEA	1.00	2.07		0.97	2.14		...	...	
AA (1947 or before)	1.92	5.84		1.75	4.88		2.42	3.03	
AA (1948–54)	1.62	7.27	.3	1.20	3.65	.14	1.81	5.70	.36
AA (1954 or later)	3.44	11.11		...	...		3.57	9.32	
EA (1947 or before)	0.23	1.33		0.23	0.91		0.00	0.00	
EA (1955 or later)	−0.13	0.6		...	...		−0.09	−0.35	
Husband's years of schooling:									
0	0.07	0.36		1.13	2.00		−.29	0.67	
1–4	0.21	1.29	.0	0.02	0.96	.02	−.31	0.83	0
5–8	−0.23	0.87		0.39	1.86		0.04	0.16	
13+	0.02	0.06		0.25	1.08		−.18	0.56	
Wife's years of schooling:									
0	2.07	7.42		1.75	4.77		2.14	5.10	
1–4	0.69	2.50	.09	0.73	2.01	.10	0.63	1.55	.09
5–8	0.40	2.34		0.23	1.08		0.48	1.98	
13+	0.36	1.51		0.36	0.17		0.31	0.69	
Husband's earnings	−3.10	1.21	...	−5.70	1.8	...	−1.28	0.32	...
$\bar{R}^2$	.47	...	...	.34	...	...	.50	...	...
SEE	1.74	...	...	1.44	...	...	1.93	...	...
No. of observations	809	...	...	354	...	...	455	...	...

NOTE.—For the units for husband's earnings, divide the coefficient by 100 to get the effect for 100 IL per month. For notation of continent of birth and period of immigration, consult table 3. R_i^{*2} is $\Sigma yx_i / \Sigma y^2$ for groups of variables indicated ($\Sigma R_i^{*2} = R^2$).

ables in the regression. Some of the analysis was also performed on sub-samples selected by age of wives (40 plus) without a length-of-marriage variable. The "time" variables in the cross section capture, of course, not only the stage in the life cycle but also differences among cohorts.

Education and Earnings—Additive Regressions

The origin and "time" variables enter the discussion mostly as controls. Our main interest is in exploring the performance of parents' education and earnings as variables.

According to the model presented earlier, husband's education is expected to be associated with weaker substitution effects and stronger income effects than is wife's education (see eqq. [10], [11]). In the regression for MAB the husband's education does not seem to play any role. In the MIS sample men with no schooling report more children than the rest, while the other differentials in fertility by male education have no clear direction. When the European and oriental groups are examined separately (not shown), one can see among the oriental group a vague (low t-values) U-shaped pattern, while among the European groups the couples with a husband of little education have somewhat lower fertility than those with higher education.

Husband's current earnings are a difficult variable to interpret. We know how crude a proxy they can be for permanent income. Where education of husband is held constant, it can perhaps be argued that the remaining variation in earnings has an important transitory element that is likely to express deviations of actual earnings from the expectations that were held at the beginning of married life. If these deviations are not a matter of the given sample year but represent a persistent position, they could affect the actual number of children. The coefficients here are negative and often not distinguishable from zero (tables 4, 5). The source of the negative association is the oriental group, both MIS and MAB, while among couples of European origin there is practically no relationship.

The most interesting question has to do with the pattern of coefficients of wife's schooling. Table 5 shows the following:

a) For the whole sample and for the two subsamples, MIS and MAB, a similar pattern is observed: the "net" relation between fertility (number of children-ever-born) and education of wife is mostly negative, with a slight inflection at the top, suggesting a transpose-J shape. The sharpest decline in fertility is between women with no schooling and women with some schooling—a difference of 1.0–1.4 children.

b) Within the European group the relation between fertility and education is much steeper and more statistically significant among MAB than among MIS. Both share, however, the flattening at the top.

c) The most striking feature about the oriental group is the very sharp

TABLE 5

COEFFICIENTS OF WIFE'S EDUCATION (DEVIATION FROM 9–12 YEARS OF SCHOOLING) AND HUSBAND'S EARNINGS FROM REGRESSIONS ON COUPLES MARRIED 11+ YEARS

	I. ALL COUPLES (MIS + MAB)			II. MARRIED IN ISRAEL (MIS)			III. MARRIED ABROAD (MAB)		
	All (1)	European (EA + ISEA) (2)	Oriental (AA + ISAA) (3)	All (4)	European (EA + ISEA) (5)	Oriental (AA + ISAA) (6)	All (7)	European (EA + ISEA) (8)	Oriental (AA + ISAA) (9)
Constant term	2.70 (6.6)	2.77 (9.4)	4.67 (4.1)	2.56 (5.2)	3.07 (7.9)	2.01 (1.0)	2.69 (4.2)	2.61 (5.8)	6.83 (4.5)
Wife's years of schooling:									
0	2.08 (8.1)	1.73 (3.7)	2.16 (3.3)	1.75 (4.9)	0.57 (1.1)	2.97 (3.0)	2.13 (5.1)	3.92 (4.8)	1.04 (1.0)
1–4	0.70 (2.6)	0.65 (2.9)	0.81 (1.1)	0.73 (2.1)	0.27 (0.7)	2.47 (2.5)	0.63 (1.6)	0.91 (3.1)	−0.84 (0.7)
5–8	0.40 (2.4)	0.23 (1.9)	0.75 (1.1)	0.23 (1.1)	0.00 (0.0)	1.49 (1.7)	0.48 (1.9)	0.42 (2.6)	−0.09 (0.1)
13+	0.36 (1.5)	0.06 (0.4)	3.81 (2.2)	0.36 (1.4)	−0.01 (−0.1)	4.54 (2.0)	0.31 (0.7)	−0.02 (0.1)	4.52 (1.7)
Husband's earnings	−3.11 (1.2)	1.50 (.8)	−14.32 (1.6)	−5.70 (1.8)	0.26 (0.1)	−29.96 (1.7)	−1.28 (0.3)	0.19 (0.1)	−6.51 (0.6)
SEE	1.73	1.11	2.73	1.44	1.03	2.10	1.93	1.13	2.97
$\bar{R}^2$	.47	.07	.18	.34	.10	.28	.50	.10	.10
No. of observations	809	547	239	354	250	81	455	297	158

NOTE.—"All" includes, in addition to EA, ISEA, AA, and ISAA, also ISIS—second-generation Israelis. The numbers in parenthesis are *t*-values of the corresponding regression coefficients. Other variables in the regressions are age, years married, and education of husband. In cols. (1), (4) and (7) continent of birth and period of immigration are also included.

increase in fertility at the top schooling category (both for MIS and MAB). A clearer relation with education emerges in the MIS oriental than in the MAB oriental.

In examining the evidence, one should recognize that there are very few oriental women with thirteen or more years of schooling and European women with zero years of schooling, so that one should not place much confidence on the results for these categories.

Because of the possible biases arising from the role of the marriage variable, I have also looked at a subsample selected by the age of wife (40 plus, table 6). The number of observations is smaller and thus restricts comparability. The general pattern of sharp decline in fertility at the bottom of the education ladder and a flattening at the top shows up also in this subsample. The relation is steeper among the oriental than the European group. Contrary to the results reported in table 5, there is no sharp upturn at the top educational category within the oriental group.

How plausible is it to regard the general pattern of education coefficients as primarily a reflection of the hypothesis presented earlier?

V. Probing

The Interaction Model: Who Is on Which Margin?

The fertility model developed by Willis (1971) focuses on one aspect of the fertility decision that I have ignored so far. Willis's argument can be paraphrased in the following way: the simple model presented earlier

TABLE 6

NUMBER OF CHILDREN-EVER-BORN TO WOMEN AGE 40+: COEFFICIENTS OF WIFE'S EDUCATION (DEVIATIONS FROM 9–12 YEARS OF SCHOOL) AND HUSBAND'S EARNINGS

	ALL		MARRIED IN ISRAEL (MIS)		MARRIED ABROAD (MAB)		ORIENTAL (AA + ISAA)		EUROPEAN (EA + ISEA)	
	b	t	b	t	b	t	b	t	b	t
Constant term	3.39	4.76	2.84	2.32	3.71	4.04	6.74	1.74	2.88	5.53
Wife's years of schooling:										
0	2.36	5.50	1.66	2.48	2.81	4.98	2.85	1.68	0.76	1.07
1–4	1.05	2.42	3.16	3.18	0.64	1.25	1.73	0.76	0.95	3.04
5–8	0.18	0.80	—0.04	—0.12	0.34	1.17	0.10	0.06	0.18	1.18
13+	0.03	0.08	0.15	0.40	—0.14	0.27	0.19	0.04	—0.03	—0.13
Husband's earnings	—3.51	0.96	—1.60	0.31	—4.50	0.89	—2.36	—0.14	—1.95	—0.70
R^2	0.44	...	...	0.35	...	0.49	...	0.09	...	0.04	0.04
SEE	1.87	...	...	1.64	...	1.95	...	3.53	...	1.20	1.20
No. of observations ..	497	...	182	...	315	...	100	...	389	...

NOTE.—Other variables in the regressions are: age of women, years of schooling of husband, and origin dummies.

applies to households where the wife plans to work part of her lifetime. Only then is the market wage (or education as an indication of market productivity) a correct measure of what she is foregoing by devoting time to her children.[6] Women who do not plan to work at all presumably have a nonmarket valuation of their time higher than the market wage. Variations in the potential market wage for such women do not correspond to variations (over individuals or over time) in the marginal value of time. But higher full income of the household, by increasing the demands on women's time in all household uses, raises the shadow price of this fixed constraint and gives rise to a substitution effect away from children. Therefore, one would expect husband's higher earnings to be associated with higher probability of the wife being a permanent nonparticipant in the labor force. Empirically Willis worked with an interaction model of the form

$$N = b_1 W_f + b_2 W_m + b_3 W_f W_m, \quad b_1 < 0, b_2?, b_3 > 0. \quad (12)$$

This formulation implies the following derivatives:

$$\frac{\partial N}{\partial W_f} = b_1 + b_3 W_m, \quad \frac{\partial N}{\partial W_m} = b_2 + b_3 W_f. \quad (13)$$

As shown in table 7, this model, which Willis has successfully applied to U.S. data, also works quite well in the Israeli case. The coefficient of the value of wife's education (i.e., the average wage for the level of schooling) comes out negative and significant; the coefficient of husband's earnings, or alternatively husband's schooling, turns out to be negative and significant but of smaller absolute value, and a positive and significant interaction term emerges.

In interpreting the findings, one should distinguish between the estimating equation and the hypothesis behind it. The estimating equation under the present conditions may be an expression of the same nonlinearities noted before. In our sample, and probably everywhere, there is a positive association between wife's education and husband's education, or earnings. The pattern depicted by the education-of-wife dummies could have been captured by a parabola:

$$N = b'_1 W_f + b'_2 W_m + b'_3 W_f^2 + \ldots. \quad (14)$$

The effect of wife's potential wage is:

$$\frac{\partial N}{\partial W_f} = b'_1 + 2b'_3 W_f, \quad b'_1 < 0, b'_3 > 0. \quad (15)$$

---

[6] Michael and Lazear (1971) have recently argued that market wages of married women do not correspond exactly to opportunity cost because of the foregone (net) return to investment in human capital.

TABLE 7

INTERACTION MODEL: COUPLES MARRIED IN ISRAEL

Married 11+ years (354)	b_i (t) (1)	$\left.\dfrac{\partial N}{\partial w_i}\right\vert \overline{w_j}$ (2)	η_{Nw_i} (3)	$\overline{X}$ (4)
W_f	−104.70 (5.5)	−24.92	−0.335	.0363
W_m	−59.76 (5.4)	−10.17	−0.220	.0584
$W_f W_m$	1,366.18 (5.1)	...	...	...
$\overline{R}^2$			.323	
R^{*2}			.166	
SEE			1.458	

NOTE.—The regression is eq. (12) in the text; variables included and not reported here are: age, years since marriage, and dummies for place of birth and period of immigration. The number of observations is in parentheses. Col. 2: the derivative of fertility with respect to one variable evaluated at the mean of the other variable. Col. 3: elasticity of fertility with respect to w_i evaluated at the means (col. 4) using the partial derivatives of col. 2. The mean number of children is 2.7. W_f = an estimate of monthly full-time earnings of women by education, using the following estimates of hourly earnings by years of schooling—0: 1.28 IL; 1–4: 1.46 IL; 5–8: 1.70 IL; 9–12: 2.36 IL; 13+: 3.14 IL—and 172 monthly hours of work (units: 1/10,000 · monthly IL). W_m = earnings of husband (units: 1/10,000 monthly IL). $\overline{R}^2 = R^2$ corrected for degrees of freedom. $R^{*2} = \Sigma x_i N / \Sigma N^2$, where $x_i = w_f, w_m, w_f w_m$.

If the correlation between W_m and W_f is positive and high (but not too high), the interaction term $W_m W_f$ may be acting as a proxy for W_f^2.

One experiment along these lines is presented in table 8. Regression 2, where W_f^2 appears, seems slightly more appealing than regression 1, with $W_f W_m$; in regression 3, where both appear, the former drives the latter out. No strong statement is called for, but it is not impossible that what the interaction regression is capturing is mostly a curvilinear association of fertility with the wife's education, which is independent of the (anyhow questionable) effect of husband's earnings.[7]

Given the similarity between the phenomena, the question is whether the hypothesis presented by Willis is the major quantitative determinant of the empirical relation observed.

If we could classify women by their permanent work status and identify the women who do not work in the market in the permanent sense, we would expect no association within this group between fertility and

[7] As Robert Willis and Jacob Mincer indicated, if one starts by assuming linear functions relating fertility to the relevant variables among working and nonworking women and also relating the probability of work to the relevant variables, a full quadratic results. One would assume that the resulting collinearity would make full estimation impossible, but the suggestion is that the coefficients in eqq. (12) and (14) should be interpreted as arising from an estimation where some relevant variables were left out.

TABLE 8

EXPERIMENTS CONCERNING SOURCE OF NONLINEARITY FOR WOMEN 40+ YEARS OLD
(MARRIED IN ISRAEL)

	1	2	3
W_f	−47.21	−223.38	−210.21
	(1.44)	(1.96)	(1.78)
W_m	−26.77	−2.44	−12.08
	(1.38)	(0.41)	(0.55)
$W_m W_f$	547.97	...	229.65
	(1.28)		(0.45)
W_f^2	...	2,632.00	2,289.54
		(1.89)	(1.43)
$\bar{R}^2$	.306	.313	.310
SEE	1.692	1.683	1.687
$\dfrac{\partial N}{\partial W_f}$	−11.91	−23.66	−15.78
$\dfrac{\partial N}{\partial W_m}$	−4.96	−2.44	−3.28

NOTE.—Other variables in the regressions are: age, continent of birth, and period of immigration. See notation in table 7. Data include 182 observations.

women's wages (or education). On the other hand, a negative relation would be observed among those working part of the time. The actual work status in the year of the survey is affected by many random factors and also reacts differently at different times to the presence of children. Classification by present work status is thus a poor substitute on many grounds for the classification by permanent work status. Still, one would expect the group of currently working women to be dominated by those who had planned and expected to participate at least part of the time, while those who are not currently working comprise those not participating because of stage in the life cycle and random factors.

In table 9 the coefficients of wife's education for working and non-working women are presented. The steep decline in fertility from 0 to 1–4 years of schooling is observed among both working and nonworking women. Working women now show a monotonic decline of fertility by education, while in the case of nonworking women the relation is of the transpose-J shape. The upturn in fertility at top education levels among the nonworking has also been observed among orientals and disappears when a sample of women 40 years of age and older is considered (not shown). What remains with us is the sharp decline in fertility between 0 and 1–4 years of schooling, among both working and nonworking women; this, among

TABLE 9

COEFFICIENTS OF WIFE'S EDUCATION (DEVIATIONS FROM 9–12 YEARS OF SCHOOLING)
AND HUSBAND'S EARNINGS: WORKING AND NONWORKING WOMEN
(COUPLES MARRIED 11+ YEARS)

	ALL (MIS + MAB)		MARRIED IN ISRAEL (MIS)		MARRIED ABROAD (MAB)	
	Working	Non-working	Working	Non-working	Working	Non-working
Constant term	3.28	2.45	3.18	2.6	4.68	2.25
	(4.9)	(4.9)	(4.8)	(4.0)	(3.5)	(3.0)
Wife's years of schooling:						
0	2.56	2.01	1.37	1.84	4.06	1.96
	(3.9)	(6.3)	(1.7)	(4.2)	(3.5)	(4.7)
1–4	0.86	0.68	0.08	0.97	1.61	0.46
	(1.7)	(2.1)	(0.1)	(2.2)	(2.0)	(1.0)
5–8	0.46	0.35	0.05	0.20	0.75	0.41
	(1.5)	(1.7)	(0.1)	(0.7)	(1.5)	(1.4)
13+	−0.14	0.61	−0.03	0.65	−0.26	0.62
	(0.4)	(1.7)	(0.1)	(1.7)	(0.4)	(1.0)
Husband's earnings ...	2.32	−3.79	6.00	−11.75	−9.32	1.28
	(0.5)	(1.3)	(1.5)	(2.0)	(0.8)	(0.3)
SEE	1.40	1.82	1.06	1.51	1.56	2.00
R^2	.37	.48	.42	.35	.45	.51
No. of observations ...	183	626	99	255	84	371

NOTE.—Other variables in the regressions are: age, years married, education of husband, continent of birth, and period of immigration.

working MIS women, represents all of the variation in fertility by education.[8]

The coefficients of husband's earnings are consistent with Willis's hypothesis among MIS but not among MAB. (This is true also in regressions where husband's education is not included.)

On Labor Supply and the Demand for Domestic Help

As figure 1 shows, rough estimates of the hourly wage by education level indicate that, contrary to the response of fertility, the larger relative response of wages to schooling is at the top education level. Let us examine how labor supply is related to education.

The sample does not provide detailed information on the work status of women. Women are merely classified as "working" and "nonworking," and

[8] Regressions by Willis on U.S. data suggest also that the steep decline in fertility by education is concentrated at the bottom of the education scale, among both working and nonworking women. At the top among working women there is a big difference in fertility between women with 5 or more years of college and those with less schooling. No such difference, however, emerges for nonworking women.

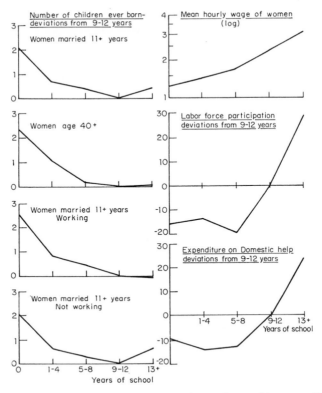

FIG. 1.—Fertility, hourly wages, labor supply, and monthly expenditures on domestic help, by education of women. (Curves on the left-hand side refer to all women married in Israel and married abroad. The coefficients are taken, going from top to bottom, from tables 4, 6, and 9. Curves on the right-hand side are based on table 7 [note], and tables 10 and 12. The last two curves refer only to women married in Israel [MIS].)

this binary variable is the dependent variable in the regressions in table 10.

The pattern of coefficients of wife's education is depicted in figure 1. It is quite different from what has been observed for fertility: the sharp differences in the proportion working are at the top levels of education, while there are no significant differences at the low levels (0, 1–4, 5–8 years of school).

This seems to be corroborated in a study of labor-force participation of women in Israel based on another source of data, the 1956–57 Saving Survey (Fishelsohn 1972).[9]

_____

[9] In a regression where annual participation is the dependent variable, and age, birthplace, and various income and employment characteristics of husbands are controlled, the following pattern of dummy coefficients for women's education earnings emerges (each coefficient should read as the fraction of women who participated at any time during the year):

TABLE 10

Labor Supply of Married Women (MIS)

	All b (t)	European (EA + ISEA) b (t)	Oriental (AA + ISAA) b (t)
Constant term	.53	.52	.59
Husband's earnings	−.92	−.48	−.35
	(1.4)	(0.6)	(0.2)
Wife's years of schooling:			
0	−.14	−.22	−.07
	(2.4)	(1.3)	(0.8)
1–4	−.14	−.20	.01
	(2.1)	(1.8)	(0.1)
5–8	−.20	−.26	−.05
	(5.2)	(5.2)	(0.7)
13+	.28	.28	.32
	(5.9)	(5.0)	(2.6)
Has one child aged 0–5	−.14	−.10	−.26
	(3.9)	(2.2)	(4.4)
Has 2+ children aged 0–5 ...	−.29	−.27	−.34
	(6.5)	(4.1)	(5.5)
Has children aged 6–13	−.07	−.07	−.11
	(2.2)	(1.7)	(2.2)
$\bar{R}^2$	.17	.17	.14
SEE	.42	.44	.37
$\bar{L}$	.30	.36	.20
No. of observations	737	450	249

Note.—"All" includes ISIS. Dependent variable $L =$ the binary classification, work-nonwork; L is the proportion working. The bases for the dummy variables are women with 9–12 years of schooling, and women with no children less than 14 years old in the house.

These regressions ignore the problems that arise when the dependent variable is of a binary nature (see Theil 1971, pp. 632–36). It is useful to examine also the relative change in the odds of working (number of working/number of nonworking) as education increases. When all couples in the sample are classified by the presence of children aged 0–5 (table 11, cols. 3, 4), we find that the relative increase in the odds of working with education are appreciably larger at the top of the educational ladder than at the bottom. (Husband's earnings are not held constant.)

	LFPR*
1. Did not go to school	.301
2. Elementary schooling incomplete	.328
3. Elementary schooling complete	.341
4. High school incomplete	.405
5. High school complete	.474
6. Higher education incomplete	.641
7. Attending	.656
8. Graduated	.789

* Labor force participation rate.

I thank Dr. Fishelsohn for letting me quote his as yet unpublished results.

TABLE 11

ODDS OF WOMEN WORKING (NO. WORKING ÷ NO. NONWORKING) BY EDUCATION
AND THE PRESENCE OF CHILDREN AGED 0–5

	ODDS		RATIO OF SUCCESSIVE ODDS BY EDUCATION		RATIO OF ODDS BY PRESENCE OF CHILDREN
	Without Children Aged 0–5 (1)	With Children Aged 0–5 (2)	With Children Aged 0–5 (3)	Without Children Aged 0–5 (4)	(1) ÷ (2) (5)
All:					
Wife's years of schooling:					
0	0.21	0.05	1.8	1.9	4.2
1–4	0.37	0.08	0.8	1.2	4.1
5–8	0.26	0.11	2.0	2.5	2.3
9–12	0.52	0.28	3.3	3.6	1.8
13+	1.72	1.10			1.5
European (EA + ISEA) ..					
0–8	0.23	0.08	3.0	9.2	2.9
9+	0.69	0.74			0.9
Oriental (AA + ISAA) ...					
0–8	0.28	0.10	3.1	1.6	2.8
9+	0.93	0.16			5.8
MIS:					
Wife's years of schooling:					
0	0.37	0.08	2.0	0.7	4.6
1–4	0.72	0.06	0.3	2.0	12.0
5–8	0.24	0.12	3.5	2.6	2.0
9–12	0.88	0.29	2.3	4.4	3.0
13	2.00	1.27			1.6
European (EA + ISEA) ..					
0–8	0.24	0.07	4.7	9.3	3.4
9+	1.14	0.65			1.7
Oriental (AA + ISAA) ...					
0–8	0.67	0.11	2.0	1.8	6.1
	1.33	0.20			6.6

The other piece of information that seems relevant here is expenditures on hired maids in the home. Certainly, this purchased input is a close substitute for the wife's time in the household both in child raising and in other activities. Again, the pattern of the coefficients seems to indicate large differences at the top of the educational range—between 13 plus and 9–12, and between 9–12 and 5–8 years of schooling, and small differences in the lower levels (table 12).[10]

Another question that bears on the subsequent discussion is: How is the presence of children associated with work reduction by women? It is clear in this sample (as was found in other studies) that it is the presence of very young children (0–5 years old) that matters. It is important also to

[10] I have not checked here the effects of the constraint of zero expenditure, and in this sense the results are tentative and may prove wrong.

TABLE 12

EXPENDITURES ON DOMESTIC HELP

	All	European (EA + ISEA)	Oriental (AA + ISAA)
Constant	—.07	.09	—.00
Husband's earnings	4.00	4.84	1.67
	(7.3)	(6.2)	(2.4)
Wife's years of schooling:			
0	—.09	—.04	—.08
	(1.7)	(0.3)	(2.0)
1–4	—.14	—.13	—.10
	(2.7)	(1.3)	(2.7)
5–8	—.13	—.14	—.08
	(4.1)	(2.9)	(2.8)
13+	.24	.21	.05
	(6.0)	(4.1)	(0.9)
Has one child aged 0–5	.08	.13	—.00
	(2.7)	(3.1)	(0.0)
Has 2+ children aged 0–5 ...	.05	.10	.01
	(1.4)	(1.6)	(0.5)
Has children aged 6–13	—.00	—.00	.05
	(0.1)	(1.1)	(2.0)
$\bar{R}^2$	.23	.22	.08
SEE	.34	.41	.17
$\bar{Y}$	.16	.23	.38
No. of observations	737	450	249

NOTE.—The dependent variable is the monthly expenditure on domestic help in 100 IL.

know whether the "effect" (ignoring the simultaneity aspect) of the presence of young children is larger among educated than noneducated women. In ordinary least-squares (OLS) regressions with a binary working-nonworking variable, the "effect" is larger among educated women (table 13); a similar result has been reported by others. Consider, however, figure 2. Let curve I be the density function of the shadow price of time in nonmarket activities, assuming that this curve applies to all women, irrespective of education. Let W_L be the low wage rate of the uneducated; the proportion of working women is the cumulative distribution up to W_L; W_H is the wage of the educated, and the same applies. Let the presence of young children shift the distribution of the shadow price of time to the right to the same degree for educated and uneducated women (II). The "effect" of the presence of children is the shaded area in figure 2, up to W_L for uneducated women and up to W_H for educated women. Thus, we observe a larger "effect" for educated than for uneducated women, even though we have a case of equal shift in the shadow-price-of-time curve. (Of course, if we let W_H be much farther to the right, this would not be the case.) If one wants to make inferences from partici-

TABLE 13

"Effect" of the Presence of Children on the Percentage of Women Working,
by Schooling—Coefficients from OLS Regression
(Women Married in Israel)

	All (1)	0–8 (2)	9+ (3)
All:			
1 child aged 0–5	−.25 (6.5)	−.21 (4.3)	−.28 (4.7)
2+ children aged 0–5	−.39 (8.6)	−.28 (5.2)	−.47 (6.4)
Children aged 6–13	−.11 (2.8)	.10 (2.1)	−.13 (2.6)
No. of observations	737	354	383
Oriental (AA + ISAA):			
1 child aged 0–5	−.32 (5.3)	−.24 (3.5)	−.48 (4.0)
2+ children aged 0–5	−.41 (6.3)	−.30 (4.1)	−.65 (4.7)
Children aged 6–13	−.07 (1.0)	−.07 (1.0)	−.13 (0.9)
No. of observations	249	186	63
European (EA + ISEA):			
1 child aged 0–5	−.24 (4.7)	−.19 (2.7)	−.26 (3.9)
2+ children aged 0–5	−.40 (5.8)	−.32 (3.0)	−.42 (4.6)
Children aged 6–13	−.14 (2.8)	−.15 (2.0)	−.14 (2.1)
No. of observations	450	149	301

Note.—Other variables in the regressions are: age, (age)², and total household expenditures on consumption. The bases for the dummy variables are couples with no children below 14 years of age.

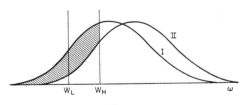

Fig. 2

pation data on differences in the effect of children on the value of time,[11] an explicit distribution has to be assumed; adopting the logic of the logit model (with the underlying logistic distribution), it is more useful to examine the *ratio* of odds-of-work status. In table 11, column 5, we see

[11] Gronau (1973) has discussed the relation between participation and the value of time.

that the *relative* effect of the presence of children aged 0–5 on the odds of working is smaller among the more educated.[12]

An interesting difference emerges, however, between women of oriental and European origin in this respect: educated oriental women let the presence of children limit their labor-market activity much more than European women. This is reflected not only in the regression coefficients of table 13, column 3, but also in the odds in table 11.

Substitution in Production and Factor Intensity

Speculation about functional form is somewhat risky. The fertility-education relation, together with what we know on the education-wage relation, suggests a declining elasticity of fertility with respect to the woman's wage. Examine equation (11) (after dividing through by η_{WE}): one source of decline in the wage elasticity of children with wages is the higher weight of the income elasticity (η_{NI}) with higher wage and employment of women. What makes this argument weak is the uncertainty about the sign and the size of the income elasticity.

Alternatively one can examine the substitution effect. The assumption on which the initial model rests is a greater time intensity of mothers in child raising than in other activities. The size of the compensated elasticity of demand for children with respect to the wage rate (and therefore education) of women depends on elasticities of substitution, both in consumption and in production. The compensated elasticity of fertility with respect to the wife's wage rate is

$$\eta^*_{NW_f} = \eta^*_{N\pi_N} (\alpha_{fN} - \alpha_{fS})$$
$$= -\sigma(1 - \gamma) (\alpha_{fN} - \alpha_{fS}), \qquad (16)$$

where α_{fi} is the share of the value of wife's time in the full price of i, σ is the elasticity of substitution in the utility function, and γ is the share of full expenditure on children in full income $(\pi_N N)/I$. Let σ_N, σ_S be the elasticities of substitution in production of N and S between wife's time and purchased inputs. They determine the sign of the relation between the α's and W. If $\sigma = \sigma_N = \sigma_S = 1$, $\eta^*_{NW_f}$ is independent of the level of wages.

Consider a case where $\sigma_N > 1$ and $\sigma_S = 0$; α_{fN} then declines with W, α_{fS} increases, the difference in factor intensities can narrow or even be reversed. Thus if the elasticity of substitution between wife's time and purchased inputs is high enough in child raising relative to all other

[12] This is a tentative examination of this question. Time-budget data on time devoted to children, other housework activities, and leisure, when analyzed, could show something different. In a recent paper Hill and Stafford (1971) show that U.S. women of high socioeconomic status spend more time with their children than do low-SES women. Leibowitz (1974), using both labor force and time-budget data, shows the same thing about education.

activities, the relative time intensity of children diminishes as women's cost of time rises, and factor intensity may even be reversed; correspondingly, the curve relating fertility to education can flatten or even rise. The observed relation could also be generated by other price differences correlated with education and not explicitly accounted for.

In discussing labor supply, we noted at the top education levels a sharp increase in labor supply, with a comparatively large wage differential, coexisting with a modest or even "wrong" fertility differential, and a relatively large increase in expenditure on domestic help. This all fits the story of a relatively high elasticity of substitution in child raising.

We also noted that education and the presence of children interact differently in affecting the labor supply where oriental and European couples are concerned, the former constraining labor-force participation more than the latter when small children are present. A priori speculation on the differences in the ease with which time of mothers could be substituted under these conditions could go both ways. Larger families in the oriental group provide for flexibility in this respect. On the other hand, high school–educated oriental women may regard the opportunities for substitution at a given level of quality as much more restricted.

This kind of speculation emphasizes the importance of some of the properties of the initial model. The assumption that children are relatively intensive in the time of the mother has not really been explored enough. It is certainly true immediately after birth. Beyond that we observe large variations in behavior. Many Israeli women who had worked steadily before birth stay a few months at home, draw from the social security service a large fraction of their usual pay, and then come back to their steady job which the law has guaranteed for them, entrusting their baby to the care of family or domestic help and later to a variety of child-care services, often subsidized. The American situation seems to be different. The Israeli institutional setup seems to involve less contradiction between child raising and work of women, and was created partly because of a pronatal bias.

If one considers subsequent stages in child raising, including expenditure on education, the need for more careful examination of the relative time-intensity assumption is clear. Bringing in expenditure raises, however, more than one problem and is discussed in the next section.

VI.   Quality of Children and Parents—Issues for Future Work

Before concluding and summarizing, I am taking the liberty of speculating a little more about one of the issues mentioned in the introduction. It is not a direction dictated by the preceding analysis, but it is one challenging and inviting possible extension of the analysis of fertility. Discussions of the secular decline in fertility as well as of cross-section differences have often referred to the changing characteristics of children; the rising expenditure, mainly on education; and the postponement of labor-force entry of children. Large variations in these are evident in the Israeli data (Ben-Porath 1970a). There is also growing evidence on a negative association in the cross section between the number of siblings and various quality dimensions. (Leibenstein [1971] has recently alerted economists to some of these findings. See also Blau and Duncan 1967.)

Becker (1960), who introduced the analogy between various characteristics of children and the quality of other goods, urged the need to recognize the voluntary element in the determination of these characteristics; and recent studies have incorporated a "quality" dimension into formal fertility models (De Tray 1972b; Willis 1971).

The introduction of child characteristics (I hope we can find a substitute for the word quality) as a decision variable into the utility function, as well as the corresponding expansion of the production side, makes the problem more dramatically underidentified, given the limited number of truly exogenous variables around. The theory of the household still provides a useful organizing principle, but when specific models are carved out of it by imposing enough restrictions, they need to be examined simultaneously on several aspects of behavior and compared with alternatives. Lancaster (1966) has suggested that we think of any observed good as an input into some basic commodities. Preferences can be constant in terms of the basic commodities, but the goods inputs may change. Children and their various characteristics can also be viewed as such "goods" servicing various "basic" parental needs.

One can think of several "motives" for having children, starting from various psychological needs and ending with children as a source of old-age security. Each of the motives may have a different income elasticity and is affected by different sets of substitutes and complements. Presumably the "quality" required for each of them may be different so that the nature of the qualities and their relation to numbers varies. For certain motives it is appealing to regard the number of children and some index of quality as substitutes in the provision of "child services" (as suggested by De Tray [1972b]). Thus, if "quality" is future earning power of children, then from the point of view of the old-age security motive,[13] quality and numbers can be substitutes—two or three well-educated children can provide the same future income that several uneducated children would. I leave to introspection the judgment of how much substitution there is between the number of children and their "quality" in serving companionship or entertainment values.

These two examples have to do with cases where both the number and characteristics of children serve what might be called egoistic motives. But it must be clear that while the decision to have children may serve

[13] An interesting study of this motive is in Caldwell (1968).

one set of motives, their characteristics may be involved with another. In particular, the characteristics of children may have to do with altruistic motives: my utility function includes the number of children, my standard of living, and what I take as a proper utility function for each of my children (that is if they would have the sense to have my preferences). While I have children for my sake, my utility depends on what I conceive to be their long-term happiness, and I decide on their standard of living while at home and on their schooling according to this consideration. What is important here is the link that this creates between the parents' own consumption level and education and those of their children. The link does not necessarily take the form of perfect complementarity (Willis 1971); there may be some sensitivity to relative prices, but one can see that there would be limits to the desired intergenerational inequalities to income and opportunities, even without assuming taste dependence on parents' education. In terms of this story, the decision between the number of children and their "quality" is inconceivable without reference to the parents' standard of living. It is evident that postulating such a link does not have to rest on arguments of social pressure (see the Becker [1960]-Duesenberry [1960]-Okun [1960] discussion and the subsequent paper by Blake [1968]) coercing the rich to spend much on their children. While such pressures may exist, they depend presumably on prevalence of a desire by most rich persons to spend much on their children.

As indicated, the weight of different motives changes as income and the relative costs of fulfilling them change. Every textbook in demography mentions social security as a substitute for old-age security. Also, the feeling of parents that they have an opportunity to affect their children's future depends not only on the supply conditions of education but also on the parents' evaluation of how the labor market works. How important, for example, is social origin versus schooling?[14] This varies between markets and among individuals, depending on their own experiences.

The other part of this question has to do with the production side. How important is the jointness in production between the "standard of living" of parents and children? To what extent can certain parents achieve certain characteristics of children "costlessly"? This is where the hereditary argument may affect family size (for a recent survey of the controversy, see Scarr-Salapatek [1971]). To what extent can parents (necessarily mothers?) with certain characteristics (IQ, schooling?) produce higher "quality" children more efficiently?[15] Is this efficiency in terms more of their time or of purchased inputs? These considerations open up many possibilities. No wonder that one can find a set of assumptions to accom-

[14] This point was made by Simon Kuznets.
[15] Michael (1969) has examined implications of education effects on household production both in general and with respect to fertility (1970). I have dealt with the effects of human capital on further production of human capital (Ben-Porath 1970c).

modate any facts. For example, one central set of facts is that the negative relation between fertility and education of women tends to diminish, disappear, or even reverse at the upper range of education or among groups of higher social and economic position. Elsewhere, in looking at aggregate Israeli census data by age, I have also noted a sharp decrease of fertility differentials by education of women (Ben-Porath 1970a). The consideration of the quality dimension can generate rationalization of these facts. The ingredients of the arguments are the following: (1) Quality, the desired "standard of living" of children while at home, and the stock of their human capital are income-elastic. (2) In producing quality, the educated and/or rich have a lower marginal cost for quality. If $\pi(Q_i)$ is the "full price" of a child of a given "quality," then

$$\frac{\pi(Q_1)}{\pi(Q_0)} \bigg|\, \text{rich/educated} \;<\; \frac{\pi(Q_1)}{\pi(Q_0)} \bigg|\, \text{poor/uneducated,}$$

where $Q_1 > Q_0$.

The grounds for this may be the following: (a) There may be some joint production between parents' and children's standards of living, so that parents as they raise their own standard of living can raise that of their children at less cost than if they had to raise their children's standard of living alone. (b) As suggested earlier, educated mothers (or parents!) may be more efficient in producing human capital in their children. (c) The importance of parents' time in the total cost of children may be low for "high-quality" children.

These ingredients could be combined into the statement that at higher levels of income the desired quality of children is such that the cost differentials by education or income diminish or disappear. But of course equally plausible ingredients could be combined to explain some other evidence.

VII. Conclusion

I have examined cross-section evidence on differential fertility in Israel, focusing on the relation between education and fertility. The interpretation of this relation as reflecting the relation between education and the cost of women's time and the relation between cost of time and the "price" of children is helpful in understanding some of the phenomena; what is left unexplained is the large decline in fertility at the bottom of the education ladder.

This sharp decline may be dominated by informational and cultural differences concerning family planning, of the sort suggested by sociologists (see, e.g., the evidence presented by Bachi and Matras [1962], Matras and Auerbach [1962], and Peled [1969]). Several pieces of evidence are consistent with a view that most of the cross-section and time-series variation in fertility reflects differential movement to a low level of fertility where the long-term optima do not vary much. (Thus, see the very flat curve relating fertility to education among couples of European origin married in Israel.)

Even if such a view were to be accepted, the need for explaining the mechanisms of transition remains. The possibilities of the simple cost-of-time hypothesis are far from exhausted in this paper: a more explicit treatment of the cost of time (see Gronau's paper herein), a more satisfactory treatment of husbands' lifetime or permanent income, and a fertility variable that takes timing and survival into account are some of the more immediate needs. What seems to be quite important is a simultaneous examination of several aspects of behavior.

In the specific Israeli context, I regard as the main challenge the understanding of the differentials between those born in Europe-America, Asia-Africa, and Israel and the linking of the cross section to the changes over time. The unexplained differences between these groups are partly a result of measurement problems of the economic variables. Better understanding may involve following some suggestions made by Professor Lewis and, beyond that, a study of the behavior over time of cohorts of immigrants.

In terms of further development of the hypothesis, I have suggested that an adequate analysis of fertility declines and differentials has to be more concerned than I have been here with the joint determination and interdependence between the number of children and their quality (chiefly their education) with a somewhat more explicit link with the theory of investment in humans than has hitherto been made. One additional reason why I think this is a useful direction is that it bridges the dichotomy between economic determinants and economic consequences of population change. Studying the economic corollaries of changes in fertility may turn out to be quite important in understanding the interrelations of demographic and economic transition and understanding better those cases where changes in fertility actually take place.

Comment

H. Gregg Lewis

University of Chicago

Most of what I have to say in comment on Professor Ben-Porath's paper he would have said himself had he lengthened his paper by a few pages. My remarks consist mainly of conjecture.

First, I consider the question of the "power" of the budget-restraint or opportunity factors in the "new home economics" to explain fertility differences in Israel's population. It is certainly true that, in his fertility regressions across individual Jewish households, the budget-restraint factors (I include here everything except the birthplace, place of marriage, and migration-period variables) do not explain much—about 20 percent at most—of the total fertility variance. Yet mother's schooling, age, and duration of marriage together with father's schooling and earnings not only are imperfect proxies for the underlying wage, income, household-productivity, and price-of-contraception variables embedded in the budget restraint, but also the extent to which they are so differs, I conjecture, by birthplace, migration date, place of marriage, and even the parents' schooling. The consequences are biased estimates of regression coefficients and, I suspect, overestimation of the importance of the place-of-birth, place-of-marriage, and migration-date variables, and underestimation of the importance of the opportunity factors in explaining fertility differences.

But what can be done about these problems, especially without asking for unavailable data? I have a hunch that the ratio of years of schooling to the natural logarithm of wages for which schooling in one of its roles is serving as a proxy is greater: (1) for immigrants who completed their schooling before migrating to Israel than for native-born Israelis and for immigrants who completed their schooling in Israel, partly because, I think, that schooling is somewhat country-specific, especially, of course, with respect to language; (2) for more recent than for earlier immigrants; and (3) for immigrants who live in "settlements" chiefly populated by immigrants of like origin than for others, especially settlements well outside of the urban centers. These differences, furthermore, may vary by place of origin, sex, age, and years of schooling. Checking these hunches, of course, does require wage data, though not necessarily the presently unavailable wage data by sex for individual households. In the absence of the relevant wage data, these conjectures contain only the suggestion that Ben-Porath include, in one way or another, among the independent variables in his household regressions the place of schooling and the place of settlement in Israel. Of course, even though wages are unavailable by household, if wage averages are available by years of schooling, sex, and place of residence in Israel (and perhaps other relevant characteristics), it would be useful to construct from these data an estimate of the wage by sex for each household and to include these variables in the household-fertility regressions.

Schooling quite possibly plays a significant second role in the budget restraint, namely, as a proxy for the "price of contraception"; and here, as in its wage role, its imperfections may be correlated with the amount of schooling and the other independent variables. But here, too, is there anything useful that can be done about it? I have only one suggestion. Let me assume that a person's knowledge of contraceptive technique is, say, a positively inclined linear function of both his schooling and the average schooling of the communities in which he has lived. Data on schooling by community, I assume from Ben-Porath's table 2, may be available for Israel's communities. Similarly, at least rough estimates of schooling might be available for the immigrants by country of origin. And, of course, date of immigration is known. Thus I think that it is possible to construct an estimate of the average schooling of the communities in which each parent in the household has lived, for use as independent variables.

I suspect that the errors in schooling in its third role as a proxy for household productivity may be less importantly related to the independent variables.

The power of the budget-restraint factors to explain fertility differences, of course, depends on what differences are to be explained. In particular, a little aggregation of households often helps, as Ben-Porath's regressions in table 2 tend to confirm. In the first of the regressions, which is across Jewish communities except the kibbutzim and which has only two independent variables, the median schooling of men and the median schooling of women, the coefficient of determination (R^2) is 53 percent. Furthermore, the contribution of the budget-restraint factors to explaining time-series variations in aggregate fertility of Israel's Jewish population, I conjecture, will be considerably larger than it appears to be in the household cross-section regressions. I hope that when Ben-Porath has completed his work on the latter, he will apply the results to the time-series data.

The central finding in his paper is the sharp decline in fertility with additions in schooling at low levels of schooling of the mother, and the much more modest declines from additional schooling at higher levels. (Indeed, there is a suggestion that fertility may even be positively related to mother's schooling at high levels of schooling.) I regard this finding that fertility apparently is not linearly related to schooling of the mother as important, in part because it may help to reconcile apparently divergent findings from regressions in which wage, income, and/or schooling variables enter linearly. Furthermore, despite my earlier comments about the danger of biased coefficient estimates resulting essentially from left-out variables, I would be surprised if this result is seriously changed. More work on the data, of course, may flatten the fertility-education curve somewhat, possibly eliminate the suggestion of positive inclination at high levels of schooling, and, I would hope, reduce some of the differences between place-of-origin groups in their fertility-schooling curves. But I doubt that the sharp drop at low schooling levels will disappear, simply because it is too marked to be eliminated easily.

In his section on "Substitution in Production and Factor Intensity" and also in the following section on "Quality of Children and Parents," Ben-Porath speculates about what lies behind or explains the shape of the fertility-education or fertility-wage curve (and, related to it, the curve of labor-force participation and wage and that of domestic services expenditures and wage). He is disinclined, and so am I, to give much weight to an income-effect explanation. The sign of the relevant income elasticity is ambiguous even though the income elasticity of demand for number of children embedded in the utility function is positive. He suggests that the curve shape may be rationalized in part by factor- (time-) intensity reversals accompanying increases of the mother's potential wage if the elasticity of substitution in household production between mother's time and purchased inputs is higher in child raising than in other activities. I would add that the tendency of the elasticity of fertility with respect to the mother's wage to increase algebraically as the mother's wage increases will be accentuated if the elasticity of substitution in the utility function between number of children and parents' standard of living is less than unity. Then, as the mother's wage increases, the fraction of income allocated to the parents' standard of living $(1 - \gamma)$ will be positively correlated with the time-intensity difference $|\alpha_{fN} - \alpha_{fS}|$ in his equation (16).

Once the quality versus quantity distinction is made in the analysis of fertility behavior, and I think that it should be, our degrees of freedom to rationalize data expand rather substantially. I would put child quality (per child) in the utility function (as Willis does) along with child number and the parental "standard of living":

$$U = U(N, Q, S),$$

where Q is child quality, and I would be willing to assume, as Ben-Porath does, that in this utility function child quality has a high income elasticity

224 H. GREGG LEWIS

relative to those for child quantity and the parents' "standard of living." In the budget restraint I would add at least one term on the expenditure side of Ben-Porath's equation (6):

$$I = S\Pi_s + N\Pi_N + NQ\Pi,$$

where $N\Pi_N$ consists of expenditures on children that do not depend on their quality, such as contraception costs (which enter negatively) and $NQ\Pi$ are expenditures that depend on both quality and quantity. (It can, of course, be argued that there are still other expenditures on children, as long as there are any, that depend on child quality but not on number of children.) Earlier in this volume, Gary Becker and I discussed some of the implications of such a model.

Economics of Postwar Fertility in Japan

Masanori Hashimoto

University of Washington and National Bureau of Economic Research

I. Introduction

Japan experienced a precipitous decline in fertility during the decade following the postwar baby boom of 1947–49, and then her fertility rates leveled off. The rapid decline in fertility paralleled liberalization of abortion laws and an active campaign to disseminate contraceptive information. Given these developments and the apparent subordination of women in Japanese culture, one might be inclined to ascribe the fertility decline to increased availability of abortions and other means of birth control and to doubt the explanatory relevance of economic theory which emphasizes the effects of rising wages and educational attainment of women on fertility. The conclusion that emerges from this study, however, is that the basic economic forces identified by the new economic theory of household decision making have been operating to produce a considerable part of the observed differentials and trends in Japanese fertility.[1] Indeed, increased use of abortion and contraceptive devices appears to have been induced to some extent by economic forces.[2]

I benefited greatly from comments and suggestions made by Gary S. Becker, Margaret L. Hashimoto, Masatoshi Kuratani, H. Gregg Lewis, Gail Makinen, Jacob Mincer, Marc Nerlove, Douglas S. Paauw, Gary Saxonhouse, T. W. Schultz, T. Paul Schultz, Miron Stano, Kozo Yamamura, and Dennis Zimmerman. Haeng-Ja Song's research assistance is gratefully acknowledged. Sachio Kohjima of the Bank of Tokyo obtained some data for me. This paper was written while I was at Wayne State University. I thank the Economics Department at Wayne State University, where this research was performed, for providing resources for my research. Finally, I alone am responsible for the contents of this paper.

[1] Silver (1966) found that births, and to a somewhat lesser extent marriages, responded positively to both ordinary and Kuznets cycles between 1878 and 1957, and that the magnitudes of the cyclical responses of births were similar to those in the United States and Britain.

[2] It would be premature, however, to look for exact magnitudes of the parameters of the Japanese fertility function or for a complete explanation of fertility trends. The statistical model employs only a few key variables and is still formulated in static terms. The statistical analysis is performed mainly on cross-section data which are highly aggregated. Further refinements of the model and the data base are both desirable and possible.

II. Differentials and Trends in Japanese Fertility: Background

The phenomenal growth of the Japanese economy during the postwar years has been widely noted. Between 1950 and 1969, real gross national product grew at an average annually compounded rate of close to 10 percent, while the comparative rate for the United States was 4 percent. Real gross national product per capita grew at 9 percent, contrasted with 2 percent for the United States. The rapid industrialization of the Japanese economy is documented in the share of agricultural employment, which fell from about 49 percent in 1950 to 30 percent in 1960 and then declined to less than 18 percent in 1970. Employment opportunities for women grew also; the proportion of women in nonagricultural employment increased from 29 percent in 1950 to 35 percent in 1960 and to 37 percent in 1970.

Against this background of rapid economic development, Japanese fertility dropped sharply (fig. 1). The crude birth rate, which had been about 35 in the late 1940s, first dipped below 30 in 1950; 5 years later it fell below 20 and stayed there. Fertility decline in Japan began about 1920, but the rate of decline accelerated after 1950.[3] By the early 1960s the persistent decline appears to have ended, and then the leveling off began. A sharp drop in fertility in 1966 in response to the superstition of *Hinoeuma* vividly underscores that fertility is very much within the realm of deliberate control.[4] Birth rates just before and after 1966 were to some extent adjustments to the 1966 phenomenon.

Rural regions experienced a more rapid and a more persistent birth rate decline than industrial areas (see table 1). Only part of this difference is accounted for by shifts in age composition as women of childbearing age migrated from rural to urban regions.[5] Until 1962, the average number of children ever born by duration of marriage for women married before they were 30 years old continuously declined for all groups (see table 2). There was a slight increase between 1962 and 1967 among women married less than 10 years. But completed fertility measured approximately by the fertility of women married more than 10 years continued to decline. Table 3 provides more direct evidence on the decrease in desired completed fertility during the postwar years, 1950–67.

[3] Between the two periods, 1920–22 and 1940–42, the crude birth rate declined from 35.2 to 30.7 (7.1 percent per decade), and the total fertility rate declined from 5.21 in 1920 to 4.11 in 1940 (11.2 percent per decade). Between the 1949–51 and 1959–61 periods, the crude birth rate dropped from 28.8 to 17.2 (40.3 percent), and the total fertility rate from 3.72 to 1.99 (46.5 percent).

[4] *Hinoeuma* takes place every 60 years. The superstition is that a woman born in that year will "eat men alive," which is to say that she will be very aggressive and no man will want to marry her.

[5] According to Japan's Institute of Population Problems, holding constant the age composition of the population at 1930 values, the birth rate in urban areas (*shi*) dropped from 26.4 in 1950 to 17.8 in 1960 and then rose to 19.0 in 1965. The birth rate in rural areas (*gun*) continued to drop from 32.7 in 1950 to 19.0 in 1960 and to 17.6 in 1965. These results were reported in Aoki (1970, table 24).

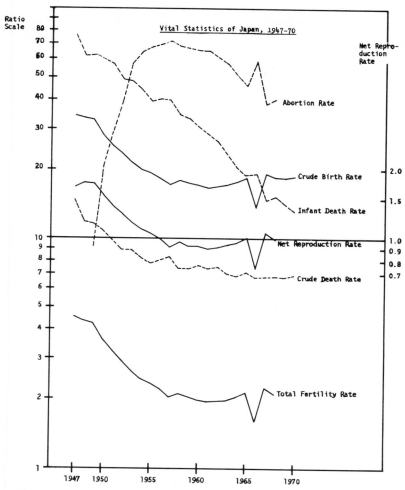

FIG. 1.—Infant death rate is deaths at ages 0–1 per 1,000 live births. Abortion rate is number of registered abortions per 100 live births. Other vital statistics have their usual definitions. (Data on births, deaths, and infant deaths are from Japan Ministry of Health and Welfare [1970]; abortion rate, total fertility rate, and net reproduction rate are from Mainichi Newspaper Company [1970, p. 246]).

For families already having two children, the proportion desiring no additional children increased throughout the years, while the proportion desiring two and three or more additional children continued to decline. Moreover, the percentage of couples with "no idea" how many additional children they wanted tended to decline, suggesting an increased

TABLE 1

CRUDE BIRTH RATES BY REGIONS

	% TOTAL EMPLOYMENT IN AGRICULTURE, 1960	CRUDE BIRTH RATES						% CHANGE IN CRUDE BIRTH RATES	
		1950	1955	1960	1965	1970		1950–60	1960–70
All Japan	30.0	28.1	19.4	17.2	18.6	18.8		−38.8	9.3
Industrial regions	11.7	25.6	16.8	16.8	20.1	20.7		−33.9	23.2
Rural regions...........	49.6	31.0	22.1	18.0	19.0	16.2		−42.6	−7.9

SOURCES.—Japan Ministry of Health and Welfare (1970, vol. 1) and Japan Prime Minister's Office (1970).
NOTE.—Industrial regions included are Tokyo, Kyoto, Osaka, Kanagawa, Fukuoka, and Aichi prefectures. Rural regions included are Aomori, Yamagata, Niigata, Ibaragi, and Kumamoto prefectures. Classification of prefectures as industrial or rural-farm is from Honda (1959). Crude birth rates for regions are simple averages of birth rates in each prefecture. Percent changes in crude birth rates for regions are simple averages of the percent changes in each prefecture.

TABLE 2
AVERAGE NUMBER OF CHILDREN EVER BORN
(WIFE MARRIED BEFORE AGE 30)

MARRIAGE DURATION (YEARS)	SURVEY YEARS			
	1940	1957	1962	1967
1–4	0.98	0.93	0.87	1.06
5–9	2.34	2.16	1.92	1.95
10–14	3.55	2.92	2.46	2.28
15–19	4.39	3.62	2.85	2.66
20+	5.17	4.72	3.90	3.43
All groups	3.49	2.86	2.37	2.28

SOURCES.—Aoki and Nakano (1967, table 3) and Japan Ministry of Health and Welfare (1968, table 24B).
NOTE.—Includes married women with husband present.

awareness of family planning in later years. My estimates of completed fertility (table 3) also show a pronounced decline over the years.[6]

The rapid decline in fertility in the postwar years coincided with the liberalization of policies on abortions and contraceptive use. Abortion was first legalized in September 1948, and in June 1949, grounds for abortion and sterilization were extended. After May 1952, abortion could be obtained with only the consent of man and wife. Alarmed at the increased number of abortions and possible health hazards from abortion, the government in 1952 initiated programs to disseminate birth control information through local agencies. Resort to abortion continued to increase, however, until 1957, when the number of abortions per 100 live births reached its peak of 71.6.

III. Economic Framework for Fertility Analysis

The following discussion will emphasize the effect of parental education on fertility. The testing of economic hypotheses about the effect of parental education on fertility also provides a test of the usefulness of economic theory in interpreting Japanese fertility behavior.

The basic proposition in the economic theory of fertility is that observed changes and differentials in fertility reflect to a large extent changes and differentials in the demand for fertility and that resource constraints on

[6] The true decline is likely to have been even more rapid than these estimates suggest because my calculations may underestimate completed fertility to a greater extent in earlier years. First, the true mean of the open-ended class would be larger than three, the figure used for my calculations, by a larger amount in earlier years if completed fertility declined over time. Second, the group with "no idea" as to number of additional children desired was omitted from the calculations. If people gave the "no idea" answer because of greater ignorance (lower level of education) than other respondents, then economic analysis predicts their desired completed fertility to be greater than that of others. This omission would have mattered less in recent years because of general declines in fertility and because this group made up a smaller fraction of respondents in more recent years.

TABLE 3

ADDITIONAL CHILDREN DESIRED AND ESTIMATED DESIRED COMPLETED FERTILITY, BY COUPLES WITH TWO CHILDREN
(WIFE'S AGE LESS THAN 50)

Number of Additional Children Desired	1950	1952	1955	1957	1959	1961	1963	1965	1967
0	29.8	39.3	42.7	56.4	57.7	64.2	71.7	70.5	71.1
1	32.8	35.2	32.3	30.0	25.5	19.3	22.3	23.5	20.0
2	19.2	14.7	15.8	6.9	7.2	4.0	3.2	2.4	3.1
3+	6.9	5.4	3.2	0.9	1.4	3.2	0.6	0.4	0.8
No idea	11.3	5.4	6.0	5.8	8.2	9.3	2.2	3.2	5.0
Estimated desired completed fertility	3.04	2.85	2.78	2.49	2.48	2.41	2.31	2.30	2.30

SOURCE.—Aoki and Nakano (1967, p. 44).
NOTE.—Estimated desired completed fertility was calculated as 2 plus the average number of desired additional children. Respondents with "no idea" were not included, and the 3+ group was assigned a value of 3. Figures are shown as percentages.

households exert appreciable effects on fertility demand. Following Becker (1960), most economic models of fertility view children as primarily consumer durables. In this conception, a flow of services emanates from the stock of children, and these services enter the parents' utility function. Since parents must make outlays (e.g., food, clothing, housing, and, most important, their time) to obtain child services, they are not free goods, but command a price. To be quite general, therefore, demand for fertility is determined by the preferences of parents, the resources available to parents, and the cost of producing child services relative to the cost of other commodities (usually identified collectively as the standard of living) that also yield utility.[7]

Typically, the fertility rate has declined in countries experiencing sustained growth in real income. Since growth in real income is usually brought about by growth in real wages, this phenomenon may be interpreted as reflecting the dominance of substitution over income effects. An increase in real income would, other things being equal, increase the number of children per family unless the number of children was an "inferior good."[8] Assuming that child services are more time-intensive for mothers than the standard of living, an increase in the wife's wage rate would raise the relative price of child services, imparting a substitution effect away from them.[9] Relying on income and wage rates alone, one may, therefore, interpret the decline in fertility accompanying growth in real income as reflecting the dominance of the substitution effect of a rise in the wife's wage rate over the combined income effects of increases in both spouses' wage rates. However, both income and wage rates are correlated with the educational levels of the parents and the level of contraceptive knowledge, relationships which complicate the empirical estimation of the magnitudes of the income and substitution effects.

The effect of educational attainment of parents on fertility has been investigated more thoroughly than that of income or wage rates by Ben-Porath herein (also 1970a, 1970b) and Michael (1974) among others. Educational attainment of parents is typically negatively associated with

---

[7] Most models use the time-allocation framework (Becker 1965) and they are usually cast in a lifetime dimension, thereby avoiding the complexities of timing and spacing of births (see, for example, the papers herein by Ben-Porath and Willis; also DeTray [1972a] and Michael [1974]). Some problems with the use of static models are discussed by T. Paul Schultz in his paper in this book.

[8] Also relevant to the decline in fertility are changes in the quality of children as real income rises. Research on the demand for consumer durables suggests that the effect of income on the demand for quality is greater than on the demand for quantity. Even assuming numbers of children are not inferior, parents would tend to a greater extent to spend more per child than to have more children as real income rises.

[9] An increase in the husband's wage rate, however, is expected to produce mainly income effects because his time intensities are assumed to differ little between child services and the standard of living and because his wage income constitutes a large proportion of family income (see, for example, Ben-Porath's paper above).

their fertility. Proposed explanations of this relationship fall generally into three groups: the tastes hypothesis, the cost-of-fertility-control hypothesis, and the cost-of-time hypothesis.

According to one version of the tastes hypothesis, parents with higher education may be more "rational" than others in that they tend to regard the number of children as a decision variable, while less educated parents regard it as something beyond their control (Ben-Porath 1970b). Therefore, parents with higher levels of education would control fertility more and have fewer children than other parents. Another version is that education affects the perception of child quality (Ben-Porath 1970b, Gardner 1972). Parents with more education may desire a greater expenditure per child to obtain a given level of child quality. Other things being equal, they will have a smaller number of children. Economists have not succeeded in incorporating such taste factors in their theory in ways that generate testable hypotheses. Such taste factors are still regarded as residuals.

The second explanation hypothesizes that parents with more education have better access to information about birth control devices and are more efficient at using them. In other words, education lowers the cost of fertility control. More educated parents would engage in fertility control to a greater extent than other parents, other things, particularly the benefit of control, being the same. This hypothesis may partly explain the negative association between education and fertility.[10]

The third explanation emphasizes the effect of education on fertility through its effects on the cost of time. In the time-allocation framework of the fertility model, education is assumed to raise the productivity of time spent at home in the production of commodities (such as child services and the standard of living) as well as that of time spent in the labor force. An increase in the productivity of time at work leads to an increased real wage rate, thereby raising the relative prices of time-intensive commodities. An increase in the productivity at home, say, at the same rate for all commodities, lowers the relative prices of time-intensive commodities. An increased productivity at home or market also results in increased real income, imparting income effects. The full effect of education on the demand for children is the net of these forces. To rely on the cost-of-time hypothesis to explain the negative correlation between education and fertility, one must argue that the substitution

[10] More educated people may also use birth control more than others because they desire fewer children, i.e., the benefit of birth control is greater for them. Both Becker (1960, p. 218) and Ben-Porath (1970b, p. 6) propose a test of the hypothesis that education lowers the cost of fertility control. If improvement in birth control techniques comes as a once-and-for-all change, then fertility differentials among educational groups would widen at first but would tend to narrow over time as information on birth control measures became more diffused (see Section IV below for some evidence of a differential rate of diffusion among educational groups of birth control techniques in Japan after 1948–52).

effect imparted by education outweighs the income effect. One plausible case is that education, especially of the wife, raises the productivity of time spent in the market more than that of time spent in producing child services or the standard of living. In this case, the relative price of child services rises, causing substitution effects away from them.[11] The substitution effect of the husband's education is likely to be small, assuming that time intensity varies little between the two commodities for him. The husband's education is expected, therefore, to exert mainly income effects (see Ben-Porath above).

The cost-of-time hypothesis has played a central role in the economic analysis of fertility. It emphasizes the role of the relative price of child services, and its predictions are empirically distinguishable, at least for Japan, from those of the tastes and the cost-of-fertility-control hypotheses. The latter two hypotheses predict that the education of either parent will be negatively associated with fertility, but they leave the relative importance of the effects of each parent's education an empirical question. In Japan, where the husband apparently dominates family decision-making,[12] one would expect his education to be at least as important as the wife's education, if not more so. The cost-of-time hypothesis predicts that the negative association between education and fertility is more strongly manifested when the education variable refers to the wife's rather than the husband's education. The husband's education would be positively correlated, if anything, with fertility when other things, in particular the level of contraceptive knowledge, are the same. In other words, husband's education serves as a proxy for family wealth, while wife's education represents the price of child services.

These three hypotheses, however, are not necessarily mutually exclusive. They help identify possible mechanisms through which parents' education affects fertility. For example, the cost-of-time and the cost-of-fertility-control hypotheses would best be viewed not as alternatives but as complementary hypotheses. The cost-of-time hypothesis emphasizes forces affecting the demand for the service of birth control, a demand which is derived from the desired reduction in births, given the level of fecundity. Underlying this demand is the demand for fertility. The cost-of-fertility-control hypothesis emphasizes the supply side, or the cost of

---

[11] Even if the wife does not work in the market in her lifetime, her shadow price of time could be increased by education, making child services more expensive (see Gronau [1973]).

[12] A survey of 422 couples in the Saitama prefecture in 1960 showed that 78 percent were using condoms, a device for the husband's use, and that 62 percent had the husband obtain the contraceptives. The same study showed that for 70 percent of white-collar workers, 52 percent of farmers, and 51 percent of laborers, the husband was responsible for obtaining contraceptive devices (Muramatsu 1962). Matsumoto, Koizumi, and Nohara (1972, p. 254) also report that husbands are primarily responsible for decisions concerning family limitation.

achieving the desired reduction in births. The cost-of-time hypothesis has been the most useful to economists for analyzing information on fertility behavior.

IV. Empirical Analysis

Study of Japan appears to offer an opportunity to obtain evidence concerning both the effects on fertility of decreases in the cost of preventing births and changes in fertility demand. Thus, I want below first to examine evidence concerning the proposition that both decreased demand for fertility and increased access to abortions and contraceptive techniques contributed to the phenomenal postwar decline in Japanese fertility.

Abortion, Contraceptive Use, and Fertility

The rapid decline in Japanese fertility in the postwar decade coincided, as I have stated, with abortion liberalization measures and the subsequent dissemination of information about other means of fertility control. It is tempting to explain the rapid decline in fertility as simply the result of a widespread resort to abortion. According to this view, many births prior to abortion legalization were unwanted: the liberalization of birth-control policies simply eliminated this excess fertility. In other words, if abortion had not been legalized, fertility would not have declined appreciably. But since fertility in Japan had been declining persistently since around 1920, there is a presumption that it would have declined even in the absence of abortion reform.

Since abortions and other fertility-control measures entail costs, both monetary and nonmonetary, the extent of use of these measures presumably was influenced by considerations of gains and costs. Abortion legalization and birth control information programs certainly decreased the costs of fertility control, leading to increased use of control measures. On the demand side, as discussed in Section III, the main determinant of the demand for fertility control is the demand for fertility. A fuller interpretation of the developments in Japan would be that the price of child services increased and demand for fertility declined, leading to an increased demand for fertility control, and that the increased availability of birth control measures and abortions facilitated the attainment of lower fertility. Put differently, even without the liberalization of abortion and other control policies, resort to illegal abortion and the use of contraceptives would have grown because of the increase in the price of child services. In fact, the availability of illegal abortions had been growing before 1948, and the Eugenics Law of 1948 was motivated by hygienics, not by intent of population control (Muramatsu 1967). In short, legalization and liberalization of control measures were not so much autonomous events as responses by authorities to increased demand for fertility control and the health hazards of illegal practices.

How much did legalization of abortion contribute to the rapid decline in fertility? To answer this question accurately, one would have to estimate (1) the increase in the number of abortions caused by abortion legalization, and (2) the proportion of those abortions that would have terminated in births had there been no legal abortions. Since such estimates are beyond the scope of this paper,[13] I report the results of a crude calculation. Assuming that all pregnancies aborted legally would have terminated in live births if abortions had been illegal, I calculated, for each year from 1949 to 1961, the "maximum" general fertility rate as births plus abortions per 1,000 women of ages 10–49.[14] The excess of actual fertility decline over any decline in the "maximum" fertility rate can be viewed as a measure of fertility decline due to abortion.

Between the 1949–51 and 1959–61 periods, the actual general fertility rate dropped by 44 percent, from 93 to 52. According to my calculations, the "maximum" general fertility rate decreased by 22 percent, from 111 to 87. Thus, it would appear that abortions about doubled the rate of decline in the general fertility rate during the decade after 1950.[15] But resort to abortion by no means accounted for the entire fertility decline. Indeed, the rate of decline in the estimated "maximum" rate is still substantially greater than the rate of decline in the actual fertility rate during the prewar years.[16] This evidence of a substantial fertility decline—indeed, a possible acceleration of the prewar decline—after adjusting for the effect of abortions suggests that the actual fertility decline partly represents decreases in the demand for fertility.

[13] In principle, effects of legal abortions on fertility in any year could be assessed from a simultaneous-equations model in which key endogenous variables would be the fertility rate and prices of abortions and of contraceptive measures. Once the effect of legalization on the prices of abortions and contraceptive measures was estimated, the ultimate effect on fertility could be obtained from the demand-for-fertility function.

[14] These are maximum estimates for each year of the fertility rate in the absence of legal abortions because, if abortions had been illegal, some pregnancies would have been aborted illegally or prevented by other means. In other words, the abortions in each year were not solely due to decreases in costs but also to increases in the demand for fertility control. On the other hand, these estimates may understate the true maximum values because of underreporting of abortions. Muramatsu (1960) estimated that in 1955 at most 77 percent of induced abortions performed were reported. He also estimated that in 1955 the number of live births in the absence of abortion would have been twice (or more) the number actually registered. I calculated the ratio of the maximum to the actual general fertility rate to be 1.68 in 1955.

[15] Because of the underreporting of abortions, my calculations may overstate the effect of abortions on fertility decline. Since the underreporting was probably greater in earlier years, the actual drop in the max mum fertility rates would have been greater, and the effect of abortions on fertility decline smaller than I calculate.

[16] Between 1920 and 1940, the rate of decline per decade in the general fertility rate was about 13 percent.

TABLE 4
RATE AND COMPOSITION OF PREGNANCIES BY REGIONS,
1955, 1960, AND 1965

	1955	1960	1965	RELATIVE CHANGE		AVERAGE 5-YEAR-PERIOD CHANGE (%)
				1955–60 (%)	1960–65 (%)	
Rate of pregnancy:						
All Japan........	223.32	187.01	166.01	− 16.26	− 11.23	− 13.74
Industrial regions .	206.25	191.23	183.00	− 7.28	− 4.30	− 5.80
Rural-farm regions	251.14	191.30	155.59	− 23.83	− 18.67	− 21.29
Share of births (in %):						
All Japan........	57.96	58.14	66.04	0.31	13.59	6.74
Industrial regions .	54.59	56.79	65.91	4.03	16.06	9.88
Rural-farm regions	59.58	59.85	65.28	0.45	9.07	4.67
Share of abortions (in %):						
All Japan........	39.17	38.49	30.53	− 1.74	20.68	− 11.71
Industrial regions .	42.24	39.40	30.42	− 6.72	− 22.79	− 15.14
Rural-farm regions	37.79	37.01	32.22	− 2.06	− 12.94	− 7.66
Percentage of females (Ages 15+) of childbearing age (20–34) (in %):						
All Japan	36.88	35.73	34.21	− 3.12	− 4.25	− 3.69
Industrial regions .	39.28	38.95	39.29	− 0.84	0.87	0.01
Rural-farm regions	35.66	34.06	30.17	− 4.49	− 11.42	− 8.02

SOURCES.—Pregnancies, births, and abortions from Shinozaki (1971); female population composition from Japan Prime Minister's Office (1955, 1960b, 1965).
NOTE.—Rate of Pregnancy = 1000 × (births + fetal deaths + abortions)/married women of childbearing age with husband present. Share of births = (births/pregnancies) × 100. Share of abortions = (abortions/pregnancies) × 100. Regions are the same as in table 1.

Dissemination of birth-control measures other than abortions undoubtedly played some role in the decline in actual fertility rates, but in the absence of estimates of the number of pregnancies prevented by the use of modern contraceptive measures, one cannot directly assess its impact on fertility. Since the efforts to disseminate birth-control information started only in 1952, the major effects of birth control on fertility were probably felt during the late 1950s. Assuming that most couples with accidental pregnancies turned to abortion as a last resort to control fertility, the share of abortions compared with the share of actual births in total pregnancies may provide information on the trend of fertility demand and the use of contraceptives. Since abortions had already become widespread by the middle of the 1950s, subsequent changes in the share of abortions would reflect, to a large extent, an increased use of contraceptives. Table 4 summarizes trends and differentials in the rate of pregnancy and in the shares of abortions and births in pregnancies after 1955. There was a general increase of the share of births and a decrease of the share of abortions in total pregnancies. For Japan as a whole, the pregnancy rate among fertile women declined at an average 5-year rate of 14 percent from 1955 to 1965. The rate of decline was greater in the rural regions (21 percent) than in the industrial regions (6 percent). Indeed, by 1960 the pregnancy rate in rural regions had dropped below that in industrial regions. During the 10-year period, the rate of increase in the share of births and the rate of decrease in the share of abortions were both greater in industrial than in rural regions, suggesting that "unwanted" pregnancies declined more rapidly in industrial areas.

What can one infer from these regional differences? Suppose that all these differences are attributable to the differential spread of contraceptive methods (i.e., differential reduction in costs of control). Then the implicit assumption would be either that there was no change in demand for fertility in industrial and rural regions, or that the decline in demand for fertility did not vary systematically between the two types of regions. The slower rate of increase in the share of births and the slower rate of decrease in the share of abortions in rural regions would then presumably be attributable mostly to a slower spread of contraceptive measures in these regions. The more rapid decline of the pregnancy rate in rural regions, however, is the opposite of what one would expect if contraceptive measure did spread more slowly in these regions. Therefore, a more plausible interpretation of these differences would rely on a combination of differential change in fertility demand and differential spread of contraceptive knowledge. One interpretation would be that fertility demand declined more rapidly in rural than in industrial regions, resulting in a more rapid decline of the pregnancy rate, but that the spread of contraceptive knowledge was not rapid enough in rural regions to diminish rapidly the use of abortions as a last resort to control fertility.

Although the changing age composition of females precludes a firm judgment about the validity of the above interpretation,[17] this interpretation is supported by a comparison of the 1955–60 and 1960–65 periods. The pregnancy rate dropped more rapidly during 1955–60 than it did during 1960–65 in both regions. If this was attributable entirely to the spread of contraceptive measures, one would also expect to observe more rapid changes in both the share of births and the share of abortions in the earlier period. Indeed, given the early 1950s' reforms regarding the use of contraceptives, this expectation would appear to be quite plausible, but the course of events was just the opposite as both shares changed more rapidly in the later period (table 4). Again, a more plausible interpretation would be that demand for fertility continued to decline in both periods; that the spread of contraceptives increasingly facilitated effective

[17] The industrial prefectures experienced a slight increase and the rural prefectures a rather large decrease in the proportion of women of childbearing age (table 4). These changes in age composition undoubtedly explain in part the more rapid decline in the pregnancy rate in the rural than in the industrial prefectures.

TABLE 5
DIFFUSION OF CONTRACEPTIVE USE BY EDUCATION LEVEL
(PERCENTAGE OF COUPLES USING CONTRACEPTIVE DEVICES)

	1950	1952	1955	1957	1959
All.................	19.5	26.3	33.6	39.2	42.5
Husband's education:					
<9	14.2	18.2	28.2	33.4	37.6
10–12	25.4	37.0	37.7	46.5	43.9
13+	37.3	47.0	48.8	52.5	54.0
Range.............	23.1	28.8	20.6	19.1	16.4
(MAD/mean)	30.31	31.03	18.39	16.25	13.06
Wife's education:					
<9	13.0	20.1	28.2	33.3	35.0
10–12	32.4	38.7	46.1	48.1	51.6
13+	36.0	59.1	47.8	53.2	51.9
Range.............	23.0	29.0	19.6	19.9	16.9
(MAD/mean)	34.75	33.59	20.47	17.16	16.09

SOURCE.—Japan Ministry of Health and Welfare (1959).
NOTE.—Range is the difference between the largest and the smallest values. The MAD is the mean absolute deviation. In all years except 1959, the data refer to couples with wife under age 49. For 1959, wife's age is less than 50. The sample size varies from 3,500 couples in 1952 to 3,835 couples in 1959.

fertility control, thereby reducing unwanted pregnancies; and that the role of abortion continued to diminish in importance as a control measure.

The above evidence documents an increased use of contraceptive measures from 1955 to 1965. The relationship between parents' education and the use of contraceptives was discussed in Section III in the form of the cost-of-fertility-control hypothesis. If there was a period in which the use of birth control techniques was introduced or improved once and for all, then this hypothesis predicts that differences among education groups in the extent of use of birth control would widen at first, then narrow gradually. In Japan, a marked increase in the availability of abortions and birth control information occurred after 1948–52, so this period would appear to provide a reasonably proper setting for testing this hypothesis.

Table 5 presents the percentage of families within education class (husband's or wife's) that reported using some birth-control technique. The data are taken from surveys conducted in selected years to determine the attitudes of Japanese families of various socioeconomic classes toward contraceptive usage. In most education classes, the proportion of families using birth-control techniques increased over the years, presumably because costs of control declined and benefits increased. The differences across education groups in the extent of contraceptive usage as measured by either the range or the mean absolute deviation (relative to the mean) varied most in the early 1950s and persistently declined after 1952. One detects a slight increase in these measures of dispersion in 1952 with the

TABLE 6

COMPLETED FERTILITY BY EDUCATION LEVEL
(AVERAGE NUMBER OF CHILDREN EVER BORN PER COUPLE)

	1940	1952	1962	1967
All.........................	5.10	4.47	3.91	3.36
Husband's education:				
Low	5.19	4.62	4.05	3.45
Middle	4.81	3.62	3.60	3.27
High.....................	4.17	3.47	3.21	2.92
Wife's education:				
Low	5.19	4.57	4.04	3.48
Middle	4.39	3.58	3.47	3.14
High.....................	4.74	3.13	3.09	2.69

SOURCES.—Aoki and Nakano (1967, table 11) and Japan Ministry of Health and Welfare (1968, various tables).
NOTE.—For 1940, the figure is for couples married more than 21 years; for 1952, couples with wife age 45 or older; and for 1962 and 1967, couples married more than 20 years. Schooling definitions are: low, less than 10 years; middle, 10–12 years; and high, 13 years or more.

start of the campaign to disseminate birth-control information. These findings, though based on sparse information, agree with the predictions of the cost-of-fertility-control hypothesis.

Education and Fertility

The preceding discussion suggests that a decline in fertility demand and increased access to abortions and birth-control information played a joint role in producing the observed decrease in fertility in Japan. 1 now explore the relationship between fertility and parental education in the light of the hypotheses discussed in Section III.

According to the tastes and cost-of-fertility-control hypotheses, education of either parent is expected to be negatively associated with fertility. For Japan, education of the husband, because of his dominant family role, is likely to be a more significant explanatory variable than is the wife's education. The cost-of-time hypothesis predicts that the husband's education will be weakly, but positively, associated with fertility and that the wife's education will have a strong negative association with fertility.

Table 6 presents a measure of completed fertility by education groups for 1940, 1952, 1962, and 1967. The data are from Institute of Population Problems surveys. Education of either parent generally is negatively associated with fertility, in agreement with findings for other countries. These data also document the persistently declining trend in completed fertility at all levels of parental education, underscoring that education is by no means the only factor contributing to the decline in completed fertility over time.

TABLE 7
TRENDS IN COMPLETED FERTILITY STANDARDIZED BY EDUCATION

	SURVEY YEARS				MEAN ABSOLUTE DEVIATION
	1940	1952	1962	1967	
Actual.................	5.10	4.47	3.91	3.36	0.85
Standardized:					
Husband's education ...	4.99	4.21	3.84	3.36	0.75
Wife's education	4.93	4.22	3.84	3.36	0.72

SOURCE.—Calculated from table 6.
NOTE.—Standardized rates were calculated by using the 1967 distribution of couples by education of husband and wife. The mean absolute deviation was calculated as the average of absolute deviations of annual values from the 1967 value.

The negative association of fertility and the education of either parent may at first appear to agree with the prediction of the tastes and the cost-of-fertility-control hypotheses. Unfortunately, these data are not cross-classified by education of parents, so that one cannot discern the "pure" relationship between the fertility rate and the wife's and husband's education separately. Since the levels of husband's and wife's education are (positively) correlated, table 6 reflects the joint influence of both levels of education. Since the correlation is not perfect, one may still attempt (see table 7) to determine the relative importance of the education of either parent in "explaining" observed differences in fertility.

Table 7 presents the observed completed fertility in the 4 survey years and estimates of completed fertility obtained by using the 1967 distribution of educational attainment of husband and wife. That the general increase in the level of school attainment played a role in the decline in observed fertility is demonstrated by standardized rates which are consistently lower than actual rates in every year. The difference between standardized fertility rates using husband's and wife's education appears to narrow in later years. One reason for this tendency may be the increased correlation of husband's and wife's educational attainment accompanying a general increase in the dispersion and level of women's educational attainment. According to the mean absolute deviation of yearly values from the 1967 value (shown in table 7), the year-by-year differences in the fertility rate are decreased when yearly rates are standardized by education of either parent, but the reduction is somewhat greater when the distribution of the wife's rather than of the husband's education is used. Standardizing by the husband's education reduces the mean absolute deviation by 12.8 percent; standardizing by the wife's education decreases it by 15.3 percent. Thus, the trend in the distribution of the wife's education appears to have been more important than that of the husband's in the fertility trend.

Since the data for table 7 were not cross-classified by parents' education, one could not directly observe the "pure" effect of the education of either parent. To determine the relative magnitudes of the pure effects of parents' education on fertility, multiple regressions of the following form were estimated using cross-section data for 46 prefectures: $C = a + b_1(Ed_{HN}) + b_2(Ed_{HH}) + c_1(Ed_{WN}) + c_2(Ed_{WH}) + f$ (other variables) $+ u$, where C = fertility rate; Ed_{HN} = proportion of males who never attended school; Ed_{HH} = proportion of males who completed approximately 10 or more years of schooling; Ed_{WN} = the same as Ed_{HN}, for females; Ed_{WH} = the same as Ed_{HH}, for females; other variables = other standardizing variables discussed in the text; and u = disturbance term. Since time-series data on education and other variables are lacking for Japan, as for many other countries, the regression analysis was restricted to cross-section data. Regressions reported in table 8 use the average number of children ever born for selected age groups of women (completed fertility) as the dependent variable; in regressions in table 9 the live birth rate is the dependent variable. The Japanese census presents the distribution of educational attainment in four categories—none, elementary, middle, and high. Instead of estimating a single measure of educational attainment, such as the mean or median, I used two categories of the education variable for each parent. One advantage in using these measures is that the coefficients, that is, b_1 and b_2 for the husband and c_1 and c_2 for the wife, may reveal differential effects on fertility of a shift in the education distribution between the lower and the upper segments of the distribution. The expected signs of the regression coefficients according to the hypotheses discussed earlier are shown below:

Tastes and Cost of Fertility Control*		Cost of Time†	
$b_1 > 0$	$b_2 < 0$	$b_1 \leq 0$	$b_2 \geq 0$
$c_1 > 0$	$c_2 < 0$	$c_1 > 0$	$c_2 < 0$

* A weaker version of the above: $-b_1 + b_2 < 0$ and $-c_1 + c_2 < 0$.
† A weaker version of the above: $-b_1 + b_2 \geq 0$ and $-c_1 + c_2 < 0$.

Regressions of Completed Fertility

For the regressions of completed fertility reported in table 8, each observation was weighted by the square root of the number of age-specific ever-married women in each prefecture. In addition to the education variables, standardizing variables included in these regressions are the percentage of persons, age 15 and older, employed in agriculture, forestry, and fisheries, and the percentage of the population living in urban areas. These variables refer to 1960 and therefore do not reflect accurately the background in which the couples made fertility decisions. For these variables to have substantive meaning, one must assume that the majority of couples have lived in the prefecture they resided in in 1960 for most of their married lives and that the rankings of prefectures by these variables have not changed significantly over time. Unfortunately,

TABLE 8

REGRESSIONS OF COMPLETED FERTILITY, 46 PREFECTURES IN JAPAN:
1960 CENSUS (WEIGHTED REGRESSIONS)

REGRESSION NUMBER	AGE COHORT OF WIFE	% EMPLOYED		EDUCATION (MALE)		EDUCATION (FEMALE)		$\bar{R}^2$/S.E.
		Agriculture	Urban	None	High	None	High	
1............	(40–49) (n = 46)	0.006	−0.010	−0.179	−0.011	0.191	0.019	.938
		(0.71)	(−1.30)	(−1.07)	(−0.52)	(1.87)	(0.21)	.297
			$F(2, 39) = 5.64^*$	$F(2, 39) = 0.64$		$F(2, 39) = 2.05$		
2............	(50–59) (n = 46)	0.009	−0.009	−0.378*	0.006	0.213*	−0.099	.945
		(1.07)	(−1.16)	(−2.95)	(0.21)	(4.60)	(−0.84)	.325
			$F(2, 39) = 7.96^*$	$F(2, 39) = 5.03^*$		$F(2, 39) = 11.38^*$		
3............	Pooled (n = 92)	0.006	−0.011	−0.307*	−0.001	0.209*	−0.043	.941
		(1.16)	(−2.01)	(−3.17)	(−0.06)	(5.25)	(−0.62)	.608
		$F(2, 84) = 14.18^*$		$F(2, 84) = 5.18^*$		$F(2, 84) = 14.19^*$		
4............	Pooled	0.004	−0.012	−0.311*	−0.004	0.201*	−0.038	.942
		(0.51)	(−1.62)	(−3.15)	(−0.22)	(4.85)	(−0.55)	.612
		0.009	−0.010					
		(1.16)	(−1.17)					
		$F(4, 82) = 7.28^*$		$F(2, 82) = 5.03^*$		$F(2, 82) = 12.12^*$		

SOURCE.—Japan Prime Minister's Office (1960b, various volumes.)

NOTE.—Student's t-values are in parentheses. Intercepts are not reported. Regression 3 allows only the intercept to vary between the two cohorts, while 4 allows the regression coefficients of "agriculture" and "urban" as well as the intercept to vary between the two cohorts. The dependent variable (average number of children ever born) and the education variables are age-specific.

* Significant at 1%.

242

TABLE 9

REGRESSIONS OF LIVE BIRTHS PER 1,000 MARRIED WOMEN, AGES 15+
(46 PREFECTURES IN JAPAN: 1960 CENSUS)

Regression Number	Age Composition	% Employed		Education (Male)		Education (Female)		Log of Monthly Earnings		Labor-Force Participation Rate		$\bar{R}^2$/S.E.
		Agriculture	Urban	None	High	None	High	Male	Female	Male	Female	
1	2.765** (8.34)	0.189 (1.35) $F_{(2,38)} =$	−0.184 (−1.29) 3.29*	0.647 (0.17) $F_{(2,38)} =$	1.729 (1.27) 0.83	3.279* (2.34) $F_{(2,38)} =$	−6.322 (−1.67) 4.30*	...	...	...	...	0.739 5.411
2	2.339** (6.78)	0.148 (1.04) $F_{(2,36)} =$	−0.039 (−0.27) 0.82	−5.287 (−1.31) $F_{(2,36)} =$	−0.565 (−0.38) 0.84	5.008** (3.26) $F_{(2,36)} =$	−0.659 (−0.16) 6.05**	13.422 (1.28)	−9.624** (−2.74)	...	...	0.790 4.981
3	2.618** (6.12)	0.262 (1.35) $F_{(2,36)} =$	−0.138 (−0.88) 2.33	−0.855 (−0.20) $F_{(2,36)} =$	1.518 (1.03) 0.57	3.743* (2.35) $F_{(2,36)} =$	−6.111 (−1.58) 4.51*	...	...	−0.063 (−0.07)	−0.189 (−1.90)	0.744 5.502
4	2.325** (5.74)	0.158 (0.87) $F_{(2,34)} =$	0.021 (0.14) 0.40	−7.208 (−1.59) $F_{(2,34)} =$	−1.131 (−0.69) 1.30	5.430** (3.33) $F_{(2,34)} =$	−0.263 (−0.06) 6.20**	13.799 (1.23)	−10.045** (−2.87)	−0.635 (−0.72)	−0.062 (−0.54)	0.797 5.043

SOURCES.—Earnings: Japan Prime Minister's Office (1960a). Other variables: Japan Prime Minister's Office (1960b, various volumes).

NOTE.—Student's t-values are in parentheses. Age-composition variable is birth-rate-constant age distribution of women calculated by

$$\sum_{i=1}^{9} B_i W_{ij},$$

where B_i is the birth rate in the ith age class for all women in Japan, W_{ij} is the proportion of women in the ith age class in the jth prefecture (i = 15–19, 20–24, 25–29, 30–34, 35–39, 40–44, 45–49, 50–54, 55+). Monthly earnings are average monthly contract wages and salaries for household head (male) and average monthly contract wages and salaries for wife and other household members (female) in 1959; each is deflated by a regional price index. Labor-force participation rates are percentages of populations ages 15+ in the labor force in 1960.

* $p < .05$.
** $p < .01$.

243

neither income nor earnings is held constant in these regressions for lack of data pertaining to these age groups.

Regressions 1 and 2 were run for married women, ages 40–49 and 50–59, respectively. No coefficient in regression 1 is significant. The ambiguous result obtained for this cohort may be partly because the majority of these women were married during World War II times. Uncertainty about the future and participation by males in war activities may have distorted family-size decision making. The sizes of the regression coefficients for the education variables satisfy the weaker prediction of the cost-of-time hypothesis, however. For regression 2, the results are less ambiguous. Judging from the t-values, both Ed_{HN} and Ed_{WN} are significant at the 1 percent level, and the F-values for the education variables indicate that both the husband's and the wife's education are statistically significant at better than 1 percent. Both husband's and wife's education obtain regression coefficients that are largely consistent with the cost-of-time hypothesis.

To determine if the fertility relationships for the two groups of married women were different, I tested three null hypotheses using Chow's (1960) test for equality of two regressions. The three null hypotheses were that (1) the two relationships are completely the same; (2) the two relationships are the same except for the intercept; and (3) the two relationships are the same only with respect to the education variables. The first null hypothesis was rejected ($F_{7,78} = 10.93$), but the latter two were accepted. Based on these findings, I pooled the observations for the two groups and obtained regressions 3 and 4. Regression 3 assumes that only the intercept differs, while regression 4 assumes that everything except the education coefficients differs between the two groups. The results for pooled regressions 3 and 4 are quite similar. Both husband's and wife's education are statistically significant at better than 1 percent, with regression coefficients as expected from the cost-of-time hypothesis.

The results of these regressions clearly support the economic framework based on the cost-of-time hypothesis. According to the coefficients of the pooled regressions, male education variables higher by one standard deviation unit, holding female education constant, are associated with higher fertility by about 0.13 children. Holding male education constant, female education variables higher by one standard deviation are associated with about 0.30 fewer children. However, the relationship between education and fertility is apparently nonlinear. The distribution of either parent's educational attainment has a greater effect on average completed fertility when it shifts from no education to some education than when it shifts from some to high education.[18] While influences of

[18] Ben-Porath, above, reported a similar finding for Israel. In particular, the sharpest decline in fertility was observed between women with no education and women with some education.

education on fertility through tastes and the cost of fertility control are undoubtedly present, the dominant influences appear to be through income and prices.

These regressions refer to families which made fertility decisions before and during World War II. One would expect the decision-making process to have been more male-dominated in these than in postwar years. Yet female education is one of the most important variables in these regressions, a finding which strongly supports the relevance of the economic analysis of fertility. For this paper, regressions of completed fertility could not be run for families making fertility decisions during the postwar years, since the 1970 census was not available for all prefectures. As an alternative, I now turn to regressions of live birth rates in 1960.

Regressions of Live-Birth Rates

Multiple regressions of the number of live births in 1960 per thousand married women, age 15 or older, are reported in table 9. In addition to the percentage employed in agriculture and the percentage living in urban areas, these regressions hold constant the age composition of women and, in some cases, wage rates and labor-force participation rates. The age-composition variable is a weighted average of age-specific birth rates for Japan, the weights being the percentage of women in each age class in each prefecture. The percentage distributions of all women rather than of only married women were used because the latter may reflect endogenous decisions about the timing and duration of marriage. Both the female wage rate and the female labor-force participation rate are expected to affect fertility negatively. The male wage rate and the male labor-force participation rate would capture income effects and are expected, therefore, to obtain positive regression coefficients.

The results for the birth-rate regressions are largely consistent with the predictions of the cost-of-time hypothesis. An increase in male education, holding constant female education, increases, and an increase in female education, holding constant male education, decreases the birth rate. Female education is always more significant than male education. Female education tends to remain statistically significant with negative effects on fertility even after the female wage rate and labor-force participation rate, either separately or together, are introduced in the regressions. As expected, the female wage rate obtains negative and significant regression coefficients. The male wage rate obtains coefficients that are insignificant, though with expected signs. Neither the agricultural employment nor the urbanization variable has significant coefficients, perhaps because urban-rural differences in birth rates had largely disappeared by 1960 (see table 1).

Adding wage-rate variables to the regressions greatly reduces the effect of female education on the birth rate. Without the wage-rate variables in regressions 1 and 3, a uniform percentage shift upward in the female education distribution reduces the birth rate by about 10, for example, $-3.279 - 6.322 = -9.6$ for regression 1, but the magnitude drops to about five when the wage-rate variables are introduced in regressions 2 and 4. This finding is not surprising since the cost-of-time effects are likely to be captured jointly by female education and wage rates. The female wage rate also reduces the magnitude and significance of the female labor-force participation rate, as expected if decisions about fertility and labor supply are made simultaneously on the basis of the wage rate.[19] The nonlinearity usually observed in the effects of female education is observed only when wage rates are held constant. Otherwise, the results are ambiguous: the deterrent effect of female education appears greater when education increases from some to high than from none to some schooling, though the regression coefficients for "high" are never statistically significant.

These regressions suggest that area differences in the birth rate reflect differences in the female variables more than in the male variables. For example, according to regression 2, increasing all the male variables by one standard deviation unit, holding constant other variables, increases births per thousand married women by about three, but similar increases in female variables decrease the birth rate by 10. Calculations for regression 4 show the effect of male variables to be $+1.2$ and the effect of female variables to be -10.9.

V. Summary and Agenda

Increased access to abortions in Japan undoubtedly contributed to the post–World War II acceleration of that country's decline in fertility. But I conclude that fertility would still have declined at a more rapid rate than in the prewar period, which had been characterized by a mild and rather monotonic decline, if abortion had not been legalized. Therefore,

---

[19] A rise in the female wage rate, other things being equal, increases the attractiveness of labor-force participation relative to home production, including child rearing. Therefore, increased female wage rates not only directly reduce fertility demand but also increase labor-force participation, which in turn indirectly reduces fertility still more. Moreover, the direction of causation may also run from higher birth rates in an area to lower female labor-force participation there. To allow for such simultaneity, regressions 3 and 4 were also estimated by two-stage least squares, treating female labor-force participation as endogenous. However, these estimates did not substantially differ from the ordinary least-squares estimates. The labor-force participation regressions seem to have been plagued by multicollinearity. Although the regressions were statistically significant, judging by the F-values, with coefficients of determination above 0.70, they did not successfully disentangle the effects of the exogenous variables.

dissemination of contraceptive information and/or an accelerated decline in the demand for fertility must also have contributed to the trend.

Cross-section analyses of 1960 data reveal that the economic theory of fertility, with its emphasis on the effects of female education and earning power on fertility demand, provides a useful framework for analyzing fertility differentials in Japan. In particular, regressions of completed fertility and live birth rates in 1960 show that female education and earnings affect fertility negatively and are the most significant variables in the regressions. Male education and earnings tend to have positive but less significant effects. On the basis of only sociological, demographic, or taste considerations, one would not necessarily expect to find female education more important than male education in explaining fertility differentials. Indeed, in Japan, because of the male's generally dominant role in household decisions, one would have expected to find male education to be at least as relevant as female education, if not more so, in explaining fertility differences.

How useful are these results in interpreting the fertility trends in Japan? A tentative answer can be obtained from the regressions in table 9. Assuming that the parameter estimates remain stable over time and using the observed magnitudes of change between 1950 and 1960 for all the explanatory variables except for the age-composition variable, my results predict the decline of births per thousand married women to be only 4 percent at the mean according to regression 2, and 3 percent according to regression 4. The actual decline between 1950 and 1960 was about 42 percent, of which one would hope to explain about half if legalization of abortion explains another half. For the period 1960–70, both regressions predict a decline, while in fact births per thousand married women increased somewhat. On the basis of these results, one may be inclined to doubt the usefulness of cross-section regressions in interpreting the trend.[20]

However, since the regression models and the economic hypotheses underlying them pertain to long-run adjustments, one would expect from these regressions better predictions of longer-term changes in fertility. It is possible that the sharp decline of fertility during the 1950s and the subsequent leveling off in the 1960s represent swings around a longer-term trend that has persisted since 1920.[21] If so, a more appropriate comparison of actual and predicted declines might be made between 1950 and 1970. The predicted decline for this period was 19 percent according to regression 2 and 15 percent according to regression 4. The actual decline was about 30 percent. These regressions appear, therefore, to be more helpful in providing an interpretation of the longer-term fertility

[20] T. Paul Schultz in his study of Taiwan, below, discusses problems in the interpretation of time series from cross-section estimates of parameters. Here I ignore the kinds of problems he raised.

[21] A similar observation is made by Okazaki (1970, p. 26).

TABLE 10

A Comparison of Trends in Fertility and Economic Variables: 1950–69
(Japan and United States)

	1950	1960	1969	1950–60 (%)	1960–69 (%)	1950–69 (%)
				Rates of Change		
Crude birth rate:						
Japan	28.1	17.2	17.9*	−38.8	4.1	−36.3
U.S. (white)	23.5†	23.2‡	16.6	−1.3	−28.5	−29.4
Total fertility rate:						
Japan	3.63	1.99	2.10§	−45.2	1.05	−44.6
U.S. (white)	3.05†	3.56‡	2.37‖	16.7	−33.4	−22.3
Real GNP per capita: (1950=100)						
Japan	100	247.4	529.3	147.4	114.0	429.3
U.S.	100	115.2	152.7	15.2	32.5	52.7
Real wage (1950=100):						
Japan	100	170.2	253.9	70.2	49.2	153.9
U.S.	100	136.2	177.3	36.2	30.2	77.3
Percentage employed in agriculture:						
Japan	48.7	30.0	17.8	−38.4	−40.7	−63.4
U.S.	12.1	8.3	4.6	−31.4	−44.6	−62.0
Percentage female in non-agricultural employment:						
Japan	29.0	35.1	36.6	21.0	4.3	26.2
U.S.	31.3	34.6	38.3	10.5	10.7	22.4

Sources.—U.S. data: U.S. Bureau of the Census, *Statistical Abstract of the United States* (various issues) and U.S. Department of Health, Education, and Welfare (1968*a*); Japanese data: Japan Prime Minister's Office, *Statistical Yearbook of Japan* (various annual issues) and Mainichi Newspaper Company (1970).
  * Average between 1965 and 1970.
  † Average between 1949 and 1951.
  ‡ Average between 1957 and 1960.
  § Average between 1965 and 1968.
  ‖ For 1968.

decline in terms of price and income variables, but they are not likely to facilitate understanding of the shorter-term movements by which the decline may actually occur.

In table 10 some of the salient features of the United States and Japanese experiences during the postwar years are compared. If the economic framework for fertility analysis has general validity, it would predict more rapid fertility changes for countries experiencing more rapid changes in their economies. Clearly, both the economic variables examined and fertility rates changed more rapidly in Japan than in the United States during 1950–69. A similar point is observed if one confines the comparison to the periods in which fertility declined: 1950–60 for Japan and 1960–69 for the United States.

Much more work is needed before we fully understand the reasons for the possible acceleration in the decline of fertility demand in Japan in the 1950s and the leveling off in the 1960s. A promising area for investigation is the interaction of the demands for quality and quantity of children in Japan. There may have been an accelerated substitution of quality for quantity during the postwar years because of income effects.

Also, the prospect of future economic growth may have raised the expected return to education and rising family income increasingly facilitated the financing of children's education beyond the level required by law. It is noteworthy that the enrollment rate in kindergarten (which is not compulsory) increased more sharply between 1950 and 1960 (by 95 percent per 5 years) than between 1960 and 1965 (by 58 percent). Also, the enrollment rate in senior high school (not compulsory) rose more rapidly between 1950 and 1960 (by 26 percent per 5 years) than between 1960 and 1965 (by 20 percent). The model may also be extended to include such interrelated aspects of behavior as marriage and female labor-force participation. Such a model may be estimated using more disaggregated data, say by age, than I use here. The rapid decline in Japanese fertility from 1950 to 1960 coincided with an increase in the labor-force participation of females and a decrease in the proportion of married women among women of childbearing age. For example, among females, ages 20 to 39, living in urban areas, the labor-force participation rate increased from 38 percent in 1950 to 43 percent in 1960, and the proportion ever married decreased from 75 to 70 percent. The most dramatic changes occurred for females, ages 20 to 24, among whom the proportion ever married dropped from 43 percent in 1950 to 31 percent in 1960 but showed no appreciable change in the 1960s. The pace of all these developments appears synchronous with the fertility history of postwar Japan, and possible relationships among them deserve rigorous analysis.

Finally, it would greatly enhance the scope and accuracy of analysis to have micro, or household, data for Japan on such related characteristics as fertility; wage rates and family wealth, age, and work experience; parents' and children's education; and contraceptive use. Ideally, such data would be collected longitudinally for a given set of families and made available to interested researchers in raw rather than summarized form.

Comment

Gary R. Saxonhouse

University of Michigan

At a conference of distinguished specialists on human capital theory my comparative (absolute?) advantage is in the study of the Japanese economy. Much the same can be said for Hashimoto's paper. No attempts at any significant new departures in human capital theory or in the testing of such theory are made in this paper. Rather, one finds here an extension of a now-familiar approach to Japanese data with now-familiar results.[1] This is a study that can stand alongside the Israel and Taiwan studies by Ben-Porath and T. Paul Schultz, respectively. Hashimoto's paper is another line, and an admirably executed line at that, in T. Paul Schultz's table A1 below.

Hashimoto's ultimate concern is in explaining the acceleration in the 1950s of the long-term decline in Japanese fertility and the subsequent bottoming out of this decline in the 1960s. The achievements of this particular paper are more modest. An attempt is made to challenge what Hashimoto finds is a simplistic overemphasis on the diffusion of abortion and contraceptive practice after 1948 (i.e., a downward shift in the supply of birth-control schedules). As an alternative, Hashimoto stresses outward shifts of the demand schedule for birth control resulting from the increasing cost of female time in postwar Japan.[2]

---

[1] Hashimoto states that, previous to this paper, there had been but one other economic study of fertility in Japan. This is a bit unfair. Only if the literature is restricted to that in English and one assumes the economic study of fertility starts with Becker is this statement true. Unlike the United States, in Japan throughout the twentieth century demographic study remained within the province of economists. For a sample of Japanese work, see Tachi and Arao (1935) and Tachi (1946).

[2] My reading of the Japanese literature suggests that most Japanese demographers would applaud Hashimoto's stress on changes in both the demand and supply schedules. Some Japanese demographers do appear to part company with Hashimoto when it comes to a discussion of the determinants of the demand-schedule shifts. There is a Japanese emphasis on the role of wealth. Relative to the period prior to World War II, Japan of the early 1950s is seen as a poor country.

I am much in sympathy with Hashimoto's hypotheses. There is considerable evidence to suggest that control of fertility within marriage was widespread long before 1948, and I do find stress on the cost of female time provocative.[3] At the same time, I do not think Hashimoto's various analyses are altogether persuasive. For example, if instead of using maximum crude birth rates and maximum general-fertility rates, maximum total-fertility rates for 1950 and 1960 are calculated, it appears that the practice of abortion might very well have tripled the rate of fertility decline.[4] The decline in the estimated maximum total-fertility rate between 1950 and 1960 is 16.8 percent. This is only a modest acceleration of the 12.6 percent rate of decline exhibited in the actual fertility rates between 1930 and 1940. An acceleration of this magnitude might easily be explained by the diffusion of modern contraceptive techniques during the 1950s. This mild acceleration might also be viewed as a reaction to the much higher-than-trend total-fertility rates between 1940 and 1950. Thus, it would appear that if Hashimoto wishes to stress the role of demand factors in the acceleration of Japanese fertility decline, he more than likely cannot avoid an inquiry into the extent to which legal abortions were substitutes for older forms of birth control.

Regardless of the magnitude of the acceleration remaining to be explained by some factor other than the legalization of abortion, I am not satisfied with Hashimoto's analysis of the spread of contraception. That the share of abortions in total births is high and rising in the rural regions of Japan in the presence of a sharply declining pregnancy rate can be taken as evidence that the spread of contraception is not sufficient to explain fertility changes unexplained by the legalization of abortion only if (1) abortion as a technique of birth control is already completely diffused, and (2) abortion is viewed as a technique of last resort.[5]

I doubt either of the above conditions held for Japan during the 1950s. Abortion diffused throughout Japan in much the same manner and only slightly in advance of modern contraception. At any point during that decade, for any age cohort, the better educated a couple and the larger the city in which a couple lived, the higher the probability they had experienced an abortion. Among couples who had never practiced contraception, the probability of an abortion experience was relatively low. Significantly, high rates of abortion were found among couples who had practiced contraception and for one reason or another discontinued

---

[3] For a discussion of the history of birth control in Japan, see Honjo (1941).

[4] The maximum total fertility rates in 1950 and 1960 are 4.16 and 3.46. I have calculated these rates with data taken from Japan Ministry of Health and Welfare (1967) and Aoki (1967).

[5] The industrial-rural dichotomy presented in Hashimoto's table 4 is based on a comparison of six urban prefectures with five rural ones. As an alternative, the share of induced abortions among pregnancies of Japanese women not living in cities of 50,000 or more (the rate typically regarded as the rural rate) can be examined. This rate rose throughout the 1950s, reaching a peak in 1961 (see Aoki [1967, p. 44]).

this practice.[6] I would conclude that abortion was not necessarily a birth-control technique of last resort and that the rising share of abortions in total pregnancies in rural areas during the 1950s might very well reflect a positive reaction to the diffusion of a new technique.[7]

While Hashimoto does not make manifest the need for a new demand variable to explain the movement of postwar Japanese fertility, the final section of his paper does stand on its own as a test of competing hypotheses in explaining regional differentials. The results reported in tables 8 and 9 tend to support Hashimoto's de-emphasis of the role of the cost of fertility control. In both sets of regressions, I have a particular problem with the education variables Hashimoto chooses to use as explanatory variables. The male education variables in the completed-fertility regressions are based on the assumption that Japanese women are marrying Japanese men of the same age. Actually, Japanese women of the age cohorts in question were marrying men who were, on the average, 4 to 5 years older than themselves.[8] The peculiarities of the Japanese enforcement of their compulsory-education legislation make it a matter of some importance whether a male reached school age before 1900 (as a substantial proportion of the husbands of the women in these cohorts did) or after 1905. There was considerable variability among prefectures in the degree of male compliance with the compulsory education laws before 1900. After 1905, compliance was almost complete among the prefectures.[9] The degree of compliance across prefectures is only weakly correlated between the two periods. Interestingly enough, noncompliance for males in the earlier period is rather strongly correlated with noncompliance for females in the later period.[10] It follows that if one is a believer in the cost-of-fertility hypothesis (and only if one is a believer in the cost-of-fertility hypothesis), it is possible to argue that the errors in the male education variable are imparting a positive bias to the estimate of the

---

[6] The surveys on which the above analysis is based were conducted and periodically published by the Mainichi Newspaper Company (1950); see also Taeuber (1958, p. 282).

[7] There is every reason to believe that the spread of contraceptive methods in rural Japan was rapid in the late 1950s. The aforementioned Mainichi surveys indicate a better-than-25-percent increase in contraceptive practice between 1955 and 1959. These same years saw family-planning expenditures by Koseisho (Ministry of Health and Welfare) at their real height. Also, survey evidence analyzed by Aoki (1967, p. 57) suggests that increases in contraceptive efficiency were also greatest during this period.

[8] Summary statistics on the average age at first marriage, by sexes, are available in the annual reports, *Descriptive Materials on Japanese Vital Statistics*, published by the Japan Prime Minister's Office (1917f).

[9] In 1900, the percentage of the male school-age population attending primary school or otherwise complying with the compulsory-education laws ranged across prefectures from 79.1 to 97.5 percent. By 1905 the degree of compliance varied from 94.7 to 99.5 percent. These statistics are from annual reports published by Japan Ministry of Education (1904f).

[10] Using the 1960 census data, the simple correlation coefficient between the prefectural pattern of males with no education, age cohorts 50–59 and 60–69, is .39. The simple correlation coefficient between the prefectural pattern of males with no education in the age cohort 60–69 and females with no education in the age cohort 50–59 is .83.

coefficient of the no-education variable for females and a negative bias to the estimate of the coefficient of the no-education variable for males. These biases could be quite substantial and might account for Hashimoto's interesting results.

Unlike the completed-fertility regressions, Hashimoto's regressions reported in table 9 deal entirely with postwar reproductive activities and specifically with 1960 live births. The education variables in these regressions refer to the entire (over age 15) prefectural population. Unfortunately, virtually the entire interprefectural variation in the proportion in the no-education variables relates to the experience of age cohorts that in 1960 were well beyond their reproductive years! I do not doubt that, inspired by Leibowitz's paper in this volume, work can be done on how a mother's education affects a daughter's fertility, but this is not the hypothesis in question.[11]

Also with respect to these same regressions, I am a bit puzzled by the use of the logarithm of earnings rather than arithmetic earnings. I suspect one gets a higher t-statistic on female wages when this form is used, but when using what should be thought of as grouped data, I am unsure of the theoretical justification.

In concluding my remarks, I would like to offer a suggestion for future research. Notwithstanding Hashimoto's very useful analysis, I do not find the postwar period to be the most interesting stretch of Japanese demographic history. While there are many instances of fertility decline in the context of rapid economic growth, the experience of Japan between 1875 and 1920 appears to be unique. There was rapid economic growth starting from a relatively high income base, a declining agricultural labor force, a revolution in female education coexisting with a high and, as recent research indicates, very likely a rising level of fertility.[12] Further, in view of the Japanese experience after 1920, I

---

[11] Nationwide, 82 percent of men with no education and 96 percent of women with no education came from the age groups 50 and older and 40 and older, respectively. The simple correlation by prefecture for never-educated men above age 50 and younger than age 50 is .25. The simple correlation by prefecture for never-educated women above and below age 40 is .21.

[12] The official statistics collected for Japan suggest rising fertility throughout most of this period. These statistics have been traditionally treated with considerable skepticism on account of underreporting in the earliest periods. Taeuber, in analyzing these statistics, suggests that fertility probably rose substantially during the first part of this period and subsequently declined slowly (see Taeuber [1958, pp. 52–54]). Estimates which allow for the traditional criticisms of the official statistics have been prepared by Okazaki (1965). Okazaki estimates that the Japanese population in 1875 was almost 2 million above the official statistics. More recently, Akasaka Keiko has provided another series of alternative estimates. Somewhat surprisingly, in view of the earlier criticisms, she finds that the official statistics overestimate population by 600,000 in 1875 and understate the rate of population growth at least through 1910. For Akasaka's estimates, see Hitotsubashi University Institute of Economic Research (1968). For an informative discussion of the alternative estimates, see Umemura (1969).

would submit that this episode constitutes a fascinating and important puzzle for those who would stress the role of economic factors in general, and the cost of time, in particular, in the explanation of fertility history.

Birth Rate Changes over Space and Time: A Study of Taiwan

I. Introduction

A number of recent empirical investigations have concluded that economic variables account for a statistically significant share of cross-sectional variation in aggregate and individual fertility. Though the models underlying these studies differ in terms of analytical complexion and econometric complexity, their empirical findings are nonetheless similar.[1] Theories of household behavior derived from generally accepted economic tenets alone, however, do not yield many refutable propositions with regard to fertility, unless additional constraints are imposed. The choice of a formulation to the economic theory of fertility may therefore have to rely more heavily on the weight of empirical evidence as to how this decision-making process is constrained than other fields of applied economics, where joint production is less essential and consumption and production are more readily dis-

The research underlying this paper was supported in part by a Rockefeller Foundation grant to study the economics of fertility determination and family behavior and is related to research supported by the Agency for International Development under contract csd-2355. Views expressed in this paper are mine and not those of any organization with which I am affiliated. I acknowledge the able research assistance of Kenneth Maurer, and the help and advice extended by persons too numerous to mention in both Taiwan and the United States. A first draft benefited from the comments of Yoram Ben-Porath, Jacob Mincer, T. W. Schultz, and Finis Welch, and my RAND colleagues, William Butz, Julie DaVanzo, Dennis De Tray, and Charles Phelps. In particular, I acknowledge the comments of James Tobin that helped to improve an earlier draft and correct an embarrassing error in computation. Only I am responsible for remaining deficiencies.

[1] A review of empirical findings presently available to me is provided in appendix tables A1 and A2, where in tabular form the sign and statistical significance of the regression coefficients estimated for each class of economic variable are reported. It is, of course, crucial for the interpretation of these summarized findings to also know, in addition to the nature of the data, what other variables were included in the regression equation, and, in simultaneous-equations estimates, the estimation techniques used and the structure of the rest of the system. Table A1 reviews studies of medium- and low-income countries; table A2 is confined to studies of the U.S. population.

tinguished. Most current evidence on these constraints derives from
analyses of single cross sections; change in reproductive behavior over time
is undoubtedly the dimension of fertility that economists have studied
least. It is, therefore, the focus of this paper.

Economic theories of fertility determination generally presuppose an
equilibrium relationship between permanent or lifetime conditions and
completed fertility, whereas empirical verification is often based on observations of either conditions prevailing sometime after the arrival of the last
child or current conditions in conjunction with an incomplete stock or rate
of addition to an unobserved stock of children. Moreover, unbiased
estimates of cause and effect relations are difficult to obtain from a single
cross section in which most economic and demographic aspects of the
household are jointly dependent on prior conditions that have also influenced fertility. Thus, little is known about the time required for reproductive behavior to adapt to unanticipated change in environmental constraints, for example, how parents react to policy measures that seek to
provide family-planning information and reduce the supply costs of modern
birth control. To cope intelligently with rapid rates of population growth
occurring in most low-income countries one needs an understanding of
precisely this process of behavioral adjustment to demographic and
economic change and the resulting disequilibrium that it introduces into
the family formation process.

The factors affecting the timing of births over a lifetime may differ fundamentally from those affecting completed fertility. In high-income countries, short-run changes in completed fertility are generally moderate in
comparison with changes in birth rates induced by variation in the timing of
births (Ryder 1969). In low-income countries where completed fertility is
falling rapidly but unevenly, changes in the timing of births seem of much
less consequence in accounting for changes in birth rates over time. Economic models of change in fertility over time, whose primary implications
relate to lifetime reproductive goals, may, therefore, be tested more accurately using data on birth rates if the data are drawn from this second
environment. The choice is made here to study a low-income country for
which fairly reliable demographic time series are available. To satisfy these
conditions, I have had to sacrifice detail of an economic nature and deal
with aggregate data when information on individuals would be preferable.

In this paper I investigate approaches to the interpretation of 6 years of
aggregate economic and demographic data for the populations of 361 small
administrative regions of Taiwan. My purpose is to obtain more information on the dynamic structure of a model of fertility variations, disequilibria, and changes that will make better sense of population problems
and policy options in low-income countries. Although not wholly unexpected, given the scarcity of analytical tools and the shortage of data
relevant to this task, few firm conclusions emerge.

The setting of Taiwan is sketched in Section II. In Section III I briefly review the implications of economics for reproductive behavior and specify a model within the data constraints for Taiwan that can test several of these implications. Cross-sectional estimates of this model are reported in Section IV, and several approaches for combining time series and cross sections are explored in Section V to obtain a more satisfactory picture of the time dimension of the responsiveness of birth rates in Taiwan to changing economic, demographic, and policy constraints.

II. The Setting: Taiwan, 1950–70

To aid in interpreting the subsequent econometric results, I shall outline some major features of Taiwan's recent past. Taiwan's postwar economic progress is notable by any standards: real national income doubled from 1951 to 1961 and doubled again by 1968; growth in per capita income deflated by consumer prices has annually averaged about 5 percent since 1962; the share of employment in agriculture fell from 57 percent of the male labor force in 1951 to 36 percent by 1967, while the number of persons engaged in agriculture remained practically constant. Until 1961 the number of women employed in agriculture also remained virtually constant, and little growth in employment for women occurred elsewhere in the economy. From 1961 to 1967, however, the number of women in agriculture decreased by 30 percent, and nonagricultural employment of women increased about 130 percent. In terms of the opportunity value of a woman's time in child rearing, almost three-fourths of the women in the agricultural labor force in 1967 were classified as engaged in housekeeping activities, which one might surmise need not have curtailed their family commitments. The shift in the allocation of women's time out of the home, therefore, coincides with the acceleration in the decline in crude birth rates after 1961 (see fig. 1).

Taiwan's population reached 13 million in 1966 and has grown at the rapid rate of about 3 percent per year for most of the postwar period (see fig. 1). Registered crude death rates declined after the war from 18.2 per 1,000 in 1947 to 11.5 by 1950, and decreased to 5.0 as the population became increasingly concentrated in low-mortality age groups. Registered crude birth rates increased after the postwar readjustment period, peaking in 1951 at 50.0 per 1,000; only after 1956 did a secular downward trend emerge clearly. This significant turning point is seen more clearly in figure 2, where the age composition of the population is held constant by examining birth rates for women of specific age groups. The decline in birth rates did not occur uniformly across age groups; it is accentuated among women over 29 years of age but not yet substantial among women less than 30.

According to the 1967 census, women 35 years of age or older averaged between five and six live births. For women aged 35–39, 93 percent of these

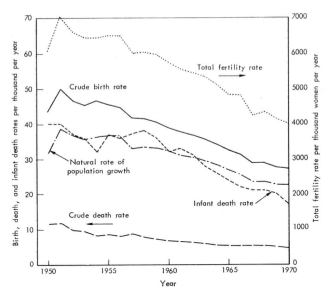

FIG. 1.—Annual registered vital statistics: Taiwan 1950–70 (source: Taiwan Dept. of Civil Affairs 1970, tables 1, 9, 10, and 17).

children were living, whereas only 80 percent of the children of women 20 years older were living. This difference in child-survival rates is in small part due to the greater age to which the older women's children have

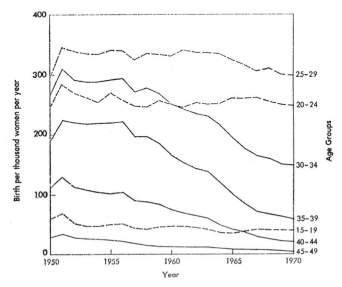

FIG. 2.—Age-specific birth rates: Taiwan (source: Taiwan Dept. of Civil Affairs 1970).

survived. More important, it is related to the decline in child mortality that has taken place in Taiwan and in most low-income countries during the last 20–40 years.

A large-scale family-planning program was launched on an experimental basis in Taichung City in 1963 (Freedman and Takeshita 1969) and in the following year in the majority of Taiwan's communities. Two types of fieldworkers were trained and coordinated to spread information about family planning and to promote the subsidized adoption of related services. The assignment of these workers across regions and over time is not obviously related to readily distinguished socioeconomic features of these regions or their resident populations.

III. Economic Hypotheses

According to the theory of consumer choice, quantity of a good demanded is constrained by available resources and relative prices, with associated "income" and "substitution" effects. When this framework is used to study factors influencing parent demand for children, however, well-known difficulties arise. First, parametrically given prices are not readily isolated or satisfactorily measured. Second, although additions to household resources relax the family's budget constraint, they also tend to change relative prices, depending upon their source, with offsetting effects on the demand for children (Schultz 1969). There are few instances, therefore, where either pure price or income effects can be identified and estimated from existing data.

A closely related problem stems from the interrelated nature of life-cycle choices, many of which bear upon reproductive behavior (Nerlove and Schultz 1970). Proxies that might at first appear useful as measures of the opportunity cost of a child, such as years of schooling completed by the child, must be treated as endogenous variables in a broader system of behavioral relationships. This household decision-making system also interacts with such public sector choices as the allocation of educational and family-planning expenditures. Simultaneous-equations estimation techniques are required to obtain asymptotically unbiased estimates of interactions among these classes of behavior; the consistency of ordinary least-squares estimates of a "demand" equation for fertility depends critically on the predetermined nature of all explanatory variables. Neither theory nor data are now adequate to identify and estimate the underlying structural demand and supply equations for both the number and the resource intensity of children.

Nonetheless, under a variety of assumptions explored in several papers in this volume, a reduced-form "demand" equation can be expressed for numbers of children that contains explanatory variables assumed to be outside of parents' control.[2] Since the implications of these alternative models do not differ with respect to the variables observed for Taiwan, no test of the adequacies of their underlying assumptions can be proposed. At least one dimension of public policy, however, will be explored as it might affect fertility, namely, the allocation of field personnel to family-planning activities.

Empirical Formulation of the Model for Taiwan

Only the rudiments of a formal model of fertility determination can be tested against Taiwan data. The object is to specify a relation between the birth rate parents want and the price, income, and information constraints that are not themselves determined simultaneously with, or subsequently by, the objective number of births. A single reduced-form equation is therefore analyzed here: that between birth rate in year t, b_t, and the lagged values of (1) the reciprocal of the child-survival rate, D (*return* and price effects); (2) the proportion of the male labor force employed in agriculture, A (relative *price* effects); (3) male school attainment, E^m (*income*, price, and information effects); (4) female school attainment, E^f (*price*, income, and information effects); and (5) two classes of family-planning fieldworkers employed by the health and family-planning programs, H and F (*information* and price effects). These variables and the time lags τ and τ' are defined more precisely in table 1, where data sources are given. The correlations among the variables and their means and standard deviations are shown in table 2. Unfortunately, none of the explanatory variables is available on an age-specific basis. Assuming the relation is approximately linear,[3] the equation to be estimated is of the following form:

$$
\begin{aligned}
b_t = {}& \alpha_0 + \alpha_1 D_{t-\tau} + \alpha_2 A_{t-\tau} \\
& + \alpha_3 E_{t-\tau}{}^m + \alpha_4 E_{t-\tau}{}^f \\
& + \alpha_5 H_{t-\tau'} + \alpha_6 F_{t-\tau'} + e_t.
\end{aligned} \tag{1}
$$

The expected signs and relative magnitudes of the parameters, α's, and the choice of lags are discussed below. The disturbance term, e_t, when the

[2] More formally, ordinary least-squares estimates of the parameters to the equation are asymptotically unbiased only when all explanatory variables are predetermined. Lagged values of endogenous variables cannot, in general, be treated as independent of the disturbances in relationships accounting for the same or related forms of current behavior. Omitted variables pertaining to both the "quality" demand equation and the "quality" and "quantity" supply equations must also be assumed uncorrelated with observed explanatory variables considered in the "quantity" demand equation.

[3] Alternative nonlinear formulations of similar models are discussed and estimated for the Taiwan data elsewhere (Schultz 1971a). Cross-sectional findings do not change substantially nor do the tests of hypotheses depend on which of these functional specifications of the model is adopted.

TABLE 1

DEFINITIONS OF VARIABLES FOR 361 ADMINISTRATIVE REGIONS OF TAIWAN

b_t = The number of births per thousand women of specific age group in year t.

D_t = The reciprocal of the probability of survival from birth to age 15 estimated from age-specific death rates in year t.

A_t = The proportion of the male labor force employed in the agricultural sector in year t.

E_t^m = The proportion of men 12 years and over with at least a primary school certificate in year t.

E_t^f = The proportion of women 12 years and over with at least a primary school certificate in year t.

H_t = Number of man-months of VHEN (Village Health Education Nurse) employed by the family-planning program per thousand women aged 15–49 from 1964 to year t.

F_t = Number of man-months of PPHW (Pre-Pregnancy Health Workers) employed by the family-planning program per thousand women aged 15–49 from 1964 to year t.

e_t = Independently, normally distributed random disturbance until assumed to be otherwise in Section V.

τ = Combined behavioral and biological lag between the change in an environmental constraint on desired fertility and the change in birth rates.

τ' = Biological lag between change in birth control practice and birth rate.

α's = Parameters of the model to be estimated.

SOURCES.—Taiwan Department of Civil Affairs, *The Taiwan Demographic Factbook*, various annual issues since 1961; Taiwan Population Studies Center, *The Demographic Reference: Taiwan*, various years since 1956; and Taiwan Provincial Institute of Family Planning, *Family Planning Reference Book*, vol. 1, 1969.

observations are appropriately weighted is assumed to be normally distributed with zero mean, constant variance, and uncorrelated with the explanatory variables.

The dependent variable in the fertility equations estimated in the next section is birth rates for an age group of women for the years 1964–69. This is not the dimension of fertility underlying the theoretical basis for equation (1), namely the number of children born to an individual women. Formally, several unverified assumptions are required to assure that the aggregate flow of births across groups of women of different ages responds in the same way to differences in the determinants of fertility as does the stock of children-ever-born across individual women. Yet if one is not to wait decades until today's younger parents in Taiwan have completed their childbearing years in order to estimate the effects of changing environmental constraints on their completed fertility, research must in the interim analyze current birth rates for evidence of the contribution of specific dimensions of economic change and population policies. Thus the closest approximation to the economically prescribed dependent variable is the birth rate among women at least 30 years of age. Because these women are frequently completing the formation of their families, they are pri-

TABLE 2

SIMPLE CORRELATIONS AMONG VARIABLES*

					VARIABLE DIFFERENCES 1969-64									
	Total Fertility Rate† (1)	Age-Specific Birth Rates 15-19 (2)	25-24 (3)	25-29 (4)	30-34 (5)	35-39 (6)	40-44 (7)	45-49 (8)	Child-Death Adjustment (Ratio) (9)	Agricultural Composition (Proportion) (10)	Male Education (Proportion) (11)	Female Education (Proportion) (12)	VHEN (13)	PPHW (14)
VARIABLE LEVELS														
1966:														
(1)	...	.262	.214	.393	.611	.489	.351	.229	.084	−.037	−.041	−.095	−.076	−.003
(2)	.374	...	.427	−.131	−.149	−.159	−.119	−.017	−.074	−.064	.056	.114	.096	.026
(3)	.594	.465	...	.123	−.366	−.464	−.497	−.409	−.083	−.097	.169	.208	.084	.173
(4)	.699	−.195	.317	...	.050	−.155	−.216	−.268	−.047	.033	.108	−.004	−.028	−.006
(5)	.851	.127	.184	.594	...	.548	.403	.353	.098	.026	−.176	−.234	−.081	−.059
(6)	.890	.318	.295	.506	.855	...	.581	.369	.192	.028	−.205	−.212	−.154	−.124
(7)	.836	.345	.265	.424	.801	.878	...	.566	.151	.000	−.119	−.111	−.090	−.135
(8)	.416	.146	−.026	.120	.459	.518	.545	...	.054	−.020	−.073	−.147	−.068	.037
(9)	.583	.307	.366	.317	.493	.527	.553	.187	...	−.009	−.090	−.019	.023	−.087
(10)	.567	−.077	.384	.646	.429	.433	.397	.138	.379	...	−.118	−.128	−.122	−.058
(11)	−.735	−.123	−.555	−.646	−.579	−.582	−.498	−.198	−.404	−.659	...	.352	.138	.092
(12)	−.643	.063	−.507	−.719	−.507	−.451	−.362	−.078	−.321	−.673	.909	...	.079	.069
(13)	.046	−.075	.053	.158	.008	.004	−.011	−.126	.063	.215	−.120	−.173	...	−.270
(14)	−.113	.017	.160	.066	−.012	.000	−.003	.009	.070	.181	−.113	−.158	−.299	...
Mean	4,835.0	40.7	275.	328.	189.	90.8	37.7	5.89	1.06	.440	.694	.484	.256	1.36
Standard deviation ..	806.0	21.2	45.9	45.9	44.6	38.7	22.4	6.84	0.0242	0.291	0.104	0.146	0.330	1.38
1969-64 differences:														
Mean	−948.0	2.31	−8.11	−35.0	−61.6	−55.0	−28.3	−3.92	−0.0296	−0.0166	0.0628	0.0884	0.574	4.72
Standard deviation ..	366.0	17.2	45.0	35.9	33.0	31.1	20.7	10.3	0.0411	0.0248	0.0460	0.0555	0.601	2.66

NOTE.—Variable levels in 1966 appear below the diagonal; variable differences, 1969-64, appear above it.

* Weighted by the number of women between the ages of 15 and 49 in each observed region.

† The total fertility rate (which is five [the age interval] times the sum of the age-specific birth rates) represents a cross-sectional proxy for completed fertility expected per thousand women surviving to age 50. It is not a longitudinal measure of completed fertility for any specific group of women, but rather an expected measure of fertility that would occur if current age-specific birth rates persisted for all childbearing years of a surviving cohort.

marily engaged in the marginal childbearing decisions for which the economic model is relevant.

Child mortality appears to increase the cost of rearing a child to maturity. If we can assume that parents feel themselves better off, all things considered, the longer their child survives (O'Hara 1972), an overall decline in mortality should make childbearing more attractive. But if the marginal return from having additional surviving children diminishes and becomes negative for small increases in the size of surviving family, the relation between child mortality and fertility will embody two partially offsetting price changes—a decline in the cost of rearing a surviving child and a decline in the marginal return. Economics does not tell us the magnitude of the net effect or even its sign. The observed behavior of parents will provide information on the relative weight parents attach to the costs of rearing a child who dies compared with the elasticity of their demand for surviving children. Highly inelastic demand for surviving offspring implies that there should exist in equilibrium a positive association between birth rates and anticipated or experienced child-death rates (or the reciprocal of survival rates). Changes in this child-death adjustment ratio would also affect the returns to human capital investments in a child, increasing the probability that a positive association will exist between child-death and birth rates (Schultz 1971c; O'Hara 1972).

Agricultural composition of the male labor force is intended to capture relative price effects. The cost of rearing any specific number of children might be lower in rural than in urban areas (the prices of food and housing might be lower), while, in traditional agriculture, the rate of return to schooling children may be depressed relative to the return anticipated by parents in the more dynamic urban sectors of the economy. This disparity in the returns to education could arise from higher direct and opportunity costs of obtaining schooling for the dispersed farm population, or from lesser productivity gains for the better-educated in agricultural in comparison with nonagricultural activities. The reduced-form equation discussed here cannot attribute a partial association between economic sector and fertility to any particular class of differential input prices or to differential returns to schooling, but both sets of relative prices might account for higher fertility in rural regions of many low-income countries when other demographic and economic factors were held constant. However, it need not follow that marriage and childbearing would occur earlier in the agricultural sector, for quite to the contrary, the scarcity of land and capital has often been attributed a role in delaying marriage in the rural sector when the urban sector is prospering.

The value of the time of each spouse is assumed to be equalized at the margin between market and nonmarket work. This would be the case if each spouse is engaged in both market and nonmarket activity, or if the wife specializes entirely in nonmarket production she is assumed to produce within the household some perfect substitutes for market goods.[4] I will assume, in other words, that the implications of "corner solutions" considered by Gronau (1973) and Willis (1971) are not here an important factor in accounting for the household allocation of time between market and nonmarket activities.

The measure of schooling considered here approximates the median accomplishments of the adult population. If this variable adequately reflects the lifetime value of husband and wife time in market and nonmarket activities,[5] plausible assumptions regarding the relative value of sex-specific

---

[4] This may sound like a strong assumption, but I think it is more realistic than the converse that stresses "corner solutions" to the household time-allocation problem in which the woman allocates all of her time to nonmarket work that has no meaningful market substitute. First, in a cross section only a proportion of the population is in the paid labor force at any one time. Over a lifetime a much larger fraction would have entered the labor force, equalizing market and nonmarket opportunities at various points in their life cycles. Second, a wide range of nonmarket production directly substitutes for market goods, services, and labor; unpaid family labor can at times be replaced by hired labor; much of household production is virtually interchangeable with goods and services that could be purchased from or bartered for in the market. I conjecture that over a woman's lifetime, even if she is a most productive homemaker situated in a remote labor market that does not offer her an attractively paying job, she will nonetheless allocate her time according to the relative prices of market goods and services she can replace by home-produced ones. If her household develops a comparative advantage in the production of some of these fringe "market" goods and services, this may induce her to become a petty trader or participate in a "home industry," as occurs frequently throughout much of Africa and Southeast Asia. A continuum of market and nonmarket activity exists, and the overlap is sufficient to equilibrate market and nonmarket productivity in most instances. My hunch is that the "corner solution" may be of interest in some highly developed societies, where the comparative advantage of home production is being eroded except in final consumption activities, and perhaps in the Muslim Middle East where very few employment options are open to the woman outside of the home.

[5] Observed wages, however, may differ from the opportunity cost of time because the market wage rate is net of investment in on-the-job training (Mincer 1962a); because depreciation in specific types of human capital may be modified by shifting time between market and nonmarket activities (Michael and Lazear 1971); and because the market wage may include a premium for the utility (or disutility) of market work. For example, the wife who allocates her time to nonmarket activities may accelerate depreciation on her stock of market-specific human capital. The downward bias on market wages as a measure of the current price of time would tend to be serious during the first decade after school completion for men, but it is not clear whether this is also true for women. More generally, the variable that is predetermined with respect to the fertility decision is not the current potential market wage but a potential lifetime wage stream (Mincer 1974b). How people redistribute that wage stream by *all* forms of human capital investments will be jointly determined with their desired number and timing of births. Only this preinvestment potential wage can be viewed as uncontaminated by life-cycle goals and unobserved factors, such as tastes. If this interpretation has merit, the contemporaneous association between wages and completed fertility contains a serious simultaneous-equations bias that is very difficult to isolate completely. The first step would appear to be to estimate wage functions separately and use them to predict potential lifetime wage opportunities as explanatory variables in the derived demand-for-children equation. For these reasons, schooling might be preferable to current market wages as a proxy for potential lifetime wages.

time inputs into the rearing of numbers of children[6] imply $\alpha_4 < \alpha_3$, and past studies of fertility might lead one to conjecture that $\alpha_3 \geqslant 0$, and $\alpha_4 < 0$. A serious practical problem with joint estimation of the partial association between birth rates and male and female schooling is the collinearity between the sex-specific schooling rates.[7]

Information about the nature and local availability of modern birth control methods is provided by the two classes of family-planning field personnel; this should reduce birth rates among older women by reducing the information costs of avoiding additional unwanted or ill-timed births. But the reverse effect might occur among younger women, who may adopt a more concentrated pattern of childbearing when they are provided with a reliable means of birth control (Keyfitz 1971). Activities that seek to spread a given set of information to a fixed population of potential de- manders are likely eventually to experience decreasing returns to effort. This anticipated nonlinearity in the relation between family-planning activity and its effect on birth rates is documented in another study (Schultz 1971a) but is neglected here for simplicity. The regression co- efficients α_5 and α_6 should, therefore, be interpreted with caution as only approximations for the *average* effectiveness of a personnel man-month of local activity per 1,000 women of childbearing age.

The impact of personnel allocated to family planning on completed fertility will depend upon at least three factors: (1) the elasticity of parent demand for numbers of children; (2) the advantage of the pro- gram's new birth control technology compared with that indigenously available, in terms of individual search and use costs; and (3) the distribu- tional efficiency of the program imparting new knowledge of birth control and subsidizing its use among those segments of the population with a more elastic demand for children and least initial access to adequate (modern) birth control technology.

Temporal Specification

Anticipations about the future are not always fulfilled; it takes an un- certain amount of time to have a child, and children die unpredictably.

---

[6] This conclusion is derived rigorously in the model presented in this volume by Ben-Porath, in which the variable resource intensity of children is omitted. It is implied as well by Gardner (1972) and assumed by Willis (1971). In De Tray's (1972a) model the female time-value intensity is assumed greater than the male's for numbers (C) of children, leading to the prediction of an algebraically smaller coefficient for the female than for the male wage variable in the equation for derived demand for children.

[7] The simple correlation (weighted by number of women aged 15–49 in the relevant region and time period) between the male and female primary school variables is very high, .91. Between the change variables the correlation is, of course, less, .35 (see table 4). I have not uncovered any good reasons why the regional sex-specific schooling variables should be so highly correlated in a country, such as Taiwan, that is experiencing substantial migration and other rapid changes, such as those in educa- tional attainment.

Consequently, lags and adjustments of a biological and behavioral nature interpose themselves between the observed environment characterized in the model and the observed birth rate the model seeks to predict. In other words, what should be the values of τ and τ' in equation (1)? Most environmental conditions that modify parents' preferences for children change slowly, at least at the regional level considered here. Death rates, on the contrary, are subject to substantial year-to-year variation and cannot be predicted accurately within a small community, to say nothing of the family unit. Short-run reaction to replace recent child losses may therefore permit identification of the speed and magnitude of parent reaction to unanticipated changes.

Some sequential models of fertility determination would imply a mechanism by which the unanticipated death of a child to a still-fertile mother may influence her to have a somewhat higher birth rate than she would otherwise have had. Although the death of a child may motivate the mother to seek an additional offspring, the effect on her actual reproductive behavior is difficult to distinguish in the *short run* if she is young, for members of her age cohort will probably continue having additional desired children for some time, regardless of their personal experience of child mortality. If, on the other hand, the mother of the deceased child is older, say in her late thirties, when a sizable proportion of her cohort intends to avoid further births, her seeking another birth will sharply distinguish her from others in her cohort within a relatively short time. Experimentation with various discrete (see τ in eq. [1]) and simple distributed lags for Taiwan suggests the association between regional child-death rates and subsequent birth rates is statistically strongest after the lapse of 2–4 years, particularly among women 30–44 years of age (Schultz 1971a). These findings, that a pronounced 2–4-year average behavioral-biological lag exists between child deaths and subsequent births, are generally consistent with other evidence on the mean length of closed birth intervals for women not practicing modern contraception (Potter 1963). Lacking better evidence, not only the child-death ratio but also the schooling and agricultural variables that must affect birth rates with a behavioral-biological lag are lagged 3 ($\tau = 3$). The bias introduced by this approximation for what undoubtedly should be a more complex distributed-lag formulation is discussed in Section V.

Family-planning program inputs represent a still more complex problem of measurement and dynamic model specification. The temporal link between environmental conditions and fertility and that between birth control information and fertility should differ. Current practice of birth control influences birth rates 9 months hence; the lag between adoption of more effective birth control methods and their maximum impact on birth rates is likely to be no more than 1 year, not the 2 or 3 required, on average, for a woman to deliver a child. Therefore, program inputs are lagged only 1 year ($\tau' = 1$). Furthermore, the program is likely to have a persisting effect on contraceptive knowledge in the community, slowly "depreciating" as people forget or move away and as new generations of parents grow up or move in. Thus, all past program inputs must be considered as possible determinants (with perhaps exponentially diminishing weights) of the target population's current knowledge of birth control methods. Time series as yet are too short for an empirical exploration of the declining time dimension of program input effectiveness. A first approximation is simply to ignore the depreciation effect and treat the total of all past program inputs as a determinant of current effective knowledge of birth control in the community.

IV. Cross-sectional Evidence

Ordinary least-squares estimates on equation (1) are reported for 1965 and 1969 in table 3, for which the moment matrices were weighted by the observed number of women in the specific age group in the region;[8] only selected implications of these results are discussed below.

In each year from 1964 to 1969 (not shown), between 48 and 65 percent of the interregional variation in total fertility rates is accounted for by equation (1). There is substantial variation in the explanatory power of the model across years and age groups and in the size and statistical significance of the regression coefficients of each explanatory variable.[9]

The coefficient for the child-survival factor is positive and substantial relative to the magnitude of birth rates in every year and age group, although this pattern is most pronounced among older women and teenagers. For example, for the age group 40–44 the ratio of the coefficient of the child-survival factor to the mean value of the birth rate approaches 15 by 1969, and even for the total fertility rate this ratio increases to more than three by 1969. These estimates imply parent demand for surviving children is inelastic.

[8] Disturbances in the birth-rate equation are likely to have differing variances. The expected variance of the estimate of a population mean (the frequency of births in this case) is inversely proportional to the size of the sample population. Therefore, the observations on which the regression is based are weighted by the square root of the regional population of women of the specific age group in the relevant year. Neglect of heteroscedasticity of disturbances asymptotically biases upward the estimated variance of the parameters, reducing their t-ratios. However, in the case at hand, it seems likely that the variance of the disturbances may not be independent of other variables in the model, which implies the ordinary least-squares estimates of the parameter means may also be biased. Similar reasoning often leads to respecifications of estimation equations to obtain approximately constant-variance disturbances (Malinvaud 1970, pp. 302–6).

[9] The t-ratios reported in parentheses beneath each regression coefficient in all of the tables are used to test statistical confidence in rejecting the null hypothesis that there appears to be no particular association between the variable and the birth rate. Since most of the parameters have a predicted sign, the one-tailed test is generally appropriate. For a large n (degrees of freedom), a t-ratio exceeding 1.65 satisfies a confidence level of 95 percent, and one exceeding 2.34 satisfies a confidence level of 99 percent.

TABLE 3

CROSS-SECTIONAL REGRESSIONS ON BIRTH-RATE LEVELS

DEPENDENT VARIABLE	CONSTANT TERM	CHILD-DEATH ADJUSTMENT (RATIO)	AGRICULTURAL COMPOSITION (PROPORTION)	MALE EDUCATION (PROPORTION)	FEMALE EDUCATION (PROPORTION)	FAMILY-PLANNING PROGRAM MAN-MONTHS (CUMULATIVE INPUTS TO PRIOR YEAR) VHEN	PPHW	R^2/SEE
Total fertility rate:*								
1965	2148. (2.70)	4567. (7.15)	535. (3.76)	−4156. (6.53)	913. (1.95)	−93.7 (0.71)	−136. (2.58)	.529 (546.)
1969	−699. (4.35)	13,150. (9.20)	189. (1.67)	−4944. (7.78)	1372. (3.29)	190. (4.39)	18.7 (1.89)	.588 (455.)
Age-specific birth rates for ages:								
15–19								
1965	−65.1 (2.56)	135. (6.57)	−11.0 (2.41)	−116. (5.69)	90.1 (6.04)	−7.92 (1.90)	−2.78 (1.66)	.271 (17.5)
1969	−232. (4.22)	327. (6.70)	−11.9 (3.15)	−168. (8.00)	98.5 (7.10)	5.12 (3.55)	.542 (1.65)	.317 (15.2)
20–24								
1965	169. (2.94)	172. (3.68)	−10.1 (0.98)	−136. (3.03)	6.47 (0.20)	6.00 (0.64)	−2.64 (0.70)	.159 (38.9)
1969	−373. (2.55)	739. (5.63)	−.858 (0.09)	−244. (4.51)	7.01 (0.20)	14.8 (3.97)	2.95 (3.41)	.453 (38.3)
25–29								
1965	255. (5.81)	92.8 (2.63)	49.2 (6.29)	−5.87 (0.17)	−97.3 (3.79)	12.1 (1.67)	−3.14 (1.08)	.492 (29.7)

* See definition note to table 2.

268

TABLE 3 (*Continued*)

Dependent Variable	Constant Term	Child-Death Adjustment (Ratio)	Agricultural Composition (Proportion)	Male Education (Proportion)	Female Education (Proportion)	Family-planning Program Man-Months (Cumulative Inputs to Prior Year)		R^2/SEE
						VHEN	PPHW	
1969	121. (1.05)	215. (2.10)	37.3 (4.71)	.124 (0.00)	−127. (4.37)	5.38 (1.77)	.794 (1.13)	.480 (31.0)
30–34								
1965	101. (1.97)	181. (4.43)	27.4 (2.98)	−188.0 (4.57)	38.0 (1.26)	−5.20 (0.62)	−5.76 (1.71)	.363 (35.0)
1969	−312. (2.81)	539. (5.50)	6.77 (0.83)	−192. (4.22)	67.0 (2.25)	6.61 (2.14)	−.146 (0.20)	.278 (32.3)
35–39								
1965	−19.1 (0.43)	216. (6.00)	30.5 (3.80)	−233. (6.49)	79.6 (3.02)	−14.0 (1.89)	−9.31 (3.14)	.462 (30.7)
1969	−438. (5.33)	568. (7.81)	2.19 (3.63)	−229. (6.85)	134. (6.12)	4.55 (2.04)	−.0819 (0.16)	.346 (24.0)
40–44								
1965	−26.0 (0.98)	115. (5.43)	16.7 (3.46)	−120. (5.56)	41.6 (2.65)	−6.94 (1.55)	−3.93 (2.18)	.397 (18.5)
1969	−251. (5.36)	301. (7.26)	6.21 (1.83)	−113. (5.94)	71.9 (5.83)	2.18 (1.72)	−.127 (0.43)	.323 (13.5)
45–49								
1965	12.0 (1.23)	7.70 (1.00)	3.17 (1.81)	−43.3 (5.35)	30.7 (5.19)	−3.23 (1.93)	.0613 (0.09)	.132 (6.94)
1969	9.09 (0.51)	5.65 (0.36)	−.637 (0.49)	−35.9 (4.69)	28.3 (5.53)	−.125 (0.24)	.115 (0.99)	.093 (5.58)

In the short run, it was anticipated that the link between child mortality and fertility would be more pronounced among older mothers; this seemed plausible because they were more likely already to have the number of surviving offspring they wanted and would, therefore, weigh heavily the survival or death of these earlier children in their decision whether to have an additional child. The strong statistical association between child-death rates and birth rates of women aged 30 and over confirms this hypothesis; the strength of the association with teen-age birth rates suggests two subsidiary tentative hypotheses.

Life-cycle commitments of a mother may depend to a substantial degree upon the survival of her first born. The dislocation of her life may be somewhat less if a subsequent child dies later in the formation of her family. It may be assumed that teen-age mothers more frequently experience the loss of their first born than other age groups and are thus motivated more strongly, on average, to shorten the interval to their next birth.[10] This logic could account for a strong replacement link at the family level between child mortality and the teen-age birth rate.[11]

Societies also traditionally adjust to the heavy incidence of childhood mortality by promoting early marriage, and though this pattern may stem from desired fertility goals, it is likely to become institutionalized and only slowly adapt to sudden changes in death rates or in other constraints on the family formation process. The aggregate association observed in Taiwan between child-death rates and subsequent teen-age birth rates may, therefore, represent *long-term* regional differences in the proportion of married teen-age women (see Schultz 1971b). Examination (in the next section) of time series may help to determine whether this relation observed in the cross section of aggregates is due to misspecification of the model's temporal dimensions or neglect of intermediary causal relations involving, for example, the timing of first marriage.

Local reliance on agricultural employment is often positively associated with total fertility rates, except in 1967, but t-ratios are not substantial. Differences in the age pattern of fertility in agricultural regions are more pronounced, however. Birth rates among teen-age women are decidedly lower in agricultural areas, but distinctly higher among women aged 25–29, and somewhat higher during the first half of the period among all women over age 29. These findings do not confirm the importance of

[10] First, it is a medical fact that infant mortality is greater among the children of teen-age mothers and among firstborn. It is also true that a greater proportion of a teen-age mother's children at risk of dying are firstborn, compared with older groups of mothers. Since the child-death rates cannot be linked to the age of the child's mother, the child-death rate is likely to reflect disproportionately the family mortality experience of the youngest group of mothers.

[11] A similar pattern of stronger reproductive replacement response was observed among teen-age married women (and married women between the ages of 30 and 39) to the loss of their own child in a study of household survey data from Bangladesh (Schultz and DaVanzo 1970, table 12).

relative price effects operating between the agricultural-nonagricultural sectors of Taiwan, but they do suggest that the timing of marriage and births may be modified by the availability of complementary agricultural resources.

A puzzling result from these cross-sectional regressions is the consistently negative coefficient of male schooling and the positive coefficient of female schooling. Although collinearity may be called upon to excuse these unexpected results, and the schooling variable may be criticized as a proxy for the value of parent-time, the results nonetheless cast doubts on the adequacy of static cross-sectional evidence of the economic determinants of fertility in a rapidly changing environment.

Except for birth rates among women aged 25–29, the negative partial association with male schooling is statistically notable in every year and age group. Increasing the proportion of men with a primary school certificate from 50 to 60 percent in a community is associated with approximately a 10 percent reduction in births, with the greatest proportionate declines occurring among women aged 15–19 and over 30.

Increased schooling for women is associated with lower teen-age birth rates, but noticeably higher birth rates among women over the age of 35. Although the teen-age pattern might have been predicted, the expectation from economic theory is for educated women to have fewer births after age 30. As industrialization has proceeded, the historic tendency has been for the value of women's time to increase relative to market goods and for women's participation in the paid labor force to increase. If proper controls were available for husband's wage rate, nonhuman wealth, and child-survival rates in a regression model accounting for variation in fertility, better-educated women would tend to have fewer births in their lifetimes. But in all likelihood, the better-educated women would concentrate these fewer births in the first decade of their marriages and possibly exhibit higher birth rates in their mid- and late twenties compared with less educated women. These expectations are not confirmed by the cross-sectional estimates based on the levels of birth rates in Taiwan.

The nationwide family-planning program initiated in 1964 appears to have reduced the total fertility rate in 1965 and 1966, but thereafter program efforts are *positively* associated with total fertility rates. An explanation for this weakening and eventually reversed relationship between program information inputs and the level of total fertility is found in the sharply diminishing returns to scale experienced by the program and the differential effects of the program on women of different ages. The former attribute of the program's effectiveness has been treated elsewhere, and an unnecessary digression would be required here to introduce nonlinear production functions for family-planning activities (see Schultz 1971a). Suffice it to say that the marginal effect of program personnel at average employment levels diminished from 1965 to 1969 as the cumulative level of program activity increased, while in each single year the marginal effect of personnel was relatively less in regions where past program activity was relatively intense. The differential age effects, however, are visible, even from the simple linear estimates of the family-planning program reported in table 3.

Program inputs are most consistently linked to lower birth rates among women 30 years old and over. Among these prime candidates for family-planning assistance, the distribution of field personnel is strongly associated with substantial declines in age-specific birth rates.

A very different pattern of program effectiveness emerges from the study of birth rates among women less than 30 years old. In the first year or two of the national program, field personnel elicited several reductions in these younger age-specific birth rates. After 1966 the tendency became increasingly statistically significant for birth rates among women aged 15–29 to be *higher* in regions intensively canvassed by family-planning program fieldworkers. This evidence is consistent with the hypothesis advanced earlier that where reliable birth control methods are understood and made more accessible, marriage may not be further delayed; and child spacing, if more widely practiced at all, may produce oscillations in birth rates among younger women.

Another implication of these results that is seen more clearly in the nonlinear formulation of the model (Schultz 1971*a*) is that one class of fieldworker—the Village Health Education Nurse (VHEN)—was more effective in reducing birth rates in the early years of the program than the other class of fieldworker—the Pre-Pregnancy Health Worker (PPHW). (The PPHW is trained in the family-planning program to systematically contact and recruit mothers, generally in their thirties, with a recently recorded birth; the VHEN, on the other hand, is instructed to disseminate the principles and practices of home economics, family sanitation and hygiene, and family planning to the entire village population. The observed pattern of differing age-specific effectiveness of these two classes of fieldworker is, therefore, not implausible.)

The major puzzle embodied in these cross-sectional findings attaches to the estimates for the male and female schooling variables. The paradox is not resolved by indirectly adjusting the variables for regional differences in age composition, nor by adopting alternative measures of educational attainment. Inclusion in the model of a proxy for male income, derived from the regional structure of male employment and national estimates by industry of value added per worker, reduces the size and significance of the coefficient on the male schooling variable but does not change the signs on male or female schooling. Reversal of this unexpected finding is discussed in the next section, where analysis deals with time series and cross sections together.

V. Time Series of Cross Sections

Economic models of the determinants of fertility tend to be formulated and tested in static terms. Parents are viewed as deciding in a single period on the appropriate number of births needed to yield them an optimal lifetime number of children. Though these abstractions have proved a powerful generalizing device where none has existed before, little attention has been given to the question of what economic theory and statistical techniques can say about models of dynamic behavior that might be confirmed or refuted by empirical evidence (Nerlove 1972a). Reproductive behavior occurs sequentially, and the constraints on child-bearing exert diverse influences on many other areas of economic and demographic decision making in the household sector. Exploration of the time dimension of this process and its complex ramifications on other household choices is warranted.

In the preceding section, cross-sectional variation in the level of *birth rates* was analyzed, although the implicit economic model set forth earlier was framed in terms of completed lifetime fertility. This unavoidable change in the measurement of the dependent variable provides certain advantages, however, when the temporal dimension of parent reaction to changing economic and demographic constraints is the object of analysis. Discrete lags between fertility and the explanatory variables were introduced to approximate the average time for reproduction to respond and for birth control information to take effect. But the stochastic nature of the reproductive process and the numerous neglected features of the individual that could affect reaction times suggest that a *distributed* lag would be more appropriate to the study of changes in fertility. Yet identification and estimation of these lag structures are difficult because of the limited availability of time-series information and the strong positive serial correlation of such relevant characteristics of regional populations as wages, nonhuman wealth, industrial structure, and schooling.

The cross-sectional findings in Section IV are, as a result, not to be interpreted as estimates of the impact of slowly changing environmental constraints on birth rates during the 3-year lag interval. For example, the systematic portion of the regime of mortality is determined by such slowly changing factors as long-term investments in public health, sanitation, water supplies, transportation, geography, climate, and socioeconomic characteristics of the population; thus interregional differences in child mortality contain a relatively stable component over time. High positive serial correlation in regional differences in mortality implies that cross-sectional observations on mortality in any single time period contain substantial information about the interregional differences that existed 5, 10, and perhaps even 20 years earlier (see Griliches [1961] for a discussion of this type of bias).

The estimates from cross sections using discretely lagged levels will tend to understate long-run responses because a single annual observation approximates the appropriate weighted distribution of past observations with substantial error. On the other hand, a discrete 3-year lag overstates short-run responses and creates the erroneous impression that the estimated response would occur in 3 years, whereas in all likelihood it would take longer. To improve the temporal specification and estimation of the dynamic behavioral relationship accounting for reproductive behavior, one needs the combined information of time series and cross sections. Below, I report estimates from the pooled time series of cross sections, assuming a Nerlovian two-component model of the stochastic structure of the disturbance (Nerlove 1971a). Then, first-differences of the cross section are estimated and related to disequilibrium in the family formation process.

A Two-Component Model of Disturbances

The statistical properties of the estimates of equation (1) are determined by the nature of the disturbances in the model, e_{it}, where i refers to region. The disturbance term presents both the net effects of numerous factors that have unavoidably been omitted from the analysis and errors of measurement and approximation in the form of the behavioral relationship. It is reasonable to assume that many of these effects are specific to regions and relatively time-invariant. As a first approximation, then, the disturbance term might be decomposed following Nerlove (1971b) into two independent elements, a region-specific time-invariant effect, μ_i, and a region- and time independent effect, ν_{it}. The stochastic structure for the disturbance in equation (1) might then be expressed:

$$E\, e_{it}e_{i't'} = \begin{cases} \sigma^2 = \sigma_\mu^2 + \sigma_\nu^2 \,, i = i', t = t' \\ \sigma_\mu^2 \qquad\qquad , i = i', t \neq t' \\ 0 \qquad\qquad\quad , \text{otherwise,} \end{cases}$$

$$E\, e_{it} = 0, \text{ all } i \text{ and } t.$$

Let the parameter $\rho = \sigma_\mu^2/\sigma^2$ be defined as the proportion of the variance of the disturbances accounted for by the region-specific component. It may be shown (Nerlove 1971a) that generalized least squares for a model with this form of variance-covariance matrix amounts to using transformed values of the variables, which are a weighted combination of the original observations and the deviations from regional means. These weights can be expressed as a simple function of ρ. Several methods for estimating ρ have been considered; the two-stage method used here appears to show least bias, least mean-square error, and greatest overall robustness against specification error (Nerlove 1971b). The procedure has been used by Schultz (1967) and Nerlove and Schultz (1970) in the study of birth rates in Puerto Rico.

Fitting equation (1) to the pooled time series of cross sections, weighted estimates are reported in table 4, part A for the levels of the original variables, in table 4, part B for the deviations of these variables from regional means, and in table 4, part C for the transformed variables based on the values of ρ reported in the last column of the table.

Between 57 and 84 percent of the variation in the residuals from the pooled regression on the original variable levels is attributable to the region-specific component (see values of ρ in table 4, part C). The estimates based directly on the variable levels are similar whether analysis is limited to individual years (table 3) or the pooled timed series of cross sections (table 4, part A). Additional information contained in the time-series dimension of these data is extracted only when the relative importance of the two disturbance components is estimated and used to obtain the transformed variable estimates of the model parameters. In the total fertility equation based on the transformed variables, the coefficients for the child-survival factor and male schooling remain significantly different from zero and of the appropriate sign, but their size is about half of those implied by the analysis of levels. This confirms that *direct cross-sectional estimates of short-run responses are seriously biased upward.* The total fertility effect from agricultural composition is no longer significant, although there is a tendency for agricultural regions to have higher birth rates for women between the ages of 25 and 29 and somewhat lower birth rates thereafter.

Of greater importance is the shift in sign of the coefficients estimated for female schooling. In the total-fertility-rate equation, female schooling now depresses fertility as does male schooling, but elasticities calculated at regression means are still greater for male than for female schooling ($-.32$ versus $-.17$). In all but the teen-age birth-rate equation, female schooling is associated with lower birth rates. Although the puzzling behavior of the estimates for female schooling has been partially resolved by the analysis of pooled time series of cross sections, the economic prediction that the coefficient on women's schooling, as a proxy for the value of their time, should algebraically be less than the coefficient on men's schooling is confirmed by the transformed estimates *only* for the birth-rate equation for women aged 25–29.

The transformed variable estimates based on the time series of cross sections also indicate that family-planning information has twice the effect on birth rates as that implied by the estimates based on the levels, reducing total fertility rates 8 percent rather than 4 percent. This should also have been anticipated, for these program inputs are not subject to the same dynamic specification errors that biased upward the coefficients on gradually changing environmental constraints. Among all women over the age of 24, birth rates are significantly inversely related to the allocation of both classes of family-planning field personnel. Among the younger women,

TABLE 4

REGRESSION ON POOLED TIME SERIES OF CROSS SECTIONS

A. LEVELS, 1964–69

DEPENDENT VARIABLE	CONSTANT TERM	CHILD-DEATH ADJUSTMENT (RATIO)	AGRICULTURAL COMPOSITION (PROPORTION)	MALE EDUCATION (PROPORTION)	FEMALE EDUCATION (PROPORTION)	FAMILY-PLANNING PROGRAM MAN-MONTHS (CUMULATIVE INPUTS TO PRIOR YEAR)		R²/SEE
						VHEN	PPHW	
Total fertility rate	−2,246. (4.40)	9,067. (20.7)	234. (4.17)	−4,500. (16.5)	714. (3.74)	−23.9 (0.94)	−38.3 (7.86)	.567 (544.)
Age-specific birth rates for ages:								
15–19	−87.0 (5.04)	182. (12.3)	−14.2 (7.72)	−171. (18.9)	110. (17.4)	6.14 (7.64)	1.27 (8.23)	.237 (17.8)
20–24	56.4 (1.45)	303. (9.03)	−5.88 (1.36)	−182. (8.95)	4.66 (0.34)	19.9 (5.05)	−.0592 (0.07)	.242 (41.2)
25–29	116. (3.71)	220. (8.22)	37.3 (10.8)	53.0 (3.19)	−167. (14.3)	−1.48 (0.94)	−1.34 (4.41)	.482 (32.8)
30–34	−129. (3.91)	408. (14.5)	10.7 (2.90)	−188. (10.4)	23.8 (1.90)	−7.53 (4.48)	−4.18 (13.0)	.424 (35.6)
35–39	−243. (8.61)	432. (17.9)	10.3 (3.26)	−247. (16.2)	98.2 (9.23)	−8.42 (5.98)	−3.53 (13.0)	.461 (30.4)
40–44	−148. (8.97)	232. (16.6)	9.27 (5.03)	−130. (14.5)	57.1 (9.04)	−9.18 (5.71)	−3.51 (10.1)	.414 (17.9)
45–49	−6.09 (1.04)	24.7 (4.97)	−.740 (1.18)	−33.9 (10.4)	20.2 (8.91)	−.999 (3.30)	−.175 (3.12)	.092 (6.47)

TABLE 4 (*Continued*)

B. Deviations from Regional Means, 1964–69*

Dependent Variable	Child-Death Adjustment (Ratio)	Agricultural Composition (Proportion)	Male Education (Proportion)	Female Education (Proportion)	Family-planning Program Man-Months (Cumulative Inputs to prior Year)		R^2/SEE
					VHEN	PPHW	
Total fertility rate	2,142. (6.53)	−918. (2.19)	−2,159. (5.62)	−2,875. (9.68)	−219. (9.85)	−56.1 (12.3)	.568 (271.)
Age-specific birth rate for ages:							
15–19	−16.5 (1.43)	−14.4 (1.01)	5.41 (0.40)	23.1 (2.21)	.494 (0.64)	.113 (0.71)	.026 (9.29)
20–24	−23.3 (0.73)	−56.4 (1.37)	−9.44 (0.26)	1.68 (0.06)	−.250 (0.12)	−1.33 (2.95)	.008 (26.3)
25–29	112. (3.87)	−5.81 (0.16)	−4.84 (0.14)	−140. (5.44)	−9.71 (4.98)	−1.90 (4.75)	.192 (23.5)
30–34	152. (6.33)	−58.9 (1.87)	−159. (5.56)	−210. (9.58)	−13.5 (8.20)	−3.31 (9.90)	.519 (20.0)
35–39	132. (6.47)	−23.2 (0.89)	−185. (7.70)	−136. (7.30)	−14.1 (10.3)	−3.02 (10.7)	.549 (16.9)
40–44	67.4 (5.43)	−16.3 (1.01)	−65.7 (4.48)	−72.5 (6.39)	−6.66 (7.91)	−1.87 (10.8)	.447 (10.4)
45–49	10.9 (1.96)	−5.46 (0.74)	−12.5 (1.85)	−24.9 (4.73)	−.316 (0.82)	.0102 (0.13)	.071 (4.73)

* Intercept suppressed.

TABLE 4 (*Continued*)

C. Transformed Variables, 1964–69

Dependent Variable	Constant Term	Child-Death Adjustment (Ratio)	Agricultural Composition (Proportion)	Male Education (Proportion)	Female Education (Proportion)	Family-Planning Program Man-Months (Cumulative Inputs to Prior Year)		R^2/SEE	$\hat{\rho}$
						VHEN	PPHW		
Total fertility rate ..	4,471. (9.83)	2,748. (8.06)	74.4 (0.53)	−2,454. (6.78)	−1,860. (6.91)	−218. (10.1)	−60.6 (14.5)	.553 (288.)	.840
Age-specific birth rates for ages:									
15–19	55.5 (3.52)	−2.22 (0.19)	−3.42 (0.76)	−45.1 (3.62)	35.4 (3.83)	1.85 (2.50)	.450 (3.19)	.027 (9.90)	.815
20–24	321. (7.70)	1.35 (0.04)	17.0 (1.50)	−88.1 (2.77)	−23.8 (1.01)	4.13 (2.04)	−.149 (0.38)	.027 (27.4)	.769
25–29	223. (6.35)	136. (4.76)	38.9 (5.47)	18.9 (0.74)	−151. (8.12)	−7.71 (4.45)	−1.81 (5.64)	.271 (24.8)	.566
30–34	144. (4.43)	192. (7.79)	−13.3 (1.47)	−136. (5.24)	−110. (5.79)	−15.6 (9.92)	−4.37 (14.6)	.494 (21.2)	.788
35–39	64.4 (2.32)	172. (8.19)	−8.80 (1.10)	−174. (7.88)	−45.4 (2.78)	−16.1 (12.2)	−3.92 (15.4)	.523 (17.9)	.809
40–44	2.10 (0.13)	93.2 (7.33)	3.14 (0.71)	−73.3 (5.59)	−18.6 (1.94)	−7.46 (9.28)	−2.25 (14.7)	.426 (11.0)	.763
45–49	1.10 (0.16)	16.5 (3.02)	−2.67 (1.84)	−17.0 (3.18)	−1.15 (0.30)	−.978 (2.81)	−.205 (3.20)	.058 (4.96)	.619

278

the reverse is indicated. On balance, the program's effect has been to reduce the number of births even though it may accelerate the "tempo" of fertility among some younger women, at least in the short run.

First-Difference Model

Another approach to the analysis of time series where omitted variables are thought to bias estimates of short-run response is to assume that region-specific, relatively time-invariant effects can be removed by first-differencing the basic model over time. Assume a model of the form

$$
b_{it} = \alpha_0 + \sum_{k=1}^{n} \alpha_k X_{ikt}
$$
$$
+ \sum_{j=1}^{m} \beta_j Y_{ijt} + e_{it}, \tag{2}
$$

where the X_{ikt} are n observed short-run determinants of birth rates and the Y_{ijt} are m unobserved long-run determinants of birth rates, and e_{it} is a normal random error independently distributed with respect to time and region. If the Y_{ijt} do not change, say within a 5-year period, but tend to be correlated with specific X_{ikt}, which do change, then the cross-sectional regression on levels will spuriously attribute the effect of Y_j's to X_k's and bias estimates of the short-run response of birth rates to the observed short-run factors.

Absolute differences between cross sections several years (δ) apart provide, then, another test of the model's specification and a further procedure for evaluating how rapidly reproductive behavior responds to specific short-run changes in economic and demographic determinants of the desired number of children. The estimated equation becomes

$$
b_{it} - b_{i.t-\delta} = \sum_{k=1}^{n} \alpha_k
$$
$$
(X_{ik,t-\tau} - X_{ik,t-\tau-\delta}) + V_i,
$$

where $V_i = e_{it} - e_{i.t-\delta}$.

Using the maximum available value of δ for the Taiwan data of 5 years, this reformulation of equation (1) states that only changes experienced in the explanatory variables from 1961 to 1966 (or to 1968 for family-planning inputs) affect changes in birth rates from 1964 to 1969.[12] This

[12] Because of greater year-to-year variability of a stochastic nature in child-death rates estimated for small communities, the first-differenced child-death adjustment factor is based on 2-year averages at the beginning and end of the 5-year period, i.e., $[(D_{1961} + D_{1962}) - (D_{1966} + D_{1967})]/2$. Death rates were first published in 1961.

procedure sharply reduces multicollinearity among the explanatory variables (see table 2) and the statistical significance of regression coefficients
for the reasons mentioned earlier (see also Fisher 1962). Comparisons
across methods of estimation may rely on the standard error of estimate
(SEE), given the maintained model specification, since when the intercept
is forced through the origin no obvious interpretation attaches to R^2.[13]

The weighted estimates of the first-differenced form of equation (1) are
reported in table 5, part A. The child-survival factor is positively associated with birth rates to a statistically significant extent *only* among
women aged 30–44—those in the groups thought to be most responsive,
in the short run, to such changes in the regime of child mortality. Changes
in agricultural composition of the labor force are not apparently related
to changes in birth rates. For the first time the coefficient of male schooling is positive for birth rates between ages 20 and 29, which is consistent
with expectations that the income effect would exceed the substitution
effect for the value of male time. Women's schooling may increase birth
rates from ages 15 to 24, but it substantially reduces those rates thereafter.
From 25 years of age and over, the algebraic value of the coefficient on
women's schooling is less than that on men's schooling, as expected on
economic grounds. The family-planning personnel may contribute to a
slight increase in birth rates among women aged 15–19, but reduce birth
rates substantially among women aged 25–44, as anticipated.

The predictions of the general economic model that can be tested with
these data for Taiwan are confirmed when the initial static model is differenced over time, although the magnitudes of the response estimates are
smaller than those based on the individual cross sections and similar to
those based on the combined time series of cross sections (see table 6).
Since first-differencing an economic behavioral relationship is often a
severe econometric test for specification error, I conclude from this evidence that reproductive behavior does systematically respond in the *short*

[13] Indeed, in half of the regressions reported in table 5, the standard error of estimate exceeds the standard deviation of the dependent variable. This may appear to
cast doubt on the maintained hypothesis that the intercept of the first-differenced
equation equals zero or, in other words, that the birth-rate equation does not shift
over time independently of the six specified explanatory variables. Relaxing this
constraint and permitting the intercept to assume a nonzero value tends to reduce
somewhat the size of the regression coefficients and their t-statistics, but not their
signs or relative magnitudes. If the hypothesis of the zero intercept is maintained, a
summary statistic in place of R^2 might be defined with respect to both the variance
of the (first-differenced) dependent variable and the variance of the level of the ap-
propriate birth rate. Hence, $S^2 = 1 - (\Sigma V_i^2)/\{N \ [\text{var} \ (b_{it} - b_{i,t-\delta}) + \text{var} \ (b_{it})]\}$,
where S is the new summary statistic, N is the number of observations, and var()
is the variance of the respective variables. In this case, for example, the first-differenced relationship estimated over the total sample for the birth rate of women aged
30–34 yields an $S^2 = 0.592$, where the $R^2 = -.062$ (see table 5, part A). Relaxing the
maintained hypothesis that the intercept is zero, the standard error of estimate falls
to 31.97 and $S^2 = 0.647$ and $R^2 = .0812$.

TABLE 5
Regression on Absolute Differences of Birth Rates: 1969 Less 1964

Dependent Variable	Child-Death Adjustment (Ratio)	Agricultural Composition (Proportion)	Male Education (Proportion)	Female Education (Proportion)	Family-planning Program Man-Months (Cumulative Inputs to prior Year)		R^2/SEE
					VHEN	PPHW	
A. Total Sample							
Total fertility rate	4,748. (5.14)	−680. (1.15)	−922. (1.65)	−2,482. (5.72)	−248. (6.41)	−66.0 (8.63)	−.519 (455.)
Age-specific birth rates for ages:							
15–19	−27.7 (0.80)	−14.8 (0.68)	−10.9 (0.51)	24.2 (1.45)	1.67 (1.18)	−.0638 (0.22)	.022 (17.0)
20–24	92.1 (0.95)	−68.4 (1.12)	18.1 (0.33)	23.1 (0.55)	−3.85 (0.96)	−.753 (0.95)	−.024 (46.5)
25–29	102. (1.30)	19.5 (0.40)	65.5 (1.43)	−102. (2.87)	−12.1 (3.75)	−3.46 (5.41)	−.101 (37.1)
30–34	284. (4.05)	−25.4 (0.55)	−104. (2.46)	−196. (6.02)	−14.2 (4.84)	−3.71 (6.49)	−.062 (34.3)
35–39	330. (5.33)	−25.7 (0.65)	−103. (2.73)	−141. (4.80)	−13.7 (5.37)	−3.46 (6.82)	.052 (30.7)
40–44	168. (4.08)	−16.2 (0.59)	−41.6 (1.64)	−56.2 (2.87)	−7.30 (4.21)	−2.19 (6.38)	.025 (20.7)
45–49	5.30 (0.28)	−8.88 (0.66)	−7.49 (0.59)	−29.2 (2.93)	−1.32 (1.53)	.0500 (0.29)	.027 (10.2)

TABLE 5 (*Continued*)

Dependent Variable	Child-Death Adjustment (Ratio)	Agricultural Composition (Proportion)	Male Education (Proportion)	Female Education (Proportion)	Family-planning Program Man-Months (Cumulative Inputs to prior Year)		R²/SEE
					VHEN	PPHW	
B. Subsample for Which 1964 Birth Rates Tended to be Less than Predicted by the Cross-sectional Model							
Total fertility rate	3,895. (2.77)	−1,219. (1.33)	−74.3 (0.08)	−3,297. (4.65)	−161. (2.79)	−65.4 (5.63)	−.795 (432.)
Age-specific birth rate for ages:							
15–19	−82.1 (2.46)	−57.1 (2.75)	−47.9 (2.42)	32.0 (1.89)	2.94 (2.36)	.775 (2.95)	.155 (10.3)
20–24	84.7 (0.64)	−249. (2.54)	−52.8 (0.68)	32.0 (0.54)	14.6 (2.44)	.0157 (0.01)	.095 (46.3)
25–29	−11.8 (0.13)	−11.9 (0.15)	4.35 (0.07)	−155. (2.81)	.780 (0.16)	−.967 (1.02)	−.057 (34.2)
30–34	270. (2.90)	−6.60 (0.11)	−141. (2.59)	−157. (3.43)	−9.14 (2.52)	−2.10 (2.71)	−.062 (30.9)
35–39	236. (3.80)	44.1 (1.11)	−80.2 (2.13)	−160. (4.78)	−9.52 (3.89)	−2.24 (4.61)	.309 (20.5)
40–44	112. (3.60)	−13.5 (0.60)	−46.6 (2.42)	−46.9 (2.99)	−3.91 (3.30)	−1.42 (5.34)	.132 (10.3)
45–49	−16.3 (1.87)	−1.81 (0.23)	1.37 (0.19)	2.33 (0.39)	−.332 (0.70)	−.125 (1.36)	.020 (3.57)

TABLE 5 (Continued)

Dependent Variable	Child-Death Adjustment (Ratio)	Agricultural Composition (Proportion)	Male Education (Proportion)	Female Education (Proportion)	Family-Planning Program Man-Months (Cumulative Inputs to prior Year)		R²/SEE
					VHEN	PPHW	
C. Subsample for Which 1964 Birth Rates Tended to be More than Predicted by the Cross-sectional Model							
Total fertility rate	5,905. (4.87)	−54.7 (0.07)	−2,298. (3.09)	−1,807 (3.27)	−302. (5.68)	−63.6 (6.03)	−.336 (464.)
Age-specific birth rate for ages:							
15–19	29.5 (0.53)	11.0 (0.31)	−22.3 (0.61)	39.1 (1.48)	.884 (0.36)	−.884 (1.90)	.020 (20.8)
20–24	185. (1.53)	12.8 (0.19)	−34.7 (0.52)	−11.4 (0.22)	−14.6 (3.12)	−.283 (0.31)	−.021 (39.4)
25–29	485. (4.19)	10.9 (0.20)	91.4 (1.63)	−112. (2.78)	−15.2 (3.96)	−4.15 (5.47)	−.124 (33.1)
30–34	356. (3.92)	−53.5 (0.88)	−77.6 (1.39)	−241. (5.91)	−16.8 (4.04)	−5.61 (7.61)	−.020 (32.3)
35–39	460. (4.62)	−42.6 (0.66)	−187. (2.95)	−108. (2.45)	−13.6 (3.15)	−4.97 (5.66)	−.328 (36.4)
40–44	237. (3.49)	21.7 (0.50)	−95.4 (2.23)	−60.1 (1.92)	−9.37 (2.92)	−2.64 (4.68)	.001 (25.5)
45–49	68.8 (1.81)	1.00 (0.05)	−32.9 (1.55)	−28.3 (1.78)	−1.99 (1.38)	−.0119 (0.04)	.090 (12.8)

TABLE 6

Elasticity of Birth Rates with Respect to Explanatory Variables

| | | Estimation Technique and Sample Composition | | | | |
| | | Time Series of Cross Sections | | Cross Section of First-Differences | | |
Dependent Variable	Independent Variable	Levels (1)	Transformed (2)	Total (3)	"Equilibrium" (4)	"Disequilibrium" (5)
Total fertility rate	Child-death adjustment*	1.9	.58	1.0	.85	1.2
Total fertility rate	Female schooling	.064	—.17	—.22	—.30	—.15
Total fertility rate	Male schooling	—.59	—.32	—.12	—.01	—.27
Birth rate, 35–39†	Child-death adjustment*	3.9	1.5	3.0	2.6	3.3
Birth rate, 35–39†	Female schooling	.37	—.17	—.53	—.76	—.32
Birth rate, 35–39†	Male schooling	—1.4	—.98	—.58	—.57	—.81

Sources.—Evaluated at regression means in 1964. Coefficients for col. 1 from table 4, part A; col. 2, table 4, part C; col. 3, table 5, part A; col. 4, table 5, part B; and col. 5, table 5, part C.
* The average child-death adjustment ratio in 1961 (3-year lag appropriate for the 1964 birth-rate regression) was about 1.073, which implies a child-death rate to age 15 of about 68 per 1,000 live births, i.e., child-death adjustment ratio = [1/(1-child-death rate)]. The elasticity of birth rates with respect to the child-death rate would be 0.073 times the elasticity with respect to the child-death adjustment ratio reported above.
† Age group of women.

run to the evolving configuration of economic and demographic constraints that I could observe in Taiwan.

Disequilibrium and Change in Birth Rates

If elements of an economic theory of fertility have some empirical validity in predicting long-run desired equilibrium levels of fertility toward which parents gravitate, then unexplained deviations of birth rates from those predicted by the theory should contain information about the magnitude of reproductive disequilibrium present across populations. In a period of secularly decreasing fertility, which has been pronounced in Taiwan among women over the age of 30 since the mid-1950s (see fig. 2), positive residuals in a cross-sectional regression of birth-rate levels should constitute evidence of disequilibrium and perhaps imply a relative inability to control reproductive behavior at a tolerable individual cost, to correspond to the rapidly changing environment. More specifically, let me propose that in regions in which actual birth rates (particularly among older women) exceed the model's predicted birth rates, the information disseminated by the family-planning program is likely to be in greater demand. These disequilibrium regions are likely to experience more substantial declines in birth rates as a function of the subsequent allocation of family-planning personnel.

A second, more tentative, hypothesis would suggest that where positive disequilibrium was substantial initially, a greater response of birth rates could be expected to subsequent changes associated with a further reduction in desired birth rates. This conjecture would be consistent with the assumption that the rate of adjustment in birth rates was a positive function of the extent of disequilibrium between actual birth rates in the previous period and desired birth rates in the current period.

To test these simple concepts of disequilibrium and change in birth rates, the 361 regions of Taiwan were divided in half, based on the algebraic size of their residuals from regressions on 1964 birth-rate levels (not reported). The absolute differences in birth rates between 1964 and 1969 were then regressed on the differenced explanatory variables. The regression results for the half of the sample with primarily negative residuals (below the regression plane), which I will call the "equilibrium" regions, and those for the sample with primarily positive 1964 residuals (above the regression plane),[14] which will be called the "disequilibrium" regions, are shown in table 5, parts B and C, respectively.

The first hypothesis is confirmed; the regression coefficients for the family-planning personnel variables are algebraically smaller for the disequilibrium regions than for those regions presumed to be closer to equilibrium. In six of the 10 possible comparisons for the birth-rate equations for women between the ages of 20 and 44, the regression coefficients differ significantly in the anticipated direction between the two subsamples, based on a one-tailed t-test at the 5 percent confidence level. It is also interesting to note that the effect of the program personnel *to increase* the teen-age birth rates is also greater across the disequilibrium regions.

The second hypothesis is more difficult to assess, largely because the data are less appropriate. To test the stock-adjustment model, information is required on the initial stocks or number of living children of women of specific ages. Since these data are not published by small regions in Taiwan, I have assumed that the regional variation in birth rates in 1964 closely parallels the regional variation in completed fertility at that date, and positive discrepancies between observed and predicted birth rates reflect in part "unwanted" births. Changes in child mortality elicit a 50 percent greater response in birth rates in the disequilibrium regions than they do across the equilibrium regions (see table 6). Male and female schooling coefficients for the equilibrium regions conform to the pattern observed in most cross-sectional studies of fertility; female schooling is the more significant and sizable deterrent to high birth rates among women

[14] Of course, to obtain subsamples of approximately equal size, i.e., 180 and 181, the dividing line between the two groups of residuals does not turn out to be exactly zero.

aged 25–44. In the total-fertility equation, the schooling of men is hardly associated with birth rates, whereas the elasticity of total fertility rates with respect to women's schooling is −0.30. In the disequilibrium regions, the implied effects of changes in male schooling achievement are greater than those of changes in female schooling; the elasticity of total fertility with respect to male schooling is −0.27 and for female schooling, −0.15. This reversal in the relative importance of schooling of men and women on fertility between the equilibrium and disequilibrium subsamples is also evident in the older age-specific birth-rate equations, as illustrated in table 6 with reference to women 35–39 years old. Although these tentative findings may be rationalized, they raise more questions in my mind than they answer. Explicit stochastic models of dynamic behavior are now needed to make sense of these results and to proceed with the analysis of other time-series evidence on reproductive behavior that will permit economic analysis to be beyond the static notion of long-run equilibrium.

VI. Conclusions

Age-specific birth rates for a cross section of small communities over time were analyzed to infer the responsiveness of birth rates in Taiwan to changing economic, demographic, and policy constraints. There are sound reasons to also consider information on individual reproductive behavior over time, since most models of fertility determination presuppose a relation between fertility and the number of living children parents have and the immediate and lifetime circumstances of the parents. Lacking longitudinal data for individuals, I have explored two methods for extracting information about the dynamic process of birth-rate determination from an integrated treatment of a time series of aggregate cross sections.

Two issues were raised. The first is the traditional concern of economists with separating short-run reactions from long-run adjustments toward equilibrium. Evidence from the analysis of the time series of cross sections, assuming a two-component variance model and the first-differenced cross section over time, implied that estimates based on a single cross section are seriously biased. Slowly changing constraints in the parents' environment, such as the regime of child mortality, agricultural composition, and male schooling, are attributed, in the cross section, an exaggerated and distorted role in affecting birth rates. Both approaches to time series and cross-sectional variation in birth rates, however, continue to imply that child mortality and adult schooling exert strong and statistically significant effects on birth rates within the relatively short 3–5-year time horizon examined here.

More curious, the effect of female schooling is obscured entirely in the cross-sectional estimates, whereas either approach to the time series provides indications that increased schooling for women in Taiwan is associated with markedly lower birth rates, especially among older women who are concluding their childbearing. Also, the effect of the family-planning program on birth rates is biased downward by about 50 percent in cross-sectional estimates compared with those obtained from the time series. Such important shifts in the model's parameters do not give one confidence in analyses that stop with estimates from a single cross section.

The second issue is how to treat disequilibrium in reproductive behavior within an economic framework, especially where this phenomenon must be quantitatively important, as in low-income countries in which fertility has been high and birth rates are beginning to decline rapidly. Evidence was presented that a rudimentary theory of variation in birth rates might help to isolate communities where birth rates were atypically high given the configuration of environmental constraints. Allocations of family-planning field personnel were shown to have exerted twice the effect in reducing birth rates among older women in these "disequilibrium" communities than in the "equilibrium" communities. Evidence of "disequilibrium" in reproductive behavior derived from analyses of residuals might prove to be a useful method, therefore, for the stratification and study of change in fertility over time, and as a guide for the efficient allocation of policy resources.

Priority should be given to extending the static equilibrium theory of household time allocation and decision making to allow the introduction of dynamic elements of innovation, search and information costs, the biological and behavioral constraints on the supply of children, and the longitudinal complexities of intergenerational savings and transfers. Theoretical progress in these directions and more extensive empirical analyses of aggregate and individual time series might improve substantially our understanding of both the economic and demographic behavior of the household sector during the process of economic development.

Appendix

TABLE A1

SUMMARY OF EMPIRICAL RESULTS FROM STUDIES OF ECONOMIC DETERMINANTS OF FERTILITY IN LESS DEVELOPED COUNTRIES

Country/Time	Equation/ Data Type	Dependent Variable	Adult Education Male (1)	Adult Education Female (2)	Adult Education All (3)	Wage Rate Male (4)	Wage Rate Female (5)	Family Income (6)	Child Schooling (7)	Child Labor (8)	Child Mortality (9)	Rural or Agriculture (10)	Sample Size
1. Puerto Rico, 1950–57	Single aggregate	Crude birth rate	...	...	−**	...	...	−*	−**	+**	+**	+	75
2. Egypt, 1960	Reduced form aggregate	Child/woman ratio	...	−a	...	...	...	...	...	+a	...	−a	41
3. Israel,[b] 1961 Jewish non-kibbutz	Single aggregate	Adjusted birth rate	±	−**	...	...	...	...	...	...	...	=	431
Kibbutzim			++	+	...	...	...	...	...	...	...	...	180
Non-Jewish			++	−**	...	...	...	...	...	...	...	−**	133
4. Philippines, 1968	Structural micro	Children born to women, 35–39[c]	...	−*	...	...	...	...	...	+	++**	+**	250

SOURCES.—Study 1, Schultz 1969, p. 175; study 2, Schultz 1970, p. 44; study 3, Ben-Porath 1970a, p. 30; study 4, Harman 1970, p. 29-D-1; study 5, Nerlove and Schultz 1970, p. 45; study 6, Schultz 1971a, p. 61; study 7, Da Vanzo 1971, p. 78; study 8, Maurer, Ratajczak, and Schultz 1972, table 9; and study 9, Schultz 1972b.

a No confidence intervals are reported for reduced-form coefficients derived from estimates of structural equations.
b Treated as endogenous and estimated with simultaneous-equations techniques.
c Fertility for women aged 35–39 or 35–44 is used for comparative purposes.
* Regression coefficient exceeded 1.65 times its standard error, i.e., 5 percent one-tailed t-test of statistical significance.
** Regression coefficient exceeded 2.37 times its standard error, i.e., 1 percent one-tailed t-test of statistical significance.

TABLE A1 (Continued)

Country/Time	Equation/Data Type	Dependent Variable	Adult Education			Wage Rate		Family Income (6)	Child Schooling (7)	Child Labor (8)	Child Mortality (9)	Rural or Agriculture (10)	Sample Size
			Male (1)	Female (2)	All (3)	Male (4)	Female (5)						
5. Puerto Rico, 1950–60	Structural aggregate	Crude birth rate	...	...	−**	...	...	+	−	−**	+**	...	825
6. Taiwan, 1964–68	Single aggregate	Birth rate for women, 35–39c	...	±	...	...	...	...	−**	...	+**	±	361
7. Chile, 1960	Structural aggregate	Children born to women, 35–39c	...	...	+	−*b	...	...	...	+*b	+**	...	50
8. Thailand, 1960	Reduced form aggregate	Children born to women, 35–39c	+a	−a	...	−a	...	...	−a	+a	...	...	71
9. Bogota, Colombia, 1965	Structural micro	Children present, women, 30–34	−	+*	−b	−*b	+	...	...	...	...	...	63

289

TABLE A2

SUMMARY OF EMPIRICAL RESULTS FROM STUDIES OF ECONOMIC DETERMINANTS OF FERTILITY IN UNITED STATES

INDEPENDENT VARIABLES	EQUATION/DATA TYPE	DEPENDENT VARIABLE	Adult Education Male (1)	Adult Education Female (2)	Wage or Earnings Male (3)	Wage or Earnings Female (4)	Family Income (5)	Non-human Wealth (6)	Interaction (2)·(3) (7)	SAMPLE SIZE
1. 1960 census, SMSA:										
White	Single aggregate	Children born per married woman, 35–44	—	—*a	+*	—**	...	...	...	100
Nonwhite			—	—***a	+*	—**	...	...	...	
2. 1960 census grouped:										
Married 14–21	Single aggregate[b]	Children born per married woman, 35–44	—**	—**	—	...	...	...	...	480
Married 22 years or more			—**	—**	—**	...	...	...	...	
3. 1940 and 1960, grouped census:										
Without interaction	Single aggregate	Children born per married woman, 40–44[c]	—**	—**	+*	...	...	...	...	35
Without interaction	1960	35–44[c]	—**	—**	+	...	...	...	...	98
With interaction	1940	40–44[c]	—**	—**	—**	...	...	...	...	35
With interaction	1960	35–44[c]	—**	—**	—**	...	...	...	+**	98
4. 1960 census states:										
Rural-farm	Single aggregate	Children born per married woman, 40–44	+**	—**	...	—**	+	...	...	40
Urban			+	—	...	—**	+**	...	...	

SOURCES.—Study 1, Cain and Weininger 1967 (rev. 1971), tables 3 and 4; study 2, Willis 1971, p. 61a; study 3, Sanderson and Willis 1971, tables 2 and 3; study 4, Gardner 1972, table 2; study 5, De Tray 1972a, p. 36; study 6, Michael 1974; study 7, Schultz 1972a.

a The education variable was the percentage of women 23 years of age and over with *less than* 5 years of schooling. The sign of the regression coefficient is reversed here for comparative purposes.

b Equation is fit in logarithmic form in terms of dependent fertility variable, and those explanatory variables measured in money terms, i.e., incomes.

c Women's potential wage was constructed from 1959 earnings of employed wives adjusted for hours worked per week (see D. Tray 1972a, p. 29).

d Median value of housing used as a proxy for nonhuman wealth (see Willis 1971, pp. 117 ff.).

e South and nonsouth residence at age 16 was used to divide black population according to the quality of schooling received.

† Treated as endogenous and estimated with simultaneous-equations techniques.

* Regression coefficient exceeded 1.65 times its standard error, i.e., 5 percent one-tailed t-test of statistical significance.

** Regression coefficient exceeded 2.37 times its standard error, i.e., 1 percent one-tailed t-test of statistical significance.

TABLE A2 (*Continued*)

Independent Variables	Equation/Data Type	Dependent Variable	Adult Education Male (1)	Adult Education Female (2)	Wage or Earnings Male (3)	Wage or Earnings Female (4)	Family Income (5)	Non-human Wealth (6)	Interaction (2)·(3) (7)	Sample Size
5. 1960 census counties	Single aggregate[b]	Children born per married woman, 35–44	+	−**	+*	−**	...	+*d	...	519
6. 1968 suburban household survey	Single micro	Children born per married woman, 35–39	−	−*	...	...	+*	...	...	513
7. 1967 survey of economic opportunity:	Structural micro	Children born per married woman,								
White married, husband present		35–39	−**	−	+**f	−**f	...	−	...	1,098
Black married, husband present		35–39	−**	−	− f	−**f	...	−	...	475
Black not resident in South at age 16[e]		35–39	−**	+**	+**f	−**f	...	−	...	158
White married, husband present		40–44	−**	+	+**f	−**f	...	+	...	1,138
Black married, husband present		40–44	+	+	−**f	− f	...	−	...	441
Black not resident in South at age 16[e]		40–44	−**	+**	+**f	−**f	...	−	...	116

291

Comment

James Tobin
Yale University

Paul Schultz's paper provides a very useful summary of current economic hypotheses about human fertility, with succinct commonsense versions of their theoretical rationales. I was grateful also for his account of past empirical attempts to test these hypotheses and estimate their parameters. The paper then turns to the regional time series available for Taiwan, which Schultz analyzes with great ingenuity and methodological sophistication.

Over the period 1964–69 in Taiwan, fertility declined about 20 percent. Age-specific birth rates fell in all age brackets except the youngest, 15–19. The declines, in percentage of the 1966 levels, were systematically related to age, ranging from 3 percent for 20–24-year-old women to 75 percent for 40–44-year-old women. The association of larger relative declines with higher age is virtually monotonic.

How are these facts to be explained? Certain possible explanatory variables have been trending in the "right" directions. Public birth control program inputs have greatly risen. Child-survival rates have increased, diminishing the occasion for replacement births. The agricultural proportion of the population has diminished, and the conventional hypothesis is that industrialization and urbanization bring lower fertility. The educational attainments of women have increased; the hypothesis is that education raises the opportunity cost of childbearing and child rearing. On the other hand, male educational attainment has also grown, though by less than female, and the new standard hypothesis is that this trend should increase the birth rate.

Paul Schultz's study may be viewed as an attempt to see whether these possible explanatory trends do in fact account for the observed declines in birth rates. If they do, he reasons, the fertility declines should be most pronounced in those geographical areas where the trends are most pronounced. Schultz has districtwide data for 361 administrative regions.

His presumption that these are useful data is consistent with current population microeconomics. The presumption is that aggregate fertility is the summation of individual behavior and decision.

An alternative hypothesis would be that individual fertility responds to changing national, even international, cultural norms, which are not to be understood by studying individual or regional differences. I find it hard to imagine that differences between U.S. states or counties would do much to help us understand the decline in age-specific birth rates in this country in the 1960s, or their rise in the 1940s. But as an amateur in the field, I should eschew such speculations and return to considering Schultz's paper on its own grounds.

Unfortunately, table 5, part A, indicates that interregional differences in the listed explanatory trends did little to explain interregional differences in birth-rate declines. The standard errors of estimate of the regressions are as often as not larger than the standard deviations of the dependent variable. However, the signs of the coefficients generally conform to the hypotheses.

The most encouraging statistical results are those reported in table 5, parts B and C. Schultz divides the regional observations for each regression evenly between those for which birth rates were high in 1964 and those for which they were low in 1964. Of high 1964 birth-rate regions, those with the stronger birth control programs had the largest declines. Moreover, birth control inputs made more of a difference where the need and opportunity for them was greater, in the "high" rather than the "low" regions. With respect to the other explanatory variables, the partitioning seems to be of little significance.

I am sure Paul Schultz has already thought of better ways of testing the hypotheses that led him to this partitioning. It does make sense that the absolute change in birth rate depends on the initial rate—perhaps the initial rate for the next younger age group would be better—in order to capture cohort effects. It does make sense that the marginal efficacy of family-planning programs depends on the interaction of initial birth rates and program inputs. The initial levels of the independent variables, as well as that of the dependent variable, would enter if one had in mind a stock-adjustment model. But I am not sure I see the logic of using the residuals from the 1964 cross section as an interactive factor with *all* the independent variables in the regressions of 1964–69 differences.

A stock-adjustment model is what one would come up with if he really allowed himself to be infected by the spirit of this meeting, namely that children are durable goods that yield utility-generating services in amounts that depend on certain input flows. But before we ask Dale Jorgensen or his equivalent to apply neoclassical investment theory to these durable goods, we might remind him of some of their peculiar properties. They come in discrete integral lumps; they cannot be bought or sold in the used-child market or scrapped at will; the rental market is highly imperfect; delivery time is more than normally uncertain; their qualities are very uncertain ex ante, and ex post control of quality is quite limited; their own requirements and tastes alter the household utility function, and so on. Suppressing these concerns and looking at the problem as one of durable goods investment, I am led to some other questions about Schultz's specifications.

The first concerns the treatment of the survival rate. The rate used is the theoretical probability of survival to age 15, calculated from specific age-mortality rates for each year. Choice of this variable seems to imply that families calculate changes of survival ex ante, and beget extra children in advance to allow for expected attrition. Given that the mean survival rate appears to be 0.94 in 1966 and given the discreteness of choices available to an individual family, I find this description of behavior implausible.

In the text Schultz suggests a different scenario—specific replacement of lost children by subsequent births. The opposite hypothesis would be discouragement, in the literal sense of loss of heart. This matter could be tested directly if individual observations were available, but here Schultz has only regional aggregates. A low survival rate in the past may have contributed to an aggregate stock of children below desired stocks, but unexpected or regretted births may have contributed to the opposite. In any case, the logical variable would seem to be the number of living children per 1,000 mothers in the region, parceled out by age of mother if possible.

If the replacement scenario is correct, one could expect the elasticity of the birth rate with respect to the survival rate to be greater the older the mother. An older woman has less time to make the replacement. Schultz's tables do disclose some tendency in this direction.

My second question concerns the interpretation of the regional proportions of persons in agriculture or with education. Movements over time in these proportions occur mainly through the young, who adopt or attain different characteristics from their elders. How does the fact that the region is becoming less agricultural and better educated affect the behavior of families whose occupation and education were already fixed long ago? I would have more confidence in estimates of the effects of these variables on birth-rate declines if the significant coefficients were systematically concentrated on the younger age brackets.

In the level cross-section regressions, these proportions presumably represent mainly long-standing differences among regions, differences which may well affect family size targets. The appropriate dependent variable is then the *stock* of children per 1,000 women, age-corrected, not the birth rate. Clearly an interregional difference in such a proportion is not the same thing as an intertemporal change in the proportion for a given region. If region A is and always has been better educated than region B, the difference is diffused over all age brackets. If region B becomes better educated in 1969 than it was in 1964, the difference is concentrated in the younger brackets.

In a similar vein, it is one thing to find that educated women have fewer children than their less-educated contemporaries. It is another thing to expect that this difference will predict how much a general increase over time in women's education in a country or a region will diminish overall fertility. The second effect will be weaker than the first. This follows on purely economic grounds, since a general advance in educational attainment cannot increase women's wages as much as a similar advance concentrated on a few women puts them ahead of their peers. In any case, the opportunity cost of child rearing depends not only on the market value of women's time but also on the time required for child rearing, and education may diminish the latter at the same time that it raises the former.

We must be careful not to prove too much. Human reproduction will continue, I suspect, even if all women are college educated. At least equal in importance to the calculations of the new home economics, it seems to me, is the general social definition of the appropriate role of women, determining simultaneously how much schooling they get, how much work they do outside the home, and how many children they have.

Part Three

Economics of Marriage

A Theory of Marriage

Gary S. Becker

University of Chicago and National Bureau of Economic Research

I

1. Introduction

In recent years, economists have used economic theory more boldly to explain behavior outside the monetary market sector, and increasing numbers of noneconomists have been following their examples. As a result, racial discrimination, fertility, politics, crime, education, statistical decision making, adversary situations, labor-force participation, the uses of "leisure" time, and other behavior are much better understood. Indeed, economic theory may well be on its way to providing a unified framework for *all* behavior involving scarce resources, nonmarket as well as market, nonmonetary as well as monetary, small group as well as competitive.

Yet, one type of behavior has been almost completely ignored by economists,[1] although scarce resources are used and it has been followed in some form by practically all adults in every recorded society. I refer to marriage. Marital patterns have major implications for, among other things, the number of births and population growth, labor-force participation of women, inequality in income, ability, and other characteristics among families, genetical natural selection of different characteristics

I benefited from the discussion of several earlier drafts of this paper at the Workshop in Applications in Economics of the University of Chicago and in seminars at the National Bureau of Economic Research, Northwestern University, and the Population Council. Very helpful suggestions were received from William Brock, Isaac Ehrlich, Alan Freiden, H. Gregg Lewis, Robert T. Michael, Marc Nerlove, Richard Posner, George J. Stigler, T. W. Schultz, and two referees. Michael Keeley provided valuable research assistance. Research was supported by a grant from the Ford Foundation to the National Bureau of Economic Research for the study of the economics of population. This paper is not an official NBER publication since it has not been reviewed by the NBER Board of Directors.

[1] To the best of my knowledge, the only exception prior to my own work is an unpublished paper by Gronau (1970*a*). His paper helped stimulate my interest in the subject.

over time, and the allocation of leisure and other household resources. Therefore, the neglect of marriage by economists is either a major oversight or persuasive evidence of the limited scope of economic analysis.

In this essay, it is argued that marriage is no exception and can be successfully analyzed within the framework provided by modern economics. If correct, this is compelling additional evidence on the unifying power of economic analysis.

Two simple principles form the heart of the analysis. The first is that, since marriage is practically always voluntary, either by the persons marrying or their parents, the theory of preferences can be readily applied, and persons marrying (or their parents) can be assumed to expect to raise their utility level above what it would be were they to remain single. The second is that, since many men and women compete as they seek mates, a *market* in marriages can be presumed to exist. Each person tries to find the best mate, subject to the restrictions imposed by market conditions.

These two principles easily explain why most adults are married and why sorting of mates by wealth, education, and other characteristics is similar under apparently quite different conditions. Yet marital patterns differ among societies and change over time in a variety of ways that challenge any single theory. In some societies divorce is relatively common, in others, virtually impossible, and in Western countries it has grown rapidly during the last half-century. Some societies adjust to legal difficulties in receiving divorces by delaying marriage, whereas others adjust by developing more flexible "consensual," "common-law," or "trial" marriages. In many the bride brings a dowry, in others the groom pays a bride-price, and in still others couples marry for "love" and disdain any financial bargaining. In some the newly married usually set up their own household, in others they live with one set of parents.

I do not pretend to have developed the analysis sufficiently to explain all the similarities and differences in marital patterns across cultures or over time. But the "economic" approach does quite well, certainly far better than any available alternative.[2] It is hoped that the present essay will stimulate others to carry the analysis into these uncharted areas.

Section 2 of Part I considers the determinants of the gain from marriage compared to remaining single for one man and one woman. The gain is shown to be related to the "compatibility" or "complementarity" of their time, goods, and other inputs used in household production.

Section 3 of Part I considers how a group of men and women sort themselves by market and nonmarket characteristics. Positive assortative mating— a positive correlation between the values of the traits of husbands and wives —is generally optimal, one main exception being the sorting by the earn-

---

[2] Some of the best work has been done by Goode (1963), but there is no systematic theory in any of his fine work.

ing power of men and women, where a negative correlation is indicated. Empirically, positive assortive mating is the most common and applies to IQ, education, height, attractiveness, skin color, ethnic origin, and other characteristics.

Section 4 of Part I considers how the the total output of a household gets divided between the husband and wife. The division is not usually fixed, say at 50–50, or determined mechanically, but changes as the supply of and demand for different kinds of mates changes.

Part II develops various extensions and modifications of the relatively simple analysis in this part. "Caring" is defined, and some of its effects on optimal sorting and the gain from marriage are treated. The factors determining the incidence of polygamous marital arrangements are considered. The assumption that the characteristics of potential mates are known with certainty is dropped, and the resulting "search" for mates, delays in marriage, trial marriage, and divorce are analyzed. Divorce and the duration of marriage are also related to specific invest-ments made during marriage in the form of children, attachments, and other ways. Also briefly explored are the implications of different marital patterns for fertility, genetical natural selection, and the inequality in family incomes and home environments.

2. The Gain from Marriage

This section considers two persons, M and F, who must decide whether to marry each other or remain single. For the present, "marriage" simply means that they share the same household. I assume that marriage occurs if, and only if, both of them are made better off—that is, increase their utility.[3]

Following recent developments in the theory of household behavior, I assume that utility depends directly not on the goods and services purchased in the market place, but on the commodities produced "by" each household.[4] They are produced partly with market goods and services and partly with the own time of different household members. Most important for present purposes, commodities are not marketable or transferable among households, although they may be transferable among members of the same household.

Household-produced commodities are numerous and include the quality of meals, the quality and quantity of children, prestige, recreation, companionship, love, and health status. Consequently, they cannot be

---

[3] More precisely, if they *expect* to increase their utility, since the latter is not known with certainty. Part II discusses some consequences of this uncertainty, especially for the time spent searching for an appropriate mate and the incidence of divorce and other marital separations.

[4] An exposition of this approach is given in Michael and Becker (1973).

identified with consumption or output as usually measured: they cover a much broader range of human activities and aims. I assume, however, that all commodities can be combined into a single aggregate, denoted by Z. A sufficient condition to justify aggregation with fixed weights is that all commodities have constant returns to scale, use factors in the same proportion, and are affected in the same way by productivity-augmenting variables, such as education. Then different commodities could be converted into their equivalent in terms of any single commodity by using the fixed relative commodity prices as weights.[5] These weights would be independent of the scale of commodity outputs, the prices of goods and the time of different members, and the level of productivity.

Maximizing utility thus becomes equivalent for each person to maximizing the amount of Z that he or she receives. Moreover, my concentration on the output and distribution of Z does not presuppose transferable utilities, the same preference function for different members of the same household, or other special assumptions about preferences.

Each household has a production function that relates its total output of Z to different inputs:

$$Z = f(x_1, \ldots, x_m; t_1, \ldots, t_k; E), \tag{1}$$

where the x_i are various market goods and services, the t_j are the time inputs of different household members, and E represents "environmental" variables. The budget constraint for the x_i can be written as:

$$\sum^m p_i x_i = \sum^k w_j l_j + v, \tag{2}$$

where w_j is the wage rate of the jth member, l_j the time he spends working in the market sector, and v property income. The l_j and t_j are related by the basic time constraint

$$l_j + t_j = T \qquad \text{all } j, \tag{3}$$

where T is the total time of each member. By substituting equation (3) into (2), the goods and time constraints can be combined into a single "full" income constraint:

$$\sum^m p_i x_i + \sum^k w_j t_j = \sum^k w_j T + v = S, \tag{4}$$

where S stands for full income, the maximum money income achievable, if the w_j are constants.

I assume that a reduction in the household's total output of Z makes

---

[5] One serious limitation of these assumptions is that they exclude the output of commodities from entering the production functions of other commodities. With such "joint production," the relative price of a commodity would depend partly on the outputs of other commodities (Grossman 1971). Joint production can result in complementarity in consumption, and thereby affect the gain from marriage and the sorting of mates. See the brief discussion which follows in section 3.

no member better off and some worse off.[6] Consequently, each member would be willing to cooperate in the allocation of his time and goods to help maximize the total output of Z. Necessary conditions to maximize Z include

$$\frac{MP_{t_i} \equiv (\partial Z/\partial t_i)}{MP_{t_j} \equiv (\partial Z/\partial t_j)} = \frac{w_i}{w_j}, \qquad \text{for all } 0 < t < T. \tag{5}$$

If the household time of the kth member $= T$, then

$$\frac{MP_{t_k}}{MP_{t_j}} = \frac{\mu_k}{w_j}, \tag{6}$$

where $\mu_k \geq w_k$ is the "shadow" price of the time of k. Also

$$\frac{MP_{x_i}}{MP_{t_j}} = \frac{p_i}{w_j} \qquad \text{for all } x_i > 0 \text{ and } 0 < t_j < T. \tag{7}$$

Each member must cooperate and allocate his time between the market and nonmarket sectors in the appropriate proportions.

If M and F are married, their household is assumed to contain only the two time inputs t_m and t_f; for simplicity, the time of children and others living in the same household is ignored. As long as they remain married, $T_m = T_f = 24$ hours per day, 168 hours per week, and so forth, and conditions (5) to (7) determine the allocation of the time of M and F between the market and nonmarket sectors. More time would be allocated to the market sector by M than by F (less to the nonmarket sector) if $w_m > w_f$ and if $MP_{t_f} \geq MP_{t_m}$ when $t_f = t_m$. Indeed, F would specialize in the nonmarket sector ($l_f = 0$) if either w_m/w_f or MP_{t_f}/MP_{t_m} were sufficiently large.

A singles household is taken to be exactly the same as a married one except that $T_f = 0$ when M is single and $T_m = 0$ when F is single. A singles household allocates only its own time between the market and nonmarket sectors to satisfy equation (7). Single persons generally allocate their time differently than married persons because the former do not have time and goods supplied by a mate. These differences depend partly on the elasticities of substitution among the x_i, t_f, and t_m, and partly on the differences between the market wage rates w_m and w_f. For example, single F are more likely to "work" more than married F and single M less than married M, the greater the percentage excess of w_m over w_f. Empirically, single women clearly "work" more than married women and single men less than married men.[7]

If Z_{m0} and Z_{0f} represent the maximum outputs of single M and F, and m_{mf} and f_{mf} their incomes when married, a necessary condition for

[6] This assumption is modified in the following section and in Part II.

[7] See, e.g., *Employment Status and Work Experience* (U.S., Bureau of the Census 1963c), tables 4 and 12.

M and F to marry is that

$$m_{mf} \geq Z_{m0}$$
$$f_{mf} \geq Z_{0f}. \qquad (8)$$

If $m_{mf} + f_{mf}$, the total income produced by the marriage, is identified with the output of the marriage,[8] a necessary condition for marriage is then that

$$m_{mf} + f_{mf} \equiv Z_{mf} \geq Z_{m0} + Z_{0f}. \qquad (9)$$

Since most men and women over age 20 are married in all societies, equation (9) must generally hold because of fundamental reasons that are not unique to time or place. I have a useful framework for discovering these reasons.

The obvious explanation for marriages between men and women lies in the desire to raise own children and the physical and emotional attraction between sexes. Nothing distinguishes married households more from singles households or from those with several members of the same sex than the presence, even indirectly, of children. Sexual gratification, cleaning, feeding, and other services can be purchased, but not *own* children:[9] both the man and woman are required to produce their own children and perhaps to raise them. The physical and emotional involvement called "love" is also primarily between persons of the opposite sex. Moreover, persons in love can reduce the cost of frequent contact and of resource transfers[10] between each other by sharing the same household.

Economies of scale may be secured by joining households, but two or more males or females could equally well take advantage of these economies and do so when they share an apartment and cooking. Consequently, the explanation of why men and women live together must go beyond economies of scale.

The importance of own children and love implies that, even with constant returns to scale, M (now standing for a man) and F (now standing for a woman) gain from marriage because t_m and t_f are not perfect substitutes for each other or for goods and services supplied by market firms or households. When substitution is imperfect, single persons cannot produce small-scale equivalents of the optimal combination of inputs achieved by married couples.

Consequently, the "shadow" price of an hour of t_f to a single M—the price he would be willing to pay for t_f—would exceed w_f, and the "shadow" price of t_m to a single F—the price she would be willing to pay

---

[8] Income and output can differ, however, because some output may be jointly consumed. See the discussion in the following section and in Part II.

[9] The market in adoptions is used primarily by couples experiencing difficulties in having their own children and by couples paid to raise other persons' children.

[10] The relation between love and such transfers is discussed in Part II.

for t_m—would exceed w_m. Both gain from marriage because M then, in effect, can buy an hour of t_f at w_f and F can buy an hour of t_m at w_m, lower prices they then would be willing to pay. Of course, this is also why married households use positive amounts of t_f and t_m.

My explanation of the gain from marriage focuses on the complementarity between M and F. The gain from complementary can be illustrated in much-exaggerated measure by assuming that the production function relating Z to t_m, t_f, and x has the Cobb-Douglas form

$$Z = kx^a t_m{}^b t_f{}^c. \tag{10}$$

Clearly, $Z_{m0} = Z_{0f} = 0$ since both t_m and t_f are needed to produce Z ($Z = 0$ if t_m or $t_f = 0$), whereas Z_{mf} can take any value. Other functions have less extreme "complementarity" and permit positive production when some inputs are absent but less "efficiently" than when all are present.

Some sociological literature also suggests that complementarity between men and women is the major source of the gain from marriage (Winch 1958, 1967; Goode 1963), but the meaning of "complementarity" is left rather vague and ill defined. By building on the substantial economic literature that analyzes complementarity and substitution in production, I have shown how "complementarity" determines the gain from marriage.

Can this analysis also explain why one man is typically married to one woman, rather than one man to several women, several men to one woman, or several men to several women? The importance of own children is sufficient to explain why marriages of several men to one or several women are uncommon since it would be difficult to identify the father of a child if many men had access to the same woman, whereas the identity of the mother is always known. The marriage of several women to one man does not suffer from this defect, and, indeed, such marriages have been more common. However, if the sex ratio equalled about unity, each household having several women and one man would have to be balanced by households having only men. If I assume that all men and all women are identical, and if I make the rather plausible assumption of "diminishing returns" from adding persons to a household having one man and one woman, the total output from say two single male households and one household with three women and one man would be smaller than the total output from three households each having one man and one woman.[11] Consequently, monogamous unions—one man married to one woman—predominate because it is the most efficient marital form.

---

[11] For example, assume that singles households have an output of 5 units of Z, one man and one woman 13 units, one man and two women 20 units, and one man and three women 26 units. Three households each with one man and one woman would produce 39 units, whereas two single male households and one household having three women and one man would produce only 36 units.

Polygamy is encouraged when the sex ratio is significantly different from unity and when men or women differ greatly in wealth, ability, or other attributes.[12]

My definition of marriage in terms of whether a man and a woman share the same household differs from the legal definition because my definition includes persons in "consensual" and casual unions and excludes legally married persons who are separated. However, my analysis does have useful implications about the choice between legally recognized and other unions (Kogut 1972), as well as about the decisions to remain married, divorce, remarry legally, remarry "consensually," remain single, and so forth, that must be made in the course of a lifetime (see Part II).

The gain from marriage has to be balanced against the costs, including legal fees and the cost of searching for a mate, to determine whether marriage is worthwhile. The larger the gain is relative to costs, the larger the net gain from marriage; presumably, therefore, the larger too is the fraction of persons who marry. I now consider the more important determinants of this net gain.

The gain is greater the more complementary are the inputs: the time of spouses and market goods. Since I have argued that these inputs are complementary in good part because of the desire to raise own children, the gain would be positively related to the importance of children. Hence, persons desiring relatively few or low-"quality" children either marry later, end their marriages earlier, or do both.[13]

The gain from marriage also depends on market opportunities. The effect of a change in opportunities can be analyzed most easily by equating the maximum output of any household to its full income deflated by the average cost of producing a unit of output. For example, with constant returns to scale, the output of a married household with both members participating in the labor force can be written as

$$Z_{mf} = \frac{\text{full income}}{\text{average cost of production}} \equiv \frac{S_{mf}}{C_{mf}(w_m, w_f, p)} \equiv \frac{S_m + S_f}{C_{mf}},$$

$$(11)$$

where C_{mf} depends on the wage rates of t_m and t_f and the price of x.[14] The output of a singles household can be written in the same form except that only one price of time enters the average cost functions C_m and C_f.[15]

What is the effect of an increase in income on the incentive to marry? If only the property incomes of M and F, v_m and v_f, rose exogenously

[12] See the more extensive discussion of polygamy in Part II.

[13] A further discussion can be found in Keeley (1974).

[14] Duality theory shows that C is the dual of the production function.

[15] Or, alternatively, the shadow price of F to M enters C_m, and the shadow price of M to F enters C_f.

by the same percentage, and if $v_m/S_m = v_f/S_f$, then S_m, S_f, and S_{mf} would all rise by the same percentage. With constant returns to scale, Z_{m0}, Z_{0f}, and Z_{mf}, and thus the absolute gain from marriage, would also rise by the same percentage as full income since neither C_{mf}, C_m, nor C_f would be affected by the rise in property incomes, as long as both M and F continue to participate in the labor force,[16] and assuming that property income is unaffected by the allocation of time.[17] Since a rise in property income should not greatly affect the cost of getting married, the incentive to marry would also rise.

The effect of a rise in wage rates alone[18] on the incentive to marry is less clear-cut. A rise in the wage rates of M and F by the same percentage would increase outputs by smaller percentages than full incomes, even with constant returns to scale, because costs of production also rise.[19] Moreover, the cost of getting married rises to the extent that the own time of M and F enters into search and other marital costs. Consequently, the effect on the net gain from marriage is not clear a priori and depends on the relative importance of own time in marriage costs and in the production of output in single and married households.

Consequently, my analysis predicts that a rise in property income, necessarily, and a rise in wage rates, possibly, increase the incentive to marry. This implication runs counter to the popular opinion that poor persons marry earlier and divorce less than rich persons but is consistent with the empirical evidence. In the United States, at least, the probability of separation and divorce is negatively related to income (U.S., Bureau of the Census 1971). Keeley (1974) finds too that when years of schooling and a few other variables are held constant, higher-wage persons appear to marry earlier than others.

My analysis implies that a rise in w_f relative to w_m, F's wage rate relative to M's, with the productivity of time in the nonmarket sector held constant, would decrease the gain from marriage if w_f were less than w_m: the gain from substituting M's time in the market for F's time (and F's time in the household for M's time) is greater the lower w_f is relative to w_m. As a proof, consider an increase in w_f "compensated" by a sufficient decrease in w_m to maintain constant the combined output of the two singles households. The increase in w_f would not increase married output as

---

[16] Even if married F did not participate in the labor force, the percentage rise in Z_{mf} would still equal the share of property income in full income (see section 2, Part I of the Appendix).

[17] The gain from marriage would increase even more if the income from nonhuman capital, i.e., property income, was positively related to the time allocated to "portfolio management" (see the discussion in the following section).

[18] By alone is meant in particular that the productivity of time in household production or marital search is unchanged.

[19] The percentage rise in output equals the percentage rise in wage rates multiplied by the ratio of total earnings to full income. Although this relation holds whether or not married F is in the labor force (see section 2, Part I of the Appendix), the ratio of total earnings to full income can depend—positively or negatively—on her participation.

much as the decrease in w_m would decrease it if married F worked sufficiently fewer hours in the market sector than single F, and married M worked at least as much as single M. Since married women do work much less than single women and married men work more than single men, an increase in the wage rate of women relative to men would decrease the incentive to marry.[20] As supporting evidence, note that American states that have higher wage rates of women relative to men also have smaller fractions of men and women who are married (Santos 1970; Freiden 1972).

The gain from marriage also depends on traits, such as beauty, intelligence, and education, that affect nonmarket productivity as well, perhaps, as market opportunities. The analysis of sorting in section 3b implies that an increase in the value of traits that have a positive effect on nonmarket productivity, market productivity held constant, would generally increase the gain from marriage. Presumably this helps explain why, for example, less attractive or less intelligent persons are less likely to marry than are more attractive or more intelligent persons.[21]

3. The Marriage Market and Sorting of Mates

a) Optimal Sorting

I now consider not one M and F who must decide whether to marry or remain single, but many M's and F's who must decide whom to marry among numerous potential candidates, as well as whether to marry. If there are n M's and n F's (unequal numbers of M and F are discussed in section 4), each is assumed to know all the relevant[22] entries in an $n + 1 \times n + 1$ payoff matrix showing the maximum household commodity output that can be produced by any combination of M and F:

$$
\begin{array}{c|ccc}
 & F_1 & \cdots & F_n \\
\hline
M_1 & Z_{11} & \cdots & Z_{1n}\ Z_{10} \\
 & & Z_{ij} & \\
M_n & Z_{n1} & \cdots & Z_{nn}\ Z_{n0} \\
 & Z_{01} & \cdots & Z_{0n}
\end{array}
\qquad (12)
$$

The last row and column give the output of single M and F. Each person has $n + 1$ possibilities and the $2n$ persons together have $n^2 + 2n$ pos-

[20] A fortiori, if married women were not in the labor force, a compensated increase in their wage rate would decrease the incentive to marry since an increase in their wage rate would not affect married output, whereas a decrease in the male wage rate would decrease output. This footnote as well as the text assumes that compensated changes in w_f and w_m do not much affect the cost of getting married.

[21] Evidence on marriage rates by intelligence can be found in Higgins, Reed, and Reed (1962) and Bajema (1963). The statement on marriage rates by attractiveness is not based on any statistical evidence.

[22] That is, all the entries relevant to their decisions. This strong assumption of sufficient information is relaxed in Part II, where "search" for a mate is analyzed.

sibilities. I assume that each person gains from marriage, so that the singles row and column of the payoff matrix can be ignored.

There are $n!$ different combinations that permit each M to marry one F and vice versa; that is, there are $n!$ ways to select one entry in each married row and column. The total output over all marriages produced by any one sorting can be written as

$$Z^k = \sum_{i \in M, j \in F} Z_{ij}, \qquad k = 1, \ldots, n!. \tag{13}$$

Number one of the sortings that maximizes total output so that its entries lie along the diagonal and write

$$Z^* = \sum_{i=1}^{n} Z_{ii} = \max_k Z^k \geq Z^k \qquad \text{all } k. \tag{14}$$

If the total output of any marriage is divided between the mates,

$$m_{ij} + f_{ij} = Z_{ij}, \tag{15}$$

where m_{ij} is the income of the ith M from marriage to the jth F, and similarly for f_{ij}. If each chooses the mate who maximizes his or her "income," the optimal sorting must have the property that persons not married to each other could not marry and make one better off without making the other worse off. In game theoretic language, the optimal sorting is in the "core" since no "coalition" outside the core could make any of its members better off without making some worse off.

Persons entering noncore marriages could not produce more together than the sum of their incomes in the core. For, if they could, and if any division of output between mates were feasible, they could find a division of their output that would make each better off, a contradiction of the definition of the core. If the sorting along the diagonal were in the core, this condition states that

$$m_{ii} + f_{jj} \geq Z_{ij} \qquad \text{all } i \text{ and } j. \tag{16}$$

Conditions (15) and (16) immediately rule out any sorting that does not maximize the total output of commodities over all marriages, for at least one M and one F would then be better off with each other than with their mates.[23] Moreover, the theory of optimal assignments, which has

---

[23] If M_i married F_j and F_i married M_p in an optimal sorting that did not maximize total output, condition (16) requires that $m_{ij} + f_{pi} \geq Z_{ii}$, all ij, pi, or, by summation,

$$Z_p = \sum_{\text{all } ij, \, pi}^{n} m_{ij} + f_{pi} \geq \sum_i Z_{ii} = Z^*.$$

Since Z^* is the maximum total output, it must exceed Z_p, by assumption less than the maximum. Hence, a contradiction, and a proof that the optimal sorting cannot produce less than the maximum total output.

the same mathematical structure as the sorting of persons by marriage, implies the existence of a set of incomes that satisfy conditions (15) and (16) for sortings that maximize total output.[24]

The solution can be illustrated with the following 2×2 matrix of payoffs:

$$\begin{matrix} & F_1 & F_2 \\ M_1 & \begin{bmatrix} 8 & 4 \\ M_2 & 9 & 7 \end{bmatrix} \end{matrix} \tag{17}$$

Although the maximum output in any marriage is between M_2 and F_1, the optimal sorting is M_1 to F_1 and M_2 to F_2. For, if $m_{11} = 3$, $f_{11} = 5$, $m_{22} = 5$, and $f_{22} = 2$, M_2 and F_1 have no incentive to marry since $m_{22} + f_{11} = 10 > 9$, and neither do M_1 and F_2 since $m_{11} + f_{22} = 5 > 4$. In other words, the marriage market chooses not the maximum household commodity output of any single marriage but the maximum sum of the outputs over all marriages, just as competitive product markets maximize the sum of the outputs over all firms. Let me stress again that the commodity output maximized by all households is not to be identified with national output as usually measured, but includes conversation, the quantity and quality of children, and other outputs that never enter or enter only imperfectly into the usual measures. Put still differently, the marriage market acts as if it maximizes not the gain from marriage compared to remaining single for any particular marriage, but the average gain over all marriages.[25]

Each marriage can be considered a two-person firm with either member being the "entrepreneur" who "hires" the other at the "salary" m_{ij} or f_{ij} and receives residual "profits" of $Z_{ij} - m_{ij}$ or $Z_{ij} - f_{ij}$. Another interpretation of the optimal sorting is that only it enables each "entrepreneur" to maximize "profits" for given "salaries" of mates because only the optimal sorting satisfies condition (16). With all other sortings, some "entrepreneurs" could do better by "hiring" different mates than those assigned to them.

---

[24] For a proof, see Koopmans and Beckman (1957).

[25] Clearly,

$$\left[\sum_i^n Z_{ii} - \sum_{j=1}^n (Z_{0j} + Z_{j0}) \right] \bigg/ n = \left\{ \sum_i [Z_{ii} - (Z_{0j} + Z_{j0})] \right\} \bigg/ n$$

is maximized if

$$\sum Z_{ii}$$

is, since Z_{0j} and Z_{j0} are given and independent of the marital sorting.

b) Assortive Mating

I now consider the optimal sorting when M and F differ in a trait, or set of traits, such as intelligence, race, religion, education, wage rate, height, aggressiveness, tendency to nurture, or age. Psychologists and sociologists have frequently discussed whether likes or unlikes mate, and geneticists have occasionally assumed positive or negative assortive mating instead of random mating. But no systematic analysis has developed that predicts for different kinds of traits when likes or unlikes are motivated to mate.[26] My analysis implies that likes or unlikes mate when that maximizes total household commodity output[27] over all marriages, regardless of whether the trait is financial (like wage rates and property income), or genetical (like height and intelligence), or psychological (like aggressiveness and passiveness).

Assume that M differs only in the quantitative trait A_m, and F only in A_f, that each trait has a monotonic effect on the output of any marriage, and that higher values have the larger effect:

$$\frac{\partial Z_{ij}(A_m, A_f)}{\partial A_m} > 0, \qquad \frac{\partial Z_{ij}}{\partial A_f}(A_m, A_f) > 0. \tag{18}$$

If increasing both A_m and A_f adds the same amount to output as the sum of the additions when each is increased separately, all sortings of M and F would give the same total output. On the other hand, if increasing both adds more to output than the sum of the separate additions, a sorting of large A_m with large A_f and small A_m with small A_f would give the greatest total output since an increase in A_m reinforces the effect of an increase in A_f. The converse holds if increasing both adds less to output than the sum of the separate additions. Mathematically, this states that positive or negative assortive mating—mating of likes or unlikes—is optimal as

$$\frac{\partial^2 Z(A_m, A_f)}{\partial A_m \, \partial A_f} \gtrless 0 \tag{19}$$

(proofs in Appendix, Part I, section 1).

Consider, as an example, a matrix of outputs when $n = 2$:

$$\begin{array}{c} \\ A_1 \\ A_2 \end{array} \begin{array}{c} A_1 \quad A_2 \\ \begin{bmatrix} Z_{11} & Z_{12} \\ Z_{21} & Z_{22} \end{bmatrix} \end{array}, \qquad \text{with } A_2 > A_1. \tag{20}$$

---

[26] Winch (1958) essentially assumes that each person tries to maximize utility ("In mate selection each individual seeks within his or her field of eligibles for that person who gives the greatest promise of providing him or her with maximum need gratification" [pp. 88–89]) and stresses complementary needs as a prerequisite for mating (especially in chap. 4), but he only considers psychological traits, brings in "eligibles" as a deus ex machina, and nowhere shows how mating by complementary needs brings equilibrium into the marriage market.

[27] Let me emphasize again that commodity output is not the same as national product as usually measured, but includes children, companionship, health, and a variety of other commodities.

If $Z_{22} - Z_{12} > Z_{21} - Z_{11}$, if equality (19) is positive, then obviously $Z_{11} + Z_{22} > Z_{12} + Z_{22}$, and a positive correlation between A_m and A_f maximizes total output, as predicted from (19).

One tradition in production theory distinguishes substitution from complementarity by the sign of the cross-derivative of output with respect to different inputs into a production function. Although condition (19) is not defined in terms of household production functions, duality theory implies that the same condition holds when A_m and A_f are treated as inputs into these production functions.[28] Condition (19) says, therefore, that the association of likes is optimal when traits are complements and the association of unlikes is optimal when they are substitutes, a plausible conclusion since high values of different traits reinforce each other when they are complements, and offset each other when they are substitutes.

Economists have generally considered the sorting of different *quantities* of different traits, such as labor and capital, not different *qualities* of the same trait. Although sorting by quantity and quality are related analytically, many applications of sorting by quality are also directly available in economics, such as the optimal sorting of more able workers and more able firms,[29] more "modern" farms and more able farmers, or more informed customers and more honest shopkeepers. As already mentioned (n. 26 above), some sociologists have considered "complementarity" to be an important determinant of sorting, but have not given a rigorous analysis of the effects of "complementarity" or embedded their discussions in the context of a functioning marriage market.

Mating of likes—positive assortative mating—is extremely common, whether measured by intelligence, height, skin color, age, education, family background, or religion, although unlikes sometimes also mate, as measured, say, by an inclination to nurture or succor, to dominate or be deferential. This suggests that traits are typically but not always complements.

The determinants of complementarity and substitutability are best discovered by going explicitly to the household production function and the maximization process. All households are assumed to have the same production *function*; that is, if the inputs of time, goods, and *all* traits were exactly the same, the output of commodities would be exactly the same. Different families can, of course, produce different outputs from the same input of goods and time if their education, ability, and so forth, differ.

I consider a number of determinants in turn. First, if M and F differ *only* in their market wage rates—each M and each F are identical in all

---

[28] Wage rates or other monetary variables, however, cannot be treated as productive inputs.

[29] This sorting is discussed for Japanese firms by Kuratani (1972). Hicks (1948, chap. 2, sec. 3) asserts that more able workers work for more able firms without offering any proof. Black (1926) discusses the sorting of workers and firms with a few numerical examples.

other market and in nonmarket traits—according to equation (11), the optimal output between M and F who are both participating in the labor force can be written as

$$Z = \frac{S}{C(w_m, w_f, p)}, \qquad (21)$$

where the subscripts on Z, S, and C have been omitted and constant returns to scale assumed. Then, by differentiation and by using equation (4),

$$Z^m = \frac{T}{C} - \frac{S}{C^2} C^m,$$

where

$$\left.\begin{array}{c} \\ Z^m = \dfrac{\partial Z}{\partial w_m} \quad \text{and} \quad C^m \equiv \dfrac{\partial C}{\partial w_m} \end{array}\right\} \qquad (22)$$

Since

$$C^m = t_m Z^{-1}, \qquad (23)$$

where t_m is the time spent by M in the household,

$$Z^m = l_m C^{-1} > 0 \qquad (24)$$

if l_m, the time spent at work, is greater than zero. Similarly,

$$Z^f = \frac{T}{C} - \frac{S}{C^2} C^f = l_f C^{-1} > 0. \qquad (25)$$

Positive or negative assortive mating by wage rates is optimal as

$$\frac{\partial^2 Z}{\partial w_m \, \partial w_f} \equiv Z^{mf} \equiv Z^{fm} \gtrless 0. \qquad (26)$$

Differentiate Z^f with respect to w_m to get

$$Z^{fm} = -C^{-2} C^m l_f + C^{-1} \frac{\partial l_f}{\partial w_m}. \qquad (27)$$

The first term on the right is clearly negative, so Z^{fm} will be negative if the second term, $\partial l_f / \partial w_m \leq 0$, is nonpositive, that is, if t_m and t_f are not gross complements, as these terms are usually defined.[30] Consequently, a perfectly negative rank correlation between w_m and w_f would maximize total commodity output if the time of M and F were not such gross

---

[30] This definition is different from the one given earlier in terms of the sign of the cross-derivative of profit or production functions. The definition in equation (28) is preferable, at least as a predictor of responses to changes in input prices. By "gross" rather than "net" complements is meant in the usual way that the income effect is included along with the substitution effect. Even if t_m and t_f were net complements they could still be gross substitutes since the income effect of an increase in w_m would tend to increase t_f.

complements as to swamp the first term in (27). Considerable empirical evidence supports the conclusion that t_m and t_f are not gross complements (Ofek 1972; Smith 1972a).

A negative correlation between w_m and w_f maximizes total output because the gain from the division of labor is maximized. Low-wage F should spend more time in household production than high-wage F because the foregone value of the time of low-wage F is lower; similarly, low-wage M should spend more time in household production than high-wage M. By mating low-wage F with high-wage M and low-wage M with high-wage F, the cheaper time of both M and F is used more extensively in household production, and the expensive time of both is used more extensively in market production.

All persons have been assumed to participate in the labor force. During any year, however, most married women in the United States do not participate, and a significant number never really participate throughout their married life. My analysis does predict that many women would have only a weak attachment to the labor force since low-wage women would be discouraged from participation both by their low wage and by the high wage of their husbands.[31]

If some women are not in the labor force, however, the wage rates of men and women need not be perfectly negatively correlated to maximize total output. For assume that all women with wage rates below a certain level would not participate in the labor force with a perfectly negative correlation between the wage rates of men and women. These women have $\partial Z/\partial w_f = 0$,[32] and, thus, $Z^{fm} = 0$; therefore, up to a point, they could switch mates without lowering total output. Consequently, other sortings having weaker negative, and conceivably even positive, correlations would also maximize total output; that is, many sortings would be equally good, and wage rates would not be a decisive determinant of the optimal sorting.

If M and F differ only in their stock of nonhuman capital, K_m and K_f, and if everyone participates in the labor force, $\partial C/\partial K_m = \partial C/\partial K_f = 0$ since the value of time is measured by the market wage rates. If the rate of return on K, denoted by r, depended positively on the amount of time allocated to "portfolio management," r would be positively related to K.[33] It then follows that

---

[31] Low-wage men also would be encouraged to work less both because of their low wage and the relatively high wage of their wives. They would not leave the labor force in large numbers, however, partly because average wage rates of men are so much higher than those of women and partly because the nonmarket productivity of women is higher than that of men.

[32] As long as they are not indifferent at the margin to working in the market sector.

[33] For this result and a more complete analysis of the allocation of time to portfolio management, see Ben-Zion and Ehrlich (1972).

$$\frac{\partial Z}{\partial K_m} = \frac{\partial Z}{\partial K_f} = rC^{-1} > 0$$

and

$$\frac{\partial^2 Z}{\partial K_m \, \partial K_f} = \frac{dr}{dK} C^{-1} > 0$$

(28) [34]

A perfectly positive correlation between the nonhuman capital of M and F would be optimal, an implication that is consistent with evidence on sorting by, say, parental wealth.

If some F did not participate in the labor force, the value of their time would be measured by a "shadow" price that exceeded their wage rate and was not constant but positively related to the sum of their nonhuman capital.[35] Moreover, a perfectly positive correlation of this capital is no longer necessarily optimal because of diminishing returns to an increase in the time of M and goods for a given amount of the time of F (for proof, see Appendix, Part I, section 2).

All differences in the output of commodities, by assumption the only determinant of behavior, not related to differences in wage rates or nonhuman capital are, by definition, related to differences in nonmarket productivity.[36] The widespread differences between men and women in nonmarket productivity are caused by differences in intelligence, education, health, strength, height, personality, religion, and other traits. I now consider the optimal sorting of traits that affect nonmarket productivity, while assuming that wage rates and nonhuman capital are the same for all M and for all F.

To demonstrate the tendency toward complementarity of nonmarket traits in the context of household commodity outputs, rewrite the optimal output equation given by (21) as

$$Z = \frac{S}{C(w_m, w_f, p, A_m, A_f)},$$

(29)

where A_m and A_f are the traits of M and F. Then using the assumption that w_m, w_f, and the rate of return on nonhuman capital are independent of A_m and A_f,

---

[34] If time is allocated to portfolio management, $S = wT + Kr(\ell_p) - w\ell_p$, where ℓ_p is the time so allocated. Then $\partial S/\partial K = r + (K \, dr/d\ell_p)(d\ell_p/dK) - w(d\ell_p/dK) = r + d\ell_p/dK[(K \, dr/d\ell_p) - w]$. Since, however, $K \, dr/d\ell_p = w$ is one of the first-order maximization conditions, then $\partial S/\partial K = r$.

[35] See the discussion in section 2, Part I of the Appendix.

[36] Differences in the earning power of children are assumed to be derived from differences in either the nonmarket productivity or incomes of their parents, and are not considered separately.

$$
\left.\begin{aligned}
\frac{\partial C}{\partial A_m} &\equiv C_{a_m} \\[2mm]
\frac{\partial C}{\partial A_f} &\equiv C_{a_f}
\end{aligned}\right\} < 0 \quad \text{and} \quad \frac{\partial S}{\partial A_f} = \frac{\partial S}{\partial A_m} = 0. \tag{30}
$$

Then,

$$
\left.\begin{aligned}
\frac{\partial Z}{\partial A_m} &= -SC^{-2}C_{a_m} \\[2mm]
\frac{\partial Z}{\partial A_f} &= -SC^{-2}C_{a_f}
\end{aligned}\right\} > 0, \tag{31}
$$

and

$$
\frac{\partial^2 Z}{\partial A_m\,\partial A_f} > 0 \quad \text{if } 2C^{-1}C_{a_m}C_{a_f} > C_{a_m,a_f}. \tag{32}
$$

Since the term on the left is positive, equation (32) necessarily holds if A_m and A_f have either independent or reinforcing effects on productivity, for then $C_{a_m,a_f} \leq 0$; moreover, (32) might hold even if they had offsetting effects. Therefore, perfectly positive assortive mating is definitely optimal if the traits have reinforcing effects; less obvious and more impressive, however, is the conclusion that positive assortive mating is also optimal if they have independent effects because C enters inversely in the equation for Z, or even if they have offsetting effects if these are weaker than a multiple of the direct ones.[37]

The reasons for the prevalence of a complementary relation between traits that raise nonmarket productivity can be seen more transparently by considering a couple of special cases. If the percentage effect on output of a trait were independent of the quantities of goods and time, the optimal output equation could be written as

$$
Z = \frac{S}{b(A_m, A_f)K(w_m, w_f, p)}, \tag{33}
$$

where $\partial b/\partial A_m \equiv b_{a_m} < 0$, and $\partial b/\partial A_f \equiv b_{a_f} < 0$. Hence,

$$
\frac{\partial^2 Z}{\partial A_m\,\partial A_f} > 0 \quad \text{as } 2b^{-1}b_{a_m}b_{a_f} > b_{a_m,a_f}, \tag{34}
$$

---

[37] Equation (32) can be written as

$$
2|\varepsilon_{c_{a_m}}| > \varepsilon_{c_{a_f},a_m},
$$

where $\varepsilon_{c_{a_m}} = (C_{a_m} \cdot A_m)/C < 0$, and $\varepsilon_{c_{a_m},a_f} = C_{a_f,a_m} \cdot A_m/C_{a_f} > 0$ if the effects are offsetting. The cross-elasticity must be smaller than twice the absolute value of the direct elasticity.

which must hold if $b_{a_m,a_f} \leq 0$ and can easily hold even if $b_{a_m,a_f} > 0$. Positive assortative mating is optimal even when these productivity effects are independent because productivity is raised multiplicatively: higher A_m (or A_f) have bigger *absolute* effects when combined with higher A_f (or A_m). A fortiori, this multiplicative relation encourages the mating of likes when the effects are reinforcing and can do so even when they are offsetting.[38]

The effect of most traits on nonmarket output is not independent of goods and time, but generally operates through the time supplied to the household; for example, if the time supplied became zero, so would the effect. A simple way to incorporate this interaction is to assume that each trait affects outputs only by augmenting the effective amount of own household time. It is shown in section 3, Part I of the Appendix that positive assortative mating would still be optimal as long as the elasticity of substitution between the household time of M and F was not very high.[39] Negative assortative mating can be expected for own-time-augmenting traits only if they augment dimensions that are easily substitutable between M and F. Dominant and deferential persons tend to marry each other (Winch 1958), perhaps, therefore, because the dominant person's time can be used when households encounter situations calling for dominance and the deferential person's time can be used when they call for deference.

Note that it is shown in section 2 that the gain from marriage is also greater when substitution between the time of M and F is more difficult. Therefore, the mating of likes should be more common when marriage is more attractive, an important and subtle implication of the analysis.

How do the nonmarket traits of one sex combine with the market traits of the other? In particular, does my analysis justify the popular belief that more beautiful, charming, and talented women tend to marry wealthier and more successful men? Section 4 in Part I of the Appendix shows that a positive sorting of nonmarket traits with nonhuman wealth always, and with earning power usually,[40] maximizes commodity output over all marriages. The economic interpretation is basically that nonmarket productivity and money income tend to combine multiplicatively, so that higher values of a trait have larger absolute effects when combined with higher income.

Scattered references have been made to the empirical evidence on sorting, and this evidence is now considered a little more systematically. The simple correlations between the intelligence, education, age, race,

---

[38] Section 3, Part I of the Appendix shows that positive assortative mating of A_m and A_f is still optimal even when F do not participate in the labor force.

[39] The elasticity estimates of Ofek (1972) and Smith (1972a) are only of modest size.

[40] By "usually" is meant that a positive sorting with earnings always maximizes total output when an increase in a trait does not decrease the spouses' hours worked in the market sector and *could* maximize output even when they do decrease.

nonhuman wealth, religion, ethnic origin, height, and geographical propinquity of spouses are positive and strong.[41] A small amount of evidence suggests that the correlations between certain psychological traits, such as a propensity to dominate, nurture, or be hostile, are negative.[42] The correlation by intelligence is especially interesting since, although intelligence is highly inheritable, the correlation between mates is about as high as that between siblings (Alstrom 1961). Apparently, the marriage market, aided by coeducational schools, admissions tests, and the like, is more efficient than is commonly believed.

This evidence of positive simple correlations for a variety of traits, and of negative correlations for some, is certainly consistent with my theory of sorting. A more powerful test of the theory, however, requires evidence on partial correlations, when various other traits are held constant. For example, how strong is the correlation by intelligence, when years of schooling and family background are held constant? I do not yet have results on partial correlations by intelligence, but do have some on years of schooling, wage rates, and age, for samples of white and black families.[43] Even when age and wage rates are held constant, the correlation between years of schooling is high, $+.53$ for whites and virtually the same $(+.56)$ for blacks. Although the partial correlations between wage rates are much lower, they are also positive, $+.32$ for whites and a bit lower $(+.24)$ for blacks.

The strong positive partial correlation between years of schooling is predicted by the theory, but the positive correlation between wage rates is troublesome since the theory predicts a negative correlation when nonmarket productivity is held constant. Note, however, that the sample is biased because it is restricted to women in the labor force in a particular year. Since the higher the husband's wage rate the higher must be his wife's wage rate to induce her to enter the labor force, a negative correlation across all mates is consistent with a positive one for those having wives in the labor force.[44] Indeed, Gregg Lewis has shown[45] that a correlation of about $+.3$ for mates who are participating almost certainly implies a negative one (about $-.25$) for all mates, given the relatively small

[41] Many of the relevant studies are listed in Winch (1958, chap. 1).

[42] See Winch (1958, chap. 5). Deference is treated as negative values of dominance, succorance as negative values of nurturance, and abasement as negative values of hostility.

[43] A 20 percent random sample of the approximately 18,000 married persons in the 1967 Survey of Economic Opportunity was taken. Families were included only if the husband and wife both were less than age 65 and were employed, the wife for at least 20 hours in the survey week.

[44] Also, nonmarket productivity varies even when years of schooling and age are held constant. If investments that raise nonmarket productivity also raise, somewhat, market earning power (Heckman [1974] finds that the education of women raises their nonmarket productivity almost as much as their market earning power), the positive correlation between wage rates may really be picking up the predicted positive correlation between husband's wage rate and wife's nonmarket productivity.

[45] Via an unpublished memorandum extending some work of Gronau (1972).

fraction of married women who participate. If his calculations hold up, this would be striking confirmation of my theory since it is counter to common impressions and is one of the few examples (and a predicted one!) of negative associative mating.

Other evidence, probably less affected by unobserved differences in nonmarket productivity, does suggest that the gain from marriage is greater when differentials between male and female wage rates are greater. For example, a larger percentage of persons are married in American states that have higher wages of males and lower wages of females, even when age, years of schooling, the sex ratio, the fraction Catholic, and other variables are held constant (Santos 1970; Frieden 1972). Or a larger fraction of black households are headed by women in metropolitan areas with higher earnings of black women relative to black men (Reischauer 1970).

Quantitative evidence on the association of traits that affect nonmarket productivity with earnings and other income is scarce. The evidence I put together and referred to earlier indicates that husband's wage rate and wife's education are significantly positively correlated, even when husband's education and wife's wage rate are held constant.[46] One interpretation, stressed by Benham in his paper which follows, is that a wife's education contributes to her husband's earnings, just as a mother's education is said to contribute to her children's earnings (Leibowitz 1972). An alternative suggested by our theory of sorting is that a wife's education is a proxy for traits affecting her nonmarket productivity, especially when her wage rate is held constant[47] and that women with higher nonmarket productivity marry men with higher earning power. Although the relative importance of these alternative interpretations has not been determined, Benham does find that hours worked by husbands are positively related to wife's education, a sufficient condition for positive sorting (see n. 40 above).

My analysis of mating and sorting has assumed perfect certainty in the production of household commodities. Uncertainty surrounds the production of many commodities, but my concern here is only with uncertainty about the "quality" of own children since children are a major source of the gain from marriage. An important result in population genetics is that positive assortive mating of inheritable traits, like race, intelligence, or height, increases the correlation of these traits among siblings; the increase would be greater the more inheritable the trait is and the greater the degree of assortive mating (Cavalli-Sforza and Bodmer 1971, chap. 9, sec. 7). Therefore, inheritable traits of M and F

[46] In his more detailed analysis in this book, Benham finds similar results, after several additional variables are also held constant. Note, however, that the husband's wage rate is much more strongly related to his own than to his wife's education.

[47] I argued earlier that her wage rate also is a proxy for such traits, when her education is held constant.

can be said to be complements in reducing the uncertainty about one's children. Positive assortative mating of inheritable traits would increase the utility of total output if more certainty about the "quality" of children is desirable—perhaps because friction between siblings or the cost of raising them is increased by uncertainty.

My analysis of sorting is based on several other simplifying assumptions that ought to be modified in a fuller treatment. For example, the conclusion in section 2, that the gain from marriage is independent of preferences, assumes, among other things, no joint production and constant returns to scale in households. With beneficial joint production[48] or increasing returns, mating of persons with similar preferences would be optimal and conversely with detrimental production or decreasing returns. Similarly, the conclusion in section 2, that a monogamous union is always optimal, which is taken for granted in the discussion of sorting, should be modified to consider polygamy (I do this in Part II) and remaining single (see the discussion of search in Part II). Further, I have considered only one trait at a time, holding all other traits constant. But since people differ in many interdependent traits, optimal sortings should be determined for a set of traits, perhaps using the canonical correlation coefficient or related statistics as the measure of association.

Probably the assumption that would be most questioned is that any division of output between mates is feasible. Some of the output may not be divisible at all and may constitute a "public," or better still, a "family" commodity. Children might be said to be largely a family commodity, and, as shown in Part II, "caring" can convert the whole output into family commodities. Or some divisions may not be feasible because they are not enforceable. For example, even though the marriage market might dictate a 2/5 share for a particular husband, he may receive a 3/5 share because his wife cannot "police" the division perfectly.

Although the rigidities resulting from family commodities and enforcement problems can often be overcome (through dowries and other capital transfers), it is instructive to consider a model of sorting that incorporates these rigidities in an extreme fashion. How robust are the conclusions about optimal sorting when complete rigidity in the division of output replaces the assumption of complete negotiability?

Rigidity is introduced by assuming that M_i would receive a constant fraction e_i of commodity output in *all* marriages, and F_j receive d_j. Note that e_i and e_k $(k \neq i)$ or d_j and d_k $(k \neq j)$ need not be equal, and that

$$e_i + d_j \gtrless 1, \tag{35}$$

as family commodities or enforcement costs were dominant. The matrix showing the incomes for all combinations of M and F would then be

---

[48] Grossman (1971) distinguishes beneficial from detrimental production by the effect of an increase in output of one commodity on the cost of producing others.

$$
\begin{array}{c|ccc|}
 & F_1 & F_j & F_n \\
\hline
M_1 & e_1 Z_{11}, d_1 Z_{11} & \cdots\cdots\cdots & e_1 Z_{1n}, d_n Z_{nn} \\
M_i & & e_i Z_{ij}, d_j Z_{ij} & \\
M_n & e_n Z_{nj}, d_1 Z_{n1} & \cdots\cdots\cdots & e_n Z_{nn}, d_n Z_{nn} \\
\hline
\end{array}
\qquad (36)
$$

If

$$
\hat{Z}_1 \equiv Z_{st} > Z_{ij}, \qquad \text{all } i \neq s, \text{ all } j \neq t, \qquad (37)
$$

were the maximum output in any possible marriage and if each person tried to maximize his commodity income, M_s would marry F_t since they could not do as well in any other marriage.[49] Now exclude M_s and F_t from consideration, and if

$$
\hat{Z}_2 = Z_{uv} > Z_{ij}, \qquad \text{all } i \neq u \text{ or } s, \text{ all } j \neq v \text{ or } t, \qquad (38)
$$

were the maximum output in all other marriages, M_u would marry F_v. This process can be continued through the $\hat{Z}_3, \ldots, \hat{Z}_n$ until all the M and F are sorted.

How does this sorting, which combines the various maxima, compare with that obtained earlier, which maximizes total output? As the example in (17) indicates, they are not necessarily the same: combining the maxima in that example sorts M_2 with F_1 and M_1 with F_2, whereas maximizing total output sorts M_1 with F_1 and M_2 with F_2. Yet, in perhaps the most realistic cases, they are the same, which means that the sum of the maxima would equal the maximum of the sums.

Assume that an increase in trait A_m or A_f always increases output and that M and F are numbered from lower to higher values of these traits. Then, $\hat{Z}_1$ is the output of M_n with F_n, $\hat{Z}_2$ is that of M_{n-1} with F_{n-1}, and $\hat{Z}_n$ that of M_1 with F_1. Consequently, when traits have monotonic effects on output, the most common situation, combining the various maxima implies perfectly positive assortive mating.

I showed earlier that, in a wide variety of situations, namely, where traits are "complementary," maximizing total output also implies perfectly positive assortive mating. In these situations, permitting the market to determine the division of output and imposing the division a priori gives exactly the same sorting. Therefore, the implication of the theory about the importance of positive assortive mating is not weakened, but rather strengthened, by a radical change in assumptions about the determinants of the division of output.

When maximizing total output implies negative assortive mating, as it does between wage rates (with nonmarket productivity held constant), and between own-time augmenting traits that are close substitutes, these assumptions about the division of output have different implications. The

---

[49] Clearly, $e_s Z_{st} > e_s Z_{sj}$, all $j \neq t$, and $d_t Z_{st} > d_t Z_{it}$, all $i \neq s$ by condition (37).

empirical evidence on sortings cannot yet clearly choose between these assumptions, however, because positive sortings are so common: perhaps the positive correlation between observed wage rates is evidence of rigidities in the division, but several alternative interpretations of this correlation have been suggested that are consistent with a negative "true" correlation, and some psychological traits are apparently negatively correlated. Moreover, dowries and other capital transfers provide more effective fluidity in the division than may appear to the casual observer.

4. The Division of Output between Mates

With complete negotiability the division of output is given by condition (15) and (16). The m_{ii} and f_{ii} are determined by their marginal productivity in the sense that if $Z_{ki} > Z_{kk}$, necessarily $f_{ii} > f_{kk}$,[50] and similarly for the m_{ii}. Also, if $f_{ii} > f_{kk}$, necessarily $Z_{ii} > Z_{ik}$.[51] The following limits are easily derived:

$$\left. \begin{array}{l} Z_{ii} - \mathrm{Max}_k \, (Z_{ki} - Z_{kk}) \geq m_{ii} \geq \mathrm{Max}_k \, (Z_{ik} - Z_{kk}) \\ Z_{ii} - \mathrm{Max}_k \, (Z_{ik} - Z_{kk}) \geq f_{ii} \geq \mathrm{Max}_k \, (Z_{ki} - Z_{kk}) \end{array} \right\} \, [52] \qquad (39)$$

The division of output resulting from conditions (15) and (16) is not unique, however. For if a set of m_{ii} and f_{ii} satisfies these conditions with all $0 < m_{ii} < Z_{ii}$, a positive quantity λ exists, such that $m_{ii} + \lambda$ and $f_{ii} - \lambda$ also satisfy these conditions. The range of indeterminacy in the division would narrow as the sum of $\mathrm{Max}_k \, (Z_{ik} - Z_{kk})$ and $\mathrm{Max}_k \, (Z_{ki} - Z_{kk})$ approached closer to Z_{ii}.

Clearly, the indeterminacy would vanish if the distribution of Z_{ik} became continuous. It could also vanish in a second case to which I turn. Assume v_i identical M_i and u_i identical F_i; by identical is meant that they would produce the same output with any mate or while single, so that they would receive the same income in market equilibrium. If the number of v_i were sufficiently large for a competitive equilibrium, there would be a supply curve of M_i to the marriage market: it would be horizontal at the singles income Z_{io} until all $v_i{}^o$ were married, and then would rise vertically (see S_o in fig. 1). Similarly, if the number of u_i were sufficiently large, there would be a market supply curve of F_i: it would be horizontal at Z_{oi} until all $u_i{}^o$ were married, and then would rise vertically. If initially I assume, for simplicity, that the M_i and F_i either marry each other or remain single, the supply curve of F_i would

---

[50] Since $f_{kk} + m_{kk} = z_{kk}$, all k, and $f_{ii} + m_{kk} \geq z_{ki}$, all i and k, then $f_{ii} - f_{kk} \geq z_{ki} - z_{kk} > 0$ by assumption.

[51] That is, if $f_{ii} > f_{kk}$, then $Z_{ii} = m_{ii} + f_{ii} > m_{ii} + f_{kk} \geq Z_{ik}$.

[52] Given conditions (15) and (16), $m_{ii} - m_{kk} \geq Z_{ik} - Z_{kk}$, all k, or, since $m_{kk} \geq 0$, $m_{ii} \geq Z_{ik} - Z_{kk}$, all k. The other conditions in (39) can be proved in a similar way.

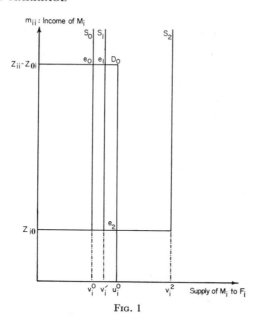

FIG. 1

also be a derived demand curve for M_i that would be horizontal at $Z_{ii} - Z_{oi}$ until all u_i^o were married, and then would fall vertically (D_o in fig. 1); moreover, the supply curve of M_i to the market would be its supply curve to F_i.

The equilibrium income to each M_i is given by point e_o, the intersection of S_o and D_o. If the sex ratio (v_i^o/u_i^o) were less than unity, the equilibrium position is necessarily on the horizontal section of the derived demand curve, as is e_o. All the M_i would marry and receive the whole difference between their married output and the singles output of F_i. All the F_i would receive their singles output and, therefore, would be indifferent between marrying and remaining single, although market forces would encourage v_i^o of them to marry.

An increase in the sex ratio due to an increase in the number of M_i would lengthen the horizontal section of the supply curve and shift the equilibrium position to the right, say, to e_1. All the M_i would continue to marry and a larger fraction of the F_i also would. If the sex ratio rose above unity, equilibrium would be on the horizontal section of the supply rather than the derived demand curve (see e_2). Now all the F_i would marry and receive the whole difference between their married output and the singles output of M_i; market forces would induce u_i^o of the M_i to marry, and $v_i^2 - u_i^o$ to remain single.

The importance of sex ratios in determining the fraction of men and women who marry has been verified by numerous episodes and in several studies. An aftermath of a destructive war is many unmarried young women pursuing the relatively few men available, and men usually either marry late or not at all in rural areas that have lost many young women to cities. Statistical studies indicate that the fraction of women currently married at different ages is positively related to the appropriate sex ratio.[53]

I know of only highly impressionistic evidence on the effects of the sex ratio, or for that matter any other variable, on the division of output between mates. This division usually has not been assumed to be responsive to market forces, so that no effort has been put into collecting relevant evidence. Admittedly, it is difficult to separate expenditures of goods and time into those that benefit the husband, the wife, or both, but with enough will something useful could be done. For example, the information giving the separate expenditures on husband's and wife's clothing in some consumer surveys, or on the "leisure" time of husbands and wives in some time budget studies could be related to sex ratios, wage rates, education levels, and other relevant determinants of the division of output.

If I drop the assumption that all the M_i and F_i must either marry each other or remain single, M_i's supply curve to F_i would differ from its market supply curve because marriage to other persons would be substituted for marriage to F_i; similarly, F_i's supply curve to M_i would differ from its market supply curve. To demonstrate this, suppose that, at point e_0 in figure 1, M_i does better by marrying F_i than by marrying anyone else; that is, condition (16) is a strict inequality for M_i. If M_i's income from marrying F_i were less than at e_0, the difference between the sum of M_i's income and that of other $F_j \neq F_i$, and what they could produce together would be reduced. At some income, this difference might be eliminated for an F, say, F_k: then all the M_i would be indifferent between marrying F_i and F_k.

At lower values of M_i's income from marrying F_i, some of the M_i would try to marry F_k. The increase in the supply of mates to F_k would raise M_i's income and reduce that of M_i's mates. In equilibrium, just enough M_i would marry F_k to maintain equality between the income M_i receives with F_i and F_k. The important point is that if some M_i marry F_k, the number marrying F_i would be less than the number supplied to the marriage market (v_i). Moreover, the number marrying F_i might fall still further as M_i's income with F_i fell further because some might marry, say, F_p, if they could then do as well with F_p as with F_i or F_k.

The net effect of these substitutions toward other F is a rising supply curve of M_i to F_i, shown by S_o in figure 2, with an elasticity determined both by the distribution of substitute F and by the effect on the income of

[53] See the studies essentially of whites by Santos (1970) and Freiden (1972), of blacks by Reischauer (1970), of Puerto Rico by Nerlove and Schultz (1970), and of Ireland by Walsh (1972). By "appropriate" is meant that a group of women must be matched with the men they are most likely to marry, e.g., college-educated women with college-educated men, or women aged 20–24 with men aged 25–29.

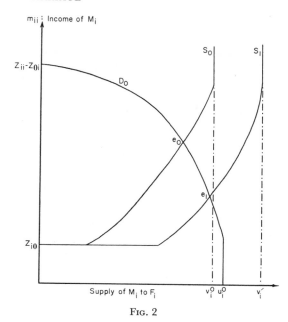

FIG. 2

these F of a given increase in the number of M_i available to marry them. Since F_i would also substitute toward other M, its derived demand curve for M_i would also fall, as D_o does in figure 2. The equilibrium position e_o determines both the division of output between M_i and F_i and the number marrying each other. The difference between the total number of M_i, v_i^o, and the number marrying F_i no longer measures the number of M_i remaining single, since at e_o all M_i marry, but rather it measures the number marrying other F and receiving the same income as the M_i marrying F_i; similarly, for the F_i.

An increase in the number of M_i from v_i^o to v'_i would shift their supply curve to F_i to the right and lower the equilibrium position to e_1 in figure 2. The reduction in M_i's income (equal to the increase in F_i's income) is negatively related to the elasticities of the demand and supply curves, which are determined by the availability of substitute M and F. The additional M_i all marry, some to F_i and some to other F; a larger fraction of the F_i are induced to marry M_i by the increase in F_i's income.

An increase in the sex ratio between M_i and F_i would not necessarily increase the fraction of F_i or decrease the fraction of M_i who marry since all can marry if some marry other F or M. However, if all F_i and M_i married, an increase in their sex ratio would tend to decrease the number of other M or increase the number of other F who marry, if the quantity of other M and F were fixed. For an increase in the ratio of M_i to F_i not only lowers M_i's and raises F_i's income, but also lowers the incomes of substitute M and raises those of substitute F. Some of these M

would thereby be induced not to marry because their gain from marriage would be eliminated, and some F would be induced to marry because a gain from marriage would be created. Consequently, an increase in the ratio of M_i to F_i would still decrease the fraction of M and increase the fraction of F marrying, if substitute M and F as well as M_i and F_i were considered.

To illustrate these effects, assume an autonomous increase (perhaps due to selective immigration) in the size of a group of identical men, aged 24, who initially were indifferent between marrying women aged 22 and those slightly older or younger, although most married 22-year-olds. The increase in their numbers would decrease their income and the proportion marrying women aged 22. For if the percentage increase in the number marrying women aged 22 were as large as the increase in the number marrying other women, the income of those marrying 22-year-olds would fall by more than others, since men aged 24 are a larger fraction of all men marrying women aged 22 than of all men marrying women of other ages. Moreover, the income of women aged 22 would increase and more of them would marry men aged 24; the income of older or younger men marrying women aged 22 would fall and they would be encouraged to marry women of other ages; the income of women somewhat older or younger than 22 would increase too, and so on.[54]

5. Summary

In Part I above I have offered a simplified model of marriage that relies on two basic assumptions: (1) each person tries to find a mate who maximizes his or her well-being, with well-being measured by the consumption of household-produced commodities; and (2) the "marriage market" is assumed to be in equilibrium, in the sense that no person could change mates and become better off. I have argued that the gain from marriage compared to remaining single for any two persons is positively related to their incomes, the relative difference in their wage rates, and the level of nonmarket-productivity-augmenting variables, such as education or beauty. For example, the gain to a man and woman from marrying compared to remaining single is shown to depend positively on their incomes, human capital, and relative difference in wage rate.

The theory also implies that men differing in physical capital, education or intelligence (aside from their effects on wage rates), height, race, or many other traits will tend to marry women with like values of these traits, whereas the correlation between mates for wage rates or for traits of men and women that are close substitutes in household production will tend to be negative.

[54] The permanence of these effects depends on whether the immigration continues or is once and for all.

My theory does not take the division of output between mates as given, but rather derives it from the nature of the marriage market equilibrium. The division is determined here, as in other markets, by marginal productivities, and these are affected by the human and physical capital of different persons, by sex ratios, that is, the relative numbers of men and women, and by some other variables.

II

1. Introduction

In the discussion which follows I extend the simplified analyses in Part I in several directions. My purpose is both to enrich the analysis in Part I and to show the power of this approach in handling different kinds of marital behavior.

The effect of "love" and caring between mates on the nature of equilibrium in the marriage market is considered. Polygamy is discussed, and especially the relation between its incidence and the degree of inequality among men and the inequality in the number of men and women. The implications of different sorting patterns for inequality in family resources and genetic natural selection are explored. The assumption of complete information about all potential mates is dropped and I consider the search for information through dating, coeducational schools, "trial" marriages, and other ways. This search is put in a life-cycle context that includes marriage, having children, sometimes separation and divorce, remarriage, and so forth.

2. Love, Caring, and Marriage

In Part I, I ignored "love," that cause of marriage glorified in the American culture. At an abstract level, love and other emotional attachments, such as sexual activity or frequent close contact with a particular person, can be considered particular nonmarketable household commodities, and nothing much need be added to the analysis, in Part I, of the demand for commodities. That is, if an important set of commodities produced by households results from "love," the sorting of mates that maximizes total commodity output over all marriages is partly determined by the sorting that maximizes the output of these commodities. The whole discussion in Part I would continue to be relevant.

There is a considerable literature on the effect of different variables such as personality, physical appearance, education, or intelligence, on the likelihood of different persons loving each other. Since I do not have anything to add to the explanation of whether or why one person would love another, my discussion concentrates on some effects of love on marriage. In particular, since loving someone usually involves caring about what happens to him or her, [55] I concentrate on working out several implications, for marriage, of "caring."

An inclusive measure of "what happens" is given by the level of commodity consumption, and the natural way for an economist to measure "caring" is through the utility function. [56] That is, if M cares about F, M's utility would depend on the commodity consumption of F as well as on his own; graphically, M's indifference curves in figure 3 are negatively inclined with respect to Z_m and Z_f, the commodities consumed by M and F respectively. [57] If M cared as much about F as about himself (I call this "full" caring), the slopes of all the indifference curves would equal unity (in absolute value) along the 45° line; [58] if he cared more about himself, the slopes would exceed unity, and conversely if he cared more about F.

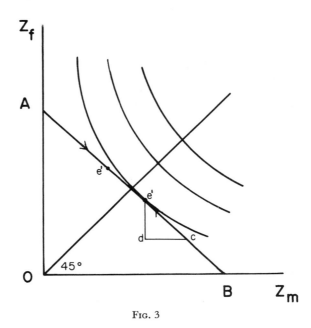

FIG. 3

[55] The *Random House Dictionary of the English Language* includes in its definitions of love, "affectionate concern for the well-being of others," and "the profoundly tender or passionate affection for a person of the opposite sex."

[56] This formulation is taken from my paper, "A Theory of Social Interactions" (1969).

[57] Since there is only a single aggregate commodity, saying that M's utility depends on F's consumption is equivalent to saying that M's utility depends on F's utility (assuming that F does not care about M). If many commodities $Z_1, \ldots, Z_q$, were consumed, M's utility would depend on F's utility if $U^m = U^m[Z_{1m}, \ldots, Z_{qm}, g(Z_{1f}, \ldots, Z_{qf})]$ where g describes the indifference surface of F. Hence $(\partial U^m/\partial Z_{if})/(\partial U^m/\partial Z_{jf}) = (\partial g/\partial Z_{if})/(\partial g/\partial Z_{jf})$; this ratio is F's marginal rate of substitution between Z_i and Z_j.

[58] "Full" caring might also imply that the indifference curves were straight lines with a slope of unity, that Z_f was a perfect substitute for Z_m.

Point c in figure 3 represents the allocation of commodities to M and F that is determined by equilibrium in the marriage market. Only if M were married to F could he transfer commodities to F, since household commodities are transferable within but not between households. If the terms of transfer are measured by the line AB, he moves along AB to point e: he transfers cd and F receives de. Presumably commodities can be transferred within a household without loss, so that AB would have a slope of unity. Then the equilibrium position after the transfer would be on the 45° line with full caring, and to the right of this line if M preferred his own consumption to F's.

Most people no doubt find the concept of a market allocation of commodities to beloved mates strange and unrealistic. And, as I have shown, caring can strikingly modify the market allocation between married persons. For example, the final allocation (point e) after the transfer from M to F has more equal shares than does the market allocation (point c).[59] Moreover, if F also cared about M, she would modify the market allocation by transferring resources to M from anywhere in the interval Ae' until she reached a point e',[60] generally to the left of e. The market completely determines the division of output only in the interval $e'e$: positions in Be are modified to e, and those in Ae' are modified to e'. Furthermore, if each fully cares for the other, points e and e' are identical and on the 45° line. Then the total amount produced by M and F would be shared equally, regardless of the market-determined division. This concept of caring between married persons, therefore, does imply sharing—equal sharing when the caring is full and mutual—and is thus consistent with the popular belief that persons in love "share."

Sharing implies that changes in the sex ratio or other variables considered in section 4 of Part I would not modify the actual distribution of output between married M and F (unless the market-mandated distribution were in the interval ee'). This is another empirical implication of caring that can be used to determine its importance.

I indicated earlier that total income would be less than total output in a marriage if resources were spent "policing" the market-mandated division of output, whereas total income would exceed total output if some output were a "family" commodity, that is, were consumed by both mates. Caring raises total income relative to total output both by reducing policing costs and by increasing the importance of family commodities.

Consider first the effect of caring on policing costs. "Policing" reduces the probability that a mate shirks duties or appropriates more output than is mandated by the equilibrium in the marriage market.[61] Caring reduces

[59] Provided it were in the interval Ae, M would not modify the market allocation.
[60] I assume that AB also gives the terms of transfer for F, and that e' is the point of tangency between AB and her indifference curves.
[61] Policing is necessary in any partnership or corporation, or, more generally, in any cooperative activity (see Becker 1971b, pp. 122–23; Alchian and Demsetz 1972).

the need for policing: M's incentive to "steal" from his mate F is weaker if M cares about F because a reduction in F's consumption also lowers M's utility. Indeed, caring often completely eliminates the incentive to "steal" and thus the need to police. Thus, at point e in the figure, M has no incentive to "steal" from F because a movement to the right along AB would lower M's utility.[62] Therefore, if M cares about F sufficiently to transfer commodities to her, F would not need to "police" M's consumption.[63] Consequently, marriages with caring would have fewer resources spent on "policing" (via allowances or separate checking accounts?) than other marriages would.

M's income at e exceeds his own consumption because of the utility he gets from F's consumption. Indeed, his income is the sum of his and F's consumption, and equals OB (or OA), the output produced by M and F. Similarly, F's income exceeds her own consumption if she benefits from M's consumption.[64] Caring makes family income greater than family output because some output is jointly consumed. At point e, all of F's and part of M's consumption would be jointly consumed. Since both e and e' are on the 45° line with mutual and full caring, the combined incomes of M and F would then be double their combined output: all of M's and all of F's consumption would be jointly consumed.

Love and caring between two persons increase their chances of being married to each other in the optimal sorting. That love and caring cannot reduce these chances can be seen by assuming that they would be married to each other in the optimal sorting even if they did not love and care for each other. Then they must also be married to each other in the optimal sorting if they do love and care for each other because love raises commodity output and caring raises their total income by making part of their output a "family" commodity. Hence, their incomes when there is love and caring exceed their incomes when there is not. Consider the following matrix of outputs:

$$
\begin{array}{c}
 \\
M_1 \\
\\
M_2 \\
\end{array}
\begin{array}{c}
F_1 \qquad F_2 \\
\left[
\begin{array}{cc}
8 & 4 \\
(3, 5) & \\
9 & 7 \\
& (5, 2)
\end{array}
\right].
\end{array}
\qquad (1)
$$

[62] A fortiori, a movement along any steeper line—the difference between AB and this line measuring the resources used up in "stealing"—would also lower M's utility.

[63] With mutual and full caring, neither mate would have to "police." On the other hand, if each cared more about the other than about himself (or herself), at least one of them, say M, would want to transfer resources that would not be accepted. Then F would "police" to prevent undesired *transfers from* M. This illustrates a rather general principle; namely, that when the degree of caring becomes sufficiently great, behavior becomes similar to that when there is no caring.

[64] F's income equals the sum of her consumption and a fraction of M's consumption that is determined by the slope of F's indifference curve at point e. See the formulation in section 1 of the Mathematical Appendix.

With no caring, this is also the matrix of total incomes,[65] and M_1F_1 and M_2F_2 would be the optimal sorting if incomes were sufficiently divisible to obtain, say, the division given in parenthesis. With mutual and full caring between M_1 and F_1, m'_{11}, the income of M_1, would equal $8 > 3$, and f'_{11}, the income of F_1, would equal $8 > 5$;[66] clearly, M_1 would still be married to F_1 in the optimal sorting.

That love and caring can bring a couple into the optimal sorting is shown by the following matrix of outputs:

$$
\begin{array}{c}
 \\
M_1 \\
\\
M_2 \\
\\
M_3 \\
\end{array}
\begin{bmatrix}
\begin{array}{ccc}
F_1 & F_2 & F_3 \\
10 & 6 & 5 \\
(4, 6) & & \\
9 & 10 & 4 \\
& (6, 4) & \\
2 & 3 & 10 \\
& & (5, 5) \\
\end{array}
\end{bmatrix}. \tag{2}
$$

Without love and caring the optimal sorting is M_1F_1, M_2F_2, and M_3F_3, with a set of optimal incomes given in parenthesis. If, however, M_1 and F_2 were in love and had mutual and full caring, the optimal sorting would become M_1F_2, M_2F_1, and M_3F_3 because the incomes resulting from this sorting, $m_{12} = f_{21} = k > 6$,[67] and, say, $m_{21} = f_{21} = 4\frac{1}{2}$, and $m_{33} = f_{33} = 5$, can block the sorting along the diagonal.

Does caring per se—that is, as distinguished from love—encourage marriage: for example, couldn't M_1 marry F_1 even though he receives utility from F_2's consumption, and even if he wants to transfer resources to F_2? One incentive to combine marriage and caring is that resources are more cheaply transferred within households: by assumption, commodities cannot be transferred between households, and goods and time presumably also are more readily transferred within households. Moreover, caring partly results from living together,[68] and some couples marry partly because they anticipate the effect of living together on their caring.

Since, therefore, caring does encourage (and is encouraged by) marriage, there is a justification for the economist's usual assumption that even a multiperson household has a single well-ordered preference function. For, if one member of a household—the "head"—cares enough about all other members to transfer resources to them, this household would act as if it maximized the "head's" preference function, even if the preferences of other members are quite different.[69]

[65] I abstract from other kinds of "family" commodities because they can be analyzed in exactly the same way that caring is.

[66] The output of love raises these incomes even further.

[67] The difference between k and 6 measures the output of love produced by M_1 and F_2.

[68] So does negative caring or "hatred." A significant fraction of all murders and assaults involve members of the same household (see Ehrlich 1970).

[69] For a proof, see section 1, Part II of the Appendix; further discussions can be found in Becker (1969).

Output is generally less divisible between mates in marriages with caring than in other marriages[70] because caring makes some output a family commodity, which cannot be divided between mates. One implication of this is that marriages with caring are less likely to be part of the optimal sorting than marriages without caring that have the same total *income* (and thus have a greater total output).[71]

Another implication is that the optimal sorting of different traits can be significantly affected by caring, even if the degree of caring and the value of a trait are unrelated. Part I shows that when the division of output is so restricted that each mate receives a given fraction of the output of his or her marriage, beneficial traits are always strongly positively correlated in the optimal sorting. A negative correlation, on the other hand, is sometimes optimal when output is fully divisible. Caring could convert what would be an optimal negative correlation into an optimal positive one because of the restrictions it imposes on the division of output.

For example, assume that a group of men and women differ only in wage rates, and that *each* potential marriage has mutual and full caring, so that the degree of caring is in this case uncorrelated with the level of wage rates; then the optimal correlation between wage rates would be positive, although I showed in Part I that it is negative when there is no caring.[72] The (small amount of) evidence presented there indicating that wage rates are negatively correlated suggests, therefore, that caring does not completely determine the choice of marriage mates.

3. Polygamy

Although monogamous unions predominate in the world today, some societies still practice polygamy, and it was common at one time. What determines the incidence of polygamous unions in societies that permit them, and why have they declined in importance over time?

I argued in Part I that polyandrists—women with several husbands—have been much less common than polygynists—men with several wives—because the father's identity is doubtful under polyandry. Todas of India did practice polyandry, but their ratio of men to women was much above

---

[70] See the proof in section 2, Part II of the Appendix.

[71] See the example discussed in section 2, Part II of the Appendix.

[72] As an example, let the matrix of outputs from different combinations of wage rates be

$$
\begin{array}{c}
 & F_{w_1} & F_{w_2} \\
M_{w_1} & \begin{bmatrix} 5 & 10 \\ (5, 5) & (10, 10) \\ 12 & 15 \\ (12, 12) & (15, 15) \end{bmatrix}
\end{array} .
$$

If outputs were fully divisible, the optimal sorting would be $M_{w_1}F_{w_2}$ and $M_{w_2}F_{w_1}$, since that maximizes the combined output over all marriages. With mutual and full caring in all marriages, the income of each mate equals the output in his or her marriage; these incomes are given in parenthesis. Clearly, the optimal sorting would now be $M_{w_2}F_{w_2}$ and $M_{w_1}F_{w_1}$.

one, largely due to female infanticide.[73] They mitigated the effects of uncertainty about the father by usually having brothers (or other close relatives) marry the same woman.

I showed in Part I that if all men and all women were identical, if the number of men equaled the number of women, and if there were diminishing returns from adding an additional spouse to a household, then a monogamous sorting would be optimal, and therefore would maximize the total output of commodities over all marriages.[74] If the plausible assumption of diminishing returns is maintained, inequality in various traits among men or in the number of men and women would be needed to explain polygyny.

An excess of women over men has often encouraged the spread of polygyny, with the most obvious examples resulting from wartime deaths of men. Thus, almost all the male population in Paraguay were killed during a war with Argentina, Brazil, and Uruguay in the nineteenth century,[75] and apparently polygyny spread afterward.

Yet, polygyny has occurred even without an excess of women; indeed, the Mormons practiced polygyny on a sizable scale with a slight excess of men.[76] Then inequality among men is crucial.

If the "productivity" of men differs, a polygynous sorting could be optimal, even with constant returns to scale and an equal number of men and women. Total output over all marriages could be greater if a second wife to an able man added more to output than she would add as a first wife to a less able one. Diminishing marginal products of men or women within each household do not rule out that a woman could have a higher marginal product as a second wife in a more productive household than as the sole wife in a less productive household.

Consider, for example, two identical women who would produce 5 units of output if single, and two different men who would each produce 8 and 15 units, respectively, if single. Let the married outputs be 14 and 27 when each man has one wife, and 18 and 35 when each has two.[77] Clearly, total output is greater if the abler man takes two wives and the other remains single than if they both take one wife: $35 + 8 = 43 > 14 +$

---

[73] See Rivers (1906). Whether the infanticide caused polyandry, or the reverse, is not clear.

[74] An optimal sorting has the property that persons not married to each other could not, by marrying, make some better off without making others worse off. I show in Part 1 (1973) that an optimal sorting maximizes total output of commodities.

[75] After the war, males were only 13 percent of the total population of Paraguay (see *Encyclopaedia Britannica*, 1973 ed., s.v. "Paraguay"). I owe this reference to T. W. Schultz.

[76] See Young (1954, p. 124). The *effective* number of women can exceed the number of men, even with an equal number at each age, if women marry earlier than men and if widowed women remarry. The number of women married at any time would exceed the number of men married because women would be married longer (to different men— they would be sequentially polyandrous!). This apparently was important in Sub-Saharan Africa, where polygyny was common (see Dorjahn 1959).

[77] These numbers imply diminishing marginal products, since $18 - 14 = 4 < 6$, and $35 - 27 = 8 < 12$.

27 = 41. If the abler man received, say, 21 units and each wife received, say, 7 units, no one would have any incentive to change mates.

My analysis implies generally that polygyny would be more frequent among more productive men—such as those with large farms, high positions, and great strength—an implication strongly supported by the evidence on polygyny. For example, only about 10–20 percent of the Mormons had more than one wife,[78] and they were the more successful and prominent ones. Although 40 percent of the married men in a sample of the Xavante Indians of Brazil were polygynous, "it was the chief and the heads of clans who enjoyed the highest degree of polygyny" (Salzano, Neel, and Maybury-Lewis 1967, p. 473). About 35 percent of the married men in Sub-Saharan Africa were polygynous (Dorjahn 1959, pp. 98–105), and they were generally the wealthier men. Fewer than 10 percent of the married men in Arab countries were polygynous, and they were the more successful, especially in agriculture (Goode 1963, pp. 101–4).

I do not have a satisfactory explanation of why polygyny has declined over time in those parts of the world where it was once more common.[79] The declines in income inequality and the importance of agriculture presumably have been partly responsible. Perhaps the sex ratio has become less favorable, but that seems unlikely, wartime destruction aside. Perhaps monogamous societies have superior genetic and even cultural natural selection (see the next section). But since more successful men are more likely to be polygynous, they are more likely to have relatively many children.[80] If the factors responsible for success are "inherited," selection over time toward the "abler" might be stronger in polygynous than in monogamous societies. I have even heard the argument that Mormons are unusually successful in the United States because of their polygynous past! However, if the wives of polygynous males were not as able, on the average, as the wives of equally able monogamous males, selection could be less favorable in polygynous societies.

The decline in polygyny is usually "explained" by religious and legislative strictures against polygyny that are supposedly motivated by a desire to prevent the exploitation of women. But the laws that prevent men from taking more than one wife no more benefit women than the

[78] Young (1954, p. 441) says that "in some communities it ran as high as 20–25 percent of the male heads of families," but Arrington (1958, p. 238) says about 10 percent of all Mormon families were polygynous.

[79] Polygyny was more common in Islamic and African societies than in Western and Asian ones, although in China and Japan concubines had some of the rights and obligations of wives (see Goode 1963, chap. 5).

[80] Salzano, Neel, and Maybury-Lewis (1967, p. 486) found evidence among the Xavante Indians of "similar means but significantly greater variance for number of surviving offspring for males whose reproduction is completed than for similar females." This indicates that polygynous males (the more successful ones) have more children than other males.

laws in South Africa that restrict the ratio of black to white workers (see Wilson 1972, p. 8) benefit blacks. Surely, laws against polygyny reduce the "demand" for women, and thereby reduce their share of total household output and increase the share of men.[81]

4. Assortive Mating, Inequality, and Natural Selection

I pointed out in Part I that positive assortive mating of different traits reduces the variation in these traits between children in the same family (and this is one benefit of such mating). Positive assortive mating also, however, increases the inequality in traits, and thus in commodity income, between families. Note that the effects on inequality in commodity and money incomes may be very different; indeed, if wage rates, unlike most other traits, are negatively sorted (as argued in Part I), assortive mating would reduce the inequality in money earnings and increase that in commodity income.

Positive sorting of inherited traits, like intelligence, race, or height, also increases the inequality in these traits among children in different families, and increases the correlation between the traits of parents and children (see proofs in Cavalli-Sforza and Bodmer [1971, chap. 9]). Moreover, positive sorting, even of noninherited traits such as education, often has the same effect because, for example, educated parents are effective producers of "education-readiness" in their children (see Leibowitz [1972] and the papers by her and Benham in this volume). The result is an increase in the correlation between the commodity incomes of parents and children, and thereby an increase in the inequality in commodity income among families spanning several generations. That is, positive assortive mating has primary responsibility for noncompeting groups and the general importance of the family in determining economic and social position that is so relevant for discussions of investment in human capital and occupational position.

Since positive assortive mating increases aggregate commodity income over all families, the level of and inequality in commodity income are affected in different ways. Probably outlawing polygyny has reduced the

---

[81] An alternative interpretation of the religious and legislative strictures against polygyny is that they are an early and major example of discrimination *against* women, of a similar mold to the restrictions on their employment in certain occupations, such as the priesthood, or on their ownership of property. This hypothesis has been well stated by (of all people!) George Bernard Shaw: "Polygamy when tried under modern democratic conditions as by the Mormons, is wrecked by the revolt of the mass of inferior men who are condemned to celibacy by it; for the maternal instinct leads a woman to prefer a tenth share in a first rate man to the exclusive possession of a third rate." See his "Maxims for Revolutionists" appended to *Man and Superman* (Shaw 1930, p. 220). Shaw was preoccupied with celibacy; he has three other maxims on celibacy, one being "any marriage system which condemns a majority of the population to celibacy will be violently wrecked on the pretext that it outrages morality" (1930, p. 220).

inequality in commodity income among men at the price of reducing aggregate commodity income. Perhaps other restrictions on mating patterns that reduce inequality would be tolerated, but that does not seem likely at present.

Since positive assortive mating increases the between-family variance, it increases the potential for genetic natural selection, by a well-known theorem in population genetics. [82] The actual amount of selection depends also on the inheritability of traits, and the relation between the levels of the traits of mates and the number of their surviving children (called "fitness" by geneticists). For example, given the degree of inheritability of intelligence, and a positive (or negative) relation between number of children and average intelligence of parents, the rate of increase (or decrease) per generation in the average intelligence of a population would be directly related to the degree of positive assortive mating by intelligence.

Moreover, the degree of assortive mating is not independent of inheritability or of the relation between number of children and parental traits. For example, the "cost" of higher-"quality" children may be lower to more-intelligent parents, and this affects the number (as well as quality) of children desired. [83] In a subsequent paper I expect to treat more systematically the interaction between the degree of assortive mating and other determinants of the direction and rate of genetic selection.

5. Life-Cycle Marital Patterns

To life-cycle dimensions of marital decisions—for instance, when to marry, how long to stay married, when to remarry if divorced or widowed, or how long to stay remarried—I have paid little attention so far. These are intriguing but difficult questions, and only the broad strokes of an analysis can be sketched at this time. A separate paper in the not-too-distant future will develop a more detailed empirical as well as theoretical analysis.

A convenient, if artificial, way to categorize the decision to marry is to say that a person first decides when to enter the marriage market and then searches for an appropriate mate. [84] The age of entry would be earlier

---

[82] This theorem was proved by Fisher (1958, pp. 37–38) and called "the fundamental theorem of natural selection." For a more recent and extensive discussion, see Cavalli-Sforza and Bodmer (1971, sec. 6.7).

[83] For a discussion of the interaction between the quantity and quality of children, see Becker and Lewis in this book.

[84] This categorization is made in an important paper by Coale and McNeil, "The Distribution by Age of the Frequency of First Marriage in a Female Cohort" (1972). They show that the frequency distribution of the age at first marriage can be closely fitted in a variety of environments by the convolution of a normal distribution and two or three exponential distributions. The normal distribution is said to represent the distribution of age at entry into the marriage market, and the exponential distributions, the time it takes to find a mate.

the larger the number of children desired, the higher the expected lifetime income, and the lower the level of education.[85]

Once in the marriage market, a person searches for a mate along the lines specified in the now rather extensive search literature.[86] That is, he searches until the value to him of any expected improvement in the mate he can find is no greater than the cost of his time and other inputs into additional search. Some determinants of benefits and costs are of special interest in the context of the marriage market.

Search will be longer the greater the benefits expected from additional search. Since benefits will be greater the longer the expected duration of marriage, people will search more carefully and marry later when they expect to be married longer, for example, when divorce is more difficult or adult death rates are lower. Search may take the form of trial living together, consensual unions, or simply prolonged dating. Consequently, when divorce becomes easier, the fraction of persons legally married may actually *increase* because of the effect on the age at marriage. Indeed, in Latin America, where divorce is usually impossible, a relatively small fraction of the adult population is legally married because consensual unions are so important (see Kogut 1972); and, in the United States, a smaller fraction of women have been married in those states having more-difficult divorce laws (see Freiden [1972] and his paper in this volume).[87]

Search would also be longer the more variable potential mates were because then the expected gain from additional "sampling" would be greater. Hence, other determinants being the same, marriage should generally be later in dynamic, mobile, and diversified societies than in static, homogeneous ones.

People marry relatively early when they are lucky in their search. They also marry early, however, when they are unduly pessimistic about their prospects of attracting someone better (or unduly optimistic about persons they have already met). Therefore, early marriages contain both lucky and pessimistic persons, while later marriages contain unlucky and optimistic ones.

The cost of search differs greatly for different traits: the education, income, intelligence, family background, perhaps even the health of persons can be ascertained relatively easily, but their ambition, resiliency under pressure, or potential for growth are ascertained with much greater difficulty.[88] The optimal allocation of search expenditures implies that marital decisions would be based on fuller information about more-easily searched traits than about more-difficult-to-search traits. Presumably,

[85] For a theoretical and empirical study of these and other variables, see Keeley (1974).

[86] The pioneering paper is by Stigler (1961). For more recent developments, see McCall (1970) and Mortensen (1970).

[87] These results are net of differences in income, relative wages, and the sex ratio.

[88] In the terminology of Nelson (1970), education, income, and intelligence are "search" traits, whereas resiliency and growth potential are "experience" traits.

therefore, an analysis of sorting that assumes perfect information (as in Part I) would predict the sorting by more-easily searched traits, such as education, better than the sorting by more-difficult-to-search traits, such as resiliency.[89]

Married persons also must make decisions about marriage: should they separate or divorce, and if they do, or if widowed, when, if ever, should they remarry? The incentive to separate is smaller the more important are investments that are "specific" to a particular marriage.[90] The most obvious and dominant example of marriage-specific investment is children, although knowledge of the habits and attitudes of one's mate is also significant. Since specific investments would grow, at least for quite a while, with the duration of marriage, the incentive to separate would tend to decline with duration.

The incentive to separate is greater, on the other hand, the more convinced a person becomes that the marriage was a "mistake." This conviction could result from additional information about one's mate or other potential mates. (Some "search" goes on, perhaps subconsciously, even while one is married!) If the "mistake" is considered large enough to outweigh the loss in marriage-specific capital, separation and perhaps divorce will follow.

The analysis in Part I predicts sorting patterns in a world with perfect information. Presumably, couples who deviate from these patterns because they were unlucky in their search are more likely than others to decide that they made a "mistake" and to separate as additional information is accumulated during marriage. If they remarry, they should deviate less from these patterns than in their first marriage. For example, couples with relatively large differences in education, intelligence, race, or religion, because they were unlucky searchers, should be more likely to separate,[91] and should have smaller differences when they remarry. Subsequently, I plan to develop more systematically the implications of this analysis concerning separation, divorce, and remarriage, and to test them with several bodies of data.

6. Summary

The findings of Part II include:

a) An explanation of why persons who care for each other are more likely to marry each other than are otherwise similar persons who do not.

---

[89] See the discussion in section 3, Part II of the Appendix.

[90] The distinction between general and specific investment is well known, and can be found in Becker (1964, chap. 11). Children, for example, would be a specific investment if the pleasure received by a parent were smaller when the parent was (permanently) separated from the children.

[91] If they have relatively large differences because they were less efficient searchers, they may be less likely to separate.

This in turn provides a justification for assuming that each family acts as if it maximizes a single utility function.

b) An explanation of why polygyny, when permitted, has been more common among successful men and, more generally, why inequality among men and differences in the number of men and women have been important in determining the incidence of polygyny.

c) An analysis of the relation between natural selection over time and assortive mating, which is relevant, among other things, for understanding the persistence over several generations of differences in incomes between different families.

d) An analysis of which marriages are more likely to terminate in separation and divorce, and of how the assortive mating of those remarrying differs from the assortive mating in their first marriages.

The discussion in this paper is mainly a series of preliminary reports on more extensive studies in progress. The fuller studies will permit readers to gain a more accurate assessment of the value of our economic approach in understanding marital patterns.

Mathematical Appendix

I

1. Optimal Sorting[92]

Given a function $f(x,y)$, I first show that if $\partial^2 f/\partial x \partial y < 0$,

$$\frac{\partial [f(x_2, y) - f(x_1, y)]}{\partial y} \equiv \frac{\partial Q(x_2, x_1, y)}{\partial y} < 0 \qquad \text{for } x_1 < x_2. \qquad \text{(A1)}$$

Since $\partial Q/\partial y = (\partial f/\partial y)(x_2, y) - \partial f/\partial y(x_1, y)$, $\partial Q/\partial y = 0$ for $x_2 = x_1$. By assumption, $(\partial/\partial x_2)(\partial Q/\partial y) = (\partial^2 f/\partial x \partial y)(x_2, y) < 0$. Since $\partial Q/\partial y = 0$ for $x_2 = x_1$ and $\partial Q/\partial y$ decreases in x_2, $\partial Q/\partial y < 0$ for $x_2 > x_1$; hence (A1) is proved. It follows immediately from (A1) that if $y_2 > y_1$,

$$f(x_2, y_1) - f(x_1, y_1) > f(x_2, y_2) - f(x_1, y_2). \qquad \text{(A2)}$$

A similar proof shows that if $\partial^2 f/\partial x \partial y > 0$,

$$f(x_2, y_1) - f(x_1, y_1) < f(x_2, y_2) - f(x_1, y_2). \qquad \text{(A3)}$$

I now am prepared to prove the following theorem: Let $f(x,y)$ satisfy $\partial^2 f/\partial x \partial y > 0$. Suppose $x_1 < x_2 < \cdots < x_n$ and $y_1 < y_2 < \cdots < y_n$. Then,

$$\left. \begin{array}{c} \displaystyle\sum_{j=1}^{n} f(x_j, y_{ij}) < \sum_{i=1}^{n} f(x_i, y_i) \\[2mm] \text{for all permutations} \\[2mm] (i_1, i_2, \ldots i_n) \neq (1, 2, \ldots n) \end{array} \right\}. \qquad \text{(A4)}$$

---

[92] I owe the proofs in this section to William Brock.

Assume the contrary; namely, that the maximizing sum is for a permutation $i_1 \cdots i_n$, not satisfying $i_1 < i_2 < \cdots < i_n$. Then there is (at least) one j_o with the property $i_{j_o} > i_{j_o+1}$. Therefore,

$$f(x_{j_o}, y_{i_{j_o}}) + f(x_{y_o+1}, y_{i_{j_o}+1}) < f(x_{j_o}, y_{i_{j_o}+1}) + f(x_{j_o+1}, y_{i_{j_o}}), \qquad (A5)$$

by (A3) since $y_{i_{j_o}+1} < y_{i_{j_o}}$. But this contradicts the optimality of $i_1, \ldots i_n \cdot QED$.

A similar proof shows that if $\partial^2 f/\partial x \partial y < 0$, then

$$\left. \begin{array}{c} \displaystyle\sum_{j=1}^{n} f(x_j, y_{i_j}) < \sum_{i=1}^{n} f(x_i, y_{n+1-i}) \\[20pt] \text{for all permutations} \\[10pt] (i_1, i_2, \ldots i_n) \neq (n, n-1, \ldots, 1) \end{array} \right\}. \qquad (A6)$$

2. Women Not in the Labor Force

If F did not participate in the labor force,

$$S = T w_m + T \hat{w}_f + r(l_{pm}, l_{pf})(K_m + K_f) - l_{pm} w_m - l_{pf} \hat{w}_f, \qquad (A7)$$

where $\hat{w}_f$, the "shadow" price of F, is greater than w_f, her market wage rate, unless F is at the margin of entering the labor force,[93] and l_{pm} and l_{pf} are the time allocated to portfolio management by M and F, respectively. If the production function for Z were homogeneous of the first degree in time and goods, $Z = S/C(p, w_m, \hat{w}_f, A_f, A_m)$.

Then,

$$\frac{\partial Z}{\partial K_i} = C^{-1} \left[r + K \left(\frac{\partial r}{\partial l_{pm}} \frac{\partial l_{pm}}{\partial K_i} + \frac{\partial r}{\partial l_{pf}} \frac{\partial l_{pf}}{\partial K_i} \right) - \frac{\partial l_{pm}}{\partial K_i} w_m - \frac{\partial l_{pf}}{\partial K_i} \hat{w}_f \right]$$

$$+ TC^{-1} \frac{d\hat{w}_f}{dK_i} - SC^{-2}C^f \frac{d\hat{w}_f}{dK_i} - C^{-1}l_{pf} \frac{\partial \hat{w}_f}{\partial K_i} \qquad (A8)$$

$$= rC^{-1} > 0, \qquad i = m \text{ or } f \qquad (A9)$$

since $C^f = t_f Z^{-1} = (T - l_{pf})Z^{-1}$, $K_m + K_f = K$, and $\hat{w}_f = (\partial r/\partial l_{pf})K$ and $w_m = (\partial r/\partial l_{pm})K$ with an optimal allocation of time. Similarly,

$$\frac{\partial Z}{\partial w_m} = TC^{-1} + \frac{TC^{-1}d\hat{w}_f}{dw_m}$$

$$+ C^{-1} \left(\frac{\partial r}{\partial l_{pm}} \frac{\partial l_{pm}}{\partial w_m} K + \frac{\partial r}{\partial l_{pf}} \frac{\partial l_{pf}}{\partial w_m} K - l_{pm} - \frac{\partial l_{pm} w_m}{\partial w_m} - l_{pf} \frac{d\hat{w}_f}{dw_m} - \frac{\partial l_{pf}}{\partial w_m} \hat{w}_f \right)$$

$$- SC^{-2}C^m - SC^{-2}C^f \frac{\partial \hat{w}_f}{\partial w_m} = l_m C^{-1} > 0, \qquad (A10)$$

and

$$\frac{\partial Z}{\partial A_i} = -SC^{-2}C_{a_i} + TC^{-1} \frac{\partial \hat{w}_f}{\partial A_i} - SC^{-2}C^{\hat{f}} \frac{\partial w_f}{\partial A_i} - l_{pf} \frac{\partial \hat{w}_f}{\partial A_i}$$

$$+ \text{ terms whose sum is zero}$$

$$= -SC^{-2}C_{a_i} > 0 \qquad i = m \text{ or } f, \qquad (A11)$$

---

[93] An earlier draft of this section developed the analysis using the shadow price of F, but contained some errors. I owe the present formulation to H. Gregg Lewis.

if A_i does not directly affect r. Note that equations (A9)–(A11) are exactly the same as those when F does participate—equations (24), (28), and (31).
    Then,

$$\frac{\partial^2 Z}{\partial K_f \, \partial K_m} = C^{-1} \begin{vmatrix} \dfrac{\partial r}{\partial l_{pm}} & \dfrac{\partial l_{pm}}{\partial K_m} + \dfrac{\partial r}{\partial l_{pf}} & \dfrac{\partial l_{pf}}{\partial K_m} \end{vmatrix} - rC^{-2}C^f \frac{\partial \hat{w}_f}{\partial K_m}. \tag{A12}$$

The first term is positive, but the second one is negative since

$$\frac{\partial w_f}{\partial K_m} > 0, \qquad \frac{\partial \hat{w}_f}{\partial K_f} > 0, \qquad \left(\text{and } \frac{\partial \hat{w}_f}{\partial w_m} > 0\right). \tag{A13}$$

A proof of (A13) follows from the derived demand equation for t_f. Of course,

$$\frac{\partial^2 Z}{\partial w_m \, \partial w_f} = 0. \tag{A14}$$

Moreover,

$$\frac{\partial^2 Z}{\partial K_m \, \partial A_f} = -rC^{-2}C_{af} - C^{-2}C^f \frac{\partial \hat{w}_f}{\partial A_f}. \tag{A15}$$

The first term is necessarily positive and the second would be nonnegative if $\partial \hat{w}_f / \partial A_f \leq 0$. It can easily be shown that $\partial \hat{w}_f / \partial A_f = 0$ if A_f has a factor-neutral effect on output and $\partial \hat{w}_f / \partial A_f < 0$ if A_f is own-time augmenting. Consequently, there is some presumption that

$$\frac{\partial^2 Z}{\partial K_m \, \partial A_f} > 0. \tag{A16}$$

    The general expression for the cross-derivative of Z with respect to A_m and A_f can be found by differentiating equation (A11). I consider here only the case where the effects are factor-neutral, so that

$$Z = g(A_m, A_f) f(x, t_m, t_f), \tag{A17}$$

or the optimal Z is $Z = gS/[K(p, w_m, \hat{w}_f)]$, with

$$g_i = \frac{\partial g}{\partial A_i} > 0, \qquad \text{and} \qquad g_{mf} = \frac{\partial^2 g}{\partial A_m \, \partial A_f} > 0. \qquad i = m, f. \tag{A18}$$

By substituting into (A11),

$$\frac{\partial Z}{\partial A_i} = Z \frac{g_i}{g} > 0. \tag{A19}$$

Therefore,

$$\frac{\partial^2 Z}{\partial A_m \, \partial A_f} = \frac{g_m}{g^2} g_f Z + \frac{g_{mf} Z}{g} - \frac{g_m g_f Z}{g^2} = \frac{g_{mf} Z}{g} > 0. \tag{A20}$$

3. Own-Time-Augmenting Effects

By own-time augmenting is meant that the household production function can be written as $Z = f(x, t'_f, t'_m)$, where $t'_f = g_f(A_f) t_f$, and $t'_m = g_m(A_m) t_m$ are the time inputs of F and M in "efficiency" units, and

$$\frac{dg_f}{dA_f} = g'_f > 0, \qquad \text{and} \qquad \frac{dg_m}{dA_m} = g'_m > 0, \tag{A21}$$

indicates that an increase in the trait raises the number of efficiency units. The optimal Z can be written as $Z = S/C(p, w'_m, w'_f)$, where $w'_m = w_m/g_m$ and $w'_f = w_f/g_f$ are wage rates in efficiency units. Therefore,

$$\frac{\partial Z}{\partial A_m} = -t'_m C^{-1} \frac{\partial w'_m}{\partial A_m} > 0, \tag{A22}$$

since $\partial w'_m/\partial A_m < 0$. Hence,

$$\frac{\partial^2 Z}{\partial A_m \, \partial A_f} = -\frac{\partial w'_m}{\partial A_m} C^{-1} \left(\frac{\partial t'_m}{\partial A_f} - \frac{\partial w'_f}{\partial A_f} t'_m t'_f S^{-1} \right). \tag{A23}$$

The term outside the parenthesis and the second term in it are positive. The first term in the parenthesis might well be negative,[94] but Gregg Lewis has shown in an unpublished memorandum that $\partial^2 Z/\partial A_m \, \partial A_f$ is necessarily positive if the elasticity of substitution between the time of M and F is less than 2.

4. Sorting by Income and Nonmarket Productivity

If M differed only in K_m and F only in A_f, and if all M and F participated in the labor force, $\partial Z/\partial K_m = rC^{-1} > 0$, and

$$\frac{\partial^2 Z}{\partial K_m \, \partial A_f} = -rC^{-2}C_{a_f} > 0 \qquad \text{since } C_{a_f} < 0. \tag{A24}$$

If M differed only in w_m, $\partial Z/\partial w_m = C^{-1}l_m > 0$, and

$$\frac{\partial^2 Z}{\partial w_m \, \partial A_f} = -C^{-2}C_{a_f}l_m + C^{-1} \frac{\partial l_m}{\partial A_f}. \tag{A25}$$

The first term on the right is positive, and the second would also be if $\partial l_m/\partial A_f \geq 0$, that is, if an increase in A_f does not reduce the time M spends in the market sector. Even if it does, the cross-derivative is still positive if the first term dominates. In particular, equation (A25) is necessarily positive if the effect of A_f is independent of the input of goods and time. For, if A_f were independent, $C = b(A_f)K(p, w_m, w_f)$. Since $l_m = (\partial C/\partial w_m) Z = (\partial K/\partial w_m)SK^{-1}$, then,

$$\frac{\partial l_m}{\partial A_f} = 0. \tag{A26}$$

II

1. Formally, M (or F) maximizes his utility function

$$U_m = U_m(Z_m, Z_f) \tag{A1}$$

subject to the constraints

$$\left. \begin{array}{l} Z_m^0 - C_m = Z_m \\ Z_f^0 + C_m = Z_f \\ C_m \geq 0 \end{array} \right\}, \tag{A2}$$

where Z_m^0 and Z_f^0 are the market allocations of output to M and F, and C_m is the amount transferred by M to F. If $C_m > 0$, these constraints can be reduced to a single income constraint by substitution from the Z_f into the Z_m equation:

[94] There is some evidence suggesting, e.g., that men with more educated wives generally work more hours (see Benham's paper in this book).

$$m_{mf} = Z_{mf} = Z_f^o + Z_m^o = Z_m + Z_f, \qquad (A3)$$

where Z_{mf} is the output produced by M and F, and m_{mf} is M's income. Maximization of U_m subject to this single income constraint gives

$$\frac{\partial U_m}{\partial Z_m} = \frac{\partial U_m}{\partial Z_f} . \qquad (A4)$$

If $C_m = 0$, U_m is maximized subject to the two constraints $Z_m^o = Z_m$ and $Z_f^o = Z_f$. The equilibrium conditions are $\partial U_m / \partial Z_m = \lambda_m$, $\partial U_m / \partial Z_f = \mu_m$, where λ_m and μ_m are the marginal utilities of additional Z_m^o and Z_f^o, respectively. The income of M would then be

$$m_{mf} = Z_m^o + (\mu_m/\lambda_m)Z_f^o, \qquad (A5)$$

where μ_m/λ_m is the "shadow" price of Z_f to M in terms of Z_m.
  Since $\mu_m/\lambda_m < 1$ (otherwise $C_m > 0$),

$$Z_m^o + \frac{\mu_m}{\lambda_m} Z_f^o < Z_{mf} = Z_m^o + Z_f^o. \qquad (A6)$$

If $C_m > 0$, the "family" consisting of M and F would act as if it maximized the single "family" utility function U_m subject to the single family budget constraint given by (A3), even if F's utility function were quite different from U_m. In effect, transfers between members eliminate the conflict between different members' utility functions.
  2. Total income in a marriage between M and F is

$$m_{mf} + f_{mf} = I_{mf} = Z_{mf} + p_m Z_{mf}^f + p_f Z_{mf}^m,$$

where I_{mf} is the total income in the marriage, Z_{mf}^m and Z_{mf}^f are the outputs allocated to M and F, $Z_{mf} (= Z_{mf}^f + Z_{mf}^m)$ is total output, p_m is the shadow price to M of a unit of Z_m^f, and p_f is a shadow price to F of a unit of Z_{mf}^m. Their incomes must be in the intervals

$$Z_{mf}^m + p_m Z_{mf}^f = m_{mf} \leq Z_{mf},$$
$$Z_{mf}^f + p_f Z_{mf}^m = f_{mf} \leq Z_{mf}. \qquad (A7)$$

If $p_m = p_f = 0$—no caring—m_{mf} and f_{mf} can be anywhere between 0 and Z_{mf}. But if $p_m = p_f = 1$—mutual and full caring—then $m_{mf} = f_{mf} = Z_{mf}$. And, more generally, if p_m and $p_f > 0$, then

$$Z_{mf}^m < m_{mf} \leq Z_{mf} < I_{mf},$$
$$Z_{mf}^m < f_{mf} \leq Z_{mf} < I_{mf}. \qquad (A8)$$

Consider the following matrix of total *incomes*:

$$
\begin{array}{c}
 \\
M_1 \\
\\
M_2 \\
\\
\end{array}
\begin{array}{cc}
F_1 & F_2 \\
\left[\begin{array}{cc}
8 & 8 \\
& (4, 4) \\
7 & 7 \\
(3, 4) &
\end{array}\right].
\end{array}
\qquad (A9)
$$

On the surface, both sortings are equally optimal, but this is not so if only M_1 and F_2 have a marriage with caring, say full and mutual, so that $m_{12} = f_{12} =$

4.[95] The sorting M_1F_2 and M_2F_1 is not as viable as the sorting M_1F_1 and M_2F_2 because income is more divisible between M_1 and F_1 than between M_1 and F_2.[96] For if, say, $m_{11} = 4\frac{1}{2}, f_{11} = 3\frac{1}{2}, m_{22} = 4\frac{1}{2},$ and $f_{22} = 2\frac{1}{2}$, no two persons have an incentive to change mates and marry each other.[97] On the other hand, since $m_{12} = f_{12} = 4$, unless $m_{21} = 3$ and $f_{21} = 4$, either M_1 and F_1, or M_2 and F_2 would be better off by marrying each other. If $m_{21} = 3$ and $f_{21} = 4$, M_1 and F_1, and M_2 and F_2 could be just as well off by marrying each other. Therefore, this sorting is not as viable as the sorting that does not have any marriages with caring.

3. Assume that the gain from marriage of a particular person M is positively related to the expected values of two traits of his mate, as in $m = g(A_1, A_2)$, with $\partial g/\partial A_i = g_i > 0, i = 1, 2$. If the marginal costs of search were c_1 and c_2 for A_1 and A_2, respectively, equilibrium requires that

$$\frac{g_1}{g_2} = \frac{c_1}{c_2}. \tag{A10}$$

The lower c_1 is relative to c_2, the higher generally would be the equilibrium value of A_1 relative to A_2, since convexity of the isogain curves is a necessary condition for an internal maximum.

If g_1 and g_2 were invariant when search costs changed to all participants in the marriage market, not an innocuous assumption, then $A_1^{\max}$ and $A_2^{\max}$ would be the equilibrium values of A_1 and A_2 to M when everyone had perfect information about all traits. A reduction in the cost of searching A_1, therefore, would move the equilibrium value of A_1 to M closer to $A_1^{\max}$, its value with perfect information.

---

[95] The *output* between M_1 and F_2 also equals four, half that between M_1 and F_1.

[96] Or, put differently, the output between M_1 and F_1 exceeds that between M_1 and F_2.

[97] F_2 would prefer to marry M_1, but could not induce M_1 to do so because m_{12} cannot exceed four, the output produced by M_1 and F_2 (see eq. [A7]), which is less than $m_{11} = 4\frac{1}{2}$.

Comment: The Economics of Nonmonetary Variables

William J. Goode

Columbia University

In the history of science researchers have often borrowed theories, analogies, or metaphors from other fields, usually the better-developed ones; in economic terms, they invested their human capital by acquiring new and presumably more-advanced intellectual tools. The most conspicuous borrowing in nineteenth-century social science was the unfortunately imaginary set of the developmental sequences of societies, worked out by anthropology and sociology on the basis of findings from biological evolution. It is less often that scientists in a relatively developed field become restive with its constraints and invade another with the aspiration that their more powerful technical and theoretical tools will solve problems with which the less-developed field has not adequately coped. (This is a challenge I have sometimes hurled at physicists who believe that the findings of sociology are simple-minded.) Over the past two decades, physicists tried this successfully in their contributions to molecular biology, and now economists have been expanding their world by attempting to analyze problems usually brooded over by sociologists, social psychologists, anthropologists, and political scientists.

In this case, interestingly enough, they will encounter colleagues in these fields who have themselves been moving toward economic or quasi-economic analysis of the same phenomena, though to be sure they have not attempted many social analyses of purely market processes. Especially in social psychology and sociology, a small group of theorists have for nearly two decades been working out exchange and allocational problems with the aid of economic ideas.

They have been hampered by their lack of mastery over the tools of economics, their failure to use economics explicitly, and their unwillingness—thus shouldering a burden economists of the past did not wish to carry—to do much theorizing without the facts. In my own case, I have

345

been trying to understand social-control systems, of which monetary controls form one set, by considering how prestige, force and force threat, and love or affection are accumulated, allocated, or lost. Even in my monograph on divorce, written two decades ago, I was the first both to demonstrate rather fully the inverse relationship between class position and divorce rates (a prediction now made by Becker) and to give an essentially economic explanation for it (see Goode 1956, 1962).

The differing styles of economics and sociology prevent me from making an adequate, brief analysis of Becker's paper. I perceive many tautologies in the paper, but I know that disturbs an economist less than a sociologist. Where economists may be content with certain types of summary indexes, I want to see a large cross-table of percentages. Often I must respond by saying, in answer to an elegant set of mathematical formulas: "It is a beautiful flight but it is not reliable for transportation"; that is, it simply is not true—though that may seem to an economist only a crude answer. An example of this would be Becker's formulation that late marriage and the difficulty of divorce will be correlated. India, for example, has an early age of marriage but very difficult divorce; in the West the main line of division is between Catholic and non-Catholic countries, and in general Catholic countries have almost no divorce but a slightly earlier age at marriage (except for Ireland) than other Western countries; and so on. Of course, to an economist, that may seem at best an unimaginative answer.

In any event, though I am nervous about this invasion, I welcome it. In these few pages I shall look at only a few minor points in Becker's paper to illustrate a somewhat general problem that is often encountered in some explorations by economists.

A major source of weakness in this bold foray into intellectual fields such as sociology and political science that have been trying for generations to create an autonomous noneconomic body of theory is Becker's failure to be daring enough in a critical question, that is, whether any non-monetary variables actually enter the calculations. In fact, as we see in Part I, section 2, both the market and nonmarket variables are aggregated to explain S, which is the "full income, the maximum money attainable if the w_j [i.e., wage rates, of the jth member] are constants."

Although I believe this monetary emphasis may ultimately be a weakness, since the noncontractual structure of exchanges in those sectors may create different behaviors than in the monetary sector,[1] we are left with no assurance that the broadened economic formulation will be adequate, since in fact it has not been fully built into the equations or tested. That

---

[1] This matter is analyzed at length in my *The Celebration of Heroes: Prestige as a Control System* (forthcoming). Meanwhile, see my *Explorations in Social Theory* (1973).

is, the nonmonetary variables have not been given due weight, but have been monetized.

That monetary equivalent, so tempting to the economist because of his past training, can create both obstacles and factual errors in the analysis. Perhaps I should add a theoretical point, that since the income figure is purely hypothetical or imaginary, it has no greater degree of reality than an apparently subjective factor such as prestige.

To take a minor example, education *is* worth something on both the market and nonmarket exchange systems, and for some purposes a high education can be given an equivalent monetary value, but for a man with *little* education, a wife with very *much* education is *not* worth as much as one would suppose from her money value on the larger market. She is a less-fit wife for him, by nonmonetary calculations—which would still be economic—and he would be supported in this low evaluation by his social circle.

Let us consider at length a more elaborate instance of the problems this failure creates, specifically the lines of reasoning as to whether and why polygyny occurred and why it has usually been the upper-strata men who could or did take advantage of this opportunity. The case is instructive, for the focus on total monetary income leads to factual errors and obscurities, but a general focus on nonmarket economic analysis would clarify some of the facts we do know and leave one question unsolved but at least not obscure.

Becker reasons—correctly, I think—that the total monetary output of monogamy would be higher than that of either polyandry or polygyny. Here the facts are more powerful than he supposes, for whether or not multiple marriage was permitted or encouraged, it has not been common in any society, except under very special conditions. For most men, in all societies over time, polygyny was a statistically unlikely delight.

Obviously, a very low ratio of men to women—caused by successful conquests or by high death rates in war—might permit polygyny for a while, but such conditions are not likely to continue for long. Late marriage for men and early marriage for women raise the chances somewhat, but high mortality among women keeps the total number of woman-years available to each man rather limited. As a consequence, polygyny has not been general even where it is approved.

A purely market explanation may yield this aggregate result even if, as I believe, the reasoning in its favor (see Part II, section 3) is tautological. That is, for most men and women the net market payoff is higher if they pair together rather than make other types of arrangements. However, this reasoning fails at the next step, the explanation for the unequal distribution of women among men even where polygyny is permitted.

At this next step it is necessary to give due weight to strictly nonmonetary factors. First, Becker argues, in the same section, that the "total output over all marriages could be greater if a second wife to an able man added more to output than she would add as a first wife to a less able one." Again leaving aside the tautological reasoning, this hypothetical result, an increase in total output over all marriages, is essentially empty as a motivating personal or social force in marital decisions.

As in many family decisions, especially those concerning fertility, the individual who decides does not ordinarily concern himself very much with his or her effects on the total output, or society as a whole. Thus, whether total output over all marriages is greater does not motivate people to enter polygyny. If Becker disclaims this as a motive, it is nevertheless obvious from the context that it is viewed as a partial explanation for the distribution of wives in a society.

Nevertheless, if we ask only about higher or lower monetary output of individual marriages, under Becker's assumptions we could expect that able men would try to get a second wife, and their chances of success would be greater than those of less able men.

If nothing else were involved, we could be satisfied that the unequal distribution of wives among the total number of husbands is now explained, at least from the man's side (from the woman's side, the matter is less clear, since under polygyny the husband takes a much larger share than the wife does). Indeed we might then take a step further and predict which economic strata of men would be able to reap this advantage, and even how much they would pay in order to make this investment in a wife, as compared with alternative investments in other types of capital goods. Where, for example, as in much of Central Africa, women may earn money by engaging in small-scale trading, or by tilling their own gardens for the family, we might even be able to put real monetary values on this kind of investment. Moreover, we might even give a better explanation for polyandry than Becker essays, since for the most part such systems occur where the productivity of a given man is low and he has little to invest in a wife, so that a set of men (often brothers) pool their assets in order to enjoy the benefits of one wife.[2]

However, reasoning from market or monetary total output, whether of the marriage or of all marriages, would miss the importance of women as goods, of women as producers of children, of women as links in purchasing political power, of women as prestige commodities, for monetary reasoning would *not* predict that women would be added where their monetary market output drops or almost stops upon entering marriage. For the stubborn fact remains that multiple marriage is most common among the

[2] In polyandry these are often brothers, perhaps because this causes less strife; and this alleviates somewhat the problem of producing one's *own* children, which Becker speaks of as a goal in marriage. In any event, whether or not the husbands are brothers, there are usually rules to decide who is sociologically defined as father of a given child.

stratum that gets the least monetary economic output from wives, that is, the most powerful and rich, who are most likely to wall them up and use them as pets, display them as objects that prove the man's high position, use them in power linkages, or even allow them to become parasites who destroy the family wealth by their extravagance. Indeed, it seems reasonable to assert that the higher the class position, the greater the likelihood of some polygynous arrangements, but equally the greater the likelihood that wives represent net losses, except in purely nonmarket goods. Like some other monetary goods, they are in part "bought in special markets"; they are also like such goods in another respect, for instance, furs, polo ponies, Rolls Royces, in that they can be put to other practical uses, and in revolutions sometimes are.

Thus, I am asserting that the reasoning of Becker's paper sometimes goes awry not because it uses economic reasoning in nonmarket areas, but because it fails to take note of the powerful nonmarket variables, whose effects may run counter to those of income variables, however these latter are aggregated. Nor am I as yet sure that market prices or decisions "prove" the total output is greater, whether of general nonmonetary or monetary goods, under these arrangements. As Frederick Knight said more than half a century ago, all suppliers are partially monopolies; and we know that these markets are rigged.

In a parallel fashion, the reasoning fails in its attempt to explain the decline of polygyny, that is, the system, in our time and to some extent (although the facts are less clear) over a longer period of time—less clear because we suppose that never in the history of the recent world have most nations been polygynous except under rare conditions.

After flirting with a biological explanation, Becker involves himself in a complex refutation of the claim that women would be better off economically if polygyny were abolished (see Part II, section 3). But his argument, and those he tries to refute, are essentially irrelevant, because all of them still seem to refer to the total market output of the household. It is much more likely that nonmonetary variables shape this decline in polygyny.

Here, as so often in such ventures into why social structures assume their sometimes peculiar shape, we have to ask, not merely about the non-market variables, but *who decides*: who organizes the market. In spite of Becker's graceful reference (n. 81) to Shaw's clever comment, the fact is that we have no evidence from any time or place that *women* ever created a polygynous system. It was *men* who established them, men whose command of force and force threat, prestige, and wealth was paramount in all the societies we know. Doubtless, some women did better economically under such systems, as some women in the United States would if they joined with other women to marry one rich and powerful man, but the system as a whole was not created by women; and wherever new laws, social movements, revolutionary ideologies, industrialization, urbanization, or religion permit them a free market choice they move away from polygyny.[3]

I shall not presume, especially in the midst of our contemporary turmoil about who has the right to report what women feel, to know precisely why women object to this system, although I think Becker's earlier, excellent analysis of caring and sharing is relevant. From the known fact that the birth rate under polygyny is less than under monogamy, and from the rules about equal sexual rights in polygynous systems, we must infer that women do not get as much tenderness, affection, and sexual enjoyment in those systems—again, we can use economic theory to reason about these variables, but they are not monetary. Men are in a much more influential position in such systems, and do not have to share as much of the physical output of the family, as indeed they also monopolize much of the prestige-esteem output of the family. They have the power to impose their own prices, in such systems. Thus, when external constraints, including money-market constraints, permit, women decline to enter such unions, even when they are still permitted.

I suggested earlier that after this critical commentary an important puzzle would still remain, although it is one that Becker has really not perceived clearly. It is why some social *systems* are polygamous, and others are not. An explanation of a *system* may not be adequate as an explanation of how some individuals act within it. The possibility that some men will benefit from taking more than one wife does not explain why polygyny occurs here rather than there—and it especially fails if we remember that even in most such systems the typical marriage is a pairing, one man to one woman. Why are such systems approved and viewed as an *ideal*, though few can attain it?

I do not think that any current explanations work well, though doubtless when one does it will be some sort of nonmarket economic analysis. That explanation would have to confront the fact that Western societies, including Latin America, of course, have not been polygynous in any historical period—and of course I do not mean only in the statistical or distributional sense, but in the normative sense, that polygyny was never a socially approved pattern of marriage. Both Japan and China have been mainly monogamous, though in both cases wealthy or powerful men could purchase additional concubines, and in China some of these came close to being recognized as "secondary wives" with specific rights. India, similarly, has been mainly monogamous, though again with a much more open acceptance of concubines. Perhaps most societies outside those great civilizations—but remember they encompass most of the

---

[3] See in this connection the relevant sections of my *World Revolution and Family Patterns* (1963), esp. chap. 4 on Sub-Saharan Africa.

world's population—have been polygamous in the specific but narrow sense that some form of polygamy was normative, something to which men and families aspired.

Whatever those explanatory variables will turn out to be when we locate them, I rather suppose they will not be monetary, and—more important—their impact will be seen primarily among the people who dominated those sociopolitical systems and those marriage markets, that is, the upper-strata men. Upper-strata men created a set of constraints that defined the marriage and family market so as to yield great monetary and nonmonetary advantages to them.

Few good theories in the history of science "fitted the facts" very well, and the "facts" at any given time were partly wrong, so that each explorer must follow his or her temperament rather than a rule which would ground new thinking only on the facts or only on free speculation. I do suspect, however, that a deeper sense of the crude regularities would not hinder these elegant flights, but might pose still more interesting puzzles for the imaginative economist. More fundamentally, I am at least partly persuaded by the work before us that in several fields we are moving toward a single structure of hypotheses about social behavior, hypotheses supported by research in several different fields under different labels; and that two decades hence we may discover we have created a rather impressive body of social science—if not "unified," at least mutually confirmatory. Becker's explorations are an important step in that progress.

The U.S. Marriage Market

Alan Freiden

Virginia Polytechnic Institute and State University

I. Introduction

The empirical implementation of theoretical contributions in the social sciences usually rests on variables defined and measured by persons other than the theorist. Such is the case with the theory of marriage. For the United States, the only relevant demographic quantity measured with accuracy is two-person, male-female legal marriage. Thus, my decision to study legal marriage was imposed by the Bureau of the Census and the inherent difficulties of measuring other forms of communal living. This does not seem to be restrictive for the United States, where consensual marriage is often a prelude to legal marriage, but it may be important in countries such as those in Latin America, where legal and other social institutions (i.e., divorce laws) differ.[1]

That a model of marriage based on rational choice has substantial explanatory power is demonstrated in this study. Three factors—the ratio of the sexes, the potential returns to marriage, and the cost of divorce—explain many of the areal differences in marital behavior in the United States. It is also evident that the marriage market has important indirect effects on the reproduction rate.

II. The Marriage Market

People decide to marry when they expect to enjoy some flow of "real" income, denoted by Z, which is greater than that which they could receive

I thank Gary Becker, H. Gregg Lewis, Marc Nerlove, Margaret Reid, T. W. Schultz, and T. Dudley Wallace for their many helpful suggestions, not all of which have been incorporated in this paper. I, of course, am solely responsible for any errors. The work for this paper was financed in part by grants to the University of Chicago from the National Institutes of Mental Health and the Rockefeller Foundation.

[1] For an analysis of the three forms of marriage recognized in Brazil, see Kogut (1972). Cheung (1972) has described the structure of property rights within marriage in China.

if single.[2] The Z represents an abstract commodity, produced within households, which is the true source of personal satisfaction. Let

$$Z^{mf} = Z_m^{mf} + Z_f^{mf}{}^3$$

represent the yield to marriage, where the right-hand side is the distribution of this "real" income between the married partners. With Z^{mf} taken as given, this distribution of married real income is determined by the supply of husbands and wives to the marriage market. The qualitative results derived holding Z^{mf} constant are not altered when couples are sorted in a manner which optimizes the total output of Z within the community.

If unmarried, the ith male would obtain the real income Z_{mi} and the ith single female would obtain Z_{fi}. Either would prefer marriage if and only if

$$Z_{mi} \leq Z_m^{mf}$$

or

$$Z_{fi} \leq Z_f^{mf}.$$

Since no male will accept less than his single income, the first male desiring marriage will be forthcoming at some level of married income, Z_m^{mf}, which is equal to the minimum single income, Z_{mi}, taken over all males. By ordering males with respect to their single incomes, the supply curve of males in the marriage market is equivalent to the cumulative distribution of males with respect to the Z_{mi}. In figure 1, this distribution has been drawn as if the maximum single income were undefined, that is, the supply curve asymptotically approaches the boundary set by the total number of males (which initially equals the number of females). The qualitative results derived here do not depend on this particular distribution. Similarly, the supply curve of females is the cumulative distribution of the Z_{fi}. Now, since

$$Z_f^{mf} = Z^{mf} - Z_m^{mf},$$

the supply of females is a negatively inclined function of the male marital income, Z_m^{mf}, and can be viewed as the derived demand for husbands by females.[4] No women can be found who would offer more than Z^{mf} less the minimum of Z_{fi} for a husband, so the supply-of-potential-wives curve begins at

$$Z^{mf} - Z_{fi} \text{ (min)}$$

and falls to the right.

---

[2] This section is based on Part I of Becker's paper in this volume. For another application of the general model see Keeley (1974).

[3] The superscript mf denotes a married couple. The subscripts m and f refer to single males and females.

[4] The analysis is, of course, perfectly symmetrical for the derived demand for wives by males.

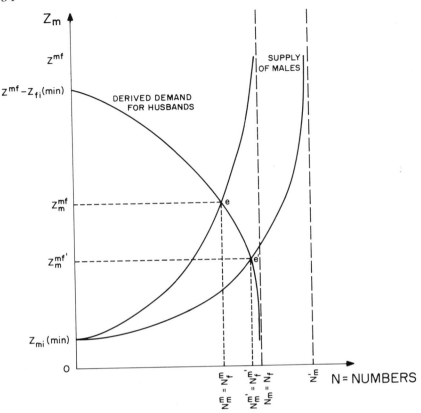

FIG. 1.—The marriage market

The intersection, e, of the supply curves in figure 1 gives the number of men and women marrying as well as the distribution of income within marriage. The proportion of females married will be N_f^{mf}/N_f, and their real income will be $Z_f^{mf} = Z^{mf} - Z_m^{mf}$.

Now, consider an increase in the number of men to N_m'. This will shift the equilibrium to e', raising the real income of married women to

$$Z_f^{mf'} = Z^{mf} - Z_m^{mf'} > Z_f^{mf} = Z^{mf} - Z_m^{mf}.$$

This increase is not directly observable, but the coincident increase in the number of females married, from N_f^{mf} to $N_f^{mf'}$, will raise the proportion of women married to

$$\frac{N^{mf'}}{N_f} > \frac{N^{mf}}{N_f}.$$

Thus, the model predicts that the proportion of women married should be positively related to the ratio of men to women.

To derive further implications, the nature of the household production process generating Z^{mf} (and the single real incomes) must be made explicit. Let

$$Z = g(X, T_m, T_f)$$

represent the household production function for the flows of real income previously denoted by Z^{mf}, Z_m, and Z_f. The X represents goods and services purchased in the market, T_m is male time, and T_f, female time. The g is then the household production function which summarizes the technology available for converting market goods and time into the actual source of utility, namely, Z. As increasing returns to scale would always result in a gain to marriage regardless of the number or sex of the participants, g will be a function such that economies of scale are ruled out.[5]

A single male would maximize his production of Z subject to the constraint that $T_f = 0$, that is, Max $Z = g(X, T_m, T_f)$, subject to (1) $T_m + L_m = T$, L_m = market work; (2) $PX = W_m L_m + V_m$, P = index of prices, W_m = wage rate, V_m = nonmarket income; and (3) $T_f = 0$. The maximized value of Z is Z_m. Similarly, a single female would Max $Z = g(X, T_m, T_f)$, subject to (1) $T_f + L_f = T$; (2) $PX = W_f L_f + V_f$; and (3) $T_m = 0$. The maximized value of Z is Z_f. In either case, one person must substitute his own time to make up for the absence of the other's. A married couple would maximize Z without the third constraint: Max $Z = g(X, T_m, T_f)$, subject to (1) $T_m + L_m = T$, $T_f + L_f = T$; and (2) $PX = W_m L_m + W_f L_f + V_m + V_f$. The maximized value of Z is Z^{mf}. The gain to marriage is then

$$G = Z^{mf} - (Z_m + Z_f).$$

A more convenient form of this expression is obtained as follows. If $Z = g(X, T_m, T_f)$, where g is a function of factor inputs, then there exists a function $c = c(P, W_m, W_f)$, a function of factor prices, which gives the minimum average cost of producing units of Z in the household (this is the cost dual of the household production function). For married couples this function is $c^{mf}(P, W_m, W_f)$; for single males it is $c_m(P, W_m)$; and so on. The maximized value of Z is then total resources available divided by this average cost of production. Resources available, called full income, can be obtained by combining the time and goods constraints. For a married couple these constraints are (1) $T_m + L_m = T$, $T_f + L_f = T$, and (2) $PX = W_m L_m + W_f L_f + V_m + V_f$.

---

[5] Note that a gain to marriage is not ruled out by decreasing returns to scale.

Let
$$L_m = T - T_m \quad \text{and} \quad L_f = T - T_f,$$
then
$$PX = W_m(T - T_m) + W_f(T - T_f) + V_m + V_f, \text{ or}$$
$$PX + W_m T_m + W_f T_f = (W_m + W_f)T + V_m + V_f.$$

The left-hand side is the total monetary equivalent of time and market-goods expenditures, while the right-hand side is full income. Thus,

$$G = \frac{(W_m + W_f)T + V_m + V_f}{c^{mf}(P, W_m, W_f)} - \left[\frac{W_m T + V_m}{c_m(P, W_m)} + \frac{W_f T + V_f}{c_f(P, W_f)} \right].$$

By totally differentiating G, further implications of the model may be derived.[6]

First, consider the wage rates. If

$$W_m = W_f,$$

$$MP_m = \frac{\partial Z}{\partial T_m} = MP_f = \frac{\partial Z}{\partial T_f}, \quad \text{and}$$

$$V_m = V_f, \quad \text{then}$$

$$Z_m + Z_f = 2Z = Z^{mf}.$$

This means that if male and female time are perfect substitutes in both household and market production, there is no gain from marriage. However, in all other cases Z^{mf} will exceed the combined single incomes. Note that the marginal products must be equal throughout the range of inputs and not just at a point. In particular, the combined gain would be greater the larger the difference between W_m and W_f. If, as is usually the case, $W_m > W_f$, then the husband will specialize in market production while the wife concentrates her time in the home. Therefore, the gains from marriage and the proportion of females married should be positively related to the relative wage rate, W_m/W_f. However, the effect of equal proportionate increases in the male and female wage rates is ambiguous. On the one hand, there is a positive income effect associated with the rise in full income. But on the other hand, there is a negative cost-of-production effect due to the elasticity of the cost dual of the household production function with respect to the wage rates. If this elasticity is sufficiently large (in absolute value), the net effect of equiproportionate increases in male and female wages may be negative. Note that equal percentage increases in the nonlabor incomes V_m and V_f do not generate a negative cost-of-production effect, so the gains to marriage are expected to rise with such a change.

[6] This approach is equivalent to a comparative statics analysis of the market-supply curves, since an increase in the gain to marriage shifts both curves to the right in figure 1.

The manner in which education affects the household production function is not obvious, so the prediction of this factor's effects on the gains to marriage is unclear. For example, consider the following two ways of looking at education: first as factor-neutral technological change and then as factor-augmenting. In the first case, education uniformly reduces the amount of each input required to produce units of Z, that is,

$$Z^{mf} = \frac{(W_m + W_f)T + V_m + V_f}{A_m(E_m)A_f(E_f)c^{mf}(P, W_m, W_f)}, \text{ and so on,}$$

where E stands for education and the A's are functions whose first derivatives are negative. It can be shown that the gain to marriage is positively related to increases in education in this case. If treated as factor-augmenting technical change, education improves the efficiency of the time input independently, that is,

$$Z^{mf} = \frac{(W_m + W_f)T + V_m + V_f}{c^{mf}[P, B_m(E_m)W_m, B_f(E_f)W_f]},$$

where B_m and B_f are functions similar to the A's. Special conditions must hold to obtain the same results as above. If education raises the non-market productivity relative to the market productivity of the mate specializing in household production, or the relative market productivity of the market specialist, then it increases the gains to marriage. However, either of these possibilities may prove difficult or impossible to distinguish empirically.

Until this point, an implicit assumption was made that perfect information and certainty held for persons in the marriage market. Clearly, this is not the case. The high divorce rate of persons married 2 years or less is evidence that uncertainty plays an important role. This divorce behavior may be interpreted as the correction of mistakes. Then a lowering of the cost of correcting a mistake (the difficulty of divorce) should induce people to marry more readily. The effect of the cost of divorce on the stock of marriages, however, is uncertain since a fall in the cost of divorce also encourages the dissolution of existing marriages. The former is likely to dominate the behavior of the young, while the latter is more relevant for older couples.

III. Empirical Implementation

Three sets of data—state, county, and Standard Metropolitan Statistical Area (SMSA) aggregates—are used to evaluate the model's predictions. Since no single set of data is completely satisfactory, this test rests on evidence accumulated from several sources. The most complete data are at the state level, but the variables are highly collinear. Heterogeneity among the observations is increased by using a random sample of United States counties, but the federal census compilations are insufficiently detailed, especially with regard to age-specific and female wage data.

The method used is to estimate an ordinary least-squares regression with a measure of the proportion of females married (FEMMAR) as a dependent variable and the relative wage (RELWG), the ratio of the sexes (SXRT), the cost of divorce (DCOST), and a measure of income as independent variables.[7] All observations are weighted by the appropriate number of females. For the states and SMSAs, equations are estimated for each of the 5-year age cohorts between ages 15 and 39. The actual variables used are described below and listed in table 1.

1. FEMMAR. The proportion of females married is the number of women married, with spouse present, divided by the total number of women. There is a small error due to the exclusion of married women having a spouse absent for reasons other than separation, but this is insignificant. More important, however, is the treatment of widows. On the average, males die earlier than females (especially married males), so there will be some widows who should be considered "involuntarily" single. Investigating a revised figure for females married, one that included widows, showed little difference in the results, so this factor is ignored.

2. RELWG. Three alternative measures of male and female wage rates are available. The best is the annual earnings of full-time wage and salary workers as estimated by the Social Security Administration. These figures represent the marginal (and here average) opportunity cost of time to a prospective labor-market participant. It is likely that these values approximate the permanent wage rates for workers by state. The relative wage is simply male earnings divided by female earnings. The mnemonic for the Social Security wage is RELWGSS. A second measure of the full-time wage is the United States Census figure for median earnings of persons working 50–52 weeks in the previous years. Since this is available for both states and SMSAs, direct comparisons between the results are feasible. The symbol for a measure of the male-female relative wage based on census data is RELWGCN. Finally, it is most unfortunate that neither of these measures is compiled at the county level. The only sex-specific earnings data are the median annual earnings of persons. This value is quite sensitive to labor-force participation rates, so it is a biased measure for the purpose of explaining marriage. Suppose the full-time relative wage is high, then the gains to marriage are highest with husbands

---

[7] Education could not be investigated at this time. In aggregate data, the relationship between income and education is very close, so multicollinearity is a severe problem. The 1970 Public Use Samples of Basic Records from the Bureau of the Census were not available when this paper was written.

TABLE 1
VARIABLES AND DATA SOURCES

Symbol	Description	Source
FEMMAR*.....	Proportion of females married, spouse present	U.S. Bureau of the Census (1962; 1963b, tables 59 and 105)
RELWGCN	Male/female relative wage, persons working 50–52 weeks in 1959	U.S. Bureau of the Census (1963b, table 134)
RELWGSS	Male/female relative wage, full-time annual earnings	U.S. Department of Health, Education, and Welfare (1968b, table V-17)
RELWGAE.....	Male/female relative median annual earnings	U.S. Bureau of the Census (1963b tables 134 and 136)
SXRT*	Sex ratio, number of males/number of females	U.S. Bureau of the Census (1963b, table 59)
DCOST	Index of ease of divorce	Table 2 (below)
CATH	Proportion of population Catholic	National Council of Churches (1956, table 4)
HSEVAL.......	Median value of owner-occupied housing	U.S. Bureau of the Census (1962; 1963b, table 20)
RENT	Median gross monthly rental	U.S. Bureau of the Census (1962; 1963a)
BIRRATE......	Births per 1,000 women	U.S. Bureau of the Census (1962)
AGRI..........	Proportion of the labor force employed in agriculture	U.S. Bureau of the Census (1962; 1963b, tables 82 and 128)
NONWT	Proportion of the population non-white	U.S. Bureau of the Census (1962)
FEMEARN.....	Median annual earnings of females	U.S. Bureau of the Census (1963b, tables 86 and 136)
FEMSCH	Median school years completed, females, 25 years and older	U.S. Bureau of the Census (1963b, table 83)
MALSCH	Median school years completed, males, 25 years and older	U.S. Bureau of the Census (1963b, table 83)
AGE..........	Index of age distribution based on national age-specific rates	†

* Age-specific data.

$$\dagger \qquad AGE = \frac{\sum\limits_{k=1}^{15} w(k) * NF(k)}{\sum\limits_{k=1}^{20} NF(k)},$$

where $NF(k)$ is the number of females in the kth age group.
$k = 1, 2, \ldots, 20$ for ages 0–4, 5–9, . . . , 95–99,

k	w(FEMMAR)	w(BIRRATE)
1	0	0
2	0	0
3	0.2	0.8
4	15.7	89.1
5	69.5	258.1
6	86.2	197.4
7	88.7	112.7
8	88.2	56.2
9	85.9	0.9
10	82.5	0
11	77.0	0
12	69.9	0
13	61.4	0
14	51.6	0
15	65.0	0

specializing in market labor and wives in household production. This implies a lower female labor-force participation rate and lower median annual female earnings. Therefore, if the model is correct, the observed annual earnings of females will be negatively correlated with the proportion of females married. With this caveat, a relative wage based on annual earnings (RELWGAE) is used for the counties.

The preceding analysis brings to light an interesting question about the interpretation of observed wage differentials and also their relation to education. If formal schooling primarily acts to raise market-earning potential, then the measured effects of education, holding the market wage constant, must be picking up something else, that is, on-the-job training. Suppose husbands and wives specialize as predicted. For a time men are receiving on-the-job training which raises their market age-earnings profile above that which would hold in the absence of such training. At the same time, their wives would experience depreciation of their stocks of market-specific human capital (but an increase in the nonmarket component) which lowers their permanent market wage. Therefore, even the full-time wage is somewhat biased as a predictor of marital behavior.[8] It is true that a "pseudo wage" estimated from the demand side of the market would be more appropriate, but this approach will not be followed at present.

3. SXRT. The ratio of the sexes is simply the number of males in each age group divided by the number of females. For the counties it is the number of males 15 years and older divided by the equivalent number of females. A minor concern with this definition is that males tend to marry females a few years younger than themselves. Redefining the sex ratio to take account of this does not affect the results appreciably.

4. DCOST. The measure of the cost of divorce is not a quantitative variable. It is an index of the ease of divorce legislation as compiled through questionnaires and other data in 1959.[9] However, an attempt was made to achieve cardinality, so the actual values used are probably at least highly correlated with the true values. Note that it is an index of the ease or permissiveness of the law and represents the inverse of the cost of divorce. Table 2 lists the values used. Religion may also be a relevant psychic cost of divorce for Catholic couples, so a set of regressions including the percentage of the population Catholic (CATH) in place of DCOST is estimated for the states.

5. INCOME. The appropriate income measure is full family income, including labor and nonlabor components. The census value, median family income, is subject to the same measurement problems mentioned above for the female wage and is, therefore, unacceptable. An alternative,

---

[8] This may be added to Gronau's list of applications (1972) in which observed female wages are biased predictors of behavior.

[9] See Rheinstein (1972) and Broel-Plateris (1961) for details.

TABLE 2
CLASSIFICATION OF STATES BY THE EASINESS OF THEIR DIVORCE LAWS, 1959

Category and State	Easiness Score	Category and State	Easiness Score
Very permissive:		Medium:	
Nevada	95	Nebraska................	49
Florida	90	Ohio	48
Arkansas	85	North Dakota............	46
Idaho	81	Delaware	45
New Mexico	77	Vermont	44
Alabama	76		
California	74		
Wyoming	72	Strict:	
		Maryland	42
Permissive:		Minnesota................	41
Kentucky	69	West Virginia............	40
Georgia	67	Maine	39
Arizona	66	Illinois	37
Oklahoma	64	Lousiana................	36
Utah....................	63	Virginia	34
Washington	62	Wisconsin	33
Mississippi	60	New Hampshire..........	32
South Dakota	59	Michigan	29
Oregon.................	59	Dist. of Columbia	28
Kansas	58		
Indiana	57	Very strict:	
		North Carolina	25
Medium:		Pennsylvania	22
Montana	55	Rhode Island	19
Tennessee...............	54	Connecticut	16
Colorado	53	New Jersey	13
Missouri	52	Massachusetts...........	9
Texas	50	New York...............	4
Iowa	49	South Carolina	1

SOURCE.—Broel-Plateris 1961, table 12, p. 149.

on the expenditure rather than the receipt side of family accounts, has been suggested (Margaret Reid 1962). This is the median value of owner-occupied housing (HSEVAL). Since a large proportion of urban dwelling units are not occupied by owners, the median monthly gross rental (RENT) will also be used for the SMSAs. There are two reasons for using these measures. First, the observed positive income elasticity of demand for housing guarantees that a family's housing expenditure is positively correlated with income so HSEVAL and RENT will be unbiased surrogate measures. Second, these expenditures are not sensitive to the transitory component of income.[10]

IV. Results

There is a problem interpreting the regression results reported below. The FEMMAR is a limited dependent variable, that is, a proportion bounded by zero and one (0–100 in percentages). This complicates the evaluation of elasticities but not the estimation technique, since no estimated values

[10] There may be a bias due to a price component.

of the dependent variable violated these boundary constraints [11] Consider a given percentage change in a bounded variable. If the variable is already near its upper bound, then a small change is also a large change relative to the distance to the upper bound. For example, suppose FEMMAR is 90. A 1 percent increase to 90.9 is the same as a 9 percent decrease in the distance between the initial value and the upper bound. Therefore, elasticities for the older age groups, those with an average proportion of married women greater than 80 percent, should be interpreted with this in mind.

Tables 3 and 4 are the ordinary least-squares results from the state and SMSA data, respectively. Two alternative measures of relative wages are shown for the states and two of income for the SMSAs. Results for one set of equations from each data source are summarized in elasticity form in table 5. The explanatory power of the four independent variables is quite good, with $R^2 > .5$ in all but one case and with the vector of estimated coefficients significantly different from zero at the 5 percent level of confidence in every case. However, there are a number of parameter estimates with large standard errors; this is not unusual, given the level of aggregation employed here. Two approaches to this problem will be described later.

The data support the hypothesis that the proportion of females married is positively related to the ratio of the sexes. Only one coefficient is not significantly greater than zero at the 5 percent level.[12] Evidence on the effect of the cost of divorce is that the incidence of marriage rises as divorce becomes easier. Table 6 contains the regression results for a replication of one set of the state equations using the proportion of the population Catholic (CATH) in place of DCOST. Here a negative sign on CATH is equivalent to a positive one on DCOST, so the coefficients (all significant) are consistent with theory.[13] Note that for all five sets of regressions (state, SMSA, and state with CATH) the elasticity of marriage with respect to the cost of divorce declines monotonically with age. The decline is greater than that which is generated by the effect discussed at the beginning of this section. This indicates that of the two effects mentioned earlier, encouraging new marriages and lowering the cost of dissolving existing ones, the former is more relevant for young couples. The influence of income is puzzling. Where significant, the coefficients of both RENT and HSEVAL are negative. This contradicts Silver's finding (1965) that the flow of new marriages (i.e., the marriage rate) conforms to the business cycle. Of course, if the income elasticity of the divorce

---

[11] Elsewhere I have used the logit transformation in this context (1972).

[12] Of course, one coefficient out of 20 will randomly fail the 5 percent t-test when the null hypothesis is true.

[13] Multicollinearity prohibits including CATH along with DCOST and HSEVAL in the same equation.

TABLE 3
Regression of FEMMAR, 1960 State Data

INDEPENDENT VARIABLE	AGE									
	15–19	15–19	20–24	20–24	25–29	25–29	30–34	30–34	35–39	35–39
RELWGCN	...	−0.078 (0.03)	...	3.55 (0.84)	...	8.06 (2.57)	...	4.97 (2.55)	...	5.22 (3.14)
RELWGSS	−2.76 (1.26)	4.59 (1.37)	7.15 (3.16)	...	...	...	3.32 (2.08)	...	3.74 (2.74)	...
SXRT	22.28 (2.72)	28.24 (3.66)	13.10 (1.85)	11.01 (1.55)	43.59 (3.68)	52.26 (3.99)	60.55 (6.92)	68.19 (8.05)	62.72 (7.63)	71.72 (9.05)
DCOST	0.099 (7.68)	0.094 (7.29)	0.137 (6.67)	0.140 (6.72)	0.026 (1.50)	0.018 (1.01)	0.016 (1.50)	0.012 (1.16)	0.009 (0.99)	0.004 (0.47)
HSEVAL	−0.484 (4.54)	−0.489 (4.36)	−0.501 (3.02)	−0.449 (2.60)	−0.754 (5.10)	−0.702 (4.65)	−0.580 (5.90)	−0.565 (5.87)	−0.325 (4.21)	−0.293 (3.85)
CONSTANT	−0.929 (0.08)	−11.52 (1.06)	46.45 (4.20)	49.96 (4.01)	36.58 (3.23)	27.20 (1.90)	28.41 (3.71)	18.66 (2.12)	22.99 (3.17)	12.16 (1.49)
R^2	.82	.81	.72	.71	.60	.57	.70	.71	.73	.74
$F(4, 43)$	47.53	45.45	27.00	26.02	16.04	14.31	24.86	26.51	28.37	30.19

Note.—t-values in parentheses.

TABLE 4
Regression of FEMMAR, 1960 SMSA Data

INDEPENDENT VARIABLE	AGE									
	15–19	15–19	20–24	20–24	25–29	25–29	30–34	30–34	35–44	35–44
RELWGCN	−0.640	0.041	2.19	9.31	6.04	10.98	1.65	4.43	1.48	2.70
	(0.20)	(0.01)	(0.47)	(1.99)	(1.85)	(3.07)	(0.91)	(2.11)	(1.35)	(2.30)
SXRT	8.27	8.87	7.05	10.10	28.48	27.71	31.30	33.03	42.91	50.99
	(2.95)	(3.18)	(1.98)	(2.76)	(3.23)	(2.61)	(4.74)	(3.41)	(9.49)	(9.15)
DCOST	0.125	0.137	0.183	0.191	0.084	0.100	0.014	0.025	−0.015	−0.015
	(8.48)	(9.34)	(9.09)	(8.94)	(5.13)	(5.42)	(1.47)	(2.38)	(2.54)	(2.15)
HSEVAL	−0.395	...	−0.546	...	−0.584	...	−0.452	...	−0.242	...
	(2.84)		(2.80)		(4.35)		(5.31)		(4.98)	
RENT	...	−0.121	...	0.005	...	−0.035	...	−0.072	...	−0.057
		(2.69)		(0.08)		(0.67)		(2.38)		(2.88)
CONSTANT	7.55	8.81	56.49	33.21	51.95	38.00	60.52	52.67	46.90	37.97
	(0.94)	(1.03)	(4.91)	(2.66)	(4.31)	(2.83)	(8.42)	(6.18)	(9.38)	(7.33)
R^2	.67	.67	.70	.66	.68	.58	.56	.38	.73	.66
$F(4, 58)$	30.1	29.5	34.1	28.34	30.6	19.78	18.26	8.74	38.76	28.18

Note.—t-values in parentheses.

TABLE 5
SUMMARY OF REGRESSION RESULTS

| INDEPENDENT VARIABLES | ELASTICITIES AT MEANS | | | | |
| | Age | | | | |
	15–19	20–24	25–29	30–34	35–39
	State Data				
RELWGCN	...	...	...	...	...
RELWGSS	−0.33	0.12	0.15	0.07	0.08
SXRT	1.48	0.20	0.52	0.70	0.73
DCOST	0.28	0.09	0.013	0.008	0.005
HSEVAL...........	−0.38	−0.09	−0.11	−0.08	−0.04
RENT	...	...	...	...	...
	SMSA Data				
RELWGCN	−0.005	0.24	0.22	0.09	0.05
RELWGSS	...	...	...	...	...
SXRT	0.63	0.15	0.33	0.38	0.59
DCOST	0.41	0.12	0.05	0.012	−0.007
HSEVAL...........	...	...	...	...	...
RENT	−0.64	0.01	−0.03	−0.06	−0.05

TABLE 6
REGRESSION OF FEMMAR, 1960 STATE DATA

| INDEPENDENT VARIABLE | AGE | | | | |
	15–19	20–24	25–29	30–34	35–39
RELWGSS	6.90	19.0	9.59	4.34	3.82
	(2.36)	(4.67)	(3.94)	(2.43)	(2.73)
SXRT	46.2	32.3	49.7	56.3	52.3
	(4.85)	(4.79)	(5.34)	(7.14)	(7.91)
CATH	−0.191	−0.303	−0.095	−0.065	−0.048
	(4.47)	(5.02)	(2.41)	(2.35)	(2.24)
HSEVAL...........	−0.110	0.096	−0.629	−0.497	−0.307
	(0.62)	(0.38)	(3.76)	(4.15)	(3.43)
CONSTANT........	−38.8	5.31	28.5	32.8	36.1
	(2.89)	(0.42)	(2.93)	(4.59)	(5.97)
R^2	.70	.64	.64	.70	.73
$F(4, 43)$	25.3	18.7	17.8	26.3	29.9

NOTE.—t-values in parentheses.

rate exceeds that of the marriage rate, then the cross-sectional and time-series results are consistent.

A strong theoretical result is that the potential gain to marriage and, therefore, the proportion of women married, is positively related to the sex-specific relative wage. This is confirmed for persons age 25 and older but not for the young. Suppose that the benefits to marriage as perceived by teenagers differ from those of adults. Then the gains to specialization may not be relevant although other market factors (sex ratio and cost of divorce) are. If so, then as these people mature, many of the "irrational" marriages will dissolve, leaving in the stock of married persons only those enjoying gains to specialization. While ad hoc, this argument is plausible given the substantially higher divorce rate among couples married as teenagers.[14] Also, suppose the costs of marriage for teenagers differ from those for adults. This is obviously the case, since the age of consent is 21 for males and 18 for females in most states. Then a measure of the cost of marriage as well as of the cost of divorce is necessary in the regressions for the group of persons ages 15–19. Unfortunately, no such measure is readily available, but the states with a substantial Catholic population seem to have the strictest marriage laws.[15] If the results for persons ages 15–19 in table 6 are interpreted with CATH viewed as a measure both of the cost of divorce and the cost of marriage, the relative wage effect is substantiated.

The evidence presented so far would have been more convincing had the estimates been more accurate. Imprecise parameters may be improved through the application of additional sample information. Here two techniques are employed to make better use of the data available. First, it is obvious that the division of the population into 5-year age cohorts is arbitrary. Therefore, one would expect the behavior of adjacent age groups to be similar. For the regression model used here, the correlations of the residuals of adjacent age groups is very high. There is information in the set of residual correlations which can be used to obtain more efficient estimates of the coefficients of all five equations through the seemingly unrelated regressions technique (Zellner 1962). The results for the state data (table 7) are as expected. The standard errors of the coefficient estimates are improved, especially those for DCOST. Since there are no qualitative changes in the coefficients, the discussion of the ordinary least-squares results need not be amended.

A second way to improve the information content of the sample is to expand the number of observations. Roughly a tenfold increase in sample size occurs through use of a random sample of 530 United States counties.[16] Unfortunately, no age-specific marriage data are compiled by the United States Bureau of the Census at this level, so the analysis must be restricted to a single equation aggregated over age. To standardize the age structure of the county populations, an index (AGE) was constructed which has the value of FEMMAR if the proportion of women

[14] Education must be the next factor to be examined in this area. It is likely that something related to schooling, such as differential human capital investments or the more efficient college marriage market, explains this poor result.

[15] This is based on the casual observation of age of consent, medical requirements, and waiting periods by state. Note that the two non-Catholic states with strict divorce laws—North and South Carolina—seem to have very liberal marriage laws.

[16] I wish to acknowledge the contribution of Donald Bogue in the preparation of these data.

TABLE 7
Regression of FEMMAR, 1960 State Data, Efficient Estimates

Independent Variable	Age					Age				
	15–19	20–24	25–29	30–34	35–39	15–19	20–24	25–29	30–34	35–39
RELWGCN	−0.65 (2.5) [0.3]	4.2 (3.9) [1.1]	6.0 (3.0) [2.0]	4.0 (1.9) [2.1]	4.5 (1.7) [2.7]	⋯	⋯	⋯	⋯	⋯
RELWGSS	⋯	⋯	⋯	⋯	⋯	−3.0 (2.0) [1.5]	4.2 (3.1) [1.4]	6.7 (2.3) [3.0]	4.3 (1.6) [2.7]	4.5 (1.3) [3.3]
SXRT	25.4 (6.5) [3.9]	13.2 (4.7) [2.8]	28.4 (7.2) [3.9]	42.7 (6.3) [6.8]	51.4 (6.0) [8.5]	21.3 (6.7) [3.2]	11.9 (4.7) [2.5]	23.7 (6.5) [3.7]	35.2 (6.2) [5.7]	42.1 (6.1) [6.9]
DCOST	0.10 (0.01) [7.7]	0.14 (0.02) [7.0]	0.04 (0.02) [2.4]	0.02 (0.01) [2.4]	0.01 (0.01) [1.7]	0.10 (0.01) [8.1]	0.14 (0.02) [7.2]	0.04 (0.02) [2.7]	0.03 (0.01) [2.7]	0.02 (0.01) [2.2]
HSEVAL	−0.50 (0.11) [4.6]	−0.43 (0.17) [2.5]	−0.57 (0.14) [4.1]	−0.44 (0.09) [4.7]	−0.24 (0.08) [3.2]	−0.49 (0.11) [4.6]	−0.49 (0.16) [3.0]	−0.62 (0.13) [4.7]	−0.45 (0.09) [4.8]	−0.27 (0.08) [3.5]
CONSTANT	−7.7 (9.5) [0.8]	46.7 (9.8) [4.8]	51.2 (9.1) [5.6]	42.7 (7.0) [6.1]	31.6 (6.5) [4.8]	0.46 (9.2) [0.1]	48.1 (8.3) [5.8]	54.3 (7.2) [7.6]	48.9 (5.8) [8.4]	40.1 (5.6) [7.1]

Note.—Standard error in parentheses. Absolute value of the coefficient estimate divided by its standard error shown in brackets.

TABLE 8
REGRESSION OF FEMMAR (WOMEN, 15 YEARS AND OLDER),
1960 STATE AND COUNTY DATA

Independent Variable	State Data	County Data	Elasticities from County Data
RELWGAE	...	2.93 (7.37)	0.091
RELWGSS	4.08 (2.57)	...	...
SXRT	55.89 (5.67)	11.22 (4.66)	0.165
DCOST	0.022 (2.35)	0.041 (6.56)	0.026
HSEVAL.....................	−0.220 (1.86)	−0.315 (6.65)	−0.061
AGE	0.548 (1.99)	1.30 (12.38)	...
AGRI.......................	0.005 (0.09)	0.092 (5.25)	0.010
NONWT	0.028 (0.93)	−0.117 (9.69)	−0.020
CONSTANT..................	−28.23 (1.26)	−34.19 (5.28)	
R^2	.72	.52	...
F............................	12.66	79.56	...
(df)	(8,39)	(7,520)	...

NOTE.—t-values in parentheses.

married in the county in each age group was identical to the national average (see table 1). Counties differ in many other ways which may influence marital behavior, but only two factors, the importance of agriculture (AGRI) and the relative size of the nonwhite population (NONWT), will be included. The regression results for the county data are in table 8. For comparison, a similar regression for age-aggregated state data is included. The results are consistent with the predictions of theory and those reported above. As expected, the parameter estimates are much more accurate. An interesting finding is that, *ceteris paribus*, nonwhites have a lower propensity to marry. Of course, everything is not being held constant, since what is being measured here is the effect of the lower male/female relative wage that is known to exist among blacks.[17]

[17] An analysis of SMSA data disaggregated by race is in progress. The county data were also used for a preliminary analysis of education. In the South, the education of women has by tradition been oriented toward household production. Then higher female education with the schooling of males held constant should increase the gains to marriage in the southern states. The following results were obtained by including median male and female schooling completed (MALSCH and FEMSCH) in the equation for FEMMAR. The absolute value of the t-statistic is in parentheses:

$$FEMMAR = -6.8 + 1.8 \, RELWGAE + 9.4 \, SXRT + 0.04 \, DCOST$$
$$\quad (1.11) \quad (4.98) \qquad\qquad (4.91) \qquad\qquad (4.81)$$
$$\quad - 0.62 \, HSEVAL + 0.09 \, AGRI - 0.11 \, NONWT + 0.74 \, AGE$$
$$\quad (5.69) \qquad\qquad (5.37) \qquad (8.67) \qquad\qquad (7.73)$$
$$\quad - 0.13 \, MALSCH + 1.8 \, FEMSCH, \; R^2 = .72, \; F(9,238) = 66.7.$$
$$\quad (0.26) \qquad\qquad (4.22)$$

TABLE 9
REGRESSIONS OF FEMMAR AND BIRRATE,
1960 COUNTY DATA, 2SLS (WOMEN, 15 YEARS AND OLDER)

EXPLANATORY VARIABLE	DEPENDENT VARIABLE	
	FEMMAR	BIRRATE
FEMMAR	...	0.33
	...	(0.15)
	...	[0.335]
BIRRATE	−0.009	...
	(0.02)	
	[0.009]	
RELWGAE	3.03	...
	(0.45)	
	[0.094]	
SXRT	11.5	...
	(2.5)	
	[0.167]	
DCOST	0.04	...
	(0.006)	
	[0.026]	
HSEVAL	−0.3	1.1
	(0.04)	(0.2)
	[−0.062]	[0.221]
AGE	1.33	1.03
	(0.12)	(0.05)
AGRI	0.095	0.063
	(0.02)	(0.041)
	[0.011]	[0.007]
NONWT	−0.11	0.09
	(0.01)	(0.04)
	[−0.020]	[0.016]
FEMEARN	...	−7.0
		(1.0)
		[−0.263]
FEMSCH	...	−1.15
		(0.39)
		[−0.188]
CONSTANT	−35.89	−8.2
	(7.46)	(9.5)
F	16.2	11.7
(df)	(8,2)	(7,3)
α	0.06	0.06

NOTE.—Standard error in parentheses. Elasticity at mean in brackets.

The county data offer an opportunity to investiate another proposition mentioned by Becker. Suppose that a major component of family utility is the consumption of own child services.[18] Then a direction of causation running from marriage to fertility may not be appropriate. It is the demand for children which is most relevant, and observed marital behavior is partially a derived demand. Table 9 lists two-stage least-squares estimates from a two-equation model treating births and marriage simultaneously.[19] Here FEMMAR is a function of the birth rate

[18] This terminology arose in recent economic research on fertility.
[19] The first attempt to deal with simultaneous family decisions empirically was by Nerlove and Schultz (1970).

(BIRRATE) and vice versa.[20] The other explanatory variables in the birth rate equation are those suggested by the new economic approach to fertility. Clearly, the proportion of females married and, therefore, factors influencing the marriage market, contributes significantly to the explanation of observed fertility. On the other hand, there is a small elasticity of the proportion of females married with respect to the birth rate. This can be explained in two ways. First, child services may not, in fact, constitute a dominant portion of couples' consumption bundles. Alternatively, this small elasticity may be a statistical anomaly caused by comparison of a change in a stock to a change of a flow. Regressing the rate of new marriages on the birth rate may prove more satisfactory. These results do, however, suggest the fruitfulness of the simultaneous analysis of family decisions.

The decision to marry is only one of a set of interrelated family choices that influence both the observed proportion of women married and the variables chosen to explain this proportion. In a sense, the marriage equation is partially a reduced form from a simultaneous system in which all of the right-hand variables are the result of choices made in the past. This possibility has already been introduced with regard to the relative wage effect, and it applies to the other variables as well. The sex ratio, for instance, is determined by migration decisions. If unmarried females decide to leave a region (as is true for a rural population), then a greater proportion of the females remaining are married, not simply because the sex ratio is higher, but also because unmarried women have left. Much more complete data are required, however, before the nature of these reverse causations can be investigated.

V. Conclusions

Data from the 1960 census yield substantial empirical support for the economic interpretation of the marriage market. Two factors, the ratio of the sexes and the cost of divorce, influence observed marital behavior as expected. This is also true of the gains to specialization, but the results are somewhat tenuous for teenagers. The evidence also suggests the tentative conclusion that long-term economic growth may result in more people desiring to remain single. Finally, it is shown that the analysis of simultaneous family decisions is empirically feasible.

[20] Means and standard deviation of these and all other variables used are given in table 10.

TABLE 10
Means of Variables Used in Regression Equations

Variable	State Data, Ages						SMSA Data, Ages					County Data
	15t	15–19	20–24	25–29	30–34	35–39	15–19	20–24	25–29	30–34	35–44	
FEMMAR	65.9 (1.9)	15.1 (4.0)	67.1 (5.1)	83.5 (3.3)	86.1 (2.6)	85.7 (2.3)	14.1 (4.6)	66.4 (6.4)	84.5 (4.4)	87.3 (2.3)	85.9 (1.7)	65.8 (4.5)
RELWGSS	1.81 (0.14)	...	...	...	...	...	...	...	...	...	...	...
RELWGCN	1.69 (0.12)	...	...	...	...	...	...	...	1.69 (0.13)	...	...	...
RELWGAE	...	...	...	...	...	...	...	...	...	...	...	2.04 (0.37)
SXRT	0.96 (0.03)	1.01 (0.04)	0.95 (0.03)	0.96 (0.03)	0.96 (0.03)	0.95 (0.03)	0.97 (0.13)	0.89 (0.15)	0.95 (0.05)	0.95 (0.04)	0.95 (0.03)	0.98 (0.07)
DCOST	42.2 (24.0)	...	...	...	...	...	...	...	41.9 (24.4)	...	...	43.9 (22.4)
CATH	19.4 (12.0)	...	...	...	...	...	...	...	...	...	...	...
HSEVAL	11.9 (2.7)	...	...	...	...	...	...	...	14.3 (2.9)	...	...	12.7 (4.5)
RENTAL	...	...	...	...	...	...	...	...	75.2 (8.5)	...	...	...
AGE (marriage)	62.3 (1.4)	...	...	...	...	...	...	...	...	...	...	65.9 (2.0)
AGE (birth rate)	...	...	...	...	...	...	...	...	...	...	...	63.4 (8.3)
AGRI	6.7 (5.2)	...	...	...	...	...	...	...	...	...	...	7.4 (11.5)
NONWT	11.0 (8.4)	...	...	...	...	...	...	...	...	...	...	12.0 (12.2)
BIRRATE	...	...	...	...	...	...	...	...	...	...	...	65.6 (12.4)
FEMEARN	...	...	...	...	...	...	...	...	...	...	...	2.3 (0.7)
FEMSCH	...	...	...	...	...	...	...	...	...	...	...	10.7 (1.2)

Note.—Standard deviation in parentheses.

Comment

T. Dudley Wallace

North Carolina State University

Alan Freiden has been reasonably faithful to the Becker marriage model in his attempt to estimate the reduced-form equation explaining variation in the proportion of females married. His observational units are regional subaggregates in cross-section data. Thus, the Freiden paper represents a commendable attempt to evaluate the usefulness of the model.

The major problem arising in going to the data is in translating and measuring full income. Full income is a precise concept in the theory but is made up of two main components, one of which is ambiguous in its effect upon marriage. The two components of full income are (1) nonlabor income, and (2) full labor earnings if both male and female were completely occupied in the market. Variation in the first component, nonlabor income, is unambiguous. Marriage should vary directly with it. Variation in "full wages" affects both implicit costs of time and full income and therefore is ambiguous. Thus, full income, in sum, is ambiguous, and Freiden chose a proxy for full income that enters his regressions as a single variable.

In all his regressions, Freiden obtained a negative sign on his proxy for full income and in many cases the t-statistics indicate that the results are not solely due to a lack of richness in the data.

Returning to the Becker theory, male and female wages and nonlabor income all enter the reduced-form relationship explaining marriage. Variational effects of wage ratios and nonlabor earnings are clear; variation in the wage sum (full earnings) is not. Nevertheless, all three enter and have separate effects. Therefore, it seems that Freiden should have introduced an additional explanatory variable, namely, the sum of male-female wages. According to the theory, the relative-wage results should hold up in the presence of full earnings. If Frieden's proxy for full income is appropriate, its net effect, holding full earnings constant, should be positive. Given the generality of the theory that guided the empirical work, one cannot anticipate the sign on "full earnings" as measured by the sum of the wages. Moreover, the data may not be rich enough to yield significant results on relative wages, full earnings, and full income. Thus, such results would be revealed by the data. It may also be the case that less generality in the theory would further clarify the role of full earnings in its relationship to marriage. For example, I investigated a Cobb-Douglas production function with unit scale for the joint household.[1]

The main additional result gained by this specificity was the delineation of the effect of a change in the sum of male and female wages (full earnings), holding the wage ratio constant. For a Cobb-Douglas household production function, an increase in full earnings due to equiproportionate changes in the male and female wages reduces the gain from the marriage whenever the ratio of full earnings to nonlabor income is less than the ratio of labor cost to market-goods cost. Conversely, when the source of full income from labor relative to nonlabor income is larger than the relative share of labor-to-goods cost in production, an equal increase in both wage sources increases the attractiveness of marriage, given the Becker framework. Whether this type of inference, or something similar, holds for more general production functions and whether data can be found to test more specific hypotheses about the role of full earnings are open to question.

Not considering product allocation within the household contributes to a failure to sort out variables into cost-returns (supply-demand) boxes that have been found so useful in most work in economics. The impression left in both the Freiden paper and the Gary Becker paper is that one can say something about the incidence of marriage but, because of symmetry, little can be said about such matters as the demand for wives by males or the supply of wives. If one took the simple and obvious expedient of assuming equal sharing of household production, the demand for wives could be represented by the optimal joint-product function less twice the single-male production, and the demand for husbands by women could be similarly represented by joint production minus twice the single-female production. These are the returns. On the cost side there are costs of search, measured in some sense by the relevant sex ratios, and costs of correcting mistakes, as reflected by ease of divorce. Whether one could construct meaningful models that are identifiable in this way, given the sorts of data which are available, is moot. If such

---

[1] For good reason, Becker wanted to avoid increasing returns to scale. Scale less than or equal to unity leaves the burden of the theory to complementarity in production. As Becker has pointed out, Cobb-Douglas (C-D) implies zero productivity in the singles cases. Our sense of description may thus be offended by using the C-D function, but if we accept the notion that marriage is more attractive, the larger the difference in joint and individual household production, the general theory is not crucially violated by zero product in the households of single individuals.

constructions are possible, the link between model and data would be clarified. As an example, in both the Freiden paper and that by Becker, the sex ratio and the divorce-cost variables are brought in by ad hoc argument rather than as an integral part of the theory. This makes for a *ceteris paribus* problem in interpreting results. The equations that Freiden fits with data are reduced forms of two sorts of considerations.

What follows are a few additional comments that may have marginal value. (1) Certainly the existence of marriage predates progressive income tax and joint returns. Nevertheless, levels of marriage incidence in modern society should depend on tax structure. (2) Divorce costs probably vary directly with the number of immature children; thus, the index used by Freiden is not so appropriate for his higher-age groups. Divorce costs in some states vary greatly, depending upon real assets. Also, lowering the probability of dissolution of long-standing marriages is the effect of the household equivalent of on-the-job training specific to the individual household. One might expect considerable differences in the analysis of survey data where one could obtain, for example, specific information about household wealth, number of dependent children, or length of time of current marriage. Survey data should also be amenable to resolution of the importance of household productivity of the less intensive wage earner. (3) The notion that the "likelihood" of marriage increases the greater the difference in joint and individual household production is appealing but somewhat lacking in rigor. The basic Becker theory is completely deterministic. Therefore, in speaking of "likelihood," one leaps from the basic theory into an area still to be explored. Whether beginning with a probabilistic framework is of practical value is not clear, but it should be recognized that there is here a methodological problem which is not usually present in microeconomic modeling.

Lest the critical tone of these comments be misleading, it is worth saying again that carrying economic analysis into unexplored terrain is exciting and of potentially great value. The Becker theory and the Freiden empirics are steps into a new area for economists. The steps are worthwhile and will not end here.

Benefits of Women's Education within Marriage

Lee Benham

University of Chicago

Studies of the returns to education have generally investigated the relationship between individuals' investments in formal education and on-the-job training and their labor-market productivity. It is well recognized, however, that other factors besides formal education and training contribute to a person's effective stock of human capital (and hence to productivity); these factors include early childhood environment, parents' behavior (see Dugan 1969), and associations with other individuals. There is general agreement, for example, that a child's development is affected by the ability and performance of peers in school. At a later stage, a significant part of an individual's college and graduate education appears to result from association with fellow students, the more able students contributing to the education of all. After formal schooling is completed, close associates are likely to continue to affect an individual's further educational development and to influence the rate of depreciation of the individual's stock of knowledge.

One of the more persuasive explanations of the observed strong positive relationship between formal education and labor-market productivity is that, in addition to providing specific skills, formal education improves the individual's ability to acquire and assimilate information, to perceive and understand changing conditions, and to respond effectively.[1] From

I thank Alexandra Benham for comments and substantial assistance throughout this study; Gary Becker, Solomon Polachek, Robert Michael, and T. W. Schultz for helpful comments; and Elayne Howard for analyzing the data. The investigation was partly supported by PHS grant HS00080 from the National Center for Health Services Research and Development.

[1] In his study of migration, Aba Schwartz (1968) found results consistent with the hypothesis that one effect of education is to reduce the cost of obtaining information. The responsiveness of individuals to lifetime-earnings differentials was found to increase monotonically with education. Finis Welch (1970) distinguishes between the worker effect and the allocative effect of education. He argues: "Much of the 'leverage' associated with added schooling is drawn from the dynamic implications of changing technology." That is, education enables an individual to adapt more rapidly to changing conditions.

this perspective, associates can contribute to a person's effective stock of education in at least three ways: (1) by providing a close substitute for the person's own formal education by extending information and advice, (2) by helping the person acquire specific skills, and (3) by helping the person acquire general skills related to information acquisition and assimilation and coping with change.

There are obvious limitations to the extent to which one person can benefit from another's experience and advice. Some individuals are better able than others to reap such benefits. Nevertheless, persons having exposure to individuals with a greater or different stock of knowledge should on average benefit from such exposure.[2] To the extent that this is true, an individual's effective stock of acquired abilities will be a function not only of his own formal education and job experience but also of associates' education, the incentives the associates have to share their knowledge, and the length of the association. This paper investigates this transmission of educational benefits in one type of association: marriage.

Marriage is distinguished from most other nonmarket associations in that there are greater incentives to share acquired abilities within the household: both current and future benefits of increased knowledge by either family member are typically shared. The costs of sharing would also appear to be lower because the transactions cost of communication within the household, given the proximity of spouses, is likely to be less than in other types of associations. For these reasons, the household would appear to provide a good opportunity to examine the benefits of association.

In the traditional human capital literature, the individual is viewed as a firm whose earnings (E_t) at time t are a function of the individual's stock of human capital (H_t), which in turn is composed of two elements, the individual's net investment in formal education (S_t) and net investment in postschool on-the-job training (P_t): $E_t = E(S_t, P_t)$.

In the present study, the household firm composed of husband and wife is investigated rather than the individual. The assumption is made that the effective stock of human capital for each marriage partner $(H_t^{h*}$ or $H_t^{w*})$ is a positive function of the individual stock of human capital of each spouse within the household:

$$H_t^{w*} = H(H_t^w, H_t^h) \text{ and}$$
$$H_t^{H*} = H(H_t^w, H_t^h),$$

where $\partial H_t^{i*}/\partial H_t^j > 0$ for $i, j = h, w$. Both the market and the nonmarket

[2] The market provides this type of advisory service. Lawyers and professional counselors are among those whose stock in trade is advice. Actors, politicians, and athletes frequently hire managers to guide their careers.

productivity of individuals within the household are functions of H_t^*.[3] Therefore, increments to the capital stock of either spouse should be reflected in the productivity of both. While this model could thus be used to examine both market and nonmarket productivity of husband and wife, the following analysis is limited to an examination of the relationship between husband's market productivity and both spouses' capital stock.[4] The initial relationship examined is the extent to which the earnings of a married man are positively related to his wife's stock of human capital, measured here by the wife's years of schooling. To investigate this, education of wives is incorporated into the model developed by Mincer (1970a) to estimate the returns to men's education.[5] The logarithm of husband's earnings is given as a function of the years of formal education of each spouse and the years of employment experience of the husband.

The specification of the model is as follows:

$$\ln \text{EARN} = \alpha + \beta_1 \text{EDH} + \beta_2 \text{EDW} + \beta_3 \text{EXP} + \beta_4 \text{EXP}^2 + \mu,$$

where $\ln \text{EARN} = \log_e$ annual earnings of husband in family with husband and wife present, EDH = years of schooling completed by husband, EDW = years of schooling completed by wife, and EXP = years of work experience of husband.[6] The coefficients β_1 and β_2 are estimates of the percentage earnings differentials to husband's and wife's formal education, respectively, in terms of husband's market earnings, given the other spouse's years of formal education and the husband's work experience.[7] Husband's work experience is entered in quadratic form to approximate the postschool investment pattern usually assumed.

Data

To estimate this model, data from three samples of the population of the United States were used: the 1/1,000 sample of the U.S. Census for 1960 (U.S. Bureau of the Census 1964), a 1963 health survey conducted by the

---

[3] For a survey of current work on nonmarket productivity within the family, see T. W. Schultz (1972a).

[4] Sorting out the impact of household capital on the wife's market productivity appears to be considerably more difficult than doing so for the husband's. Women have a lower labor-force participation rate than men, and their participation is negatively related to husbands' earnings (which are in turn positively related to husbands' education). A lower participation rate means less job experience and lower market earnings. It is beyond the scope of this paper to separate the effect of husband's human capital on her market productivity.

[5] This model is restrictive in that, for each spouse, the same percentage earnings differentials are assumed for all years of schooling.

[6] The number of years of job experience is here estimated as age minus years of schooling minus 6.

[7] Under a set of assumptions discussed in Mincer (1970a), β_1 is an estimate of the rate of return to men's formal education.

Center for Health Administration Studies of the University of Chicago
and the National Opinion Research Center (Andersen and Anderson
1967), and the 1967 Survey of Economic Opportunity (SEO) conducted
by the Bureau of the Census for the Office of Economic Opportunity.
The subsamples used in this study include only married white males with
spouse present, not living on farms, and having positive earnings in the
survey year.[8]

Results

Table 1A shows the estimates of this model obtained from the three data
sets. The coefficient of wife's education is positive and significantly greater
than zero in all cases. The simple null hypothesis that education of wife is
unrelated to husband's earnings can be rejected. Considering that three
separate data sources are used, the absolute value of β_2 and the ratio
β_2/β_1 are remarkably stable. Given the level of husband's education and
his years of work experience, his earnings increase between 3.0 and 4.1
percent for each year of his wife's education.[9]

To examine the effects of wife's education on her husband's wages and
on his work time separately, the basic equation was reestimated using the
Census data with ln weekly wage rather than ln annual earnings as the
dependent variable.[10] An additional estimate of this type was made
excluding husbands who were not working full time. The results, shown
in table 2, suggest that from 20 to 25 percent of the increase in a husband's
earnings is due to increases in weeks worked, and the remainder is due
to higher wages.

While these results are open to alternative interpretation, the observed
associations are hardly negligible, and they would appear to merit further
inquiry. If it can be established that all or even a substantial part of these
returns through a husband's earnings are due to the benefits of his wife's

---

[8] The characteristics of the subsamples differed in some minor details. See notes to table
1 for subsample descriptions.

[9] For purposes of comparison, β_1 is also calculated in table 1B with wife's education
excluded from the estimating equation. In these estimates, the percentage differentials
in husbands' earnings associated with their own education range from 8.1 to 9.0 percent.
These estimates are lower than others have made. Part of the reason is that earnings
differentials associated with the education of never-married men and divorced men are
higher, although their absolute earnings are lower.

[10] It is not obvious a priori whether a wife's education is positively or negatively
associated with a husband's market-work time. An increase in a wife's education leads to
increases in her own market and nonmarket productivity. Specialization within the
family between market and nonmarket activity will depend in part on the comparative
advantage of each spouse in these activities. If education increases the wife's market
production relative to her nonmarket productivity, this will increase the incentive for her
to specialize more in market activities and raise the incentive for her husband to spend
more time in nonmarket production. However, insofar as a wife's education increases
her husband's market productivity, an opposite effect occurs.

TABLE 1
A. ESTIMATED PERCENTAGE DIFFERENTIALS IN HUSBAND'S EARNINGS ASSOCIATED WITH HUSBAND'S AND WIFE'S EDUCATION
(*t*-Statistic in Parentheses)

Sample	Dependent Variable	Husband's Education	Wife's Education	Husband's Experience	Husband's Experience Squared	Constant	R^2	N
1/1,000 Census, 1960*	ln EARN	0.070 (19.0)	0.041 (9.7)	0.052 (18.6)	−0.00081 (−16.1)	6.625	.222	4,780
CHAS, 1963†	ln EARN	0.064 (9.8)	0.035 (4.3)	0.029 (6.6)	−0.00045 (−4.9)	7.198	.22	967
SEO, 1967‡	ln EARN	0.063 (24.3)	0.035 (11.5)	0.035 (18.3)	−0.00064 (−15.9)	7.292	.201	8,055

B. ESTIMATED RETURNS TO HUSBAND'S EDUCATION IN TERMS OF HUSBAND'S EARNINGS
(WIFE'S EDUCATION OMITTED; *t*-Statistic in Parentheses)

Sample	Dependent Variable	Husband's Education	Husband's Experience	Husband's Experience Squared	Constant	R^2	N
1/1,000 Census, 1960*	ln EARN	0.090 (29.0)	0.053 (16.0)	−0.00085 (−17.0)	6.857	.207	4,780
SEO, 1967‡	ln EARN	0.081 (37.8)	0.035 (18.4)	−0.00066 (−16.3)	7.493	.188	8,055

* These data are from a 20 percent random subsample of the 1/1,000 sample of the U.S. Census for 1960. The data used here are for males ages 18–64, married once with spouse present, husbands of once-married women, non-Negro, nonfarm residents, not in school, having positive number of weeks worked, positive earnings, and positive total income in 1959.

† These data are from a 1963 national survey conducted by the Center for Health Administration Studies of the University of Chicago and the National Opinion Research Center. The subsample used here includes only males ages 18–64, married with spouse present, heads of household, nonfarm residents, and having positive number of weeks worked and positive earnings in 1963. Observations were excluded if there were indeterminant values for any of these variables. Information was not included in this survey which would allow estimation of length of marriage or exclusion of those individuals who had remarried.

‡ These data are from the 1967 Survey of Economic Opportunity conducted by the Bureau of the Census for the Office of Economic Opportunity. The subsample used here includes only males ages 18–64 married with spouse present, white, nonfarm residents, not in school, not in army, and having positive earnings in 1966. Observations were excluded if there were indeterminant values for any of these variables. The observations were unweighted.

TABLE 2

ESTIMATED PERCENTAGE DIFFERENTIALS IN HUSBAND'S WEEKLY WAGES AND FULL-TIME EARNINGS
ASSOCIATED WITH HUSBAND'S AND WIFE'S EDUCATION
(t-STATISTIC IN PARENTHESES)

Sample	Dependent Variable	Husband's Education	Wife's Education	Husband's Experience	Husband's Experience Squared	Constant	R^2	N
1/1,000 Census, 1960*	ln WEEKLY WAGE†	0.065 (19.5)	0.035 (9.4)	0.044 (17.1)	−0.0007 (−13.0)	2.9765	.22	4,780
1/1,000 Census, 1960‡	ln EARN FULL TIME	0.074 (21.1)	0.030 (7.5)	0.042 (15.5)	−0.0007 (−13.0)	6.8629	.22	4,293

* See table 1 for description of sample.
† Weekly wage is calculated as annual earnings/weeks worked.
‡ See table 1 for general description. The subsample used here includes only husbands who worked 48 weeks or more in 1959.

education, this has important implications both for our interpretation of the returns to education for men and women and for our understanding of the market returns to marriage.

The assumption underlying the previous specification is that a wife's education has a constant percentage impact on earnings over the life cycle. If the view is taken that the husband's earnings reflect an accumulation of the stock of acquired abilities (human capital) within the household, there are several reasons for expecting earnings to be a function not only of the wife's education but also of the length of marriage. First, the incentives for the husband to acquire on-the-job training are a positive function of the expected time in labor-market activities. Since his labor-market time is positively related to his wife's education, as shown in table 2, his incentive to invest in on-the-job training should also be associated with his wife's education.[11] Second, if the complementarity between formal education and postschool investment also holds between a wife's formal education and her husband's postschool investment, this would also tend to raise the husband's postschool investment as a function of his wife's education. Third, if a wife's education increases her husband's earnings by reducing the depreciation rate of his stock of knowledge, then the full impact of the wife's education would not be observed immediately upon marriage but only over time as different rates of depreciation resulted in different earnings patterns. Further, if costs of communicating knowledge or learning are inversely related to the time span available, then a husband is not likely to gain the full benefit of his wife's education at the start of marriage.[12]

Although the quantitative importance of each of these arguments in postmarriage capital accumulation is not known, they all imply that the husband's absolute earnings should increase, at least initially, as a function of the length of marriage. While the a priori case is less clear for the percentage differentials in earnings, these arguments suggest increasing percentage differentials during the first years of marriage. To examine the life-cycle pattern of husband's earnings as a function of wife's education,

---

[11] Since the labor-force participation of wives and the interval between marriage and first births are positively correlated with wives' education, women could also be financing more on-the-job training for their husbands.

[12] Even the benefits provided by the wife's direct advice and knowledge (rather than by her increasing her husband's stock of knowledge and skills) are not necessarily realized at the time the information is available to her husband. The economic consequences of many career decisions are observable only after several years. This point could also be made concerning the benefits of one's own education. Even with no postschool investment, the better-educated person will presumably be better able to anticipate events. Since the benefits derived from this improved ability to predict are observed only after some period of time (i.e., after the person has been able to profit as a result of his earlier decisions), the relative (observed) earnings over time should reflect these differential abilities in anticipating change, and those who anticipate better may have increasing relative earnings over time.

TABLE 3

ESTIMATED PERCENTAGE DIFFERENTIALS IN HUSBAND'S EARNINGS ASSOCIATED
WITH WIFE'S EDUCATION BY LENGTH OF MARRIAGE
(t-STATISTIC IN PARENTHESES)

Sample	0–10 Years of Marriage	10–20 Years of Marriage	20–30 Years of Marriage	30–40 Years of Marriage
1/1,000 Census, 1960*	0.032	0.041	0.060	0.024
	(4.1)	(6.5)	(5.9)	(2.1)
	$N = 1,549$	$N = 1,614$	$N = 980$	$N = 558$
SEO, 1967*	0.031	0.044	0.036	0.031
	(6.0)	(8.3)	(5.6)	(3.0)
	$N = 2,610$	$N = 2,432$	$N = 2,056$	$N = 833$

NOTE.—Given education of husband, husband's years of experience, and square of husband's years of experience.
* See table 1 for description.

the basic equation was estimated for four 10-year length-of-marriage intervals (table 3).

In both estimates[13] of β_2 the differential increases after the first decade of marriage and declines again during the latter years. The full benefits from association within the household are, therefore, not observed at the time of marriage. These results are consistent with the hypothesis that the rate of postschool capital accumulation within the family during the first years of marriage is a positive function of the wife's education and that the incentives to maintain investment within the family diminish as the working life shortens.[14]

Selective-mating Hypothesis

Perhaps the principal alternative argument to the family-firm hypothesis for the observed relationship between husband's earnings and wife's education is the hypothesis of selective mating, which in this context asserts that, in an education cohort of males, the more productive males marry more highly educated females. Unfortunately, devising a test which provides clear evidence concerning the relative importance of selective mating versus household-capital formation does not appear straightforward. One difficulty is that, while the household hypothesis has some

[13] Only the SEO and U.S. Census data contain information on length of marriage.

[14] Since cross-sectional data are used here, there are several problems associated with inferences drawn about life-cycle behavior. The prior lifetime circumstances of younger and older adults were in many ways very different. The younger persons with 12 years of schooling not only had more days in school per year but presumably had better-quality instruction than the older persons. Other characteristics also differed over the age groups, including the proportion who came from agricultural backgrounds and the size of city of residence. It is noteworthy, however, that the pattern was generally the same in 1959 as in 1967. For both dates, husband's earnings as a function of wife's education were higher for the second than for the first decade of marriage, and they declined between the third and fourth decades. This is not consistent with a pure cohort effect. I appreciate the assistance of T. W. Schultz on this point.

relatively unambiguous implications concerning earnings patterns, almost any result is consistent with some variant of the selective-mating hypothesis. The problems here are similar to those faced in the human capital literature with regard to alternative explanations for the positive correlation between schooling and earnings. Schooling could be either serving as a screening device or augmenting human capital. Our understanding of this latter issue has been due primarily to the accumulation of evidence on the consistency of earnings patterns with implications of the theory of human capital rather than to tests which clearly distinguish between the two hypotheses. Similarly, no clear tests of the household-capital versus the selective-mating hypothesis are examined here, but some evidence can be brought to bear on this issue.

If the selective-mating hypothesis is refined to mean that, within a given education cohort of males, the more productive males marry females who are more highly educated at the time of marriage, it implies that a husband's earnings should be much more strongly associated with his wife's premarriage education than with her postmarriage education, *ceteris paribus*. The educational attainment of the wife at the time of marriage is not indicated in any of the data samples used, but the wife's age at the time of marriage is included in the U.S. Census and SEO data, and from this two indirect tests can be made. First, an examination is made of the relationship between the wife's age at marriage and her husband's earnings. The argument is that, for any given level of a wife's schooling, the younger she is at the time of marriage the less likely she is to have completed her education, and hence, according to the variant of the selective-mating hypothesis proposed above, the less likely she is to marry a highly productive male. This hypothesis is not supported by table 4, which shows the partial relationship between wife's age at marriage and husband's earnings to be consistently negative.[15]

An alternative way of examining this same question is to estimate the years of education completed by the wife at the time of marriage and to examine the husband's earnings differentials associated with his wife's pre- and postmarriage education. The estimates in table 5 suggest that the relationships between wife's pre- and postmarriage education and husband's earnings are very similar,[16] that women's postmarriage

[15] Several alternative forms of the variable "age of wife at marriage" were considered. These included dummy variables for each marriage age (18–25) and combinations of continuous and dummy variables. For those women marrying either at a relatively young age (18 or under) or at a relatively late age (25 and over), husband's earnings were generally lower than for women married between ages 18 and 25. For the intervening years, the association between wife's age at marriage and husband's earnings was either negative or essentially zero. An alternative hypothesis consistent with results in table 4 is that wife's age at marriage is serving as a proxy for husband's work experience.

[16] These estimates should be viewed somewhat cautiously, since a purely random division of education would push the pre- and postmarriage coefficients toward equality.

TABLE 4

ESTIMATED EFFECT OF WIFE'S AGE AT MARRIAGE ON HUSBAND'S EARNINGS

(t-STATISTIC IN PARENTHESES)

Sample	Dependent Variable	Husband's Education	Wife's Education	Husband's Experience	Husband's Experience Squared	Wife's Age at Marriage	Constant	R^2	N
1/1,000 Census, 1960*	ln EARN	0.076	0.032	0.042	−0.00070	−0.0061	6.995	.207	4,625
		(21.2)	(7.7)	(15.9)	(−12.8)	(−3.1)	(117.0)		
SEO, 1967*	ln EARN	0.065	0.036	0.036	−0.00064	−0.0034	7.337	.202	8,055
		(24.7)	(11.6)	(18.6)	(−16.0)	(−3.2)	(180.7)		
SEO, 1967†	ln EARN	0.066	0.032	0.037	−0.00070	−0.0032	7.354	.207	7,052
		(23.4)	(9.6)	(18.9)	(−16.4)	(−2.2)	(166.4)		

* See table 1 for description.
† Same as table 1 description except that families were included only if husbands were married only once.

TABLE 5

Estimated Percentage Differentials in Husband's Earnings Associated with Wife's Premarriage and Postmarriage Education
(t-Statistics in Parentheses)

Dependent Variable	Husband's Education	Wife's Years of Premarriage Education	Wife's Years of Postmarriage Education	Husband's Experience	Husband's Experience Squared	Constant	R^2	N
1) ln EARN..........	0.070 (17.5)	0.041 (10.3)	0.043 (6.1)	0.052 (17.3)	-0.001 (14.1)	6.625	.222	4,780
2) ln EARN for subset of husbands whose wives have some post-marriage education	0.079 (8.9)	0.043 (3.6)	0.044 (3.1)	0.077 (12.8)	-0.001 (10.5)	6.289	.273	982

NOTE.—Data are from a 20 percent subsample of the 1/1,000 sample of the 1960 U.S. Census, further restricted to include only males of ages 18–64, married once with spouse present, husbands of once-married women, non-Negro, nonfarm residents, not in school, having positive number of weeks worked, positive earnings, and positive total income in 1959. Wives' years of pre- and postmarriage education were determined by comparing their age at marriage with an age assigned to their corresponding level of education completed. Values were assigned as follows: for years of wife's education ≤ 16.5, age at completion = years of education + 6. For years of wife's education > 16.5, age at completion = 22.5 + 2 (years of education − 16.5). (The highest category for schooling completed is 18 years.) In the subsample used for (1) above, for husband's education, wife's premarriage education, and wife's postmarriage education, means are 11.328, 11.056, and 0.341 and standard deviations are 3.521, 3.126, and 1.63, respectively. In the subsample used for (2) above, the corresponding means are 12.589, 11.507, and 1.660 and standard deviations are 3.232, 3.930, and 3.274.

385

education is at least as strongly associated with husbands' earnings as is their premarriage education.[17]

Another variant of the selective-mating hypothesis states that a wife's education is only a proxy for other background characteristics of both spouses, such as intelligence and social class. Should these latter variables be associated both with husband's earnings and with wife's own educational attainment, then the association noted between the wife's education and the husband's earnings may be spurious. This argument has its counterpart in the recurring question of the extent to which an individual's education itself results in higher earnings versus the extent to which education is merely a proxy for intelligence, social background, and so forth.

Data on background variables were not available in the samples used for tables 1–5. However, this issue has been examined in another context by Duncan, Featherman, and Duncan (1972, p. 178) in a study of the relationship between the occupational status of husbands and the background characteristics (including education) of both spouses.[18] A multiple regression was computed of husband's occupational status in 1956 on his background characteristics, including his education, his occupational status at marriage and his father's occupational status, and his wife's background characteristics, including her education, her father's occupational status, her intelligence, and a psychological index of her drive to get ahead. All the coefficients for wife's characteristics *except education* were less than two times their standard error. This is consistent with the hypothesis that the wife's education has a significant independent effect on the husband's career development.

These results, however, are not directly comparable to those presented in tables 1–5, since occupational status rather than earnings is the dependent variable. By using another data set developed by Blau and Duncan (1967), it is possible to obtain more directly comparable results by estimating the relationship between husband's income in 1961 and both spouses' education, given several of the husband's background

---

[17] An alternative explanation concerning the strong relationship between wife's postmarriage education and husband's earnings is that husbands with higher earnings purchase more postmarriage education for their wives. To examine this question, a sample was drawn of husbands of ages 20–30 having 12 or more years of school who were employed full time during the week of the 1960 U.S. Census survey. For this group, median income was calculated for husbands whose wives were in school and for those whose wives were not in school. Only 2.4 percent of the men in this sample had a wife in school, so results should be viewed with appropriate caution; but in all men's education categories except 12 years, the median income was *lower* for those men with wives in school.

[18] The data used for these estimates were for couples who had recently had a second child at the time of the survey in 1957 (see Duncan et al. [1972, p. 34] for a more complete description).

characteristics, including occupational status of his first job and his father's occupation and education.[19]

The following three specifications were used to estimate the impact of including husband's background characteristics using these data:

$$\text{INCOME} = \alpha_1 + \beta_1 \text{ EDH} + \beta_2 \text{ EDW} + \mu,$$

$$\text{INCOME} = \alpha_1 + \beta_1 \text{ EDH} + \beta_2 \text{ EDW}$$
$$+ \beta_3 \text{ EDHF} + \beta_4 \text{ OCHF} + \mu, \text{ and}$$

$$\text{INCOME} = \alpha_1 + \beta_1 \text{ EDH} + \beta_2 \text{ EDW}$$
$$+ \beta_3 \text{ EDHF} + \beta_4 \text{ OCHF} + \beta_5 \text{ OCHJ} + \mu,$$

where INCOME = husband's income in 1961, EDH = husband's education, EDW = wife's education, EDHF = husband's father's education, OCHF = husband's father's occupation, and OCHJ = husband's occupational status on his first job. Due to the nature of the available data,[20] these specifications differ from the earlier ones in this paper in that income rather than ln earnings is the dependent variable and husband's work experience is not included.[21] Nevertheless, they provide qualitative estimates of the relative importance of husband's background characteristics.

Table 6 shows the relative impact of wife's education as compared with husband's education on husband's income (β_2/β_1) by age of wife. These estimates are consistent with those presented earlier. There is a substantial relationship between wife's education and husband's income in most years. For wives of ages 22–26, husband's income increases 37 percent as much with an increase in wife's education as with a similar increase in husband's own education. This ratio increases to 80 percent for wives ages 32–36 and then declines at older ages, a pattern similar to that shown in table 3.

When husband's father's occupation and education are included, the pattern is very similar.[22] Except for the oldest group, these results are not consistent with the hypothesis that the association between wife's education

---

[19] Data were collected from 20,700 respondents representing men in the U.S. civilian noninstitutional population between the ages of 20 and 64 in March 1962 (see Duncan et al. 1972, p. 32).

[20] Professor Otis Dudley Duncan generously provided the correlation matrices which he had developed for table 8.16 in Duncan et al. (1972, p. 240). The estimates shown here were calculated from those matrices.

[21] The consequences of excluding the husband's work-experience variables are less severe here since separate estimates are made for each of eight age-of-wife categories.

[22] Inclusion of father's education and occupation reduces the education coefficient for both spouses. The ratio of the husband's education coefficient when his father's education and occupation are included to the husband's education coefficient when they are excluded, by wife's age, is as follows: wife's age 22–26 (.91), 27–31 (.81), 32–36 (.80), 37–41 (.82), 42–46 (.87), 47–51 (.85), 52–56 (.85), and 57–61 (.80).

TABLE 6

RATIO OF INCREASE IN HUSBAND'S INCOME AS A FUNCTION OF WIFE'S EDUCATION
TO INCREASE IN HUSBAND'S INCOME AS A FUNCTION OF HUSBAND'S EDUCATION,
FOR INTACT WHITE COUPLES, BY AGE OF WIFE IN 1962

INDEPENDENT VARIABLES INCLUDED	AGE OF WIFE							
	22–26	27–31	32–36	37–41	42–46	47–51	52–56	57–61
Husband's and wife's education	.37*	.51†	.80†	.46†	.25†	.35†	.16†	.14*
Husband's and wife's education, husband's father's education and occupation	.36*	.57†	.93†	.49†	.24†	.33†	.14*	.05
Husband's and wife's education, husband's father's education and occupation, and husband's occupation at first job	.41*	.62†	1.22†	.52†	.26†	.37†	.18*	.04

NOTE.—The ratio β_2/β_1 is given in this table.
* Coefficient of wife's education greater than its standard error but less than twice as great (in absolute value).
† Coefficient of wife's education greater than twice its standard error (in absolute value).

and husband's income is predominantly due to selective mating based on wife's education and these background characteristics of husband.

When the husband's occupational status on his first job is included, the wife's education remains statistically significant for wives between ages 27 and 51.[23] Selective mating based on the husband's occupational status on his first job does not explain the association between his income and his wife's education.

Obviously, other evidence will be required before the relative importance within the family of selective mating versus benefits of wife's education can be determined. However, a significant positive relationship between husband's earnings and wife's education, given the husband's own education and job experience, has been found, and further evidence has been examined which might have contradicted the household hypothesis but which instead was found to be consistent with it.

Conclusions

Several tentative conclusions may be drawn from the results above:

1. A shift in emphasis from the individual to the family unit may not only facilitate understanding of productivity and efficiency within the

---

[23] Not surprisingly, when husband's occupational status on his first job is entered, the coefficient of husband's education is reduced. The ratio of husband's education coefficient when father's background characteristics and husband's occupational status on first job are included to husband's education coefficient when only the spouses' own educations are included, by age of wife, is as follows: wife's age 22–26 (.67), 27–31 (.70), 32–36 (.57), 37–41 (.69), 42–46 (.72), 47–51 (.66), 52–56 (.67), and 57–61 (.57).

home but also usefully extend our understanding of the effects of education on labor-market productivity.

2. The traditional human capital literature has emphasized formal schooling and on-the-job training as the locations where individuals accumulate their human capital. The results in this paper are consistent with the view that there is substantial capital accumulation within the household.

3. Labor-market benefits to men appear to be associated with their marrying well-educated women. These benefits have implications not only for earnings but also for the characteristics of marriage partners selected and the stability of marriages.

4. The wife's education provides substantial labor-market benefits to the family beyond increments to her own earnings. Both the private and social market returns to women's education may be higher than has been generally believed. The flavor of some past discussions of women's education has suggested that it is an indulgence of an affluent society. Perhaps the affluence has been more a function of women's education than has been heretofore realized.

Comment

Finis Welch
City University of New York and National Bureau of Economic Research

I have been tempted to write a note on the social cost of the "marriage-go-round." In a nutshell, the idea is that more productive marriage partners are preferred and that, on balance, net productivity in marriage is positively related to education. Increased education serves to increase an individual's chance of a good marriage, of marriage to a "more" educated spouse. If an individual's social product is independent of his spouse's education, then the marriage-go-round results in overinvestment in education. Benham's view that a person's own productivity depends on attributes of the spouse is a clear alternative.

My skepticism concerning Benham's hypothesis that a husband's earning capacity is positively related to his wife's schooling is not qualitative but quantitative. How important are these (very likely positive) cross-productivity effects? I was not surprised to hear of the positive association between wife's schooling and husband's earnings. I was surprised that most emphasis is on productivity instead of selective mating.

Benham points out that, since his measures are of annual earnings, there may be labor-supply effects submerged in the estimated relationship between husband's earnings and wife's schooling. He notes (correctly) that the direction of this effect is unclear on a priori grounds, but finds empirically that an extra year of wife's schooling has only a slightly smaller percentage effect on husband's weekly wage than on annual earnings. In tabulations using a different body of data, I have verified this result. I will briefly describe these computations.

I used the NBER-Thorndike sample of 4,519 white married males (wife present) who entered the U.S. Air Force in 1943 and who were examined as navigators and pilots at that time. Earnings are for 1969. Experience is the number of years since the individual was last in school. The geometric mean of earnings is over $13,000,[1] and logarithmic variance is 0.24.

---

[1] Earnings for 1969 are deflated to the 1958 value so as to allow life-cycle comparisons. In the regressions below, I did not rescale this variable.

The advantage of this sample is that data are available to permit explicit consideration of the possible effects of selective mating. For example, information on husbands includes: (1) schooling, (2) a measure of IQ, (3) father's schooling and occupation, and (4) religion. It is clear that the sample is rarefied, and it is consequently hard to judge how much confidence should be placed in results contained within. For example, essentially all respondents are white, completed high school, and on armed forces intelligence tests scored in the upper one-half of the distribution. On the other hand, in one important dimension, this sample is superior to the national probability samples for isolating "pure" productivity effects of wife's schooling. It is likely that the World War II marriage market functioned somewhat differently from that in normal times— possibly a careful matching of family background was less important during the war. If so, then in this sample, containing a disproportionately large number of men who were married during the war, there should be less "pollution" with covariance between wife's schooling and husband's family background.[2] For example, Benham, in an unpublished table, shows that, in the U.S. Census sample, the zero-order correlation between husband's and wife's schooling is 0.65. In the NBER-Thorndike sample the correlation is 0.38.

It is true that this lower correlation in the NBER-Thorndike sample could be the result of truncation in the husband's schooling variable, but it is important that if truncation reduces correlations it does not change biases due to omitted variables. Yet, if the reduced correlation follows from reduced covariance between wife's schooling and omitted variables such as husband's IQ or family background, which may themselves affect earnings, then the reduced correlation reduces coefficient bias. Table 1 reports regression results for this sample.

Regression 1 is equivalent to regressions Benham presents in table 1A, and the results agree that there is a "significant" association between wife's schooling and husband's earnings. There is a quantitative difference, however; while a year of schooling for the husband has the same estimated effect (6–7 percent) on earnings, the coefficient for wife's schooling is less than one-half as high in the NBER-Thorndike sample as in the samples used by Benham. Regression 2 includes the length-of-marriage variables à la Benham's table 3. Here no evidence of a statistically significant relationship exists. The computed F-statistic (2; 4,512 degrees of freedom) is only 1.16. In any case, it is hard to interpret Benham's results vis-à-vis length of marriage, for the marriage can itself be considered as a short "period of investment."

Regression 3 introduces a decomposition of the wife's schooling variable into two parts. The first part includes those components of a wife's

[2] Roughly 17.5 percent of the NBER-Thorndike sample of men who had wives in 1969 had married those particular spouses between 1941 and 1944. Of this group of men, 8 percent were married in 1944.

TABLE 1
Regression Estimates of Relationship between Husband's Earnings and Wife's Schooling
(t-Ratios in Parentheses)

A. Dependent Variable: Log_e (Husband's Annual Earnings)

Independent Variables	Regression No.		
	1	2	3
Intercept	7.04	7.02	6.45
Husband's schooling	0.067	0.067	0.061
	(18.4)	(18.4)	(16.5)
Experience	0.014	0.015	0.013
	(4.6)	(4.6)	(4.1)
(Experience)^2	−0.0002	−0.0002	−0.0002
	(−2.7)	(−2.8)	(−2.4)
Wife's education:			
a) Observed	0.015	0.015	...
	(4.2)	(4.3)	
b) Predicted by husband's IQ and background	...	...	0.144
			(11.9)
c) Observed-predicted	...	...	0.007
			(1.9)
Length of marriage	...	−0.002	...
		(−0.4)	
(Length of marriage)^2	...	0.00012	...
		(0.8)	
R^2	.113	.114	.137

B. Dependent Variable: Wife's Schooling

Independent Variables	Regression No. 4
Intercept	12.1
Husband's IQ	0.11
	(6.4)
Husband's father's schooling	0.12
	(13.5)
Husband's father's occupation status:	
a) High	0.23
	(3.3)
b) Low	−0.03
	(−0.33)
Husband's religion	
a) Jewish	0.44
	(3.2)
b) Catholic	−0.27
	(−3.7)
R^2	.078

schooling that are correlated with (and presumably would be predicted by) her husband's IQ, religion, and his father's schooling and occupation. The intention is simply that these variables would be among the most obvious predictors of wife's schooling, based on a sociological "network" or an assortive-mating frame of reference. The second part of the wife's education is that which is orthogonal to the above list and is simply the residuals between observed schooling and schooling predicted by regression 4. It is this part of a wife's schooling that is independent of her husband's background, religion, and measured IQ which is the obvious candidate for the "pure" productivity effect posited by Benham. But in these data there is little independent role for wife's education. Most of the effect is channeled through the independent variables of regression 4.

To summarize these results, note first that the effect of a year of a wife's schooling is 22 percent of the estimated effect of her husband's schooling. Further, after "partialing out" effects of a husband's IQ and background on his wife's schooling, the net effect of the wife's schooling is reduced to slightly less than half its original level and the coefficient estimate is of marginal statistical significance. The estimated net effect of a wife's schooling is roughly one-tenth of the estimated effect of her husband's schooling and is only one-fifth of Benham's estimate.

Does this then prove that the pure productivity effect is unimportant? Clearly not. Aside from the peculiarities of this particular set of data, the identification problems surrounding the Benham hypothesis are probably insurmountable. For example, consider models of selective mating. If forces for selectivity exist in the absence of this cross-productivity (cross-fertilization?) effect, they are clearly magnified by its existence.

Part Four

Family Human Capital

Family Investments in Human Capital: Earnings of Women

Jacob Mincer

Columbia University and National Bureau of Economic Research

Solomon Polachek

University of North Carolina

I. Introduction

It has long been recognized that consumption behavior represents mainly joint household or family decisions rather than separate decisions of family members. Accordingly, the observational units in consumption surveys are "consumer units," that is, households in which income is largely pooled and consumption largely shared.

More recent is the recognition that an individual's use of time, and particularly the allocation of time between market and nonmarket activities, is also best understood within the context of the family as a matter of interdependence with needs, activities, and characteristics of other family members. More generally, the family is viewed as an economic unit which shares consumption and allocates production at home and in the market as well as the investments in physical and human capital of its members. In this view, the behavior of the family unit implies a division of labor within it. Broadly speaking, this division of labor or "differentiation of roles" emerges because the attempts to promote family life are necessarily constrained by complementarity and substitution relations in the household production process and by comparative

Research here reported is part of a continuing study of the distribution of income, conducted by the National Bureau of Economic Research and funded by the National Science Foundation and the Office of Economic Opportunity. This report has not undergone the usual NBER review. We are grateful to Otis Dudley Duncan, James Heckman, Melvin Reder, T. W. Schultz, and Robert Willis for useful comments, and to George Borjas for skillful research assistance.

advantages due to differential skills and earning powers with which family members are endowed.

Though the levels and distribution of these endowments can be taken as given in the short run, this is not true in a more complete perspective. Even if each individual's endowment were genetically determined, purposive marital selection would make its distribution in the family endogenous, along the lines suggested by Becker in this volume. Of course, individual endowments are not merely genetic; they can be augmented by processes of investment in human capital and reduced by depreciation. Indeed, a major function of the family as a social institution is the building of human capital of children—a lengthy "gestation" process made even longer by growing demands of technology.

Optimal investment in human capital of any family member requires attention not only to the human and financial capacities in the family, but also to the prospective utilization of the capital which is being accumulated. Expectations of future family and market activities of individuals are, therefore, important determinants of levels and forms of investment in human capital. Thus, family investments and time allocation are linked: while the current distribution of human capital influences the current allocation of time within the family, the prospective allocation of time influences current investments in human capital.

That the differential allocation of time and of investments in human capital is generally sex linked and subject to technological and cultural changes is a matter of fact which is outside the scope of our analysis. Given the sex linkage, we focus on the relation within the family between time allocation and investments in human capital which give rise to the observed market earnings of women. Whether these earnings, or the investments underlying them, are also influenced or reinforced by discriminatory attitudes of employers and fellow workers toward women in the labor market is a question we do not explore directly, though we briefly analyze the male-female wage differential. Our major purposes are to ascertain and to estimate the effects of human-capital accumulation on market earnings and wage rates of women, to infer the magnitudes and course of such investments over the life histories of women, and to interpret these histories in the context of past expectations and of current and prospective family life.

The data we study, the 1967 National Longitudinal Survey of Work Experience (NLS), afford a heretofore unavailable opportunity to relate family and work histories of women to their current market earning power. Accumulation of human capital is a lifetime process. In the post-school stage of the life cycle much of the continued accumulation of earning power takes place on the job. Where past work experience of men can be measured without much error in numbers of years elapsed since leaving school, such a measure of "potential work experience" is clearly inadequate for members of the labor force among whom the length and continuity of work experience varies a great deal. Direct information on work histories of women is, therefore, a basic requirement for the analysis of their earnings. To our knowledge, the NLS is the only data set which provides this information, albeit on a retrospective basis. Eventually, the NLS panel surveys will provide the information on a current basis, showing developments as they unfold.[1]

II. The Human-Capital Earnings Function

To the extent that earnings in the labor market are a function of the human-capital stock accumulated by individuals, a sequence of positive net investments gives rise to growing earning power over the life cycle. When net investment is negative, that is, when market skills are eroded by depreciation, earning power declines. This relation between the sequence of capital accumulation and the resulting growth in earnings has been formalized in the "human-capital earnings function." A simple specification of this function fits the life cycle "earnings profile" of men rather well. The approach to distribution of earnings among male workers (in the United States and elsewhere) as a distribution of individual earnings profiles appears to be promising.[2]

For the purpose of this paper, a brief development of the earnings function may suffice:

Let C_{t-1} be the dollar amount of net investment in period $t - 1$, while (gross) earnings in that period, before the investment expenditures are subtracted, are E_{t-1}. Let r be the average rate of return to the individual's human-capital investment, and assume that r is the same in each period. Then

$$E_t = E_{t-1} + rC_{t-1}. \tag{1}$$

Let $k_t = C_t/E_t$, the ratio of investment expenditures to gross earnings, which may be viewed as investment in time-equivalent units. Then

$$E_t = E_{t-1}(1 + rk_{t-1}). \tag{2}$$

[1] For a description of the NLS survey of women's work histories, see Parnes, Shea, Spitz, and Zeller (1970). For an analysis of earnings of men, using "potential" work-experience measures, see Mincer (1974b). Though less appropriate, the same proxy variable was used in several recent studies of female earnings. Direct information from the NLS Survey was first used by Suter and Miller (1971). The human-capital approach was first applied to these data by Polachek in his Columbia Ph.D. thesis, "Work Experience and the Difference between Male and Female Wages" (1973). This paper reports a fuller development of the analysis in that thesis.

[2] See, for instance, Rahm (1971), Chiswick and Mincer (1972), Chiswick (1973), Mincer (1974b), and a series of unpublished research papers by George E. Johnson and Frank P. Stafford on earnings of Ph.D.'s in various fields.

By recursion $E_t = E_0(1 + rk_0)(1 + rk_1)\ldots(1 + rk_{t-1})$. The term rk is a small fraction. Hence a logarithmic approximation of $\ln(1 + rk) \simeq rk$ yields

$$\ln E_t = \ln E_0 + r \sum_{i=0}^{t-1} k_i. \tag{3}$$

Since earnings net of investment expenditures, $Y_t = E_t(1 - k_t)$, we have also

$$\ln Y_t = \ln E_0 + r \sum_{i=0}^{t-1} k_i + \ln(1 - k_t). \tag{4}$$

Some investments are in the form of schooling; others take the form of formal and informal job training. If only these two categories of investment are analyzed, that is, schooling and postschool experience,[3] the k terms can be separated, and

$$\ln E_t = \ln E_0 + r \sum_{i=0}^{s-1} k_i + r \sum_{j=s}^{t-1} k_j \tag{5}$$

where the k_i are investment ratios during the schooling period and the k_j thereafter. With tuition added to opportunity costs and student earnings and scholarships subtracted from them, the rough assumption $k_i = 1$ may be used.[4] Hence,

$$\ln E_t = \ln E_0 + rs + r \sum_{j=s}^{t-1} k_j. \tag{6}$$

The postschool investment ratios k_j are expected to decline continuously if work experience is expected to be continuous and the purpose of investment is acquisition and maintenance of market earning power. This conclusion emerges from models of optimal distribution of investment expenditures C_t over the life cycle (see Becker 1967 and Ben-Porath 1967). A sufficient rationale for our purposes is that as t increases, the remaining working life $(T - t)$ shortens. Since $(T - t)$ is the length of the payoff period on investments in t, the incentives to invest and the magnitudes of investment decline over the (continuous) working life. This is true for C_t and a fortiori for k_t, since with positive C_t, E_t rises, and k_t is the ratio of C_t to E_t.

In analyses of male earnings, a linearly (or geometrically) declining approximation of the working-life profile of investment ratios k_t appears to be a satisfactory statistical hypothesis.

---

[3] The inclusion of other categories in the earnings function is an important research need, since human capital is acquired in many other ways: in the home environment, in investments in health, by mobility, information, and so forth.

[4] According to T. W. Schultz, this assumption overstates k, especially at higher education levels, leading to an understatement of r.

It will be useful for our purpose of studying earnings of women to decompose net investments explicitly into gross investments and depreciation. Let C_{t-1}^* be the dollar amount of gross investment in period $t - 1$, δ_{t-1} the depreciation rate of the stock of human capital, hence of earnings E_{t-1} during that period, and $k_t^* = C_t^*/E_t$, the gross investment ratio. Hence

$$E_t = E_{t-1} + rC_{t-1}^* - \delta_{t-1}E_{t-1}$$

and

$$\frac{E_t}{E_{t-1}} = 1 + rk_{t-1}^* - \delta_{t-1} = 1 + rk_{t-1}, \quad \text{by equation (2),} \quad \text{(1a)}$$

thus

$$rk_t = rk_t^* - \delta_t. \tag{2a}$$

The earnings function (3) can, therefore, be written as

$$\ln E_t = \ln E_0 + \sum_{i=0}^{t-1} (rk_i^* - \delta_i). \tag{3a}$$

In transferring the analysis to women, we face two basic facts: (1) After marriage, women spend less than half of their lifetime in the labor market, on average. Of course, this "lifetime participation rate" varies by marital status, number of children, and other circumstances, and it has been growing secularly. (2) The lesser market work of married women is not only a matter of fewer years during a lifetime, and fewer weeks per year, or a shorter work week. An important aspect is discontinuity of work experience, for most of the married women surveyed in 1967 reported several entries into and exits from the labor force after leaving school.

The implications of these facts for the volume and the life-cycle distribution of human-capital investments can be stated briefly:[5]

1. Since job-related investment in human capital commands a return which is received at work,[6] the shorter the expected and actual duration of work experience, the weaker the incentives to augment job skills over the life cycle. With labor-force attachment of married women lasting, on average, about one-half that of men, labor-market activities of women are less likely to contain skill training and learning components as a result both of women's own decisions and decisions of employers, who may be expected to invest in worker skills to some extent.

2. Given discontinuity of work experience, the conclusion of optimization analysis to the effect that human-capital investments decline

[5] For a mathematical statement of the optimization analysis applied to discontinuous work experience, see Polachek (1973, chap. 3).

[6] For the sake of brevity, the term "work" refers to work in the job market. We do not imply that women occupied in the household do not work.

TABLE 1
LABOR-FORCE PARTICIPATION OF MOTHERS: PROPORTION WORKING,
WHITE MARRIED WOMEN WITH CHILDREN, SPOUSE PRESENT

| | PROPORTION WORKING (%) | | | |
AGE	In 1966	After First Child	Ever	SAMPLE SIZE
30–34	43	64	82	925
$S < 12$	46	71	75	294
$S = 12$	43	63	84	446
$S > 12$	40	59	88	185
35–39	47	67	87	945
$S < 12$	45	66	82	336
$S = 12$	49	68	88	422
$S > 12$	47	67	92	187
40–44	53	70	88	1,078
$S < 12$	52	72	78	465
$S = 12$	54	70	91	446
$S > 12$	51	68	93	167

SOURCE.—NLS, 1967 survey.
NOTE.—S = years of schooling.

continuously over the successive years of life after leaving school is no longer valid. Even a continuous decline over the years spent in the job market cannot be hypothesized if several intervals of work experience rather than one stretch represent the norm.

3. The more continuous the participation, the larger the investments on initial job experience relative to those in later jobs.

Women without children and without husbands may be expected to engage in continuous job experience. But labor-force participation of married women, especially of mothers, varies over the life cycle, depending on the demands on their time in the household as well as on their skills and preferences relative to those of other family members. The average pattern of labor-force experience is apparent in tables 1–3, which are based on the NLS data reported by women who were 30–44 years of age at the time of the survey. According to the data:

1. Though less than 50 percent of the mothers worked in 1966, close to 90 percent worked sometime after they left school, and two-thirds returned to the labor market after the birth of the first child (table 1). Lifetime labor-force participation of women without children or without husbands is, of course, greater.

2. Never-married women spent 90 percent of their years after they left school in the labor market, while married women with children spent less than 50 percent of their time in it. In each age group, childless women, those with children but without husbands (widowed, divorced, or separated), and those who married more than once spent less time in the market than never-married women, but more than mothers married once, spouse present (table 2).

TABLE 2
Work Histories of Women Aged 30–44 by Marital Status (Average Number of Years)

Group	Variable										Sample Size
	h_1	e_1	h_2	e_2	h_3	e_3	Σe	Σh	S	N_c	
White, with children:											
Married once, spouse present	0.57	3.55	6.71	1.14	1.22	1.69	6.4	10.4	11.8	3.16	2,398
Remarried, spouse present	0.54	2.43	7.85	2.60	2.02	2.00	7.1	10.3	10.6	3.28	341
Widowed	1.11	4.25	9.37	1.51	1.44	2.56	8.4	11.9	12.0	2.44	45
Divorced	0.94	2.96	6.54	4.24	2.38	2.92	10.1	9.8	10.8	2.98	133
Separated	0.74	3.97	7.81	2.71	1.14	2.08	8.7	9.6	10.1	2.86	65
White, childless:											
Married once, spouse present	1.01	5.18	…	4.39	3.35	4.90	14.5	3.3	11.7	…	147
Never married	…	7.08	…	…	1.46	7.48	14.5	1.5	12.9	…	153
Black, with children:											
Married once, spouse present	1.12	3.00	7.12	2.95	2.14	3.26	9.1	10.3	10.0	4.59	563
Remarried, spouse present	0.96	2.44	7.43	4.93	2.05	3.36	10.7	11.7	9.6	4.22	170
Widowed and divorced	1.19	2.23	7.67	4.36	1.90	3.68	10.3	10.8	9.8	4.20	149
Separated	1.28	2.86	6.24	5.57	2.38	2.81	11.2	9.8	9.4	4.22	191
Black, childless:											
Married once, spouse present	2.33	4.75	…	3.83	4.58	4.77	13.4	6.9	10.9	…	71
Never married	…	7.15	…	…	4.74	6.45	13.6	4.7	10.9	…	47

Note.—h_1 = years not worked between school and first marriage; e_1 = years worked between school and first marriage (for never-marrieds, = years worked prior to current job); h_2 = interval of nonparticipation following birth of first child; e_2 = years worked after h_2 prior to current job; h_3 = interval of nonparticipation just prior to current job; e_3 = years on current job; Σe = years worked since school; Σh = years of nonparticipation since school; S = years of schooling; N_c = no. of children.

3. Table 3 shows the characteristic work histories of mothers,[7] spouse present (MSP), who represented over two-thirds of the women in the sample. We show chronologically the length of nonparticipation (h_1) during the interval between leaving school and marriage; the years of market work between school and the birth of the first child (e_1); an uninterrupted period of nonparticipation, h_2, starting just before the first child was born, followed by e_2 and h_3, which sum intermittent participation and nonparticipation, respectively; and finally e_3, the present job tenure of women working at the time of the survey.

It is clear from the tabulations that, after their schooling, the life cycle of married women features several stages which differ in the nature and degree of labor-market and home involvement. There is usually continuous market work prior to the birth of the first child. The second stage is a period of nonparticipation related to childbearing and child care, lasting between 5 and 10 years, followed by intermittent participation before the youngest child reaches school age. The third stage is a more permanent return to the labor force for some, though it may remain intermittent for others. In our data, which were obtained from women who were less than 45 years old, only the beginning of the third stage is visible.

The following conjectures about investment behavior in each of these stages are plausible in view of the described patterns which are to some extent anticipated by the women.

1. Prospective discontinuity may well influence many young women during their prematernal employment (e_1) to acquire less job training than men with comparable education, unless they do not expect to marry or have an overriding commitment to a work career.

2. During the period of childbearing and child care, prolonged nonparticipation may cause the skills acquired at school and at work to depreciate. Some revisions of expectations and of commitments may also take place.[8] Little investment, if any, can be expected during the episodic employment period e_2.

3. There is likely to be a stronger expectation of prospective continuity of employment after the children reach school age. To the extent that the current job (e_3) is more likely to represent this more-permanent return to the labor force than e_2 does, strong incentives to resume investments in job-related skills should reappear.

---

[7] The six intervals shown in table 3 are aggregated from eight available ones. Both sets are described in the Appendix.

[8] We are reminded by T. W. Schultz that erosion of market skills during periods of nonparticipation is likely to be associated with growth in nonmarket productivity. If so, the longer the time spent out of the labor force the greater the excess of the reservation or "shadow" price over the market wage, hence the smaller the probability of subsequent labor-force participation.

TABLE 3

WORK HISTORIES OF MARRIED WOMEN BY AGE, EDUCATION, AND CURRENT WORK STATUS

AGE AND CATEGORY	VARIABLE									SAMPLE SIZE
	h_1	e_1	h_2	e_2	h_3	e_3	Σe	Σh	N_c	
30–34:										
Worked in 1966:										
$S < 12$	1.93	2.37	5.80	3.18	2.20	1.90	7.45	9.93	3.42	135
$S = 12$–15	0.90	2.84	5.41	2.21	1.39	2.31	7.36	7.70	2.89	233
$S \geq 16$	0.37	2.57	2.65	2.22	1.22	2.00	6.79	4.24	2.39	35
Did not work in 1966, but worked since birth of first child:										
$S < 12$	1.67	2.23	6.29	1.31	5.09	...	3.54	13.05	3.50	68
$S = 12$–15	0.81	2.90	4.65	1.23	4.75	...	4.13	10.21	3.49	93
$S \geq 16$	0.50	1.85	3.57	1.71	3.57	...	3.56	7.64	3.00	14
Has not worked since birth of first child:										
$S < 12$	4.54	1.42	9.64	...	...	...	1.42	14.18	3.24	85
$S = 12$–15	2.28	3.21	7.93	...	...	...	3.21	10.21	3.03	211
$S \geq 16$	1.95	1.11	7.20	...	...	...	1.11	9.15	3.14	34
35–39:										
Worked in 1966:										
$S < 12$	1.94	2.78	7.98	3.47	2.78	3.40	9.65	12.70	3.37	152
$S = 12$–15	0.98	3.42	6.85	3.09	2.01	3.70	10.21	9.84	2.99	250
$S \geq 16$	1.01	2.95	4.72	2.04	1.25	5.46	10.45	6.98	2.72	43
Did not work in 1966, but worked since birth of first child:										
$S < 12$	2.15	2.96	9.00	1.80	6.40	...	4.76	17.55	3.70	65
$S = 12$–15	1.20	3.74	7.42	1.18	5.94	...	4.92	14.56	3.51	101
$S \geq 16$	0.38	5.75	6.50	1.15	2.62	...	6.90	9.50	2.87	8
Has not worked since birth of first child:										
$S < 12$	4.23	3.54	13.53	...	...	...	3.54	17.76	3.58	113
$S = 12$–15	2.97	3.85	11.62	...	...	...	3.85	14.59	3.16	170
$S \geq 16$	1.88	2.65	10.15	...	...	...	2.65	12.03	3.50	26

TABLE 3 (*Continued*)

Work Histories of Married Women by Age, Education, and Current Work Status

Age and Category	Variable									Sample Size
	h_1	e_1	h_2	e_2	h_3	e_3	Σe	Σh	N_c	
40–44:										
Worked in 1966:										
$S < 12$	2.41	3.29	10.38	3.94	2.95	4.93	12.16	15.74	3.18	240
$S = 12$–15	1.55	4.16	8.74	3.57	2.63	4.43	12.16	12.92	2.72	297
$S \geq 16$	0.93	3.20	6.89	3.06	1.86	4.89	11.15	9.68	3.65	29
Did not work in 1966, but worked since birth of first child:										
$S < 12$	2.35	3.31	12.95	1.51	6.89	…	4.82	22.19	3.41	89
$S = 12$–15	1.39	3.68	10.43	1.24	8.23	…	4.92	20.05	3.36	82
$S \geq 16$	3.19	1.19	9.80	1.34	4.80	…	2.53	17.79	3.59	5
Has not worked since birth of first child:										
$S < 12$	6.23	2.63	17.66	…	…	…	2.63	23.89	3.93	130
$S = 12$–15	3.36	4.88	15.12	…	…	…	4.88	18.48	3.12	141
$S \geq 16$	3.03	2.67	13.35	…	…	…	2.67	16.38	2.96	31

Note.—See notes to table 2 for explanation of variables.

These conjectures imply that the investment profile of married women is not monotonic. There is a gap which is likely to show negative values (net depreciation) during the childbearing period and two peaks before and after. The levels of these peaks are likely to be correlated for the same woman, and their comparative size is likely to depend on the degree of continuity of work experience. The whole profile can be visualized in comparison with the investment profiles of men and of single women. For never-married women, stage 1 (e_1) extends over their whole working life, and the investment profile declines as it does for men. To the extent, however, that expectation of marriage and of childbearing are stronger at younger ages and diminish with age, investment of never-married women is likely to be initially lower than that of men. At the same time, given lesser expectations of marriage on the part of the never-married, their initial on-the-job investments exceed those of the women who eventually marry, while the profile of the latter shows two peaks.

The implications for comparative-earnings profiles are clear: Greater investment ratios imply a steeper growth of earnings, while declining investment profiles imply concavity of earnings profiles. Hence, earnings profiles of men are steepest and concave, those of childless women less so, and those of mothers are double peaked with least overall growth.

III. Women's Wage Equation

To adapt the earnings function to persons with intermittent work experience we break up the postschool investment term in equation (6) into successive segments of participation and nonparticipation as they occur chronologically. In the general case with n segments we may express the investment ratio $k_i = a_i + b_i t$, $i = 1, 2, \ldots, n$, and

$$\ln E_t = \ln E_0 + rs + r \sum_{i=1}^{n} \int_{ti}^{t_{i+1}} (a_i + b_i t)\, dt. \qquad (7)$$

Here a_i is the initial investment ratio, b_i is the rate of change of the investment ratio during the ith segment: $(t_{i+1} - t_i) = e_i$ = duration of the ith segment. Note that in (7) the initial investment ratio refers to its projected value at $t_1 = 0$, the start of working life. In a work interval m which occurs in later life there is likely to be less investment than in an earlier interval j, though more than would be observed if j continued at its gradient through the years covered by m. In this case, a_m in equation (7) will exceed a_j.

Alternatively, a_j and a_m can be compared directly in the formulation

$$\ln E_t = \ln E_0 + rs + r \sum_{i=1}^{n} \int_{0}^{e_i} (a_i + b_i t)\, dt, \qquad (8)$$

since a_i is the investment ratio at the beginning of the particular segment i.

While the rate of change in investment b_i is likely to be negative in longer intervals, it may not be significant in shorter ones. Since the segments we observe in the histories of women before age 45 are relatively short, a simplified scheme is to assume a constant rate of net investment throughout a given segment, though differing among segments. The earnings function simplifies to

$$\ln E_t = \ln E_0 + rs + r \sum_i a_i e_i. \tag{9}$$

Whereas $(ra_i) > 0$ denotes positive net investment (ratios), $(ra_i) < 0$ represents net depreciation rates, likely in periods of nonparticipation.

The question whether the annual investment or depreciation rates vary with the length of the interval is ultimately an empirical one. Even if each woman were to invest diminishing amounts over a segment of work experience, those women who stay longer in the labor market are likely to invest more per unit of time, so that a_i is likely to be a positive function of the length of the interval in the cross section.

Thus, even if $k_{ij} = a_{ij} - b_{ij}t$ for a given woman j, if $a_{ij} = \alpha_j + \beta_j t$ across women, on substitution, the coefficient b of t may become negligible or even positive in the cross section. On integrating, and using three segments of working life as an example, earnings functions (7), (8), and (9) become:

$$\begin{aligned} \ln E_t = a_0 + rs + r[a_1 t_1 + \tfrac{1}{2}b_1 t_1^2 + a_2(t_2 - t_1) \\ + \tfrac{1}{2}b_2(t_2^2 - t_1^2) + a_3(t - t_2) + \tfrac{1}{2}b_3(t^2 - t_2^2)], \end{aligned} \tag{7a}$$

$$\begin{aligned} \ln E_t = a_0 + rs + r(a_1 e_1 + \tfrac{1}{2}b_1 e_1^2 + a_2 e_2 \\ + \tfrac{1}{2}b_2 e_2^2 + a_3 e_3 + \tfrac{1}{2}b_3 e_3^2), \end{aligned} \tag{8a}$$

$$\ln E_t = a_0 + rs + r(a_1 e_1 + a_2 e_2 + a_3 e_3). \tag{9a}$$

In this example, t is within the last (third) segment, and the middle segment, $e_2 = h$, is a period of nonparticipation or "home time." The signs of b_i are ambiguous in the cross section, as already indicated; the coefficients of e_1 and of e_3 are expected to be positive, but those of e_2 (or h) negative, most clearly in (9a).

The equations for observed earnings ($\ln Y_t$) differ from the equations shown above by a term $\ln (1 - k_t)$—as was shown in the comparison of equations (3) and (4). With k_t relatively small, only the intercept a_0 is affected, so the same form holds for $\ln Y_t$ as for $\ln E_t$.

It will help our understanding of the estimates of depreciation rates to express earnings function (9a) in terms of gross-investment rates and depreciation rates:

$$\begin{aligned} \ln E_t = \ln E_0 + \sum_i (rk_i^* - \delta_i) \\ = \ln E_0 + (rs - \delta_s) + (rk_1^* - \delta_1)e_1 \\ + (rk_h^* - \delta_h)h + (rk_3^* - \delta_3)e_3. \end{aligned} \tag{9b}$$

This formulation suggests that depreciation of earning power may occur not only in periods of nonparticipation (h), but at other times as well. On the other hand, market-oriented investment, such as informal study and job search, may take place during home time, so that $k_h^* > 0$. Positive coefficients of e_1 and e_3 would reflect positive net investment, while a negative coefficient of h is an estimate of net depreciation. If $k_h^* > 0$, the absolute value of the depreciation rate δ_h is underestimated.

IV. Empirical Findings

Tables 4–8 show results of regression analyses which apply our earnings function to analyze wage rates of women who worked in 1966, the year preceding the survey. The general specification is $\ln w = f(S, e, h, x) + u$, where w is the hourly wage rate; S is the years of schooling; e is a vector of work-experience segments; h is a vector of home-time segments and x is a vector of other variables, such as indexes of job training, mobility, health, number of children, and current weeks and hours of work; u is the statistical residual.

The findings described here are based on ordinary least-squares (OLS) regressions. The tables show shorter and longer lists of variables without covering all the intermediate lists. In view of a plausible simultaneity problem we attempted also a two-stage least-squares (2SLS) estimation procedure, which we describe in the next section. Since the 2SLS estimates do not appear to contradict the findings based on OLS, we describe them first below.

1. *Work History Detail and Equation Form*

When life histories are segmented into five intervals (eight is the maximum possible in the data), three of which are periods of work experience and two of nonmarket activity,[9] both nonlinear formulations (equation forms [7] and [8]) are less informative than the linear specification (9). Rates of change in investment (coefficient b) are probably not substantial within a short interval, and the intercorrelation of the linear and quadratic terms hinders the estimation. Dropping the square terms reduces the explanatory power of the regression slightly but increases the visibility of the life-cycle investment profile. Conversely, when the segments are aggregated, the quadratic term becomes negative but does not quite acquire statistical significance by conventional standards. The quadratic term for current work experience is negative and significant. In the case

[9] Tables 2 and 3 show six intervals, including a very short nonparticipation interval h_1 between school and marriage. This interval is aggregated in other home time in the regressions.

of never-married women, one segment of work experience usually covers most of the potential working life. Here the nonlinear formulation over the interval is as natural and informative as it is for men.

2. *Investment Rates*

Table 4 compares earnings functions of women by marital status and presence of children, tables 5 and 6 by level of schooling, and table 7 by lifetime work experience. In each table we can compare groups of women with differential labor-force attachment. According to human-capital theory, higher investment levels should be observed in groups with stronger labor-force attachment.

We can infer these differences in investment by looking at the coefficients of experience segments, e_1 (prematernal), e_2 (intermittent, after the first child), and e_3 (current). These increase systematically from married women with children to married women without children to single women in table 4, and from women who worked less than half to those who worked more than half of their lifetime in table 7. An exception is the coefficient of e_3 which appears to be somewhat higher for the group who worked less (see table 7). Note, however, that these coefficients are investment ratios (to gross wage rates), not dollar volumes. Since wage rates are higher in the groups with more work experience, the conclusions about increasing investment hold for dollar magnitudes, a fortiori, and the anomaly in table 7 disappears.[10]

Classifications by schooling show mixed results. In table 5, where schooling is stratified by <12, 12–15, and 16+, investment ratios (coefficients of e_i) are lower at higher levels of schooling (with the exception of the coefficient of e_1). Translated into dollar terms,[11] no clear pattern emerges. At the same time in table 6, where the schooling strata are ≤ 8, 9–12, and 13+, a positive relation between investment volumes and levels of schooling is somewhat better indicated. Note that the sample size for the highest-schooling groups (10+) is quite small in table 5, as is that for the lowest-schooling groups (≤ 8) in table 6.

3. *Investment Profiles*

Another implication of the human-capital theory refers to the shape of the investment profile: it is monotonically declining in groups with continuous participation, hence earnings are parabolic in aggregated

---

[10] The coefficient of e_3, calculated as $\partial \ln W/\partial e$, is 15 percent higher in the right-hand group. However, the wage rate of this group is about 25 percent lower.

[11] Wage rates are roughly 30 percent higher in successive schooling groups.

TABLE 4
EARNINGS FUNCTIONS, WHITE WOMEN

With Children

Var.	b (1)	t	Var.	b (2)	t
C	.38	...	C	.21	...
S	.076	11.5	S	.063	10.5
(A-S-6)	.014	3.8	e	.012	1.6
(A-S-6)²	-.001	-4.2	e²	-.0002	-0.5
			e₃	.021	2.8
			e₃	-.0008	-1.9
			h	-.007	-1.5
			h²	.000	0.2
R²	.16	...	R²	.25	...

Var.	b (3)	t	No Children b (4)	t	Never Married b (5)	t
C	.09	12.0	-.42	...	.55	...
S	.064	2.8	.081	4.4	.077	4.9
e₁	.008	0.3	.014	1.6	.026*	1.5
e₂	.001	2.7	.011	1.3	-.0007†	-1.1
e₃	.012	-2.5	.015	2.2	.009	1.5
h₁	-.012	-0.7	-.005†	-1.5	-.009‡	-0.6
h₂	-.003	1.5	.0028§	0.7		...
etr	.0002	3.2	.0003	2.4	.0003	1.7
ect	.010	-1.3	-.003	-1.2	-.011	-1.8
hlt	-.0003	-1.2	-.002	-1.3	-.0008	-1.2
res	.001	2.7	.006	1.7	-.012	-2.2
loc	.044	-3.7	-.021	-0.4	-.02	-0.3
ln Hr	-.11	1.6	-.15	-1.6	-.43	-4.4
ln Wk	.03	-1.0	.25	2.2	.21	1.4
Nc	-.008		...		...	
R²	.28	...	.39	...	.41	...
N	993	...	147	...	138	...

Note.—Var. = variable; C = intercept; S = years of schooling; A = age; e = total years of work; e₁ = years of work before first child; e₂ = years of work after first child; e₃ = years of work after first child; h₁ = home time after first child; h₂ = other home time; etr = experience × training (months); ect = experience × certificate (dummy); hlt = duration of illness (months); res = years of residence in county; loc = size of place of residence at age 15; ln Hrs = (log of) hours of work per year on current job; ln Wks = (log of) weeks per year on current job; Nc = no. of children; b = regression coefficient; t = t-ratio; R² = coefficient of determination; N = sample size.

* e^2.
† e_3.
‡ Total work experience, e.
§ Total home time, h.

TABLE 5

Earnings Functions of WMSP, by Schooling

VAR.	S < 12 b	t	b	t	S = 12-15 b	t	b	t	S = 16+ b	t	b	t
C	−.095	...	−.98	...	−.61	...	−.03	...	.86	...	.36	1.1
S	.046	4.7	.039	3.8	.105	5.1	.086	4.0	.038	0.4	.107	0.5
e_1	.016	3.1	.015	2.2	.012	1.7	.008	1.3	.023	1.5	.010	−3.0
e_2	.014	2.8	.012	1.8	.006	1.2	0	0	−.013	−2.3	−.016	2.4
e_3	.021	4.7	.019	3.2	.015	3.7	.011	1.9	.002	1.6	.004	−1.7
h_1	−.002	−0.6	.001	0.2	−.013	−3.4	−.018	−2.8	−.023	−2.2	−.012	1.0
h_2	.002	0.5	.003	0.5	−.001	−0.2	−.006	−1.0	.006	0.4	.002	0.5
etr			.0004	1.2			.0004	2.0			.0007	2.1
ect			.016	2.4			.008	1.9			.032	0
hlt			−.0006	−1.7			0	0			0	1.2
res			.001	0.5			.002	1.3			.008	0.8
loc			.06	2.4			.036	1.6			.05	−3.4
ln Hrs			−.044	−0.9			−.11	−3.9			−.16	0.7
ln Wks			.045	1.5			.031	1.2			−.05	−1.5
N_c			−.004	−0.4			−.002	−0.2				
R^2	.17		.22		.14		.18		.16		.39	
N	435		...		622		...		83		...	

Note.—WMSP = white married women, spouse present. See table 4 for key to symbols.

TABLE 6

EARNINGS FUNCTIONS OF WMSP (WITH CHILDREN), BY SCHOOLING

VAR.	$S \leq 8$				$S = 9\text{-}12$				$S = 13+$			
	b	t	b	t	b	t	b	t	b	t	b	t
S	.049	1.6	.044	1.3	.051	3.2	.055	3.4	.068	2.8	.079	2.7
e_1	.007	0.4	-.002	-0.4	.013	1.7	.012	1.5	.021	1.4	.018	1.2
e_2	-.004	-2.1	-.028	-1.8	.009	1.6	.003	0.6	-.020	-1.5	-.020	-1.4
e_3	-.002	-0.3	-.008	-0.5	.013	0.7	.009	0.5	.009	2.0	.011	2.2
h_1	-.011	-1.5	-.007	-1.2	-.014	-1.8	-.010	-1.6	-.043	-3.1	-.031	-2.8
h_2	-.006	-0.4	-.003	-0.2	-.002	-0.4	-.002	-0.4	-.005	-0.4	-.004	-0.3
hlt	...	...	-.0007	-0.7	...	...	-.0011	-2.3	...	...	-.009	-0.6
$\ln Hrs$	...	...	-.050	-0.7	...	...	-.090	-1.8	...	...	-.130	-1.1
$\ln Wks$	...	...	-.070	-0.6	...	...	.060	1.6	...	...	.090	1.2
N_c	...	...	-.008	-0.2	...	...	-.019	-0.4	...	...	-.010	-2.0
R^2	.26	...	.32	...	.21	...	.26	...	.27	...	.33	...
N	182	...			593	...			218	...		

NOTE.—WMSP = white married women, spouse present. See table 4 for key to symbols.

TABLE 7
EARNINGS FUNCTIONS OF WMSP BY LIFETIME WORK EXPERIENCE

VAR.	WORKED MORE THAN HALF OF YEARS			WORKED LESS THAN HALF OF YEARS		
	b	t	M	b	t	M
C	−.28	...	...	−.10	...	...
S	.073	9.4	11.8	.059	7.9	11.0
e_1	.009	2.1	4.9	.003	0.4	2.2
e_2	.006	1.4	5.6	−.005	−0.6	1.5
e_3	.017	2.0	4.9	.022	3.8	1.6
e_3^2	−.0002	−0.7	...	−.001	−1.5	...
h_1	−.014	−2.3	2.2	−.010	−2.6	10.7
h_2	.011	1.7	2.1	−.004	−0.9	4.7
hlt	−.0008	−2.1	10.8	−.0001	−0.3	13.7
res	.002	1.1	12.1	.002	1.0	11.8
loc	.064	2.8	0.97	.024	1.0	0.90
ln Hrs	−.08	−2.0	3.52	−.13	−4.4	3.40
ln Wks	.07	1.9	3.71	.023	1.0	3.29
N_c	−.015	−1.4	2.21	−.001	−0.2	3.18
R^2	.22	...	...	.21	...	...
N	536	...	...	604	...	...

NOTE.—WMSP = white married women, spouse present. See table 4 for key to symbols.

experience for men and never-married women.[12] In the groups with discontinuous participation, the profiles are not expected to be monotonic.

We can summarize the implicit profiles schematically, in terms of the coefficients of e_1, length of work experience before the first child, h_1, uninterrupted nonparticipation after the first child, and e_3, the current work interval. We find (table 4, col. 3) that white married women with children (with spouse present) have current investment (ratio which exceeds the investment (ratio) incurred in experience before the first child.[13] Presumably, current participation in the labor force, which takes place when most of the children have reached school age, is expected to last longer than the previous periods of work experience. This is certainly true of women over age 35, and it holds in regressions with or without standardization for age.

Looking at regressions within three education levels (tables 5–6), we find that coefficient of prematernal experience (e_1) exceeds the coefficient of current work experience (e_3) at the highest level of schooling (in the short equations, though not in the long ones), and the opposite is true at lower levels. For women without children the coefficient of prematernal work experience equals that of current work experience. The investment profile of never-married women has a downward slope. Comparable

[12] In the earnings regressions, the quadratic term of aggregated experience is often negative, but not significant statistically.
[13] All statements about differences in coefficients refer to point estimates. The differences are mentioned because they are suggestive, though they would not pass strict tests of statistical significance within a given equation.

early segments of their post school job experience contain higher investment ratios—indeed, the fit implies a linear decline of such ratios over the life cycle. Evidently, women who intend to spend more time in the labor force invest more initially. This is true, presumably, even if their plans are later changed following marriage and childbearing.

4. *Depreciation Rates*

The coefficient of home time is negative, indicating a net depreciation of earning power. During the home-time interval (h_1), associated with marriage or the birth of the first child, this net depreciation amounts to, on average, 1.5 percent per year. In table 5 the depreciation rate is small $(-0.2$ percent$)$ and insignificant for women with less than high school education, larger $(-1.3$ percent$)$ for those with 12–15 years of schooling, and largest $(-2.3$ percent$)$ for those with 16+ years of schooling. In table 6, the net depreciation rate is -1.1 percent for women with elementary schooling or less, -1.4 percent for women with some high school, and -4.3 percent for women with at least some college. Sampling differences probably account for the different estimates in the two tables. The depreciation rate also appears higher in the group who worked more than half the years (table 7).

It would seem that the depreciation rate is higher when the accumulated stock of human capital is larger. An exception appears in the comparison of women without children (married and single) with women with children. The former have a lower depreciation rate. Of course, these women spend much less time out of market work, and some of this time might be job-oriented (e.g., job search).

It is useful to return to the formulation (9b) of the earnings function for a closer analysis of the depreciation rates: $\ln E_t = \ln E_0 + (rs - \delta_s) + (rk_1^* - \delta_1)e_1 + (rk_h^* - \delta_h)h + (rk_3^* - \delta_3)e_3$. Our coefficient of home time measures the depreciation rate only if market-oriented investment k_h^* is negligible. This is likely to be true for the period of child caring, the period defined as h_1 in the regression (h_2 in the tabulations).

An interesting question is whether the depreciation rate (δ_h) during nonparticipation is different from the depreciation that occurs at work as well. The question is whether depreciation due to nonuse of the human capital stock (atrophy?) exceeds the depreciation due to use (strain?) or to aging (?). We are inclined to believe that depreciation through nonuse ("getting rusty") is by far more important, particularly in groups of the relatively young (below age 45). Moreover, the atrophy aspect suggest that depreciation due to nonparticipation is strongest for the market-oriented components of human capital acquired on the job, and weakest for the inborn, initial, or general components of the human-capital stock. If so, a fixed rate of "home-time depreciation" applicable to on-the-job accumulation of human capital would appear as a varying rate in the earnings function: given the volume of other human capital, the larger the on-the-job accumulated component of human capital, the higher the observed (applied to the total earning power) depreciation rate.[14]

This may be an explanation of the observed higher depreciation rates at higher schooling and experience levels of mothers. In particular, there is a positive relation between the coefficients of h_1 (in absolute value) and of e_1 across schooling groups (table 6), experience groups (table 7), and race groups (compare tables 4 and 8).

5. Effect of Family Size

Do family size and number of children currently present affect the accumulation of earning power beyond the effect on work experience? The answer is largely negative: when numbers of children and some measures of their age are added to work histories in the equations, the children variables are negative but usually not significant statistically. Their inclusion reduces the absolute values of the coefficients of experience and of home time and does not add perceptibly to the explanatory power of the regression. Note, however, that the children variable does approach significance in the relatively small groups of highly educated women (tables 5–6), and more generally among women with stronger labor-force attachment (table 7). Possibly, shorter hours or lesser intensity of work are, to some extent, the preferred alternatives to job discontinuity.

6. Formal Postschool Training

The coefficients of experience, a_i, represent estimates of rk_i, where k_i is the average investment ratio across women over the segment and r is the average rate of return. Individual variation in k_i is not available to us. We have some individual information, however, on months of formal job training received after completion of schooling as well as on possession of professional certificates by, among others, registered nurses, teachers, and beauticians. If the length of training and possession of a certificate are positive indexes of k, we may represent $a_i = a_0 + \beta \cdot tr$, where tr is the length of training. The term $a \cdot e$ in that equation becomes

$$(a_0 + \beta tr) \cdot e = a_0 \cdot e + \beta(tr \cdot e).$$

Thus, an interaction term $(tr \cdot e)$ can be added to the equation, and if the hypothesis is correct, the coefficient β should be positive. This is indeed

[14] Where δ is the observed depreciation rate, δ_J the rate applicable to job-accumulated capital H_J, and H_0 the volume of other human capital, $\delta = (\delta_J H_J)/(H_J + H_0) = \delta_J/[1 + (H_0/H_J)]$. With a fixed rate δ_J for all individuals, the larger H_J the larger δ.

the case in most of our equations, confirming the training interpretation of the experience coefficients in the earnings function. Both interactions with months of job training and with possession of a certificate are significant for married women. The training interaction variable is also positive in the earnings function of single women, but the certificate variable is negative. Whereas the negative coefficient of the certification-experience variable implies less than average investment behavior among persons who work continuously, the corresponding positive coefficient for intermittent workers implies more than average investment behavior.

7. Effects of Mobility

Research in mobility has shown that, so long as mobility is not in-voluntary—resulting from layoffs—it is associated with a gain in earnings. However, geographic labor mobility of married women is often exogenous, due to job changes of the husband. In that case, it may militate against continuity of experience and slow the accumulation of earning power. We used the information on the length of current residence in a county or a Standard Metropolitan Statistical Area (SMSA) as an inverse measure of mobility. This variable has a small positive effect on wage rates of white MSP women and a significant negative effect for single women. To the extent that mobility is job oriented for single women and exogenous for married women, the differential signs provide a con-sistent interpretation.

8. Hours and Weeks in Current Job

When (logs of) weeks and hours worked in the survey year are included in the regression, a negative sign appears for the weekly-hours coefficient and a positive but less significant one for the weeks-worked coefficient. The hours' coefficients are smaller for married women than for single women and smaller for white than for black women. The negative sign of weekly hours may be partly or wholly spurious since some pay periods indicated by respondents were weeks or months and the hourly wage rate was obtained by division through hours. Of course, the direction of causality is suspect: it is more likely that women with lower wage rates work longer hours than the converse. Deletion of the variables, however, has a minimal effect on the equations.

9. Other Variables

Three other variables were included in the equations:

1. Twenty percent of the married women who worked in 1966 dropped out of work in 1967. We used a dummy variable with value 1 if persons

TABLE 8
EARNINGS FUNCTIONS OF BLACK WOMEN

MSP WITH CHILDREN			NEVER MARRIED		
Var.	b	t	Var.	b	t
C	−.02	...	C	−.48	...
S	.095	11.2	S	.110	3.7
e_1	.005	0.8	e	.004	0.1
e_2	.001	0.3	e^2	−.0003	−0.2
e_3	.006	1.4	e_3	.001	0.2
h_1	−.006	−1.2	h	−.02	−.05
h_2	−.005	−0.9	h^2	.001	1.1
etr	.0005	1.3	etr	.0006	1.4
ect	.008	1.9	ect	.003	0.4
hlt	−.0002	−0.5	hlt	−.001	−1.8
res	.002	0.9	res	.001	0.2
loc	.11	4.0	loc	.23	2.7
ln Hrs	−.30	−7.4	ln Hrs	−.13	−0.7
ln Wks	.08	2.2	ln Wks	.03	0.2
N_c	.005	0.6	N_c	...	...
R^2	.39	...	R^2	.46	...
N	550	...	N	70	...

NOTE.—MSP = white married women, spouse present. See table 4 for key to symbols.

working in 1966 stopped working in 1967, and 0 otherwise.[15] This variable had a negative sign, since it indicated a shorter current job experience compared with the prospective work interval of others who continued to work in 1967—the completed interval of those dropping out was not longer than the interval of stayers. In effect, women who dropped out of the labor force in 1967 had wage rates about 5 percent lower than women who continued working, given the same characteristics and histories.[16] The proportion of dropouts is somewhat larger at lower education levels.

2. The size of community in which the respondent lived at age 15 had a positive effect on earning power of married women but no effect on that of single women.

3. Duration of current health problem in months was used as a measure of health levels. It is an imperfect measure for retrospective purposes and shows a very small negative effect on the wage rate.

10. *Black Women*

The regressions for black MSP (table 8) show experience coefficients about half the size of the corresponding white population. Home time or depreciation coefficients are not significant; neither are the children

[15] Not shown in the tables.
[16] Without standardization, women who had dropped out had wage rates about 10 percent lower than women who continued working.

variables. The implication is that there is less investment on the job, even though black women spent more time than white women in the labor market. They had more and younger children, on average. The other variables behave comparably with those in the white regressions except that hours of current work and location at age 15 show stronger effects. In contrast to white women, the size of community of residence at age 15 has a positive effect for never-married women as well. Again, the experience coefficients are smaller for black single women than for whites. Perhaps contrary to expectations, neither health problems nor rates of withdrawal from the labor force in 1966 differ for black as compared to white married women with children, spouse present. Rates of return to schooling appear, if anything, to be higher for black women.

V. Lifetime Participation and the Simultaneity Problem

The earnings function, as we estimate it, relates wages of women to investments in schooling and on-the-job training and to a number of additional variables already discussed.

The interpretation of some of the independent variables as factors affecting earning power may be challenged on the grounds that they may just as well be viewed as effects rather than causes of earning power. Presumably, women with greater earning power have stronger job aspirations and work commitments than other women throughout their lifetimes. Hence, what we interpret as an earnings function may well be read with causality running in the opposite direction—as a labor-supply function. This argument is most telling for concurrent variables, such as last year's hours and weeks worked in relation to last year's wage rate. But these variables are of only marginal importance in the wage equation of married women. All other independent variables temporally precede the dependent variable (current wage rate), which makes the earnings function interpretation less vulnerable, though not entirely so for there is a serial correlation between current and past work experience and current and past earning power. Since lifetime work experience depends, in part, on prior wage levels and expectations, our experience variables are, in part, *determined* as well as *determining*. If so, the residual in our wage equations is correlated with the experience variables, and the estimates of coefficients which we interpreted as investment ratios are biased.

How serious this problem is for our analysis depends on the strength of individual correlations between current and past levels and expectations of earning power and on the strength of effect of these prior levels on subsequent work histories of individuals. Of course, when the data are grouped these correlations and effects are likely to be strong. Better-educated women tend to have higher wage rates than less educated women throughout their working lives, (see, for instance, Fuchs 1967) and as our table 3 shows, they spend a larger fraction of their lives in the labor force. Table 3 also shows that married mothers who currently do not work, spent, on average, less of their lifetime working than those who currently work.

One econometric approach to an estimation of the earnings function in the presence of endogeneity of "independent" variables is the two-stage least-squares (2SLS) approach. We estimate work experience as a variable dependent on exogenous variables, some of which are in the earnings function and others outside of it. In effect, we estimate a "lifetime labor-supply function." The second step is to replace the work-experience variables (e) in the earnings function by the estimated work experience($\hat{e}$) from the labor-supply function. Parameter estimates in this revised earnings function are theoretically superior to the original, simple least-squares estimates.[17]

Our application of a 2SLS procedure is far from thorough, for two reasons:

1. It is difficult to implement it on the segmented function, since each of the segments would have to be estimated by exogenous variables. For this purpose we aggregate years of work experience and compare the reestimated earnings function with the original, using aggregated experience.

2. One of the variables in our lifetime labor-supply function is the number of children, which is not exogenous. In principle, we should expand the equation system to three to include the earnings function, the labor-supply function, and the fertility function. At this exploratory level we prefer not to do it, particularly since the fertility function would be estimated by the same variables as the labor-supply function.

The supply function obtained for all white MSP women was

$$\frac{e}{e_p} = \underset{(5.1)}{.514 + .020\ S_F} - \underset{(1.8)}{.0064\ S_M} - \underset{(12.0)}{.062\ N_c,}$$

where e is total years of work, e_p is "potential job experience," that is, years since school, S_F is education of wife, S_M is education of husband, and N_c is number of children. The addition of earnings of husband reduced the coefficient of S_M to insignificance without changing the coefficient of determination, which was $R^2 = .14$.

Estimated values of the numerator ($\hat{e}$) are used to reestimate the earnings function. A comparison of 2SLS and OLS estimates of the earnings function is shown in table 9. If anything, the reestimated function shows larger positive coefficients for (total) experience and stronger negative coefficients for home time. The children variable becomes even less significant (in terms of t-values) than before. The reestimation leaves our conclusions, based on the OLS regressions, largely intact.

---

[17] Since $\hat{e}$ is a function of exogenous variables, it is not correlated with the stochastic term in the reestimated earnings function.

TABLE 9
EARNINGS FUNCTION, WMSP WOMEN, OLS AND 2SLS

VAR.	OLS		2SLS		OLS		2SLS	
	b	t	b	t	b	t	b	t
C	−.20	...	−.06	...	.19	...	.26	...
S	.069	12.8	.063	12.0	.053	9.4	.048	8.5
e	.010	3.2	.012	2.7	.008	2.8	.010	1.9
h_1	−.008	−3.0	−.015	−7.7	−.007	−1.9	−.013	−5.5
h_2	.0006	0.2	−.006	−2.3	.001	0.5	−.006	−1.9
e_3	.009	3.2	.009	3.5	.009	3.4	.010	3.7
tr	...	...	...	...	.005	2.2	.006	2.2
$cert$	...	...	...	...	.18	5.1	.18	5.1
hlt	...	...	...	...	−.0003	−1.3	−.0003	−1.4
res	...	...	...	...	.001	1.3	.021	1.4
loc	...	...	...	...	.044	2.8	.042	2.5
ln Hrs ...	...	...	...	...	−.11	−5.0	−.11	−4.9
ln Wks...	...	...	...	...	.03	1.5	.03	1.6
N_c	...	...	...	...	−.010	−1.3	.003	0.3

NOTE.—WMSP = white married women, spouse present; tr = months of training; $cert$ = certification (dummy); see table 4 for key to other symbols.

VI. Prediction

A test of the predictive power of the earnings function was performed on a small sample of women who did not work in 1966 but were found in the same first NLS survey to have returned to work in 1967. They were not included in our analyses, but their life histories and 1967 wage rates are available. The latter were predicted with several variants of the earnings function and compared to the reported wage rates. On average, the prediction is quite close, and the mean-square error is even smaller— relative to the variance of the observed wage rates—than the residual variance in the regressions.[18] In other words, the predictive power outside the data utilized for the regressions is no smaller than within the regressions. The test, however, is weak, because the sample is so small (45 observations). Similar tests will be performed on larger samples of women who return to the labor market in subsequent surveys.

VII. Earnings Inequality and the Explanatory Power of Earnings Functions

As table 10 indicates, the earnings function is capable of explaining 25–30 percent of the relative (logarithmic) dispersion in wage rates of white married women and about 40 percent of the inequality in the rather small sample of wage rates of single women in the 30–44 age group who worked in 1966. The earnings function is thus no less useful in understanding the structure of women's wages than it is in the analysis of wages of males.

[18] The (squared) correlation between predicted and actual wage rates was .37. The mean of actual rates was 5.196, with σ = .335; the mean of predicted wages was 5.187, with σ = .204.

TABLE 10
EARNINGS INEQUALITY AND EXPLANATORY POWER OF WAGE FUNCTIONS, 1966

Group	$\sigma^2 (\ln W)$	R_W^2	$\sigma^2 (\ln Y)$	R_Y^2	$\sigma^2 (\ln H)$	N
Married women by education (yrs):						
< 12	.17	.21	.81	.76	.64	435
12–15	.18	.17	.92	.78	.74	622
+ 16	.17	.16	.77	.74	.60	83
Total.	.22	.28	.97	.78	.75	1,140
Single women	.30	.41	.62	.66	.32	138
Married men	.32	.30	.43	.50	.11	3,230

NOTE.—$\sigma^2 (\ln W)$ = variance of (log) wages; $\sigma^2 (\ln Y)$ = variance of (log) annual earnings; $\sigma^2 (\ln H)$ = variance of (log) annual hours of work; R_W^2 = coefficient of determination in wage rate function; R_Y^2 = coefficient of determination in annual earnings function.

The dispersion of hours worked during the survey year is much greater among married women, $\sigma^2 (\ln H) = .75$, than among men, $\sigma^2 (\ln H) = .11$. The (relative) dispersion in annual earnings of women is, therefore, dominated by the dispersion of hours worked. This factor is also important in the inequality of annual earnings of single women and of men of comparable ages, but much less so. It is not surprising, therefore, that the inclusion of hours worked in the earnings function raises the coefficient of determination from 28 percent in the hourly-wage equation to 78 percent in the annual-earnings equation of married women, from 41 percent to 66 percent for that of single women, and from 32 to 50 percent for that of men.

The lesser inequality in the wage-rate structure of working married women than in the structure of male wages is probably due to lesser average, and correspondingly lesser variation in, job investments among individuals. At the same time, the huge variation in hours, reflecting intermittency and part-time work as forms of labor-supply adjustments, creates an annual earnings inequality among women which exceeds that of men. However, the meaning of that inequality, both in a causal and in a welfare sense, must be seen in the family context. As was shown elsewhere (Mincer 1974b), the inclusion of female earnings as a component of family income narrows the relative inequality of family incomes compared with that of incomes of male family-earners.

VIII.   Some Applications

1.   The Wage Gap

To compare wage rates of women with wage rates of men, we analyzed earnings of men from the Survey of Economic Opportunity (SEO) for the same year (1966). We find that the average wage rate of white married men, aged 30–44, was $3.18, compared with $2.09 for white married women and $2.73 for white single women in our NLS data.

TABLE 11
EXPERIENCE AND DEPRECIATION COEFFICIENTS, 1966, AGES 30–44

VAR.	MARRIED WOMEN		SINGLE WOMEN		MARRIED MEN	
	b	M	b	M	b	M
S	.063	11.3	.077	12.5	.071	11.6
$\hat{e}$	.012	9.6	...	...	...	...
e	...	...	.026	15.6	.034	19.4
e^2	...	...	−.0006	258	−.0006	409
e_3	.009	3.2	.009	8.0	...	...
h_c	−.015	6.7	...	...	...	...
h_0	−.006	3.5	...	...	...	...

SOURCES.—Women: NLS, 1967; men: SEO, 1967.
NOTE.—S = years of schooling; h_c = home time following birth of first child; h_0 = other home time; e = years of work experience since completion of schooling; e_3 = current job tenure; $\hat{e}$ = 2SLS estimate of total work experience; b = regression coefficient; M = means.

TABLE 12
EFFECTS OF WORK EXPERIENCE ON WAGE RATES

	RELATIVE CONTRIBUTIONS OF		PERCENT OF WAGE GAP EXPLAINED	
	Actual Experience (1)	Men's Experience (2)	(3)	(4)
Married women	+.02	+.26	45	42
Single women	+.32	+.33	7	40
Married men	+.42	...	...	...

We inquired to what extent the larger wage ratio (152 percent) of married men to married women and the smaller one (116 percent) of married men to single women can be explained by differences in work histories and by differences in job investment and depreciation. For this purpose we estimated a single earnings function of men, aged 30–44, in SEO. The coefficients and means of the variables for these men are shown in table 11, which also gives the NLS estimates for both married and single women.

Note that married men and married working women have just about the same average schooling, while never-married women are somewhat better educated (by 1 year, on average). The coefficients of schooling are somewhat lower for married women but higher for single women. The big differences are in years of work experience since completion of schooling. These are 19.4 for men, 15.6 for single women, and 9.6 for married women. The coefficients of initial experience are .034 for men, .026 for single women, and about half as much for married women.

Multiplying the coefficients by the variables (table 11) and summing yields contributions of postschool investments to the (log of) wage rates as shown in table 12. These differences, roughly 40 percent between husbands and wives and 10 percent between married men and single women, are about 70 percent of the observed difference in wage rates between married men and married women and a half of the difference between married men and single women.

If one prefers to be agnostic about the human-capital approach, one can treat the earnings function simply as a statistical relation and the regression coefficients as average "effects" of work experience and of nonparticipation on wages, without reading magnitudes of investment or depreciation into them. In that case we may ask how much the sex differential in wage rates would narrow if work experience of women were as long as that of men, but the female coefficients remained as they are. A multiplication of the female coefficients by the male variables in table 11 yields the following answers: for married women, 45 percent of the gap would be erased; for single women, only 7 percent of the much smaller gap (table 12, col. 3). The answer is similar for married women if the converse procedure is used, that is when the work experience of women is multiplied by the male coefficients (table 12, col. 4). For single women, the reduction of the gap is larger than in the first procedure.

We believe, however, that the weight of the empirical analysis of female earnings supports the view that the association of lower coefficients with lesser work experience is not fortuitous: a smaller fraction of time and energy is devoted to job advancement (training, learning, getting ahead) per unit of time by persons whose work attachment is lower. Hence, the 45 percent figure in the explanation of the gap by duration-of-work experience alone may be viewed as an understatment.

Indeed, comparing the annual earnings of year-round working women and men in the 30–40 age groups, Suter and Miller found a female-to-male earnings ratio of 46.7 percent. However, the ratio rose to 74 percent for women in this group who worked all their adult lives. The same comparison for high school educated persons yielded 40.5 as against 74.9 percent. Thus lifelong work experience reduces the wage gap by 51 or 58 percent, respectively.[19]

At this stage of research we cannot conclude that the remaining (unexplained) part of the wage gap is attributable to discrimination, nor, for that matter, that the "explained" part is not affected by discrimination. More precisely, we should distinguish between the concepts of direct and indirect effects of discrimination. Direct market discrimination occurs when different rental prices (wage rates) are paid by employers for the same unit of human capital owned by different persons (groups). In this sense, the wage-gap residual is an upper limit of the direct effects of market discrimination. Indirect effects occur in that the existence of

---

[19] Suter and Miller (1971, table 1). Their figures are not quite comparable with ours: their male data come from the Current Population Survey (CPS), and ours from SEO. They compare full-time earnings rather than wage rates, and they compare men and women without regard to marital status.

market discrimination discourages the degree of market orientation in the expected allocation of time and diminishes incentives to investment in market-oriented human capital. Hence, the lesser job investments and greater depreciation of female market earning power may to some extent be affected by expectations of discrimination.

Of course, if division of labor in the family is equated with discrimination, all of the gap is by definition a symptom of discrimination. Otherwise, the analyses of existing wage gaps and of their changes over time remain meaningful, not tautological.

Our data on work histories show some interesting trends which suggest a prospective narrowing of the wage differential. Table 3 shows that the uninterrupted period of nonparticipation which starts just prior to the birth of the first child has been shrinking when older women are compared with younger ones. Women aged 40–44 who had their first child in the late 1940s stayed out of the labor force about 5 years longer than women aged 30–34 whose first child was born in the late 1950s. Family size is about the same for both groups, but higher for the middle group (35–39) whose fertility marked the peak of the baby boom. Still, the home-time interval in that group is shorter (by about 2 years) than in the older group and longer than in the younger. Thus, the trend in labor-force participation of young mothers was persistent. If, by the time the 30–34-year-old women get to be 40–44 (i.e., in 1977), they will have had 4 years of work experience more than the older cohort, and their wage rates will rise by 6 percent on account of lesser depreciation and by another 2–4 percent due to longer work experience. Thus, the total observed wage gap between men and women aged 40–44 should narrow by about one-fifth, while the gap due to work experience should be reduced by one-quarter.[20]

2.   The Price of Time and the Opportunity Costs of Children

The loss or reduction of market earnings of mothers due to demands on their time in child rearing represents a measure of family investment in the human capital of their children. This investment cost has been measured by valuing the reduction of market time at the observed wage rate. As pointed out by Michael and Lazear (1971), this valuation is incomplete for two reasons. First, if job investments take place at work, the observed wage rate understates the true foregone wage (gross or capacity wage) by the amount usually invested during the period when

[20] Two opposing biases mar this conjecture: The shorter home-time interval for younger women is an average duration for those who already returned to work. It will lengthen with the passage of time as additional women return to the labor force. It can be shown, however, that the apparent trend is genuine. At the same time, the assumption of unchanged job-investment behavior leads to an understatement.

earnings are foregone. Second, as is clear from earnings-function analysis, the reduction of market time in turn reduces future wage rates because of a depreciation in earning power during the period of nonparticipation. The present value of future earnings lost through depreciation is a component of the opportunity cost of time, hence of children.[21]

The data and the estimated wage functions permit a tentative, perhaps only an illustrative, empirical assessment of the opportunity cost of women's time and of children. Specifically, the marginal opportunity cost per hour of a year spent at home—rather than in the market— consists of (1) the gross wage rate (W_g), that is the observed but foregone wage (W) augmented by currently foregone investment costs, and (2) the present value of the reduction of the future gross wage through current depreciation:[22]

1. We can estimate W_g since $W = W_g(1 - k)$, and rk is estimated in the earnings function by a_1, the coefficient of work experience (e_1) preceding the interruption $k = a_1/r$, where r is the rate of return.

2. The present value of the reduction in W_g due to depreciation, using r as the discount rate, is $d/r \cdot W_g$, where d is the (depreciation) coefficient of home time in our wage equations.[23]

The estimates of marginal opportunity costs of a year (in dollars per hour) are shown in panel I of table 13 for three education groups of white mothers, aged 35–39. In panel II we calculate total opportunity expenditures incurred during the nonparticipation period following the birth of the first child. This is the period for which the earnings functions show significant depreciation coefficients. The length of the period depends, in part, on the number of children. Though interpreting all of the foregone earnings this period as an opportunity expenditure on children may be an overstatement, we impose an opposite bias by ignoring subsequent periods of non participation[24] which may also be child induced. Figures in panel II are the marginal costs per hour (per year) multiplied by h, the duration of home time. Figures in panel III are average opportunity expenditures per child (N_c) in each group. Since h is in years, the dollar figures in panels II and III should be multiplied by annual hours of work. For example, with 1,500 hours of work per year, the opportunity investment expenditures per child range from about $8,000 spent in 8.8 years by mothers with less than high school education to $17,000 spent in 5.2 years by mothers with college education or more.

---

[21] As Robert Willis suggested to us, this is strictly correct for the excess of depreciation during home time over the depreciation at other times. As we stated earlier, we believe that the latter is negligible in our age groups.

[22] Note that we are looking at household productivity as the return, the purpose of reducing market work, not as a negative element in costs.

[23] A 10 percent discount rate was used in these calculations.

[24] Inclusion would lead to a 20–25 percent increase in expenditures for the age group.

TABLE 13

MARGINAL PRICE OF TIME AND OPPORTUNITY COSTS OF CHILDREN, 1966, WORKING WHITE MOTHERS (AGED 35–39)—BY YEARS OF SCHOOLING ($)

	PRICE OF TIME PER HOUR			TOTAL OPPORTUNITY EXPENDITURES ON CHILDREN			OPPORTUNITY EXPENDITURES PER CHILD		
	<12	12-15 (I)	16+	<12	12-15 (II)	16+	<12	12-15 (III)	16+
1. Observed wage	1.66	2.25	3.54	14.60	16.33	18.51	4.23	5.52	6.60
2. Capacity wage	1.96	2.59	4.60	17.25	18.87	24.05	5.00	6.41	8.57
3. Depreciation	0.05	0.30	1.40	0.44	2.18	7.32	0.13	0.73	2.63
Sum (2 + 3)	2.01	2.89	6.00	17.69	21.05	31.37	5.13	7.14	11.20
Assuming 1,500 hr work per year	...	...	...	...	...	...	7,740	10,710	16,800
h_c	...	...	...	8.80	7.26	5.23	...	...	...
N_c	...	...	...	3.45	2.96	2.81	...	...	...
h_c/N_c	...	...	...	2.55	2.45	1.86	...	...	...

Note.—h_c = duration of home time; N_c = no. of children.

Only panel I represents the marginal price of time. Note that the observed wage rate[25] represents 80 percent of the marginal price of an hour below college levels and only 60 percent at higher levels. The same proportions hold in the other two panels. However, figures in these panels are not prices but expenditures which depend on both the price of time and the number of children and the average home-time interval per child. Both of these variables can be viewed as responses to the marginal price of time. As the table indicates, observed wage rates and, even more so, marginal prices of time (panel I) increase with education. Lesser fertility and closer spacing of children are the responses:[26] both numbers of children and interval of home time per child diminish. Consequently, the differences in total expenditures by education level are reduced. While the marginal price of time of the highest education group is three times as high as that of the lowest, the expenditures per child are a little over twice as high, and total expenditures are only 70 percent higher.

Since the opportunity costs of labor-force withdrawal ("home time") are not quite the same thing as the opportunity costs of children, we again caution the reader to view the estimates of table 13 as largely illustrative. They clearly illustrate the point which the title of this paper intends to convey: foregone market-oriented human capital of mothers is a part of the price of acquiring human capital in children, and more generally, a price exacted by family life. Of course, the greater market specialization, longer hours, and greater intensity of work and of job training on the part of husbands and fathers can be viewed as a "price exacted by family life" in exactly the same sense.

Implicitly, families balance such prices against perceptions of received benefits.[27] Of course, both perceptions of net benefits and prices change. While perceptions are matters of individual psychology and of cultural climate, the marginal opportunity cost of time has risen secularly with the rise in real wages and with the growth of human capital. It is natural for economists to connect to this basic fact both upward trends in labor-force participation of women and downward trends in fertility,[28] changes in the family, and even some of the rhetoric which accompanies these developments.

[25] In principle, wage rates just before the period h are required. The wage at ages 35–39 represents, on average, a small overstatement: wage profiles of married women with children are relatively flat in the age span 25–39 within education groups.

[26] Direct evidence on closer spacing at higher levels of education is shown in a Columbia Ph.D. dissertation by Sue Ross (1974). In the NLS data, there is a strong correlation between the length of home time and the birth interval from oldest to youngest child.

[27] Some of these benefits are analyzed in the papers of Lee Benham and Arleen Leibowitz in this volume.

[28] For economic analyses which bear on the upward secular trends in labor-force participation of married women, see Mincer (1962a) and Cain (1966).

Appendix

Note on the Construction of Work-Experience Intervals

The 1967 NLS survey of women aged 30–44 permits a division of time elapsed since leaving school into, at most, eight intervals. The following information was used in constructing these intervals: (a) Dates were available for school leaving (S), first marriage (M), birth of first child (C), start of first job, return to labor force after birth of first child, start of current job, and end of last job, if currently not working. (b) Number of years during which the woman worked at least 6 months between: (1) school leaving and first marriage, (2) marriage and birth of first child, (3) return to labor force after the first child, and (4) the start of current job.

On this basis, we describe the intervals in the order of their chronological placement: interval h_1 (on average, half a year) is the interval between school and first job; e_1 is the number of years of work between school and marriage. The placement and continuity of this interval checks rather closely with the data, though direct statements are absent; e_2 is years worked (similarly defined) between first marriage and birth of first child; h_2 is the residual home time, given information on the length of interval between first marriage and birth of first child. The assumption of continuity and order of placement of e_2 and h_2 are somewhat arbitrary. They are justified by evidence of frequent identity of job e_1 and e_2 and the plausibility of h_2 starting during pregnancy. Indeed, h_2 is a fraction of a year, on average; h_3 is the uninterrupted interval of home time following the birth of the first child. It is placed by direct information; e_3 is years of work and h_4 the residual amount of time in the interval between returning to the labor force at the end of h_3 and start of current job. However, neither e_3 nor h_4 needs to be continuous. The succession of h_4 after e_3 is more plausible than the converse. Also $(e_3 + h_4)$ is, on average, about 3 years altogether; e_4 is clearly defined and placed as the current job interval.

In tables 2 and 3 we aggregate $(e_1 + e_2)$ and call it e_1, $(h_2 + h_3)$ is h_2, and the other intervals are correspondingly renamed.

In the regressions we added h_1 to h_3 to get h_2 other home time. Separately, or together, these intervals are quite short and show little effect in our analysis.

Comment

Otis Dudley Duncan

University of Michigan

For readers, other than economists specializing in studies of human capital, the most controversial sections of Mincer and Polachek's paper are likely to be the introductory statements of the motivation of the research and the authors' calculation which suggests that not less than half the wage gap between married women and men is due to sex differences in length and continuity of work histories.

To their initial rationalization of the division of labor within the family in terms of "complementarity and substitution relations in the household production process" and "absolute and comparative advantages due to differential skills and earning powers," the authors quickly add the disclaimers that sex linkage of intrafamily role differentiation is "subject to technological and cultural changes" and that such changes along with "discriminatory attitudes . . . in the labor market" are outside the scope of the study. Most feminists and many sociologists would presumably respond that with this much of the problem out of scope, what remains is likely to be misleading.

In technical terms, the issue is whether the "statistical residual" u in the general specification of the model is indeed uncorrelated with the vector e so that the coefficients of e_i (experience segments) in the earnings function are unbiased estimates of the investment in human capital appropriate to the wife's role in the household. Mincer and Polachek do address the problem of bias in their somewhat cursory treatment of two-stage least-squares estimation of the earnings function. But there the concern is with possible simultaneity of wage levels and experience variables. The more serious question may be whether such institutional and cultural factors as discrimination and employers' unwillingness to invest in training female workers—all taken to be beyond the scope of the study and presumably captured only in the residual u—act as common causes of wage levels and work experience.

Indeed, in the remarks appended to the calculations on the wage gap, Mincer and Polachek come perilously close to a premature closure of their conceptual scheme. Having attributed half the gap to sex differences in work experience they go on to observe that the lower coefficient for that experience among women may also be attributable to lower work attachment on the women's part. But the sex difference in work experience and the sex difference in coefficient for work experience provide an exhaustive decomposition of the sex difference in wages, net of initial endowment as of the beginning of the work history. Hence, the paper seems to be saying that women get about what they deserve in the job market.[1]

Many technical and conceptual improvements are required if the strategy opened up by this paper is to be productive. Mincer and Polachek seem amply aware of the frailty of their estimates, due to sample size and crudity of measurement. The hypercritical reader, however, will not fail to note various places where the authors seemingly read their tables a little too smoothly.

On the conceptual side, much work remains to be done before a serviceable model emerges from this kind of work. Treatment of the "activities, and characteristics of other family members," mentioned at the outset, is underdeveloped in the present formulation, while the labor-supply function is admittedly inadequate and a fertility function is lacking. More directly to the point of the inquiry at hand, one is disappointed to find no effort to include the quality of the work experience, and this is perhaps a more serious omission than the parallel inattention to quality of schooling. One indication that investigation of this facet of the problem could be productive is given by table 4.7 in *Dual Careers* (Parnes, Shea, Spitz, and Zeller 1970, p. 114), wherein it appears that the effect of the rate of lifetime labor-force participation on the wage rate is substantially greater for white-collar than for blue-collar workers among currently employed women. In this connection Mincer and Polachek do investigate the interaction of work experience and schooling with respect to wage rate. Close inspection of their tables 5 and 6 turns up some disconcerting variations in coefficients by years of schooling. At this point errors in the data and misspecifications of the model are hard to tell apart.

One can surmise that when all the truly endogenous and relevant causes and effects of the earnings of women are explicitly represented in the model, it will either be underidentified or else have been broadened to include the "sociological" exogenous variables ruled out of scope in this initial and productive foray. In trying to get the model properly specified, however, one need not expect too much help from the discipline of sociology as such, geared as it is to the production of dialectic rather than discovery.

---

[1] The authors' own views on the points at issue are made much clearer in their revision, which was not available when this comment was prepared.

Home Investments in Children

Arleen Leibowitz

National Bureau of Economic Research and Brown University

By the time children enter first grade, significant differences in verbal and mathematical competence exist among them.[1] These differences reflect variations in (1) inherent ability, and (2) the amounts of human capital acquired before the children reach the age of six.[2] The stocks of acquired human capital reflect, in turn, varying inputs of time and other resources by parents, teachers, siblings, and the child. The process of acquiring preschool human capital is analogous to the acquisition of human capital through schooling or on-the-job training.

Assuming a constant rental rate for human capital, earnings can be interpreted as a measure of capital stocks at later ages. The IQ also can be interpreted as such a measure of human capital stocks. It is related to some commonly used inputs of human capital, for it is well known that measured IQ is not independent of years of schooling acquired before the age of testing. At preschool ages IQ measures should be related to human capital inputs in early childhood as well as to inherent genetic ability.

Viewing measured ability as an index of the stock of human capital puts a different light on earnings functions which include ability and schooling. If contemporaneous ability and schooling measures are used to predict earnings (as in Hansen, Weisbrod, and Scanlon 1970), it is not surprising to find that earnings are more closely related to an ability measure, which

This research has been supported by grants to the National Bureau of Economic Research from the Office of Economic Opportunity and the National Institutes of Health. A National Science Foundation grant to the National Bureau of Economic Research funded the data preparation. I gratefully acknowledge the very competent research assistance of David L. Lindauer and Arun K. Mukhopadhyay. For helpful comments on a previous draft of this paper I thank Charles Betsey, Barry Chiswick, John Hause, Jacob Mincer, and Finis Welch.

[1] This is one of the important findings of the Coleman Report (see Mosteller [1972, p. 49]).

[2] Genetic factors cannot account for the entire difference, as studies of identical twins show. In one such study, identical twins raised apart showed an average difference in IQ of 14 points (Kagan 1969, p. 275).

is an index of human capital stocks, than to years of schooling, which is merely a partial measure of one of the inputs. In this respect family-background variables included in an earnings function may be interpreted as proxies for early investments in human capital if characteristics of the father and mother are systematically related to the investments in time and goods that they make in their children.

I. A Causal Model

Consider a model in which earnings depend upon human capital stocks which are built up over the life cycle through schooling, on-the-job training, and home investment.

By adapting Ben-Porath's well-known model of the acquisition of human capital over the lifetime through investments, we postulate a variant of the Ben-Porath production function for human capital (Ben-Porath 1967, p. 360):

$$Q_t = \beta_0 S_t^{\gamma_1} K_t^{\gamma_2} D_t^{\beta_1}, \tag{1}$$

where Q_t = gross additions to human capital stock in time t; K_t = the stock of human capital existing at t; S_t = the proportion of K_t allocated to producing Q_t, $0 \leq S_t \leq 1$; D_t = the quantity of goods inputs allocated to producing Q_t; and β_0 = the Hicks neutral-efficiency parameter for producing human capital, $0 < \gamma_1, \gamma_2, \beta_1 < 1$. The rate of change in the capital stock is given by

$$\dot{K}_t = Q_t - \delta K_t, \tag{2}$$

where δ is a constant depreciation rate. The stock at time T can be defined as

$$K_T = K_0 + \int_{t=0}^{T} \dot{K}_t \, dt, \tag{3}$$

where K_0 = the initial stock or inherent genetic ability.

The marginal-cost curve which corresponds to human capital production function (1) is shown by Ben-Porath to be

$$MC_t = \frac{a_0}{\beta_0 \gamma_1} \left(\frac{\gamma_1}{\beta_1} \frac{P_d}{a_0} \right)^{\beta_1/\theta} \cdot \left(\frac{Q_t}{\beta_0} \right)^{\theta} \cdot K_t^{(\gamma_1 - \gamma_2)/\theta}, \tag{4}$$

where $\theta = (\gamma_1 + \beta_1)$. Thus, the marginal cost of acquiring human capital is a function of existing stocks if $\gamma_1 \neq \gamma_2$. If $\gamma_1 > \gamma_2$, MC rises with the level of existing stocks, and human capital increases the productivity of time in the market more than the productivity of time in producing new capital. However, if $\gamma_1 < \gamma_2$, the marginal cost of producing new capital falls with existing stocks. The "demand price" depends, however, only on the rental price for human capital, the rates of interest and depreciation, and on the time remaining in the working

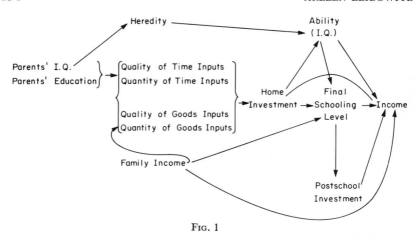

FIG. 1

lifetime. Thus, we would expect persons with greater initial levels of human capital to demand more additions to the stock if $\gamma_1 < \gamma_2$.

Figure 1 helps us to visualize the process. Parents' genetic characteristics determine the heredity of the child. I have shown (Leibowitz 1972) that the quantity of time devoted to children is positively related to parents' education, and there is evidence that the quality of time inputs is also positively related to education (Schoggen and Schoggen 1968). Thus, parents' genetic endowment and their education determine the quality and quantity of time inputs to the child. Parents' attributes also determine family income, which affects the amount and quality of time and goods inputs. These inputs comprise home investment, which, along with heredity, determines IQ. Final schooling level is determined by family income and stocks of human capital. Home investments may affect capital stocks in a manner not reflected in measured IQ. Thus, a variable such as the education of a mother may affect a schooling level both directly and through heredity. Income, which is a rent on the stock of human capital, depends on the four major sources of capital: home investment, measured ability, final schooling level, and postschool investment. This model can be written as a recursive system:

$$IQ = f_1(G, I_1),$$
$$I_2 = f_2(IQ, I_1, Y_f),$$
$$Y = f_3(I_1, I_2, I_3, IQ),$$

where G = genetic factors, I_1 = home investment, I_2 = schooling investment, and I_3 = postschool investment.

Clearly, in this system variables which are endogenous in one equation are predetermined in equations of higher number. This is true because the endogenous variables are determined at various early stages of the life cycle. That is, childhood IQ is determined prior to schooling, which is determined prior to earnings. If we assume that disturbances from each pair of equations are uncorrelated in the probability limit, this system may be estimated consistently by the use of ordinary least squares.

The rest of this paper reports an investigation of the possible returns to home investment, concentrating on the following questions:

1. Do home investments add to preschool stocks of human capital, as measured by IQ?

2. Is the amount of schooling achieved affected by early stocks of human capital and by later home investments?

3. Do home investments affect earnings if other forms of human capital are held constant? What is the bias to the coefficient on schooling (the rate of return to schooling) if home investments are omitted from the earnings function?

4. Does an early measure of ability affect earnings if schooling and home investments are held constant? What is the bias to the coefficient on schooling if ability is omitted from the earnings function?

To investigate these questions a unique data set called the Terman sample is used; it is described in Section II. In Sections III–V, the estimation of the childhood human capital, education, and earnings functions is discussed.

II. The Nature of the Data[3]

In 1921, Lewis M. Terman, a Stanford University psychologist, initiated a study to evaluate the physical, mental, and personality traits of California school children who scored in the top 1 percent of the national IQ distribution, and to follow those children as far into adult life as possible to see if high IQ was a good predictor of success in later life. (The data generated will be referred to hereafter as the Terman sample.) In 1921 when Terman began to test the children, he selected 1,528 of them with IQ scores of 140 or above, corresponding to the top 1 percent of the intelligence distribution.

The original sample consisted of 857 boys and 671 girls. The larger proportion of males among the group can probably be accounted for by the larger variability in tested IQ among boys than among girls.

[3] The data description in this section draws heavily upon discussion in Terman and Oden (1959). I am indebted to Susan Crayne of the National Bureau of Economic Research for devising an ingenious method for decoding the column binary tape of the data and for doing the decoding.

The method of selection was not free from bias. Budget constraints precluded testing every child in the California schools. Rather, in grades three through eight of schools in urban areas, each classroom teacher listed the three brightest children in the class and the youngest child. These children were further screened by a group IQ test, and the "promising" candidates were given the Stanford-Binet test. The original criterion for inclusion in the study group was a Binet IQ score of 140 or above, although 65 pupils who tested between 135 and 139 were also included. High school students nominated by their teachers as being bright were chosen if their score on the Terman group test fell within the top 1 percent of the distribution. From later evaluations, it was estimated that 90 percent of the eligible children had been included in the sample. The mean IQ of the students on the Stanford-Binet test was 151.5 for boys and 150.4 for girls at the time they were included in the study. Average age of Binet-tested pupils was 9.7 years and that of group-tested high school students was 15.2 years at the time they were selected.

The sample is thus not in any sense representative of California school children in the 1920s. The children were atypical physically and socially as well as intellectually. They tended to be taller and stronger and to mature earlier than their classmates. Fathers of the students had a median 12.4 years of schooling and the mothers, 11.7 years—nearly 4 years above the average for their generation in the United States.

The achievement of sample members also was above average. About 70 percent of the students in the sample finished college as contrasted with 8 percent of the United States population in their cohort. The average earnings of males in the sample in 1960 exceeded those of men of equivalent age and years of schooling by 30–50 percent.

At the outset, in 1921, in addition to IQ scores, many data about the home backgrounds of the students were collected. Information on the test group members was updated in 1929, 1940, 1950, 1954, and 1960 to include current data on schooling, earnings, occupation, and data on other variables. Although the data collection spanned almost 40 years, the retention rate in the sample was very high. Of the original 1,528[4] sample members, 104 (6.8 percent) died by 1955; after 1928 only 28 were lost track of until, following 1945, six more were not heard from.

III. Determinants of Ability

Our discussion up to this point has emphasized that ability as measured by IQ or other similar tests is not only the result of inherited attributes but also of acquired human capital. Although schooling level may affect measured ability, this will not be the case in our analysis, where ability is

---

[4] Regressions in this paper are based on the 821 males and 643 females for whom complete childhood records were available. Sample sizes may be further reduced in certain regressions due to missing data.

the childhood IQ score determined in 1921–22. The IQ measure is the score on the Stanford-Binet or Terman group test (TGT).

Several measures of home investment are readily available in the data. The respective educations of the father and the mother are important indices of the quality of the time spent with the child and should be positively related to IQ. In addition, as I have shown elsewhere (Leibowitz 1972), education is also positively related to the quantity of time spent with the child. Since mothers' time expenditures on children exceed those of fathers by at least a factor of 4,[5] we would expect the significance and size of the coefficient of mother's education to exceed that of father's education. However, education of the parents may be a proxy for the quality of genetic inheritance—if intelligence of the parents and their own education are positively correlated, and if intelligence can be transmitted genetically. If education is acting as a proxy for heredity, the coefficient of each parent's education on child's IQ should not differ significantly. A comparison of the size and significance of these two variables will indicate whether parents' schooling is influencing IQ directly through the quality and quantity of time spent with children or whether it is a proxy for inherited ability.

A more direct measure of the quantity of time spent with children in preschool investment results from the parents' estimate in 1922 of how much home instruction they provided their child. Two dummy variables were generated: HOMETR2 = one if parents conducted "an appreciable amount of instruction along particular lines," and zero if they did not; HOMETR1 = one if parents spent a "considerable number of hours, but chiefly reading, telling stories, and writing," and zero if they did not do so. The omitted category covered "no instruction, other than usual amount of reading and telling stories."

It is a consistent finding of psychological studies that first children and children from smaller families score higher on IQ tests and achieve more (for instance, get more schooling). The analysis of family investment presents a rationale for this phenomenon, since the more children there are, the less time input parents have available per child. For the same reason children of lower birth order can be expected to receive more time inputs. Both the number of siblings and birth order have been included as proxies for home investments.

In addition, the regressions included a dummy variable equal to one if the IQ test was the Terman group test rather than the Stanford-Binet test. About 33 percent (268) of the male subjects and 26 percent (168) of the females had taken the TGT, in which average scores were 8.5 points below the Stanford-Binet version of the IQ test. Terman's analysis showed

[5] This is based on 1967 data (Leibowitz 1972). It appears unlikely that in 1922 fathers spent more time with children than mothers did.

the TGT-tested students were at least as select a group as the Binet-tested ones, but scores were shifted down. The assumption is made that the two tests are identical in all other respects. Means and standard deviations of the variables are presented in Appendix C.

A. *Estimation for Males*

In table 1 the regression of family-investment variables on IQ measured at age 11 is presented for the 821 males in the sample. Both home-investment variables were positive, with HOMETR2 having a stronger positive impact on IQ than HOMETR1. Thus, the quality of time inputs by parents did raise measured IQ and special instruction had more of an impact than generalized time inputs. Since this holds the quantity of time inputs constant, the education variables can be taken to measure the quality of time. The mother's education is a very significant predictor of IQ, while the coefficient for father's education is not significantly different from zero. This suggests, as argued above, that education is a proxy for home investment and not solely for inherited factors. Psychologists have also shown (Kagan and Moss 1959) that correlation between child's IQ and maternal education is greater than that between child's IQ and paternal education, while the correlations between child's IQ and those of mother and father do not differ significantly.

Birth order is represented by the variable BORDER, which was coded 1 for a first-born child, 2 for the second-born, and so on. This variable thus contains some information about number of siblings as well as about birth order. The negative effect of birth order, while quantitatively small, is quite significant. If, instead of birth order, number of siblings is used, its coefficient is significantly different from zero only at the 10 percent level of significance. If both are included in the equation, birth order's coefficient remains significantly different from zero, while number of siblings does not. Estimated family income in 1922 (YK) did not prove to be a significant predictor of childhood IQ, as seen in table 1, column 2.

When the equations are based on the 553 boys who took the Stanford-Binet test, thus allowing us to dispense with the TGT dummy variable, the coefficients are substantially the same (see col. 3, table 1).

B. *Estimation for Females*

The same variables which accounted for 18.6 percent of the variance in IQ of males in the sample account for only 13 percent of the variance of females' IQ (see table 1, col. 4). Apart from the TGT dummy and family income, none of the variables meets conventional levels of significance. Neither the direct measures of the quantity of time inputs (HOMETR1 and HOMETR2) nor the parents' education variables have coefficients

TABLE 1
Determinants of Childhood IQ

Independent Variable	Males			Females				
	(1)	(2)	(3)	(4)	(5)	(6)	(7)	(8)
TGT	−8.468	−8.498	...	−7.82	−7.77	−7.80	...	...
	(−12.23)	(−12.19)		(9.30)	(9.28)	(9.29)		
EDMOT	0.3475	0.332	0.420	0.160	...	0.163	0.115	0.317
	(2.42)	(2.29)	(2.03)	(0.98)		(1.00)	(0.52)	(2.13)
BORDER	−0.561	−0.568	−0.689	0.0008	...	...	−0.055	0.299
	(−2.13)	(−2.16)	(−1.92)	(0)			(0.14)	(1.08)
HOMETR2	2.400	2.42	2.86	−0.958	...	...	−2.00	2.14
	(2.61)	(2.63)	(2.21)	(0.86)			(1.37)	(1.93)
HOMETR1	1.593	1.593	1.654	0.431	...	...	0.344	0.443
	(1.89)	(1.89)	(1.40)	(0.44)			(0.26)	(0.50)
EDFAT	0.065	0.008	0.128	−0.123	...	−0.135	−0.103	−0.124
	(0.60)	(0.05)	(0.81)	(0.85)		(0.94)	(0.53)	(1.09)
YK	...	3.79	...	10.85	9.57	10.97	13.96	0.002
		(0.80)		(2.01)	(2.32)	(2.04)	(1.98)	(0)
C	147.1	144.6	145.6	140.4	141.9	140.3	138.2	139.3
R^2	.186	.186	.040	.130	.126	.129	.017	.047
Number of observations	821	821	553	643	643	643	475	168

Note.—t-values are in parentheses.

significantly different from zero. Birth order and number of siblings have no significant impact on measured IQ. The only other variable which was significantly related to IQ was YK, a measure of relative family incomes, generated from data on the father's occupation in 1922. (The construction of this latter variable is described in Appendix A.)

When the equation is estimated for only those subjects who took the Stanford-Binet test, the only significant variable is family income (table 1, col. 7). However, when the sample covers only the girls who took the Terman group test (as in table 1, col. 8), mother's education and HOMETR2 are positively related to childhood IQ as is the case for males, while family income is not significantly related to IQ. It should be noted that the girls chosen by the TGT were older, and probably constituted a more selective group than the girls chosen by the Stanford-Binet test. The ratio of boys to girls in the TGT group was 1.83 and in the Stanford-Binet group 1.16 (Terman 1925, p. 560). The greater selectivity of the older group is consistent with the fact that IQ of girls falls more than that of boys over time (Sontag, Baker, and Nelson 1958, pp. 22–32). The TGT group had high abilities which endured at least until their adolescence.

Although a drop in IQ on retest is expected on statistical grounds due to regression toward the mean, girls showed greater decreases in IQ than boys when their IQs were retested after an interval of several years. In this sample, 54 children younger than age 13 in 1927–28 were again given the Stanford-Binet test. The 13-point average decrease in IQ for girls was significantly different from the three-point average drop for boys.[6]

These results suggest that the kind of intelligence that endures through adolescence (as was the case with the TGT-selected girls) is systematically related to home investments. However, in the younger group the factors which account for their scoring in the top 1 percent of the IQ distribution are more evanescent and are not related to home investments. Home investments were related to older girls' IQ differences that were stable over time, but only income was related to younger girls' IQs which faded over time.

IV. Determinants of Schooling Level

The model postulates that final schooling level depends on ability, family income, and home investments. If human capital is not equally productive in the market and in the acquisition of new human capital, measures of human capital stock (such as childhood IQ) should be related to years of schooling.

___

[6] The approximate standard deviation of the difference is two (Terman, Burks, and Jensen 1930, p. 25). Four hundred older students also were retested in 1927–28, but the difference by sex was not significant (ibid., p. 33).

The impact of family income on schooling attainment may be quite attenuated in this sample. First, all sample members were residents of California and had access to the "free" state university system, which is of high quality. Second, because of their demonstrated scholastic aptitude, the students without sufficient family resources to finance the indirect costs of schooling would have been eligible for scholarships. Two alternative estimates of parental income were constructed (as described in Appendix A). Further, additional numbers of siblings in a family are assumed to have the effect of reducing the amount of family support for schooling and to indicate lower levels of home investments. The effects of the quantity of preschool home investments (the HOMETR variables) should have been captured in the childhood IQ measure, but measures of home investments made after the childhood IQ test was taken can be expected to have a positive impact on schooling levels. Later home investments may be assumed to be positively correlated with early home investments as well as with parents' education. If the constructed income variable measures family income imperfectly, father's education may be a proxy for income as well as for home investment. (Definitions of schooling levels and their frequencies are given in Appendix B.)

A. Estimation for Males

Table 2 presents the equations estimating education levels for the 780 males for whom we had 1940 data and the 781 males for whom we had complete 1950 data.

The regressions for both years show that childhood ability is positively related to schooling level. This fact indicates that the kind of human capital that IQ represents enhances productivity in acquiring schooling more than it does productivity in the labor market. This is consistent with the general finding of psychologists that the one thing IQ predicts best is success in school.

Both the education of the mother and of the father are positively and significantly related to schooling achieved, and the coefficients are not significantly different from each other. The effect of other children in the family (SIBS) is negative and significant at the 10 percent level in 1940. By 1950, the subjects were nearly 40 years old, and the effect of siblings in restricting resources available for schooling seems to have leveled off as other sources of funding were developed.

The quantity-of-home-investment variables are not significantly different from zero at the 10 percent level. Since these variables were important determinants of IQ their negative signs may indicate that intensive training may temporarily boost IQ (as measured at age 11), but that this increase fades as time passes. This, the quantity-of-home-investment variables are correlated with a transitory increase in IQ

TABLE 2
YEARS OF SCHOOLING OF MALES IN TERMAN SAMPLE

INDEPENDENT VARIABLE	1940		1950	
	(1)	(2)	(3)	(4)
EDMOT	0.124	0.131	0.134	0.141
	(3.05)	(3.18)	(3.35)	(3.47)
EDFAT	0.110	0.122	0.149	0.163
	(3.51)	(3.22)	(4.82)	(4.35)
CIQ	0.021	0.023	0.024	0.025
	(2.16)	(2.29)	(2.46)	(2.57)
TGT..................	0.753	0.765	0.500	0.511
	(3.54)	(3.59)	(2.38)	(2.43)
HOMETR1.............	...	−0.192	...	−0.124
		(0.80)		(0.53)
HOMETR2.............	...	−0.293	...	−0.248
		(1.13)		(0.96)
SIBS	−0.118	−0.123	−0.058	−0.063
	(2.01)	(2.09)	(1.01)	(1.08)
YK	...	−0.782	...	−0.929
		(0.58)		(0.69)
C.....................	10.03	10.38	9.39	9.85
R^2	.078	.080	.102	.104
Number of observations ...	780	780	781	781

NOTE.—t-values are in parentheses.

which has faded by the time schooling decisions are made.[7] Family income was not significantly related to schooling levels.

In summary, these regressions indicate that the schooling level for males is positively related to ability, that larger numbers of siblings may cause schooling to take longer to complete due to the difficulty of financing it (or the obligation to put younger brothers and sisters through school), but the final level of schooling is independent of family size. Finally, the levels of parent's education, representing the quality and quantity of home investments, have a positive effect on schooling levels, while the quantity of preschool investments does not. Mother's and father's education have equal impacts on schooling, while mother's education was much more important in determining IQ. Father's education may be a proxy for income, although a more direct measure of income was not significantly related to schooling levels.

B. Estimation for Females

In contrast to males, schooling levels of females are not significantly related to ability (see table 3, cols. 1 and 4.) They are, however, related

[7] This transitory effect on IQ of intensive preschool programs has also been seen in programs outside the home, such as Head Start. Finis Welch pointed out this analogy to me.

TABLE 3
YEARS OF SCHOOLING OF FEMALES IN TERMAN SAMPLE

INDEPENDENT VARIABLE	1940			1950		
	(1)	(2)	(3)	(4)	(5)	(6)
EDMOT	0.163	0.180	0.161	0.158	0.180	0.152
	(4.67)	(2.89)	(3.77)	(4.73)	(3.01)	(3.70)
EDFAT	0.085	0.085	0.112	0.073	0.043	0.113
	(2.73)	(1.52)	(3.55)	(2.43)	(0.79)	(3.70)
CIQ	0.011	−0.011	0.014	0.009	−0.019	0.012
	(1.28)	(0.36)	(1.51)	(1.15)	(0.63)	(1.44)
TGT	0.669	...	...	0.491	...	...
	(3.47)			(2.65)		
SIBS	−0.136	−0.152	−0.146	−0.126	−0.131	−0.143
	(2.42)	(1.62)	(2.08)	(2.34)	(1.47)	(2.12)
YK	1.524	0.682	0.076	1.705	1.034	0.083
	(1.30)	(0.31)	(1.30)	(1.51)	(0.48)	(1.44)
FIRSTBORN	0.349	0.513	0.274	0.232	0.340	0.164
	(1.97)	(1.60)	(1.26)	(1.36)	(1.10)	(0.79)
C	9.311	13.637	10.004	9.817	14.978	10.531
R^2	.166	.177	.153	.154	.145	.152
Number of observations	606	158	448	615	158	457

NOTE.—*t*-values are in parentheses.

to parents' schooling levels. Although the difference between the coefficients on mothers' and fathers' education is greater for the girls than for the boys, this difference is not significant at the 5 percent level. As with males, the more children in the family, the less schooling achieved, but for women the negative effect of a larger family on schooling attainment is not overcome by 1950. Girls who were the oldest child in their family got more schooling, as seen by the positive effect of the variable FIRSTBORN. For boys, once number of siblings was held constant, birth order did not matter. Family income and quantity of home investment in preschool years are not strongly related to years of schooling achieved.

In table 3, columns 2 and 5 refer to the girls selected in high school by the TGT and columns 3 and 6 refer to the Stanford-Binet-selected girls. The mother's education seems to be relatively more important in determining schooling attainment of TGT-girls, while father's education, family income, and number of siblings are relatively more important determinants of schooling for the Stanford-Binet group.

In summary, there is some evidence here that a mother's characteristics have a stronger impact on schooling achieved by females than by males, particularly for the girls chosen in high school. Further, number of siblings and family income are more closely related to females' schooling levels than to those of males, while ability is more strongly related to the males' schooling levels than to those of females. If we apply Becker's analysis (1967, p. 17), these results suggest that for girls the supply curve of funds shifts relative to a comparatively stable demand curve for schooling, while the opposite is true for males. This implies that males face greater equality of opportunity for schooling than do females.

C. Total Effect of Mother's Education

The total effect of mother's education on schooling achieved is composed of the direct effect and the indirect effect via IQ. For a male, each year of mother's education results in an addition of .14 of a year of schooling in 1940 and .15 of a year in 1950. Thus, the effect of having a mother who is a college graduate compared to one who is a high school graduate is to increase schooling attainment by .6 of a year.

For girls who took the TGT, each additional year of a mother's schooling resulted in .18 of a year of schooling attained in 1940 and .17 of a year in 1950. For the girls who were selected through the Stanford-Binet test, an additional year of mother's schooling added .16 of a year to schooling attained by 1940 and .15 of a year to schooling attained by 1950.

V. Determinants of Income

A. Schooling and Postschool Investments

According to the model presented in figure 1, income is derived from the rent on different forms of human capital: ability and home, school, and postschooling investment. The relation to be estimated is of the form $Y = \beta_1 + \beta_2 I_2 + \beta_3 I_3 + \beta_4 (I_3)^2 + u$, where $Y = $ log of earnings in a given year, $I_2 = $ years of schooling, $I_3 = $ years of experience, and $u = $ other income-affecting factors which are uncorrelated with the investment variables

Using the approximation that $\log (1 + r) \cong r$, and assuming that rates of return are constant over time, the coefficient β_2 can be interpreted as equal to rK, where r is the rate of return to investments made in schooling and K is the ratio of investment costs to gross potential earnings during the schooling period.[8]

A common assumption in interpreting human capital earnings functions is that $K = 1$, since opportunity costs probably account for the major part of investment costs and part-time earnings are assumed to offset tuition charges. Under these conditions, β_2 can be interpreted as the rate of return to schooling. The inclusion of the number of years of experience and its square results from a Taylor series expansion of a series of on-the-job investments whose ratio to earnings declines linearly with time (see Mincer 1974b, pp. 3–6).

The parameters of the above equation were estimated using data on income earned by men in the sample in 1939, 1949, and 1959. Since

---

[8] This approach is fully developed by Becker and Chiswick (1966).

labor-supply data were never obtained, the earnings functions could not be estimated for women in the Terman sample. Only males who were no longer students and who were not unemployed were included in order to achieve as nearly as possible a sample of men who were employed full time.

The dependent variable in 1939 was the full-time monthly wage or salary. For 1949 and 1959, the dependent variable was annual earned income. Years of schooling were assigned to correspond to rather detailed descriptions of schooling level given in the questionnaires (see Appendix B). Experience was calculated as: age − age at high school graduation − (final education level − 12). If we employ the useful assumption that $K = 1$, the regression results presented in column 1 of tables 4–6 imply a rate of return to schooling of between 5.6 and 6.7 percent. This is low compared with other estimates of rates of return to college graduates.

Rates of return calculated for graduate training are usually lower than those for bachelor of arts degree holders, and 44 percent of this sample had more than 16 years of schooling. There is also reason to believe that the assumption that $K = 1$ is less tenable for this sample than for the average college graduate, since 24 percent of the Terman undergraduates had scholarships or fellowships amounting to $200 or more and 10 percent had received $1,000 or more in support of their studies. If $K < 1$, $\beta_2 < r$, thus coefficients on years of schooling appear to be underestimates of the rate of return to education for this sample.

TABLE 4
EARNINGS FUNCTIONS FOR MALES IN 1940

	LOG OF MONTHLY EARNINGS ($)			
	(1)	(1a)	(2)	(3)
Years of schooling in 1940	0.056	0.056	0.063	0.063
	(5.18)	(5.18)	(5.77)	(5.22)
Years of experience in 1940	0.004	0.019	0.019	0.026
	(0.07)	(2.70)	(2.75)	(2.87)
(Years of experience)^2	0.0003	...	...	...
	(0.27)			
Mother's education.............	...	...	−0.016	...
			(−1.52)	
Father's education	...	...	−0.009	...
			(−0.91)	
YK	...	...	0.85	...
			(2.41)	
Family income adequacy........	...	...	0.050	...
			(3.40)	
CIQ	...	...	...	−0.001
				(−0.46)
TGT..........................	...	...	...	−0.10
				(−1.36)
Intercept	4.424	4.247	3.529	4.169
R^2	.036	.036	.063	.038

SOURCE.—Calculated from the Terman sample; includes 724 observations.
NOTE.—t-values are in parentheses.

TABLE 5
EARNINGS FUNCTIONS FOR MALES IN 1950

	LOG OF ANNUAL EARNINGS ($100)		
	(1)	(2)	(3)
Years of schooling in 1950	0.062	0.064	0.064
	(6.14)	(6.29)	(5.79)
Years of experience in 1950	0.131	0.138	0.128
	(2.39)	(2.52)	(2.34)
(Years of experience)^2	−0.0018	−0.0019	−0.0017
	(−2.19)	(−2.32)	(−2.06)
Mother's education	...	−0.026	...
		(−2.56)	
Father's education	...	0.00075	...
		(0.08)	
YK	...	0.655	...
		(2.00)	
CIQ	...	...	0.00049
			(0.20)
TGT	...	...	−0.033
			(−0.52)
Intercept	1.02	0.567	0.905
R^2	.061	.073	.062

SOURCE.—Calculated from the Terman sample; includes 731 observations.
NOTE.—t-values are in parentheses.

TABLE 6
EARNINGS FUNCTIONS FOR MALES IN 1960

	LOG OF ANNUAL EARNINGS ($100)		
	(1)	(2)	(3)
Years of schooling in 1950	0.067	0.067	0.075
	(6.81)	(6.63)	(6.93)
Years of experience in 1960	0.097	0.104	0.089
	(1.44)	(1.54)	(1.31)
(Years of experience)^2	−0.001	−0.001	−0.001
	(−1.45)	(−1.54)	(−1.18)
Mother's education	...	−0.016	...
		(−1.58)	
Father's education	...	0.001	...
		(1.05)	
YK	...	0.263	...
		(0.84)	
CIQ	...	...	0.002
			(0.86)
TGT	...	...	−0.096
			(−1.54)
Intercept	1.722	1.411	1.33
R^2	.091	.097	.097

SOURCE.—Calculated from the Terman sample; includes 701 observations.
NOTE.—t-values are in parentheses.

There is, however, a striking constancy in the schooling coefficients from decade to decade. The experience variables are not significant in explaining 1940 incomes (the subjects were, on the average, 29 years old). At this stage in the life cycle, experience may be exerting a linear rather than parabolic effect on earnings, as indicated in column 1a, table 4.

B. Home Investments

What is the effect of expanding this earnings function to include home investment variables? The equation to be estimated is of the form

$$Y = \beta_1' + \beta_2' I_2 + \beta_3' I_3 + \beta_4' (I_3)^2 + \beta_5 I_1 + V, \tag{5}$$

where $I_1 =$ the amount of home investment and all other variables are defined as above.

It is clear that if home investments affect income and if home investment and schooling are positively correlated, then the simple regression of income on schooling results in a coefficient on schooling which is biased upward from β_2' by a factor equal to $\beta_5 r_{I_1, I_2}$, where $r_{i,j}$ is the regression coefficient of variable i on variable j in the sample. However, if home investments do not directly influence income, but affect it only indirectly by influencing schooling levels, then the coefficient β_2 is not biased upward from β_2'.

Estimates of equation (5) for 1940, 1950, and 1960 are presented in column 2 of tables 4–6. Father's education was not significantly related to earnings in any one of the three years. Mother's education was negatively related to earnings in all 3 years, and in 1950 this coefficient was significantly different from zero. Mother's education was positively correlated with the two family-income measures (correlation with YK = .43, correlation with family income adequacy =.16). Both family-income measures were quite significantly related to 1940 income. In 1950, only YK was significantly related to income, and by 1960 neither income measure was. Thus, the effect of parents' income on earnings is attenuated over the life cycle. Family-income variables are related to quality of college attended, and this may, in turn, affect earnings (see Wachtel 1974). Of those who had "abundant incomes," 63 percent attended Stanford; in contrast, only 27 percent of those with "limited" incomes and 36 percent of those with "adequate" incomes did so. Greater percentages of the lower-income groups attended state colleges rather than the higher-quality state universities.

Mother's education and YK are positively correlated with own years of schooling ($\rho = .23$, $\rho = .17$, respectively) and FAMINC is negatively related ($\rho = -.02$). The net effect of the home-background variables is to increase the coefficient on years of schooling from .056 to .063 in 1940, although the YK variable is significantly related to 1940 income. The years-of-schooling coefficient is virtually unchanged by the inclusion of background variables in 1950 and 1960.

These findings provide some evidence against the hypothesis advanced by Bowles (1972) that specification errors and errors in measurement of family-background variables lead (because these variables are positively correlated with schooling level) first to overestimating the importance of schooling; and second, to underestimating the importance of background variables in the earnings function.

Bowles maintains that because data on parents' education, occupations, and incomes are obtained from questionnaires administered many years after the fact "the degree of error in the measurement of the father's occupation and education variable greatly exceeds that in the respondent's own years-of-schooling variable" (1972, p. S227). Consequently, the importance of background variables will be underestimated, while that of the respondent's own schooling will be overestimated. The Terman data allow a simple test of the proposition that if background and the sample member's own data were subject to similar levels of error, the background variables would increase in significance while the member's own variables would fall. In the Terman sample, data on parents' education and home investment were supplied by parents when the child was 11 years old. Yet, in spite of the significance of some of these variables, the importance of the years-of-schooling variable was not reduced.

C. *Ability*

Using the same reasoning applied to the home-investment variables, we can say that if ability affects earnings and if it is positively correlated with schooling achieved, omitting this variable in the earnings function results in biasing upward the rate of return to schooling.

Income in 1940, 1950, and 1960 is not significantly related to IQ, holding schooling and experience constant (see col. 3 of tables 4–6). The IQ variables remain insignificant if both home investment and IQ variables are included in the earnings function, while the coefficients on the schooling and experience terms are virtually unchanged. We conclude that childhood ability has very little independent effect on earnings. It is to be expected that earnings are related to contemporaneous stocks of human capital. In this sample, years of schooling in 1940 is no doubt a better index of human capital in 1940 than is IQ measured in 1922.

Furthermore, it must be recalled that due to the nature of the sample, we are considering marginal differences in ability within the top 1 percent of the ability distribution. Yet, IQ scores varied for this group from 135 to 200, while a standard deviation for the IQ distribution is 15 points and IQ was a significant determinant of schooling.

With a less restricted sample, Griliches and Mason (1972) who used data on United States military veterans who were younger than 35 years, also found the inclusion of an ability measure did not greatly change the coefficient of schooling. Using the change in schooling level after military service, they concluded that the bias in this coefficient due to the omission of an ability variable (AFQT) was only about 12 percent. In their sample, in contrast with this study, the ability variables were significant, although they did not greatly change the schooling coefficient.

Several other studies have also found relatively small bias due to omission of ability variables. Ashenfelter and Mooney (1968, p. 86), in a study of past recipients of Woodrow Wilson fellowships, found that the "inclusion of an ability measure affected the estimates of the coefficients for the other education related variables only in a very marginal fashion." Weisbrod and Karpoff (1968), roughly controlling for ability in a sample of employees of the American Telephone and Telegraph Company, estimate that only one-fourth of the earnings' differences between high school and college graduates is attributable to nonschooling factors rather than to differences in schooling level.

Taubman and Wales (1973) found, after testing several ability measures, that in the NBER-Thorndike sample of United States Air Force volunteers for certain programs, only the omission of mathematical ability affected the schooling parameters. They estimate that the bias to the education coefficient from omitting the mathematical-ability variable was about 25 percent for 1955 incomes and 15 percent for 1969 incomes. Using unpublished data from Dael Wolfle on Minnesota high school graduates, Taubman and Wales found a bias of "no more than four per cent at the various educational levels" from omitting ability measures from the earnings function.

John Hause (1972) found that the effect of ability on log of income remained small at all schooling levels when he used data from Project Talent which tested a sample of high school students and later surveyed their earnings. He calculated upward bias in the education coefficient, if ability is omitted, at 13–18 percent in Daniel Rogers's (1969) data based on a sample of Connecticut school boys, and at 3–11 percent in the Thorndike data.

VI. Summary

Because of the unique nature of the sample, the findings on the Terman data cannot be readily generalized to the population as a whole. However, several conclusions can be drawn:

1. It has been demonstrated that home investments do increase measured stocks of childhood human capital. Even within a sample of

very able children, home-investment variables were positively and significantly related to a measure of human capital, IQ, for boys and for a subset of older girls. A mother's education was significantly related to IQ, while the father's was not, thus indicating that home investments rather than wholly genetic factors underlie the relationship.

2. Education achieved by age 29 and age 39 by men and women in the Terman sample did depend on parents' education and on family size, but not on a more direct measure of the quantity of preschool time inputs or on family income. Boys' achievement also depended on ability, indicating greater equality of opportunity for boys to get schooling than for girls.

3. Men's earnings at ages 29, 39, and 49 were strongly related to schooling and experience variables. The addition of home-investment and ability variables did not significantly decrease the coefficients on schooling and experience, although family income was positively and significantly related to earnings in the early years of the life cycle.

Appendix A

Measures of Family Income

Two measures of family income were examined in this study. One was a subjective measure; the other was constructed from data on fathers' occupations in 1922.

A. The subjective measure, family income adequacy, resulted from the answer given in 1950 to the following question: "How adequate were family finances during your childhood and youth?" Answers were coded as follows:

Coding	Frequency (in %)
1 = limited or very limited	20.9
2 = adequate	75.0
3 = abundant.....................	4.1

B. An alternative estimate of 1922 family income was derived from the father's 1922 occupation, reported as one of six categories. Estimates of income for various occupation groups were derived from King (1923, p. 111) since the United States Census did not collect income data by occupation until 1940. King's estimates were based on average earnings for a sample of 436 employed males between December and February 1922.

The ratio of income in each category to the income of professional workers is presented below:

Terman Category	YK
1. Professional.................................	1.00
2. Semiprofessional, higher business	0.90
3. Clerical, skilled trades, retail business..........	0.82
4. Farming and agriculture	0.78
5. Semiskilled trades, minor clerical, or business ...	0.72
6. Slightly skilled trades, little training...........	0.64

TABLE B1
Years of Schooling in the Terman Sample, Description, and
1950 Frequencies for Males and Females

Years of School Coded	Highest Level of Schooling	Males		Females	
		Number	%	Number	%
10	High school, 1–3 years	7	0.9	9	1.4
12	High school, 3 years plus business or trade school; high school graduate	59	7.2	63	9.8
13	High school graduate plus 1–2 years of art, music, business, normal, technical, or trade school, or less than 2 years of college	65	7.9	54	8.4
14	High school graduate plus pharmacy, chiropractic, accounting, or nursing school or $2\frac{1}{2}$–3 years of college	86	10.5	70	10.9
15	High school plus 3–4 years of art or music school or college	5	0.6	1	0.2
16	B.A. or L.L.B. or D.D.S. without B.A.	200	24.3	186	28.9
17	Masters' degrees or 5–6 year engineering or architecture degrees	138	16.8	213	33.1
18	D.D.S. with B.A., M.B.A., graduate work of 2 years	20	2.4	1	0.2
19	J.D. or L.L.B with B.A.	87	10.6	2	0.3
20	Ph.D., Ed.D., L.L.D., etc.	74	9.0	13	2.0
21	M.D.	45	5.5	6	0.9
. . . .	Incomplete information	36	4.4	25	3.9

Appendix C

Variable	Mean	Standard Deviation
A. 1922 data—821 observations:		
CIQ	148.88	10.36
EDMOT	11.74	2.71
EDFAT	12.36	3.53
SIBS	1.85	1.58
ORIGTEST	0.33	0.47
BORDER	1.89	1.24
HOMETR1	0.19	0.40
HOMETR2	0.15	0.36
YK	0.88	0.09
FAMINC	1.82	0.48
B. 1940 data—724 observations:		
LWAGE40	5.60	0.67
ED40	16.11	2.65
EX40	8.82	3.90
EX40SQ	92.92	75.63
YK	0.88	0.09
FAMINC	1.81	0.48
C. 1950 data—742 observations:		
LINC50	4.30	0.81
ED50	16.38	2.59
EX50	18.18	4.27
EX50SQ	348.69	155.79
D. 1960 data—699 observations:		
LINC60	4.91	0.60
EX60	28.16	4.31
EX60SQ	811.51	243.27

TABLE C2
MEANS AND STANDARD DEVIATIONS—FEMALES

Variable	Mean	Standard Deviation
A. 1922 data—643 observations:		
CIQ	148.33	9.96
EDMOT	11.88	2.67
EDFAT	12.09	3.55
SIBS	1.88	1.60
ORIGTEST	0.26	0.44
BORDER	1.98	1.33
HOMETR1	0.19	0.39
HOMETR2	0.13	0.34
YK	0.89	0.09
FAMINC	1.83	0.51
B. 1940 data—606 observations:		
ED40	15.34	2.12
C. 1950 data—615 observations:		
ED50	15.50	2.03

Comment

Frank P. Stafford

University of Michigan

The Leibowitz study is important because, through the use of home-investment variables, it goes beyond the usual practice of recording that parental education and income should in some fashion influence the lifetime-earnings potentials of individuals. As the study suggests, data requirements for research on home investments are rather demanding because such final output measures as adult earnings are not often available along with measures of home and school investments. Moreover, the position advanced and given considerable empirical support is that the family investments end up as being a type of intermediate good. The intermediate-good argument is crucial to the analysis, for it suggests that simply taking measures of human capital for adults (education and labor-market experience) and tacking on variables for home investments may suggest only a minor influence of the latter which would likely be subsumed in measures of adult skills.

While the author has demonstrated that home investments substantially affect adult earnings, there are several theoretical and empirical problems with the current effort which may be remedied in future research.

It would seem that to pursue seriously the specification of a dynamic accumulation model starting at childhood (even given an exogenous family size and earnings potential of the parents) would require something more than Ben-Porath's model of investment in human capital. For if K_0 is the initial condition of "inherent genetic ability," it seems unlikely that preschoolers choose, or that parents can make them choose, a time path of training so as to maximize the present value of net earnings. To a large extent, the investments in preschoolers are organized by their parents, and this preschool investment determines an intermediate good. This intermediate good then contributes to the learning process at the point when the child begins to make independent investment decisions with his parents' resources defining a financial constraint or marginal cost of funds. A variety of specifications, such as having the intermediate good an argument in the production function or altering the efficiency parameter, could be used. This general specification would be more in keeping with the empirical work in the paper and would separate conceptually the role of parents and children in determining educational attainment.

A more difficult theoretical problem is hidden in the recursive model used. While a model of this type has much to recommend it on grounds of estimation, the critical factors influencing home investment in children include number of children in the family and the quantity and quality of home investments as well as other training given to particular children. That is, the process of investment in children is bound up with the family decision on number of children. On a descriptive level it may be sufficient to treat the number of children as exogenous and observe how variations in parental input influence educational attainment, given family income. Yet, the decision making by the family requires a delicate balancing of number of children and lifetime family income by virtue of the very high (dynamic) shadow price of the wife's withdrawal from the labor force, particularly for highly educated young women. Although these decisions can be portrayed by a complex model, there is much merit in a less ambitious (realistic?) approach which takes the family size and home investments per child as given. The point of reference to a model with a demographic sector is to emphasize that the approach in the Leibowitz paper must be utilized with some uneasiness insofar as it glosses over a large and important question of family behavior: How do parents decide number of children and home inputs per child?

On the empirical side, the major data limitations are that in the Terman sample there is only minimal variation in several of the critical variables (IQ has a mean of 149 with a standard deviation of only 10) and that the variables measuring home training, HOMETR1 and HOMETR2, are rather vague. It seems tenuous to argue that the difference between (1) "no instruction, other than usual amount of reading and telling stories" and (2) "considerable number of hours, but chiefly reading, telling stories and writing" or between (1) and (3) "an appreciable amount of instruction along particular lines" really constitutes a measure of the quantity of time inputs by the parents. Yet, this is in fact assumed because use of these variables, it is argued, "holds the quantity of time inputs constant, [and] the education variables can be taken to measure the quality of time." This is all the more difficult to believe since recent work (Leibowitz 1972; Hill and Stafford 1974) strongly suggests that quantity of time inputs to children by more-educated women is greater than for less-educated women within a lifetime income group.

Without distinguishing between quality or quantity of home inputs per child, the finding, verified in other studies, that education of the wife is much more important than education of the husband (or IQ of the mother) in determining IQ of the child implies that there is a large nongenetic component to IQ. More significantly, this nongenetic component which can be related to home investment influences educational attainment. This is a first major step in the direction of showing that home investments constitute an intermediate form of human capital which influences education. The second step is the demonstration that the IQ and parental-education variables (home investment proxies) influence educational attainment. The third step is to show that education influences earnings but that the home investment variables have no direct influence on earnings. This finding corroborates recent work for a national probability sample wherein each year of a father's education results in a .3 increase in the years of schooling of his sons, but the earnings of sons are not directly influenced by education of the father (Johnson and Stafford 1973, pp. 145 and 151).

A secondary theme developed in the paper is the issue of upward bias in educational variables owing to measurement error attributable to imperfect memory or subjective recall in background variables. With minor error in the background variables because the information was obtained from parents when the child was 11 years old, it is found that the influence of the child's own schooling is not appreciably lowered. These results are interpreted as contradicting the contention that most research understates the importance of background variables (Bowles 1972). Yet, aside from the issue of measurement errors, the model used here specifies that parental variables influence home investment and therefore have a major, though indirect, influence on adult earnings. This and other research (Griliches and Mason 1972; Johnson and Stafford 1973) constitute an empirical link in understanding the rule of intergenerational influences on the income distribution.

To conclude, let me mention two topics on which this study has a bearing. The observed positive correlation between spouses' educations can be interpreted as a mutual consumption choice and the return to education of women is, under this view, partly realized in this fashion (though Veblen interpreted this consumption as a vestigial form of predatory activity). In the Leibowitz study, one of the major returns to education of women is in the form of home investments in children. An interesting study would be to develop value-added figures and combine these with earnings data to calculate returns to schooling for women. This would show, I believe, that earnings differentials between educated men and women are considerably offset by nonmarket productivity differences.

The efficacy of public policy as a vehicle for altering the income distribution is limited since, it is said, income is so strongly influenced by parental background that opening better schooling opportunities will not have any appreciable effect on earnings for those born into low-income families. In this light, do the different forms of income maintenance, by

allowing more home time by the mother, result in larger home investments in the children? If the answer is yes, there is reason to believe that
public policy can influence what appears to be an important source of
human capital formation.

The Effect of Children on the Housewife's Value of Time

Reuben Gronau

The Hebrew University and University of Chicago

Much recent economic literature on the socioeconomic factors affecting fertility has focused on the "price" of children. A good bit of attention has been paid to the effect of the price the woman assigns to her time. It is argued that these time inputs constitute a predominant part of the costs of production of "child services," in particular while the child is young.[1] The price of time has figured as a main determinant of almost every dimension of fertility: the amount of child services produced, the trade off between the quality of children and the number of children, the timing of the first child, and the spacing of the various children.

The first endeavors were to associate the woman's price of time with the wage rate of working women who have the same market characteristics. An objection to this procedure is that the wage rate of working women is net of her general on-the-job training costs and that a true measure of the price women have to pay for having children should include the costs of depreciation of their market skills as well as the value of appreciation of their nonmarket skills (Michael and Lazear 1971). Furthermore, over three-fifths of all American married women as yet abstain from entering into the labor force in any given week, implying in their behavior that they reject the wage offered to them by the market as an adequate compensation for the loss of nonmarket productivity (Willis 1969 [rev. 1971]; Gronau

I benefited from suggestions by Gary Becker, Barry Chiswick, Stanley Diller, Robert Hall, James Heckman, William Landes, Arleen Leibowitz, Gregg Lewis, Robert Michael, Jacob Mincer, Marc Nerlove, T. W. Schultz, and Robert Willis. I wrote this paper while I was a postdoctoral fellow at the University of Chicago. I acknowledge the financial support of the Rockefeller Foundation through a grant to the University of Chicago for research on the economics of population and family decision making. Finally, I want to express my thanks to my research assistant, Randall Olsen, whose devoted help made this paper possible.

[1] An incomplete list of the studies analyzing the effect of the price of time on fertility includes Ben-Porath (1970*b*), De Tray (1972*b*), Michael (1970, 1971), Willis (1969 [rev. 1971]), and of course Mincer's seminal paper (1963).

1973). This is particularly true in the case of mothers of young children. Thus, while 68 percent of all urban white American married women stayed out of the labor force during the 1960 census week, over 85 percent of all white mothers with one child and over 90 percent of all white mothers with two or more children under 3 years old found that their value of marginal product at home exceeded that of the market.[2] Any evaluation of the price of children has to start, therefore, with the evaluation of the price of time of those mothers who devote their whole time to the home, the housewives.

There is little direct evidence on the price families place on the housewife's time. Admittedly, one may find some indirect evidence in studies of the labor-force participation of married women (e.g., Mincer 1962a; Cain 1966); but most of these studies, though recognizing the importance of children to the participation decision, did not investigate the effect of children in sufficient detail to allow any inference on the effect of children on the housewife's value of time. Some more recent studies (Smith 1972b and, in particular, Leibowitz 1972) contributed significantly to the discarding of the notion that children can be treated as a homogeneous commodity, but these studies still did not provide direct evidence on the price of the women's inputs in the production of child services. Likewise, an attempt to measure directly the change, explained by presence of children, in time inputs involved in housework (Hill and Stafford 1974; Leibowitz 1972) is only circumstantial evidence, serving as a complement rather than a substitute to a direct evaluation of the housewife's value of time.

I have tried in the past to estimate the price of time of nonworking women (Gronau 1973, 1974). These estimates were based on aggregate data, a method that proved expensive both in computation and in terms of loss of information. Thus, I was able to examine only the effect of income and young children on the housewife's shadow price of time, leaving out variables such as the woman's age, education, and number and age composition of children. The inclusion of these variables in the analysis called for a method of estimation utilizing disaggregate data. The description of this method and the new estimates of the factors effecting the shadow price of time occupy most of this paper.

I analyze herein the woman's age and education, her family income, her husband's age and education, and the number and the age composition of her children. It is found that education has a considerable effect on the woman's value of household productivity: the shadow price of time of college graduates exceeds that of elementary school graduates, other things being equal, by over 20 percent. Husband's characteristics (age and education) have a much smaller effect on the price of a wife's time (e.g., the

---

[2] These data are based on the 1960 Census 1/1,000 sample and refer to urban white married women belonging to primary families only. These rates would, of course, have been somewhat higher had they referred to annual participation rates.

price of time of women married to college graduates exceeds the price of time of those married to elementary school graduates, other things being equal, by less than 10 percent). The income elasticity of the price of time is relatively low (less than 0.15) but seems to increase with income. The effect of children on the shadow price of time of their mothers seems to vary with the child's age and the mother's education. The existence of children tends to increase the value placed on their mother's time, but this effect diminishes with the child's age. Moreover, given the child's age, the effect of a child on his mother's value of time is not uniform but varies with her education. The effect of a young child (less than 3 years old) increases with the mother's level of education. A child older than 3 years seems not to have any effect on the price of his mother's time if her formal schooling ended at the elementary level, and has almost the same effect on his mother's price of time regardless of whether she finished only high school or whether she continued her studies in college. A child over 11 years old maintains his positive effect if his mother is a high school graduate but may have even a negative absolute effect if his mother is a college graduate. These last results are highly tentative and call for additional investigation.

Economic theory is of little help in predicting the direction and magnitude of the effects of most of the variables discussed above. The evaluation and interpretation of our results must, therefore, rest to a large extent on the indirect evidence, on the evidence collected by scientists in some related fields of social science (e.g., educational psychology), and, at least partly, on intuitive observations.

I. The Shadow Price of Time

The adage "time is money" has, since Becker's pathbreaking article of 1965, become a part of economic theory. The answer to the question, "How much money is time?" leads, however, a shaky life within the framework of economic analysis. More and more economists, in particular those interested in transportation, have come to question the traditional answer that the value one places on his time is equal to the person's marginal wage rate. This contention drew increasing fire from two directions—from those arguing that this equality ignores any possible differentials between the direct utilities associated with work and nonwork activities, and from those attacking the presupposition that time can be shifted freely between the market and nonmarket sector. Addressing ourselves to the latter reservation, if the number of working hours is fixed institutionally, or, in particular, if the person does not work at all, one is faced with a "dual economy" in which input prices in the two sectors need not necessarily be equal.

Formally, let there be two commodities (or activities), say "standard of living" (S) and "child services" (C),[3] each being produced by combining the household members' time (T_i) and market goods (X_i)

$$S = S(X_s, T_{sm}, T_{sf}),$$

$$C = C(X_c, T_{cm}, T_{cf}),$$

(1)

where it is assumed for simplicity that the family consists of two adults, husband (m) and wife (f), and that children do not contribute to household production. Given perfect foresight, the family maximizes its intertemporal welfare function U:

$$U = U(Z_1, \ldots, Z_n),$$

(2)

where the utility in any given period Z_j is a function of the quantities of S_j and C_j consumed during that period:[4]

$$Z_j = Z_j(S_j, C_j).$$

(3)

The maximization of welfare takes place under two kinds of constraints: (a) the intertemporal wealth constraint,

$$\sum_{j=1}^{n} \alpha_j(X_{sj} + X_{cj}) = \sum_{j=1}^{n} \alpha_j(W_{mj} T_{wmj} + W_{fj} T_{wmj}) + V,$$

(4)

where T_{wij} denotes the time spent in work by person i in period j, W_{ij} is the wage rate, V is the initial endowment of nonhuman capital, and α_j is a discount factor; and (b) the temporal time constraints

$$T_{sij} + T_{cij} + T_{wij} = T \qquad i = m, f \qquad j = 1, \ldots, n.$$

(5)

The maximization of the welfare function subject to these constraints yields the optimal life-cycle pattern of consumption—for example, the optimal timing and spacing of children—as well as the optimal combination of inputs required in the production of each commodity. One of these interior equilibrium conditions is the familiar equality of the value of the marginal productivity of time in all its uses with price-time charges in the market, namely, the wage rate W_{ij}.[5]

There is nothing, however, in the model that will rule out corner solu-

---

[3] Both S and C are in effect vectors of commodities. In particular, C is a vector describing the "quality" of the children in the various age groups.

[4] In this formulation the utility derived from a child may vary over time both because of the aging of the parents (a change in the function Z_j) and because of the aging of the child (a change in the composition of the vector C_j).

[5] Note that this method commits the same sin I mentioned earlier. The utility derived from S and C is independent of the way these commodities are produced, and T_{wi} does not figure in the welfare function altogether. Thus, I rule out any psychic income (positive or negative) associated with work or child care.

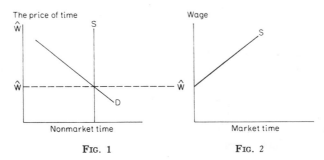

FIG. 1   FIG. 2

tions, and in particular the corner solution $T_{wfj} = 0$, that is, the wife does not work in the market in period j. It can be easily shown that in this case the woman's price of time ($\hat{W}_j$) becomes an endogenous variable being determined by the familiar equation stating that the input price should equal its value of marginal product:

$$\hat{W}_{fj} = \hat{\pi}_{sj} S_{Tfj} = \hat{\pi}_{cj} C_{Tfj}, \tag{6}$$

where S_{Tfj} and C_{Tfj} denote the marginal product of the wife's time in the production of S and C in period j, respectively, and the commodity price $\hat{\pi}_{ij}$ is itself an endogenous variable:

$$\hat{\pi}_i = x_i + W_m t_{im} + \hat{W}_f t_{if} \qquad i = S, C, \tag{7}$$

x_i, t_{im}, and t_{if} being the marginal inputs of goods, husband's time, and the wife's time in the production of commodity i, and the subscript j being omitted for clarity.[6] The price of time changes over the life cycle. For some periods, when the woman works, it equals the marginal wage rate, and for other periods, when the woman stays out of the labor force, it exceeds the wage rate.

The supply of women's time is infinitely inelastic (fig. 1). The shadow price of her time, in the absence of market opportunities, is therefore demand determined. The demand for her time consists of the derived

[6] Differentiating U with respect to T_{if} subject to the time and budget constraints yields

$$U_{sj} S_{Tfj} = U_{cj} C_{Tfj} = \lambda_{Tfj}, \tag{6'}$$

where U_{ij} is the marginal utility of commodity i and λ_{Tfj} denotes the marginal utility of T_f in period j. Equilibrium in the commodity "market" implies

$$U_{ij} = \lambda_x \pi_{ij}, \tag{6''}$$

λ_x being the marginal utility of wealth. Combining (6') and (6'') yields (6) where $\hat{W}_{fj} = \lambda_{Tfj}/\lambda_x$ is the shadow price of the wife's time in period j.

demand for T_{if} in each of its uses, which in turn depends on the commodity prices ($\hat{\pi}_s$ and $\hat{\pi}_c$), the price of other inputs (W_m), and the technology employed. A change in any one of these parameters will shift the derived demand curve D_{Tf} and change the shadow price of time.

Assuming that the production functions (eq. [1]) are linear homogeneous, it has been shown that an increase in the initial endowment of nonhuman capital V increases the demand for both commodities (ruling out inferior commodities and inferior outputs) and raises the demand for all inputs and the shadow price $\hat{W}_f$ (Willis 1969 [rev. 1971]; Gronau 1973).

An increase in the husband's wage rate W_m gives rise to a substitution of market goods and the wife's time for the husband's time. An increase in the demand for the wife's time is enhanced by an income effect and, possibly, by a substitution between commodities. The wage increase raises both full income and real full income and, thus, increases the demand for all commodities and inputs. The same change raises the relative price of the activity that is husband's-time-intensive and leads to a substitution of the less husband's-time-intensive commodity for the more time-intensive commodity. This substitution increases the demand for the wife's time to the extent that husband's time intensity and wife's time intensity are negatively correlated.

The most ambiguous of all changes is the change in productivity. This change may take many forms. It may be commodity biased, input biased, both commodity and input biased, or neutral in all respects. Moreover, even if the nature of the technological change is known, one can rarely predict its effect on the value of the wife's time without making additional assumptions about factor intensities and the income and substitution elasticities. The analysis of these factors becomes quite elaborate. Sufficient, therefore, to say that, in general, the tendency of an increase in the wife's productivity to be accompanied by an increase in the demand for her time is greater when there is a positive correlation between the commodities' time intensities and their income elasticities, and when there is a negative correlation between the husband's time intensities and the wife's time intensities.

Formal education is considered the prime source of changes in productivity in the market sector and may very well play a similar role in the nonmarket sector (though it would be difficult to isolate the contribution of education to home productivity from that of "natural ability"). "Home experience" is the variable one would like to use to capture the effect of on-the-job training on the wife's value of time. In the absence of this information one may have to revert to a measure of "years married," or simply "age." Given the ambiguity surrounding the productivity effect, it would be difficult, however, to predict the effect of age and education on the wife's value of time.

Age and education assume an additional dimension if one considers the intertemporal aspects of our model. The present value of the commodity prices changes over time because of (1) changes in input prices and technology and (2) the existence of a positive interest rate. The change in commodity and input prices gives rise to a substitution both in production and in consumption, resulting in changes in the demand for inputs over time (Ghez and Becker 1972). If the husband's wage rate is held constant, the demand for the wife's time and her shadow price of time will change with her age both because of the effect age may have on productivity and because of the family's incentive to delay its consumption activity when the rate of interest exceeds the rate of time preference. Moreover, in this context husband's education not only plays the role of a proxy for nonmarket productivity but also assumes some of the explanatory power of the missing "permanent income" variable.

Finally, it is often claimed that women's behavior is dictated by their environment. To the extent that the wife's environment is associated with her husband's age and education, one would like to control these factors so as to isolate, at least partially, this taste effect.

A natural question at this point is, What role do children play in determining their mother's price of time? In a world where all families have the same welfare function, where the production functions are sole functions of age and education, and where the measurement of all variables is not marred by errors, the answer to this question, which is the crux of this paper, is that children have no independent effect on $\hat{W}_f$. In this model, the shadow price of time and the amount of child services are mutually determined. Given the age and education of the parents, the husband's wage rate and the family's nonhuman wealth, the family's rate of interest, and its rate of time preference, all families are supposed to consume the same amount of "child services," have the same number and quality of children, and the same price of time $\hat{W}_f$.

In a less deterministic world where one allows for differences in the utility function and the production functions among families with seemingly identical characteristics, differences in the number of children may reflect differences in underlying factors that may also have some bearing on the wife's value of time. Other things being equal, the difference in the number of children may be associated with a difference in tastes for "child services" and a difference in the efficiency of production of this commodity, either because of more efficient methods of controlling quantity (information about methods of contraception) or because of more efficient methods of producing quality. An increase in the consumption of child services due to tastes or productivity is associated with a higher value of the mother's shadow price of time if the production of child services is more intensive in wife's time than the other commodity. An increased consumption (or production) of child services does not necessarily imply a larger number of children. On the other hand, given the parents' characteristics and family income, a larger number of children would imply, in general, a greater consumption of child services. A positive correlation between child services and the price of time implies, therefore, a positive correlation between the number of children and price of time. Since the size of the correlation depends on the time intensity of the production of child services, we should expect the correlation between number of children and $\hat{W}_f$ to weaken the less time-intensive child services become. Thus, if the time intensity changes with the child's age, so should his mother's price of time.

II. The Estimation of the Price of Time

Figure 1 suggests that in estimating the housewife's price of time one has to trace her derived demand for time D_{Tf}. Alternatively, if one is ready to contend that there is no inherent difference between housewives and their counterparts who work in the market as long as they share the same socioeconomic characteristics, one should be able to impute the housewife's value of time from data on women's supply of hours to the market. A woman's labor supply is the mirror image of her derived demand for time at home, and hence her price of time in the absence of market opportunities $\hat{W}$ corresponds to her "entry wage"—the wage at which she is ready to supply the first unit of labor (see fig. 2). Thus, by estimating women's labor supply, one should be able to derive the "entry wage" and the housewife's value of time. To estimate the effect of, say, income or children on the housewife's value of time, one has to measure the effect of shifts in the labor supply function due to these factors on the "entry wage."

This method, so alluring in its simplicity, runs into some overwhelming difficulties. Economic theory does not specify which of the following is the "true" dimension of labor supply: weekly hours, weeks worked, annual hours, and so on. Furthermore, theory supplies very few clues as to the mathematical function providing the best description of labor supply.[7] The estimates turn out to be very sensitive both as to the nature of the dependent variable and to the choice of functional form.[8] Finally, one has to reject the underlying assumption concerning the lack of difference be-

---

[7] One would expect the "entry wage" to be positive. Thus, the intercept in a regression of the amount of labor on the wage rate is supposed to be negative. This prior assumption rules out a certain class of mathematical functions (e.g., the double-log used in the estimation of some aggregate supply functions) but still leaves a wide scope for choice.

[8] Fitting a linear reciprocal function and a semilog function to data on weekly hours, weeks worked, and annual hours of working women resulted in extremely low values of the price of time (about 10 percent of the wage rate) and a large dispersion in the estimates. (The data were derived from the 1960 Census 1/1,000 sample.) The use of a linear function resulted in significant positive estimates of the intercept even when the data were restricted to women who worked only part time (say less than 35 hours a week or less than 1,000 hours annually).

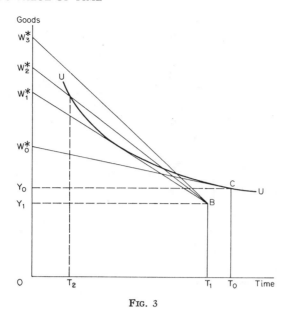

Goods

W_3^*
W_2^*
W_1^*
W_0^*
Y_0
Y_1

U

U

C

B

O T_2 T_1 T_0 Time

FIG. 3

tween working and nonworking women with the same characteristics. The mere fact that they differ in their labor-force behavior indicates that there are some unobserved fundamental differences between the two groups, and there are good reasons to suspect that these differences may be related to the price the women assign to their time (Ben-Porath 1973; Gronau 1974). Because of these difficulties it seems advisable to reject this simple method in favor of a method which focuses on a different dimension of labor supply—labor-force participation.

Let it be assumed that the family is fully aware of the wife's potential wage in the market, W^*; that this wage is insensitive to the number of hours worked; and that the search for the employer who will offer this wage is costless in terms of both time and pecuniary costs.[9] A necessary and sufficient condition for search (the necessary and sufficient condition for the wife's entry into the labor force) is that her potential wage (W^*) exceeds her value of time in the nonmarket sector ($\hat{W}$).[10]

Let family income when the woman abstains from entering the labor force be $0Y_0$ (fig. 3); then the housewife's value of time can be measured by the slope of her indifference curve UU at the point C. Assuming other

[9] The analysis will not change significantly if I adopt a somewhat more sophisticated search model (McCall 1970; Mortensen 1970) where the job-offer distribution consists of more than one point and the optimal strategy consists of a determination of a critical value W^*, so that the job seeker accepts a job if the wage offer exceeds W^* and continues his search otherwise.

[10] For a more general discussion of the labor-force participation decision, see Lewis (1971).

sources of income (including husband's earnings) do not change as a result of her decisions, the woman will decide to look for a job actively if her potential wage exceeds CW^*_0 and will decline to enter the labor market otherwise. Comparing the reactions of women who are supposed to have the same price of time but who have different potential wages should give some indication as to the potential wage at which these women are indifferent to whether they enter the market, thus yielding an estimate of their price of time.

This method may yield a biased estimator if some of our basic assumptions are violated. For example, if work involves a fixed cost (such as search costs) consisting of T_0T_1 units of time and Y_0Y_1 units of income the woman does not enter the labor force unless her potential wage exceeds BW^*_1. This wage overstates the woman's value of time. This overestimate may be inflated by deviations of the measured wage rate from the "true" wage. Discrepancies of this kind may originate in taxes, variable costs associated with work, and psychic income. For example, given a proportional tax rate, the net wage affecting the woman's participation decision may be BW^*_1 but the measured wage before taxes is BW^*_3. Similarly, if work involves time and pecuniary costs (such as commutation) that vary proportionally with the amount of work, or if work involves a proportional negative psychic income component, the measured wage exceeds the true wage (psychic income has an opposite effect when it is positive). Further distortions in the measurement of the "true" wage rate occur when the average wage deviates from the marginal wage because of an increasing marginal wage rate, progressive taxation, changes in the psychic income, and costs per unit of work, or changes in the husband's supply of work, resulting in a nonlinear price line. Finally, there may exist a minimum amount of work demanded by the employers (say, T_0T_2). This minimum requirement may increase the wage rate at which women enter the labor market (BW^*_2) and the upward bias in the estimated price of time. Bearing these reservations in mind we continue the analysis.

It is clear that even women who seem to have the same market characteristics (say education and age) may differ randomly in their potential wage. Similarly, women who seem to have the same nonmarket characteristics may differ in the price they place on their time. Let it be assumed, for the sake of exposition, that the potential wage W^*_i is known, and that the women's price of time is

$$\hat{W}_{ik} = \hat{\mu}_k + \hat{\epsilon}_{ik}, \tag{8}$$

where $\hat{\mu}_k$ is the mean value of time of all women sharing the set of non-market characteristics k, and $\hat{\epsilon}_{ik}$ is the ith random deviation from this mean. The woman participates in the labor market if $W^*_{ij} \geq \hat{W}_{ik}$, that is, if

$$W^*_i - \hat{\mu}_k \geq \hat{\epsilon}_{ik}, \tag{9}$$

and she remains a full-time homemaker otherwise.

Variable $\hat{\mu}_k$ is an unobserved variable. However, one can conjecture about the variables that affect it. In the preceding section, the mean price of time of a woman was associated with her age (A_f), education (E_f), family income (Y), number of children (C), and husband's age (A_m) and education (E_m). Let it be assumed that these variables affect $\hat{\mu}$ in an additive fashion:[11]

$$\hat{\mu} = \beta_0 + \beta_1 A_f + \beta_2 E_f + \beta_3 Y + \beta_4 C + \beta_5 A_m + \beta_6 E_m. \quad (10)$$

Furthermore, let us define $\hat{\hat{\epsilon}} = \hat{\epsilon}/\hat{\sigma}$ where $\hat{\sigma}$ is the standard deviation of $\hat{W}$. The woman participates in the labor force if

$$\frac{1}{\hat{\sigma}} [W^* - (\beta_0 + \beta_1 A_f + \beta_2 E_f + \beta_3 Y + \beta_4 C + \beta_5 A_m + \beta_6 E_m)] \geq \hat{\hat{\epsilon}}_i \quad (11)$$

and stays out of the market otherwise.

When $\hat{\hat{\epsilon}}$ has a normal distribution,

$$\hat{\hat{\epsilon}} \sim N(0, 1), \quad (12)$$

the probability that a given woman participates in the labor force equals $P(X_i = 1)$

$$= (2\Pi)^{-1/2} \int_{\infty}^{(1/\hat{\sigma})[W^*_i - (\beta_0 + \beta_1 A_{fi} + \cdots + \beta_6 E_{mi})]} \exp{(-U^2/2)} dU, \quad (13)$$

where a value $X = 1$ is assigned to every woman participating in the labor force and a value of $X_i = 0$ is assigned to full-time housewives. The logarithm of the likelihood of observing a sample of n independent observations consisting of r women participating in the labor force and $(n - r)$ nonparticipants equals

$$L = \sum_{i=1}^{r} \log P(X_i = 1) + \sum_{i=r+1}^{n} \log[1 - P(X_i = 1)].$$

Given the n values of W^*_i, A_{fi}, E_{fi}, Y_i, C_i, A_{mi}, and E_{mi}, the likelihood function depends on the parameters $\beta_0, \beta_1, \ldots, \beta_6$ and $\hat{\sigma}$. Using the probit iterative method (Tobin 1955), one can obtain the maximum-likelihood estimators,

$$X_i = b_0 + b_i A_{fi} + b_2 E_{fi} + b_3 Y_i + b_4 C_i$$
$$+ b_5 A_{mi} + b_5 A_{mi} + b_6 E_{mi} + b_7 W^*_i, \quad (14)$$

b_7 serving as an estimator of the coefficient of W^* in the likelihood function, that is, of $1/\hat{\sigma}$, and $b_l (l = 0, 1, \ldots, 6)$ serving as an estimator of

[11] There is nothing in the analysis of the preceding section to indicate that this relationship is linear, and I will not try to justify it by imposing on the model a specific set of utility and production functions. The assumption of linearity is adopted merely for simplicity's sake.

$-\beta_l/\hat{\sigma}$. A consistent estimator of $\hat{\sigma}$ is therefore $1/b_7$, and a consistent estimator of β_l is $-b_l/b_7$.

The analysis is not much affected when W^*_i is unknown, but one knows the mean potential wage μ^*_j where

$$W^*_{ji} = \mu^*_j + \epsilon^*_{ji}, \tag{15}$$

ϵ^*_{ij} denoting the random deviation of the potential wage of woman i with market characteristics j from its mean. In this case the prerequisite for entry into the labor force is

$$\mu_{jk} = \mu^*_j - \hat{\mu}_k \geqslant \hat{\epsilon}_{ki} - \epsilon^*_{ji} = \epsilon_{kji}. \tag{16}$$

If ϵ has a normal distribution ($\epsilon \sim N[0, \sigma]$), one can still apply the probit analysis to obtain consistent estimators of $\beta_0, \beta_1, \ldots, \beta_6$ and σ by replacing W^* in equation (14) by μ^*.[12] Note, however, that in this case one cannot estimate separately the standard deviation of the price of time $\hat{\sigma}$, but rather σ which reflects dispersions both of the price-of-time distribution and of the wage-offer distribution.

Unfortunately, one knows neither W^* nor its mean μ^*. An inherent difficulty in the estimation of labor-supply functions is the nonexistence of data on the wage offers received (or expected) by those women who do not work. The same problem plagues our study. This problem has received very little attention in the economic literature.[13] In the past economists opted for one of two routes of escape. One way is to postulate the relationship between the mean wage offer and some measurable market characteristics, say the woman's age and education,

$$\mu^* = \alpha_0 + \alpha_1 A_f + \alpha_2 E_f, \tag{17}$$

and the introduction of these variables in equation (14). Alternatively, it was assumed that the mean wage offer (μ^*) equals the average wage of working women with the same market characteristics ($\overline{W}$). Either one of these methods is sizzling with problems which mar the reliability of the estimates of the determinants of the price of time.

If one opts for the first method, the wife belongs to the labor force if

$$\mu/\sigma = \frac{1}{\sigma} \left[(\alpha_0 - \beta_0) + (\alpha_1 - \beta_1) A_f \right. $$
$$\left. + (\alpha_2 - \beta_2) E_f - \beta_3 Y - \beta_4 C - \beta_5 A_m - \beta_6 E_m \right] \geqslant \epsilon', \tag{18}$$

---

[12] The assumption of normality is a common one in economics and does not call for much justification. It does not necessarily call for an assumption that W^* and $\hat{W}$ have an independent bivariate normal distribution. However, if one opts for that line of explanation, one can argue that the assumption of independence is justified on the ground that any positive correlation between W^* and $\hat{W}$ due to natural ability may be offset by the negative effect of specialization in the investment in human capital. It would be more difficult to justify in this case the assumption of homoscedasticity, since heteroscedasticity in the wage-offer distribution should imply heteroscedasticity of ϵ.

[13] The only exception is Lewis (1971).

where $\epsilon' = \epsilon/\sigma$ (i.e., $\epsilon' \sim N[0, 1]$). One can still apply the probit method to estimate

$$X = a_0 + a_1 A_f + a_2 E_f + a_3 Y + a_4 C + a_5 A_m + a_6 E_m \qquad (19)$$

to obtain the maximum-likelihood estimators $a_l = $ est $[1/\sigma(\alpha_l - \beta_l)]$ for $l = 0, 1, 2$, and $a_l = $ est $(-\beta_l/\sigma)$ for $l = 3, 4, 5, 6$. However, one cannot estimate the absolute effects on $\hat{\mu}$ of income, children, and husband's characteristics but only their relative effects (β_l/σ), since $\beta_l(l = 3, 4, 5, 6)$ can be estimated only up to a factor of proportionality $1/\sigma$. Moreover, one cannot separate in this case the effect of the woman's characteristics (age and education) on the mean price of time from their effect on the mean wage offer.[14]

Given the adverse circumstances, one may be ready to forego an estimate of the effect of the wife's age and education on her price of time as long as one can obtain an estimate of the (relative) effect of the other factors (income, children, and husband's characteristics). But even these estimates are not free of criticism. Objection may be raised to the specification of the wage function. A case can be made for including in the wage function all the variables that affect the price of time. Husband's income may affect the wife's potential wage in various ways. Progressive taxation makes the wife's wage rate after taxes a function of her husband's income. Income also affects the probability of the wife's past and future participation in the market, and thus affects the profitability of the investment in market skills versus nonmarket skills. The same holds for children. The number of children affects the marginal tax rate and hence the net wage rate. It may also be negatively correlated with the mother's market experience and, hence, her potential wage rate (Michael and Lazear 1971). Given age and education, variations in the husband's income may reflect variations in his natural ability. Husband's and wife's natural ability seem to be positively correlated (Becker 1971a), and thus one would expect that, other things being equal, the husband's age and education may affect his wife's asking wage.

If one expands equation (17) to include also the rest of the variables appearing in equation (10), one cannot estimate even the relative effect of income, children, and husband's characteristics on the woman's price of time. The estimates of these factors based on equation (19) should, therefore, be regarded as merely a first approximation, assuming that the effects of income, children, and husband's age and education on the wife's expected wage offer are negligible.

Some of these difficulties are removed if one opts for the alternative

[14] Note that the inclusion of a term in the wage-offer function (17) that does not appear in the price-of-time function (10) does not solve this problem and allow "identification."

method, assuming $\mu^*_j = \overline{W}_j$, but this hypothetical "gain" may be offset by acquiring new difficulties. Admittedly, the equation $\mu^*_j = \overline{W}_j$ involves a very strong assumption. Different patterns of participation behavior of women with seemingly identical market and nonmarket characteristics may be the result of different potential wages and not necessarily of different values of time (Ben-Porath 1973; Gronau 1974). A low rate of participation in group jk may be due not to a high price of time but rather to a low mean wage rate. Under these circumstances the average wage of working women clearly overestimates the mean wage offer of nonparticipants. The danger of this kind of bias is accentuated by our measure of market experience. Market experience is presented in the wage function (eq. [17]) by a proxy age. This far from ideal choice is forced upon us by the lack of a better measure. The possibility of a bias in the measurement of the mean wage offer increases the greater the variation in wages of women with a given market experience and the greater the variation in market experience of women of the same age. Thus, this bias may be relatively small for young women who are quite homogeneous in terms of their market experience but may be considerable for women beyond the age of 50.[15] This bias will enforce the upward tendency in the bias discussed above. Moreover, errors in the measurement of μ^* may result in inconsistent estimates of the other coefficients $(\beta_1, \ldots, \beta_6)$ and bias the estimated effects of the explanatory variables on the price of time. Thus, it is only with great forbearance that one would adopt the simplistic assumption $\mu^* = \overline{W}$.

However, if one is ready to overcome these misgivings, one can estimate equation (14) replacing W^* by $\overline{W}$. The mean value of time at the point of means can be estimated by

$$\hat{\mu} = -\frac{1}{b_7}(b_0 + b_1\overline{A}_f + b_2\overline{E}_f + b_3\overline{Y} + b_4\overline{C} + b_5\overline{A}_m + b_6\overline{E}_m);\quad (20)$$

$-b_l/b_7$ measures the absolute effect of factor l on $\hat{\mu}$, and $-b_l/b_7\ \hat{\mu}$ measures its relative effect.

Fortunately, if one assumes that $\hat{W}$ and W^* are independently normally distributed, one can use the information on the labor-force participation rate and the average wage of working women to obtain an estimate of μ^*_j.[16] Equations (14) and (20) provide in this case a consistent estimate of $\beta_1, \ldots, \beta_6$ and of the mean price of time.

---

[15] It was found that teen-agers who have been asked what wage they expect to receive when they start working quoted a wage that was almost equal to the average wage of working people of the same age.

[16] It can be shown (Gronau 1973, 1974) that if $\overline{W}_j = \mu^*_j + \overline{X}_j\sigma^*$,

$$\overline{X}_j = (\sigma^*/\sigma)\frac{1}{P_j\sqrt{2\pi}}\,e^{-z_j^2/2} = X^*(\sigma^*/\sigma),\quad (16')$$

where σ^* is the standard deviation of W^*, $\sigma^2 = \hat{\sigma}^2 + \sigma^{*2}$, P_j is the labor-force partici-

Finally, one can replace the assumption that $\hat{\mu}$ is an additive function of $A_f, E_f, \ldots, E_m$ by the assumption that this function is multiplicative

$$\hat{\mu} = B_0 B_1^{A_f} B_2^{E_f} B_3^{Y} B_4^{C} B_5^{A_m} B_6^{E_m}, \tag{21}$$

where $\beta_l = \log B_l$.[17] Moreover, let it be assumed that ϵ has a log-normal distribution $[\epsilon \sim \Lambda(0, \sigma)]$. Equation (14) can be estimated by substituting $\log \overline{W}$ for W^*, where $\overline{W}$ denotes the geometric rather than the arithmetic average wage rate.[18] Let M denote the mean of the logarithm of $\hat{W}$ and Σ denote the standard deviation of the logarithm of ϵ; then $(1/b_7) = \text{est}(\Sigma)$, and M can be estimated from equation (20). Variable e^M is the median of the log-normal distribution of $\hat{W}$. To obtain an estimate of the mean one has to know the dispersion of $\log \hat{W}$ (Aitchison and Brown 1963, p. 9). This calls for the additional assumption that $\epsilon^* = 0$, that is, that there is no within-group dispersion of the potential wage, the standard deviation of ϵ^* is equal to zero, and Σ measures the standard deviation of $\log \hat{W}$. Thus, the estimate of the mean price of time is

$$\hat{\mu} = e^{M + (\Sigma^2/2)}, \tag{22}$$

and the estimate of the standard deviation is

$$\hat{\sigma} = (e^{\Sigma^2} - 1)^{1/2} \hat{\mu}. \tag{23}$$

In this case $-(b_l/b_7)$ measures the percentage change in $\hat{\mu}$ as a result of a unit increase in factor l.

III.   The Data and the Results

To estimate the price of time of housewives we return to the 1960 Census $1/1,000$ sample. The sample consists of 975 observations selected randomly from all urban white married women, spouse present, who belonged to primary families (not to subfamilies) in households with no nonrelatives. The dependent variable is defined as a dummy variable (zero, one) accord-

pation rate in group j, and Z_j satisfies Prob $(Z < Z_j) = P_j$ where Z is a standardized normal variable. Given P_j one can compute X^* and regress over different income groups

$$\overline{W}_j = b'_0 + b'_1 x^*, \tag{16''}$$

where b'_0 is an estimate of μ^*_j and b'_1 is an estimate of (σ^{*2}/σ).

[17] An alternative assumption is

$$\hat{\mu} = B_0 A_f^{B_1} E_f^{B_2} Y^{B_3} C^{B_4} A_m^{B_5} E_m^{B_6}.$$

[18] Alternatively, one has to replace $\overline{W}$ by $\log \overline{W}$ in eq. (16'') to obtain an estimate of μ^*.

ing to whether the wife participated in the labor force (was employed or looked actively for a job) in the week preceding the 1960 census. By choosing this dependent variable I focus on the participation decision in the short run. To obtain some estimates of the price of time in the long run, one should use a variable that reflects the woman's participation experience over a longer period of time. Thus, a second dependent variable is defined describing the wife's work status in the previous year. This variable assumed a value of one if the woman worked at least 1 week and a value of zero otherwise.

The income variable is a continuous variable measuring family income (wife's earnings excluded) in the year 1959. It is argued that husband's earnings and other sources of income should affect the woman's price of time differently. Given the unreliability of the data on "other income" and the husband's wage rate, I did not try to ascertain these differences. The wife's age and education are defined as dummy variables so as to allow nonlinear effects of years of age and schooling on the wife's value of time. The wife's age is described by a set of three dummy variables according to whether she belonged to the age group "less than 30," "30–49," or "50 plus."[19] Similarly, education is defined in terms of whether one belonged to one of three groups: "elementary education," "high school," or "college" (the latter included people with graduate education). An identical definition is used in the case of the husband's education, while the husband's age was measured, for simplicity, as a continuous variable.

Children are not a homogeneous commodity. Their effect on their mother's price of time depends on both their number and their age composition. Thus, children were subclassified into four groups: number under age 3, number aged 3–5, number 6–11 years old, and number in the age group 11–17.[20] In some of the regressions I included a variable "children" describing the total number of children less than 18 years old, omitting the variable "number of children 6–11." In this case the coefficient of the variable "children" describes the effect of an addition of one child 6–11 years old, while all other coefficients measure the differential effect of an additional child in group l as compared with an additional child in the age group 6–11 (the net effect of an addition of one child of age l and a subtraction of one child of age 6–11).

Allowing for returns to scale in child care, I adopted a second measure of the effect of children. Using a set of 16 dummy variables, all women were classified according to whether they had zero, one, two, or three or more children under age 6, and whether they had zero, one, two, or three or more children belonging to the age group 6–11. In a second subclassifica-

[19] The iterative probit method is too expensive to allow for a greater detail in the subclassification.

[20] Note that the measure is the number of children in a given age group and not a dummy variable describing the existence of children in that age group.

tion into a set of 12 dummy variables, women were classified according to whether they had a child less than 3 years old, had a child age 3–5, and had zero, one, or two or more children belonging to the age group 6–11.

The 1960 Census does not allow for a direct estimate of the hourly wage rate. However, it provides data on the woman's annual earnings in 1959, the number of weeks she worked that year, and the number of hours she worked during the week that preceded the Census. In the absence of a better measure, the hourly wage rate of a working woman is defined as her earnings in 1959 divided by the product of weeks worked (in 1959) and weekly hours (in 1960). All white working women in the 1960 Census 1/1,000 sample were subclassified into four age groups (less than 30, 30–49, 40–49, and 50 plus) and four education groups (elementary, high school, college, and graduate education).[21] For each of the 16 classes, I computed the arithmetic and the geometric average of the hourly wage rate (see table 1), and these values were assigned to all (working and nonworking) women belonging to that class. Alternatively, I assigned to each of the 16 classes the estimated mean wage offer μ^*.[22]

To allow for comparison with past studies of labor-force participation, I estimated the determinants of the housewives' price of time using all three methods described in the previous section: (a) assuming μ^* is a function of the woman's age and education, (b) assuming $\mu^* = \overline{W}$, and (c) estimating μ^* from data on wage rates and labor-force participation rates. Since the assumption that ϵ is normally distributed led to results very similar to those obtained under the assumption that ϵ has a log-normal distribution, and since the latter assumption seemed to have a greater explanatory power, I have omitted the former results.[23]

The estimates of equations (14) and (19) for the weekly rate of participation are presented in table 2.[24] Equation (19) yields familiar results. As expected, education has a positive effect on labor-force participation; its effect on market productivity and the asking wage exceed its effect on nonmarket productivity and the housewife's price of time. Age has its custom-

[21] I ignored the effect children may have on the women's wage since, contrary to one's expectations (Michael and Lazear 1971), working women with children usually have a higher (and not a lower) arithmetic average wage rate than childless women. The explanation may be that they have a higher price of time and hence may be more selective in the wage offers they accept. The greater selectivity of these mothers may offset their lower wage-offer distribution. An attempt to include the number of young children as a determinant of the asking wage yielded estimates that were inferior to the one I have described.

[22] See n. 16. Additional information about the means of the variables in the sample is in the Appendix.

[23] The log-normal assumption may also be more appealing on theoretical grounds, since it rules out negative estimates of $\hat{\mu}$.

[24] To evaluate the reliability of the estimates, table 2 includes the likelihood-ratio statistic to test for the hypothesis $H_0: \beta_l = 0$ for all $l = 1, 2, \ldots$, and the t scores derived as the ratio of the coefficient and its standard error. The former has a χ^2 distribution while, given the size of the sample, the latter have a normal distribution.

TABLE 1

AVERAGE HOURLY WAGE RATE OF WHITE MARRIED WOMEN BY AGE AND EDUCATION

Education and Age	Arithmetic Average Wage	Arithmetic Average Log (Wage)	Geometric Average Wage
Total	2.01	0.4559	1.58
Elementary school:			
Total	1.78	0.3064	1.36
<30	1.53	0.1565	1.17
30–39	1.67	0.3168	1.37
40–49	1.70	0.3107	1.36
50+	1.98	0.3317	1.39
High school:			
Total	1.87	0.4147	1.51
<30	1.75	0.3540	1.42
30–39	1.85	0.4332	1.54
40–49	1.93	0.4346	1.54
50+	2.03	0.4494	1.57
College:			
Total	2.62	0.6897	1.98
<30	2.48	0.6308	1.88
30–39	2.55	0.6441	1.90
40–49	2.75	0.7377	2.09
50+	2.72	0.7756	2.17
Graduate:			
Total	3.17	0.9834	2.67
<30	2.70	0.8699	2.39
30–39	3.32	0.9967	2.71
40–49	3.09	0.9400	2.56
50+	3.58	1.1628	3.20

SOURCE.—1960 Census 1/1,000 sample.

ary inverted U-shape effect.[25] Income and the husband's age and education have the expected positive effect on the mean price of time (i.e., negative effect of labor-force participation), though the effect of husband's education seems to be insignificant. An increase in the number of children has a significant effect on the mother's value of time, but this effect diminishes the older the child (the differential effect of children in any two adjoining age groups is usually significant, using a one-tailed test and a level of significance of $\alpha = 0.05$).

These conclusions are reaffirmed when $\overline{W}$ and the estimated μ^* are introduced into the regression equation. An increase of $1,000 in husband's income increases the value of time of his wife (if she does not work) by 1.0–1.8 percent.[26] The elasticity of the mean price of time with respect to income estimated at the point of means equals 0.07–0.12.

[25] Note, however, that the broad classification of age groups may conceal a large part of the variation taking place within these groups (Leibowitz 1972).

[26] The lower limit refers to the estimate where W is inserted in eq. (14), and the

TABLE 2
DETERMINANTS OF THE HOUSEWIFE'S VALUE OF TIME

EXPLANATORY VARIABLES	UNITS	$\mu^* = \alpha_0 + \alpha_1 A_f + \alpha_2 E_f$		$\mu^* = \overline{W}$			$\mu^* = \text{est } \mu^*$		
		Probit Coefficients	t-Scores	Probit Coefficients	t-Scores	Marginal Effects on $\hat{\mu}$ (%)	Probit Coefficients	t-Scores	Marginal Effects on $\hat{\mu}$ (%)
Constant	...	1.651	3.07	−1.782	−1.61	...	0.879	1.50	...
Income	$10,000/year	−0.868	−4.10	−0.852	−3.91	10.0	−0.838	−3.88	17.9
Age < 30	Dummy (0, 1)	−0.378	−1.33	0.140	0.43	−1.6	−0.356	−1.23	7.6
Age ≥ 50	Dummy (0, 1)	−0.670	−2.63	−0.885	−3.35	10.4	−0.266	−0.95	5.7
Education-elem.	Dummy (0, 1)	−0.680	−3.14	0.419	1.12	−4.9	0.239	0.71	−5.1
Education-coll.	Dummy (0, 1)	0.632	2.90	−1.865	−2.59	21.8	−0.972	−1.95	20.8
Husband's age	10 years	−0.250	−2.32	−0.308	−2.75	3.6	−0.224	−2.04	4.8
Husband's educ.-elem.	Dummy (0, 1)	0.372	1.89	0.403	2.03	−4.7	0.392	1.99	−8.4
Husband's educ.-coll.	Dummy (0, 1)	−0.094	−0.45	−0.123	−0.57	1.4	−0.129	−0.60	2.8
Child < 3 (net)	No.	−0.871	−3.54	−0.870	−3.50	10.2	−0.879	−3.54	18.8
Child 3–5 (net)	No.	−0.329	−1.47	−0.312	−1.39	3.6	−0.314	−1.40	6.7
Child 12–17 (net)	No.	0.355	2.02	0.265	1.49	−3.1	0.298	1.70	−6.4
Child	No.	−0.377	−3.31	−0.325	−2.83	3.8	−0.343	−3.00	7.3
Potential wage	Dollars/hour	...	...	8.560	3.56	...	4.676	3.53	...
Likelihood ratio test	...	138.1	...	157.1	...	...	152.5	...	...
Degrees of freedom	...	12	...	13	...	...	13	...	...
σ	Dollars/hour	...	...	.206	...	...	.298	...	...
Housewives' mean value of time ($\hat{\mu}$)	Dollars/hour	...	...	1.75	...	...	1.38	...	...
Mean wage offer (μ^*)	Dollars/hour	...	...	1.55	...	...	1.13	...	...
$\hat{\mu}/\mu^*$	...	...	...	1.13	...	...	1.22	...	...

When it is assumed that $\mu^* = \overline{W}$, the housewife's value of time seems to increase with her age. There seems to be only a slight increase during the years up to the age of 50 and a sharp increase thereafter. This pattern is consistent with the life-cycle theory of consumption (when the interest rate exceeds the rate of time preference) and with the hypothesis that non-market human capital depreciates at a slower rate than market human capital, but it may also reflect a cohort effect (the older cohorts having a greater demand for home commodities relative to market commodities). However, replacing $\overline{W}$ by the estimate of μ^* indicates that these findings are merely due to an overstatement of the potential wage (the wage of working women over age 50 considerably exceeds the potential wage of nonparticipants in this age group), age having no significant effect at all on the housewife's value of time.

Education is a major determinant of the housewife's value of time, but its effect is not distributed equally among all levels of education. In the absence of market opportunities, high school graduates would not have differed significantly from elementary school graduates in terms of their price of time. It seems that if high school graduates are more productive, then the increase in productivity is offset by lower commodity prices, leaving the demand for their time unchanged. There exists, however, a significant difference (over 20 percent) between the price of time of college and high school graduates.

The education effect measures the shift in the demand function when income and husband's age and education are held constant. By holding income constant one controls the amount of goods used by the family. When "other income" is proportional to total income, and the husband's age and education determine his wage rate, then by holding income and husband's age and education constant one controls, at least partly, the amount of time the husband spends in the market and, consequently, the amount of time he spends at home. The shifts in the demand for the wife's time are measured where the total amount of other inputs is maintained constant, and reflect, therefore, the change in the "economy" productivity —the change in productivity where output prices are allowed to vary but the total amount of inputs is given. The increase in the price of time due to college education can be regarded as a lower limit of the contribution of college education to home productivity. This contribution constitutes a substantial part of the benefits of higher education and should be incorporated in the computation of the rate of return to women's education.

A husband's age has a positive effect on his wife's value of time for somewhat similar reasons to those brought to explain the correlation between the wife's age and her price of time (i.e., the life-cycle patterns of

---

upper limit is obtained when $\overline{W}$ is replaced by the estimate of μ^*. Income entered into the regression in its original form. An attempt to introduce this variable in a logarithm form resulted in inferior results.

consumption, a productivity effect, and a cohort effect). The husband's education has the positive effect one has come to expect if education is a proxy for permanent income. It is noteworthy that in this case the college/ high school differential is small and insignificant, while there is a significant difference in the price of time of women married to high school graduates versus those married to elementary school graduates. This difference may be explained by the smoothening of the life-cycle pattern of income associated with an increased level of education, and the decline in the importance of the transitory component in income, resulting in a decline in the explanatory power of education when current income is held constant. Alternatively, the difference can be explained by a larger differential in market and nonmarket productivity in the case of college-educated husbands due to specialization in the investment in human capital, reflecting a greater tendency of husbands of little education to participate in home production (Leibowitz 1972).

The positive effect of the number of children and the decline in the demand for the mother's time as the child grows older are again apparent. While one additional child younger than 3 years increases the value of his mother's time by 14–26 percent, an additional child 3–5 years old results in a gross increase of only 7–14 percent; a child of 6–11 years results in an increase of 4–7 percent, and if the child is older than 11 he does not affect his mother's price of time at all (any increase in the demand for her time is offset by the child's contribution to home production).[27]

The decline in the demand for the mother's time with the age of the child may be explained by several factors which are difficult to separate. (a) The technology of production of child services may be such that the marginal product of C of a given input unit (time and goods) increases with the child's age. Since it may be difficult to change the output per child of child services (the child's "quality") as he grows older, this technology should lead to a decline in inputs with the child's age. (b) An increase in the elasticity of substitution between the mother's time and market goods and services as the child grows, and a greater incentive to substitute goods for time if mother's age has a positive effect on her price of time, may lead to replacing the mother's time by market goods. (c) An increase in the mother's productivity in the production of child services due to on-the-job training and formal schooling (formal schooling, for instance, may contribute to a greater increase in productivity the older the child) may allow her to produce the same level of services with ever-decreasing time inputs. (d) The utility derived from a child may be directly related to the amount of time spent in the production of child services. If the psychic income associated with the production of child services declines as the child grows older, so would his mother's value of time.

[27] All the age differentials (except for the difference between a child of 3–5 years and one 6–11 years old) are significant at $\alpha = .05$ applied in a one-tailed test.

Finally, the estimated mean price of time exceeds the mean potential wage, when it is assumed that $\mu^* = \overline{W}$, by 13 percent. This margin increases to 22 percent when $\overline{W}$ is replaced by an estimate of μ^*. However, since the estimated μ^* is only two-thirds of the (geometric) average wage rate $(\overline{W})$, the estimated value of $\hat{\mu}$, adopting the latter method, falls short of the average wage rate by more than 20 percent.

The effect of education on the woman's productivity may depend on the number and age composition of her children. To investigate the interaction between children and education, I distinguish within each age group of children between children whose mothers have (1) elementary education, (2) high school education, and (3) college education. The regression results are presented in table 3.

The new specification affects neither the price-of-time/wage ratio nor the estimated effects of income, age, education, and the husband's age and education (except for a slight change in the estimated effect of elementary education on the wife's value of time).

Strictly speaking, the only statistically significant result concerning the children variable is the decline in the effect a child has on his mother's value of time as he grows older. There is a significant difference between the effect of a child less than 3 years old and the effect of a child older than 11 years within each education group. Neither the difference in the effects of children in adjoining age groups within a given education group nor the difference between the effects of children in the same age group with mothers in adjoining education groups is statistically significant (at $\alpha = .05$). Still, the differences in the implict patterns of behavior of the three education groups are such that they deserve some further discussion, even if this discussion is speculative.

The effect of additional children on the price of time of mothers with elementary education dissipates as soon as the children reach the age of 3 years. Thus, while a child less than 3 years old increases the value of his mother's time by 10 percent, children beyond that age do not have any consistent effect on $\hat{\mu}$. The effect of a child younger than 3 years on a mother's value of time when she has high school education is somewhat (though not significantly) higher than the effect in the case of a mother with elementary education (12 percent), but then the decline in this effect is much more gradual, so that even children over 11 years old exert a positive effect on their mother's value of time. Young children have the largest effect on their mother's evaluation of her time when she has a college education (an increase of over 20 percent), but this effect diminishes to the same rate as high school mothers as the child grows older, with children over 11 years of age having no effect on (or perhaps even reducing) the value of their mother's time.

To verify these impressions I ran separate regressions in each education group. Table 4 contains the results where $\overline{W}$ is omitted from the regres-

TABLE 3

DETERMINANTS OF THE HOUSEWIVES' VALUE OF TIME (AN INTERACTION MODEL)

Explanatory Variables	Units	$\mu^* = a_0 + a_1 A_f + a_2 E_f$		$\mu^* = \overline{W}$			$\mu^* = $ est μ^*		
		Probit Coefficients	t-Scores	Probit Coefficients	t-Scores	Marginal Effect on $\hat{\mu}$ (%)	Probit Coefficients	t-Scores	Marginal Effect on $\hat{\mu}$ (%)
Constant	....	1.667	3.04	−1.894	−1.58	...	0.870	1.44	...
Income	$10,000/year	−0.858	−4.07	−0.850	−3.91	9.5	−0.823	−3.86	17.1
Age ≤ 30	Dummy (0, 1)	−0.446	−1.54	0.159	0.46	−1.8	−0.346	−1.18	7.1
Age ≤ 50	Dummy (0, 1)	−0.676	−2.60	−0.870	−3.24	9.7	−0.249	−0.85	5.1
Educ. = elem.	Dummy (0, 1)	1.048	−3.95	0.081	0.19	−0.9	−0.072	−0.18	1.5
Educ. = coll.	Dummy (0, 1)	0.742	2.52	−2.138	−2.43	23.8	−1.135	−1.82	23.3
Husband's age	10 years	−0.235	−2.15	−0.296	−2.60	3.3	−0.206	−1.84	4.2
Husband's educ. = elem.	Dummy (0, 1)	0.403	2.04	0.418	2.10	−4.6	0.410	2.08	−8.4
Husband's educ. = coll.	Dummy (0, 1)	−0.077	−0.36	−0.126	−0.58	1.4	−0.128	−0.59	2.6
Child < 3:									
Educ. = elem.	No.	−1.030	−1.66	−0.861	−1.31	9.6	−0.868	−1.32	17.8
Educ. = h.s.	No.	−1.052	−4.16	−1.077	−4.20	12.0	−1.071	−4.2	22.0
Educ. = coll.	No.	−2.028	−3.86	−1.880	−3.49	20.9	−2.012	−3.71	41.4
Child 3–5:									
Educ. = elem.	No.	0.008	0.01	0.114	0.20	−1.3	0.106	0.18	−2.2
Educ. = h.s.	No.	−0.768	−3.55	−0.768	−3.53	8.5	−0.783	−3.61	16.1
Educ. = coll.	No.	−0.735	−1.64	−0.443	−0.99	4.9	−0.536	−1.19	11.0
Child 6–11:									
Educ. = elem.	No.	−0.183	0.78	−0.186	−0.79	2.1	−0.215	−0.92	4.4
Educ. = h.s.	No.	−0.377	−2.71	−0.382	−2.71	4.3	−0.389	−0.28	8.0
Educ. = coll.	No.	−0.689	−2.47	−0.364	−1.22	4.0	−0.390	−1.32	8.0
Child 12–17:									
Educ. = elem.	No.	0.356	1.37	0.275	1.05	−3.1	0.235	0.88	−4.8
Educ. = h.s.	No.	−0.253	−1.56	−0.291	−1.78	3.2	−0.256	−1.58	5.3
Educ. = coll.	No.	−0.232	0.68	0.337	0.96	−3.8	0.369	1.06	−7.6
Potential wage	Dollars/hour	...	...	8.982	3.35	...	4.866	3.29	...
Likelihood-ratio test	....	151.7		169.0			165.0		
Degrees of freedom	....	20		21			21		
σ	Dollars/hour	...		.195			.278		
Housewives' mean value of time ($\hat{\mu}$)	Dollars/hour	1.74		1.74			1.38		
Mean wage offer (μ^*)	Dollars/hour	1.55		1.55			1.28		
$\hat{\mu}/\mu^*$	...	1.12		1.12			1.08		

TABLE 4

Determinants of Married Women's Labor-Force Participation by Education Groups: $\mu^* = \alpha_0 + \alpha_1 A_f + \alpha_2 E_f$

Explanatory Variables	Units	Elementary Education		High School Education		College Education	
		Probit Coefficients	t-Scores	Probit Coefficients	t-Scores	Probit Coefficients	t-Scores
Constant	....	0.852	0.68	1.715	2.41	1.550	1.15
Income	$10,000/year	−0.098	−0.25	−0.981	−3.11	1.380	−2.74
Age < 30	Dummy (0, 1)	−0.907	−1.05	−0.540	−1.55	0.269	0.34
Age ⩾ 50	Dummy (0, 1)	−0.075	−0.15	−1.339	−3.60	0.094	0.14
Husband's age	10 years	−0.522	−2.22	−0.153	−1.04	−0.120	−0.44
Husband's educ. = elem.	Dummy (0, 1)	1.156	2.54	0.200	0.08	3.330	2.35
Husband's educ. = coll.	Dummy (0, 1)	0.646	0.48	−0.910	−0.34	0.044	0.11
Child < 3 (net)	No.	−0.972	−1.39	−0.600	−2.06	−1.925	−2.68
Child 3–5 (net)	No.	0.093	0.13	−0.361	−1.35	−0.176	−0.28
Child 12–17 (net)	No.	0.460	1.10	0.117	0.54	0.820	1.62
Child	No.	−0.114	−0.45	−0.467	−3.19	−0.389	−1.22
Likelihood-ratio test (df = 10)	....	21.4	....	85.1	....	62.3	....

sions, and table 5, where $\overline{W}$ is included. The three separate regressions suggest that σ is increasing with education, implying that the variation in the price of time and/or the asking wage varies with education (and income). Similarly, the income effect becomes more pronounced the higher the woman's level of education is. Since education and income are positively correlated, this may indicate that the elasticity of the price of time with respect to income (0.03, 0.07, and 0.17, respectively) increases with income. There exist only slight differences among the three groups in the effect of the woman's age and her husband's age and education on $\hat{\mu}$,[28] but, as was observed earlier, there are considerable differences with respect to the child effect.

The importance of the effect of an additional child on the mother's value of time declines significantly with the child's age in all three education groups. However, the extent of this decline varies widely among the three groups. A child under age 3 increases the value of his mother's time by 5 percent if she has only elementary education, by 11 percent if she possesses high school education, and by almost 30 percent if she is a college graduate. On the other hand, a child older than 11 years decreases $\hat{\mu}$ if the mother has elementary or college education (by 3 and 6 percent, respectively) but increases it if the mother is a high school graduate (neither of the first two results is statistically significant).

Further evidence on the child effect can be found in the patterns of annual labor-force participation. Thus, I recomputed the interaction equation, replacing the previous dependent variable by a dummy variable reflecting annual participation. The evidence presented in table 6 supports our previous findings concerning the effect the husband's and wife's age and education, their family income, and the child's age have on the housewife's value of time. These findings, however, blur somewhat the observed interaction between the child's age and the mother's education.

It is still evident, however, that a child affects his mother's price of time if she is an elementary school graduate only when he is very young. However, the prior observed difference between high school and college graduates in the effect of a young child on his mother's value of time almost disappears. The decline in the child effect as he grows older where the mother is a college graduate is a little less sharp, and the decline of this effect where the mother is a high school graduate is even more gradual.[29]

Given the shaky nature of our findings about the interaction between the child's age and his mother's education, one could have dismissed them as a flicker of chance—an offspring of sampling variability. Still, it is

[28] Of particular interest is the strong negative effect husband's education has on $\hat{\mu}$ when the husband has attended only elementary school while his wife is a college graduate. This may suggest a reversal of roles in the household consistent with the principle of comparative advantage.

[29] Replacing the probit method by the tobit method and estimating the equations for weekly hours and annual weeks reproduced the same two distinctive patterns.

TABLE 5

Determinants of the Housewife's Value of Time by Education Groups: $\mu^* = \overline{W}$

Explanatory Variables	Units	Elementary Education		High School Education		College Education		Marginal Effect on $\hat{\mu}$ (%)		
		Probit Coefficients	t-Scores	Probit Coefficients	t-Scores	Probit Coefficients	t-Scores	Elem.	H.S.	Coll.
Constant	...	-4.432	-0.51	-2.134	-0.59	-3.247	-1.47	...	...	...
Income	$10,000/year	-0.088	-0.23	-0.977	-3.09	-1.555	-2.69	0.5	10.5	20.3
Age ≤ 30	Dummy (0, 1)	1.615	0.37	0.090	0.13	0.494	0.59	-9.5	-1.0	-6.4
Age ≥ 50	Dummy (0, 1)	-0.382	-0.54	-1.427	-3.74	-0.459	-0.64	2.2	15.3	6.0
Husband's age	10 years	-0.530	-2.25	-0.191	-1.26	-0.229	-0.78	3.1	2.1	3.0
Husband's educ. = elem.	Dummy (0, 1)	1.147	2.52	0.400	0.16	3.072	2.22	-6.7	-4.3	-40.0
Husband's educ. = coll.	Dummy (0, 1)	0.965	0.67	-0.071	-0.27	-0.155	-0.36	-5.7	0.8	2.0
Child <3 (net)	No.	-0.754	-1.03	-0.596	-2.04	-2.099	-2.79	4.4	6.4	27.3
Child 3–5 (net)	No.	0.088	0.13	-0.352	-1.30	-0.195	-0.30	-0.5	3.8	2.5
Child 12–17 (net)	No.	0.442	1.03	0.079	0.36	0.651	1.22	-2.6	-0.9	-8.5
Child	No.	-0.119	-0.47	-0.450	-3.05	-0.191	-0.56	0.7	4.8	2.5
Potential wage	Dollars/hour	17.066	0.62	9.299	1.09	7.679	2.79	...	...	...
Likelihood-ratio test (df = 11)	...	22.1	...	86.3	...	72.9	...	...	...	...
σ	Dollars/hour	0.0270	...	0.179	...	0.297	...	...	...	...
Housewife's mean value of time ($\hat{\mu}$)	Dollars/hour	1.48	...	1.66	...	2.27	...	...	...	...
Mean wage offer (μ^*)	Dollars/hour	1.36	...	1.51	...	2.03	...	...	...	...
$\hat{\mu}/\mu^*$	...	1.08	...	1.10	...	1.12	...	...	...	...
No. of observations	...	237	...	566	...	172	...	...	...	...

tempting to rationalize these patterns even at the risk that these patterns do not exist.

It was argued earlier that an increase in education increases the productivity of the woman in the household sector. This increase in productivity favors the production of child services if the technological improvement is "child-services biased" or if it is biased in favor of inputs which constitute a large fraction of child services' costs of production, such as the mother's time. Under these circumstances, other things being equal, the consumption of child services tends to increase with the wife's education. In particular, we should expect that given the number of children, the quality of the child is positively correlated with the mother's education (the amount of child services represented by each child increases with the mother's education). The increased demand for child services is reflected in an increased demand for the mother's time when the child is young for one or more of the following reasons:

a) The mother's productivity differential changes with the age of the child. There may be only very small differences in productivity between high school and college graduates when the child is young, but these differences widen as the child grows older and the production of quality calls for ever increasing inputs of human capital services. An increase in the demand for child services leads, therefore, to an increase in the demand for the mother's time when the child is young; but the increase in the demand for time becomes less and less pronounced as the differences in productivity increase.

b) There is a low elasticity of substitution between the mother's time and other inputs when the child is young. The production function of child services may call for some invariant amounts of the mother's time that are proportional to output, the mother having to establish herself as the prime figure in the baby's life in order to be an efficient producer of quality in the future.

c) Baby care may involve a large positive psychic income component when the baby is one's own, and considerable negative psychic income when the baby belongs to someone else. Thus, a college graduate may find it cheaper to care for her baby herself, rather than enter the labor force and hire a high school graduate to fill in her post. This psychic income component may change with the child's age, giving rise to a different reaction as the child grows older.

d) Finally, it can be argued that the production function of child services varies with education, because of imperfect information. This argument has been applied in the analysis of the effect of education on the quantity of children (Michael 1970), but it may equally hold true in the case of quality, college-educated mothers being more aware of the importance of infancy to the future development of the child.

All of our findings are based on the implicit assumption that the demand

TABLE 6

Determinants of the Housewives' Value of Time (An Interaction Model):
Dependent Variable = Annual Participation

Explanatory Variables	Units	$\mu^* = \overline{W}$			$\mu^* = $ est μ^*		
		Probit Coefficients	t-Scores	Marginal Effect on $\hat{\mu}$ (%)	Probit Coefficients	t-Scores	Marginal Effect on $\hat{\mu}$ (%)
Constant	...	-1.962	-1.48	...	1.298	2.17	...
Income	$10,000/year	-0.907	-4.37	8.5	-0.893	-4.33	15.3
Age ≤ 30	Dummy (0, 1)	0.620	1.80	-5.8	0.018	0.06	-0.3
Age ≥ 50	Dummy (0, 1)	-0.960	-3.64	9.0	-0.215	-0.73	3.7
Educ. = elem.	Dummy (0, 1)	0.411	0.88	-3.9	0.252	0.61	-4.3
Educ. = coll.	Dummy (0, 1)	-2.791	-2.85	26.3	-1.653	-2.51	28.2
Husband's age	10 years	-0.344	-3.08	3.2	-0.239	-2.20	4.1
Husband's educ. = elem.	Dummy (0, 1)	0.680	0.86	-8.2	0.164	0.85	-2.8
Husband's educ. = coll.	Dummy (0, 1)	-0.005	-0.02	0.0	-0.009	-0.04	0.2
Child < 3:							
Educ. = elem.	No.	-1.512	-1.86	14.2	-1.517	-1.86	25.9
Educ. = h.s.	No.	-0.898	-4.17	8.4	-0.892	-4.18	15.2
Educ. = coll.	No.	-1.057	-2.97	10.0	-1.196	-3.26	20.4
Child 3-5:							
Educ. = elem.	No.	-0.004	-0.01	0.0	-0.006	-0.01	0.1
Educ. = h.s.	No.	-0.987	-4.87	9.3	-0.998	-4.95	17.0
Educ. = coll.	No.	-0.252	-0.69	2.4	-0.356	-0.98	6.1
Child 6-11:							
Educ. = elem.	No.	-0.346	-1.46	3.2	-0.386	-1.61	6.6
Educ. = h.s.	No.	-0.330	-2.51	3.1	-0.341	-2.62	5.8
Educ. = coll.	No.	-0.262	-0.98	2.5	-0.284	-1.07	4.8
Child 12-17:							
Educ. = elem.	No.	0.309	1.19	-2.9	0.261	0.99	-4.5
Educ. = h.s.	No.	-0.406	-2.54	3.8	-0.363	-2.29	6.2
Educ. = coll.	No.	0.113	0.33	-1.1	0.162	0.48	-2.8
Potential wage	Dollars/hour	10.616	3.44	...	5.855	3.60	...
Likelihood ratio	...	189.6			186.9		
Degrees of freedom	...	21			21		
σ	Dollars/hour	.156			.193		
Housewives' mean value of time ($\hat{\mu}$)	Dollars/hour	1.65			1.25		
Mean wage offer (μ^*)	Dollars/hour	1.56			1.13		
$\hat{\mu}/\mu^*$	...	1.06			1.11		

TABLE 7

EFFECT OF CHILDREN ON THEIR MOTHER'S VALUE OF TIME

No. of Children <6 Years		No. of Children 6–11 Years			
		0	1	2	3+
0	No. of observations	518	102	49	12
	Probit coefficients	. . .	—0.628	—1.300	—0.659
	t-scores	. . .	—2.49	—3.53	—1.02
	Marginal effect on $\hat{\mu}$ (%)	. . .	7.8	16.2	(10.7)
1	No. of observations	81	50	26	4
	Probit coefficients	—0.856	—1.492	—2.439	—0.850
	t-scores	—2.30	—3.76	—3.12	—0.70
	Marginal effect on $\hat{\mu}$ (%)	10.7	18.6	30.2	(10.6)
2	No. of observations	52	30	12	4
	Probit coefficients	—2.063	—2.320	—0.860	0.562
	t-scores	—3.59	—2.92	—1.16	0.51
	Marginal effect on $\hat{\mu}$ (%)	25.7	28.9	(10.7)	(—7.0)
3	No. of observations	21	8	3	3
	Probit coefficients	—2.588	—1.414	—0.315	—12.451
	t-scores	—2.33	—1.21	—0.23	—0.06
	Marginal effect on $\hat{\mu}$ (%)	32.3	(17.6)	(3.9)	(155.2)

NOTE.—Terms in parentheses are insignificant at $\alpha = .05$.

for the mother's time increases uniformly with the number of children in a given age group.[30] To test this assumption, a set of 16 dummy variables was defined, specifying whether the women had zero, one, two, or three or more children younger than 6 years old and whether she had zero, one, two, or three or more children in the age group 6–11. The estimated effects of income, age, education, and husband's characteristics are almost identical with those presented in table 2 and thus are not reproduced here. Estimated effects of the new children variables on the weekly rate of participation are presented in table 7. These findings demonstrate once again the effect of the child's age on his mother's value of time, but contain very little evidence to refute our prior hypothesis. Similarly, an attempt to test the validity of the assumption within the various education groups, using a somewhat different definition of the children variable, did not come up with any persuasive evidence that will call for a reformulation of the

[30] I would hesitate to interpret any change in the time input per child associated with a change in the number of children within a given age group as evidence for returns to scale in the production of child services. Even if one adheres to the traditional assumption that, other things such as parents' income, education, and age being equal, an increase in the number of children does not result in a decline in the optimal quality of the child, quality being exogeneously determined, it is dangerous to claim that an observed decline in inputs per child in families with a larger number of children attests to increasing returns to scale. Other things being equal, the difference in the number of children may be explained in terms of differences in efficiency in the production of child services. Under these circumstances the observed decline in inputs per child is a spurious result.

TABLE 8

EFFECT OF CHILDREN ON THEIR MOTHER'S VALUE OF TIME:
MOTHER'S EDUCATION = HIGH SCHOOL

NO. OF CHIL- DREN <3 YEARS	NO. OF CHIL- DREN 3–5 YEARS		NO. OF CHILDREN 6–11 YEARS		
			0	1	2+
0	0	No. of observations	254	71	38
		Probit coefficients	. . .	−0.816	−1.465
		t-scores	. . .	−2.63	−3.48
		Marginal effect on $\hat{\mu}$ (%)	. . .	7.2	12.9
0	1+	No. of observations	33	33	12
		Probit coefficients	−1.154	−2.034	−2.874
		t-scores	−2.71	−4.07	−2.67
		Marginal effect on $\hat{\mu}$ (%)	10.1	17.9	25.2
1+	0	No. of observations	49	9	10
		Probit coefficients	−2.091	−1.100	−2.368
		t-scores	−4.52	−1.46	−2.13
		Marginal effect on $\hat{\mu}$ (%)	18.4	(9.7)	20.8
1+	1+	No. of observations	30	17	10
		Probit coefficients	−2.269	−3.199	−0.912
		t-scores	−3.78	−3.01	−1.21
		Marginal effect on $\hat{\mu}$ (%)	19.9	28.1	(8.0)

NOTE.—Terms in parentheses are insignificant at $a = .05$.

estimation procedure (the estimates of the regression for mothers with a high school education are presented in table 8).[31]

IV.   Some Concluding Remarks

Given our tentative conclusions, it is of interest to compare them with the indirect evidence contained in other studies of the labor-force participation behavior of married women. Leibowitz (1972) used the same body of data I did (the 1960 Census 1/1,000 sample) but focused only on the number of weeks worked. Not surprisingly, there is a great similarity between her results and the results reported in table 6. Leibowitz reports that children under 3 years old seem to be an equally forceful deterrent to the market-labor supply of women of all three education classes (elementary, high school, and college), that the labor supply of high school and college graduates is more sensitive to the existence of children older than 3 years than is that of elementary school graduates, and that there exists no signifi-cant difference between high school and college graduates in this regard. Smith (1972b) using the Survey of Economic Opportunity data, reports

[31] Table 8 does not include the estimated effects of income, age, and the husband's characteristics, since they are almost identical with those produced in table 5. I do not present the results for the other education groups because most of the "children" coefficients are insignificant.

that he could find little to support the notion that the effect of children on time inputs at home varies with education (it is, however, worth noting that Smith investigated the difference among husband's education classes).

Hill and Stafford used in their study the University of Michigan Survey Research Center's 1965 *Productive American* survey (Morgan, Sirageldin, Baerwaldt 1966). These data allowed them to investigate not only the effect of children on the hours mothers worked in the market but also the effect of children on time spent on "housework." They observe that while the effect of children on mother's market time is usually insignificant, children have a significant effect on the amount of "housework." This effect varies with socioeconomic status groups. While for the lowest socioeconomic group only children under 3 years old have any effect on their mother's "housework," older children also have an effect when the mother belongs to the higher status groups. It seems that the effect of a young child on time spent in "housework" is greater when the mother belongs to the highest status group than when she belongs to the second highest, but that these differences tend to diminish as the child grows older (it is difficult to tell whether this result is significant).

The record does little to confirm, but also does not directly contradict, the findings reported in the last section. There is no way to strengthen the claim that the effect of a child depends on the mother's education but by further research. A sample excluding families who do not have children less than 12 years old, and data, such as those from the Ohio Survey, containing a better measure of labor-force experience should help in sharpening the conclusions.

In summary, it seems that this paper poses more new questions than the old ones it answers. What, for instance, is the production function of child services and how does it change with the age of the child? What are the elasticities of substitutions in production between time and goods and how are they affected by the child's age? How does this productivity vary with the child's age?

Economists tend to regard children as a consumption (or production) durable, but in economic literature the tendency has been to analyze the demand for child services as demand for nondurables. I hope this paper may help in reversing this trend.

Appendix

CHARACTERISTICS OF WOMEN IN THE SAMPLE BY EDUCATION GROUP

	Total	Elementary School	High School	College
No. in sample	975	237	566	172
Percentage distribution	100.0	24.3	58.1	17.6
Wife's age distribution (%)	100.0	100.0	100.0	100.0
<30	22.3	7.2	28.6	22.1
30–49	49.8	37.5	53.9	53.5
50+	27.9	55.3	17.5	24.4
Husband's average age	45.1	54.8	41.8	42.6
Husband's education distribution (%)	100.0	100.0	100.0	100.0
Elementary school	32.4	75.9	21.9	7.0
High school	44.6	22.4	58.5	29.6
College	23.0	1.7	19.6	63.4
Average no. of children:				
<18	1.29	0.81	1.47	1.34
<3	0.25	0.11	0.28	0.32
3–5	0.24	0.10	0.30	0.27
6–11	0.46	0.30	0.50	0.49
12–17	0.34	0.30	0.39	0.26
Families with child (%):				
<18	46.9	24.1	55.1	51.2
<3	19.4	8.4	41.1	25.6
3–5	19.7	8.9	23.9	20.9
6–11	31.1	19.4	35.3	33.1
Average income*	6,774	5,667	6,756	8,356
Average potential wage:				
Arithmetic mean	1.998	1.836	1.868	2.653
Geometric mean	1.551	1.363	1.508	2.032
Participation rate (%)	31.6	23.2	32.7	39.5

* Wife's earnings excluded.

Comment

Robert E. Hall
Massachusetts Institute of Technology

Most of the papers in this volume consider the value of time as one of the determinants of the size of the family, but Reuben Gronau takes the opposite view in his paper. In part, this reflects different notions of the value of time. In the economic theory of fertility, the value of time is a predetermined parameter of the family's intertemporal budget constraint, a measure of the consumption foregone by having a child. In Gronau's terminology, the value of time is at least partly a measure of the location on the budget constraint chosen by the family and is therefore a measure of preferences of the family. It is important to keep this terminological distinction in mind in comparing his paper with the others.

An important feature of Gronau's paper is its explicit treatment of variations in preferences among the population. Although the other authors generally admit the existence of a diversity of preferences with regard to childbearing and working in the market, they develop the theory and empirical applications as if all families had the same preferences. The effects of variations in preferences appear only in the random disturbance which is added to the model almost as an afterthought. Gronau treats variations of tastes (in the form of variations in the value of time) as an integral part of his model from the start. He assumes that the value of time, $\hat{w}$, has a normal distribution whose mean depends on certain observed characteristics including the number of children in the family. He then estimates the parameters of this dependence by the statistical method of maximum likelihood, using data on participation in the labor force. The results are clearly suitable for predicting whether a woman is in the labor force given her characteristics, especially the number and ages of her children. A question which deserves more attention is whether the estimated equation can be given a structural interpretation. For example, could the equation be used to predict the effect on labor-force participation of a subsidy for childbearing? Gronau's introductory remarks seem to

489

suggest that his results might answer this question, but I think considerable caution is necessary.

In my view, a better way to account for variations in preferences would recognize that the size of the family and the labor-force participation of the wife are jointly determined. Suppose, for example, that there is a single axis along which tastes vary. One end of the axis is traditional, valuing large families and domestic activities, and the other is modern, valuing activities outside the home for both wife and husband. Suppose, further, that all families face the same prices and wages. Even then we will find a strong negative relation between family size and labor-force participation of the wife. Since no part of this relation is caused by variations in prices, we cannot give a structural interpretation to the results at all.

Now, in fact, not all of the variation in Gronau's sample is caused by variations in preferences along a single axis. To the extent that other sources of variation in the number of children are independent of the sources of variation in the decision to enter the labor force, the estimates will be closer to the underlying structural relation. As Gronau pointed out in the discussion, purely random variations in family size reduce the bias in his results. Unfortunately, we do not know how much bias remains.

Gronau has made an important contribution in this and a related paper by developing a method for estimating the true mean of the wage distribution facing a group of potential workers. The naïve estimate obtained by taking the average of the wages of those who work has a serious upward bias for any group with a rate of labor-force participation much less than one. The exclusion of nonparticipants generally eliminates observations of low wages from the average.

Effects of Child-Care Programs on Women's Work Effort

James J. Heckman

Columbia University and National Bureau of Economic Research

In recent years, Congress has considered a variety of work-subsidy programs designed to encourage work among welfare recipients. Many of these programs would subsidize individuals only if they work some minimum number of hours. Commonly used techniques cannot give direct answers to relevant policy questions since a tied offer is involved, and hence the offer cannot be treated as a simple wage change. The essence of the problem involves utility comparisons between two or more discrete alternatives. Such comparisons inherently require information about consumer preferences in a way not easily obtained from ordinary labor-supply functions.

To make such comparisons, I present a method for directly estimating consumer indifference surfaces between money income and nonmarket time. Once these surfaces are determined, they can be used to compare a variety of alternative programs to investigate whether or not there is scope for Pareto-optimal redistribution of income transfers and time, improving the general level of welfare of the community at large without reducing the welfare of individuals receiving income transfers. Knowledge of these indifference surfaces allows us to estimate reservation wages to estimate the value of nonworking-women's time (Gronau herein), labor-force participation functions, hours-of-work functions, and welfare losses due to income tax programs (Harberger 1964). I demonstrate that direct estimation of indifference surfaces allows us, at least in principle, to relax

This research was sponsored by National Science Foundation and Office of Economic Opportunity grants to the National Bureau of Economic Research. I gratefully acknowledge Ralph Shnelvar's skilled programming assistance. Orley Ashenfelter, Charles Betsey, Jacob Mincer, Marc Nerlove, Mel Reder, James Smith, Finis Welch, and Robert Willis provided useful comments. I thank Elisabeth Parshley for her assistance. I retain full responsibility for all errors in the paper. This paper has not undergone NBER staff review and is not an official publication of NBER, NSF, or OEO.

the conventional assumption that the wage rate is independent of hours of work. The separation of preferences and constraints allows us to estimate labor-supply functions for individuals affected by welfare systems and progressive income taxation.

The methodology presented here is similar in spirit to the pioneering work of Wald (1940). In his neglected paper, Wald suggested that information from different price situations can determine a family of indifference curves up to a second-order approximation. In this paper, I depart from Wald's methodology and suggest a plausible estimable specification for the marginal rate of substitution function between goods and leisure, the parameters of which are estimated by maximum-likelihood methods.

The particular focus in this paper is on the effect of work-related child-care programs. However, the methodology is more general and may be applied to a variety of work-subsidy programs.

I. An Anatomy of Proposals for Child-Care Programs

Proposals designed to relieve work-related child-care expenses have received the most attention. The Nixon administration has promoted several measures of this type. In 1971, an administration bill (HR 1) was introduced as "workfare" legislation designed to vacate welfare rolls by providing child care to working women. In 1972, tax laws were modified to give generous deductions for work-related child-care expenses if a woman worked 30 hours a week or more. Since some work requirement seems likely in any future legislation, I confine my analysis to such programs.

If a child-care program gives a woman with a child an hourly supplement for each hour she works, and she is free to spend it on any child-care source, the supplement is equivalent to a wage change of equal magnitude on both her hours of work and her decision to work. Given reliable estimates of work participation and hours-of-work functions, it is straightforward to make projections of the labor-supply effects of alternative programs.

If a cash grant or tax rebate is given to working women with children, it is no longer possible to proceed so simply. Given an agreed minimum number of hours which defines the condition of working, the wage rate for hours worked in excess of the minimum is not affected by such offers although the wage rate for hours worked below the minimum is increased. For currently working women who work in excess of the minimum, there are only income effects. If nonmarket time is a normal good, such offers will diminish their hours of work. Women working below the minimum will either increase their work to the minimum number of hours or will be unaffected by the program. For nonworking women market work is

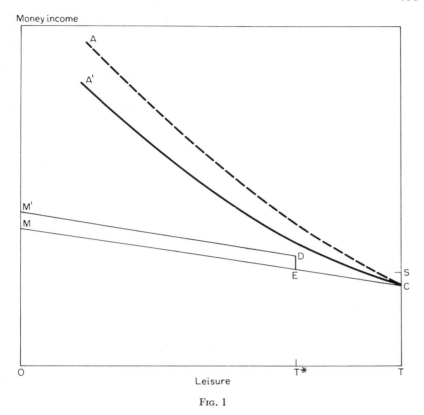

Fᴉɢ. 1

more attractive, and some portion of them will be expected to commence working.

Knowledge of the reservation wage (i.e., the minimum wage that a woman will accept to go to work) does not enable us to form estimates of program labor-supply effects. To see this, consider the familiar labor-leisure diagram reproduced in figure 1.

Since we only consider wage changes, we may compress all other goods into money income and construct an indifference curve between money income and nonmarket time or leisure. That there are many uses for nonmarket time is inessential to the argument as long as time is freely transferable among its uses.

Suppose that a woman (or family unit) can enjoy *TC* units of money consumption if she does not work and that her wage rate is independent of her hours of work so that the market opportunity line is *CM*. The individual (or family) is on indifference curve *AC* if the woman does not work. As drawn, the slope of the indifference curve at zero hours of work (i.e., the reservation wage) exceeds the offered wage rate (given by the slope of *MC*) so that the woman does not work. Suppose the government gives the woman supplement SC but requires her to work at least T^*T hours to qualify as working. As the figure is drawn, the woman will not take the offer. Her effective budget constraint becomes $M'DEC$, and the government subsidy does not improve her (or her family's) welfare. Raising the size of the subsidy or reducing the extent of required effort may reverse this conclusion.

In practice, tax rebates may be more complicated. If the "work requirement" becomes a minimum-earnings requirement which must be attained to be able to deduct child-care expenses, T^* will depend on the wage rate, shifting to the right for higher-wage women and making the program differentially more attractive to them, thus working in an opposite direction to the Nixon "workfare" proposals, *ceteris paribus*. Furthermore, since high-income families are more likely to itemize deductions, tax rebates for child care will tend to favor such families, although surely in the presence of these rebates more low-income families would find it profitable to itemize their deductions.

Suppose that the government operates on the supply side of the market by reducing the price per unit quality of work-related child care.[1] Remembering that the composite commodity theorem (Hicks 1946) allows us to aggregate all goods whose relative prices do not change into money income, a reduction in the price of work-related child care is equivalent to a shift in the indifference map of figure 1 from AC to $A'C$.[2] With lower price per unit quality, consumers can attain the same basket of market goods (including the quality of their work-related child care) with lower money income. Hence, $A'C$ lies below AC but the two curves meet at C because at this point no work is undertaken and the expenditure on work-related child care is zero. Its price is irrelevant to the height of the curve at this point but a reduction in the price of work-related child care reduces the slope of the curve at C (i.e., the reservation wage).[3]

---

[1] I ignore the practical difficulties in enforcing child-care provision solely for working time.

[2] This analysis assumes that individuals are free to choose the quality per unit hour of their child care. If for some reason the quality per hour is not an object of choice, the appropriate wage for labor-supply decisions is the wage net of hourly child-care costs. Only in this case can child care be treated as a cost of work. Since fixity here, as elsewhere, is unreasonable to impose a priori, I do not pursue this approach. However, I mention this case because it is tempting to treat child-care expense as a cost. Throughout this paper I assume that quality can be varied. That only rarely do children go unsupervised when a mother works is a statement about consumer preferences and not one about the need to consume a minimum amount of child-care quality. Using these expenditures as exogenous variables in regression analysis of labor supply when in fact they are an object of choice would bias the resulting labor-supply estimates.

[3] The proof of these propositions is relatively straightforward and is deleted for the sake of brevity. Note that, in the text, I only argue that the reservation wage for AC exceeds that for $A'C$. In general, the slope of AC might not exceed the slope of $A'C$ for any arbitrary hours-of-work position unless total expenditure on child-care quality rises with increasing hours of work along any iso-utility curve or, what amounts to an equivalent proposition, that work and quality per hour of purchased child care are Hicks-Allen substitutes.

Since the reservation wage has decreased more women will now work. If the price per unit quality is reduced for all child care, whether or not it is work related, the two curves no longer intersect at C, but if the expenditure on nonwork-related child care is small the assumption of intersection may remain plausible.

An important question for policy purposes is whether women receiving grants should be free to spend those grants on any form of child care service. In President Nixon's veto message (December 10, 1971) an unrestricted voucher scheme was proposed. However, the Secretary of the Department of Health, Education, and Welfare testified that the administration favored monitoring voucher use so that only "authorized" quality sources could be used for expenditure of child-care vouchers (March 27, 1972).[4] This distinction is quite important. It is well known that over 80 percent of working women with small children do not use formal day-care services (Low and Spindler 1968; Ruderman 1968). Since families are free to resort to the market, the implication of this fact is that the price per unit quality of these informal sources is less than that available in the market. If individuals are given cash grants or wage supplements and simultaneously are allowed to spend them only in the formal market, two offsetting effects are at work for women who have informal child-care sources available. On the one hand, a wage or income subsidy for working raises the attractiveness of work effort. On the other hand, the price change shifts the indifference curves (e.g., from $A'C$ to AC in figure 1) and tends to offset work incentives. A currently working woman who uses informal arrangements may either remain unaffected by the program or switch into the "formal" program. For policy purposes, it is important in assessing revenue costs to know how many will, in fact, switch over to formal sources.

II. Estimating Indifference Curves

If we knew a consumer's system of indifference curves and how this system shifts in response to variations in the price of child care, we could answer the policy questions raised in Section I. Since ordinary labor-supply functions are derived from indifference curves and their parameters may be used to estimate such curves, why bother to directly estimate them? My answer comes in four parts.

The first is that direct estimates of indifference curves allow us to derive the parameters of both hours-of-work and decision-to-work functions from a common set of parameters, enabling us to present a unified framework in which to interpret these two aspects of work behavior as well as giving an economy in parameters to be estimated. Second, by estimating

---

[4] Again, I abstract from the very real problem of enforcing quality standards.

indifference curves we can combine observations on all women, whether or not they work, and can avoid both the extrapolation error involved in using observations on working women to estimate the indifference surfaces appropriate to all women and the censored-sample problem that arises from estimating labor-supply parameters on a subsample of working women. A sample is censored when data are missing for some observations for reasons related to the model in question. Thus, for example, when a woman does not work we do not know what wage she would earn were she to work. The reason she does not work is that her reservation wage (i.e., the slope of the indifference curve at the zero hours-of-work position) exceeds the (unknown) available market wage. Estimates of wage functions and labor-supply functions based on subsamples of working women lead to biased parameter estimates (see Aigner 1971; Heckman 1974; Gronau, above). Third, by estimating indifference surfaces we can directly estimate reservation wages and can use these estimates as Gronau has done to estimate the value nonworking women place on their time. These estimates provide a "reasonableness" criterion with which to judge labor-supply estimates apart from the usual sign restrictions on income and substitution effects. We can further judge the desirability of any labor-supply specification by asking what reservation wage the functional form implies.

A fourth reason for directly estimating indifference curves is that the procedure allows for the separation of preferences from constraints. The ability to make this separation is less important if we are willing to make the conventional assumption that wage rates are independent of hours of work (e.g., Kosters 1966) but becomes quite important when we acknowledge the existence of progressive taxation, welfare regulations, and time and money costs of work. Thus, for example, even if the pretax wage is independent of hours of work, progressive income taxes create breaks in the budget constraint, since tax rates are set on income intervals and change discontinuously at boundaries. While it may be reasonable to assume smoothness in tastes, the resulting labor-supply functions may be quite intractable either to specify or to estimate (see Wales 1973). My procedure supplies a natural solution to this problem, and it admits of ready generalization to data from welfare populations which face similarly distorted budget lines.

A. Estimable Indifference Curves

Any indifference curve may be characterized as a locus of points or as an envelope of tangents. For my purposes, the latter characterization is more convenient. Given any initial consumption position, the reservation wage is the slope of the indifference curve at zero hours of work. If leisure is a normal good, higher initial endowments lead to higher reservation wages (Hicks 1946, pp. 28–29). We have seen that higher prices for child-care quality lead to higher reservation wages if a woman uses some child care when she works.

We may write the marginal rate of substitution function (or slope of the indifference curve) at a given level of prework income Y as

$$m = m(p_q, Y, h), \tag{1}$$

where we ignore variations in the price of other goods and where h is hours of work and p_q is the price per unit quality of child care. A consumer possesses a family of indifference curves indexed by level indicator Y, the no-work level of money income or consumption. We know that $\partial m/\partial Y > 0$ (normality of nonmarket time) and that $\partial m/\partial p_q > 0$ at the zero hours-of-work position. Moreover, it is plausible that this inequality remains valid for all values of h.[5] From diminishing marginal rate of substitution between goods and time we know that $\partial m/\partial h > 0$.

If a consumer faces a parametric wage W, at initial income position Y, she works if $W > m(p_q, Y, 0)$. If this inequality applies, the equilibrium position is characterized by

$$W = m(p_q, Y^*, h^*), \tag{2}$$

where Y^* is a level index appropriate to the equilibrium indifference curve and is nothing more than the amount of money income that would make the consumer indifferent to a choice between working h^* hours at wage rate W to gain total resources $Wh^* + Y$ or not working and re-ceiving income Y^*. As things stand, without knowledge of Y^*, we cannot deduce the equilibrium relationship between W and h. However, given Y^*, we know that equilibrium also requires that

$$Wh^* + Y = \int_0^{h^*} m(p_q, Y^*, h)dh + Y^*. \tag{3}$$

This equilibrium condition states that we may imagine moving the consumer to her final equilibrium position in one of two ways: giving her a flat hourly wage rate of W or giving her payment $Y^* - Y$ to be added to her initial resource endowment Y and compensating her by amount

$$\int_0^{h^*} m(p_q, Y^*, h)dh,$$

which is nothing more than the area under her (real) income-compensated supply curve for labor. Given W, h, Y, and p_q we may solve out for Y^*.

---

[5] Strictly speaking, it is possible that beyond certain values of h this expression becomes negative, but for this to occur would require decreasing quality expenditure on child care as hours of work increase, holding the consumer at the same level of utility (see n. 3 above).

From equation (2), if m is monotonic in Y^* we may solve for Y^* as a function of p_q, W, and h: $Y^* = g(p_q, W, h)$; using this value in equation (3), we implicitly define the labor-supply function by

$$Wh + Y = \int_0^h m[p_q, g(p_q, W, h), h]dh + g(p_q, W, h).$$

B. A Particular Functional Form for m

A wide variety of functional forms may be used to specify m.[6] One plausible specification, arrived at after considerable empirical experimentation, is to write

$$\ln m = \alpha_0 + \alpha_1 \ln p_q + \alpha_2 Y + \alpha_3 h + \alpha_4 Z + u \qquad (4)$$

where, as before, p_q is the price per unit quality of child care, Y is the prework level of income, h is hours of work, and Z is a vector of constraints to be discussed more fully below. A random variable designated "u," with zero mean and variance σ_u^2, reflects variation in preferences for work among individuals. The previous analysis leads me to the prediction that $\alpha_2 > 0$ (normality of leisure) and $\alpha_3 > 0$ (diminishing marginal rate of substitution between goods and leisure) and to the presumption that $\alpha_1 > 0$.

Manipulation along the lines discussed in section A shows that the resulting labor-supply function is implicitly defined by

$$u = \ln W - \alpha_0 - \alpha_1 P_q - \alpha_3 h - \alpha_4 Z$$

$$- \alpha_2 \left[Wh + Y - \frac{W}{\alpha_3} (1 - e^{-\alpha_3 h}) \right]. \qquad (5)$$

This labor-supply curve can become backward bending beyond a certain value for hours worked.[7]

This particular functional form is offered as a starting point. If it is grossly inconsistent with the data, either α_2 or α_3 will be negative, and the implied reservation wages, predicted from estimates of equation (4), will be unreasonable.

---

[6] One method is to let the data determine the functional form, in the manner of Box and Tidewell (1962) and Box and Cox (1964). I did not pursue that approach in this paper.

[7] Straightforward differentiation of eq. (5) shows that $\partial h/\partial W = \{(1/W) - \alpha_2[h - (1/\alpha_3)(1 - e^{-\alpha_3 h})]\}/[\alpha_2 W(1 - e^{-\alpha_3 h}) + \alpha_3]$. Clearly, $1/W$ is nonnegative; the denominator is positive, as is the first expression in brackets. To see why the latter assertion is true, note that when $h = 0$ the first bracketed expression is zero and that the partial of that bracketed expression with respect to h is $(1 - e^{-\alpha_3 h})$, which is clearly nonnegative since α_3 is positive and $h > 0$. Thus, it is possible, for suitably large values of h, for $\partial h/\partial W$ to become negative.

C. The Empirical Specification

To estimate the relevant parameters, we must specify the time dimension of the decision period and the vector of constraints (Z) which affect the marginal rate of substitution between goods and leisure. For the purposes of this paper, I use hours worked in a given year. In my judgment, this dimension is the appropriate one for analyzing the labor-supply behavior of women with children—the target population for child-care programs—since we are interested in knowing how they will respond to programs at the age when they have their children. I simplify the analysis by assuming that variations in the wife's labor supply do not affect the husband's earnings.[8]

We may follow a well-established tradition in the literature and postulate a one-period static model, or we may imagine the individual woman (or household) maximizing her lifetime utility function at each age of her life, subject to the constraints reflecting past decisions and chance events. The traditional static model may easily be shown to be a special case of a more general life-cycle model.

To simplify exposition and maintain comparability with previous studies in labor supply, I assume a one-period framework. After presenting the essential features of my procedure under this assumption, I then show how to incorporate more general intertemporal considerations.

In specifying the list of variables (Z) that would plausibly affect the marginal rate of substitution between goods and leisure, the presence of children of different ages and the price per quality unit of child care are the most obvious candidates.

Since children require time and effort, it is likely that the presence of children, especially young children, makes market work less attractive.[9] If a mother works and values her child's environment during her working hours, she will make child-care arrangements. The effect of children on the indifference system allows us to estimate what compensation is necessary to induce the woman to work and how the presence of children affects the hours worked by women.

An important empirical fact is that most working women with small children do not pay for their child care, or if they do pay they use informal sources and pay less than women using formal sources. Some economists have interpreted this fact as evidence of failure in the child-

[8] This assumption is widely used (see Gronau's paper above; Bowen and Finegan 1969), but it is clearly open to the criticism that the family labor supply is jointly determined. This assumption is equivalent to fixing the husband's nonmarket time institutionally or excluding it altogether from household preferences.

[9] For example, if children require at least some minimum amount of the mother's time, then presence of a child, viewed solely as a reduction in available time without an offsetting utility flow, would raise the reservation wage as long as consumption is a normal good.

care market.[10] I interpret these facts differently. It is plausible that some women have low-cost, nonmarket substitutes available to care for their children. Potential sources of low-cost child care are relatives living nearby, husbands with flexible working hours, and friends and neighbors. The availability of these low-cost sources lowers the reservation wage and makes it more likely that women having such sources available will work.

Unfortunately, it is not possible to directly measure the price per unit quality women must pay for their child care. It is plausible to argue that all families can resort to the market to purchase units of child-care quality but that some families have informal sources available at a lower price per unit quality than is available in the market. Measuring quality by expenditure, we may normalize the market price at unity.[11]

Suppose the distribution of informal prices among the population at large is given by

$$\ln p_q = X\beta + \varepsilon \tag{6}$$

where ε is a disturbance with zero mean and variance σ_ε^2 and where X is a vector of variables assumed to affect the price per unit quality of child care. If we assume that the family selects its source of child care by the rule $\min(0, \ln p_q)$, the marginal rate of substitution function at the prework level of utility for families using informal sources ($\ln m_I$) may be written as

$$\ln m_I = \alpha_0 + \alpha_1 X\beta + \alpha_2 Y + \alpha_3 h + \alpha_4 Z + u + \alpha_1 \varepsilon, \tag{7}$$

while the function for women using formal sources ($\ln m_{II}$) may be written as

$$\ln m_{II} = \alpha_0 + \alpha_2 Y + \alpha_3 h + \alpha_4 Z + u \tag{8}$$

where a restriction on the distribution of ε arises from the condition that

$$\ln p_q < 0 \rightarrow X\beta + \varepsilon < 0. \tag{9}$$

It is possible to estimate β/σ_ε from data on whether or not a family uses informal child care when the wife works. However, further information is required to estimate the coefficient α_1 alone,[12] although it is possible to estimate $\alpha_1\sigma_\varepsilon$. Since σ_ε is known to be positive, it is still possible to test the hypothesis that α_1 is positive.

[10] In particular, Nelson and Krashinsky (1972) argue this position.

[11] This procedure is clearly open to debate but is conventional. It assumes that quality is an objective characteristic and that units of quality are available at prices independent of the level of quality or the number of children.

[12] To see this, note that we can estimate $\alpha_1\beta$ from eq. (7) and $\alpha_1^2\sigma_\varepsilon^2$. Suppose, as is asserted in the text, we know β/σ_ε. Then, from the "intercept term" we can estimate $\alpha_1\sigma_\varepsilon$, and from the variance we can also estimate $\alpha_1\sigma_\varepsilon$ if ε is independently distributed from u, but we cannot determine α_1 independently from σ_ε unless we assume further information. One possible assumption is that $\sigma_\varepsilon = 1$.

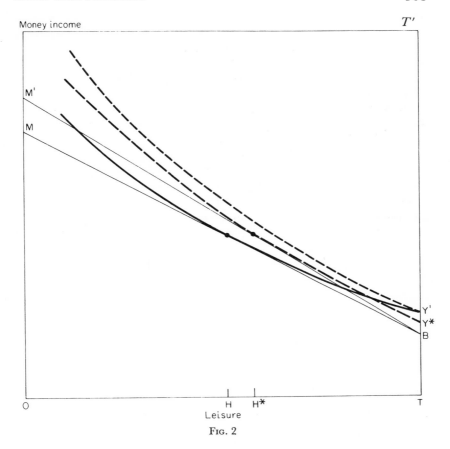

FIG. 2

Suppose that we can successfully estimate the relevant parameters of equations (7) and (8), including $\alpha_1\beta$. We can use these functions to address the problem, raised in Section I, of restricted vouchers. If a government program raises the wage rate of a woman with a child and insists that she use formal child-care sources, it is equivalent to a pure wage change for a woman already using formal sources but involves a change in p_q to unity (ln p_q to zero) for a woman not using these sources. From estimates of the indifference surfaces we can determine whether or not (on average) a woman using informal sources would switch to formal sources, because we can estimate the equilibrium position for hours of work in the case where she gets a higher wage but must pay a higher price for child care and the case where she abstains from the program. Having determined her equilibrium hours of work and wage rate in each situation, we can use equations (7) and (8) to determine the Y^* (the amount of money income without work that would put the women at the same level of utility as working would) implicit in each situation. Since Y^* serves as an index of utility, the situation with the higher Y^* is the preferred situation and will be chosen. This approach is exact only if a woman spends nothing on child care when she does not work; it is approximately correct if child care is a small fraction of family expenditure when the woman does not work.

To see this more explicitly, consider figure 2 which, is similar to figure 1. Consider a woman facing budget constraint MB and working TH hours. The government raises her wage but simultaneously increases the price of work-related child care. In terms of this diagram, the effect of the price change is to shift "preferences" as shown by the dashed lines and to raise the wage so that the new budget line becomes $M'B$. A new equilibrium position emerges along isoquant Y^*, using the "new" system of preferences. Using the estimated labor-supply curves, we can deduce that TH^* hours would be worked. Further, using the new equilibrium values, we can deduce level Y^* from equation (8). Then we can determine which situation is preferable since it is assumed that child-care expenditure is a negligible portion of consumer expenditure if a woman does not work, so that the effect of changes in the price of work-related child care is to pivot the indifference map around the intercept on the TT' axis. As the diagram is drawn, the woman abstains from the program since Y^* lies below Y'. Precisely the same methodology may be used in analyzing tied offers.

D.   Life-Cycle Modifications

Assume an additively separable lifetime-preference function which may be represented as the (time preference) discounted sum of utility functions at each age.[13] In this specification, utility at one age is not directly affected by variation in the consumption of time and goods at other ages. However, given a lifetime budget constraint, increasing consumption at one age reduces resources available at all other ages.

Within the context of this model, it is heuristically convenient (and formally correct) to imagine the consumer maximization process as a two-stage affair: subject to any income allotment, the family maximizes its utility within each period. To determine its allotment among periods, the family allocates income to equalize the marginal constribution to lifetime utility of an additional dollar of income in all periods if it is free to transfer resources among periods at a given borrowing and lending rate.

To account for the mobility of funds among periods, we must allow for saving or dissaving in a given period. For example, by borrowing against

[13] This specification is widely used in the optimal-growth literature (e.g., Shell 1967) and the operational-utility literature (e.g., Strotz 1957).

future income, households may enhance current resources. By saving, households transfer some of the current flow of resources to future time periods. Accordingly, the budget line in the conventional labor-leisure diagram (see fig. 1) must be shifted up (down) by the amount of net debt accumulation (saving) in the period. If saving is set at zero, the traditional one-period model retains its validity in a life-cycle context.[14]

Assuming that, there is no saving or borrowing is restrictive but traditional. It simplifies the analysis but is not necessary to it. Since the value of saving at any age depends on all prices, wages, and exogenous incomes, including the current wage, the current wage enters the analysis in two ways: as a direct determinant of work effort through the slope of the budget constraint, as in the traditional analysis, and as a determinant of the level of the given period's budget constraint through its effect on saving. Thus, in addition to the usual income and substitution effects confined to one period, there is an intertemporal income-transfer effect of wage change.

Introducing intertemporal considerations alters the simplicity of some of the previous analysis. In particular, consider the effect of a government program which raises the wage rate for women at an age at which children are present and simultaneously requires that the woman use approved child-care sources. In a one-period context we are able to solve the implicit level of utility, indexed by Y^*, under each program and are able to conclude whether or not a woman participates in such a program. In an intertemporal context we lose this simple feature because it is possible for Y^* to be lower in one time period but for the resulting earnings flow to be sufficiently higher to more than compensate the woman by enhancing her future utility. Thus, we encounter an intertemporal index-number problem.

To illustrate this point, consider figure 3. The dotted indifference curve represents the goods-leisure trade-off at a given period. The solid curves are the indifference system after the price per unit quality is raised. Consider a woman initially in equilibrium at point B', where TK is the flow of earnings from other sources minus saving in the period. Holding saving fixed, raise the wage so that the new equilibrium is B''. As drawn, B'' is at a lower level of current utility than B'. Yet, if earnings are increased sufficiently, the woman might still opt for the program, since she can transfer resources to future time periods and enjoy greater utility. If this is the case, the budget line shifts down by the amount of saving

[14] For a proof of these propositions, see Heckman (1971) where the Strotz "utility tree" is applied to an intertemporal labor-supply problem. The assumption of additive separability yields a traditional labor-leisure diagram for each period in the consumer's life cycle. The level of the budget constraint in each period is determined, in part, by exogenous income flows in that period and the net transfer of resources into or out of the period.

Money income

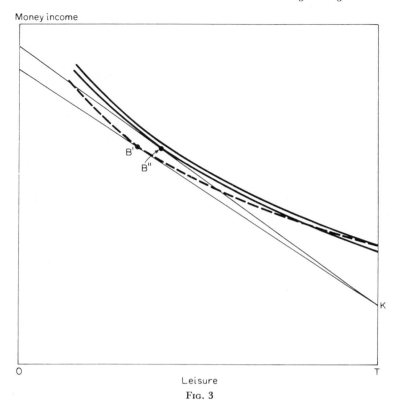

Leisure

Fig. 3

and the woman works more since leisure is a normal good in each time period. Note, however, that if saving is held fixed, and the wage increase leads to a higher level of utility in this period, the possibility of transferring funds among periods enhances the attractiveness of the program so that a woman will definitely choose to participate in it and thus we can estimate a lower bound on the number of program participants. Note, too, that we can estimate an upper bound: take all women who are made worse off in this period and assume they participate in the program. Solving their new equilibrium values, allowing for a transfer of resources among periods, we can solve for their new earnings. If we also estimate their expenditure on child care, their earnings net of child-care expenditure (in the new program) must increase for resources to be freed to transfer to subsequent periods. Then we know that only women who have such options will participate in the program, although clearly not all of these women will participate.

The only necessary modification in the previous empirical specification is the introduction of a savings function which is subtracted from the exogenous income flow Y. In the absence of data on saving, we are forced to estimate an implicit savings function.

III. Estimates

Estimates of the one-period model developed in Section II are presented below. The estimation of the complete life-cycle model is left for another occasion.[15]

Before presenting the estimates, it is useful to stress the restrictive nature of some of our assumptions. The assumption that the wage rate is independent of hours of work ignores the effect of progressive taxation. However, as noted in Appendix B, this defect can be remedied. A potentially more serious problem is our treatment of employer behavior. If firms incur fixed costs per worker, they are not indifferent to alternative combinations of men and hours per man which yield the same total man-hours (Rosen 1968). Under these circumstances, firms might pay higher hourly wage rates for longer weekly hours, at least up to certain levels of weekly hours worked. Thus, it is possible that the equilibrium condition invoked in Section II, that wage rates equal the marginal rate of substitution for working women, might not apply. This consideration creates a potentially important complication which is ignored in this paper.[16]

As Gronau notes, both the presence of fixed costs of work and the possibility of endogeneity of husband's earnings create potentially important biases. These factors could be accommodated within our framework but only at much higher computational cost.

The data used to form the estimates are from the National Longitudinal Survey (NLS) of 1966 for women aged 30–44. The functions are estimated on a subsample of women who were married, spouse present, with at least

[15] An attempt was made to estimate a full-fledged life-cycle model on a cross section of data. In principle, this is a simple exercise. In practice, since the necessary savings data are missing, it is necessary to specify a savings function, which depends on current and future wage rates and exogenous income flows and on current-asset variables. The additional wage and income variable introduced in eq. (5) as determinant of saving led to unstable estimates. In fact, plausible alternative specifications for the savings function lead to underidentification for some parameters. These results suggest that we are asking too much of the data from one cross section. When the second-year data from the National Longitudinal Survey are available, it will be possible to estimate a separate savings function and get reliable estimates of the complete model.

[16] If there were a fixed standard work week, the analysis of Section II could be generalized to accommodate this complication. For those working fixed hours, and not moonlighting, the marginal rate of substitution evaluated at the standard work week (which depends, among other things, on the income flow from work and length of time at work) is less than the potential moonlighting wage, while for moonlighters the opposite is true. Thus, as shown in Appendix B, it is possible to gain some information about consumer preferences even when the marginal equality conditions no longer apply.

one child under age 10. This subsample is chosen for two reasons. The principal reason is that it is a population obviously affected by child-care programs.[17] Previous studies (Ruderman 1968; Bowen and Finegan 1969) and Gronau's paper herein suggest that only younger children exert an important retarding effect on women's work effort. A second reason for this choice of sample is closely related to the first. The NLS data give information on the availability of informal sources of child care, defined as care by relatives or zero (dollar)-cost day care. A unique feature of these data is that, in addition to questions asked on the type of child care used by working women, questions concerning the availability of informal sources were asked of nonworking women as well. It is computationally and conceptually more difficult to incorporate in our sample women for whom child care is an irrelevant issue.

In Appendix A I present an estimation method that incorporates the information that (1) the reservation wage is less than the offered wage and (2) the price per quality unit for child care is less than that available in the market. Both types of sample-inclusion criteria create the potential of censoring bias, but this is avoided by the procedure used.

By the construction of the sample, the presence of at least one child younger than age 10 is assured. To allow for scale effects, I created separate variables for number of children aged 0–3, 4–6, and 7–10. Other children variables led to unstable estimates. Husband's earnings are added to net worth multiplied by an estimable flow coefficient to approximate the flow of exogenous income relevant to a one-period model.

Michael argued earlier in this book that education may affect the household's ability to organize and produce its final consumption. To accommodate this hypothesis, I present estimates which measure the effect of the education (in number of years) of the wife on the marginal rate of substitution between goods and leisure. I contrast these results with more conventional estimates which exclude education from household preferences.

In order to include in the sample nonworking women for whom wage data are missing, it is also necessary to estimate a function for the market wages of all women. Its specification is kept simple. The natural logarithm of wages is postulated to depend on education and labor-market experience.[18] I explicitly allow for correlation between the disturbances of the preference function and the wage function.

A novelty of the procedure used is the explicit estimation of an informal child-care price function (discussed in Section II). Previous studies (e.g.,

---

[17] However, the most relevant policy population is women on welfare who have young children. Small sample size and ignorance of the features of the welfare system confronting poor mothers precluded estimation on this sample.

[18] For a discussion of the experience variable, see the paper by Mincer and Polachek in this volume. I aggregated their segments of experience into a total-experience variable.

Bowen and Finegan 1969) have shown that children aged 14–18 serve as stimulants to married female labor-force participation, and it is plausible that they supply a ready source of child care. Similarly, it is plausible that relatives living in the home, husbands with flexible working hours, and friends serve as low-cost sources of child care (see Low and Spindler 1968; Ruderman 1968). Accordingly, these determinants of the quality-adjusted price of day care are incorporated in the estimation.

To capture the effect of relatives on the price of child care, I created a dummy variable which assumes the value of one when a sister, parent, or grandparent lives in the household. The number of children aged 14–18 is included as a variable. As a crude measure of the flexibility of the husband's hours and his availability for child care, I use the number of hours he works in a week. As a measure of the availability of low-cost care from friends and relatives living nearby, I use two variables: a dummy which assumes the value of one when a woman has lived in a Standard Metropolitan Statistical Area (SMSA) all her life and a continuous variable measuring the number of years a woman has lived in an SMSA. Both are expected to depress the price of child care.

The estimates are presented in table 1. Column 1 reports estimates of the parameters for whites obtained by excluding the effect of education from household preferences, while column 2 shows the effect of including education. Comparable results for blacks are in columns 3 and 4.

Consideration of column 1 coefficients for whites will illustrate the meaning of the coefficients. A unit increase in the logarithm of the quality-adjusted price of child care divided by its standard error raises the marginal rate of substitution by 14.3 percent. Each $10,000 of exogenous income raises the marginal rate of substitution by 22 percent. Each 1,000 hours worked raises the marginal rate of substitution by 51 percent. An additional child aged 0–3 raises the marginal rate of substitution by 24.3 percent; an additional 4–6-year-old child raises the marginal rate of substitution by 8.4 percent, while an additional child aged 7–10 raises it only 2 percent. The coefficient on assets is a number converting the stock of net worth into a flow yield. Thus, if a family has $10,000 worth of assets, the estimated income flow is $380. This flow is added to other exogenous income flows in calculating the effect of income on the marginal rate of substitution.

Similarly, the coefficients for the quality-adjusted price of child care show the effect of the associated variables on percentage changes in this price divided by the standard error of the price distribution. Older children, relatives living in the home, and length of residence in the SMSA all have the expected negative effects on this price while the other coefficients cannot be deemed significant by conventional standards.

The estimates for the market-wage function show the effect of the associated variables on the natural logarithm of market wages. The population correlation coefficient measures the interequation residual correlation between the market-wage function and unmeasured tastes for work.

In comparing columns 2 and 1, it is seen that while conventional significance tests suggest that education should be included in household preferences, its inclusion alters few coefficient estimates. The only notable exception is that the effect of education on market wages is increased and is not significantly different from the effect of education on reservation wages. This suggests that for white women with at least one child younger than age 10, better-educated women do not work in the labor force as much as less educated women. For comparable black women, better-educated women are more likely to work.

The most useful way to summarize these numbers is to consider their potential application. Making the bold assumption that the preference parameters for married black women with spouse present are those appropriate to all black women, we can investigate the possibility of using tied child-care offers to alleviate welfare dependency. Consider a group of black women currently eligible for an annual welfare payment of $3,000. For the sake of illustration, we assume that each woman has three children—one in each of our estimated age intervals. We assume that each woman uses informal child-care sources and that she has one child from 14 to 18 years old, one older relative living in the home, and that she has lived in her current SMSA for 8 years. We further assume that each woman has no asset income and 10 years of schooling.

Each woman has a choice of working or taking welfare. The geometric mean indifference curve appropriate to potential welfare recipients is sketched as AA' in figure 4. Fifty percent of the potential welfare recipients have an indifference curve emanating from A ($=\$3,000$) which lies below AA'. Twenty-five percent of the group have an indifference curve starting at A which lies below AC. This latter group may be termed the most "work prone" because they require less compensation to be induced to work. Again, solely for the sake of argument, suppose that each woman has an identical wage of $1.50 per hour which she can earn in the market. More realistically, we might assume a distribution for wages as well.

In this extreme example not all women will choose to go on welfare. The few who are not on welfare will be observed to work long hours at low wages. Again, solely for the sake of argument, suppose no women work. Suppose the government offers an unrestricted "day-care" voucher to a woman if she works 1,500 hours. From budget line OB we can see that if the woman were to work 1,500 hours at $1.50 per hour she would earn $2,250. The minimum compensation beyond her own earnings that would be necessary to induce half the women to leave welfare is the distance $B''B'$ ($=\$3,300$). Note, however, that if a $2,560 child-care subsidy were offered ($=B'B'''$) 25 percent of the women would leave

TABLE 1

PARAMETER ESTIMATES FOR BLACKS AND WHITES
(MARRIED, SPOUSE PRESENT, WITH AT LEAST ONE CHILD LESS THAN 10)

	Whites		Blacks	
	(1)	(2)	(3)	(4)
Parameters of the marginal rate of substitution:				
Intercept, α_0	-0.046 (-2.83)	-1.2453 (3.37)	0.086 (1.19)	-0.233 (-1.56)
Price effect of child care, α_1	0.143 (2.66)	0.110 (2.05)	0.297 (8.11)	0.237 (9.6)
Income term, α_2	0.22×10^{-4} (2.62)	0.198×10^{-4} (2.43)	0.13×10^{-4} (1.43)	0.12×10^{-4} (14.9)
Hours effect, α_3	0.51×10^{-3} (4.88)	0.487×10^{-3} (3.83)	0.43×10^{-3} (4.2)	0.314×10^{-3} (5.98)
No. of children aged 0–3, α_{41}	0.243 (3.32)	0.234 (2.95)	0.124 (5.26)	0.076 (5.84)
No. of children aged 4–6, α_{42}	0.084 (2.11)	0.081 (2.59)	0.040 (1.82)	0.022 (1.37)
No. of children aged 7–10, α_{43}	0.020 (0.66)	0.032 (2.09)	-0.036 (-2.1)	-0.031 (1.37)
Wife's education, α_5		0.100 (14.5)		0.054 (2.14)
Flow coefficients on assets, S	0.038 (1.29)	0.024 (0.88)	0.159 (0.05)	0.129 (0.89)
Standard deviation, σ_u	0.668 (6.73)	0.598 (5.1)	0.607 (8.4)	0.492 (14.6)
Parameters of the quality-adjusted price of child care:				
Intercept, $\beta_0/\sigma_\varepsilon$	0.063 (3.43)	0.064 (3.47)	0.023 (0.845)	0.026 (1.00)
Lived in SMSA all your life? $\beta_1/\sigma_\varepsilon$*	0.069 (0.4)	0.063 (0.365)	0.2459 (1.2)	-0.082 (-0.41)
No. of children aged 14–18, $\beta_2/\sigma_\varepsilon$	-0.283 (-4.71)	-0.279 (-4.63)	-0.084 (-1.4)	-0.106 (-1.8)
Relative living in home?, $\beta_3/\sigma_\varepsilon$†	-0.666 (-2.92)	-0.666 (-2.92)	-0.424 (-2.1)	-0.405 (-2.1)
Husband's hours of work last week, $\beta_4/\sigma_\varepsilon$	0.0012 (0.349)	0.0012 (0.334)	0.003 (0.5)	0.0001 (0.298)
Length of residence in this SMSA, $\beta_5/\sigma_\varepsilon$	-0.0122 (-2.12)	-0.0120 (-2.09)	-0.0138 (-1.69)	-0.45×10^{-2} (-0.56)
Parameters of the wage function:				
Intercept, m	-0.266 (1.49)	-0.815 (-7.99)	-0.149 (-0.99)	-0.329 (-2.22)
Education, n_1	0.059 (4.45)	0.103 (13.0)	0.0454 (3.37)	0.080 (5.6)
Market experience, n_2	0.026 (8.63)	0.027 (10.3)	0.0137 (7.2)	0.011 (8.53)
Standard deviation, σ_v	0.393 (26.01)	0.381 (28.2)	0.487 (23.2)	0.433 (33.7)
Population correlation between the disturbances of tastes (u) and wages (v), ρ	0.598 (5.36)	0.566 (3.51)	0.85 (20.1)	0.91 (70.4)

TABLE 1 (*Continued*)

	NUMBER OF OBSERVATIONS	
	Whites	Blacks
Do not work, would use formal sources‡	248	87
Do not work, would use informal sources	148	62
Work and use formal sources	104	45
Work and do not use formal sources	293	187
Total..	793	381

SOURCES.—Data are from 1967 National Longitudinal Survey of Work Experience of Women aged 30–44. For a description of these data, see *Dual Careers* (Parnes, Shea, Spitz, and Zeller 1970).
NOTE.—Numbers in parentheses are asymptotic normal statistics estimated from the information matrix.
* = 1 if yes; 0 if otherwise.
† = 1 if sister, parent, grandparent; 0 if otherwise.
‡ Formal sources are defined as paid care at child-care centers and care at a nonrelative's home. Informal sources include all other sources. Nonworking women are classified into two groups: those looking for work (group B) and those not looking for work (group C). Everyone in the first group was asked whether or not child-care arrangements would be necessary and what type of arrangements would be made if they were necessary. This allowed for a classification broadly consistent with the classification of actual use for working women. Information on the group not looking for work is more scarce. To be included in the sample they had to answer "yes" or "it depends" to a hypothetical question about whether they would work if a job were offered to them (Parnes et al. 1970, question 30a, p. 260) and a subsequent question on need for child care and what form would be used (question 31). To determine whether the composition of the sample was biased by using this inclusion criterion, separate discriminant functions were fitted by race for all married women with at least one child younger than 10 years old in group C. Respondents were distinguished from non-respondents by a set of variables including the number of children in different age intervals, assets, age and education of wife, and husband's earnings. The only significant discriminants for both races were assets and the number of children aged 0–3 years. Both variables tended to be larger for nonrespondents. Accordingly, the coefficient estimated reported in this table may be biased. In my opinion, the added information about potential child-care sources for nonworking women was worth the risk of bias.

welfare voluntarily, and the welfare cost to society at large would diminish by $440 per person who leaves welfare.[19] Clearly, in this case there is scope for using tied offers to reduce welfare dependency. The transfer-minimizing policy is Pareto optimal and is straightforward to determine.[20] Note, too, that we can determine what proportion of women will work beyond the minimum number of hours needed to qualify for the program. Consider a woman whose indifference curve is AC. At 1,500 hours of work, the slope of the indifference curve (at B''') exceeds $1.50, so that if she were given slightly more than $2,540 she would leave welfare and work

[19] Remember that it was assumed that all women were on welfare. In reality, only some fraction of this 25 percent would be.

[20] For each value for hours worked, h, a child-care bonus B determines a proportion of welfare clients $P(B)$ who will leave welfare, given that bonus. Clearly, B lies between zero and $3,000, the welfare payment. The mean transfer to the group is $P(B)B + [1 - P(B)]($3,000)$. Minimizing mean transfer is equivalent to minimizing group transfer since I assume no discrimination within the group is possible. For each h, there will exist a B which minimizes mean transfer, and the minimum mean transfer for all h can be determined. Thus, knowing the distribution of preferences, it is possible to simultaneously determine B and h. Under general conditions, there exists a unique Pareto-optimal policy for tied welfare offers which can be estimated from the data. Note that, in the example, it is assumed that no one works initially. To determine the Pareto-optimal tied offer if some work, it is necessary to subtract the transfers paid to those who would have worked without a child-care bonus. Note that Pareto optimality is used here in the restricted sense of improving community welfare from a current position; it is not the global optimality concept of general equilibrium theory.

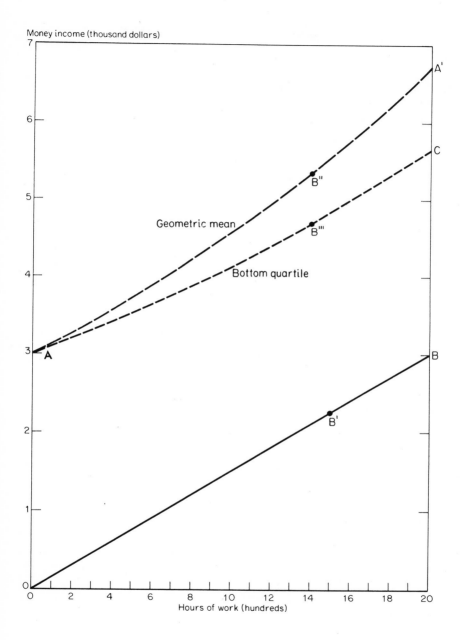

Fig. 4

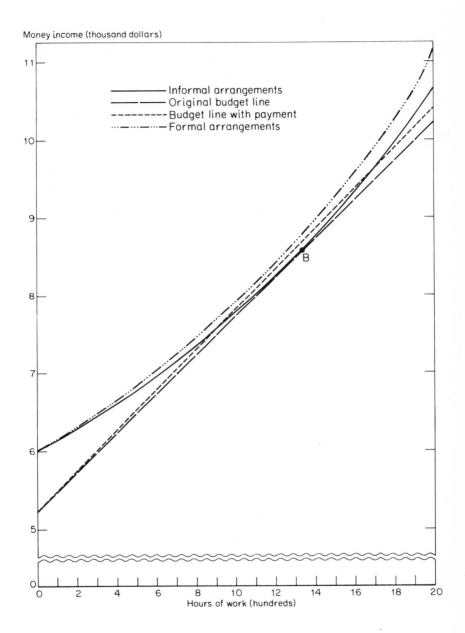

Money income (thousand dollars)

Hours of work (hundreds)

— Informal arrangements
—— Original budget line
------- Budget line with payment
·—··—··— Formal arrangements

Fɪɢ. 5

exactly 1,500 hours. The reason she would not work longer hours is that her reservation wage at 1,500 hours exceeds her offered wage of $1.50.

As a further illustration of the use of the empirical results, consider a representative working white woman, using informal child-care sources, whose husband earns $5,500 per annum. Suppose that she has 12 years of schooling, assets of $5,000, and two children, one from 0 to 3 years old and one from 4 to 6. In figure 5, we plot a solid system of indifference curves appropriate to the case of lower prices for informal child care, drawn on the assumption that the woman has not lived in the SMSA all her life, that her husband works 40 hours a week, that a relative lives in the home, and that she has lived in her current SMSA for the last 10 years. Superimposed on this system is a broken-line indifference curve appropriate to the use of child care purchased in the formal market.

As the lines are drawn, the woman is in equilibrium at point B earning $2.30 per hour. Suppose the government raises her wage to $2.40 per hour by providing a 10¢ per hour child-care subsidy conditional on her use of formal sources. Will she take the offer? In this case, the answer is no. The dashed "program budget line" lies below the iso-utility contour for formal arrangements, equivalent in utility terms to the indifference curve for informal arrangements on which she previously was in equilibrium. Hence, she abstains from the program. Given the parameters of the distributions of the curves, we can make similar statements for groups as a whole and hence can estimate the proportion of working women currently using informal child-care sources who will switch to formal sources if only restricted vouchers are available.[21]

IV. Summary and Suggested Extensions

The economics of tied work payments and methods for estimating the effect of such payments on labor supply have been discussed in this paper. It is important to distinguish the conceptually easier problem of modeling the response to tied offers from the more demanding problem of providing reliable estimates of the appropriate behavioral functions. It has been shown that knowledge of consumer preferences is necessary to estimate program effects, and methods have been suggested for determining these preferences.

By directly estimating indifference curves, hours of work and work-participation equations have been derived from a common set of parameters. The separation of preferences from constraints allows us to estimate the labor-supply parameters of individuals from data generated by non-

[21] To answer both policy questions fully would require consideration of the distributions of wage rates, preferences, and prices for child care. Such projections would be suspect at this stage of this research because the full tax-adjusted life-cycle model has not been estimated.

standard constraints, such as the broken-line budget constraints resulting from the tax system, where a tractable labor-supply function does not exist. At the cost of estimating a savings function, we can embed the traditional one-period model of labor supply into a life-cycle model. Both the distribution of tastes for work and the distribution of market wage rates for the population at large are estimated. The estimates suggest that wage rates are strongly correlated with preferences for work so that simple "reduced-form" labor-supply functions obtained by regressing hours worked on wage rates give biased estimates. In forming estimates, a statistical procedure is employed which avoids this bias and the censoring bias discussed above.

Perhaps the most controversial aspect of this study is the treatment of the choice of the mode of child care. A latent distribution of informal prices for child care is assumed to exist in the population at large. It is further assumed that a competitive market in child-care quality exists so that individuals facing informal prices in excess of the competitive price use formal child-care sources if they work. The decision to work and the decision to use formal sources are related in the sense that the price of child care is a determinant of the decision to work and of the actual hours worked. This model enables us to use information on hours of work and the decision to work, in combination with direct information on the form of child care used by working mothers, to estimate the determinants of the mode of child care mothers select. The empirical results are consistent with this model but have not been tested against possible alternative models.

If families value the development of their children, and the mother's time is an important input into this development, custodial child care might be chosen if a mother works a limited number of hours but might be unacceptable if she works full time. If formal sources provide higher-quality day care, the decision to work, the length of the work week, and the choice of the mode of child care are jointly determined and mutually dependent on the wage rate and the prices of formal and informal care. Although this alternative model is much more difficult to estimate, it is conceptually more attractive and contains the present model as a special case. For these reasons it is an approach that might prove fruitful in future research on the economics of child care.

Appendix A

The Estimation Procedure

The parameters of the marginal rate-of-substitution function (4) are estimated by a maximum-likelihood technique developed in another paper (Heckman 1974). In that paper, I present a method that permits observations on nonworking women to be pooled with observations on working women to estimate hours-of-work functions, work-participation functions, and wage functions for all women. The procedure avoids the bias that results from estimating wage and hours-of-work functions using standard regression techniques on censored subsamples of working women.

Four distinct subsamples are considered here in contrast to the two subsamples I considered earlier (1974). Some working mothers use informal child-care sources while others use formal sources. Potentially, the same dichotomy exists among nonworking women, and a unique feature of the data used here is that for many nonworking women it is possible to identify which mode of child care they would use if they were to work.

Letting W_i be the wage rate for the ith woman and using the notation of the text, woman i works and uses formal sources of child care if

$$X_i\beta + \varepsilon_i > 0 \text{ and } \ln W_i > \alpha_0 + \alpha_2 Y_i + \alpha_4 Z_i + u_i, \qquad (A1)$$

where $X_i\beta + \varepsilon_i$ is the quality-adjusted price of child care. Woman i works and uses informal sources if

$$X_i\beta + \varepsilon_i < 0 \text{ and } \ln W_i > \alpha_0 + \alpha_1 X_i\beta + \alpha_2 Y_i + \alpha_4 Z_i + \alpha_1 \varepsilon_i + u_i. \qquad (A2)$$

For nonworking women who would use formal sources,

$$X_i\beta + \varepsilon_i > 0 \text{ and } \ln W_i < \alpha_0 + \alpha_2 Y_i + \alpha_4 Z_i + u_i, \qquad (A3)$$

while for nonworking women who would use informal sources

$$X_i\beta + \varepsilon_i < 0 \text{ and } \ln W_i < \alpha_0 + \alpha_1 X_i\beta + \alpha_2 Y_i + \alpha_4 Z_i + \alpha_1 \varepsilon_i + u_i. \qquad (A4)$$

To circumvent the practical difficulty that wage rates are missing for nonworking women, I postulate a wage function for the ith individual,

$$\ln W_i = m + nk_i + v_i, \qquad (A5)$$

where k_i includes determinants of market wages such as education and labor-market experience, and where v_i is a disturbance term with zero mean and variance σ_v^2.

To derive the appropriate sample likelihood function, consider the joint density of the disturbances $h(u, v, \varepsilon)$. For a working woman who uses formal sources, the density function for u, v, and ε for the domain defined by (A1) is

$$\frac{h(u, v, \varepsilon)}{Pr(m + nk - \alpha_0 - \alpha_2 Y - \alpha_4 Z > u - v \wedge \varepsilon > -X\beta)}, \qquad (A6)$$

where $Pr(\cdot)$ denotes the probability of event "$\cdot$". Assuming independence between ε and other disturbances, but allowing for dependence between u and v, we may write $h(u, v, \varepsilon) = g(u, v)s(\varepsilon)$, so that the conditional density of u, v, and ε, given that a woman works and uses formal sources, may be written as

$$\frac{g(u, v)s(\varepsilon)}{Pr(m + nk - \alpha_0 - \alpha_2 Y - \alpha_4 Z > u - v)Pr(\varepsilon > -X\beta)}. \qquad (A7)$$

The density function for observed hours of work, wages, and the event "use of formal child-care services" is readily derived. To simplify the exposition, I present only the distribution for u, v, and the use of child care, which is

$$\frac{g(u, v) \int_{-X\beta}^{\infty} s(\varepsilon)\, d\varepsilon}{Pr(m + nk - \alpha_0 - \alpha_2 Y - \alpha_4 Z > u - v)Pr(\varepsilon > -X\beta)}. \qquad (A8)$$

For working women who use informal sources, it is more convenient to work with the density function

$$b(u + \alpha_1 \varepsilon, v, \varepsilon), \tag{A9}$$

which can easily be derived from h. For expository ease, it is convenient to define $u + \alpha_1 \varepsilon = c$. Clearly, c is not independent of ε. This implies that the conditional distribution of c, v, and the dummy variable associated with the "use of informal sources" may be written as

$$\frac{\int_{-\infty}^{-X\beta} b(c, v, \varepsilon) \, d\varepsilon}{Pr(m + nk - \alpha_0 - \alpha_1 X\beta - \alpha_2 Y - \alpha_4 Z > c\Lambda\varepsilon < -X\beta)}. \tag{A10}$$

We may combine observations described by (A8) and (A10) to form the *conditional* likelihood function for working women. To incorporate sample information for nonworking women, we know that the appropriate probability statement for nonworking women who would not use formal sources is

$$Pr(m + nk - \alpha_0 - \alpha_1 X\beta - \alpha_2 Y - \alpha_4 Z < c\Lambda\varepsilon < -X\beta), \tag{A11}$$

while for nonworking women who would use formal sources the appropriate probability statement is

$$Pr(m + nk - \alpha_0 - \alpha_2 Y - \alpha_4 Z < u - v\Lambda\varepsilon > -X\beta). \tag{A12}$$

We may combine observations described by (A8) and (A10) with observations on nonworking women by weighting the conditional densities by the probability of the conditioning event.

To form the sample likelihood function in terms of observable variables, substitute for u and v from equations (5) and (A5), respectively. The Jacobian of transformation is $|\alpha_3 + \alpha_2 W(1 - e^{-\alpha_3 h})|$. It is straightforward to verify that since $h \geq 0$, the transformation is one-to-one since $\alpha_2 > 0$ and $\alpha_3 > 0$. Ordering the observations so that the first T_{WF} work and use formal sources, the next T_{WI} work and use informal sources, the subsequent T_{NWF} do not work and would use formal sources, while the last T_{NWI} do not work and would use informal sources, the sample likelihood may be written as

$$= \prod_{i=1}^{T_{WF}} |\alpha_3 + \alpha_2 W_i(1 - e^{-\alpha_3 h_i})| g(u_i, v_i) \int_{-X_i\beta}^{\infty} s(\varepsilon) \, d\varepsilon$$

$$\prod_{i=T_{WF}+1}^{T_{WI}+T_{WF}} |\alpha_3 + \alpha_2 W_i(1 - e^{-\alpha_3 h_i})| \int_{-\infty}^{-X_i\beta} b(c_i, v_i, \varepsilon) \, d\varepsilon$$

$$\prod_{i=T_{WF}+T_{WI}+1}^{T_{WF}+T_{WI}+T_{NWF}} Pr(m + nk_i - \alpha_0 - \alpha_2 Y_i - \alpha_4 Z_i < u - v) Pr(\varepsilon > -X_i\beta)$$

$$\prod_{i=T_{WF}+T_{WI}+T_{NWF}+1}^{T_{WF}+T_{WI}+T_{NWF}+T_{NWI}} Pr(m + nk_i - \alpha_0 - \alpha_2 Y_i$$

$$- \alpha_4 Z_i < c_i - v_i \Lambda\varepsilon < -X_i\beta)$$

where $u_i = \ln W_i - \alpha_0 - \alpha_3 h_i - \alpha_4 Z_i - \alpha_2[W_i h_i + Y_i - (W_i/\alpha_3)(1 - e^{-\alpha_3 h_i})]$, $c_i = u_i - \alpha_1 X_i\beta$, and $v_i = \ln W_i - m - nk_i$. In deriving the estimates, I assume that the disturbances are jointly normally distributed, with ε uncorrelated with u and v. The precise functional forms are well known and are not presented here. Note that each term in the third group of products involves the product of two cumulative normals and hence is easily computed. The last group of products involves a bivariate normal density. Rather than using inexact and computationally expensive numerical quadrature to evaluate these expressions, I use a Chebyshev-Hermite orthogonal polynomial expansion to 100 powers (Kendall 1941). This procedure allows for a computationally simple algorithm which can readily be applied to more general multivariate probability statements arising from the normal distribution.

To perform the calculations, two algorithms were used: the Powell conjugent gradient method and GRADX. The Powell method was used for initial iterations while GRADX was used to locate final optima.[22]

Appendix B

Tax Rates and Welfare Systems

In the text, I assume that the wage rate is independent of hours of work. My approach allows me to relax this assumption. Tax laws set rising rates of taxation on income intervals. For any wage rate, the income intervals can be converted into intervals for hours of work. Given an initial position for prework income, Y, the budget line is a broken line, illustrated in figure 6.

If the wage rate is known, we know the intervals t_1, t_2, and so on. Suppose a woman's equilibrium position for hours of work is C. Since the budget constraint is concave, the slope of the first segment of the constraint must exceed the slope of the indifference curve intersecting Y for a woman to work any hours. For a woman to work beyond Tt_1 hours, exactly the same type of inequality condition must be met. The "reservation wage" for work in excess of Tt_1 hours is partly determined by the value of hours worked and the known income YM which accrues if the woman works Tt_1 hours at the given wage rate net of taxes. Thus, a second inequality must be satisfied for a woman to work beyond Tt_1 hours. We acquire as many inequalities as there are breaks in the schedule. If a woman happens to be in equilibrium exactly at a switch point, the usual marginal conditions do not apply, but we can still acquire information about consumer preferences from such observations, since at the switch point, the marginal rate of substitution must lie between the slopes of the two segments of the budget constraint.

Since wage rates are known for working women, we can avoid bias due to censoring and incorporate tax rates into the estimation procedure by maximizing the appropriate conditional likelihood function.[23] To illustrate the procedure, consider a woman in equilibrium at position C in figure 6. For the woman to be in equilibrium on this segment of the budget constraint, the marginal rate of substitution at the right boundary is less than the slope of the segment, while the marginal rate of substitution at the left boundary is greater than the post tax marginal wage rate for further hours of work. This imposes a condition on the range of the disturbances of the indifference system. It is straightforward to derive the conditional distribution for the indifference system in this segment and to form the appropriate conditional likelihood function.

Precisely the same method may be applied to welfare systems which impose similar "distortions" on the budget line.

---

[22] For a discussion of these algorithms, see chap. 1 of the excellent book by Goldfeld and Quandt (1972).

[23] It is possible to have unknown wage rates, but the distributional problems become severe and they are not discussed here.

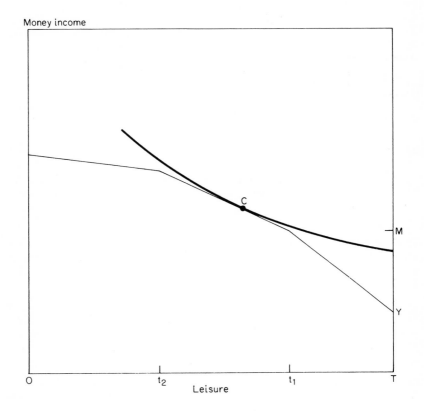

FIG. 6

Comment

Sherwin Rosen
University of Rochester and Harvard University

Heckman has applied sophisticated theory and empirical methods to an important practical problem. He uses a variant of Tobit analysis to combine qualitative data on labor-force status with quantitative data on hours of work. These methods not only take account of the usual differences in market wage opportunities confronting individuals, but also account for differences in tastes among them. Few previous labor-supply studies have attempted to incorporate variations in tastes, and virtually none has treated the problem with other than ad hoc methods. In addition, Heckman's statistical approach directly addresses a problem of interpretation raised by Lewis (1971): Cross-section regressions of labor-force participation rates on wage rates and other variables do not necessarily capture underlying substitution effects between leisure and goods. For example, suppose there are differences in preferences or home productivities among members of the population under study, over and above those represented by such exogenous variables as education and number of children. Then there is a distribution of unobserved reservation wages. Those whose reservation wage exceeds available market wages choose not to participate in the labor market. They specialize in home production and leisure instead. As wages increase, the fraction of the population satisfying this criterion decreases and labor-force participation rates rise. Therefore, wage variation in the sample sweeps out a tail of the underlying distribution of reservation prices. Regression estimates may only give us back properties of this distribution and may be uninformative with respect to the more interesting aspects of the structure of preferences. Heckman explicitly deals with this problem in his analysis. Furthermore, both labor-force status and hours-of-work data are utilized efficiently in estimating labor-supply parameters. I know of no other work that utilizes the sample information in this way.

519

Heckman does not rest content at this point. He offers some conceptual modifications as well. Predictions of labor-supply responses to child-care programs require more knowledge than the uncompensated supply function, because these programs introduce a complicated wedge between average and marginal wage rates. However, no difficulties arise if the whole preference map or, what amounts to the same thing for prediction purposes, the utility compensated supply function for hours of work is known. The paper gives the impression that parameters of indifference curves are estimated directly. However, appearances are deceiving. Under the assumptions of the model, the plain fact is that the observations are generated by an uncompensated, garden-variety supply function. Conversely, the data identify an ordinary supply function, not an uncompensated one. The latter, as well as indifference-map parameters, always must be inferred from the former, using the theory of revealed preference. Since most of this theory is found in rather inaccessible discussions of integrability and related topics, it is worthwhile to spell out some details in a simple case.

A decision maker maximizes a quasi-concave utility function $u = U(x, h)$ subject to the constraint $x = wh + y$, where h is hours of work, x is all other goods, w is the wage rate (in terms of units of x), and y is nonlabor income (also in units of x).[1] Necessary conditions are $U_x = \lambda$ and $U_h = -w\lambda$, where λ is the marginal utility of income. These conditions and the budget constraint imply a set of uncompensated demand and supply functions,

$$x = f(w, y) \tag{1}$$

and

$$h = g(w, y). \tag{2}$$

It is equation (2) that generates the labor-supply observations. Equations (1) and (2) are not independent of each other. Substituting into the budget contraint and differentiating gives

$$wg_w - f_w = -g \tag{3}$$

and

$$-wg_y + f_y = 1. \tag{4}$$

Define an indirect utility function by substituting the demand and supply functions into $U(x, h)$: $u = U[f(w, y), g(w, y)] = V(w, y)$. Totally differentiate $V(w, y)$, $du = (U_x f_w + U_h g_w)dw + (U_x f_y + U_h g_y)dy$, and sub-

---

[1] Alternatively, $U(x, h)$ can be a synthetic utility function, after optimizing out the child-care quality decision conditional on h. That is the approach followed by Heckman. Then the quality price of child care is a proper argument of U, but is suppressed in this discussion.

stitute the necessary conditions plus restrictions (3) and (4). Simplification yields the result

$$du = \lambda[g(w, y)dw + dy]. \qquad (5)$$

What combinations of wage rates and nonlabor income results in the same level of utility when consumption-labor choices are optimal?[2] Setting $du = 0$ in (5) and using the fact that $\lambda > 0$, these values must satisfy

$$dy/dw = -g(w, y). \qquad (6)$$

Equation (6) defines the marginal rate of substitution between w and y. It gives the slope of an "indifference curve" between w and y rather than between x and h. Notice that the slope only depends on $h = g(w, y)$, which is known and estimated from the data.[3] Now treat equation (6) as a differential equation in y and integrate to obtain

$$y = F(w, c), \qquad (7)$$

where c is a constant integration, dependent on the initial state (w_0, y_0). The conditions under which a solution exists are minimal and almost certain to be satisfied by any empirically tractable supply function. In fact, (7) is the equation of the indirect preference map and c is a utility indicator: $F(w, c)$ is an inverse of the indirect utility function. Once the uncompensated supply function $h = g(w, y)$ has been estimated, $F(w. c)$ can be obtained without prior knowledge of the utility function by integration, if not analytically, then with numerical methods on a computer. Finally, substitute equation (7) into equation (2),

$$h = g[w, F(w, c)] = G(w, c). \qquad (8)$$

Equation (8) is the utility-compensated supply function for hours of work and $G_w = g_w + g_y F_w = g_w - h g_y$ is the pure substitution effect. Alternatively, solving for w in terms of h and c in equation (8) yields the marginal rate of substitution function, the form used by Heckman. Note that (8) or its inverse is inferred only from knowledge of the uncompensated supply function.

The discussion above shows how it is possible to learn something about the utility function purely from observing the uncompensated supply function. Heckman's procedure is more or less the opposite. He begins with a functional form restriction on the preference map (i.e., a restriction on equation [8]—his equation [4]) and integrates back to an uncompensated supply function (his equation [5], comparable with equation [2] above). It is the latter that is estimated. His restrictions are such that

---

[2] The following development is a variant of an argument due to Hotelling (1932).

[3] Differentiation of (6) reveals that $d^2y/dw^2 = -\partial h/\partial w + h(\partial h/\partial y)$. This is the negative of the pure substitution effect and the wage-nonlabor income indifference curves are concave to the origin.

estimated parameters of the uncompensated supply function exactly identify parameters of the preference map without further manipulation. Of course the theory does not specify precise functional forms, and some prior specifications are necessary for estimation. The compensated and uncompensated supply functions stand in a one-to-one relationship, and a functional form restriction on either one implies a corresponding restriction on the other. Thus, the question boils down to where one should impose the restrictions in practice. My own preference is to put the functional form restrictions on the uncompensated supply function and work back from that to the compensated function. After all, the observations directly identify only the uncompensated supply function, and, in the nature of the revealed preference argument, the structure of preferences only can be inferred indirectly from observed behavior. There really is no way out of a specification search at the point of observations. We simply have no way of knowing whether semilog linear preference maps are appropriate. The proper specification must come from observed, uncompensated behavior.

Heckman's restriction makes the generating function of the observations (his equation [5]) nonlinear and difficult to estimate. Computational difficulties are compounded by incorporating observations on labor-force nonparticipants. On the other hand, predictions of various program effects are more easily computed. If one starts from the other end, as suggested here, estimation is far less costly, and much greater experimental flexibility is achieved at the stage where that experimentation is most desirable. But this has its costs too, for preference-map inferences and program projections become more expensive. Still, if complex numerical integrations are necessary to obtain compensated response functions, they need be computed only once, after the functional form issue has been resolved. Finally, Heckman's arguments in favor of his procedure are slightly more persuasive when income tax distortions are introduced into the analysis. However, it remains true that within the received framework the observations are generated by uncompensated structures. Therefore, most of the above applies after average wage rates have been replaced by their appropriate after-tax marginal values.

Let me now turn to the empirical estimates. If nonworking women are to provide information about the structure of preferences, it is necessary to know what market wage opportunities they have foregone. Extrapolations are made from wages of working wives with the same productivity (education and experience) characteristics. Yet there are theoretical reasons for supposing these extrapolations are biased, along the lines of the paper presented by Mincer and Polachek in this volume. Women who have more-permanent labor-force attachments engage in productivity-enhancing activities to a much greater extent than those who have less permanent attachments.

To put it another way, "Are hours 'caused' by wages, or are wages 'caused' by hours?" Heckman's method assumed an answer of "no" to the second part of this question. But Mincer and Polachek's results suggest the opposite. Women who greatly value market work or who have relatively low home productivities have prior expectations leading them to acquire labor-market skills to a much different degree than women possessing the opposite characteristics. In practice, the result is that estimated market wage opportunities of those out of the labor force tend to be overstated. Estimates of substitution terms in labor-supply equations are biased upward, resulting in upward biased projections of labor-supply responses to child-care programs. Heckman has estimated the model separately for working wives, but the comparisons do not dispose of this point because the statistical treatment of child-care sources is quite different.

My final comment concerns an anomaly in the data. The observations are very thin in the range $0 < h < 600$, and almost all women who engage in market activities work a significant amount of time during the year. It is problematic how semilog linear reservation wage functions and normally distributed unobserved differences in preferences and market opportunities can account for this gap in the observations. If there is a significant mass of individuals at a boundary solution $(h = 0)$ and the distributions are smooth, a nontrivial fraction exhibiting interior solutions close to the boundary is to be expected. This raises some questions regarding sensitivity of the estimates to alternative distributional assumptions. Considering the estimation difficulties associated with normally distributed unobserved "error" components, pursuing other distributions would appear to be infertile ground for future research.

But there is a much simpler explanation for the gap. There may be almost no jobs that offer short work schedules: Market wage opportunities in this range of hours may be nil. The point can be generalized. Most jobs outside the personal service sector offer rather inflexible work schedules (the major exception being volunteer work), with hours-of-work requirements varying from job to job. Insofar as choice of working hours is intermediated by a commensurate choice of job, there is no reason for a single hourly wage to clear all markets for jobs. That is, it may be factually incorrect to assume equality between average and marginal wage rates in the analysis. Wage-hours regressions are not readily interpreted as direct estimates of labor-supply functions in this case. They undoubtedly are related to worker preferences, but contain elements of employer demand and technological considerations as well. It is impossible to say at this point what difference such modifications will make to labor-supply estimates, since a slightly different conceptual framework is required. In any event, this issue seems well worth pursuing.

In conclusion, Heckman clearly has opened a lot of new territory in the economics of labor supply. The originality of his effort is all the more remarkable when one considers the extent to which the literature shows these grounds have been worked over. Future studies in this area are bound to be affected for many years to come by Heckman's paper.

Part Five

Household and Economy

Toward a New Theory of Population and Economic Growth

Marc Nerlove

University of Chicago

> It is somewhat unusual to begin the treatment of a subject
> with a warning against attaching too much importance to
> it; but in the case of economics, such an injunction is quite
> as much needed as explanation and emphasis of the import-
> ance it really has. It is characteristic of the age in which we
> live to think too much in terms of economics, to see things
> too predominantly in their economic aspect. . . . There is
> no more important prerequisite to clear thinking in regard
> to economics itself than is recognition of its limited place
> among human interests at large. [FRANK H. KNIGHT, 1933
> (1965)]

1. Introduction: Malthus Revised

Malthus, in essays published in 1798 and 1830, and the classical economists combined a very simple model of family decision making—
procreation without bound except possibly by "a foresight of the difficulties attending the rearing of a family . . . and the actual distresses of
some of the lower classes, by which they are disabled from giving the
proper food and attention to their children" (Malthus 1970, p. 89)—
with an equally simple model of the operation of the economy. According
to the latter, a high level of capital accumulation induced by a high level
of profits—representing the difference between output and the rent of
land (natural resources) and wages—permitted a continual increase in
output and population, albeit at the cost of resort to land of increasingly

I am indebted to Gary S. Becker, Glen Cain, Richard B. Freeman, Margaret G. Reid,
and T. W. Schultz for discussions concerning the subject of this paper and for comments
on a related paper. Virginia Thurner contributed valuable editorial advice. This research
was supported by a grant from the Rockefeller Foundation to the University of Chicago
for the study of the economics of population and family decision making.

poorer quality; it did not, as the result of the model of family decision-making, lead to a rising standard of living for most people. Thus, the classical economists achieved a very simple model of economic growth and development (Baumol 1970, pp. 13–21). Modern growth theorists in the tradition of Solow (1956) and Swan (1956) have developed theories of economic growth based on far more elaborate theories of the economy, but few theories of population growth and family decision making have gone much beyond the Malthusian model (Pitchford 1973, pp. 1–10). Although natural-resource constraints may be readily incorporated through the device of diminishing returns to scale in the variable factors (Swan 1956, pp. 340–42), it is a constant proportional rate of population growth, perhaps aided and abetted by exogenous technological progress, that essentially drives the mechanism. Discussions of the optimal rates of population growth or level of population do often attempt to integrate an endogenously determined population in the model. But none, to my knowledge, have examined the feedback from changes in the economy and changes in the relative prices and costs which families face when they decide how many children they will have and what they will invest in those children's health, nutrition, or education, although Pitchford (1973) does discuss the costs of and returns to population control at the macro level.

In recent years, the recognition, crucial to the understanding of long-term growth, that much investment which occurs in the economy is made in human beings rather than in physical capital and that fertility itself is shaped in important ways by economic considerations has led to renewed interest in the economics of the household decisions. In that type of unit, not only decisions about fertility, but also those related to investments in human capital, consumption and savings, migration, labor-force participation, and, in a sense, marriage itself, are made.

With this in mind, in Section 2 I briefly and critically describe the fundamental elements of the largely static theory of household production and choice. This theory was developed in its modern form by Gary Becker (1965) and others, but most of its essentials originated in the much earlier work of Margaret Reid (1934), and it owes a good deal to Wesley Mitchell's seminal observations in his essay (1912) on "The Backward Art of Spending Money." Section 3 concludes this paper with some speculations on how the "new home economics" may be integrated in a theory of economic growth and development through an understanding of the way in which investment in human capital increases the value of human time and thus changes over time the resource constraints and the relative costs and prices which "households" face in their decisions on the number and quality of children they attempt to produce. The question as to whether this constitutes a true economic explanation of the so-called demographic transition, and thus a revision of the Malthusian tradition, is basically an empirical one and is left open.

2. The "New Home Economics": Summary and Critique

In its most unadorned form, economics is the theory of allocation of limited resources among competing ends in order to maximize satisfactions (or utility), subject to the constraints imposed by limitations in the availability of the resources required to achieve those ends. Various elaborations and accretions are necessary to accommodate this central theoretical core to the dynamics of choices made sequentially over time and in the presence of uncertainty regarding future constraints and future preferences. At several points I shall have more to say about our present failure to reach successful accommodations in our underlying theory in these directions, as well as about our even more important limitations as economists to cope with the whole complex of issues raised by inter-generational transfers, within society as an ongoing concern, and par-ticularly within the family.

The first element in the new home economics is the utility function to be maximized. Its form and its arguments (i.e., what variables determine its level) are obviously crucial in determining the choices which result from its maximization. But whose utility function is it that is maximized in connection with choices pertinent to marriage, children, consumption of commodities, work and leisure, and investment in all forms of capital? Considering the household as already formed, much of the theoretical underpinning rests on what I have called elsewhere the "Chicago model" (Nerlove 1972*b*).[1]

The "Chicago utility function," if I may call it that, has several key characteristics. First, it does not involve nonmarket goods or physical com-modities and purchasable services as we usually think of them in eco-nomics, but its arguments are abstract goods composed of a number of "attributes" which must themselves be produced within the household (Becker 1965; Lancaster 1966; Muth 1966). The importance of this characteristic of the utility function is that it leads directly to the key questions of household technology and the composition of different types of market goods and services and physical commodities, in terms of attributes contributing to satisfactions. This, indeed, is the point made forcefully by Muth (1966) and recently emphasized by Michael and Becker (1973). Earlier (1947), Leontief pointed out that the theory of consumer behavior as then developed, although of great generality, lacked content to the extent that it gave no clue to the types of relations to be expected among different categories of goods.

> The assumption of the existence of general categories of needs, different from demands for particular individual commodities,

---

[1] At this conference, Jacob Mincer objected to this and said that the model should really be called the "Morningside Heights" model; however, force of habit leads me to persist in this terminology.

but still specific enough to be clearly distinguishable from each other, is basic to the man-in-the-street idea of consumers' demand. One speaks of the desire for food as existing behind and separately from the particular demand for bread, apples, or Lobster à la Newburg. This need for food is at the same time spoken of as something clearly distinguishable from the similarly general needs for clothing or, say, for shelter, each of the latter also thought of as existing separately although manifested through the particular demands for one-family houses, apartment flats, or woolen suits and raincoats. [Leontief 1947, p. 371]

Strotz (1957), in his introduction of the notion of a utility tree and in his later (1959) discussion with Gorman, attempted to give more empirical content to the theory of consumer demand in precisely this way, although he interpreted his results in terms of a "budgeting" process. An important aspect of the household production model, including time and market-purchasable goods, as introduced by Becker (1965), Lancaster (1966), and Muth (1966), is precisely, as Muth points out, that it does yield "a utility function which is weakly separable when viewed as a function of commodities purchased on the market" (Muth 1966, p. 700). While it is true, in a sense, that many conclusions of the "new home economics" could be derived directly from Strotzian utility trees and other specializing assumptions, the home-production aspect of the Chicago function lends an intuitive insight and empirical content which are lacking in the more abstract formulation. It suggests a more direct look at the technology of processes within the household and particularly at how such processes use household time and nonpurchased inputs in addition to market-purchasable commodities. Indeed, the supposed differences in the time intensity of the production of household goods give much of the content to recent applications of the "new home economics" to the problems of fertility and human capital formation.[2] I return to this point in Section 3 where I speculate on how the increasing value of human time works through a Chicago utility function/household-production model to alter the behavior of generations through time.

A second key characteristic of the Chicago utility function is that it is just that: one utility function—the welfare of the children and other members of the family is assumed to enter the utility function of a single decision maker (not always the husband and father!), thus obviating the assumption of a "family utility function" with all the concomitant

---

[2] Unfortunately, to date relatively little attention has been paid to the implications of the household production model for the more general composition of consumption. Time and market-purchasable-commodity intensities do differ greatly for different types of consumption (e.g., drinking beer or going to a concert), and the new home economics has implications going beyond fertility and human capital formation (see, however, Michael [1972]).

problems of social utility functions in general. It is perhaps not entirely accurate to identify this position too closely with Chicago; it should perhaps be called the "Samuelsonian finesse." Samuelson (1956) writes:

> Where the family is concerned the phenomenon of altruism inevitably raises its head: if we can speak at all of the indifference curves of any one member, we must admit that his tastes and marginal rates of contribution are contaminated by the goods that other members consume. These . . . external consumption effects are the essence of family life. . . . Such problems of home economics are, abstractly conceived, exactly of the same logical character as the general problem of government and social welfare. [P. 9]

> . . . if within the family there can be assumed to take place an optimal reallocation of income so as to keep each member's dollar expenditure of equal ethical worth, then there can be derived for the whole family a set of well-behaved indifference contours relating the totals of what it consumes: the family can be said to *act as if* it maximizes such a group preference function. [P. 21]

The problem with the Samuelsonian finesse, however, is that it assumes a fixed family membership, and a great deal of what the Chicago utility function is designed to explain is how that family composition gets determined. This requires much more than Samuelson allows for in his formulation. When, for example, are children members of the family, and thus codeterminers of the utility function, and when are they just arguments in the utility function determined for the family not including them? The full internalization argued by T. W. Schultz (1972*b*) seems a necessary addition to the argument. Yet, for this to be true, what might be called the "John Donne effect" must be extremely powerful. Casual observation suggests that each individual's concern for others diminishes with distance in both time and space. Yet it may be true under certain restrictive assumptions, as pointed out to me by Assaf Razin, that what might be called pairwise intergenerational internalization (by which I mean full internalization of the utilities of the next succeeding generation by the immediately preceding generation) would lead to essentially the same type of problem as that encountered in the discussions of optimal growth with an infinite horizon.

Morishima (1970, pp. 213–25) presents an extended discussion of some of the more technical issues involved in formulating dynamic utility functions and the conditions under which such functions can be reduced to the sum of discounted utilities of each future generation or at each future point in time, irrespective of the generation involved. In general, these conditions are highly restrictive and closely related to the conditions of Strotz (1959) and Gorman (1959) for strong separability of the utility function. But as Koopmans (1967, p. 96) points out, the problem is really in some sense an ethical one:

> What is at issue is clearly an intertemporal distribution problem: that of balancing the consumption levels of successive generations, and of successive stages in the life-cycle of a given cohort of contemporaries. The most pertinent decisions—individual, corporate, or governmental—are those that determine investment in physical capital, in human capital, and in research and development. Investments in physical capital, if well made, augment future consumption through an increase in future capital-labor ratios. Investment in human capital raises the quality of labor and, one hopes, of life. Successful research and development augment future capital and labor inputs through the development of better techniques of production.

Even regarded as a strictly behavioral model, pairwise internalization, which seems central to the Chicago utility function, has most important implications for the intergenerational transfers of material wealth and human capital which Knight (1921, pp. 374–75) has so eloquently described as central to the continuity of the social order.[3] Some of these implications bear on the issues discussed in the next section. Here, however, it seems essential to point out the profound problem in, on the one hand, internalizing all the family members' satisfactions in one utility function and, at the same time, using this same utility function to determine the number and "quality" of the family members themselves. Essentially the problem results from the condensation of a sequential, dynamic set of decisions into a theory of choice based on the maximization of a single, static, timeless utility function. In its most extreme form, the issue of the conceptual adequacy of the approach arises in connection with the application of the new home economics to household formation— a formation which in an earlier, less aberrant, and nonconformist era might have been described as "marriage"! Yet marriage, in some sense, remains very much associated with procreation; and the act of marriage, or at least of household formation, is the normal first step in the central process of choice with which the new home economics deals. Where then is the utility function? Can the entire process really be separated into two distinct parts, what the econometrician would call a recursive system? If a fundamental purpose of marriage is the procreation of a couple's own legitimate children, given a society's definition of both marriage and

---

[3] Indeed, there is good reason to suppose that the reason for many institutions of society is precisely to ensure that the interests of future generations will be adequately guarded by the present. A meaningful theory of intergenerational welfare comparisons has not yet been developed, but such a theory is surely central to our understanding of household decision making and its consequences.

legitimacy, clearly the process cannot be regarded as recursive.[4] Again, the static character of the analysis, while not necessarily limiting its usefulness in an empirical sense, introduces a conceptual difficulty of a high order.

The second element in the new home economics is the technology of household production described by a production function or functions and a list of the resources utilized in the processes involved. Typically, following Becker (1965), the inputs are time, perhaps distinguishable by household member (e.g., husband and wife) and market-purchasable commodities. These inputs are used to produce within the household the goods and services that in turn lead to satisfaction. In the simplest form in the economic theory of fertility, two time inputs (the husband's and wife's) and one general market-purchasable commodity are assumed in the household technology to produce three household goods: child numbers, child quality, and a general commodity called "other satis- factions" (see Willis and De Tray herein). In all analyses to date an impor- tant further simplification of this basic technological structure has been made: each good entering the utility function is assumed to be produced by a separate independent production process. Jointness in production arises not because of common overhead factors within the household, but because the factor inputs available to the household are subject to overall constraints.[5] Willis and DeTray, for example, both assume that child quality per child and child numbers are produced by independent production processes. Each factor separately enters the household utility function in the Willis formulation. The one is simply multiplied with the other to arrive at the final good, child services, which is assumed to enter the household utility function in DeTray's formulation. Both child numbers and child quality are generally assumed to be mother's time-intensive.

This formulation also neglects the sequential and essentially dynamic character of investments in child quality. Casual observation suggests

---

[4] Still, it may be helpful analytically to tackle the problem in a stepwise fashion (see Becker's paper in this volume). In part of his work, Becker does consider the division of the gains from marriage, the most important gains being the children, and this is, of course, a matter closely related to the utility function maximized within the marriage.

[5] A partial exception is the work of Michael Grossman (1971; 1972b, pp. 74–79). In his analysis Grossman does assume separate production processes but stipulates that the entire amounts of certain factors available to the household must enter each production function as one of its arguments. That is to say, in the standard analysis, if one could separately identify the amount of one factor—say, wife's time—used in a particular activity, one could measure the effect of a unit increase in that input on the output of that activity independently of the overall resource constraint on the wife's time to the household, whereas in Grossman's formulation the overhead factor, say, the family house, cannot in principle be allocated among the activities but must enter fully into each one. Grossman's work, however, still does lack generality in the respect discussed above, since complementarity among final goods cannot be encompassed in his formulation except through the rather Ptolemaic device of introducing some of the final outputs as inputs in the production processes of some of the other outputs.

that in many societies and families, the eldest son is often the beneficiary of the bulk of the investment in the human capital that takes place in the second generation. Indeed, Sloan's recent work (1971, pp. 31–32) suggests that in poor countries the sex, as well as birth order of a child, may be an important determinant of the infant's survival probabilities, presumably because of the differential investments in health and nutrition that take place within the family rather than for purely genetic reasons.

The restrictiveness of the rather special assumption of separability of productive activities has not been apparent in the basically two-good (child services/other satisfactions) static models usually considered, for what is ruled out is complementarity among different outputs in a multi-product context. As is well known, under conditions of variable proportions, complementarity (in the sense that the output of one good could be increased without decreasing the output of the other good and without using additional resources) cannot occur if the production unit, in this case the household, is at an optimum and using resources fully. In a three-or-more-product case, however, it is possible for several of the outputs to be complementary with each other, although substitutable jointly against the rest (Hicks 1939, p. 92).[6] In the latter case, holding available resources constant, increasing the level of one of the outputs optimally might well involve also increasing another, although clearly a third output level would have to be decreased. One can easily see how restrictive the elimination of complementarity could be in a context involving several dimensions of child quality, for example, health and physical development and intellectual achievement. In a dynamic context such potential complementarities are of even greater significance since there is, for example, some evidence that early underinvestment in nutritional capital may substantially affect the productivity of later investments in intellectual human capital (Berg 1973, pp. 9–12).[7]

The third element in the new home economics is a set of assumptions about the way in which household resources, principally time, can be transformed into market-purchasable commodities to be used in the household production process. Strictly speaking, I suppose one could consider this set of assumptions as part of the general technology of household production and subsumed under the second element of the theory. It is, however, better to treat the matter separately, since most of what is involved concerns the terms upon which household members can enter the labor market, the wages they can earn, and, somewhat secondarily, the prices at which market commodities can be purchased. It is here that the lack of dynamic character of the new home economics cuts most

[6] In Hick's argument, substitute the word "outputs" for "factors" and vice versa, and hold the factor of production (his "output") fixed.

[7] It would seem more straightforward and perhaps more desirable in future work to deal with simple forms of multiproduct production functions. For an empirical example, see Eads, Nerlove, and Raduchel (1969).

deeply into its potential implications for the central problems of fertility and female labor-force participation. The timing and spacing of children, the opportunities for part-time work and accumulation of lifetime labor market experience, and choices as to the amount of education to be invested in early in the life cycle all revolve heavily on the terms under which women can participate in the labor market and thus share in the transformation of the household's time resources into market commodities. The human capital literature (Ben-Porath 1967; Mincer 1970, 1974*b*) is, of course, replete with dynamic analyses of investment in human capital over time and the life-cycle effects of these investments on earnings. But little of this work has entered the more general framework of the "new home economics," particularly as this theory bears on decisions concerning the numbers of children and their timing and spacing within a marriage and the relation of these decisions to the accumulation of other forms of assets. The work of Heckman (1971), Ghez and Becker (1972), and unpublished work of Frank Stafford does, however, represent a notable beginning of the extension of this part of theory into more dynamically relevant realms.[8] Yet we need to understand far more than we presently do about why the labor market functions so differently for men than for women, the role of institutional constraints, discrimination, and the relation of these to women's choices of occupation and timing of labor-force participation. Once again, the simultaneities of the system severely limit our ability to break out a single segment for proper analysis.

The fourth and final element in the new home economics is the resource constraints facing the household in its production and optimization decisions. Traditionally these constraints are divided into time (husband's and wife's, although often the husband is assumed to devote full time to the market) and "other" nonwage income. While it is universally recognized that some elements of household production and consumption— sleep and food, for example—are in fact inputs into the production-of-time resources, little attention has thus far been paid to the quality of the time resources and of other family resources—both genetic and material— passed from one generation to the next. Arleen Leibowitz's study of Terman's 1921 sample of California school children, reported in this

---

[8] Much recent work, however, is dynamic only in the relatively trivial sense of involving maximization over a number of periods of time without uncertainty concerning the values of future values of exogenous constraints to future decisions. This is the sense in which a dynamic programming problem can be turned into an ordinary programming problem of much larger dimensions; apart from the computational difficulties thus introduced, the chief defect of this approach is that it fails to lay bare the sequential nature of the decision-making process in the way, for example, in which the recursive solution to the general dynamic programming problem of Bellman does. In the absence of uncertainty, however, nothing essential is lost by the straightforward multiperiod extension of the basically static framework. When values of future constraints are uncertain, then it does become essential to understand and incorporate the sequential character of the decision process (see Nerlove 1972*a*). So far this has not been done in the literature of the new home economics.

volume, bears importantly on the manner in which much human capital is passed from one generation to another, especially to a child of preschool age. The sample is very unrepresentative, but it is instructive, for the investments in her child of a mother's time and the quality of those investments, as measured by her education, are found to affect appreciably later measures of the child's ability and future earning capacity.

The resource constraints facing the household, once it is formed, are, of course, a product of the household formation itself and thus connected with my earlier remarks on the inseparability of this complex of issues, from those of family choice and decision making. But, more important it is in this area that the complex issue of intergenerational transfers figures most prominently. We live, after all,

> in a world where individuals are born naked, destitute, helpless, ignorant, and untrained, and must spend a third of their lives in acquiring the prerequisites of a free contractual existence. . . . The fundamental fact about society as a going concern is that it is made up of individuals who are born and die and give place to others; and the fundamental fact about modern civilization is that it is dependent upon the utilization of three great accumulating funds of inheritance from the past, material goods and appliances, knowledge and skill, and morale. Besides the torch of life itself, the material wealth of the world, a technological system of vast and increasing intricacy and the habituations which fit men for social life must in some manner be carried forward to new individuals born devoid of all these things as older individuals pass out. The existing order, with the institutions of the private family and private property (in self as well as goods), inheritance and bequest and parental responsibility, affords one way for securing more or less tolerable results in grappling with this problem. [Knight 1921, pp. 374–75]

So the apparently simple theoretical construct of a time budget plus other income constraint to the household conceals beneath its serene and mathematically differentiable exterior the central problem of the continuity of society itself.[9]

---

[9] Closely connected to the matter of what is inherited from the past and transferred from generation to generation is the problem of how individual tastes and preferences are formed and how they may change over time. I have not mentioned this issue lest I be excommunicated from the economics profession! It is virtually part of the definition of what an economist is that he takes tastes as given, and I sometimes suspect that many of us require all tastes to be identical and assume that all differences among individuals arise from differences in the resource constraints those individuals face. Indeed, one of the consequences of the conjectures and speculations presented in Section 3 is that the tastes and preferences of at least different generations, if not of individuals within each generation, could remain constant while the number of children per family declined over time due to changes in the value of human time induced endogenously.

By themselves the four main elements of the theoretical structure of the new home economics—(1) a utility function with arguments which are not physical commodities but home-produced bundles of attributes; (2) a household production technology; (3) an external labor-market environment providing the means for transforming household resources into market commodities; and (4) a set of household resource constraints— are incapable of yielding a series of well-defined implications about the main problems of household behavior with which we are concerned. It is only a framework within which to think about these problems. Many special additional assumptions, some of which have been mentioned, must be added to the framework to arrive at empirically refutable propositions. Moreover, the nature of the required additional specific- ations is intimately related to the peculiarities of the particular bodies of data to which the new home economics has been applied. These data range all the way from aggregate time-series data covering long periods of time, to cross-sectional census data for both large and small geographic regions at a point in time and over time, to household and family data based on individual interviews, with and without collection of retrospec- tive information.

If to the key simplification involved in the assumption of separable independent productive processes within the household, one adds the assumptions that young children are highly intensive of the mother's time in comparison with other activities within the home and older children are less intensive, and that for institutional or biological reasons the comparative advantage of the male partner in the acquisition of market-purchasable commodities significantly exceeds that of the female partner, a number of interesting implications of the theory emerge which are tolerably well supported by the empirical evidence so far analyzed. Setting aside for the moment the inadequacy of the observed market wage to measure the cost of a nonworking woman's time, the immediate implication of the theory is that a rise in cost of mother's time for the family will cause a substitution away from time-intensive goods such as children and toward those requiring more inputs of market-purchasable commodities. Indeed, if we further assume momentarily that males are completely specialized in market activities, changes in their wages represent pure income effects for the family, and we do then observe for families with working mothers positive association of family size with income and negative association with female wage rates. To the extent that education serves as a proxy for the relative costs of time which may measure some of these costs less imperfectly, or at least in a fashion different from market wages, similar differences are observed between the effects of male and female educational attainments (Mincer 1963; Nerlove and Schultz 1970; and papers by Willis, DeTray, and Ben-Porath in this volume).

The interpretation of many of the results is somewhat complicated by the effects of marriage on the association of the educational attainments of husbands and wives, and by the fact that wives and mothers for the most part specialize entirely in home activities during only varying fractions of their lifetimes. Moreover, the effects of female education seem unexpectedly and puzzlingly nonlinear (see Ben-Porath's paper herein). To illustrate the nature of the difficulty involved, consider the following simple analysis of the effects of assortive mating. We know that men of higher-than-average levels of educational attainment tend to marry women of higher-than-average levels of educational attainment. Suppose, however, that tastes for children differ among the population; women with a high taste for children and a low taste for market-related activities will tend in general to seek and to receive less formal schooling than women with the opposite preference. Presumably a man's taste for children in a society where nearly all men specialize in market-related activities will not be reflected very greatly in his formal schooling. Some effect of the amount of his formal schooling may occur through early marriage, but he will certainly seek a mate with like preferences. Thus, men with a given level of schooling with a high taste for children will tend to marry women with less schooling than the average associated with the level these men have achieved. If, as is common, a husband's educational attainment is associated primarily with permanent income effects within the household, and his wife's is associated primarily with the opportunity cost of time, one can see that the negative effect of the opportunity cost of time as measured this way on fertility will tend to be exaggerated, holding male educational attainment constant, since the difference between the two across couples partly reflects differences in tastes which are unobservable and not included in the statistical analysis (see also "The Emerging Economic Picture" in Part I of T. W. Schultz's paper in this book for a related comment).

Turning the analysis around, we can ask what implications the new home economics has for female labor-force participation. The new home economics predicts what is perhaps the obvious: the composition of a woman's family is strongly associated with her labor-force participation. Typically, the number of a family's children under the age of 18 and the age of the youngest child are both strong predictors of a woman's labor-force participation. These facts about family composition have been interpreted by Cain (1966), for example, as measures of the opportunity value of a mother's time in the home. Gronau (herein) attempted a detailed and sophisticated analysis of just this proposition, using a subsample of the 1/1000 sample from 1960 United States Census; moreover, he examined the interaction of educational attainment with family composition. Others (Smith 1972a; Leibowitz 1972) have documented that highly educated married women participate to a greater extent in the labor force and work more hours when they do work than married women with less schooling. Married women as a group also tend to withdraw from the labor force when they have children; this is an implication of the new home economics, on the assumption that children are more female time–intensive than other commodities produced within the home; but the rates at which women with different educational attainments withdraw is not the same. During the child-rearing years, more highly educated women reallocate more hours to household production than do women with less education. Ben-Porath's finding (herein) of a U-shaped relation between education and labor-force participation for Israeli women with young children strongly suggests differences in the effects of education at different levels on the relative efficiencies of home and market production and also interactions between female education and child quality. But all of this has been insufficiently explored within the presently existing framework of the new home economics. As Sweet (1968), Nerlove and Schultz (1970), and Hall (in this book), have emphasized, educational investments, labor-force participation, and fertility must be viewed, at least partly, as simultaneously determined choices. This is surely one of the most important implications of the new home economics and only partly negated by the latter's currently static character.

Finally, if we regard, as I think we must, the grand problem of the new home economics as the explanation of the demographic transition, that is, the "economic and social processes and family behavior that accounts for the marked decline from very high birth and death rates to modern very low birth and death rates" (T. W. Schultz, in Part I, "The Value of Children"), the new home economics does have some insights, albeit limited, to offer (O'Hara 1972). Clearly, a high probability of child mortality affects the costs of achieving a given family size, that is, the number of children surviving to a given age. If it is assumed that on the whole parents achieve a greater (discounted) sum of satisfactions the longer a child survives and if declines in mortality result in greater relative increases in the conditional probabilities of survival from earlier ages to successively older ages, declines in mortality should tend, according to the new home economics, to generate a greater demand for children. This need not lead to an increase in births, however, since such declines in mortality lower the cost of child quality relative to the cost of numbers of children. Of course, the net effect must depend on the technology of the production of child numbers and child quality as well as on the relative importance of these in the utility function. These factors, of course, may vary substantially from time to time, culture to culture, and place to place. The elucidation of such effects, however, must surely constitute one of the central challenges to the empirical application of the new home economics. To explore such effects fully, however, requires that the household decision-making process be accommodated in a model of economic growth and development, a subject to which we now turn.

3. Household Decision Making and Economic Growth: Speculations and Conjectures

> "Would you tell me, please, which way I ought to go from here?"
>
> "That depends a good deal on where you want to get to," said the Cat. [*Alice's Adventures in Wonderland*]

In his classic paper on "Diminishing Returns from Investment," Knight (1944) pointed out that "if new investment can be freely directed to all uses, i.e., embodied in all types of productive agents indifferently, it will not be subject to diminishing returns" (p. 33). Moreover, he stressed, as did Marshall before him, the concept of capital in human beings, and that "in the production of laborers the matter of 'quality' is far more important than that of quantity in the crude sense of numbers" (p. 35). Although investment "freely directed" might not be subject to diminishing returns, certainly, under static circumstances, continued investment in any one particular direction ought eventually to result in a declining rate of return. Yet, as T. W. Schultz has emphasized, the rate of return appears to have diminished little, if at all, in response to a high level and even accelerated pace of investment in human capital, and, indeed, it may have actually risen (T. W. Schultz 1971, p. 173).

We do not, of course, have any really accurate measure of the extent of investment in human capital as compared with investment in nonhuman capital and in the stock of knowledge through investment in research and development. Yet, there are a number of clues which suggest that the capital stock invested in human beings, even on a per capita basis, has been a steadily growing portion of the total capital stock. T. W. Schultz (1961, p. 73) suggests a rise of the value of the stock of educational human capital embodied in the stock of labor of persons age 14 and older from 18 percent in 1900 of the total educational and physical capital to 30 percent in 1957. These estimates do not include on-the-job training or investments in better health and nutrition. In terms of gross capital formation, Kuznets (1966, p. 243) calculates, on the basis of Schultz's earlier work, a rise in the share of investments in formal education alone from "about 9% in 1900 to over 38% in the 1950s." Moreover, for Western countries as a whole, Kuznets (1971) calculates the share of labor has risen from 55 to 75 percent of national income over the same period. These facts, meager as they may be, suggest two significant questions which are germane to the issue with which this paper began, namely, how can the new home economics be integrated into a general theory of economic growth and development in a manner which has some hope, at least, of bearing on the grand question of the demographic transition? These two questions are the following.

First, what accounts for the failure of the rate of return to investments in human capital, even counting educational investments, to fall, despite a high and accelerating rate of investment in this form of capital relative to other forms? In other words, why does there appear to be a persistent disequilibrium among these rates of return?

Second, quite apart from the possibility of disequilibrium rates of return (even if they are in equilibrium), what effect will increasing human capital investment per capita have on the allocation of resources within the household and what, if any, repercussions will it have for the rate of growth of population and labor force? A number of speculations and conjectures on the answers to these questions follow; they emphasize the role of the increasing value of human time over time and its relation, which is reciprocal, to the increasing level of investment in human beings.

Razin (1969, 1972) showed how, under certain circumstances, the ratio of human to total capital per capita would increase along the optimal growth path of an economy experiencing technical progress. As indicated earlier, T. W. Schultz has emphasized this aspect of the persistant failure of rates of return to investments in human capital to decline. The demand for skills and knowledge embodied in human capital does not decline because of additional investments in the stock of useful knowledge and technique (technological change) which require the continual adaptation and adjustment of the human agent to utilize efficiently this augmented stock and seek out the new sources of investment opportunities which maintain the growth process. But even in the absence of a persistent disequilibrium created by the demand for human capital, it is possible that the rates of return to such investments would fail to fall over time, or fall only slowly, in relation to the rates of return to other forms of investment because of endogenously changing relative cost of investment, that is, changes on the supply side.

One of the most important consequences of the growing "quality" of human beings as reflected in the increased stock of human capital per capita, as pointed out by T. W. Schultz herein, is the increasing value of human time per unit of such time. Many of the consequences of the increasing value of time over time are amusingly explored by Linder (1970) in his penetrating study of *The Harried Leisure Class.* Yet Linder and Schultz fail to note the important link which may exist between the increasing value of human time, due presumably to investment in human capital as well as to investment in other forms of capital and in technological change, and the terms on which investment in human capital takes place. If one assumes, as I think plausible, that children (as regards both quality and quantity) are time-intensive as compared with other goods produced within the home, it follows that unless the increasing investment of human capital increases the marginal productivity of a unit of time in the care and rearing of children within the home in an offsetting fashion, increases in the value of time will lead to a shift away from children to less time-intensive activities. To be sure, such a substitution effect may be offset by a strong income effect, but there are still further grounds to suppose that both substitution and income effects will tend to lead to an increase in child quality rather than child numbers.

Earlier in this book, Becker and Lewis explored the consequences of a simple model of the relation between the quality and quantity of a good (in this case, children) entering the utility function, under the assumption that quality per unit is the same for all units. Increases in either quantity or quality cause the shadow prices of the other to rise and if, as is plausible, the income elasticity for quality is greater than that for quantity, the resulting increase in the shadow price of numbers would reduce the apparent income elasticity for quantity, perhaps even to negative level. Thus, the income effect of the increasing value of human time should, under these circumstances, lead to a substitution of quality for quantity of children, in addition to leading to a substitution away from children altogether to less time-intensive goods. This rests of course, on the premise that the productivity of time in rearing children is unchanged or, at least, not greatly increased. Moreover, the pure price effects are likely to work in the same direction, since it is plausible that quantity is more time-intensive than quality of children per unit of equal quality time and that, indeed, the shadow price of quality is likely to be reduced by increases in the quality of the mother's time input (I refer again to Arleen Leibowitz's paper in this volume).

The investments in child quality referred to earlier take two major forms: (1) sound nutrition and health care, and (2) education, skills, or attitudes conducive to acquisition of further education and skills.

Good nutrition and health care increase youngsters' chances of survival and may also affect their ability to absorb future investments in intellectual capital. To the extent that such investments increase the life span, particularly the span of years over which a person can be economically active, such an increase in quality will raise the return to investments in human capital which sons and daughters may later wish to make in themselves. To the extent that better health and nutrition result in a reduction in child mortality, they increase the satisfactions accruing to parents from other forms of investment which also raise child quality, for the returns to these investments may then be expected to be enjoyed over a longer period of time on average. Increases in longevity, particularly of an individual's economically productive years, increase the amount of human time available without increasing population; such an increase would tend by itself to lower the value of time per unit, but, as we know, most of the effects of better health care and nutrition occur in childhood and enhance the quality of a unit of time in later years more than increasing the number of children. On net balance, therefore, I would conjecture that better health and nutrition lower the costs of further investments in human capital relative to those in other forms of capital and increase the returns therefrom.

The second main form which an increase in child quality may take is, as I have stated, through investment in the form of education, skills, or attitudes conducive to later acquisition of further education or skills. Much investment in human capital of this type tends to be time-intensive in the preschool years, although the productivity of a unit of a mother's time, as remarked, may be especially enhanced by a greater stock of human capital embodied in her, so it is not necessarily true that over time, as the result of the increasing value of human time, substitution will tend to occur away from this form of investment. Nonetheless, it is in this area that we might expect some induced "technological innovations" which could economize on a mother's scarce time. Nursery schools, day-care centers, and the proliferation of "educational" toys are perhaps examples. On the whole, then, I think we may conclude that increases in quality of children relative to their numbers take the form of investments in human capital which ultimately have the effect of raising the value of time per unit in the economically active years of adulthood.

For reasons which I feel certain we do not fully understand, but which are due in part to the presence of children's utilities in the utility function of the family to which they belong, parents do desire to bequeath a stock of capital to their children. Since the stock of capital, material and intangible, human and nonhuman, is growing per capita in Western economies, one must assume that parents desire to pass along more than that which they received from their parents, or that institutions in the economy function in such a way as to induce this outcome. Irrespective of the motivation, however, the increasing value of human time must have an effect on the form in which this capital is passed on. As long as rates of return to investments in human capital remain above, or fall more slowly than, the rates of return to investments in other forms of capital, parents will be induced to bequeath a greater part in the form of human capital. Thus, the tendency toward increasing quality of children will be intensified by the bequest motive, despite the opposite tendency, resulting from the increasing cost of time, to invest in bequests which are less time-intensive. But as rates of return tend to equality over time—if they ever do—parents should tend to bequeath less in the form of human capital and more in the form of financial and physical capital. Nonetheless, as long as investment in human capital occurs, the value of a unit of human time will continue to rise with increases in the stock of capital per capita, reinforcing the tendency to fewer children of ever-higher quality. Substitution will occur in favor of fewer children of higher quality and perhaps eventually against both quality and quantity of children in favor of commodities and knowledge. The "facts" cited at the beginning of this section, suggesting an increasing portion of total capital formation in this century has occurred in the form of human capital, however, indicate that we may be far from the point at which such substitution begins to take place against children, quality, and quantity combined.

The outlines of a revised Malthusian model begin to emerge, albeit dimly, from the foregoing conjectures and speculations. In this model, the value of human time and changes in that value over time are pivotal, and the limitations imposed by natural resources are mitigated, if not eliminated, by technological progress and increases in the stock of knowledge and of capital, both human and nonhuman. The main link between household and economy is the value of human time; the increased value of human time results in fewer children per household, with each child embodying greater investments in human capital which in turn result in lower mortality and greater productivity in the economically active years. Such greater productivity in turn further raises both the value of a unit of time and income in the subsequent generation and enables persons of that generation to make efficient use of new knowledge and new physical capital. Eventually, rates of return to investments in physical capital, new knowledge, and human capital may begin to equalize, but as long as investment occurs which increases the amount of human capital per individual, the value of a unit of human time must continue to increase. It is not possible to say whether the diminishing ability of a human being to absorb such investment would eventually stabilize the number of children per household and at what level, given the satisfactions parents obtain from numbers of children as well as their quality. Nonetheless, over time the model does predict in rough qualitative fashion declining rates of population growth (perhaps eventually zero rates or even negative rates for a time) and declining rates of infant mortality. These are the main features of the demographic transition.

Much remains to be done if this rough and speculative outline is to be translated into a true integration of the new home economics with the modern theory of economic growth, particularly as the former evolves along more dynamic and empirically relevant lines. First, the model must be mathematized—and it is clear that there are many forms in which this may be accomplished—so that the crucial parameters and behavioral relations may be isolated. These must then be studied empirically, for without quantitative knowledge of the parameters and technologies involved and the key behavioral relations the course of the important variables over time cannot be predicted or compared with past behavior.

The role of the growth theorist is apparent in the first of these tasks and those of the econometrician and economic historian in the second. Finally, the conceptual foundations of the new home economics, particularly with respect to intergenerational transfers, must be clarified if we are to understand the extent to which actual growth departs from the optimal path, the reasons for such departure, and whether collective action is either desirable or necessary to correct such departures.

I hope this paper represents at least a modest beginning in showing where it is we want to get to, if not a set of directions on which way we ought to go from here.

Comment

Zvi Griliches

Harvard University

I shall divide my comments into two parts, corresponding to Nerlove's discussion of the "new home economics" and the stylized "facts" that appear to be building blocks for a future growth model. I am very much in agreement with Nerlove's exposition of the "new home economics," but I would like to amplify a bit two of his implied criticisms of the state of this theory.

One of the major working assumptions of the theory is the existence of a common family utility function. In his paper in this volume, Gary Becker shows that by introducing the notion of "caring" (or the interdependence of utilities) one can show that the family will behave as if it has a common utility function. This will not do, I think, for the analysis of the empirical phenomena that we are really interested in. What parents care for is not the utility that their children receive, but the utility function that the children have and the resources that they control. Parents care about the consumption basket of their children; they have preferences over actual actions, not just their subjective outcomes. Much of the within-family conflict comes from different evaluations of the same consumption opportunities. For example, since many families appear to subsidize their children's higher education, and since the marginal valuation of family funds may not be the same for different family members, it may pay for the young both to pursue higher education further than appears warranted on straight rate-of-return calculations (somebody else is paying the cost), and to work less hard at it than the donors of the money would have liked them to do. In any case, a common utility function cannot explain either the growth of households or their dissolution, or indicate the point at which it pays for the young to opt out of it. It is probably also not necessary for the analysis of such questions, as is indicated by Becker's model of the marriage market.

546

The main shortcoming of the "new home economics" for the analysis of fertility decisions is that it assumes too little. The basic postulates are that children are goods, that all goods are subject to two constraints—time and money—and that children are relatively time-intensive goods. But this does not distinguish children from hi-fi sets! Adding the observation that children tend to use mother's time more than father's does not get us much further. Moreover, given the aims of the theory, this should probably come out as a conclusion, rather than be assumed from the beginning. In any case, the theory focuses on children as a good whose costs have a relatively high time component (particularly mother's time). Thus, any changes that have occurred have to be explained in terms of changes in total marginal cost (money and time) of this good (children) relative to the cost of all other consumption goods. I do not think that this is enough. The theory currently provides one explanation (among several competing ones) of the secular decline in fertility, attributing it to the rising cost of time, but it fails to provide any convincing explanation for the major fertility cycles that we have experienced. We have no economic explanation yet within the framework of this theory either for the baby boom of the 1950s or the current rather sharp decline in fertility.

My belief is that if we want to study the demand for children, we have to put more content into the theory and start asking why do people want to have children; what are the returns and not just the costs of this activity? In terms of the theoretical framework used in this volume, I am looking for shifters of the utility function, or, alternatively, for factors that change the implicit household production function. If we are studying the demand for children rather than for hi-fi sets, we have to ask ourselves what it is about children that distinguishes them from other time-intensive durable goods. Perhaps we should go back to some low-level discussions about the "motives" for having children, along the lines of the discussion of the demand for money in older textbooks. I would distinguish at least three interdependent motives: (1) economic security (current labor and old-age provisions), (2) the production of reciprocal caring, and (3) an attempt at immortality via one's offspring.

The last motive explains the attempts to impose an image on the children (an improved version of our own) and the interest in the actual basket of consumption rather than just the summary state (utility) of their well-being. The returns in terms of the first two motives have been declining secularly, perhaps even faster than the rise in costs implied by the cost-of-time hypothesis. It is my guess that part of the recent sharp decline in fertility stems from the clear recognition on the part of the current childbearing cohort of the relatively low rate of return experienced by their own parents.

Turning to the last part of Nerlove's paper, I want to take issue with the two stylized facts that appear to be empirical building blocks for his growth model: the constancy of the rate of return to schooling and a persistent disequilibrium reflected in higher rates of return to the investment in human as compared with physical capital. Both Finis Welch and I have to take some blame for popularizing the first "fact" at a time when it was beginning to cease being a "fact." The persistence of relatively high rates of return to schooling through the 1950s and 1960s in the face of rising schooling levels throughout the economy was probably the result of an accidental constellation of forces rather than the expression of an underlying constancy in the economic mechanism. The higher education boom was sustained by three forces: (1) the first round of cohorts to be educated after World War II was a relatively small and declining fraction of the population; (2) the post–World War II baby boom increased greatly the demand for teachers at all levels; and (3) at about the same time the government superimposed on all of this a space-defense-research-and-development boom, heavily human capital-intensive, resulting in a scramble for young, educated talent. Unfortunately, these fortuitous influences have run their course. The educational system has probably reached its longer-run equilibrium level, if it has not overshot it. The space research and development boom is over now, at a time when there is, and will be for the next 5 years or so, an annual wave of an additional one million highly educated workers arriving at the doors of the full-time labor force. The rates of return to schooling have already started falling and will probably fall quite a bit further before supply response catches up with them.

Also, I am not sure that I understand the disequilibrium discussion in Nerlove's paper. First, I know of no study that shows that relevant rates of return, computed in comparable terms, are significantly higher for schooling than for physical investment. The fact that human capital may have been growing faster than physical is no evidence for this proposition, and it does not require it.

References

Adelman, Irma. "An Econometric Analysis of Population Growth."
A.E.R. 53 (June 1963): 314–39.

Aigner, D. "An Appropriate Econometric Framework for Estimating
a Labor Supply Function from the SEO File." Madison: Soc. Systems Res. Inst., Univ. Wisconsin, 1971.

Aitchison, John, and Brown, J. A. C. *The Lognormal Distribution.*
Cambridge: Cambridge Univ. Press, 1963.

Alchian, Armen A., and Demsetz, Harold. "Production, Information
Costs, and Economic Organization." *A.E.R.* 62 (December 1972):
777–95.

Alstrom, C. H. "A Study of Inheritance of Human Intelligence." *Acta
Psychiatrica et Neurologica Scandinavica* (1961).

Andersen, Ronald, and Anderson, Odin W. *A Decade of Health Services: Social Survey Trends in Use and Expenditures.* Chicago: Univ.
Chicago Press, 1967.

Aoki, Hisao. *Selected Statistics concerning Fertility Regulation in Japan.* (In
Japanese.) Tokyo: Ministry Health and Welfare, 1967.

———. "A General View of Fertility and Its Regulation in Japan." (In
Japanese.) *Jinko Mondai Kenkyu* 114 (April 1970): 5–20.

Aoki, Hisao, and Nakano, Eiko. *Summary of the Fertility Surveys in 1940,
1952, 1957, and 1962.* (In Japanese.) Tokyo: Ministry Health and
Welfare, 1967.

Arrington, Leonard J. *Great Basin Kingdom.* Lincoln: Univ. Nebraska
Press, 1958.

Ashenfelter, Orley A., and Mooney, Joseph D. "Graduate Education,
Ability and Earnings." *Rev. Econ. and Statis.* 50 (February 1968):
78–86.

Auster, Richard D.; Leveson, Irving; and Sarachek, Deborah. "The
Production of Health: An Exploratory Study." *J. Human Resources* 4
(Fall 1969): 411–36.

Bachi, R., and Matras, J. "Contraception and Induced Abortions
among Jewish Maternity Cases in Israel." *Milbank Memorial Fund Q.*
40 (April 1962): 207–29.

Bajema, C. J. "Estimation of the Direction and Intensity of Natural
Selection in Relation to Human Intelligence by Means of the Intrinsic Rate of Natural Increase." *Eugenics Q.* 10 (December 1963):
175–87.

Baumol, William J. *Economic Dynamics: An Introduction.* 3d ed. New
York: Macmillan, 1970.

Becker, Gary S. "An Economic Analysis of Fertility." In *Demographic
and Economic Change in Developed Countries.* Universities–National
Bureau Conference Series, no. 11. Princeton, N.J.: Princeton Univ.
Press, 1960.

550 REFERENCES

Becker, Gary S. *Human Capital.* New York: Columbia Univ. Press (for Nat. Bur. Econ. Res.), 1964.

———. "A Theory of the Allocation of Time." *Econ. J.* 75 (September 1965): 493–517.

———. *Human Capital and the Personal Distribution of Income: An Analytical Approach.* Woytinsky Lecture no. 1. Ann Arbor: Inst. Public Admin., Univ. Michigan, 1967.

———. "A Theory of Social Interactions." Manuscript, Univ. Chicago, September 1969. Forthcoming in *J.P.E.*, vol. 82 (November–December 1974).

———. "A Theory of Marriage." Workshop paper, Univ. Chicago, October 1971. (*a*)

———. *Economic Theory.* New York: Knopf, 1971. (*b*)

Becker, Gary S., and Chiswick, Barry R. "Education and the Distribution of Earnings." *A.E.R.* 56 (May 1966): 358–69.

Ben-Porath, Yoram. "The Production of Human Capital and the Life Cycle of Earnings." *J.P.E.* 75 (August 1967): 352–65.

———. *Fertility in Israel, an Economist's Interpretation: Differentials and Trends, 1950–1970.* RM-5981-FF. Santa Monica, Calif.: RAND Corp., August 1970. (*a*)

———. "On the Association between Fertility and Education." Research Report no. 20. Mimeographed. Hebrew Univ. Jerusalem, 1970. (*b*)

———. "The Production of Human Capital over Time." In *Education, Income, and Human Capital,* edited by W. Lee Hansen. New York: Nat. Bur. Econ. Res., 1970. (*c*)

———. "Labor Force Participation Rates and the Supply of Labor." *J.P.E.* 81 (May/June 1973): 697–704.

Ben-Zion, U., and Ehrlich, I. "A Model of Productive Saving." Mimeographed. Univ. Chicago, 1972.

Berg, Alan. *The Nutrition Factor: Its Role in National Development.* Washington: Brookings Inst., 1973.

Black, J. D. *Introduction to Production Economics.* New York: Holt, 1926.

Blake, Judith. "Are Babies Consumer Durables? A Critique of the Economic Theory of Reproduction Motivation." *Population Studies* 22 (March 1968): 5–25.

Blau, Peter M., and Duncan, Otis Dudley. *The American Occupational Structure.* New York: Wiley, 1967.

Bowen, William G., and Finegan, T. A. *The Economics of Labor Force Participation.* Princeton, N.J.: Princeton Univ. Press, 1969.

Bowles, Samuel. "Schooling and Inequality from Generation to Generation." *J.P.E.* 80, pt. 2 (May/June 1972): S219–51.

Box, G. P., and Cox, D. "An Analysis of Transformations." *J. Royal Statis. Soc.* 26 (1964): 211–43.

Box, G. P., and Tidewell, P. "Transformations of Independent Variables." *Technometrics* 4 (1962): 531–42.

Broel-Plateris, Alexander. "Marriage Disruption and Divorce Law." Ph.D. dissertation, Univ. Chicago, 1961.

Bumpass, Larry L. "Age at Marriage as a Variable in Socio-economic Differentials in Fertility." *Demography* 6 (February 1969): 45–54.

Bumpass, Larry L., and Westoff, Charles F. *The Later Years of Childbearing.* Princeton, N.J.: Princeton Univ. Press, 1970.

Cain, Glen G. *Married Women in the Labor Force: An Economic Analysis.* Chicago: Univ. Chicago Press, 1966.

Cain, Glen G., and Weininger, Adriana. "Economic Determinants of Fertility: Results Using Cross-sectional Aggregate Data." Mimeographed. Madison: Univ. Wisconsin, 1967 (rev. 1971).

Caldwell, J. C. "Fertility Attitudes in Three Economically Contrasting Rural Regions of Ghana." *Econ. Development and Cultural Change* 15, no. 2 (January 1967): 217–38.

———. *Population Growth and Family Change in Africa.* Canberra: Australian Nat. Univ. Press, 1968.

Cavalli-Sforza, L. L., and Bodmer, W. F. *The Genetics of Human Populations.* San Francisco: Freeman, 1971.

Central Bureau of Statistics. *The Settlements of Israel.* Pts. 2, 3. Census Publication no. 11. Jerusalem: Central Bur. Statis., 1963.

———. "Family Expenditure Survey 1963/64." Special Series no. 200. Jerusalem: Central Bur. Statis, 1966. (*a*)

———. *The Settlements of Israel.* Pt. 4. Census Publication no. 28. Jerusalem: Central Bur. Statis, 1966. (*b*)

———. *Statistical Abstract of Israel, 1971.* No. 22. Jerusalem: Government Printer, 1971.

Cheung, Steven N. S. "The Enforcement of Property Rights in Children, and the Marriage Contract." *Econ. J.* 82 (June 1972): 641–57.

Chiswick, Barry R. *Income Inequality: Regional Analysis within a Human Capital Framework.* New York: Nat. Bur. Econ. Res., 1973.

Chiswick, Barry R., and Mincer, Jacob. "Time-Series Changes in Personal Income Inequality in the United States from 1939, with Projections to 1985." *J.P.E.* 80, pt. 2 (May/June 1972): S34–66

Chow, Gregory C. "Tests of Equality between Sets of Coefficients in Two Linear Regressions." *Econometrica* 28 (July 1960): 591–605.

Coale, A. S., and McNeil, D. R. "The Distribution by Age of the Frequency of First Marriage in a Female Cohort." *J. American Statis. Assoc.* 67 (December 1972): 743.

Cohen, Malcolm S.; Rea, Samuel A.; and Lerman, Robert J. "A Micro Model of Labor Supply." BLS Staff Report Paper no. 4, Dept. Labor Statis., Washington, 1970.

Cook, William D. "The Demand for Contraceptive Goods and Services: Low-Income Families, New Orleans." Manuscript, Tulane Univ., 1972.

Dandekar, Kumudini. "Effect of Education on Fertility." In *World*

Population Conference, 1965. Vol. 4. New York: United Nations, 1967.

DaVanzo, Julie. *The Determinants of Family Formation in Chile, 1960.* R-830-AID. Santa Monica, Calif.: RAND Corp., December 1971.

DeTray, Dennis N. *The Interaction between Parent Investment in Children and Family Size: An Economic Analysis.* R-1003-RF. Santa Monica, Calif.: RAND Corp., May 1972. (*a*)

————. "The Substitution between Quantity and Quality of Children in the Household." Ph.D. dissertation, Univ. Chicago, 1972. (*b*)

Dorjahn, V. R. "The Factor of Polygyny in African Demography." In *Continuity and Change in African Cultures,* edited by W. R. Bascom and M. J. Huskovity. Chicago: Univ. Chicago Press, 1959.

Duesenberry, James. Comment on "An Economic Analysis of Fertility" by Gary S. Becker. In *Demographic and Economic Change in Developed Countries.* Universities–National Bureau Conference Series, no. 11. Princeton, N.J.: Princeton Univ. Press, 1960.

Dugan, D. J. "The Impact of Parental and Educational Investment upon School Achievement." *American Statis. Assoc., Social Statis. Sec., Proc.* (1969).

Duncan, Otis Dudley; Featherman, David L.; and Duncan, Beverly. *Socioeconomic Background and Achievement.* New York: Seminar, 1972.

Eads, George; Nerlove, Marc; and Raduchel, William. "A Long-Run Cost Function for the Local Service Airline Industry: An Experiment in Nonlinear Estimation." *Rev. Econ. and Statis.* 51 (August 1969): 258–70.

Easterlin, Richard A. *Population, Labor Force, and Long Swings in Economic Growth: The American Experience.* General Series, no. 86. New York: Nat. Bur. Econ. Res., 1968.

————. "Towards a Socio-economic Theory of Fertility: A Survey of Recent Research on Economic Factors in American Fertility." In *Fertility and Family Planning: A World View,* edited by S. J. Behrman, Leslie Corsa, Jr., and Ronald Freedman. Ann Arbor: Univ. Michigan Press, 1969.

Ehrlich, Isaac. "Participation in Illegitimate Activities: An Economic Analysis." Ph.D. dissertation, Columbia Univ., 1970.

Fane, George. "The Productive Value of Education in Agriculture in the U.S." Ph.D. dissertation, Harvard Univ., 1972.

Farrar, Donald E., and Glauber, R. R. "Multicollinearity in Regression Analysis: The Problem Revisited." *Rev. Econ. and Statis.* 49 (February 1967): 99–107.

Fishelsohn, G. "Labor Force Participation of Married Women." Manuscript, Univ. Tel Aviv, 1972.

Fisher, F. M. *A Priori Information and Time Series Analysis.* Amsterdam: North-Holland, 1962.

Fisher, R. A. *The Genetical Theory of Natural Selection.* 2d ed. New York: Dover, 1958.

Freedman, Deborah S. "The Relation of Economic Status to Fertility." *A.E.R.* 53 (June 1963): 414–26.

Freedman, Ronald, and Coombs, L. "Childspacing and Family Economic Position." *American Sociological Rev.* 31 (October 1966): 631–48. (*a*)

―――. "Economic Considerations in Family Growth Decisions." *Population Studies* 20, no. 2 (November 1966): 197–222. (*b*)

Freedman, Ronald, and Slesinger, Doris P. "Fertility Differentials for the Indigenous Non-Farm Population of the United States." *Population Studies* 15 (November 1961): 161–73.

Freedman, Ronald, and Takeshita, John Y. *Family Planning in Taiwan.* Princeton, N.J.: Princeton Univ. Press, 1969.

Freedman, Ronald; Whelpton, Pascal K.; and Campbell, A. A. *Family Planning, Sterility, and Population Growth.* New York: McGraw-Hill, 1959.

Freiden, Alan. "A Model of Marriage and Fertility." Ph.D. dissertation, Univ. Chicago, 1972.

Friedlander, Stanley, and Silver, M. "A Quantitative Study of the Determinants of Fertility Behavior." *Demography* 4, no. 1 (1967): 30–70.

Fuchs, Victor. *Differentials in Hourly Earnings by Region and City Size, 1959.* Occasional Paper no. 101. New York: Nat. Bur. Econ. Res., 1967.

―――. "Differences in Hourly Earnings between Men and Women." *Monthly Labor Rev.* 94 (May 1971): 9–15.

Gardner, Bruce. "Measuring the Income of Rural Families: A Survey of Sampson County, N.C." Econ. Res. Report, North Carolina State Univ., Raleigh, 1971.

―――. "Economic Aspects of the Fertility of Rural-Farm and Urban Women." *Southern Econ. J.* 38 (April 1972): 518–24.

Gerschenkron, Alexander. Review of *Demographic and Economic Change in Developed Countries. J. American Statis. Assoc.* 56 (December 1961): 1006–8.

Ghez, Gilbert R. "A Theory of Life Cycle Consumption." Ph.D. dissertation, Columbia Univ., 1970.

Ghez, Gilbert R., and Becker, Gary S. "The Allocation of Time and Goods over the Life Cycle." Report no. 7217, Center Math. Studies Bus. and Econ., Univ. Chicago, April 1972.

Goldberg, David. "The Fertility of Two-Generation Urbanites." *Population Studies* 12 (July 1958): 214–22.

Goldfeld, S., and Quandt, R. *Nonlinear Methods in Econometrics.* Amsterdam: North-Holland, 1972.

Goode, William J. *After Divorce.* Glencoe, Ill.: Free Press, 1956.

Goode, William J. "Marital Satisfaction and Instability: A Cross-cultural Class Analysis of Divorce Rates." *Internat. Social Sci. J.* 14, no. 3 (1962): 507–26.

———. *World Revolution and Family Patterns.* New York: Free Press, 1963.

———. *Explorations in Social Theory.* New York: Oxford, 1973.

———. *The Celebration of Heroes: Prestige as a Control System* (forthcoming).

Gorman, W. M. "Separability and Aggregation." *Econometrica* 27 (July 1959): 469–81.

Griliches, Zvi. "A Note on Serial Correlation Bias in Distributed Lag Models." *Econometrica* 29 (January 1961): 65–73.

Griliches, Zvi, and Mason, William M. "Education, Income, and Ability." *J.P.E.* 80, pt. 2 (May–June 1972): S74–103.

Gronau, Reuben. "An Economic Approach to Marriage: The Intrafamily Allocation of Time." Paper presented at the 2d World Congress of the Econometric Society, Cambridge, 1970. (*a*)

———. *The Value of Time in Passenger Transportation: The Demand for Air Travel.* Occasional Paper no. 109. New York: Nat. Bur. Econ. Res., 1970. (*b*)

———. *The Wage Rates of Women: A Selectivity Bias.* New York: Nat. Bur. Econ. Res., 1972.

———. "The Intra-Family Allocation of Time: The Value of the Housewives' Time." *A.E.R.* 63 (September 1973): 634–51.

———. "The Measurement of Output of the Non-Market Sector—the Evaluation of the Housewife's Time." In *Measurement of Economic and Social Performance,* edited by M. Moss. Studies in Income and Wealth, no. 38. New York: Nat. Bur. Econ. Res., 1974.

Grossman, Michael. "The Demand for Health: A Theoretical and Empirical Investigation." Ph.D. dissertation, Columbia Univ., 1970.

———. "The Economics of Joint Production in the Household." Report no. 7145, Center Math. Studies Bus. and Econ., Univ. Chicago, September 1971.

———. "On the Concept of Health Capital and the Demand for Health." *J.P.E.* 80 (March/April 1972): 223–55. (*a*)

———. *The Demand for Health: A Theoretical and Empirical Investigation.* Occasional Paper no. 119. New York: Columbia Univ. Press (for Nat. Bur. Econ. Res.), 1972. (*b*)

Hansen, W. Lee; Weisbrod, Burton A.; and Scanlon, William J. "Schooling and Earnings of Low Achievers." *A.E.R.* 60 (June 1970): 409–18.

Harberger, Arnold. "Taxation, Resource Allocation, and Welfare." In *The Role of Direct and Indirect Taxes in the Federal Revenue System.* Princeton, N.J.: Princeton Univ. Press (for Brookings Inst. and Nat. Bur. Econ. Res.), 1964.

Harman, A. J. *Fertility and Economic Behavior of Families in the Philippines.* RM-6385-AID. Santa Monica, Calif.: RAND Corp., September 1970.

Hause, John. "Earnings Profile: Ability and Schooling." *J.P.E.* 80, pt. 2 (May/June 1972): S108–38.

Heckman, James J. "Three Essays on the Supply of Labor and the Demand for Market Goods." Ph.D. dissertation, Princeton Univ., 1971.

————. "Shadow Prices, Market Wages, and Labor Supply." *Econometrica* (1974), in press.

Hicks, J. R. *Value of Capital.* Oxford: Clarendon, 1939 (2d ed., 1946).

————. *The Theory of Wages.* New York: Peter Smith, 1948.

Higgins, J. V.; Reed, W. E.; and Reed, S. C. "Intelligence and Family Size: A Paradox Resolved." *Eugenics Q.* 9 (March 1962): 84–90.

Hill, C. Russell, and Stafford, Frank P. "The Allocation of Time to Children and Educational Opportunity." Discussion paper, Inst. Public Policy Studies, Univ. Michigan. Presented at the Econometric Society meetings, New Orleans, December 1971.

————. "The Allocation of Time to Preschool Children and Educational Opportunity." *J. Human Resources,* vol. 9 (Summer 1974).

Hitotsubashi University Institute of Economic Research. "National Income Study Group Materials C1, C18." Mimeographed. (In Japanese.) Tokyo: Hitotsubashi Univ. Inst. Econ. Res., 1968.

Honda, Tatsuo. "Summary of the Third Fertility Survey in 1957." (In Japanese.) *Jinko Mondai Kenkyu* 77 (August 1959): 1–24.

Honjo, Eijiro. *Nihon jinko shi* [Japanese population history]. Tokyo: Nihon Hyoron-sha, 1941.

Hotelling, Harold. "Edgeworth's Taxation Paradox and the Nature of Demand and Supply Functions." *J.P.E.* 40 (October 1932): 577–616.

Houthakker, Hendrik S. "Compensated Changes in Quantities and Qualities Consumed." *Rev. Econ. Studies* 19, no. 3 (1952): 155–61.

————. "The Pareto Distribution and the Cobb-Douglas Production Function in Activity Analysis." *Rev. Econ. Studies* 23, no. 1 (1955): 27–31.

Huffman, Wallace E. "The Contribution of Education and Extension to Different Rates of Change." Ph.D. dissertation, Univ. Chicago, 1972.

Jaffe, A. J. "Urbanization and Fertility." *American J. Sociology* 48 (July 1942): 48–60.

Japan Ministry of Education. *Yearbook of the Ministry of Education.* (In Japanese.) Tokyo: Ministry Educ., 1904 and succeeding annual issues.

Japan Ministry of Health and Welfare. *Vital Statistics of Japan.* Tokyo: Ministry Health and Welfare, 1970.

Japan Ministry of Health and Welfare, Institute of Population Problems. "Summary of the Fifth Mainichi Survey of Family Planning Opinion." (In Japanese.) *Jinko Mondai Kenkyu* 77 (August 1959): 60–88.

———. *Reproduction Indices for Japan, 1960–1965.* (In Japanese.) Tokyo: Ministry Health and Welfare, 1967.

———*Report on the Fifth Fertility Survey.* (In Japanese.) Tokyo: Ministry Health and Welfare, 1968.

Japan Prime Minister's Office. *Descriptive Materials on Japanese Vital Statistics.* (In Japanese.)Tokyo: Prime Minister's Office, 1917 and succeeding issues.

———. *Annual Statistics of Japan: 1960.* Tokyo: Prime Minister's Office, 1960. (*a*)

———. *Censuses of Population of Japan.* Tokyo: Prime Minister's Office, 1955, 1960 (*b*), 1965, 1970.

———. *Statistical Yearbook of Japan.* Tokyo: Prime Minister's Office, various annual issues.

Johnson, George E., and Stafford, Frank P. "Social Returns to Quantity and Quality of Schooling." *J. Human Resources* 8 (Spring 1973): 139–55.

Johnson, Harry G. "The Economic Approach to Social Questions." *Economica* 36 (February 1968): 1–21.

Jones, R. W. "The Structure of Simple General Equilibrium Models." *J.P.E.* 73 (December 1965): 557–72.

Kagan, Jerome S. "Inadequate Evidence and Illogical Conclusions." *Harvard Educ. Rev.* 39 (Spring 1969): 274–77.

Kagan, Jerome S., and Moss, H. A. "Parental Correlates of Child's IQ and Height." *Child Development* 30 (September 1959): 325–32.

Keeley, Michael C. "A Model of Marital Formation: The Determinants of the Optimal Age at First Marriage and Differences in Age at Marriage." Ph.D. dissertation, Univ. Chicago, 1974.

Kendall, M. G. "Proof of Relations Connected with the Tetrachoric Series and Its Generalizations." *Biometrica* 32 (1941): 196–99.

Keyfitz, Nathan. "How Birth Control Affects Births." *Social Biology* 18, no. 2 (June 1971): 109–21.

Keynes, John Maynard. *The General Theory of Employment, Interest, and Money.* New York: Harcourt Brace, 1936.

Khaldi, Nabil. "The Productive Value of Education in the U.S. Agriculture, 1964." Ph.D. dissertation, Southern Methodist Univ., 1972.

King, Willford Isbell. *Employment Hours and Earnings in Prosperity and Depression: United States, 1920–1922.* New York: Nat. Bur. Econ. Res., 1923.

Kiser, C. V. "Birth Rates among Rural Migrants to Cities." *Milbank Memorial Fund Q.* 16 (October 1938): 369–81.

Kiser, C. V.; Grabill, W. H.; and Campbell, A. A. *Trends and Variations in Fertility in the United States.* Cambridge, Mass.: Harvard Univ. Press, 1968.

Knight, Frank H. *Risk, Uncertainty, and Profit.* Boston: Houghton-Mifflin, 1921.

———. "Diminishing Returns from Investment." *J.P.E.* 52 (March 1944): 26–47.

———. *The Economic Organization.* New York: Harper & Row, 1965. (Originally published by the College of the University of Chicago, 1933.)

Kogut, E. L. "An Economic Analysis of Demographic Phenomena: A Case Study of Brazil." Ph.D. dissertation, Univ. Chicago, 1972.

Koopmans, Tjalling C. "Intertemporal Distribution and 'Optima' Aggregate Economic Growth." In *Ten Economic Studies in the Tradition of Irving Fisher,* by W. Fellner et al. New York: Wiley, 1967.

Koopmans, Tjalling C., and Beckman, M. "Assignment Problems and the Location of Economic Activities." *Econometrica* 25 (January 1957): 53–76.

Kosters, M. "Income and Substitution Effects in a Family Labor Supply Model." P-3339. Santa Monica, Calif.: RAND Corp., 1966.

Kuratani, M. "Earnings Distribution and Specific Training: The Case of Japan." Mimeographed. Univ. Chicago, 1972.

Kuznets, Simon. *Modern Economic Growth: Rate, Structure, and Spread.* New Haven, Conn.: Yale Univ. Press, 1966.

———. *Economic Growth and Nations.* Cambridge, Mass.: Harvard Univ. Press, 1971.

———. "Modern Economic Growth: Findings and Reflections." (Nobel Prize lecture, December 1971.) *A.E.R.* 63 (June 1973): 247–58.

Lancaster, Kelvin J. "A New Approach to Consumer Theory." *J.P.E.* 74 (April 1966): 132–57.

Landsberger, Michael. "An Integrated Model of Consumption and Market Activity: The Children Effect." *American Statis. Assoc., Social Statis. Sec., Proc.* (1971), pp. 137–42.

Leibenstein, Harvey. *Economic Backwardness and Economic Growth: Studies in the Theory of Economic Development.* New York: Wiley, 1957.

———. "The Impact of Population Growth on Economic Welfare —Non-traditional Elements." In *Rapid Population Growth.* Baltimore: Johns Hopkins Press (for Nat. Acad. Sci.), 1971.

Leibowitz, Arleen S. "Women's Allocation of Time to Market and Nonmarket Activities: Differences by Education." Ph.D. dissertation, Columbia Univ., 1972.

———. "Education and the Allocation of Women's Time." In *Education, Income, and Human Behavior,* edited by F. Thomas Juster. New York: McGraw-Hill (for Carnegie Commission Higher Educ. and Nat. Bur. Econ. Res.), 1974, in press.

Leontief, W. "Introduction to a Theory of the Internal Structure of

Functional Relationships." *Econometrica* 15 (October 1947): 361–73.

Lewis, H. Gregg. "On Income and Substitution Effect in Labor Force Participation." Mimeographed. Dept. Econ., Univ. Chicago, 1971.

Linder, Staffan B. *The Harried Leisure Class.* New York: Columbia Univ. Press, 1970.

Lindsay, C. M. "Measuring Human Capital Returns." *J.P.E.* 79 (November/December 1971): 1195—1215.

Low, S., and Spindler, A. *The Child Care Arrangements of Working Mothers.* Children's Bureau Publication no. 461. Washington: Government Printing Office, 1968.

McCall, J. J. "Economics of Information and Job Search." *Q.J.E.* 84 (February 1970): 113–26.

MacLeod, John, and Gold, Ruth Z. "The Male Factor in Fertility and Infertility." *Fertility and Sterility* 4, no. 1 (1953): 10–33.

Mainichi Newspaper Company. *Family Planning Survey.* (In Japanese.) Tokyo: Mainichi Newspaper Co., 1950 and succeeding years.

———. *Nihon no Jinko Kakumei* [Japan's population revolution]. (In Japanese.) Tokyo: Mainichi Newspaper Co., 1970.

Malinvaud, E. *Statistical Methods of Econometrics.* Chicago: Rand McNally; Amsterdam: North-Holland, 1966. 2d ed. Amsterdam: North-Holland, 1970.

Malthus, T. R. *An Essay on the Principle of Population and a Summary View of the Principle of Population.* Baltimore: Penguin, 1970. (Originally published in 1798 and 1830.)

Marshall, Alfred. *Principles of Economics.* 8th ed. (1st ed., 1890.) London: Macmillan, 1930.

Matras, J., and Auerbach, C. "On Rationalizations of Family Formation in Israel." *Milbank Memorial Fund Q.* 40 (October 1962): 453–80.

Matsumoto, Y. Scott; Koizumi, Akira; and Nohara, Tadahiro. "Condom Use in Japan." *Studies in Family Planning* 3 (October 1972): 251–55.

Matsunaga, Ei. "Measures Affecting Population Trends and Possible Genetic Consequences." In *World Population Conference, 1965.* Vol. 2. New York: United Nations, 1967.

Maurer, K. M.; Ratajczak, R.; and Schultz, T. Paul. *Marriage, Fertility, and Labor Force Participation of Thai Women: An Econometric Study.* R-829-AID. Santa Monica, Calif.: RAND Corp., May 1972.

Michael, Robert T. "The Effect of Education on Efficiency in Consumption." Ph.D. dissertation, Columbia Univ., 1969.

———. "Education and the Derived Demand for Children." Mimeographed. Univ. California, Los Angeles, October 1970.

———. "Dimensions of Household Fertility: An Economic Analysis." *American Statis. Assoc., Social Statis. Sec., Proc.* (1971), pp. 126–36.

———. *The Effect of Education on Efficiency in Consumption.* Occasional Paper no. 116. New York: Nat. Bur. Econ. Res., 1972.

―――. "Education in Nonmarket Production." *J.P.E.* 81, pt. 1 (March/April 1973): 306–27.

―――. "Education and Fertility." In *Education, Income, and Human Behavior,* edited by F. Thomas Juster. New York: McGraw-Hill (for Carnegie Commission Higher Educ. and Nat. Bur. Econ. Res.), 1974, in press.

Michael, Robert T., and Becker, Gary S. "On the New Theory of Consumer Behavior." *Swedish J. Econ.* 75 (1973): 378–96.

Michael, Robert T., with Edward P. Lazear. "On the Shadow Price of Children." Mimeographed. Nat. Bur. Econ. Res., December 1971. (Presented at the meeting of the Econometric Society, New Orleans, December 1971.)

Mincer, Jacob. "Labor Force Participation of Married Women." In *Aspects of Labor Economics,* edited by H. Gregg Lewis. Universities–National Bureau Conference Series no. 14. Princeton, N.J.: Princeton Univ. Press, 1962. (*a*)

―――. "On-the-Job Training: Costs, Returns, and Some Implications." *J.P.E.* 70, pt. 2 (October 1962): 50–79. (*b*)

―――. "Market Prices, Opportunity Costs, and Income Effects." In *Measurement in Economics: Studies in Mathematical Economics and Econometrics in Memory of Yehuda Grunfeld,* edited by Carl Christ et al. Stanford, Calif.: Stanford Univ. Press, 1963.

―――. "The Distribution of Labor Incomes: A Survey with Special Reference to the Human Capital Approach." *J. Econ. Literature* 8 (March 1970): 1–26. (*a*)

―――. Comment on "The Production of Human Capital over Time" by Yoram Ben-Porath. In *Education, Income, and Human Capital,* edited by W. Lee Hansen. New York: Nat. Bur. Econ. Res., 1970. (*b*)

―――. "Education, Experience, and the Distribution of Earnings and of Employment." In *Education, Income, and Human Behavior,* edited by F. Thomas Juster. New York: McGraw-Hill (for Carnegie Commission Higher Educ. and Nat. Bur. Econ. Res.), 1974, in press. (*a*)

―――. *Schooling, Experience, and Earnings.* New York: Nat. Bur. Econ. Res., 1974. (*b*)

Mitchell, Wesley C. "The Backward Art of Spending Money." *A.E.R.* 2 (June 1912): 269–81.

―――. *The Backward Art of Spending Money and Other Essays.* New York: McGraw-Hill, 1937.

Moeller, John Francis. "Household Budget Responses to Negative-Tax Simulations." Ph.D. dissertation, Univ. Wisconsin, 1970.

Morgan, James N.; Sirageldin, Ismail; and Baerwaldt, Nancy. *Productive Americans: A Study of How Individuals Contribute to Economic Progress.* Ann Arbor: Univ. Michigan Inst. Social Res., 1966.

Morishima, Michio. *Theory of Economic Growth.* 2d rev. ed. Oxford: Clarendon, 1970.

Morrison, William A. "Attitudes of Females toward Family Planning in a Maharashtrian Village." *Milbank Memorial Fund Q.* 35 (January 1957): 67–81.

Mortensen, D. T. "Job Search, the Duration of Unemployment and the Phillips Curve." *A.E.R.* 60 (December 1970): 847–62.

Mosteller, Frederick. *On Equality of Educational Opportunity.* New York: Vintage, 1972.

Muramatsu, M. "Effect of Induced Abortions on the Reduction of Birth in Japan." *Milbank Memorial Fund Q.* 38 (April 1960): 153–66.

———. "Problems in Procuring Contraceptive Materials in Rural Areas in Japan." In *Research in Family Planning,* edited by Clyde V. Kiser. Princeton, N.J.: Princeton Univ. Press, 1962.

———. "Policy Measures and Social Changes for Fertility Decline in Japan." In *World Population Conference, 1965.* Vol. 2. New York: United Nations, 1967.

Muth, Richard F. "Household Production and Consumer Demand Functions." *Econometrica* 34 (July 1966): 699–708.

National Council of Churches, Bureau of Research and Survey. *Churches and Church Membership in the U.S.* Ser. A, no. 3. New York: Nat. Council Churches, 1956.

Nelson, P. J. "Information and Consumer Behavior." *J.P.E.* 78 (March/April 1970): 311–29.

Nelson, R., and Krashinsky, S. "The Organization and Planning of Day Care for Children." Washington: Urban Inst., August 1972.

Nerlove, Marc. "A Note on Error-Components Models." *Econometrica* 39 (March 1971): 383–96. (a)

———. "Further Evidence on the Estimation of Dynamic Economic Relations from a Time Series of Cross Sections." *Econometrica* 39 (March 1971): 359–82. (b)

———. "Lags in Economic Behavior." *Econometrica* 40 (March 1972): 221–52. (a)

———. "Tuition and the Costs of Higher Education: Prolegomena to a Conceptual Framework." *J.P.E.* 80, pt. 2 (May/June 1972): S178–218. (b)

Nerlove, Marc, and Schultz, T. Paul. *Love and Life between the Censuses: A Model of Family Decision Making in Puerto Rico, 1950–1960.* RM-6322-AID. Santa Monica, Calif.: RAND Corp., September 1970.

Oaxaca, Ronald L. "Male-Female Wage Differentials in Urban Labor Markets." Ph.D. dissertation, Princeton Univ., 1971.

Ofek, H. "Allocation of Time and Goods in a Family Context." Ph.D. dissertation, Columbia Univ., 1972.

O'Hara, Donald J. *Changes in Mortality Levels and Family Decisions regarding Children.* R-914-RF. Santa Monica, Calif.: RAND Corp., February 1972.

Okazaki, Yoichi. "Meiji Period Population." (In Japanese.) *Keizai Kenkyu* 16 (July 1965): 207–13.

———. "An Analysis of the Socio-economic Factors Affecting Fertility in Japan." (In Japanese.) *Jinko Mondai Kenkyu* 114 (April 1970): 21–34.

Okun, Bernard. *Trends in Birth Rates in the United States since 1870.* Studies in Historical and Political Science, ser. 77. Baltimore: Johns Hopkins Press, 1958.

———. Comment on "An Economic Analysis of Fertility" by Gary S. Becker. In *Demographic and Economic Change in Developed Countries.* Universities–National Bureau Conference Series, no. 11. Princeton, N.J.: Princeton Univ. Press, 1960.

Parnes, Herbert S.; Shea, John R.; Spitz, Ruth S.; and Zeller, Frederick A. *Dual Careers.* Vol. 1. Manpower Research Monograph no. 21. Washington: Dept. Labor, 1970.

Peled, Z. "Problems and Attitudes in Family Planning." (In Hebrew.) Mimeographed. Jerusalem: Israel Inst. Appl. Social Res., March 1969.

Pennock, Jean L. "Cost of Raising a Child." *Family Econ. Rev.* (ARS 62-5) (March 1970), pp. 13–17.

Petersen, William. *Population.* 2d ed. London: Macmillan, 1969.

Pitchford, J. D. "Population in Economic Growth." Mimeographed. Canberra: Australian Nat. Univ., 1973.

Polachek, Solomon. "Work Experience and the Difference between Male and Female Wages." Ph.D. dissertation, Columbia Univ., 1973.

Potter, Robert G., Jr. "Birth Intervals: Structure and Change." *Population Studies* 17 (November 1963): 152–62.

Potter, Robert G.; McCann, Barbara; and Sakoda, James M. "Selective Fecundability and Contraceptive Effectiveness." *Milbank Memorial Fund Q.* 48 (January 1970): 91–102.

Potter, Robert G.; Sagi, Philip C.; and Westoff, Charles F. "Knowledge of the Ovulatory Cycle and Coital Frequency as Factors Affecting Conception and Contraception." *Milbank Memorial Fund Q.* 40 (January 1962): 46–58.

Rahm, M. "The Occupational Wage Structure." Ph.D. dissertation, Columbia Univ., 1971.

Razin, Assaf. "Investment in Human Capital and Economic Growth: A Theoretical Study." Ph.D. dissertation, Univ. Chicago, 1969.

———. "Investment in Human Capital and Economic Growth." *Metroeconomica* 24 (May/August 1972): 101–16.

Reid, Margaret G. *Economics of Household Production.* New York: Wiley, 1934.

———. "Effect of Income Concept upon Expenditure Curves of Farm Families." In *Studies in Income and Wealth,* no. 15. New York: Nat. Bur. Econ. Res., 1952.

Reid, Margaret G. *Housing and Income.* Chicago: Univ. Chicago Press, 1962.

Reischauer, R. "The Impact of the Welfare System on Black Migration and Marital Stability." Ph.D. dissertation, Columbia Univ., 1970.

Research Triangle Institute. "An Index of Economic Status of Individual Rural Families." Mimeographed. Research Triangle Park, N.C.: Res. Triangle Inst., 1971.

Rheinstein, Max. *Marriage Stability, Divorce, and the Law.* Chicago: Univ. Chicago Press, 1972.

Rivers, W. H. *The Todas.* London: Macmillan, 1906.

Roberts, G. W.; Cummins, G. T.; Bryne, J.; Alleyne, C. "Knowledge and Use of Birth Control in Barbados." *Demography* 4, no. 2 (1967): 576–600.

Rogers, Daniel C. "Private Rates of Return to Education in the U.S.: A Case Study." *Yale Econ. Essays* 9 (Spring 1969): 89–134.

Rosen, Sherwin. "Short-Run Employment Variation on Class-I Railroads in the U.S., 1947–63." *Econometrica* 36 (July/October 1968): 511–29.

Ross, Sue. "The Effect of Economic Variables on the Timing and Spacing of Births." Ph.D. dissertation, Columbia Univ., 1974.

Ruderman, F. *Child Care and Working Mothers.* New York: Child Welfare League America, 1968.

Rybczynski, T. N. "Factor Endowments and Relative Commodity Prices." *Economica,* n.s. 22 (November 1955): 336–41.

Ryder, Norman B. "The Emergence of a Modern Fertility Pattern: U.S., 1917–1966." In *Fertility and Family Planning: A World View,* edited by S. J. Behrman, Leslie Corsa, Jr., and Ronald Freedman. Ann Arbor: Univ. Michigan Press, 1969.

Ryder, Norman B., and Westoff, Charles F. *Reproduction in the United States, 1965.* Princeton, N.J.: Princeton Univ. Press, 1971.

Salzano, F. M.; Neel, J. V.; and Maybury-Lewis, D. "Further Studies on the Xavante Indians." *American J. Human Genetics* 19 (July 1967): 463–89.

Samuelson, Paul A. "International Price Equalization Once Again." *Econ. J.* 59, no. 2 (June 1949): 181–97.

———. "Social Indifference Curves." *Q.J.E.* 70 (February 1956): 1–22.

Sanderson, Warren, and Willis, Robert J. "Economic Models of Fertility: Some Examples and Implications." In *New Directions in Economic Research.* 51st Annual Report of the National Bureau of Economic Research. New York: Nat. Bur. Econ. Res., September 1971.

Santos, F. P. "Marital Instability and Male-Female Complementarity." Ph.D. dissertation, Columbia Univ., 1970.

Scarr-Salapatek, Sandra. "Race, Social Class and IQ." *Science,* December 24, 1971, pp. 1285–95.

Schoggen, P. H., and Schoggen, Maxine F. "Behavior Units in Observational Research." Paper presented at the symposium on Methodological Issues in Observational Research, American Psychological Association, San Francisco, 1968.

Schultz, T. Paul. *A Family Planning Hypothesis: Some Empirical Evidence from Puerto Rico.* RM-5405-RC/AID. Santa Monica, Calif.: RAND Corp., December 1967.

———. "An Economic Model of Family Planning and Fertility." *J.P.E.* 77, no. 2 (March/April 1969): 153–80.

———. *Fertility Patterns and Their Determinants in the Arab Middle East.* RM-5978-FF. Santa Monica, Calif.: RAND Corp., May 1970.

———. *Evaluation of Population Policies: A Framework for Analysis and Its Application to Taiwan's Family Planning Program.* R-643-AID. Santa Monica, Calif.: RAND Corp., June 1971. (*a*)

———. "The Effectiveness of Population Policies: Alternative Methods of Statistical Inference." P-4663. Santa Monica, Calif.: RAND Corp., July 1971. (*b*)

———. "An Economic Perspective on Population Growth." In *Rapid Population Growth.* Baltimore: Johns Hopkins Press (for Nat. Acad. Sci.), 1971. (*c*)

———. "Economics of Fertility and Household Behavior: United States 1967." Mimeographed. Santa Monica, Calif.: RAND Corp., 1972. (*a*)

———. "Education, Wages and Fertility in Bogota, Colombia." Mimeographed. RAND Corp., 1972. (*b*)

Schultz, T. Paul, and DaVanzo, Julie. *Analysis of Demographic Change in East Pakistan: Retrospective Survey Data.* R-564-AID. Santa Monica, Calif.: RAND Corp., September 1970.

Schultz, Theodore W. "Education and Economic Growth." In *Social Forces Influencing American Education, 1961,* edited by Nelson B. Henry. 60th Yearbook of the National Society for the Study of Education, pt. 2. Chicago: Univ. Chicago Press, 1961.

———. *Transforming Traditional Agriculture.* New Haven, Conn.: Yale Univ. Press, 1964.

———. *Investment in Human Capital.* New York: Free Press, 1971.

———. *Human Resources: Fiftieth Anniversary Colloquium 6.* New York: Nat. Bur. Econ. Res., 1972. (*a*)

———. "The Increasing Economic Value of Human Time." *American J. Agricultural Econ.* 54 (December 1972): 843–50. (*b*)

———. "Explanation and Interpretations of the Increasing Value of Human Time." Mimeographed. Woody Thompson lecture, Midwest Economics Association, Chicago, April 5, 1973.

Schwartz, Aba. "Migration and Lifespan Earnings in the U.S." Ph.D. dissertation, Univ. Chicago, 1968.

Shaw, George Bernard. *Man and Superman.* In *The Collected Works of*

Bernard Shaw. Vol. 10. Ayot St. Lawrence ed. New York: Wise, 1930.

Shell, K. *Essays on Theory of Optimal Economic Growth.* Cambridge, Mass.: M.I.T. Press, 1967.

Shinozaki, Nobuo. "Regional Problem of Population in Japan from the Viewpoint of Fertility." (In Japanese.) *Jinko Mondai Kenkyu* 118 (April 1971): 5–20.

Silver, Morris. "Births, Marriages, and Business Cycles in the United States." *J.P.E.* 73 (June 1965): 237–55.

———. "Births, Marriages, and Income Fluctuations in the United Kingdom and Japan." *Econ. Development and Cultural Change* 14 (April 1966): 302–15.

Simon, Julian. "The Effect of Income on Fertility." *Population Studies* 23 (November 1969): 327–41.

Sloan, F. "Survival of Progeny in Developing Countries: An Analysis of Evidence from Costa Rica, Mexico, East Pakistan, and Puerto Rico." R-773-AID. Santa Monica, Calif.: RAND Corp., July 1971.

Smith, James P. "The Life Cycle Allocation of Time in a Family Context." Ph.D. dissertation, Univ. Chicago, 1972. (*a*)

———. "Life Cycle Patterns." Mimeographed. Univ. Chicago, 1972. (*b*)

Solmon, Lewis C. "The Relationship between Schooling and Savings Behavior." In *Education, Income, and Human Behavior,* edited by F. Thomas Juster. New York: McGraw-Hill (for Carnegie Commission Higher Educ. and Nat. Bur. Econ. Res.), 1974, in press.

Solow, Robert M. "A Contribution to the Theory of Economic Growth." *Q.J.E.* 70 (February 1956): 65–94.

Sontag, Lester W.; Baker, Charles T.; and Nelson, Virginia L. *Mental Growth and Personality Development: A Longitudinal Study.* In *Monographs of the Society for Research in Child Development,* vol. 23, no. 68. Lafayette, Ind.: Child Development Publications, 1958.

Stigler, George J. "The Economics of Information." *J.P.E.* 69 (June 1961): 213–25.

Stolper, Wolfgang F., and Samuelson, Paul A. "Protection and Real Wages." *Rev. Econ. Studies* 9 (1941): 58–73.

Strotz, R. "The Empirical Implications of a Utility Tree." *Econometrica* 25 (April 1957): 269–80.

———. "The Utility Tree—Correction and Further Appraisal." *Econometrica* 27 (July 1959): 482–88.

Stycos, J. Mayone. "Education and Fertility in Puerto Rico." In *World Population Conference, 1965.* Vol. 4. New York: United Nations, 1967.

Suter, Larry E., and Miller, Herman P. "Components of Income Differences between Men and Women in the United States." Paper presented at the American Sociological Association meetings, Denver, 1971.

Sutton, Gordon F., and Wunderlich, Gooloo S. "Estimating Marital Fertility Rates by Educational Attainment Using a Survey of New Mothers." *Demography* 4, no. 1 (1967): 135–42.

Swan, T. W. "Economic Growth and Capital Accumulation." *Econ. Rec.* 32 (November 1956): 334–61.

Sweet, James A. "Family Composition and the Labor Force Activity of Married Women in the United States." Ph.D. dissertation, Univ. Michigan, 1968.

Tachi, Minoru. "The Relationship between Production Increase and Population Growth among Japanese Prefectures, 1925–1935." (In Japanese.) *Jinko Mondai Kenkyu* 5 (February 1946): 15–44.

Tachi, Minoru, and Arao, M. "Marriage Rate and Business Cycle in Japan." *Jinko Mondai* 2 (October 1935): 205–20.

Taeuber, Irene. *The Population of Japan.* Princeton, N.J.: Princeton Univ. Press, 1958.

Taiwan Department of Civil Affairs. *The Taiwan Demographic Fact Book.* Nantou: Taiwan Provincial Government, 1961, 1963, and subsequent years.

Taiwan Population Studies Center. *The Demographic Reference: Taiwan.* Taichung: Taiwan Population Studies Center, 1965 and subsequent years.

Taiwan Provincial Institute of Family Planning (formerly Taiwan Population Studies Center). *Family Planning Reference Book.* Vol. 1. Taichung: Taiwan Provincial Inst. Family Planning, 1969.

Taubman, Paul J., and Wales, Terence J. "Higher Education, Mental Ability, and Screening." *J.P.E.* 81 (January/February 1973): 28–55.

Terman, Lewis M. *Mental and Physical Traits of a Thousand Gifted Children.* Genetic Studies of Genius, vol. 1. Stanford, Calif.: Stanford Univ. Press, 1925.

Terman, Lewis M.; Burks, Barbara S.; and Jensen, Dortha W. *The Promise of Youth.* Genetic Studies of Genius, vol. 3. Stanford, Calif.: Stanford Univ. Press, 1930.

Terman, Lewis M., and Oden, Melita H. *The Gifted Group at Mid-Life.* Genetic Studies of Genius, vol. 5. Stanford, Calif.: Stanford Univ. Press, 1959.

Theil, Henri. "Qualities, Prices and Budget Inquiries." *Rev. Econ. Studies* 19, no. 3 (1952): 129–47.

———. *Principles of Econometrics.* New York: Wiley, 1971.

Tietze, Christopher. "Differential Fecundity and Effectiveness of Contraception." *Eugenics Rev.* 50 (January 1959): 231–37. (*a*)

———. "The Clinical Effectiveness of Contraceptive Methods." *American J. Obstetrics and Gynecology* 78 (September 1959): 650–56. (*b*)

———. "The Use-Effectiveness of Contraceptive Methods." In *Research in Family Planning,* edited by Clyde V. Kiser. Princeton, N.J.: Princeton Univ. Press, 1962.

Tietze, Christopher. "Relative Effectiveness." In *Manual of Family Planning and Contraceptive Practices,* edited by Mary Steichen Calderone. Baltimore: Williams & Wilkins, 1970.

Tobin, James. "The Application of Multivariate Probit Analysis to Economic Survey Data." Discussion Paper no. 1, Cowles Foundation, 1955.

Umemura, Mataji. "Meiji Period Population Growth." In *Keizaishi ni okeru jinko* [Population in economic history], edited by H. Komatsu. Tokyo: Keio tsushin, 1969.

U.S., Bureau of the Census. *County and City Data Book, 1962: Statistical Abstract.* Suppl. Washington: Government Printing Office, 1962.

———. *U.S. Census of Housing, 1960.* Vol. 1. *States and Small Areas.* Pt. 1. *United States Summary.* Washington: Government Printing Office, 1963. (*a*)

———. *U.S. Census of Population: 1960.* Vol. 1. *Characteristics of the Population.* Pts. 1–52. Washington: Government Printing Office, 1963. (*b*)

———. *Employment Status and Work Experience.* Washington: Government Printing Office, 1963. (*c*)

———. *U.S. Censuses of Population and Housing, 1960. 1/1000, 1/10,000: Two National Samples of the Population of the United States, Description and Technical Documentation.* Washington: Government Printing Office, 1964.

———. *U.S. Census of Agriculture: 1964.* Washington: Government Printing Office, 1967.

———. *U.S. Census of Population: 1960. Childspacing.* PC(Z)3B. Washington: Government Printing Office, 1968.

———. *Social and Economic Variations in Marriage, Divorce, and Remarriage: 1967.* Current Population Reports, ser. P-20, no. 223. Washington: Government Printing Office, 1971.

———. *Statistical Abstract of the United States.* Washington: Government Printing Office, various issues.

U.S., Department of Health, Education and Welfare. *Vital Statistics of the United States.* Vol. 1. Washington: Government Printing Office, 1968. (*a*)

U.S., Department of Health, Education and Welfare. Social Security Administration, Office of Research and Statistics. *Workers under Social Security, 1960.* Washington: Government Printing Office, 1968. (*b*)

U.S., Office of Economic Opportunity, Day Care Policy Studies Group, Institute for Interdisciplinary Studies. "Child Care Programs: Estimation of Impacts and Evaluation of Alternative Federal Strategies." Report B00-5121. Washington: Office of Economic Opportunity, December 1971.

Wachtel, Paul. "The Returns to Investments in Higher Education Revisited." In *Education, Income, and Human Behavior,* edited by F.

Thomas Juster. New York: McGraw-Hill (for Carnegie Commission Higher Educ. and Nat. Bur. Econ. Res.), 1974, in press.

Wald, A. "The Approximate Determination of Indifference Surfaces by Means of Engel Curves." *Econometrica* 8 (April 1940): 144–75.

Wales, T. "Estimation of a Labor Supply Curve for Self-employed Business Proprietors." *Internat. Econ. Rev.* 14 (February 1973): 69–80.

Walker, Kathryn E. "Time Spent in Household Work by Homemakers." *Family Econ. Rev.* (ARS 62-5) (September 1969), pp. 5–6.

Walsh, B. M. "Trends in Age at Marriage in Postwar Ireland." *Demography* 9 (May 1972): 187–202.

Watts, H., and Tobin, J. "Consumer Expenditures and the Capital Account." In *Studies in Portfolio Behavior,* edited by D. Hester and J. Tobin. New York: Wiley, 1969.

Weisbrod, Burton A., and Karpoff, Peter. "Monetary Returns to College Education, Student Ability, and College Quality." *Rev. Econ. and Statis.* 50 (November 1968): 491–97.

Welch, Finis. "Measuring the Quality of Schooling." *A.E.R.* 56 (suppl.; May 1966): 379–92.

———. "Education in Production." *J.P.E.* 78 (January/February 1970): 35–59.

Westoff, Charles F.; Potter, Robert G., Jr.; and Sagi, Philip C. *The Third Child.* Princeton, N.J.: Princeton Univ. Press, 1963.

Whelpton, Pascal K.; Campbell, Arthur A.; and Patterson, John E. *Fertility and Family Planning in the United States.* Princeton, N.J.: Princeton Univ. Press, 1966.

Willis, Robert J. "A New Approach to the Economic Theory of Fertility Behavior." Mimeographed. Nat. Bur. Econ. Res., 1969 (rev. 1971).

———. "The Economic Determinants of Fertility Behavior." Ph.D. dissertation, Univ. Washington, 1971.

Wilson, Frances. *Labour in the South African Gold Mines, 1911–1969.* Cambridge: Cambridge Univ. Press, 1972.

Winch, R. F. *Mate Selection.* New York: Harper, 1958.

———. "Another Look at the Theory of Complementarity Needs in Mate Selection." *J. Marriage and Family* 29 (November 1967): 756–62.

Wray, Joe D. "Population Pressure on Families: Family Size and Child Spacing." *Population/Family Planning,* no. 9 (August 1971).

Yaukey, David. *Fertility Differences in a Modernizing Country.* Princeton, N.J.: Princeton Univ. Press, 1961.

Young, Kimball. *Isn't One Wife Enough?* New York: Holt, 1954.

Zellner, Arnold. "An Efficient Method of Estimating Seemingly Unrelated Regressions and Tests for Aggregation Bias." *J. American Statis. Assoc.* 57 (June 1962): 348–68.

INDEX

Ability, studies of effects of, among: American Telephone and Telegraph Company employees, 449; California school children (Terman sample), 435–36, 535; Connecticut school boys, 449; Minnesota high school graduates, 449; Project Talent participants, 449; recipients of Woodrow Wilson fellowships, 449; U.S. Air Force volunteers (NBER-Thorndike sample), 390–91, 449; U.S. military veterans, 449
Abortion in Japan, 225, 227, 229, 234–39, 246–47, 250–52
Adelman, Irma, 25 n., 190 n.
Age-specific birth rates, 160 n., 245, 293; for Taiwan, 257–58, 262, 268, 276–78, 286–87
Aigner, D., 496
Aitchison, John, 471
Akasako, Keiko, 253 n.
Alchian, Armen A., 329 n.
Alstrom, C. H., 318
Andersen, Ronald, 378
Anderson, Odin W., 378
Aoki, Hisao, 226 n., 229, 230, 239, 251 n., 252 n.
Arao, M., 250 n.
Arrington, Leonard J., 334 n.
Ashenfelter, Orley, 104 n., 449, 491 n.
Auerbach, C., 219

Bachi, R., 191 n., 219
Baerwaldt, Nancy, 487
Bajema, C. J., 308 n.
Baker, Charles T., 440
Baumol, William J., 528
Becker, Gary S., 3, 7, 9, 25 n., 28, 29, 30, 32 n., 34 n., 35, 37, 81, 82, 83, 91 n., 93 n., 117, 120 n., 121, 127, 128, 131, 153, 189, 193, 217, 218, 224, 225 n., 231, 232 n., 250 n., 300 n., 328 n., 329 n., 331 n., 336 n., 338 n.,